READINGS ON TAXATION
IN DEVELOPING COUNTRIES

READINGS
ON TAXATION
IN
DEVELOPING COUNTRIES

Edited by

RICHARD BIRD AND OLIVER OLDMAN

The Johns Hopkins Press, Baltimore, 1964

Preface

INTEREST in the fiscal problems of the developing countries has been increasing rapidly in recent years. Although considerable literature on this subject now exists, much of it is not readily available to the interested student. For some time the International Program in Taxation has been collecting references and materials on taxation and economic development, largely to meet its own training and research needs, but in part also to be of service to others interested in the field. The *Bibliography on Taxation in Underdeveloped Countries,* published by the Program in 1962, was the first fruit of this effort.

The present volume, a collection of readings on taxation in developing countries, is the next result. Reproduction of most of the selections in this volume has been made possible by the generous co-operation of the authors and by special permission of the publishers. Colleagues too numerous to mention, in various universities and international organizations, have kindly expressed their views to us with respect to our tentative list of selections and have suggested a few we had failed to list in the first place. Finally, we have had the loyal and capable assistance of Miss Gretchen Hovemeyer in preparing these materials for publication.

The International Program in Taxation, a part of the Harvard Law School's broad program in International Legal Studies, offers yearly, to lawyers and public officials of foreign countries, a program of special study in the problems of taxation and fiscal administration. The Program's expanding research component is responsible for numerous publications in the fields of international taxation, taxation and the developing countries, and comparative taxation. Publication lists may be obtained by writing to the Program, Kendall House, Cambridge, Massachusetts 02138. The Program has collaborated in many of its activities with the Fiscal and Financial Branch of the United Nations and was established in 1952 with the aid of a grant from The Ford Foundation.

v

Richard Bird is assistant director, Research Program on International Economic Integration, Columbia University; Oliver Oldman is professor of law and director of training, International Program in Taxation, Harvard Law School.

December 1963
Cambridge, Massachusetts

RICHARD BIRD
OLIVER OLDMAN

Contents

vii

Part VI
Taxes on Foreign Trade

Part VII
Regional Integration, Tax Administration,
and Technical Assistance

Introduction

THE thirty-three selections contained in this book of readings vary widely in content and approach. They have been selected for the most part from English-language materials with which the editors were familiar, the main criteria of selection being significance and accessibility. One large class of publications which has not been included is the general literature of public finance. Although writings in this field contain numerous ideas relevant to the problems of the underdeveloped countries, they often do not deal explicitly with them and, hence, have been omitted here. Certain other useful items which do deal directly with taxation and development have also been omitted because they are readily available in book form; where relevant, these materials are noted in the selected and annotated bibliography at the end of this volume.

The classification scheme within which these selections have been arranged is meant only as the roughest of guides; there is, in fact, some overlapping of subject matter among the classification categories and among the items themselves and, occasionally, even some repetition. We have not attempted to remove this duplication. Our general policy has been to make as few editorial changes as possible, though we have, to some extent, restyled the subheads, tables, and footnotes of the previously printed selections. The brief editorial notes at the beginning of each section are meant only to summarize the dominant themes of the section. Since these selections often represent opposing views, inclusion of an item in this volume obviously does not mean that the editors necessarily agree with the opinions expressed. What inclusion does mean is that the views expressed are felt to be worth consideration by any student of developing countries.

Finally, the primary emphasis of this collection is clearly on the *economic* aspects of taxation for development. Evident also, however, is a concern for the legal and institutional factors which are in reality so important in shaping tax policy in underdeveloped—as well as in developed—countries. Not all of the areas of possible economic controversy have been covered, of course—for example, the tax treatment of the family. Although export taxes and other taxes on foreign trade are discussed, the often remunerative special excises are not covered. Perhaps the major omission, however, is that of a careful discussion of the problems encountered in implementing a tax reform.

The authors of most of the selections are foreign observers, partly because the selections were chosen from literature with which the editors were more familiar and partly because there is more material by foreign than by native authors. The view of an outsider is often useful—he sees problems in a different light, draws on other experiences—but it can seldom express that sense of reality which an account of the best native observer exhibits. This weakness is perhaps most evident in the contrast between prescribing a tax reform and actually implementing one. Professor Hirschman's detailed study of the Colombian experience (selection 25) provides many useful insights into the implementation of a system prescribed in many respects by foreign observers. Dr. Papanek's general discussion of the role of technical assistance (selection 33) provides a framework for future work in this field. What is lacking in this volume is a careful comparative evaluation of past efforts to change tax systems in developing countries and, more particularly, a study of the role of foreign advisers in the formulation of tax policy, the drafting and adoption of legislation, the adaptation of administration to the legislation, and the creation of institutions capable of continuing the process of tax revision and reform as it becomes necessary. In order to achieve a firm basis for future work in this field, such a study, difficult as it would be to carry out, is urgently required.

Part I

Fiscal Policy and Economic Development

THE first selection in this volume was prepared for the United Nations in 1951 by Walter W. Heller, then professor of economics at the University of Minnesota and now chairman of the President's Council of Economic Advisers in the United States. It introduces the reader to the special fiscal problems faced by the less-developed countries. In addition to surveying a number of important matters relating to the proper role of government in a developing country, such as budgeting techniques and the place of government borrowing, Heller's paper raises and places in perspective most of the tax issues which are treated in more detail in later selections.

The second item in this section, a paper by John H. Adler, director of the Economic Development Institute of the World Bank, covers more or less the same range of topics, but with so little duplication that it is a complement to rather than a substitute for Dr. Heller's paper. Dr. Adler's remarks on the level and pattern of public expenditures in poor countries and on the appropriate pricing policy for public enterprises are especially worth noting.

The third selection, an extract from Pakistan's Second Five-Year Plan, illustrates how tax policy may be related to the achievement of the goals expressed in a development plan. India's Third Five-Year Plan would have served this purpose equally well, although few other development plans would have, since they tend to be much less specific than the example offered here, vague as even it is on a number of points.

The final selection in this introductory section illustrates how the problem of financing development has been dealt with in the centrally planned economy of the Soviet Union.

1

1

Fiscal Policies for
Under-developed Countries

by *Walter W. Heller**

I. The Approach to Developmental Fiscal Policy

Fiscal policy, like other governmental policy, derives its meaning and direction from the aspirations and goals of the society within which it operates, of the people whom it serves. The aspirations of the peoples of the under-developed countries are clear: economic betterment and stability to provide the material soil within which human dignity and political freedom can grow. These aspirations are reflected in the objectives of the Charter of the United Nations "to promote social progress and better standards of life in larger freedom."[1] Pursuit of this end, in turn, involves acceptance of the following as economic objectives of tax and budgetary policy: (1) to make available for economic development the maximum flow of human and material resources consistent with minimum current consumption requirements; (2) to maintain reasonable economic stability in the face of long-run inflationary pressure and short-run international price movements; (3) to reduce, where they exist, the extreme inequalities in wealth, income and consumption standards which undermine productive efficiency, offend justice, and endanger political stability.

These objectives are not basically different from the economic goals of allocative efficiency, economic growth, stability, and optimum income distribution which guide fiscal policy in advanced countries on a free enterprise basis. Similarities in goals should not, however, be permitted to conceal the vast differences in economic conditions, in the cultural, legal, and political environment within which economic

*This paper was prepared by Dr. Heller, then professor of economics at the University of Minnesota, in his capacity as a consultant to the Fiscal Division, United Nations Department of Economic Affairs. It appeared as Part One of United Nations Technical Assistance Administration, *Taxes and Fiscal Policy in Under-developed Countries,* Sales No.: 1955.II.H.1 (New York, 1954), pp. 1–22. Reprinted with the kind permission of the United Nations Publishing Service.

policy must operate, and, indeed, in the state of development of the art of taxation and the science of government. Failure to comprehend the nature and significance of these differences could result—in fact, in the past sometimes has resulted—in mistaken and costly transplanting of inapplicable experience to the economies of under-developed countries.

Before examining these differences more closely, it may be useful to sound a note of caution. Inevitably, to classify national economies into "developed" and "under-developed" and treat them as two more or less homogeneous groups, does violence to individual countries in each group. The under-developed countries represent a wide band rather than a single color on the economic and fiscal spectrum—perhaps too wide to justify some of the generalizations that will be made in this report. Nonetheless, there are significant differences between the *bulk* of the under-developed economies and the *bulk* of the developed economies. In spite of individual variations, it is not only possible to identify these differences but essential to the success of technical assistance efforts that they be given full weight in diagnosing and seeking cures for the economic and fiscal ills of under-developed economies.

II. Fiscal Policy and Capital Formation

Many of the factors which give the tax and fiscal problem of the under-developed economies its distinctive character come to light in a consideration of the central problem of capital formation, the main key to economic development. In a highly developed economy like that of the United States, high average income almost automatically generates a large flow of business and personal savings. Fiscal policy for investment therefore consists largely in minimizing the interference of taxation with the incentives to absorb those savings in productive investment. Together with public expenditure policy, tax policy seeks also to reduce or offset the fluctuations in the volume of capital formation and the consequent destabilizing influence on the economy as a whole. Finally, tax policy concerns itself with the composition of investment, as for example, in the granting of preferential tax treatment to defense-oriented investment in foreign areas.

In the under-developed economies, taxation is increasingly assigned a far more positive role in the process of capital formation and technological change. The reason for this is implicit in the extremely low levels of income and saving which serve as the source of capital formation. Annual per capita incomes in the Middle East, in Asia, and in Latin America are typically under 200 U.S. dollars, or less than one-seventh of the United States level and one-fourth of the Canadian level.[2] Propensities to consume out of these incomes are understandably high. Little remains for saving after meeting the pressing demands of sheer subsistence in the lower income strata and of traditionally lavish living, reinforced by the "demonstration effect" of American consumption standards, in the higher income strata. The ratio of net private savings to national income falls far short of the 10 to 15 per cent or even higher levels experienced in advanced countries under non-inflationary conditions. Even worse, a considerable part of the meager savings is diverted into real estate and inventory speculation and the holding of precious metals, currency, and foreign exchange.

In contrast with the 15 to 18 per cent of national income used for net private investment in the United States and Canada in recent years, it appears that less than half of this proportion commonly prevails in the under-developed countries. Total home-financed investment in India was recently estimated to be only about 2½ per cent of the national income.[3] As a consequence, investment barely suffices to provide minimum shelter and equipment for the growing population. In contrast with increases in per capita real income from 1938 to 1948 of nearly 50 per cent in the United States and Canada and nearly 25 per cent in the Union of South Africa, per capita real income in Egypt and India did not appear to have increased at all; in fact per capita real consumption was somewhat lower than in 1938.[4]

These countries are caught in the vicious circle of extreme poverty, a circle proceeding from low incomes to high consumption propensities to low savings to low rates of capital formation to a continuation of low levels of income. To break out of this circle, apart from foreign aid, calls for vigorous taxation and government development programmes; on this point, expert opinion is nearing a consensus.[5] Fiscal policy is assigned the central task of wresting from the pitifully low output of these countries sufficient savings to finance economic development programmes and to set the stage for more vigorous private investment activity.

The problem of capital formation in the under-developed economies, as it confronts public finance, breaks down into three main parts. The first concerns the financing of social overhead investment which must be undertaken directly by government. The second deals with an intermediate zone in which the actual investment projects are in private hands but the funds are made available through government finance. The third deals with the necessary incentives to private investment, both domestic and foreign, as they are influenced by taxation and other fiscal measures. In all three categories, government effort is directed toward maximizing savings, mobilizing them for productive investment, and canalizing them so as to serve the purposes of a balanced development programme.

The discussion which follows will not pause to spell out the extent to which a lack of knowledge of basic economic facts in many under-developed economies inhibits application of the desirable fiscal principles and policies. Therefore, it may be useful at the outset to emphasize the opportunity that exists here for technical assistance to reduce the institutional barrier of ignorance. Broadly conceived, the task consists in helping the developing country (*a*) to measure the resources potentially available and actually disposable for the development programme; (*b*) to assess the competing claims on these resources; and (*c*) to delineate the alternative ways in which the claims can be reconciled with the resources in an integrated development programme. Ideally, the formulation of fiscal policy for balanced and non-inflationary development should rest on a foundation of factual knowledge concerning not only national income and such components as private consumption expenditures, private investment, and government purchases of goods and services but also the flows of resources among the key agricultural, industrial, and commercial sectors of the economy. A knowledge of these inter-sectoral flows, especially as they reveal different patterns of economic relationships than those which characterize the more advanced economies, can avoid mistakes and suggest modifications in the process of transferring fiscal policy experience (particularly in its anti-inflationary aspects) from advanced to less advanced economies. Also important in establishing a sure-footed tax and expenditure policy are data on income distribution, balance of payments, price movements, labour force, unemployment, and the like.[6]

Financing Government's Share in Economic Development

The Role of Government

Perhaps the most striking feature of the capital formation process in the under-developed economy is the large and inescapable role that government must play in providing "social overhead capital" both as a direct instrument of economic development and as a prerequisite to increased participation of private capital in the development process. In economies at all stages of development, there are investment projects which are not inherently attractive to private investment, yet promise large social gains. The unwillingness of private investors to offer their resources in spite of the large social gains involved may be based on any one of several grounds. (1) There may be a sharp divergence between the opportunity for private gain and social gain; the benefits conferred upon the direct recipient of the service, which are the basis for market pricing and private profits, may be strongly supplemented by benefits to third parties, i.e., to society as a whole. Education, health, and sanitation measures clearly fall in this category. Such investment in the formation of human capital may pay rich social and economic dividends, yet provide no opportunity for private investors to exact charges commensurate with the benefits or the costs. Development of transport, soil improvement, and river development are examples of physical investment which also fall at least partially in this category. (2) Returns from the investment may be too remote, too slow to materialize, to attract private investors. (3) The amount of investment involved in the project in question may be too large to be handled by private investors. Examples of the second and third categories are power installations, river development, and various conservation projects.

A brief consideration of the relationship of these types of investment to the development process will make clear why governments of under-developed countries have to play such a central role in the capital formation process and why, in turn, the strengthening of the tax system to yield adequate revenues is of such primary concern. Apart from its direct contribution to human well-being, the social overhead investment of government makes two essential contributions to economic development. First, large-scale improvements in health, education, and training expand productive capacity by increasing the stamina and strength of the workers on one hand and enlarging their fund of knowledge and skills on the other; this represents fully as much of an increase in the resources at the disposal of the economy as do investments which increase the fund of physical capital. Second, the foregoing increases in human capacity, combined with investments in highways, power projects, irrigation, and the like, provide the necessary economic environment—the external economies—needed to make private investments more attractive. Unlike investors in advanced countries, those in the under-developed economies cannot take for granted a supply of skilled and healthy labour, easy transport and communications, availability of power and water, and readily available supplies of raw materials. The apparent profitability of many investments in such countries is therefore cut down by the large costs that have to be incurred either to develop these prerequisites to the productive process or to operate without some of them. By utilizing their fiscal power to produce these services, governments can provide many of the external economies needed to raise rates of return to levels which will attract private investors.

Implications for Budgetary Management

The foregoing consideration of the relation of government outlays to the development process illustrates some of the difficulties involved in proper analysis and classification in governmental budget accounting. For example, outlays on teachers' and doctors' salaries, insect sprays, and medicines result in additions to the stock of human capital. Yet, they do not result in the creation of the depreciable assets which are admissible to government capital accounts. Related to this budgeting dilemma is the tendency to assign priorities to government projects on the basis of their financial return rather than their real return. From the discussion above, it is clear that the greatest real returns may be realizable in precisely those areas where there are no direct financial returns. Balanced economic development depends on assigning priorities to projects according to their contribution to the productivity of the economy rather than to their chances of being self-liquidating. Only where the financial returns add to the *total* resources available for developmental investment should the financial overtones affect the scale of priorities.[7]

Like the Geneva Conference on Comparative Fiscal Administration and most of the public finance field missions in the past, this discussion concerns itself more with taxation than with techniques of budgeting. However, an analysis of the principles of budgeting— covering such subjects as comprehensiveness in budgeting, the use of current and capital accounts, and revenue classification—has been made available by the United Nations in *Budgetary Structure and Classification of Government Accounts*[8] published in February 1951. In addition, a technical assistance workshop on problems of budgetary classification and management was held in Mexico City in September 1953 for a group of Latin American experts.[9] The brief consideration which the Geneva Conference gave to problems of budget management is summarized in Section C8 of Part Two below [not included in this volume].

Capacity for Tax Increases

The pressing need for large government outlays for economic development strongly influences the approach to the problem of determining the appropriate level of taxation in an under-developed country. In a highly developed economy, tax policy tends to accept the level of expenditures as its revenue goal (modified, of course, by considerations relating to the levels of employment, prices, and economic activity). The sequence of decision tends to run from expenditures to taxes. But in under-developed countries the level of expenditures depends much more heavily on the ability of the tax system to place the required revenues at the disposal of the government. By the same token, the size of the government's development programme depends in large part on the economic and administrative capacity of its tax system to marshal the necessary resources. In this sense, the sequence of decision tends to run from taxation to expenditures.

Recognizing the strategic importance of an adequate flow of tax revenues—and the inadequacy of their own revenues—the governments of many developing countries have sought to increase the proportion of national income collected in taxes. Much of the increased demand for technical assistance in fiscal matters since World War II apparently grows out of this desire for a more productive tax system. Under-developed countries are under no illusion that they can—or should—push their tax ratios of 10 to 15 per cent of national income to the 30 to 40 per cent levels reached in such advanced countries as Austria, Belgium, France, Germany, the Netherlands, Norway, the United Kingdom, and the United States. But they are aware that even a modest increase in taxation may be able to finance a large percentage increase in a government's contribution to the development programme. A country in which the share of the government sector in the gross national product is 12 per cent may be taken as fairly typical of low-income countries.[10] If one assumes that not more than one-third of the government's share is devoted to economic development, an increase of only 2 percentage points in the ratio of taxes to national income (to 14 per cent) would enable the government to increase its contribution to development expenditures by 50 per cent.

Does experience or informed judgment provide any reliable guide as to what level of taxation is appropriate for an under-developed economy? Experience shows, first, that the less advanced the economy of a country, generally, the lower the ratio of tax payments to national income. It shows, second, that through intensive administrative and legislative efforts (and in some cases, aided by favourable international market conditions or by foreign aid), quite a few less advanced countries have considerably increased their ratios in post-war years. For example, the Commonwealth Government of the Philippines increased its tax revenues by 80 per cent from 1950 to 1951.

The judgment of technical assistance experts in public finance, as reflected in their mission reports and other writings, appears to be that most under-developed countries could increase the proportion of their national income taken by taxation without unduly disturbing the economy and perhaps even with positive gains in the face of inflationary pressures.[11] Yet where the optimum level lies permits of no doctrinaire answer. It will differ from country to country depending on the preferences of citizens, the administrative competence in government, the relative importance of existing tax levels on one hand and undeveloped external economies on the other as barriers to private investment, and many other factors. As regards taxation, one of the key factors is whether additional taxes can be so levied as to tap funds that otherwise would have gone into such channels as luxury consumption or socially unproductive investment or foreign exchange hoarding, or whether they would simply displace private productive investment and essential consumption. No categorical answer can be given then, to this question: How far and how fast can taxes be raised? Only through a careful enquiry into economic characteristics, social and cultural institutions, and prevailing standards of tax administration and compliance can an intelligent approximation be provided for any given country.

Taxation and Private Investment

The foregoing discussion revolves around the use of taxation to mobilize the resources required by the government to carry out its share of the development programme. The discussion now turns to the impact of taxation on the flow and pattern of resources devoted to private capital formation. Even though the government may take a large hand in the financing of some of the projects, they are basically private investments undertaken for private profit.

Publicly Financed Private Investment

In view of the lack of developed capital markets in many countries, and the additional fact that controls may be necessary to divert funds from lavish consumption or speculation into productive investment in agriculture and industry, an increasing number of the less developed countries are using taxes to raise funds to be loaned to private investors. For example, "Institutos de Fomento" and specialized corporations or commissions for industrial or agricultural development have been established in Bolivia, Brazil, Chile, Colombia, India, Mexico, and Peru.[12] Some countries have also provided financial assistance to private enterprises like airlines and shipping companies whose requirements for capital are large and not easily obtainable from private sources.[13] Alternatively, governments can place tax-generated savings at the disposal of private entrepreneurs through the private banking system, e.g., by retiring bank-held debt. Such action makes room for non-inflationary extension of credit for the support of private investment projects.[14]

Privately Financed Private Investment

The final category of investment, namely, private investment undertaken without the use of government funds, involves the most difficult and delicate problems of tax composition and structure. As is brought out elsewhere in this paper, such private investment is also influenced very substantially by other aspects of governmental fiscal policy. Section I has already brought out the role of government in developing transport, power, technical training, and similar facilities to create external economies for private investment.

Section IV suggests that where deficient domestic markets are blocking the flow of private funds into desired domestic industries, governments may wish to orient their taxing and spending policies toward strengthening such markets. In addition, fiscal policy influences the level and direction of investment through its impact on inflation and economic stability; some of the possibilities and limitations of fiscal policy in this regard are examined in Section III.

The position is sometimes taken that governments should not go too far in trying to prevent inflation in an underdeveloped economy because (a) this may require unduly high taxes and (b) within bounds, inflation is itself an acceptable pragmatic instrument of a developmental policy. While the pros and cons of this position cannot be fully aired here, the implications for tax policy of this pro-inflationary position are so far-reaching that it cannot be dismissed without comment.

With respect to "unduly high taxes," a point may somewhere be reached where inflation is preferable to higher taxes, but given a reasonably well-structured tax system, this point seems rather remote at levels of taxation approximating 15 per cent of national income. Moreover, a government which is aggressively participating in the development process will have other (though related) reasons for levying higher taxes. In a developmental setting, then, higher taxes are seen not as a positive good but as the lesser of evils.

On behalf of inflation, it can be noted that where it is the only available alternative to persistent stagnation, it may be attractive as a last resort in spite of its risks. One may even contend, somewhat more positively, that inflation has an invigorating effect by loosening economic and social relationships and giving the more ingenious and enterprising elements in the population a chance to come to the fore. But even without examining the pitfalls in these positions, one is entitled to the gravest doubts, on both economic and social justice grounds, about accepting inflation as an instrument for economic development.

The process by which credit-induced inflation generates capital investment is sympathetically described in terms of three steps: (a) the credit expansion provides the initial means of diverting resources from the remainder of the community; (b) profits generated in this process yield additional savings to perpetuate the capital-forming process; (c) profits thus generated also serve as the inducement to undertake the investment. But this is a costly and inequitable way of transferring resources from consumption to capital formation. First, enlarged profits to investors combined with dissaving by consumers trying to maintain previous levels of consumption will increase rather than decrease inequalities of income and wealth. Second, inflation channels much of the resulting investment into real estate, inventories, foreign exchange, and other "riskless" holdings designed to reap capital gains from socially unproductive undertakings. Third, even where investment flows into industrial production, inflation tends to elicit investment in luxury industries rather than those producing necessities. Finally, inflation is eventually self-defeating if it discourages the voluntary savings which provide the solid foundation for economic development.[15]

Turning from the level to the structure of taxation, one finds much disagreement on what constitutes the most effective policy for maximizing private investment and guiding it into the most useful channels. On some points, of course, fairly extensive agreement has been reached among experts in public finance. It is fairly widely agreed, for example, that full use should be made of tax measures which can seek out and impound income that would otherwise be squandered on lavish living and luxury imports. Commodity taxes in the form of high import duties and excises on luxury items are widely advocated as instruments of such policy in under-developed countries. Also, personal income taxes with steeply progressive rates in the upper brackets are often favoured as instruments for tapping such income.

There is also considerable agreement that taxes should, if possible, penalize the diversion of savings into land, buildings, inventories, and similar investments held for speculative gain or prestige purposes rather than productive use. Among the tax instruments recommended for use to this end are land value increment taxes, taxes on idle land, progressive taxes on either net worth or real estate holdings, and either special capital gains taxes or inclusion of capital gains in part or in full as taxable income. At the present time, many countries—especially those following the British tax pattern—exempt capital gains on casual transactions. While some experts defend this as necessary to implement a traditional definition of income, others condemn it because it provides an incentive for speculative investments which draw savings away from the development programme.[16]

The foregoing is not meant to say that there is a complete consensus among experts on the desirability of these measures. A few would contend, for example, that exorbitant profits, luxury living, and the implicit inequalities of income and wealth are necessary as stimulants to investment and human effort, objectionable as they may be in terms of distributive justice. Others who might not go quite this far nonetheless prefer tax concessions for desirable investment activities to penalty taxes on undesirable activities. Another point of view is that the tax administrations of many of the under-developed countries are too inefficient and unreliable to practice the finer arts of taxation; where this situation prevails, only simple taxes levied at relatively low rates are said to be capable of tolerable enforcement.

Even apart from the question of administrative feasibility, there is a wide diversity of opinions concerning the desirability and effectiveness of special tax concessions for private domestic and foreign investment. One point of view is that they are relatively ineffective either because levels of taxation in the under-developed countries are not generally high enough to inhibit investment seriously or because barriers like political instability and restrictions on foreign exchange conversion loom so much larger than the tax barrier.[17]

A very different view of the matter is reflected in the tax policies of India. Very extensive income tax concessions are granted with respect to returns from certain types of economic activity. For example, new industrial undertakings are exempt from income tax for five years up to six per cent of their invested capital and accelerated depreciation is allowed on new buildings, plant, and machinery.[18]

Although preferential tax treatment does not enter into the government's budget at any point, it is nonetheless a disguised government expenditure. The use of revenues raised by taxation to grant subsidies to private investment differs in form but not in substance from subsidies granted in terms of reduced tax liabilities. The danger also exists that tax concessions will be converted into tax loopholes. Taxpayers are ever watchful to gain tax benefits by meeting the formal requirements of the concession provisions without carrying out the underlying intent. In spite of these and other defects, a considerable number of persons concerned with the formation of tax policy in under-developed countries warmly defend tax concessions as an incentive to investment. Moreover, the line between questionable tax concessions and desirable improvements in tax structure is not always easy to draw.

Among the structural improvements and incentive devices most widely supported in the field of business income taxation are the following: (1) The allowance of extensive carry-overs of net business losses in one year as off-sets against net business gains in other years; this reduces or removes the deterrent to investment that otherwise results from the lack of opportunity to deduct business outlays in full from income subject to taxation. (2) Accelerated depreciation, permitting the more rapid recapture of productive investment; this device has the effect of giving the investor an interest-free loan from the government. (3) Preferential rates for reinvested business profits or, alternatively, additional taxes on profits declared as dividends; this measure recognizes such profits as a prime source of investment funds and seeks to discourage their dissipation in consumption or their "loss" by transfer abroad.

From the foregoing discussion, it is apparent that tax policy faces a basic dilemma in its role as an instrument of capital formation for economic development. On one hand, high levels of taxation are necessary to finance that part of the developmental process which falls in the government sphere and to mobilize for investment the private resources that might otherwise be dissipated. On the other hand, the lower the taxes the greater will be the inducement to private investors, per unit of net income, to take the risks associated with investment in agricultural and industrial development. The dilemma is worsened by the fact that those taxes which are most effective in capturing a large share of the gains from economic development for further capital formation are the ones most likely to affect the returns from private investment. For it is the taxes which vary directly and rise progressively with the size of income that are most effective in absorbing the gains from development (and are generally preferred on equity grounds); yet these are precisely the ones which are likely to affect marginal effort and risk-taking.

One way out of the dilemma may be to combine high rates of taxation in general with preferential treatment for categories of desired developmental activity (and penalty taxes or rates on undesirable economic activities). To implement such a policy requires careful economic analysis and planning, skillful structuring of taxes, ruling out of political favoritism, and competent tax administration. An important function of technical assistance in public finance is to ascertain for the country in question not only what combination of tax policies might best serve the interests of economic development (in the light, always, of the country's ethical preferences) but also how those policies have to be modified in translating them into tax measures which are operational in terms of the country's capacity for tax administration and conditions of tax compliance.

III. Fiscal Policy for the "Exposed Economy"

Another factor which strongly conditions the role of fiscal policy in many under-developed countries is the vulnerability of their economies to world market developments lying outside of their control. Their exposed position grows mainly out of their heavy dependence on the exports of one or two agricultural or mineral products both as a source of national income and as a source of foreign exchange. Their exposure is increased by their dependence on foreign sources for manufactured products and often for foodstuffs as well. Finally, they often find that their attempts to maintain domestic economic stability are complicated by the dominant position of foreign investment in their primary industries combined with a tendency of both foreign and domestic investors to seek safe haven for their profits abroad. Increasingly, under-developed countries have sought to protect their "exposed economies" from the buffetings of fluctuating world market demand and prices by the use of flexible fiscal and foreign exchange measures in the short run and diversification of their economies in the long run.

Examples of countries whose productive patterns and dependence on exports put them in the category of "exposed economies" are: Bolivia where, between 1938 and 1948, exports of mineral products averaged nearly 95 per cent of the total value of exports;[19] Chile, where copper in 1950 accounted for 50 per cent and nitrates for 25 per cent of total exports;[20] Cuba, where the sugar sector contributed directly between 24 per cent (1945) and 37 per cent (1947) of the national income and where exports of sugar and sugar products account for nearly 90 per cent of total exports (1949).[21] Similar examples can be found in the Central American countries: in El Salvador, for example, coffee accounts for 12 per cent of the gross national product (1946)[22] and for 89 per cent of total exports (1950).[23] In Guatemala bananas and coffee contributed 13 per cent of the gross national product (1947–48) and more than 80 per cent of total exports (coffee: 72 per cent in 1949).[24] In the last two countries, moreover, the largest part of the active population is engaged in the production of the one or two export commodities. Further examples are provided by the oil-producing countries, such as Iran, Iraq, and Venezuela, where oil exports accounted respectively for 90 per cent (1949), 51 per cent (1950) and 97 per cent (1950) of the total value of exports.[25] In the Far Eastern countries the following countries may be mentioned: Ceylon (1951: tea 42 per cent, rubber 31 per cent of the total value of exports); Indonesia (1951: rubber 42 per cent, oil 20 per cent); Thailand (1949: rice 63 per cent).[26] In the Federation of Malaya rubber in 1948 accounted for nearly 20 per cent of the net national product.[27]

Although all of these countries depend heavily on one or two primary commodities sold in world markets, they differ both in the price they pay for such dependence—in the degree of instability to which they are exposed—and in the benefits they derive—in the degree of comparative advantage they enjoy. To take an extreme example, a one-commodity country whose main export is uranium seems assured of a strong market, favorable terms of trade, and a steady supply of dollar exchange. A less extreme example of a favored mono-cultural economy is that of Cuba, whose peculiar relation to the United States market reduces the risks involved in its reliance on sugar. Moreover, the low-income, undiversified economy is not the only one to suffer from external destabilizing influences. Any export-oriented economy runs this risk. Yet, other things being equal, a country whose economic fate depends on world markets for one or two primary products risks greater instability and finds conventional fiscal policy less effective in dealing with it than a country which is industrially more diversified. Economic exposure characterizes so many of the world's underdeveloped economies that it requires special consideration in an analysis of their fiscal policies.

Fiscal Measures for Economic Stabilization

To the extent that instability is the product of external movements of prices and demand for the export products which dominate the local economy, the applicability of generalized expansionary and contractionary fiscal policy is correspondingly limited. It does not follow that the non-industrialized country has no fiscal weapons to use in defending the domestic economy against the vicissitudes of world market fluctuations. Such specific instruments as export taxes may lend themselves more readily to this kind of stabilization activity than more general measures like sales and income taxation.

Increases in export taxes and manipulation of exchange rates were used by many primary producing countries to take advantage of the sudden shift in the terms of trade in the post-Korean spurt of world market prices. These measures were used to siphon off some of the windfall gains of the export sector and to impound a large amount of precious foreign exchange. In some cases, the proceeds were used to good advantage (*a*) in shielding the economy from the inflationary impact of rising world market prices and (*b*) in financing capital imports for the development programme. Where export levies are used to build up foreign exchange reserves or perhaps even a formal "foreign exchange stabilization fund," the effects of a subsequent worsening of the terms of trade can be cushioned by adjusting such levies downward and by drawing on exchange reserves.

The advantages to be gained in reducing the exposure of primary producers to the ebbs and flows of world markets by skillful manipulation of export and import taxes or multiple exchange rates do not, of course, wipe out the traditional objections to these fiscal devices namely, (*a*) that they may interfere with the optimum pattern of world trade; (*b*) that they are inferior in equity terms to a progressive income tax; (*c*) that they may lead to uneconomic productive practices, particularly in the extractive industries; and (*d*) that especially in the case of multiple exchange rates they may seriously inhibit foreign investment by interfering with the free flow of returns on such investment.[28] Moreover, the potential contribution to internal economic stability and development can be realized only through an uncommon fusion of political will and economic skill: (*a*) will, for example, to resist a high propensity to import consumer goods, especially luxuries; and (*b*) skill not only in managing tax and exchange rates but also in so timing the changes and channeling the proceeds as to promote stable and balanced economic development.

Without gainsaying the objectionable features of these devices, especially in their interference with international monetary flows, one may acknowledge their attractions as tax measures under certain circumstances in which under-developed countries may find themselves. First, these devices can be adjusted up or down more easily than, for example, the income tax. Second, they are better suited than general taxes like the income tax to single out the export-import sector of the economy and counteract destabilizing influences that arise from it. Finally, they are relatively simple to administer and difficult to evade. In a setting of weak administration and low tax-paying morale, this can be a decisive advantage for export and import levies as instruments for economic stabilization.[29]

The application of fiscal policy for economic stabilization in under-developed primary producing countries is also complicated by the internal characteristics of their economies. Especially in predominantly agricultural economies, supply is likely to be relatively inelastic. Moreover, the organization of production is characterized by many institutional rigidities. Custom, tradition, systems of land tenure, and the like tend to block or impede the free flow of resources, both human and material, from one use into another. Nor is economic motivation such that opportunities for profit are as quickly recognized and exploited as in industrial nations. Consequently, a cautious and segmental rather than bold and aggregative approach must be taken to the use of compensatory fiscal policy.

Economically developed countries find themselves in a very different position in this respect. They generally enjoy a considerably greater degree of insulation against external destabilizing influences and a correspondingly greater opportunity to regulate their own economies. Further, since their economies are usually diversified, industrialized, and elastic, the effects of compensatory finance transmit themselves relatively smoothly and evenly throughout the economy. In this setting, for example, reductions and increases in public works or transfer payments translate themselves rather readily into higher levels of employment and income. In the under-developed economy, in contrast, injections of purchasing power may in considerable part run off into higher prices of the inelastic domestic supplies on one hand and into larger imports on the other. Much of the multiplier effect is thus thwarted or transmitted abroad. Since deficit financing may aggravate the external trade deficit, the virtues of unbalancing the governmental accounts may have to be set off against the vices of unbalancing the external trade accounts.

One of the major attractions of industrialization in under-developed countries is apparent in the foregoing discussion. In the absence of effective international measures for economic stabilization, these countries are striving to reduce the exposure of their economies by diversification.[30] In doing so, they are also motivated by a number of other considerations which suggest that the law of comparative advantage can be pursued too far: (1) Often the mono-cultural economy is characterized by disguised unemployment in the form of redundant labor in agricultural pursuits or seasonal unemployment in those pursuits; through diversification, it is hoped that a productive outlet for this labor can be provided. (2) Where exports are the only or main outlet for increased production, the pursuit of comparative advantage may be thwarted by relatively stationary or inelastic demands on the world market. (3) Without an attempt at diversification, a country may not in fact be aware of the pursuits in which its greatest comparative economic advantage lies. (4) An economy's advantage in producing a particular good may be acquired rather than inherent, in which case the shifting of resources may result in acquiring advantages in the production of goods previously imported, thereby saving transport costs and the like. (5) Agrarian societies are often economically and sometimes culturally backward; industrialization not only releases men's skills and provides new fields for expression but tends to make the social structure more fluid.

In exploring some of the reasons why countries with exposed economies so often seek to industrialize and diversify, the foregoing discussion does not mean to suggest that economic development is synonymous with industralization. The primary purpose of economic development is, of course, the raising of per capita income and living standards rather than the promotion of economic stability. Where investment in the agricultural and other primary producing sectors clearly offers the greatest returns, it would retard economic development to make a fetish of industrialization. New Zealand and Denmark serve as examples of economic advancement primarily through agriculture.

At the same time, it is essential to count *all* the costs as well as *all* the benefits in allocating developmental resources between industry and agriculture. Where industrialization absorbs manpower that would otherwise run to waste in agricultural unemployment, where it releases latent skills, and where it reduces economic instability and its heavy attendant costs, the real balance of advantages may be tipped toward investment in industry even though the apparent balance of direct increase in productivity favors agriculture. Under these circumstances, a fiscal policy that facilitates capital formation and technological progress in industry serves the ends of both economic stability and fuller use of resources.

Finally, fiscal policy for stabilization of developing economies has to deal with their unusual susceptibility to inflation. Superimposed on the pressures of basic consumption needs are strong pressures for economic development. Even the most prudent developmental programmes have inflationary concomitants. Inflationary pressures may be concentrated in certain sectors of the economy and may therefore refuse to yield to broadside tax measures. On the other hand, the bias toward inflation in the developing economy suggests the desirability of an opposing anti-inflationary bias in fiscal and monetary policy.

In this setting, loan financing of development projects involves serious risks for the economy. Inferences drawn from budgetary classifications which segregate government expenditures into those on current account and those on capital account have sometimes led to error on this score. Such segregation is essential for clear-cut economic and fiscal analysis of the government sector, especially in the measurement and programming of the government's contribution to capital formation. The danger lies in misreading the financial implications of the capital account. It has sometimes been misinterpreted as justifying domestic loan financing of development projects (especially where these promise to be self-liquidating) even in the face of inflation. The sounder guide to the method of financing such projects is the condition of the economy as judged by such criteria as the level of employment and prices and the balance-of-payments position.[31]

As in developed countries, anti-cyclical fiscal policy must be accompanied by appropriate action on the part of the monetary authorities to limit credit expansion in inflationary periods and to make credit readily available during periods of unemployment and depression. Unless coordinated action is taken on the monetary front, fiscal efforts to stabilize the economy may be nullified.[32]

Although many of the characteristics of economic instability in the less advanced economies are known in general terms, lack of factual and statistical data still plagues those who wish to analyze the problem realistically and prescribe means for its solution. Here again enters knowledge as an institutional barrier, especially in determining the potentialities and limitations of fiscal policy. While "test tube experiments" are no more possible in the less developed than in the more developed economies, great advances in the effectiveness of tax and fiscal policy can be made by ascertaining some of the rudimentary facts cited in Section II above.

Other Fiscal Problems of the "Exposed Economy"

A somewhat different aspect of the exposure of many underdeveloped economies to external economic influence is the extensive participation of foreign investment in certain segments of the economy, especially the extractive industries. It has been estimated, for example, that local participation in the form of wages, royalties, and taxes in the Bolivian tin industry amounted to only about 20 per cent of the value of minerals exported during the 1920's and perhaps 45 per cent in recent years. While this may have the questionable virtue of transmitting more of the instability of the minerals industry abroad, it has the offsetting vice from the standpoint of the under-developed country of drawing off income and foreign exchange out of which consumption levels could be raised or investment for economic development could be expanded. This is not to say, of course, that the country is worse off than if the foreign capital had not come in at all. It merely re-emphasizes that the country seeking development faces an uncomfortable dilemma in tax policy. On one hand, it wishes to maximize total output by attracting foreign capital into the country, an objective which in appropriate cases may be advanced by low taxes or special tax incentives. On the other hand, it wishes to maximize its share of any given output, presumably by levying high taxes and royalties. It is not easy to strike the proper balance.

Foreign investment exposes the tax system of the under-developed country to other elements beyond its immediate control. For example, the credits allowed by some of the major capital exporting countries, e.g. the United States and England to their individual and corporate investors in foreign countries specify rather closely what types of foreign taxes shall be eligible under the crediting provisions. This may influence the country seeking investment from abroad to adjust its tax system so as to draw full advantage from the credit provisions both for its own revenue and for the foreign investor.

Another factor is the complication of tax administration and structure. Where profits accrue to foreign owners or where the business unit in the taxing country is integrated with one in another country, it is administratively hard to determine the base for income taxes and even in some cases for *ad valorem* export taxes. Moreover, opportunities for evasion are significantly increased. Finally, the relationship between the domestic and foreign arms of many undertakings make it more difficult to integrate corporate with individual income taxes so as to prevent both (*a*) discriminatory double taxation of distributed earnings and (*b*) avoidance of personal income tax either through unreasonable corporate accumulations or through distribution of earnings to non-resident shareholders. Such difficulties as the foregoing have undoubtedly decreased the attractiveness of income taxes relative to export and import duties in the less advanced economies.

IV. REDISTRIBUTIVE ASPECTS OF FISCAL POLICY

In advanced economies, the function of fiscal policy as it affects income and wealth distribution is largely one of attempting to attain that degree of redistribution through taxation and government spending which most neatly balances (*a*) the humanitarian interest in sharing economic well-being more equally, against (b) the efficiency interest in maintaining sufficient inequalities of reward to serve as an incentive to the exercise of special economic effort and ingenuity. Inequalities of wealth and income, while still substantial, have been narrowed in most developed economies by a combination of increases in productivity and various redistributive policies of government. The magnitudes involved in the inequalities which remain are generally large enough to offer fertile ground for progressive taxation and redistributive expenditure. In most advanced countries, the machinery of progressive income and wealth taxation is sufficiently well developed to carry out its share of a redistributive fiscal policy.

Contrast the setting, role, and magnitudes of redistributive finance in the less advanced economies. Many are characterized by extremes of wealth and poverty which, in terms of the equalitarian ethic as accepted throughout the free world, constitute a compelling case for redistributive government finance.[33] Not only is the humanitarian interest often more intense than in advanced countries, but the efficiency interest may differ sharply in both nature and emphasis, as brought out below. However extreme the existing inequalities may be, the impact of distributive considerations on fiscal policy in less advanced countries must in practice be tempered by the limits they encounter in varying degrees with respect to (a) the absolute size of existing concentrations of income and wealth and (b) the ability of their tax systems to tap these concentrations.

Within these limits, what role does redistributive finance play as an instrument of economic policy in the country seeking development? Qualitatively, the answer goes to the very root of the problem of economic productivity. Investments in human beings are an integral part of government programs for improving productivity and technology. Improvements in sanitation, health, and nutrition build up working capacity and thus increase the quantity of manpower available for economic development. Education and training programmes reduce illiteracy and increase skill and thus increase the quality of manpower. To the extent that taxation finances this process of human capital formation at the expense of lavish consumption, speculation, and foreign exchange hoarding rather than at the expense of productive private investment, it increases productivity and accelerates development.

Countries seeking to establish home industries in the interests of balanced economic growth often find that domestic markets are too limited to support such undertakings.[34] Insofar as redistributive government finance increases the productivity and real income of the bulk of the population, it tends to broaden the base of the domestic market. It may also contribute to this end by shifting demand from luxury items ordinarily imported from abroad to more needed items which can be produced domestically. How much of the purchasing power diverted from luxury consumption or created by increased productivity should be siphoned off for further capital formation and how much should be permitted to express itself in higher levels of mass consumption will depend on the stage of economic development and the preferences of the society in question. One country may wish to mobilize every available source of saving for a program of social overhead investment. Another may put more emphasis on increases in consumption as (*a*) a source of human capital formation; (*b*) an incentive to harder work; and (*c*) a method of widening markets and thereby increasing the private inducement to invest. Although redistributive government finance can be oriented toward either policy, the latter necessarily implies a combination of taxes and expenditures that will reduce economic inequalities.

In the less advanced as in the more advanced economies, adverse incentive effects on initiative, risk-taking, and managerial efforts place limits on progressive taxation. Yet, high incomes in under-developed countries may, comparatively speaking, be derived from such sources and devoted to such uses that the disincentive effects are less damaging than in developed countries. The greatest damage occurs where high marginal rates bear oppressively on incomes whose source is largely in entrepreneurial effort and whose use is largely in further investment. But where land rents and interest charges are a dominant or very important source of large income and where luxury spending, speculation, and hoarding dominate the use of such funds—a combination which describes many economically under-developed societies—the danger of discouraging private contributions to economic development by redistributive fiscal measures is considerably lessened.[35]

Redistributive finance, then, appears to offer greater gains and involve less costs to under-developed than to developed economies. Accepting this qualitative appraisal as valid does not, of course, resolve doubts concerning the quantities involved. The contribution to economic progress through human capital formation and enlarged markets depends less on the degree of economic inequality than on the absolute amounts concentrated at or near the top of the income scale. The conspicuously large fortunes in many under-developed countries may offer only a limited field for redistributive finance, both because the aggregate resources they represent may be small relative to the huge numbers at the other end of the income scale and because tax administration may not be equal to its share of the task. This hardly vitiates the economic argument, but cautions against letting it carry more weight in shaping fiscal policy than the quantities involved may justify.

Turning from economic to ethical and political interests in reduced inequality, the situation is reversed: the total sums involved are much less significant than the degree of inequality. The contribution to a sense of justice depends far more on how much the gap between the top and bottom incomes is narrowed than on how much income or wealth is transferred in the process.

Similar considerations govern the contribution of redistributive finance to political stability. Development of the backward economies does little to advance the cause of freedom and stable self-government if the benefits are concentrated in the hands of the few. Instead, such concentration polarizes interests by widening and deepening the gulf between the wealthy and powerful at one extreme, the poor and the weak at the other. Fiscal policies which reduce this gap reduce the accompanying threat to political stability.

As a country's economy develops, as the lot of its people improves through a wide sharing of benefits, and as economies of scale and adequate markets are provided to improve the climate for private investment, redistributive finance offers less benefits and higher costs per unit of income redistribution. For example, the marginal productivity of investments in human beings may gradually diminish. At the same time, as social overhead investment and widening markets remove basic economic barriers to private investment, the adverse incentive effects of progressive taxes may be felt more keenly. As an instrument of economic growth and political stability, redistributive finance will become less attractive. But in the earlier stages of development, it forms an integral part of a developmental program which seeks to achieve its goals of technical progress and economic advancement without disrupting upheavals in political and social structure.

V. FISCAL INSTRUMENTS AND INSTITUTIONS

The emphasis in the preceding sections of this chapter has been on the distinguishing features of the economic setting and aspirations of the under-developed countries as they affect the tasks which their tax systems (in combination, of course, with government spending) are called upon to perform. This section inquires whether these tax systems are equal to the modern tasks of fiscal policy as they stand or can be made equal to them by transfer of techniques from the advanced countries. Again, because of the wide diversity in the tax structures and administrations of the less developed countries, each generalization in this area is subject to significant exceptions.

The tax systems of the under-developed economies differ most noticeably from the pattern in advanced countries in their heavy emphasis on commodity taxation and the taxation of exports and imports. The dominance of *in rem* as against personal taxes is particularly marked in Latin American countries. Reflecting in part their

Spanish origins, the tax systems of these countries have traditionally relied on stamp taxes and commodity taxes. They also stressed the schedular rather than the global approach to income taxation (though several countries have in recent years superimposed a global income tax or even substituted it for the schedular tax). The net impact of this influence has been toward regressivity and retarded growth of progressive instruments of taxation. In those under-developed countries to which the British system has in part or in whole been exported, the tendency is to rely somewhat more heavily on income taxation as, for example, in India and Israel.

In analyses of the tax problems of under-developed economies, the traditional objectives of progressivity and equity in taxation, reinforced by the modern economic objectives of taxation, have pointed strongly to more aggressive use of net income and wealth taxation. Particularly before World War II, public finance missions seldom failed to urge the adoption of fuller use of net income taxes. Frequently, these recommendations seemed to reflect the ideological precepts of the technical advisers rather than an appreciation of the institutional setting of the country in which the recommendations were to be put into practice.

Fortunately, in recent years, there has been a growing sensitivity to the institutional framework within which technical assistance efforts are to be applied. There is a growing realization that conditions within which the most modern, equitable and flexible instruments of taxation thrive do not yet prevail in many of the under-developed countries and that substantial modifications of the fiscal techniques applicable in developed countries are necessary to adapt them to the under-developed economy. To translate this point into specific terms, Richard Goode, a member of the United Nations Technical Assistance Mission to Bolivia, set forth the conditions for successful use of income taxation side by side with the conditions actually found in under-developed countries. Problems involved in modernizing the tax systems of under-developed countries are brought out so effectively in his analysis that it is quoted here at some length.[36]

1. The first condition is the existence of a predominantly money economy. The subsistence farmer cannot be satisfactorily reached by an income tax, not so much because he does not have money to pay—that may mean that he cannot pay a tax of any kind—as because the greater part of his real income cannot be satisfactorily assessed. Even highly skilled administrators have made little progress toward including the value of home-produced and consumed foods in the taxable income of farmers. In many under-developed countries these products and others obtained by barter make up a major fraction of the total real income of large segments of the population. Admittedly these groups are usually the poorest in the society, and failure to subject them to direct taxation

may not be seriously objectionable from the equity point of view. It does, however, encourage use of other taxes.

2. Another condition that may not be strictly necessary but is very helpful is a high standard of literacy among taxpayers. In many under-developed countries the majority of the population is illiterate. For example, among the eleven Latin American republics for which data are readily available, seven have illiteracy ratios higher than 50 per cent.[37] In many regions of Asia and Africa the figure is higher, as it probably also is for several Latin American countries for which data are not available. Illiteracy, like exclusion from the money economy, is most characteristic of the poorest farmers, but often wage earners, independent craftsmen, and small shopkeepers cannot read and write well enough to fill out the simplest income tax return with the guidance of printed instructions. Wage earners may be covered by withholding, but in any refined system they must be able to file claims for exemptions and refunds.

3. Prevalence of accounting records honestly and reliably maintained is another prosaic but important condition for satisfactory income taxation. In most under-developed countries many businessmen keep no books at all; others maintain two or more sets. Vigorous tax administration can do much to improve accounting standards if combined with an educational campaign, but more trained personnel and office equipment are essential.

4. A fourth requirement for satisfactory income taxation is a large degree of voluntary compliance on the part of taxpayers. The best administrative organization cannot satisfactorily collect income taxes from the self-employed when, as in many countries, evasion is generally attempted and incurs little or no moral disapproval from the public. The roots of a tradition of voluntary compliance with tax laws are not easy to trace, but it is fairly clear that such a spirit does not grow up over night. Although something can be done in the short run, a long period of popular education and efficient and equitable administration of those taxes that can actually be enforced seems necessary to establish firmly the habit of general voluntary acceptance of the fiscal responsibilities of citizenship. Adoption of elaborate measures that will not be uniformly applied delays improvement in taxpayer morale.

5. The political conditions for development of income taxes into a major revenue source, like the spirit of voluntary compliance, are intangible and hard to explain. The environment most favourable to progressive taxation seems to be one of free political democracy. In many under-developed countries wealth groups have enough political power to block tax measures that they consider threats to their position. Until the popular will is stronger and more united or until the rich are ready to accept the ability-to-pay principle—whether from altruism or a sense of guilt or fear—steeply progressive taxes will not be collected.

6. Honest and efficient administration is needed for any tax, but minimum acceptable standards appear to be higher for income taxes than for many other levies. Difficult as the task of establishing a satisfactory administration may be, it is probably the condition for successful income taxation that can be met most quickly. The expert, nevertheless, must guard against the assumption that a tidy organization chart and nonpolitical staffing assure good administration. Nor can he be confident that the best obtainable administration will eliminate obstacles to heavy reliance on income taxes.

A recitation of such limitations is, of course, a counsel of caution, not of despair. It suggests the lines along which action must be taken to remove the barriers listed and underscores again the necessity of improving administration and compliance to the limits possible within the framework of existing social institutions. At the same time, it calls for ingenuity in adapting and modifying advanced fiscal instruments to the conditions existing in economically under-developed countries. In the case of the income tax, for example, the difficulties encountered in many countries do not rule out the income tax entirely but strongly suggest that it not be used as a mass tax. As may be seen in Section C1 of Part Two [not included in this volume], this seems to have been the prevailing opinion of the participants in the Geneva Conference. A personal income tax with a narrow base but high rates on large incomes, buttressed by administrative efforts concentrated on this area, may be a suitable instrument for achieving some of the ends of economic policy and distributive justice.

The types of limitations encountered in the under-developed economy may also suggest modification in the approach taken to taxation of wealth. A relatively refined form of wealth tax may be found in the net worth taxes of the Netherlands, Germany, and the Scandinavian countries. However, this requires skilled administration and conditions of compliance which generally are lacking in the underdeveloped countries. The appropriate action may be, not to abandon the attempt to tax wealth, but to determine whether a simpler tax on such outstanding sources of wealth as real property, or business assets, might yield a fairly good approximation to the refined net worth tax. If the correlation between real property holdings and net worth is reasonably close, and if the enforcement of a tax against the real property base is feasible, the indicated ends of tax policy may be served by a rough-hewn counterpart of the tax technique of the advanced country.

It is also worthy of note that the institutional limitations strike different types of taxes with substantially different force. Taxation of land, for example, is closely linked to systems of land tenure and to the agrarian structure as a whole. Consequently, techniques in land taxation are difficult to transfer from one country to another.

In contrast, transferability of techniques applicable to corporations is considerably greater. In this case, the financial institution itself—the corporate method of doing business—has been transferred to, and taken root in, the under-developed country in much the same form as in the developed country. By the same token, the common use of the corporate form may permit the imposition of substantially the same type of tax on agricultural corporations operating, e.g., large-scale sugar and rubber plantations, as is levied on corporations engaged in manufacturing or mineral extraction; here a considerable part of the corporation tax experience of advanced countries may be directly transferable to the less advanced countries.

In connexion with institutional barriers to the application of modern fiscal policy, it should not be forgotten that taxation is itself an instrument of social change. It does not need to wait passively until restrictive and binding social institutions are changed but can itself help hasten the change. For example, a tax reform which changes the relationship between landlords and tenants can be the beginning of an over-all land reform. Effective progressive taxes also can have significant distributive effects which will influence not only financial relationships but the social structure as such.

Some will argue that no matter how clearly the fiscal course toward economic development and stability may be charted, those in control of the governments in under-developed countries will not follow this course if it conflicts with their own interests. But in answer to this pessimistic appraisal, one may cite the concrete evidence of wide-spread willingness to entertain new ideas and advice as exemplified in the technical assistance programmes. One may also surmise that the pressure generated by growing aspirations of the peoples of the less advanced areas of the world and the growing realization on the part of the governing groups that their enlightened self-interest for the longer run lies in the direction of economic development have engendered a new receptivity to fiscal improvements and change. It may be concluded, then, that though the barriers are high, the portents are hopeful.

NOTES TO SELECTION 1

[1]Preamble of the Charter, paragraph 4.
[2]For detailed estimates and a discussion of the limitations of their use, see United Nations Statistical Papers, Series E, No. 1, *National and Per Capita Incomes in Seventy Countries*—1949 (ST/STAT/SER.E/1, September 20, 1950) and *National Income and its Distribution in Under-developed Countries* (ST/STAT/SER. E/3, October 9, 1951).
[3]Figures cited in E. M. Bernstein and I. G. Patel, "Inflation in Relation to Economic Development," *International Monetary Fund Staff Papers*, Vol. II, No. 3 (Washington, November, 1952), p. 364.
[4]*Ibid.*

[5]See, for example, the discussions by Ragnar Nurkse of Columbia University and John H. Adler of the International Bank for Reconstruction and Development in the *American Economic Review* (May, 1952), especially pp. 583 and 592–96; Ragnar Nurkse, *Problems of Capital Formation in Under-developed Countries* (Oxford, 1953); the discussion by Bernstein and Patel, "Inflation in Relation to Economic Development," pp. 393–95; various United Nations studies, e.g., *Domestic Financing of Economic Development*, United Nations Publications, Sales No.: 1951. II. B. 1, and *Economic Development in Selected Countries*, Vols. I and II, United Nations Publications, Sales Nos.: 1948. II. B. 1 and 1950. II. B. 1; and the recommendations of technical assistance missions as summarized in Part Three of the present report [not included in this volume].

[6]For a discussion of the relative usefulness of national income estimates and social accounting data in a setting of economic under-development, see Dudley Seers, "The Role of National Income Estimates in the Statistical Policy of an Underdeveloped Area," *The Review of Economic Studies*, Vol. XX, No. 3, (1953), pp. 159–68.

[7]Extensive discussions of the principles which govern the planning of development programmes and the participation of the government in them are contained in various United Nations studies, e.g., *Methods of Financing Economic Development in Under-developed Countries*, United Nations Publications, Sales No.: 1949. II. B. 4, *Domestic Financing of Economic Development, op. cit.; Measures for the Economic Development of Under-developed Countries*, United Nations Publications, Sales No.: 1951.II.B.2; and *Formulation and Economic Appraisal of Development Projects*, United Nations Publications, Sales No.: 1951. II. B. 4, Vols. I and II.

[8]United Nations Publications, Sales No.: 1951. XVI. 3. See also *Government Accounting and Budget Execution*, United Nations Publications, Sales No.: 1952. XVI. 3.

[9]*Budget Management, Report of the Workshop on Problems of Budgetary Classification and Management, Mexico City, 3–11 September 1953*, United Nations Publications, Sales No.: 1954. XVI. 2.

[10]See the recent article by John H. Adler, "Fiscal Problems in Economic Development," *Rapports pour le Congrès de Londres de l'Institut international de finances publiques* (Paris, 1951). In it, he concludes that for a number of under-developed countries, particularly in Latin America, "The share of the government sector in the gross national product, varies between 10 and 16 per cent and is in most countries not higher than 12 per cent."

[11]Bernstein and Patel, "Inflation in Relation to Economic Development," p. 395.

[12]See *Economic Development in Selected Countries, op. cit.*, Vols. I and II.

[13]See *Domestic Financing of Economic Development, op. cit.*, p. 44.

[14]Nurkse, *Problems of Capital Formation*, p. 151. A similar point is made in reference to the economies of western Europe since World War II in Howard S. Ellis, *The Economics of Freedom* (New York, 1950), p. 40.

[15]For a fuller development of this analysis, see Bernstein and Patel, "Inflation in Relation to Economic Development."

[16]See the discussion of capital gains taxation in Section C3 of Part Two below [not included in this volume].

[17]"There is no evidence that taxation in Colombia has tended to reduce the over-all level of investment either by cutting the supply of savings or by reducing investment returns and hence the willingness to invest." (International Bank for Reconstruction and Development, *The Basis of a Development Programme for Colombia*, Washington, 1950, IBRD Special Publication, Sales No.: IBRD. 1950. 2, p. 264.)

[18]See *Foreign Investment Laws and Regulations of the Countries of Asia and the Far East,* United Nations Publications, Sales No.: 1951. II. F. 1, p. 27, and *The Use of Taxation Techniques as Incentive to Private Investment in Far Eastern Countries,* United Nations document ECAFE/I and T/FED/19, September 8, 1953.

[19]*Report of the United Nations Mission of Technical Assistance to Bolivia,* United Nations Publications, Sales No.: 1951. II. B. 5.

[20]*International Financial Statistics,* International Monetary Fund, October, 1952, p. 140.

[21]*Report on Cuba, Findings and Recommendations by a Mission of the International Bank for Reconstruction and Development,* Washington, 1951, IBRD Special Publication, Sales No.: IBRD. 1951. 3, Chap. 40.

[22]H. D. Wallich and J. H. Adler, *Public Finance in a Developing Country, El Salvador, a Case Study* (Cambridge: Harvard University Press, 1951), p. 25.

[23]See *International Financial Statistics,* October, 1952, p. 46.

[24]*The Economic Development of Guatemala, Report of a Mission by the International Bank for Reconstruction and Development,* Washington, 1951, IBRD Special Publication, Sales No.: IBRD. 1951. 2, pp. 10 and 12.

[25]*International Financial Statistics,* October, 1952, pp. 66, 68, and 134.

[26]*Ibid.,* pp. 139, 151 and 161.

[27]See Frederick Benham, *The National Income of Malaya,* 1947–49 (Government Printing Office, Singapore, 1951).

[28]For a development of some of these points see E. M. Bernstein, "Some Economic Aspects of Multiple Exchange Rates," *International Monetary Fund Staff Papers,* Vol. I, No. 3 (Washington, September, 1950), and the section on taxation and public finance in the *Report of the United Nations Mission of Technical Assistance to Bolivia, op. cit.*

[29]See E. R. Schlesinger, *Multiple Exchange Rates and Economic Development,* (Princeton, 1952), p. 20.

[30]This view is reflected, for example, in the study, *Theoretical and Practical Problems of Economic Growth,* by the United Nations Economic Commission for Latin America (document E/CN.12/221 of May 18, 1951). It states (p. 43): "Certain productive activities, in which the level of productivity is lower than in others, may nevertheless be eminently advantageous, owing to the fact that they diminish a country's vulnerability to foreign fluctuations and contingencies." See also *The Economic Development of Latin America and its Principal Problems,* United Nations Publications, Sales No.: 1950. II. G. 2, Chap. VII.

[31]See *Budgetary Structure and Classification of Government Accounts,* United Nations Publications, Sales No.: 1951. XVI. 3, p. 12.

[32]For a discussion of both monetary and fiscal policy measures for economic stabilization in an under-developed economy, see Wallich and Adler, *Public Finance in a Developing Country: El Salvador, a Case Study.*

[33]Some statistical evidence on the commonly accepted conclusion that the inequalities are marked is provided in "National Income and its Distribution in Under-developed Countries."

[34]For a thorough discussion of this point, see Nurkse, *Problems of Capital Formation,* Chap. I, "The Size of the Market and the Inducement to Invest."

[35]Progressive taxation has, in fact, been put forward for several positive incentive uses in less advanced economies, e.g., in stimulating changes in land use and land tenure. Thus, where large landholdings are held idle or are under-cultivated, steeply graduated taxes on net wealth or property or land values may serve as an important stimulus to full utilization of the land. Progressive taxes on land value increments, or on capital gains, or on net income including capital gains have been used or recommended to discourage the holding of land for speculative purposes. Countries seeking to discourage accumulation or encourage subdivision of large landholdings may find graduated wealth or income taxes more attractive on

this account. Steeply progressive death duties can have this effect by forcing disposal of parts of large holdings in order to meet tax liabilities at death.

[36]This is an excerpt from an address by Dr. Richard Goode before the Forty-fourth Annual Conference of the National Tax Association, 1951, and is published in the *Proceedings* of that conference, pp. 212–22 [see selection 8 in this volume]. This particular quote is pp. 213–15.

[37]United Nations *Statistical Yearbook*, 1949–50, pp. 486–94. The figures are for various dates between 1930 and 1945 and refer to the population 7–10 years of age and over.

2

Fiscal Policy in
a Developing Country

by John H. Adler*

I. INTRODUCTION

THE bibliographical note appended to the last chapter in W. A. Lewis' *The Theory of Economic Growth* ends with the following sentence: "There is regrettably very little theoretical discussion of the fiscal problems of underdeveloped countries."[1] There is ample reason for this deficiency, which has not disappeared since Lewis' book was first published. The fiscal system and the fiscal policy of any country reflect its citizens' general economic views and aspirations, which it may have in common with other countries, or may be peculiar to it; but they also are the result of the country's social and cultural institutions, its resource endowment, the structure of its economy, the distribution of income, and the seat of political power, in a configuration which is inevitably unique. Any general discussion of fiscal problems is thus bound to be of limited usefulness since just below the surface of the broadest generalizations lurks a multitude of specific exceptions to the general rules. Nevertheless, some principles of fiscal policy which are pertinent to low income countries

*This paper was presented at the Round Table on Economic Development with Special Reference to East Asia, April 2–9, 1960, at Gamagori, Japan. Copyright International Economic Association. It is also included in *Economic Development with Special Reference to East Asia* (London: Macmillan, 1964), pp. 287–315; it is reprinted here with the kind permission of the author and the International Economic Association.

The views expressed in this paper are those of the author and not necessarily those of the International Bank for Reconstruction and Development—Dr. Adler was serving as director of the Bank's Economic Development Institute in 1964.

The assistance of Dr. H. H. H. Eschenberg in the preparation of the statistical tables is gratefully acknowledged.

endeavouring to advance economically at a faster pace than in the past may be derived from observation and speculation.

This paper deals with various aspects of fiscal policy under four headings. After a note on empirical evidence some general principles of government finance relevant to developing countries are presented. The next two sections discuss the revenue structure, and comment on the financing of public capital expenditure, while the last part deals with the role of deficit financing of government expenditures in low income countries.

II. NOTE ON EMPIRICAL EVIDENCE

Any attempt to present the fiscal data of a number of countries on a uniform basis runs into conceptual and statistical difficulties which can be overcome only at great expense of time and effort.[2] And even the most perfect international comparison does not prove very much, since what may be the best possible fiscal arrangement for one country may be an unworkable scheme for another. Moreover, there is a difference between the observed pattern of revenue and expenditure and what might be conceived, on the basis of some criteria, as the most desirable pattern. The data themselves do not reveal anything about the reasons for the difference between the observed and the desirable.

Nevertheless, the fiscal data which have been assembled in the appended tables permit some general observations about the major characteristics of the fiscal structure of low income countries, as compared to those of advanced countries, the differences in coverage, classification, etc., of the data notwithstanding.

Level of Revenue and Expenditure

The ratios of public revenue and public expenditure to the gross national product are substantially higher in advanced than in low income countries. There are, of course, wide variations among the countries shown within the two categories of "low income" and "high income" countries in Table 1; the variations are commented on below. But in spite of the differences from country to country and the limited comparability of the data, it is obviously significant that the unweighted average of the ratios of revenue to G.N.P. for all low income countries amounts to 14.7 per cent while that for high income countries is 22.0 per cent. The corresponding average ratios for expenditure are 16.1 per cent and 22.3 per cent. The averages include revenue and expenditure of state and local authorities only for those countries for which they are separately shown in the table. Since state and local expenditures are by and large more significant in high income countries than in low income countries, a more complete coverage of revenue and expenditure of authorities other than the central government would probably result in an even wider difference.[3]

An explanation for the differences in the ratios of public revenue and expenditure to G.N.P. must be sought both on the revenue and expenditure side. As to revenue, it is quite clear that in the low income countries the scope for taxation is smaller than in advanced countries; later on we shall have more to say on this. On the expenditure side, the difference is only in part accounted for by defence expenditures, which are considerably larger in advanced than in low income countries (Table 1). But, with the exception of those of the United States, they do not exceed 7 per cent of G.N.P. in the advanced countries compared with an average of 2.9 per cent for low income countries.[4] There is also considerable evidence suggesting that a part of the difference in public expenditure in low income and high income countries not accounted for by defence outlays is due to transfer expenditures, mainly for welfare purposes. The large amounts of transfer payments included in the public expenditures of high income countries are a reflection of the high income of these countries; they are something which less developed countries have to forgo as much as possible, and can forgo, because the social arrangements of family ties, community relations, etc., are such that the need for public welfare expenditures is smaller.

But even if transfer payments and defence expenditures account for a significant part of the difference between the ratios of government revenue and expenditure to G.N.P. in advanced and less developed countries, it may well be argued that government expenditure in low income countries is too small and that attempts should be made to increase it. The argument rests on the proposition that the unit cost of government is likely to be higher in low income than in advanced countries for a wide variety of government services. For example, in a country in which the literacy rate is low, a person qualified as a school teacher or government clerk is bound to command a higher pay relative to the average income than in advanced countries—even if by the standards of high income countries the salaries of teachers and clerks in low income countries appear to be ridiculously low. The unit cost is also likely to be higher for other kinds of expenditure—e.g. uniforms for military and police personnel, equipment for hospitals, government offices, workshops of technical service, etc., cost more or less the same in low income and high income countries and therefore require a relatively higher outlay in proportion to G.N.P. in low income countries.

Three conclusions may be drawn from these observations. First, the need for additional public revenue in low income countries is not necessarily a reflection of the need for economic development expenditure but is due in part also to the higher unit cost of public expenditure. Second, because of that, and because of the limitations on the ability to raise revenue, every effort should be made to avoid "frills" in public expenditures. Third, although the governments of many low income countries are constantly under pressure to expand the scope of their activities, the high unit cost of functions which only public authorities can perform (such as the maintenance of law and order, the provision of educational facilities, public health, and sanitation) are strong reasons for limiting the scope of government operation.

A comparison of the revenue and expenditure of low income with those of high income countries inevitably leads to the question, "What constitutes the "proper" level of government revenue?" Some experts have pointed out that the increase in the share of government revenue and expenditure in national production is a fairly recent development and that in countries in which the share of government in the national product is low, it is still appreciably higher than the ratios of government revenue to national income which prevailed a hundred years ago in countries which are now advanced.[5] But it seems quite inadmissible to conclude therefrom that low income countries nowadays should get along, or, at any rate, should attempt to get along with a level of revenue comparable to that of the United Kingdom or the United States a hundred years ago. To the contrary; it may well be argued that government expenditure is inadequate in countries in which the ratio of government revenue and expenditure is less than 10 per cent of G.N.P., and the optimum ratio of revenue to G.N.P. for low income countries may be substantially above that figure, notwithstanding the limitations on the organizational and administrative ability of the governments of many low income countries to make effective use of fiscal resources.

Revenue and Foreign Investment

The figures shown in the appended tables indicate clearly that, from a fiscal point of view, countries which are able to attract foreign investment in large-scale enterprises stand to derive considerable fiscal benefits from it. The share of government revenue in the national product of countries with large oil investment (Iraq, Venezuela), foreign-owned mining operations (Chile, Peru), and foreign investment in agriculture (Ceylon, Costa Rica, Guatemala, Panama) is substantially higher than in most other low income countries. The ratio of tax revenue to income of these companies is a multiple of the national average; therefore the burden of taxation on all other income is correspondingly smaller. Thus, from a fiscal point of view, foreign investment is to the host country's advantage, except for the not too likely event that it necessitates government expenditures which would not be required if there were no foreign investment.

Limitations of Direct Taxation

One difference between the revenues of low income and high income countries which is clearly revealed by the figures shown in Table 2 is the significantly lower proportion of total revenue derived from direct taxes in the low income countries. The reason for the lesser reliance on direct taxes in low income countries is the fact that direct taxes in general and personal income taxes in particular are *par excellence* suitable for countries with a fairly high level of economic advancement; more will be said on this subject in Part IV of this paper. The lesser role played by direct taxes in low income countries would become even clearer if the imposts on foreign enterprises could be shown separately.

Taxation of Foreign Trade

The limited use of direct taxes in low income countries is offset to a considerable extent by heavy reliance on exports and imports as a tax basis. The low income countries shown in Table 2 derive almost 30 per cent of their total revenue from taxes on exports and imports, while in advanced countries the comparable figure is 11.5 per cent.[6] A number of public finance experts have expressed misgivings about the use of taxes on exports and imports as a major instrument of taxation. Actually a fairly good case can be made for the extensive use of both export and import taxes.[7]

Pattern of Public Expenditure

While it appears possible to obtain some general impressions from a comparison of the revenue data of a number of countries with low and with high incomes, comparison of the expenditure pattern does not lead to useful generalizations.[8] To some extent the apparent lack of significant similarities and systematic dissimilarities in the pattern of expenditures is due to the vagueness and limited comparability of statistical classifications. But even if these limitations of information could be eliminated, it seems likely that the expenditure pattern would reflect differences in resource endowment, the structure of the economy, social institutions, etc., which could not readily be taken into account in a comparative study of public expenditures. Therefore it seems preferable to confine the discussion of expenditures to some general observations on capital expenditure which do not imply an even approximate similarity of the over-all expenditure structure.[9]

III. Some Principles of Public Finance

Challenge of Basic Principles

Some of the basic ideas which, in the last fifty years, had been evolved as "principles of public finance" have in recent years been questioned with increasing frequency, and challenged as to their general validity. This process of reappraisal of what was considered a generally accepted body of ideas was the logical consequence of the introduction (or, more exactly, reintroduction) of dynamic considerations into economic thinking. Three propositions in particular have been seriously challenged and, as a result, undergone considerable modification; or, to put it more cautiously, their general validity has been challenged with some success.[10]

The first principle is that the only equitable form of taxation is a tax, or a system of taxes, which is at least moderately, but preferably steeply, progressive. This principle, the fiscal application of the concept of the diminishing marginal utility of income, has been challenged on the ground that the growth of an economy requires a certain rate of capital formation and that at least private capital formation depends largely on the concentration of resources in the hands of a limited number of economic units in the system. A related argument against a progressive system of taxation is the contention that progressive taxation has serious disincentive effects on productive effort in general, and entrepreneurial willingness to take risks in particular.

True, the proponents of progressive taxation always were aware of the limits which the requirements of capital formation and economic incentives impose on the principle of progressiveness. But the renewed emphasis on capital formation as one of the basic determinants of the rate of economic growth has presumably weakened the case for a progressive tax structure, or at least thrown some doubt on the general applicability of progressive taxation to all countries in all conditions.

The second proposition which has been underlying most discussions of government finance was the at least tacit assertion that all 'normal' government expenditures were exhaustive in the sense that they did not produce any benefits comparable to the benefits which could be derived from private expenditures of the same amounts, either for consumption or investment. Only in the case of capital expenditure for self-liquidating projects was it admitted that a return for the economy as a whole could be expected.[11] The result of this way of looking at public expenditure was that it became an objective of public policy to keep government expenditure to a minimum; the smaller the share of government in the national product, the better for the economy.

The desirability of keeping government expenditure to a minimum at all times has been challenged on two grounds. In the first place, it has been argued that under some conditions the economy stands to benefit from an increase in public expenditures. For instance, even such "wasteful" outlays as those for the maintenance of law and order or for public buildings may have a favourable effect on the efficiency of the economy as a whole and enhance total output.

But even if in a particular period a certain government outlay does not produce any measurable benefits it still may be preferable for the economy as a whole to incur the expenditure if it will yield benefits in the future.[12] For instance, outlays on primary education may be completely "wasteful" in the sense that they do not immediately contribute to the efficiency of the economy, or in any other way enhance its growth, but the advantages of a literate labour force and, more generally, of a literate electorate may assert themselves in the long run and thus bring about a situation in which the advantages of increased outlays become greater than the disadvantages of an increased tax burden.

The third basic proposition of public finance which has been completely modified in the last twenty-five years is the stipulation that all expenditures other than those for self-liquidating projects must be paid for by current receipts, except in unusual circumstances such as war or a natural disaster. The sanctity of the balanced budget has been challenged by what may be termed the Keynesian principles of public finance. They suggest that within the limits imposed by balance of payments considerations the Government has the task of maintaining a level of economic activity close to full employment, and impose upon the Government the obligation to supplement by public outlays in excess of public revenues the expenditures of the private sector wherever the latter are inadequate. The logical corollary of this Keynesian concept of deficit financing is, of course, the accumulation of Treasury surpluses and the retirement of the public debt to the banking system, whenever total outlays of the private sector threaten to exceed the supply of goods and services.

There is no need in the context of this paper to comment at length on the Keynesian policy prescriptions and on their complex relations with monetary policy. It is worthy of note, however, that of the three challenges to classical principles of public finance the third has received in low income countries a great deal more attention than the first two although, as will be argued below, it is much less relevant for under-developed countries than the first two.

The Burden of Taxation and the Benefits of Expenditure: The Production Principle of Public Finance

The discussion of the "classical" principles of public finance and their recent modifications form an essential background against which the key issues of fiscal policy of low income countries can be sketched. The fiscal dilemma of less developed countries can be presented in its most general form as follows: Taxes on consumption cannot be increased because the average level of consumption is so low that even a temporary further lowering of consumption levels is socially and politically unbearable. Taxes on savings, through the imposition of progressive taxes affecting primarily the income of the well-to-do, are undesirable because they may lead to a decrease in the rate of private, and perhaps of total, capital formation. Therefore total tax revenue cannot be increased.

A resolution of this dilemma can be attempted on two grounds. In countries in which *per capita* income is rising it may be sufficient to increase taxes only to such an extent as to limit the *growth* of *per capita* consumption. If a tax increase does not adversely affect the rate of private capital formation and if the additional revenue is used to enhance the rate of economic growth, the economy as a whole benefits. The size of the tax increase is, of course, limited by the amount by which *per capita* income grows. It must be zero in countries in which the growth of aggregate income does not exceed population growth. Moreover, increased taxes on consumption are difficult in countries in which income growth is concentrated in one sector, or a group of sectors, while income stagnates in the rest of the economy. In that case an increase in taxation aiming at a curtailment of over-all consumption growth inevitably implies an absolute curtailment of consumption in some parts of the economy and may therefore become socially and politically unacceptable.

The argument for an increase in taxation can be greatly strengthened, however, by bringing into it the increase in public expenditure which is associated with the tax increase, if the additional public expenditure results in benefits greater than, or at least equal to, the burden of the additional tax, and if the incidence of the additional tax can be matched to the greatest extent possible by the incidence of additional benefits.

The relation between the burden of additional taxes and the benefits of additional public expenditures is not just a convenient piece of abstract reasoning but is likely to be of considerable practical significance. An increase in taxation of, say, agricultural production may be expected to affect adversely the level of agricultural output. However, the disincentive effect of increased taxes may be offset, or more than offset, by the stimulating effects of public expenditure on, say, farm-to-market roads which lower the cost of transport and thus leave the agricultural producer better off.

In the preceding example the incidence of increased taxes and that of increased benefits is on the same sector of the economy. The justification of an increase in taxes and a corresponding increase in expenditures becomes more uncertain, if the incidence of the tax and that of the benefits is on different groups or sectors in the economy. But the basic principle, that an increase in taxation is justified as long as the favourable effects on output (and indirectly on material well-being) of increased public services exceed the adverse effects of the tax increase, is the same.

The practical conclusion for the public finances of low income countries to be drawn from these considerations is, that the limit of public expenditure does not only depend on the ability of the public authorities to obtain revenue without curtailing consumption of low income groups and without adversely affecting private capital formation, but on the "productivity" of public expenditure in terms of increased productive efficiency and improved economic organization.

This "productivity" of additional public expenditure in turn depends to a considerable extent on the efficiency with which services are produced. The question of the efficiency in providing public services will be further explored in the next section; only one point needs stressing here. The dilemma, besetting many low income tax countries, that on the one hand production in all sectors of the economy suffers through the lack of education of the working population, while on the other hand Government does not have the means of providing such essential services as a modicum of general and technical education, or public health and medical facilities, disappears if the benefits of such services, which only Government can adequately provide, are properly appraised against the economic cost of additional taxes.

However, if the overriding objective of economic policy of a low income country is to obtain a high rate of growth of *per capita* production and income, it must also be realized that some types of public services are more conducive to increased output than others. Social welfare expenditures, for the aged, the sick, the destitute, though good and desirable on humanitarian grounds, and undoubtedly providing important benefits to the immediate beneficiaries, do not contribute to productive efficiency, and do not provide incentives to production, while the taxes, necessary to finance them, have inevitably some adverse effects on production. Therefore, low income countries are well advised to resist the tendency of emulating, on grounds of social justice, the scope of social welfare expenditures which has in recent years characterized the public expenditure pattern of advanced countries.

In more general terms, in the light of the growth objectives of low income countries, a consideration of the incidence of the tax burden and of the benefits of public expenditure leads to what might be called the Production Principle of public finance, which may be stated as follows: An increase in public expenditure is justified, as long as the stimulating effects of additional expenditure on productive effort, including capital formation, exceed the disincentive effects of additional taxes. The principle is based in part on the assumption that the most important factor enhancing the material welfare of the economy and its constituent units is the growth of total economic production;[13] it is a substitute for the static principle that because of the declining marginal utility of money an increase in welfare can be most readily achieved through a more even distribution of income, including the redistribution of income through the fiscal system.

The Redistribution of Income through the Fiscal System

It is clear that there is a close connexion between the objective of production growth and capital formation. Since in low income countries the level of private capital formation is generally determined by the income accruing to the uppermost income groups, particularly the small class of entrepreneurs, a redistribution of income through the fiscal system in favour of lower income groups and at the expense of the high income groups runs counter to the production principle of public finance, because such a redistribution affects adversely the rate of private savings and private investment, and thus conflicts with the growth objective. A certain degree of redistribution of income through the fiscal system is unavoidable, because, as indicated above, for social and humanitarian reasons a part of government expenditures has to be devoted to providing services which primarily benefit the lowest income groups without significantly affecting their contribution to total production. But, aside from that, there is no reason why the pattern of public expenditures in low income countries should be such as to result in a redistribution of income. To the contrary: if the pattern of government expenditures is designed to support the objective of production growth, it inevitably brings a large share of benefits to the entrepreneurial class. The progressive incidence of benefits—particularly of expenditures for social overhead capital but also of current "development" expenditures—is likely to offset partially, or completely, the progressive incidence of the tax system.

Thus the incidence of the benefits of public expenditures may justify some degree of progressiveness in the tax structure. But because of the importance of private capital formation in the growth process, it appears desirable to keep the degree of progressiveness moderate.

Limits of Public Expenditure: Deepening vs. *Widening of Public Operations*

The production principle of public finance not only determines the optimum level of public revenue and expenditure, but also has a direct bearing on their composition. Economists, concerned with the purely economic aspect of developments, frequently overlook that it is not only the level of production which is under-developed, but that in many low income countries administrative organization, technical competence, managerial knowledge, etc., are also under-developed, both in the public and in the private sector. Many low income countries have no roads, or bad roads, because the Government has no funds to build them, but often also because it has failed to develop an effective system of building and properly maintaining them. Educational facilities are inadequate because teacher training is inadequate; little attention is given to adapting the school curriculum to the country's specific needs. The financial administration of public enterprise is deficient, because not enough persons have been trained in accounting and bookkeeping; the goods and services which they provide are deficient because production techniques, quality controls, etc., are deficient.

The efficiency with which government services are provided is, of course, an important factor determining their unit cost, or, conversely, given an amount of public revenue to finance public services, the efficiency with which the services are provided determines their volume and their quality.

The low level of productive efficiency is not confined to the public sector but exists in the private sector as well. However, it is an essential characteristic of the working of a competitive system of enterprise, that in time inefficiency is self-correcting; the most inefficient productive units are eliminated by price and quality competition within the country or from abroad. But this mechanism does not operate over a wide range of public services which are produced by the Government only, and which are not sold and not subject to the market test. It is therefore of paramount importance for the Government to strive constantly to improve the efficiency of its operations and, if necessary, to seek foreign assistance for this purpose.[14] In order to attain improved efficiency, it is desirable for the Government to confine its range of activities to the provision of such services as cannot be, or are not likely to be, provided by the private sector. Government can contribute most to the growth of the economy by extending its operations in depth, not by widening the scope of its activities.

This conclusion runs counter to the contention that the Government of a low income country must make itself responsible for providing such goods and services which private enterprise is unable or unwilling to provide at a particular time, because the private sector either lacks the necessary technical knowledge and organizational ability, or because it lacks the capital resources necessary for those undertakings for which large-scale operations and, therefore, heavy initial capital outlays are essential (e.g. steel mills). The argument for the Government to take on the task of producing goods and services which private enterprises are unable or unwilling to produce, because they lack technical competence, is based on the assumption that somehow Government can acquire the missing competence more readily than a private firm.

Except in the most exceptional circumstances, which are hard to conceive, this assumption appears unwarranted. In most cases it is likely to be more efficient if the public authorities assist in bringing the missing technological experience from abroad to cooperate with private producers, and to provide such tax incentives and, if necessary, subsidies to private enterprise to overcome the reluctance to take risks in a hitherto untried line of production.

If private initiative for the production of some important goods and services, or for the exploitation of some natural resources, is not forthcoming, because the initial capital requirements are beyond the limits available to a private firm, then it may be preferable for the Government to lend assistance through the provision of funds (e.g. through a development bank supported by the Treasury), or a guarantee, than to enter the field itself as an entrepreneur.

There may be exceptions to this "rule of reluctance" for the Government to expand the scope of its operations into pursuits which can be left to the private sector. These exceptions may be particularly important in the field of public utilities where the argument that competition cures and prevents inefficiency does not apply because of the monopolistic or quasi-monopolistic attributes of utilities. But even in that case it must be realized that the losses of public undertakings are not a necessary cost of economic development, but that they are likely to be detrimental to the development process.[15]

IV. REVENUE STRUCTURE FOR ECONOMIC GROWTH

On the basis of what has been said in the preceding sections it is possible to develop some general notions about the most desirable characteristics of the revenue structure of low income countries, and to indicate what role should be assigned to various taxes. The tax structure must of course reflect the structure of the economy, its pattern of production and income distribution. But despite the wide variations in institutions, endowment, and economic structure among low income countries some meaningful general observations pertaining to the major types of taxes can be made.

Income Taxes

The role of income taxes, particularly of taxes based on global personal income, is necessarily more limited in low income countries than in advanced countries. In the first place, the main advantage of personal income taxes, i.e. that they make a high degree of progressivity possible, is, as has been argued before, much less important in low income countries than in high income countries. In the second place, as has been pointed out in an excellent paper by R. Goode, the effective administration of an income tax, covering a wide range of income and a large number of payers, is exceedingly difficult in low income countries.[16] An income tax can be used as a mass tax only if a large share of total income is paid out as salaries and wages, if a large proportion of income is recorded in some form, if the population is literate, and so on; these conditions are rarely fulfilled in low income countries. Conversely, an income tax is a poor instrument of taxation for agricultural producers and shopkeepers, who account for a large share of total income in many low income countries.

Nevertheless, there is a place for income taxes in the revenue structure of low income countries. The conditions making income taxes effective are likely to prevail in the highest income brackets. For them some degree of progressiveness appears desirable, or, because of the benefits which they derive from government services, at least not objectionable;[17] in the absence of some progressive taxes at the highest income levels, the incidence of total taxation may even become regressive, a clearly undesirable situation.

In a number of low income countries, particularly in Latin America, attempts have been made to expand the scope of taxes on income through the imposition of flat rate taxes on salaries and wages, dividends, interest, rents, etc. The difficulty with such schedular taxes is that they are bound to lead to a shifting from the income recipient to the source of income (e.g. from the wage earner to the enterprise employing him) and thus becomes a tax on production. In general, it is probably to a low income country's advantage to concentrate on improving the administration of income taxes affecting a limited number of taxpayers before embarking on the much more difficult task of broadening the tax base and increasing the number of persons subject to the tax.[18]

Real Property and Land Taxes

There is a good deal of evidence that suggests that real property and land taxes have been neglected as revenue sources in many low income countries.[19] The most important reasons for it are: (*a*) the political influence of landowners and owners of urban property; (*b*) the erosion of the tax base through inflation and the failure to correct the excessively low valuation bases through higher rates; and (*c*) the difficulty of making property assessments and keeping them up to date.

This neglect is the more regrettable since real property taxes are in some respects superior to taxes on income. Since the tax liability of the property owner is based on the value of the property, and not on the income derived from it, the tax does not vary with income and does not have the same disincentive effect as income taxes, and particularly high income taxes, have on productive efforts. It has even been suggested that property taxes be used as a means of insuring the efficient use of the property, either by imposing higher rates on property that is left uncultivated,[20] or by using the value of the property in its most efficient use as a basis for the tax assessment, with the value of the improvements not included in the valuation.[21] But, except in unusual circumstances, serious objections on grounds of equity may be raised against the method of "unimproved valuation."

It is frequently charged that property taxes are essentially undesirable because they are almost inevitably proportional. In the case of low income countries this deficiency—if it is one—can be overcome by exempting from the tax property below a certain value. The exemption can be devised in such a way as to spare small peasant holdings. This would also make the administration of the tax much easier.

The other shortcoming of property taxation, i.e. the difficulty of surveying and valuing property, should not be an unsurmountable obstacle. Recent technological advances of aerial photography make cadastral surveys much less expensive and much less time consuming. The uniformity of land use and crop patterns in low income countries also helps to simplify valuation.

Consumption Taxes

Because of the restricted role of income and related direct taxes, and the impossibility of obtaining more than a limited amount of revenue from property taxes, a large part of the government revenue of low income countries must inevitably consist of taxes on consumption. The disadvantage of consumption taxes, particularly of those falling on commodities and services with a high income elasticity, is their disincentive effect on productive effort. But, on balance, this disincentive effect is likely to be smaller than in the case of income taxes, which, as has been pointed out, have the additional disadvantage of also affecting private savings.

Moreover, the traditional objection against consumption taxes, i.e. that their incidence is likely to be regressive, does not apply to low income countries. The report of the Indian Taxation Enquiry Commission, and other studies concerned with the tax structure of low income countries,[22] have found that the incidence of consumption taxes is moderately progressive over a fairly wide range of income groups. This is due to the differences in consumption patterns at various income levels. At the lowest level, which prevails mainly in backward rural areas, a high proportion of consumption is consumption of subsistence production which inevitably escapes taxation. With rising income levels, encountered in more advanced rural areas and among urban dwellers, a growing proportion of consumption consists of purchased goods other than staple goods. While for reasons of equity the latter remain untaxed, the former can be taxed through excise levies or import duties.

Import duties are bound to be important in the taxation of consumption because in low income countries the income elasticity of demand for imports is high, and the collection of revenue is particularly easy in the case of imports. The imposition of high duties on "non-essential" imports may have the undesirable side effect of according protection to the domestic production of the same non-essentials, but this can be easily avoided by matching the duty by a domestic excise tax.[23]

For reasons of administrative ease it is usually advisable to devise excise duties on domestic products in such a way as to collect them, like import duties, on the narrowest point in the flow of the taxed commodities. This means that the best place to tax manufactured goods is at the plant, and agricultural products at the processing stage (e.g. cotton at the gin, oil seeds at the oil presses). Sales taxes imposed at the retail stages and turnover taxes, on the other hand, are virtually ruled out in low income countries because of the absence of sales records and cash registers.

It is impossible to indicate in general terms which commodities should be subjected to consumption taxes and which should remain untaxed. Only two broadly applicable rules may be mentioned. One is that the coverage of consumption taxes should be fairly wide because the narrower the range of coverage, the greater the avoidability. For reasons of equity, and, in the case of countries with a significant proportion of subsistence agriculture, for reasons of administrative ease as well, staple goods should not be taxed. But it would be bad practice to confine consumption taxes to "luxuries" and "non-essentials."

The second rule, which is in part a restatement of the first, is that the best revenue yield will come from commodities with a high income and a low price elasticity of demand. The combination of high income and low price elasticities explains the very sharp increases in the yield of liquor and tobacco taxes in low income countries, particularly in Latin America, in the post-war period.

Export Taxes

One of the most significant differences between the revenue structure of high income and low income countries is the virtually complete absence of export taxes in the former, and their frequency and importance in the latter. Export taxes are a source of large revenues in low income countries because they are easy to collect and because they frequently constitute a downward extension of income taxes which could not be accomplished by any other method. They are a particularly useful tax device in countries where production for export is carried on by a large number of agricultural producers.[24]

Export taxes have two disadvantages. First, they add to the instability of revenues because export proceeds, which form the tax basis, are likely to fluctuate more than total income. This volatility of yield which also characterizes import duties—they vary with the level of imports which in turn depends on the level of export earnings—is no overriding argument against the use of export taxes; but, as will be explained in the last section, it requires a fair degree of fiscal discipline to offset it.

The second drawback is more serious. Export taxes have a disincentive effect on export production, and may result in a shift of productive effort from export commodities to production for the home market. The strength of the disincentive effects depends on the responsiveness of the producers to economic incentives (and disincentives) and on the availability and attractiveness of alternatives to export production, including the alternative of a decline in productive effort.

The high degree of responsiveness to discriminatory treatment explains for example the decline in export production of Argentina in the first ten years after World War II, while the limited response, and the absence of alternative production opportunities explain, at least in part, the continued growth of export production of Nigeria in the face of exceedingly heavy export taxes and related levies on export producers.[25]

The possibility of adverse effects on the balance of payments must be taken into account in the designing of export taxes. The most effective way of doing this is to devise a sliding scale of rates which vary more than proportionately with export prices. An incidental, but exceedingly useful, effect of sliding rates is the dampening of fluctuations of receipts of the export producers.

In a number of low income countries export duties have been used instead of, or in addition to, taxes on the income of large-scale enterprises producing export commodities. The case for the use of export taxes in these circumstances is much weaker than in the case of an export sector consisting of a large number of small-scale producers. If exports are produced by large-scale enterprises it may be preferable to rely on direct taxes.[26]

V. Financing Capital Expenditure

The most important reason why in many low income countries public revenues fall short of the level which would conform to the production principle of public finance, is the large amounts of revenue required to finance capital expenditures. The need to finance capital expenditures arises for several reasons. First, although inefficiency and administrative difficulties impose limitations on the desirable level of public expenditures, there remains a volume of public capital expenditure which is an essential prerequisite for economic growth. Second, even if for reasons of efficiency it is inadvisable for the Government to proceed with certain investments, the Government may have to provide financial resources if an undertaking is to be owned and operated in the private sector.[27] And third, the volume of private savings which can be channelled through the sale of government securities into the public sector is in most low income countries small, sometimes because the total volume of transferable savings is small, and sometimes because inflationary price movements, or the fear of such movements, prevent the establishment of a market for government securities.

The resources of the governments of low income countries are frequently supplemented by grants and loans from abroad. But grant funds for economic development expenditures can take care only of a small fraction of the public capital expenditures, and loans are often limited to the cost of the import content of capital expenditures. Moreover, the debt service burden of foreign loans on the balance of payments also restricts the amount of foreign loans that a government can prudently incur. Therefore, at least a part, and in most low income countries a major part, of capital expenditures must be financed through tax receipts.

Full-cost Pricing

The problem of finding financial resources to pay for the expansion of economic overhead facilities can be greatly alleviated by systematically applying the principle of full-cost pricing to state enterprises.[28] As used here, the term full-cost pricing means that the prices charged for the goods and services sold by state enterprises must yield receipts large enough to cover operating cost, the cost of replacing capital (depreciation charges at replacement cost), and a reasonable return on the capital. Depreciation reserves and capital returns together will in most instances go a long way toward meeting the cost of modernization and expansion so that the claims on the Treasury (and perhaps on borrowings from abroad) for these purposes can be kept to reasonable amounts.

The principle of full-cost pricing should be applied not only to public enterprises which are revenue-producing (e.g. railroads, power companies, ports), but also to economic overhead facilities which provide free services (e.g. roads). In the case of the latter, the revenue which is attributable to the public facilities should be large enough to pay for them; for example, gasoline taxes, motor vehicle licence fees and other taxes attributable to motor transportation, taken together, should yield enough revenue to pay for the average annual cost of the highway system. In some instances it may be difficult to determine accurately the increase in revenue which is attributable to the services provided by public facilities; multi-purpose projects in particular, providing a variety of benefits and giving rise to some cost other than capital and operating cost proper, are likely to have revenue consequences which are difficult to assess.

Revenue Feed-back

But leaving aside these difficulties, which are theoretical-conceptual as well as statistical,[29] it is clear that in low income countries the capital projects with the higher direct or indirect revenue yields are preferable to those with lower yields, the presumption being that the level of the revenues accruing to the public enterprise or the Government is more or less proportionate to the net social yield of any given project. But even if the social yield of a project A with a low revenue "feed-back" may be somewhat higher than of a project B with a high revenue "feed-back," project B may still be preferable to project A if the revenue is conceived of as available for further public capital expenditure—or, more generally, for further expenditures enhancing economic advancement—while a large part of the social yield of project A does not accrue to the Government and only leads to an increase of private consumption.

It is quite conceivable and even likely that exceptions to the general rule of maximum revenue "feed-back" (which may be thought of as supplementing the principle of full-cost pricing, particularly for the selection of new projects) will occur and will have to be allowed for.

But it should be clear that the principle runs counter to the view, frequently held in low income countries, that low-priced public services, especially the provision of cheap public power, are a prerequisite of economic development. The view implies that the external economies which accrue to the users of public services at economic prices do not offer enough inducement to private producers, and should therefore be extended further so as to "externalize" a larger part of the social return.[30] Related to this position is the suggestion, implied in the concept of the "big push," that in low income countries social overhead facilities should be built ahead of demand, in order to have the greatest possible growth stimulating effect.[31]

If "building ahead of demand" means that the appraisal of a public investment project should take account of the growth of demand in the immediate future, rather than the present level of demand, nobody can seriously question the proposition. But if it means that economic overhead facilities should be provided even if their discounted future returns to the Government fall short of their total cost, including discounted future cost, then again a subsidization scheme, which conflicts with the rule of maximum revenue feed-back, is implied.

The difference between the "big push" strategy and the position taken here may be conveniently stated in these terms: the "big push" strategy stresses the importance of ample economic overhead facilities as indispensable for economic advancement, but is not concerned with the fiscal problem which it implies; the position taken here, while accepting the indispensability of adequate economic overhead facilities, stresses the importance of assuring a *continuous* flow of fiscal resources into the financing of economic overheads. In other words, it is based on the belief that it is more important to assure an *adequate* supply of power, transportation, etc., at an *economic* price than to provide economic overhead services at a subsidized price, but run the risk that an adequate supply cannot be sustained.

VI. Deficit Financing

So far the exposition has proceeded almost entirely on the assumption that total government revenue equals total expenditure; only in connexion with the financing of capital expenditures was the possibility mentioned that the tax revenue may be supplemented by borrowing internally or from abroad.

There is no need to labour the proposition that an increase in aggregate expenditure—presumably by an excess of government expenditure over receipts—in order to increase the volume of effective demand is not a policy prescription applicable to low income countries. This is so because the constellation of under-utilized resources does not permit an immediate response to an increased level of total demand; the response is likely to be slow and sluggish.[32] Instead of pursuing this argument further it may be more useful to indicate the conditions determining the extent to which the governments of low income countries *can* incur public expenditures in excess of public revenue.

Two methods of deficit financing may be mentioned as not likely to cause inflationary pressures although they result in an increase in the money supply and aggregate expenditure. Some increase in the money supply is necessary in order to meet the liquidity needs of a growing economy. The increased liquidity can be provided in part by deficit financing, i.e. the purchase of securities by the banking system from the Government. But in most instances it would be inappropriate for the Government to pre-empt the entire increase because such a policy may impede the functioning of the private sector, even if the increase in government expenditure leads to an increase of bank deposits and makes a secondary credit expansion possible.

Another possibility for the Government to increase the money supply through a budget deficit exists in low income countries where a part of the economy is not completely monetized. In such a country it is likely that each year another segment of the subsistence sector, where little or no money is used, becomes "converted" to holding money. If this happens the Government can again through a cash deficit claim a share of the permissible increase in the money supply.

But aside from these two limited possibilities, governments of low income countries can incur a deficit only when the deficit does not lead to an increase in the money supply. The money supply will not increase (*a*) if the private sector purchases securities from the public sector; (*b*) if government securities are sold abroad, or resources are obtained from abroad through grants; (*c*) if an increase of bank credit to the public sector is offset by a decrease of bank credit to the private sector; and (*d*) if the sales proceeds of government securities to the banking system are used to purchase goods from abroad.

Possibilities (*a*) and (*b*) have already been mentioned in the preceding section; it has also been indicated that the total flow of funds from these sources is in most countries likely to be limited.[33] Case (*c*) is of interest as an alternative to "pure" deficit financing.

If in a low income country it is considered essential that public expenditure be increased beyond ordinary revenue (and receipts from domestic and foreign borrowing), then it is preferable to attempt to determine the impact on the private sector of the Government's increased claim on resources beforehand by curtailing the volume of financial resources available to the private sector than by letting the price increases, caused by the increased money supply, determine the impact. In other words, if resources are to be "squeezed" from the private sector for the benefit of the public sector, it is better to have the squeeze accomplished by credit policy than by the mechanism of price inflation.

It is clear, however, that this method of transferring resources to the Government also cannot be used indiscriminately since, if relied upon for any prolonged period, it is bound to affect adversely the functioning of the private sector.

The last possibility of deficit financing—the sale of government securities to the banking system and the use of the proceeds to purchase goods abroad—is under certain conditions of some practical significance. If the central bank of a low income country holds foreign exchange reserves in excess of "normal" needs, and the Government can make effective use of them, for example for the purchase of capital equipment, it does not have to purchase the foreign exchange, but can borrow it. The central bank increases its holdings of government securities at the expense of foreign securities, and there is no increase in the money supply and aggregate domestic expenditures.

A type of deficit financing somewhat akin to case (d) is sound policy in a low income country with a revenue system which depends to a large extent on taxes on exports and imports. The export proceeds of such a country are bound to show wide fluctuations, reflecting price changes and, in the case of agricultural commodities, changes in the size of crops. The level of export proceeds also determines the volume and value of imports. The changes in the value of exports and imports in turn cause wide variations in the yield of taxes on exports and imports. The extent of the variations depends on the characteristics of the taxes, whether they are based on the volume or the value of the trade, and whether the rates are proportional or progressive with respect to the value.

In practice it is impossible to vary the rate of government expenditure at short notice in order to keep it in line with total revenue. Even if it were possible, it would be undesirable to do so, particularly since the main cuts and increases would have to fall on capital expenditures because a large proportion of recurrent expenditure consists of salary payments which cannot be reduced or increased at will. Therefore it is unavoidable that cash surpluses accumulate and are followed by cash deficits, if the rate of expenditures remains more or less constant.

There is a good deal to be said for this sort of cyclical sequence of surpluses and deficits because it dampens the impact of export booms and recessions on the economy. But in order that this policy be truly cyclical, it is essential that the expansion of government expenditures be controlled while export earnings and tax yields are high, that surpluses be allowed to accumulate, and that the accumulation of fiscal surpluses be matched by an increase in foreign exchange reserves. If this is done, the incurring of a cash deficit subsequently will not strain the economy too much. If the deficit is not to raise domestic prices unduly, a substantial portion of the income generated by it must be allowed to "leak out" through increased imports. Clearly, if foreign exchange reserves are not accumulated in times of high export earnings, the scope for such "leakage" will be limited and the impact of deficit financing on domestic prices will be more than is needed to keep the domestic productive resources fully employed.

Unfortunately, this apparently simple prescription of letting both "windfall" revenues and foreign exchange reserves accumulate during an export boom is not easy to carry out. Governments of low income countries, constantly under pressure to increase expenditures, find it difficult to restrain expenditures, or to refrain from entering into new expenditure commitments when export earnings and revenues increase. They may find it even more difficult to interfere with the liberal use of foreign exchange (for imports and other payments) by the private sector when exchange reserves are rising. One method of exercising fiscal and monetary discipline in such circumstances is to sterilize the cash surplus by allocating it to a "revenue equalization reserve," to hold this reserve in foreign exchange, and to make use of it only when revenues decline below their "normal" level.

But even if account is taken of all these possibilities, the fact remains that in low income countries the range of non-inflationary deficit financing is narrowly circumscribed. It is therefore of paramount importance for low income countries to conduct their fiscal operations in such a way as to assure a flow of tax revenue large enough to meet the essential requirements of public services, and to make the best possible use of fiscal resources by practising efficiency and economy in their application. If this is done, fiscal operations can make an important contribution to economic growth.

TABLE 1

SHARE OF GOVERNMENT FINANCE IN THE NATIONAL PRODUCT[a]

Low Income Countries	Fiscal Years Ending	Revenue as % of G.N.P.	Total Expenditure as % of G.N.P.	Defense Expenditure as % of G.N.P.
		(Average of Period)		
Africa				
Egypt	1954–56	21.06	21.12	5.50
Ghana	1952–58[b]	12.21	14.46	. . .
Asia				
Burma	1954–57	20.09	23.11	7.77
Ceylon	1954–57	20.23	21.20	0.60
India[b]	1956–58	7.32[f]	11.66[f]	2.15
		5.60[g]	9.20[g]	—
Iraq	1953–57	31.42	25.71	5.40
Israel	1954–59[b]	20.13	29.61	4.86
Japan	1954–58	13.28	13.17	1.94
Philippines	1954–58[d]	9.35	10.35	1.77
Latin America				
Argentina	1953–58[d]	9.58	13.14	2.91
Brazil	1953–58[d]	8.78[f]	10.29[f]	2.81
		5.71[e,g]	6.51[e,g]	—
Chile	1953–58[e]	13.03	13.96	2.77
Colombia	1953–57[e]	9.85	10.35	2.30
Costa Rica	1953–57	12.68	12.09	0.57
Ecuador	1952–57[e]	9.97	10.66	2.29
Guatemala	1953–57	13.47	14.87	1.32
Honduras	1952–57	8.59	9.47	1.22
Mexico	1953–57	8.82	9.91	0.65
Panama	1953–56	16.63	18.33	. . .
Peru	1953–56	13.86	14.48	2.78
Venezuela	1954–58[d]	18.91	16.31	1.45
Europe				
Greece	1952–57[e]	16.01	19.39	6.36
Spain	1952–57[e]	12.48	12.45	3.06
Turkey	1954–58[e]	12.74	14.44	4.17
AVERAGE				
All Low Income Countries		14.66	16.09	2.94

TABLE 1 (*continued*)
SHARE OF GOVERNMENT FINANCE IN THE NATIONAL PRODUCT[a]

High Income Countries	Fiscal Years Ending	Revenue as % of G.N.P.	Total Expenditure as % of G.N.P.	Defense Expenditure as % of G.N.P.
		(Average of Period)		
North America				
Canada	1953–58[d]	15.75	16.01	6.05
United States	1954–57	16.53[f]	16.64[f]	10.92
		8.07[g]	8.77[g]	—
Europe				
Austria	1953–58[b]	26.78	27.15	1.05
Belgium	1953–57	17.51	20.88	3.85
Denmark	1954–59[b]	17.03	17.47	3.03
Finland	1954–57	24.63	25.30	1.66
France	1953–57	19.81	21.61	6.78
Germany (F.R.)	1954–59	14.41[f]	14.39[f]	3.86
		14.90[g]	11.97[g]	—
Italy	1953–58[b]	17.05	19.61	3.40
Netherlands	1954–58	21.44	22.30	5.31
Norway	1953–58[b]	19.34	18.35	4.15
Sweden	1954–58[b]	21.62	22.75	4.73
Switzerland	1954–57	8.20[f]	7.33[f]	2.66
		7.01[g]	6.55[g]	—
United Kingdom	1954–59	26.25	27 32	7.19
Oceania				
Australia	1954–58	20.29[f]	17.44[f]	3.48
		8.00[g]	12.78[g]	—
New Zealand	1953–58	26.64	22.41	2.73
AVERAGE				
All High Income Countries		21.95	22.31	4.43

[a]Gross national product of same period, or nearest calendar year.
[b]1958 revised budget estimate.
[c]National income instead of G.N.P.
[d]1957, 1958 revised budget estimate.
[e]Includes governmental transfer payments.
[f]Central government.
[g]State and local governments.
...not available; — not applicable.
SOURCE: U.N., *Public Finance* (New York, 1959). See notes to Tables for definition of terms and coverage. *IMF International Financial Statistics*, February, 1960. *U.N. Yearbook of National Accounts Statistics*, 1958.

TABLE 2

COMPOSITION OF PUBLIC REVENUE

Low Income Countries	Fiscal Year Ending	Percentage of Total Revenue			Other Revenue
		Direct Taxes	Indirect Taxes		
			Total	Customs Duties[a]	
Africa					
Egypt	1954–59	18.82	43.24	. . .	37.93
Ghana	1952–58[b]	11.47	66.27	64.7	20.76
Asia					
Burma	1954–59	27.33	45.39	27.4	27.28
Ceylon	1954–59	23.42	66.46	54.5	11.15
India	1956–57	21.96[e]	53.28	29.1	26.00
		17.83[f]	—	—	82.19
Iraq	1953–58	7.29	25.09	18.4	67.63
Israel	1954–59[b]	37.15	48.67	22.3	14.18
Japan	1954–59	47.80	32.71	3.2	19.51
Philippines	1954–59[e]	38.79	46.40	30.2	14.81
Latin America					
Argentina	1953–58[e]	35.1	36.8	2.5[d]	28.1
Brazil	1953–57[e]	37.7[e]	51.6	. . .	10.7
		60.7[f]	19.8	—	19.5
Chile	1953–58[e]	36.9	52.3	17.1	10.8
Colombia	1953–58	46.4	42.4	31.4	11.1
Costa Rica	1953–58	17.63	72.23	58.9	10.14
Ecuador	1952–57	13.1	78.6	43.1	8.3
Guatemala	1953–57	7.90	81.25	51.5	10.85
Honduras	1952–57	17.26	76.74	51.6	5.89
Mexico	1953–58	27.10	56.8	28.6	16.1
Panama	1953–58	22.0	47.4	25.4	30.6
Peru	1953–58	23.4	59.7	32.0	16.9
Venezuela	1953–58[e]	26.9	27.6	13.4	45.5
Europe					
Greece	1952–57	17.4	54.2	21.3	28.4
Spain	1952–57	45.8	48.5	4.9	5.7
Turkey	1954–59	59.1	29.3	7.6	11.6
AVERAGE					
(Central governments only)		27.8	51.8	29.05	20.4

TABLE 2 (*continued*)

High Income Countries	Fiscal Year Ending	Percentage of Total Revenue			
		Direct Taxes	Indirect Taxes		Other Revenue
			Total	Customs Duties[a]	
North America					
Canada	1954–59[b]	57.0	36.9	10.3	6.1
United States	1954–58	80.8[e]	15.0	...	4.2
		69.4[f]	30.7	—	—
Europe					
Austria	1953–58[b]	44.10	43.92	4.7	11.98
Belgium	1953–58	41.95	20.12	6.6	37.92
Denmark	1953–58[b]	43.6	48.8	...	7.6
Finland	1954–58	22.6	52.5	13.2	24.9
France	1953–58	25.5	68.4	2.1	6.2
Germany (F.R.)	1953–58	40.0[e]	53.6	...	7.8
		92.0[f]	5.9	—	2.1
Italy	1953–58[b]	20.5	53.8	21.9	25.6
Netherlands	1954–58	56.5	43.5	10.0	—
Norway	1953–58[b]	29.6	60.0	7.4	10.4
Sweden	1954–59[b]	48.3	37.8	...	13.9
Switzerland	1954–59	25.4	58.5	28.0	16.1
United Kingdom	1954–58	49.5	41.7	...	8.8
Oceania					
Australia	1953–58	61.79	35.81	8.2	2.29
New Zealand	1953–58	61.17	31.31	14.1	7.51
AVERAGE					
(Central governments only)		44.3	43.9	11.5	12.8

[a]Mainly export taxes and import duties.
[b]1958 revised budget estimate.
[c]1957, 1958 revised budget estimate.
[d]1954–57 only.
[e]Central government.
[f]Local government.
...not available; —not applicable.
NOTE: Total may not add because of rounding.
SOURCE: U.N., *Public Finance* (New York, 1959). See notes to Tables for definition of terms and coverage. *IMF International Financial Statistics*, February 1960. *U.N. Yearbook of National Accounts Statistics*, 1958.

NOTES TO SELECTION 2

[1]W. A. Lewis, *The Theory of Economic Growth* (London: Allen & Unwin, 1955), p. 419.

[2] Cf. A. M. Martin and W. A. Lewis, "Patterns of Public Revenue and Expenditure," *The Manchester School of Economic and Social Studies*, XXIV (September, 1956), 203–44 [see selection 5 in this volume].

[3]One factor, however, may result in an understatement of the ratio of revenue to G.N.P. in less developed countries, particularly in Latin America. Exchange profits resulting from lower exchange rates applicable to exports, or certain kinds of exports, compared with rates applicable for imports, are generally not shown as

government revenue since they usually accrue to central banks. To the extent to which these profits are transferred by the central bank to the Government and used to finance public expenditures, they are very much like an export tax and therefore should be included in revenue.

[4] Which because of the inclusion of Burma, Egypt, Iraq, and Israel has probably an upward bias.

[5] A. R. Prest and I. G. Stewart, *The National Income of Nigeria* (Colonial Research Studies No. 11; London: H.M. Stationery Office, 1953), p. 83.

[6] If exchange rate profits and other measures used in lieu of export and import taxes were included, the share of these taxes in total revenue would be even larger.

[7] Cf. Part IV below.

[8] Cf., however, Martin and Lewis, "Patterns of Public Revenue and Expenditure."

[9] Cf. Part V below.

[10] The principles enumerated and discussed in the next few paragraphs are stated in their simplest form and without proper qualifications. It is realized that some of the modifications which are emphasized in the discussion were always present in the minds, and sometimes also in the writings, of the exponents of the principles. But the impact of these modifications on policy certainly has become greater in recent years and therefore the distinction made here between the "original" principles and their recent modifications may be justified.

[11] The distinction between self-liquidating capital expenditures on the one hand, and all other public expenditures on the other, was the basis of the principle that the former should be financed "below the line" through loans rather than taxation.

[12] In order to make the flow of benefits in the future comparable with its present cost it must, of course, be properly discounted.

[13] "Economic" implies that the composition corresponds to the desires of the community at the prevailing system of price relations, or at some other price relations which, for some reason, are considered more desirable than those prevailing.

[14] The fiscal section of the Secretariat of the U.N. has in recent years provided effective technical assistance for the improvement of the fiscal administration, and the U.N. Technical Assistance Administration has helped in improving administrative machinery in general. The bilateral provision of technical assistance has also made important contributions to improving the efficiency of public administration in low income countries.

[15] Cf. Part V below.

[16] "Reconstruction of Foreign Tax Systems," National Tax Association, *Proceedings of Forty-Fourth Annual Conference,* 1951, pp. 212–22.

[17] The partial substitution of an expenditure tax and a net worth tax for the personal income tax, which were advocated by N. Kaldor in *Indian Tax Reform,* Report of a Survey (New Delhi: Ministry of Finance, 1956), and *An Expenditure Tax* (London: Allen and Unwin, 1955), and which have been introduced in India and Ceylon, is an attempt to meet the main objection to taxation of high incomes at highly progressive rates, i.e. its adverse effects on private savings. It would go beyond the intended scope of this paper to comment on these fiscal innovations, and the criticisms levied against them.

[18] Because of the technical complexity of the subject no attempt is made here to discuss the role of corporate or company income taxes, or, more generally, of business income taxes, in the revenue structure of low income countries. This role depends on the importance of large-scale business enterprise, particularly of foreign-owned companies, in the economy. As a general rule, taxes on net business income are preferable to taxes on gross income, or other substitute taxes, such as export taxes, because the latter are likely to lead to certain distortions in the pattern of production and in financial arrangements.

[19]Cf. Martin and Lewis, "Patterns of Public Revenue and Expenditure," pp. 224–25; H. Wald, *The Taxation of Agricultural Land in Underdeveloped Economies* (Cambridge: Harvard University Press, 1959), *passim*.

[20]*The Basis of a Development Program for Colombia,* Report of a Mission of the International Bank for Reconstruction and Development (Washington, D.C., 1950), p. 262 [see selection 24 in this volume].

[21]This method of assessing the "unimproved" value of property was recently introduced, on an experimental basis, in Jamaica, following the example of Australia.

[22]Cf. H. C. Wallich and J. H. Adler, *Public Finance in a Developing Country—El Salvador, a Case Study* (Cambridge: Harvard University Press, 1951), p. 132. J. H. Adler, E. R. Schlesinger, and E. O. Olson, *Public Finance and Development in Guatemala* (Stanford: Stanford University Press, 1952), p. 138.

[23]This is not to say that protection of domestic production is always undesirable; this is obviously not the case. But it may be useful to distinguish rather clearly between revenue and protection objectives of import duties.

[24]E.g. Ghana, Nigeria, British West Africa, Burma, several Central American countries. Profits of monopolistic marketing boards, though originally devised for purposes of income equalization, may be considered as akin to export taxes. Exchange rates discriminating against certain exports (e.g. the coffee rates in Brazil), or exchange taxes imposed on certain exports (e.g. the recently introduced *retenciones* of Argentina), fulfil the same function. Cf. E. R. Schlesinger, *Multiple Exchange Rates and Economic Development* (Princeton: Princeton University Press, 1952), particularly p. 20.

[25]For a more extensive treatment of export taxes, cf. J. H. Adler, "The Economic Development of Nigeria: Comment," *The Journal of Political Economy,* Vol. 44 (October, 1956), pp. 425–34, and P. T. Bauer, "Reply," *ibid.* pp. 435–41. The "Comment" was in response to an article by P. T. Bauer, "The Economic Development of Nigeria," *The Journal of Political Economy,* Vol. 43 (October, 1955), pp. 398–411 [see selections 29 and 30 in this volume].

[26]Cf. R. Goode, "Reconstruction of Foreign Tax Systems," pp. 217–20.

[27]E.g. the financing of private industrial enterprises through development banks which are government-owned, or which obtain financial resources from the Government; the provision of credit facilities for agriculture.

[28]E. M. Bernstein and I. G. Patel, "Inflation in Relation to Economic Development," *IMF Staff Papers,* Vol. 2, No. 3 (November, 1951), p. 393.

[29]Cf. P. O. Steiner, "Choosing Among Alternative Public Investments," *American Economic Review,* Vol. 49, No. 5 (December, 1959), pp. 893–916.

[30]A. O. Hirschman has used the term "internalize" to describe the opposite process (*The Strategy of Economic Development* [New Haven: Yale University Press, 1958], p. 57).

[31]Cf. R. Nurkse, "Comments" (on paper by P. N. Rosenstein-Rodan), presented to Round Table of the I.E.A., Rio de Janeiro (*Economic Development for Latin America* [London: Macmillan, 1961], pp. 74–78).

[32]J. H. Adler, "Deficit Spending and Supply Elasticities," *Indian Journal of Economics,* Vol. 3, No. 144 (July, 1955), pp. 17–18.

[33]There are, of course, exceptions to the proposition that non-inflationary borrowing of funds by government from the private sector is small in low income countries. The most important exception is India, where the Government can count on a steady flow of private savings becoming available to the public sector. In recent years, foreign grants have also been an important source of financing expenditures, either directly or indirectly, through the creation of "counterpart" funds.

3

Taxation and
Economic Planning

*by the Pakistan Planning Commission**

APPROPRIATE economic policies must be pursued if the Plan is to be
fully implemented. It is intended to move away from an extensive
use of direct controls, which has tended to retard the pace of development, and to rely mainly on fiscal and monetary measures to regulate
the economy. Fiscal measures can exert a powerful influence on the
pattern of production, consumption, investment, saving and international trade. They can also be used to control possible inflationary
pressures and to mobilise resources for development by augmenting
government revenues.

Fiscal measures will be most effective if they are accompanied by
suitable monetary policies. An inflationary situation is likely to call
both for increased taxation and greater stringency in making credit
available. High levels of taxation, needed to raise resources for development, may properly be accompanied by high rates of interest
to encourage saving and economical use of capital. And policies
designed to encourage capital formation may depend for their execution on the development of financial institutions and on arrangements
to provide finance through the capital market and the banking
system.

TAXATION POLICY

Tax policy will be directed to mobilizing resources for development
and allocating them according to Plan priorities. The Taxation
Enquiry Committee, appointed by the Government in 1958, is currently engaged in an analysis of the existing structure of taxation,
with a view to suggesting necessary tax reforms. The interim reports
on Central and Provincial taxation have already been presented and

*Government of Pakistan, Planning Commission, *The Second Five-Year Plan
(1960–1965)* (Karachi, 1960), Chap. 3, pp. 47–57.

are receiving consideration from the Government. The final reports of the Committee are expected to take full account of the need for additional taxation during the Plan period.

Review of Present Tax Structure

Tax revenues are low, amounting to only 7 per cent of gross national product, or nearly 9 per cent of the income in the monetized sector. This is too small a proportion for the Government to be able to support an adequate development programme. Revenue raised from taxation is not sufficient to finance even the non-development expenditure of the Government, which is about 10 per cent of gross national product. If the Government is to be able to discharge the heavy responsibilities for development, in addition to carrying on its normal administrative functions, this state of public finances cannot be allowed to continue for long.

The yield from taxation has not shown the response that might be expected in a period of growing output. The provincial tax revenues, in particular, have been fairly inelastic. The small yield from taxes is explained partly by the limited coverage of income tax (only 0.26 per cent of the gainfully employed population pays income tax) and partly by the small yield from agriculture, which accounts for about 55 per cent of gross national product. Revenue from excise duties has also lagged, increasing by only 240 per cent against 500 per cent increase in large-scale industrial production between 1949–50 and 1959–60. This is because excise duties are largely specific in nature, and have not been adjusted with changes in prices or extended to include many new products manufactured in the country even though the latter have often replaced dutiable imports.

The country is heavily dependent on indirect taxes, which account for nearly 70 per cent of total tax revenue. There has been some shift from indirect to direct taxes during the last ten years, the share of direct taxes increasing from 25 per cent of total tax revenues in 1949–50 to 33 per cent in 1959–60.

The incidence of taxation on various income groups, economic sectors, and regions cannot be analysed very completely at present, for lack of comprehensive studies on family budgets and on distribution of personal and regional incomes. The fragmentary data available permit, however, some broad judgments. It appears that direct taxation has borne more heavily on non-agricultural than on agricultural incomes. Indirect taxes, such as import duties, excise duties and sales tax, have fallen on both the urban and rural sectors, but their incidence seems to have been greater on the urban sector in view of its consumption pattern and its monetized character. Export duties have fallen mainly on the agricultural sector. Account must also be taken, however, of a number of other government policies which have had similar effects as the imposition of taxes and subsidies. Agriculture has in effect been taxed through control of foodgrain prices and by having to surrender to the Government all the foreign exchange earned from the export of commodities at less than the scarcity value of foreign exchange to the economy. Unlike industry, agriculture has received no special tax concessions for investment. Agriculture also had to buy domestic substitutes at much higher prices than it would have paid if imports had not been restricted for balance of payments reasons, thereby providing a highly protected market for industry. Industry, on the other hand, has in effect received subsidies. Controlled prices of foodgrains have kept wages down, and foreign exchange to industry has been made available at a price much below its scarcity value. In addition, tax concessions, liberal depreciation allowances, and tax evasion have reduced the incidence of taxation on industry. Although the transfers of income from agriculture to industry were favourable for development, they also had the effect of weakening agricultural incentives by depressing prices of agricultural produce. The fact of taxation has not been so unfortunate as the form of taxation. The same contribution from agriculture could have been obtained by increasing direct taxes on agriculture, which are now too low, while maintaining incentives for agricultural production.

In the past, tax policy has been guided more by the need for revenue than by the requirements of capital formation. This has meant that the taxation system has lacked a clear focus; broader economic implication of some taxes, like export duties, were not given sufficient weight compared with their revenue-yielding aspects; tax policy was not very extensively used as an anti-inflationary device; and the role of taxes and subsidies remained limited, as against direct controls, in the allocation of resources.

Future Tax Policy

The tax system needs to be directed increasingly towards meeting the long-term needs of development. This will imply a greater use of taxes and subsidies to secure a desirable allocation of resources, instead of relying on a multiplicity of direct controls; the use of taxation as a means to control inflationary or deflationary tendencies; and the raising of more revenue to provide the means for development. The tax system will also need to be revised to broaden its coverage, make it more flexible, rationalize its incidence, and ensure the best balance between direct and indirect taxes.

The Plan proposes additional taxation of Rs. 1,000 million. It is hoped that the Taxation Enquiry Committee will make detailed proposals for raising this sum. In the following analysis, an attempt is made to indicate some of the considerations that should guide future tax increases, and to identify those sectors of the economy from which additional taxation can be raised.

i) Coverage of the tax system should be expanded in relation to national income, and the system should be made more flexible so that future economic growth may have a direct and immediate impact on public revenues. This is particularly important in the case of provincial taxation.

ii) In order to achieve the high rate of marginal savings required for the Plan, reliance will have to be placed on indirect taxes, particularly consumption taxes, which should capture a significant proportion of the increasing average incomes in the country. A progressive element can be introduced into these taxes by applying high rates to luxury goods.

iii) Direct taxes cannot be made more progressive without affecting the incentives to work and to save. The tax system should take full account of the needs of capital formation. It will be necessary to tolerate some initial growth in income inequalities to reach high levels of saving and investment. What is undesirable is a wide disparity in consumption levels. Tax policy should, therefore, be so oriented as to direct a large part of high incomes into saving and investment rather than consumption.

iv) "Disguised" taxation, particularly on agriculture, such as the compulsory procurement of foodgrains at fixed prices, reduces incentives to produce and invest and should be replaced by a more satisfactory system of direct taxation.

v) The need to raise revenue should not impede the broader objectives of the Plan. Tax policy should be closely coordinated with the development policy of the country.

Additional Taxation

The following discussion identifies the areas from which additional taxation can be raised for the Plan.

Import surcharges. Imports are being regulated at present through direct controls. Although these controls have been found necessary because of the general shortage of foreign exchange and the need to make the best use of this scarce resource, their larger implications have been unfortunate. These controls have often led to shortages of spare parts and key raw materials, and considerable windfall profits for importers. The consumers have generally been paying a high price for imports whose supply has been scarce, whereas the importers have been able to obtain unearned gains by securing "cheap" import licences.

It is desirable that a part of the windfall gains should be diverted from importers to the public coffers. This can be done by introducing a system of import surcharges. Ideally, the import surcharges should be high enough to take care of the excess market demand for broad categories of imports, to reflect the current shortage of foreign exchange, and to promote a more rational distribution of resources. Such a system can, however, be introduced only gradually; direct controls on imports will have to be retained for some time.

The system of import surcharges can take several forms. One such form can be to divide the import sector into various broad categories such as investment goods, raw materials, and consumer goods; another form can be to classify the imports according to varying degrees of essentiality. The allocation of foreign exchange to imports can then be made in line with broad national priorities, with the changing needs of the economy and requirements of the Plan. Import surcharges can be fixed in such a way as to bring into line demand and supply of foreign exchange for each category of import. An equilibrium between demand and supply can be reached only through a process of trial and error. A provision can also be made for refunds where necessary: for instance, if imports enter as inputs in an export industry, or if a so-called luxury good, such as a refrigerator, is required for an essential use, as in a hospital. Government imports should not be exempt from import surcharge, so that the public sector has a measure of the true scarcity value of the foreign exchange allocated to it.

If present import controls are replaced entirely by a system of import surcharges, the surcharges that will have to be fixed will need to be high. There may be an argument for special treatment for certain sectors of the economy, especially for the import of investment goods. It may be necessary, therefore, to operate an import surcharge system side by side with some of the present direct controls. Increasingly, these surcharges can be raised sufficiently to take care of the excess market demand for the imported category and to free various imports gradually from direct controls.

The objective of the import surcharge proposal can partly be achieved by suitably revising import duties. The merit of the import surcharge proposal, however, is that it concentrates attention on broad categories of imports; it avoids problems of valuation of imports since the surcharge is levied on the import licence itself; it withdraws purchasing power from the system before imports are made, thereby moderating inflationary pressures; and it helps focus attention on broad priorities in the import sector.

The commercial imports are around Rs. 800 million at present and are expected to increase in the next five years. The surcharge rates will vary, depending on the nature of various imports. They may vary from nil on certain categories like drugs and medicines, which are regarded as essential, to more than 100 per cent for certain consumer goods, which constitute luxury consumption. Even if the average surcharge rate is 20 per cent, it can yield as much as Rs. 1,000 million during the Plan period. This shows the potentialities of raising revenues from the import sector.

Export duties. The case for adjusting the present export duties on jute, cotton, and tea needs to be examined very carefully. The Taxation Enquiry Committee has suggested that export duties are "retrograde in principle and discourage exports, and the objective should be to replace them eventually." The case for their adjustment is strengthened by the introduction of the export bonus scheme for manufactured goods, and by the size of the export targets proposed in the Plan.

The export bonus scheme has provided a great incentive for the export of manufactured goods, but corresponding incentives are also necessary for the production of raw materials. Otherwise, an increase in semi-manufactures and manufactures is likely to occur mainly at the expense of raw material exports or adequate supplies in the home market. Basic to the success of any export drive is an abundant and increasing domestic supply of goods that can be diverted to the export market. This means that steps will have to be taken to increase the production of exportable commodities. The planned increases in cotton and jute production, of 38 per cent and 22 per cent respectively, will not be achieved without adequate incentives. Furthermore, adjustment of export duty on cotton will bring the domestic prices more in line with the international price, thereby restraining consumption at home.

A careful analysis is necessary to show how far the adjustment of export duties can help in increasing the production and export of raw materials. The case for abolishing or reducing the export duties seems to be much stronger in relation to raw cotton and tea than raw jute. These duties have not been abolished hitherto mainly for revenue considerations. However, as the Taxation Enquiry Committee has pointed out, in considering the question of export duties "the revenue aspect is no doubt important, but should not be allowed to override the objective of promoting exports." Moreover, import surcharges could more than make up the reduction in government revenues on account of the adjustment of export duties. In adjusting export duties, the impact on internal prices, the loss of subsidy for cotton and jute manufacturers, and the broader implications of a transfer of income from the non-agricultural to the agricultural sector will need to be fully considered. Such consideration may point to some related policies that will have to be followed, but will certainly not nullify the necessity for the adjustment of export duties.

The Government is expected to realize about Rs. 700 million from export duties if these are continued at the present levels during the Plan period. Of this amount, Rs. 300 million is expected from export duty on cotton and tea. Allowance must be made for possible loss from an adjustment of export duties in considering the net additional taxation of Rs. 1,000 million during the Plan period.

Excise duties. The rise in revenue from excise duties has not been proportionate to industrial growth, and there is a strong case for additional excise taxation. The Plan envisages a more extensive application of excise duties. There are several reasons for this. First, the Plan calls for a high rate of saving out of additional incomes; the desired austerity in personal consumption can be partly enforced through increases in excise duties. Second, as suggested by the Taxation Enquiry Committee, indigenous industries which have developed "under the protective wall of high import duties and quantitative restrictions must be taxed in order to replace the customs revenue on imports." Third, a greater reliance on excise duties will make the tax system more flexible and responsive to economic growth, especially if these duties are *ad valorem* in nature; it will also improve the ability of the Government to check inflationary or deflationary tendencies in the economy through appropriate changes in excise duties. It is paradoxical, but true, that the higher the excise taxation and the prices of excisable commodities, the more anti-inflationary are the effects produced. This is so because consumers are left with less purchasing power to spend on other goods and services. This consideration assumes particular importance when it is recalled that the present coverage of income tax is extremely limited, and no automatic way of influencing the income flow in the economy is available to the Government. Fourth, the present exemption limit in the case of income tax is Rs. 6,000 a year, which is high compared with the average income in the country. The administrative problems make it difficult to reach the average income groups in the country through the machinery of income tax, but it is necessary that persons with incomes below the exemption limit should also make some contribution to national development. Finally, more widespread levy of excise duties and removal of export duties will fit in with the general Plan strategy of diverting production from domestic consumption to export. It must be remembered that excise duties are easy to collect and difficult to evade.

It is not possible to indicate in detail the various commodities that might be subjected to additional excise duty. It is expected that this aspect will be fully analyzed by the Taxation Enquiry Committee in its final report. The Committee has already recommended the levy of excise duty on cement and betelnuts, and the enhancement of rates of duty on coarse cloth, tea, sugar, and vegetable products. The aim should be to bring as large a segment of the industrial sector as possible under excise duties, subject, of course, to considerations of equity and cost of collection.

If the coverage of excise taxation is broadened, it should be possible to raise additional revenues of Rs. 300 to 500 million through excise duties during the Plan period.

Sales tax. Greater reliance on consumption taxes is inevitable in order to finance the Plan. Sales tax is the closest approximation to a general consumption tax. Even a small increase in the sales tax could yield substantial revenue while the ultimate burden on the consumer would be quite light. The present basic rate of sales tax is 10 per cent for most commodities. If a surcharge of 25 per cent is added to the basic rate, it could bring in as much as Rs. 350 to 400 million over the Plan period.

Agricultural taxation. Agricultural taxation will need to be increased considerably during the Plan period, because: (*i*) The existing land revenue and water rates bear no relation to the taxable capacity of agriculture: agricultural prices have risen several times since 1939, while these rates have hardly been changed. Actually, some settlements were made even before 1939 and commutation values were based on much earlier prices. (*ii*) Additional agricultural income of more than Rs. 6,000 million will be generated during the Plan period. Because a capitalistic sector has not as yet emerged in agriculture, and traditions of reinvestment of income are on the whole lacking, consumption levels are likely to rise considerably to absorb a large part of increased productivity, unless the Government steps in and takes a part of it away for development. (*iii*) In the absence of a good system of agricultural taxation, marketable surplus may not increase much even when production does increase. (*iv*) The burden of indirect taxation on agriculture will be lessened through adjustment of export duties and decontrol of foodgrains; and (*v*) A good deal of expenditure is to be incurred by the Government on subsidizing fertilizers and seeds so that it is legitimate that a part of the cost should be recovered from increasing agricultural productivity. At the same time, the incentives for agricultural production will be maintained because agricultural taxation is intended to be of a nature which will not interfere with normal market incentives.

Gross land revenue collections (excluding water rates) in both East and West Pakistan are estimated at about Rs. 300 million at present. This is more than twice as much as was being collected in 1949–50. The increase has been made possible, however, by the collection of accumulated arrears and by the acquisition of rental interests in East Pakistan for which compensation is being paid out of extra receipts. Actually, land revenue rates have not changed much. Land revenue still constitutes only 2 per cent of the total agricultural income in the country, and contributes a mere 16 per cent to the total tax revenues of the Government although agricultural incomes are about 55 per cent of the total national income.

The low yield from land revenue in West Pakistan is explained mainly by two factors: (*i*) a long period of settlement in most cases, varying between 30 to 40 years, and (*ii*) maximum ceiling of 25 per cent on the enhancement of land revenue at the time of settlement. The Taxation Enquiry Committee has suggested the reduction of the period of settlement to 15 years, and the abolition of the legal bar on the enhancement of land revenue. As an interim measure, a 25 per cent flat increase was proposed. The objective should be to make revenue from agricultural taxation more responsive to growth in agricultural output and prices, without adversely affecting the incentives for production and investment. In Japan, where in the earlier stages of economic development, transfers from the agricultural sector cumulatively fed the process of economic growth, this purpose was achieved by a land tax which was revised every five years. In this connection, the possibility of aggregating agricultural incomes with non-agricultural incomes for the purposes of income tax also needs consideration.

Water rates have remained fixed in most cases for the last 30 years. In West Pakistan, the Irrigation Department has been running a substantial deficit which is made up by indirect credits from Land Revenue Department. A large subsidy has been implicit in the provision of water. There may be some justification for a subsidy for specific purposes and for a specific period of time, but the continuation of such a large concealed subsidy is not justified. In general, water rates need to be raised sufficiently to cover the full cost of providing water. The price of water will still be much less than the improved agricultural productivity made possible by its provision. The West Pakistan Government has already revised water rates so as to make up a part of the deficit incurred by the Irrigation Department. The rates should be increased sufficiently to run the department as nearly on commercial lines as possible. Additional revenue from agriculture can also be raised through betterment levies and the extension of estate duty to agricultural property. The First Plan recommended that a betterment tax should be levied on lands which have received improved irrigation as a result of the construction of new barrages, but very little to this effect has been done. This recommendation is repeated, especially because large new areas are going to be brought under cultivation through the completion of a number of irrigation projects in the Second Plan period. Such taxes can increase public revenues without discouraging agricultural production or causing inequities. The imposition of death duties has played an important part in some countries in reducing inequalities between the various classes of people through gradual liquidation and distribution of large accumulations of wealth, including land ownership. Hitherto, agricultural properties have been exempt from the application of the Estate Duty Act in West Pakistan. The extent to which death duties should in future be imposed on agricultural properties will require most careful consideration.

The flow of additional income to the agricultural sector and the relative absence of the tradition of private savings and investment among the farmers underline the magnitude of taxation that may have to be imposed on agriculture in order to realize Plan targets for marginal savings. Additional taxation of about Rs. 500 million can be raised from agriculture during the Plan period.

Direct taxation. Direct taxation (income tax, corporation tax, and property tax) needs to be reviewed and rationalized in the light of the final report of the Taxation Enquiry Committee. The following aspects will require particular consideration:

  i) The existing tax concessions need to be rationalized. The justification for continuing certain tax concessions to established industry is somewhat questionable, whereas the need for tax concessions to encourage a particular location (East Pakistan or the under-developed areas of West Pakistan) may deserve consideration. All general tax concessions should be examined and made more selective and discriminating. Tax concessions should also be so adjusted as to increase the bias towards the reinvestment of profits.

  ii) Taxes on property are currently imposed by a number of agencies (Central Government, Provincial Governments and municipalities). The consolidated incidence of property taxes needs to be analyzed, and thought given to the possibility of amalgamating various forms of property taxation, and reducing the combined burden. This is all the more important in view of the considerable increase in private house construction expected in the Plan period.

  iii) The desirability of introducing a capital gains tax should also be considered.

The total additional taxation proposed above adds up to more than Rs. 1,000 million, after allowance is made for a reduction in the export duties. Should other resources for the Plan not become available for any reason, higher additional taxation may have to be undertaken than is indicated here.

Growth of Tax Revenues

As a result of additional taxation and increased revenue from existing taxes, total tax revenues will increase substantially. It is estimated that the revenue from existing taxes will increase by about 25 per cent as national income increases by 20 per cent. This is so because taxes are mainly collected from sectors which will be growing at a rate faster than the national average. Besides, additional taxation of Rs. 1,000 million will add to the growth in tax revenues. It is estimated that the Government will be capturing about 8.5 per cent of gross national product through taxation by the end of the Plan period, against 7.3 per cent at present. Table 1 below summarizes the expected growth in tax revenues.

TABLE 1

ACTUAL AND EXPECTED GROWTH OF TAX REVENUE, 1949–50 TO 1964-65

(Consolidated Central and Provincial Receipts)

	1949–50 (Actuals)	1953–54 (Actuals)	1959–60 (Budget Estimates)	1964–65 (Projections) (a)	(b)
Composition of tax receipts		(Million Rupees)			
Income and corporation tax	115	212	265[c]	400	
Land revenue	134	178	295	320	
Customs	463	401	490	550	
Excise duties	99	221	310	390	
Sales tax	149	158	285	390	
Miscellaneous	108	76	205	220	
Total tax revenue	1,068	1,246	1,850	2,270	2,600
Distribution between direct and indirect taxes					
Direct taxes	269	407	602	760	
Indirect taxes	799	839	1,248	1,510	
		(Per Cent)			
Ratio of direct taxes to total tax revenue	25	33	33	33	
Tax revenue as a percentage of gross national product in current prices	6.1	6.9	7.3	7.4	8.5

[a]Excluding additional taxation during the Second Plan period.
[b]Including additional taxation during the Second Plan period.
[c]Excluding extraordinary collections of tax arrears.

Conclusion

The strategy of taxation, as outlined above, is three-fold. Firstly, excise taxation will be extended, sales tax raised and import surcharges levied to keep the increase in consumption in check and to encourage more economical use of national resources. Secondly, agricultural taxation will be increased, and direct taxation rationalized to strengthen incentives for increased production and investment. Finally, export duties will be so adjusted as to promote larger exports. The tax system will, therefore, help to strengthen the economy and raise revenues for the Plan.

4

Financing Soviet
Economic Development

*by F. D. Holzman**

THE purpose of this paper is threefold: to explain Soviet choice among sources of finance, to present and analyze the relevant data, and to evaluate the fiscal and monetary policies pursued. It should be stated at the outset that the sum of amounts collected from the various sources of finance always substantially exeeds the value of gross national investment. This is because from the same pools of funds the Soviet government finances not only investment in fixed and working capital, but government stockpiles of strategic materials, expenditures of the Ministry of Armed Forces for defense, administrative activities of the various departments of the government, expenditures on health and education, transfer payments, subsidies to state enterprises which sell their output at below-cost prices, and gross expenditures of the machine tractor station complex.[1] Since budgetary receipts, the largest single source of funds, are not earmarked for specific expenditures, there is no way of determining how the one category of expenditures which is directly relevant to economic development, viz. gross investment, was financed. We are limited to discussing the sources of finance of the whole of the "nonconsumption" activities of the Soviet state, loosely defining "nonconsumption" as the sum of goods and services purchased by the state plus transfer payments to the household. Because of our interest in how the state planned its economic expansion, investment from private profits and private depreciation funds will not be considered; private investment expenditures were, however, insignificant in all but the first year or two of the period under review. Discussion will center around the first three Five-Year Plan periods, i.e. from

*Reprinted from *Capital Formation and Economic Growth* by Moses Abramovitz (ed.), by permission of Princeton University Press. Copyright 1955 Princeton University Press. Excerpted here are pages 229–46.

Part of the research for this paper was accomplished while I was attached to the Russian Research Center, Harvard University. The financial assistance of that organization is gratefully acknowledged, as are the critical comments of Mathilda Holzman and Gregory Grossman.

1928/1929, when the first Plan went into operation, until 1940, the third and last completed year of the Third Plan (which was truncated by World War II). This period is adequate to illustrate the problems faced and policies adopted by Soviet planners.

Before turning to the sources of finance, a few words will be devoted to a consideration of the significance of money and finance for the functioning of the Soviet economy. Those unfamiliar with the Soviet economy may be misled by the emphasis on the words "planning" and "controls" into thinking that money is not important in the Soviet economy. While the Soviets rely more on direct economic controls than any other nation in the world today, and while such controls, where they are used, substitute for money and the market mechanism as the allocator of scarce resources, money has not been replaced by direct controls. There are no direct controls in large sectors of the Soviet economy. Consumer goods, for example, are distributed at present by the market mechanism; the amount of consumer goods which any household can purchase is determined by its current and accumulated earnings. The labor market, though less free than it was in the 1930's, still depends primarily on differential wage payments for the allocation of labor. Other markets (raw materials and producer goods), though on the whole more subject to direct controls, do nevertheless contain substantial areas in which free market forces are still allowed to operate. Even where allocation is accomplished directly, to the extent that prices provide the planners with a basis for allocation, money functions as a standard of value, if not as a medium of exchange.[2] Failure by the Soviets to keep their financial house in order will have a deleterious effect on the economy (through reduced incentives, misallocation of resources, etc.) so long as markets and prices are used by them to perform economic functions.

CHOICE AMONG SOURCES OF FINANCE

A listing of the major Soviet sources of finance has a conventional ring: direct taxation of the population, sales taxes, profits taxes, sales of government bonds to the population and to state institutions, retained profits of enterprises, depreciation reserves, bank credit, household savings. While there are many real similarities between the above categories and their Western counterparts, closer examination reveals substantial differences both of an institutional nature and in their relative importance. A cursory glance at Table 1 reveals that the financial path followed by the Soviet Union differs in several significant respects from the paths followed by many Western nations.

TABLE 1

SOURCES OF SOVIET FINANCE AS PERCENTAGES
OF ADJUSTED TOTAL, 1937

Major indirect or commodity taxes	71.9
Direct taxes	3.8
Sales of government bonds to population	4.1
Miscellaneous budgetary receipts	7.3
Retained profits of state enterprises	4.6
Indivisible fund of collective farms	1.7
Depreciation reserves	5.4
Voluntary household savings	1.0
Increase of currency in circulation	1.4

SOURCE: Taken from Tables 3 and 4 below [not included in this volume]. The above items total to more than 100 per cent for reasons discussed in the notes to Tables 3 and 4.

Foreign Borrowing

Outstanding for its absence from Table 1 is foreign borrowing. I do not think it would be possible to single out over the past 150 years many nations which have industrialized, especially in the early stages, without some foreign aid. The Soviets industrialized without any significant foreign aid, not because they wanted to—they did not—but because the Western World was hostile to them[3] and they, in turn, were hostile to and distrustful of Western nations. This was not a climate in which international capital was likely to flow freely and abundantly. With some minor exceptions, the Soviets paid in gold, commodities, and in imperial crown jewels for all goods purchased from other nations in the interwar period. In recent years the situation has changed somewhat. During the war, of course, the Russians received considerable help from the United States in the form of lend-lease shipments; and since the war reparations have contributed, in some years, respectable sums to budget receipts.[4] Finally, there may be considerable capital flow between the Soviet Union and the countries within its political orbit, but on this there is very little reliable information as to either amount or direction.

Voluntary Savings

The Soviets have always encouraged voluntary saving by the population. A large network of banks in both urban and rural areas has been developed to foster the saving habit; the 5 per cent interest on time deposits (six months or more) is the highest obtainable in the Soviet Union;[5] the Currency Reform of December 1947 applied a much more favorable conversion rate to savings deposits than to either cash or government bonds. Nevertheless, understandably enough, savings have never amounted to much in the Soviet Union.

The annual increment to savings deposits is only a fraction of 1 per cent of total household money income.[6] The average Soviet citizen is in much too great need of current goods and services to put aside large sums of money to meet future needs. And those future needs which induce the greatest amount of saving in Western nations (e.g. provision against sickness, accidents, old age, unemployment, etc.) are relatively well provided for in the Soviet Union by a comprehensive social security system. Furthermore, the incentive to save must certainly have been vitiated by twenty years of rapidly rising prices in the consumer goods markets, not ending until the currency reform of 1947.[7] Finally, of course, the state imposes upon the population such a high rate of compulsory saving that little is left to individual initiative.[8]

Commodity Taxes

Most of the compulsory savings of the economy are collected by the state in the form of taxes and are reflected in the budget accounts;[9] and indirect or commodity taxes are responsible for from two-thirds to three-fourths of budgetary receipts. The three principal commodity taxes are the turnover tax, deductions from the profits of state enterprises (profits tax), and the social insurance markup. The turnover tax is essentially a sales tax levied, at present, exclusively on consumer goods—except for petroleum and petroleum products, where the tax substitutes for explicit rent payments. Before 1949 it was levied on producer goods as well, but for fiscal control of the tax-paying enterprises rather than for revenue. The rates on consumer goods are highly differentiated, varying from 1 per cent of the *selling price* on some commodities to as much as 90 per cent on others.[10]

The deduction from profits is correctly not called a tax on enterprise[11] by the Soviets because it applies to nationalized industries. The state does not tax the profits of its own industries; it simply transfers money from one state account to another. From a fiscal point of view the deduction from profits, as part of profits, adds to the price paid by the consumer; in this respect it does not differ from the turnover tax and can properly be considered a commodity tax on the household. Every enterprise pays a minimum 10 per cent tax on profits for purposes of fiscal control. The remaining profits are used as needed to finance investment planned for the enterprise and to make payments into the Directors' Fund.[12] Any surplus above these needs is *deducted* into the budget.

The social insurance markup is a form of payroll tax, and for our purposes can be looked upon as adding to the price of commodities bought by the household, just like the turnover and profits taxes. The receipts from this tax are derived as additions to the wage funds of enterprises, the percentage varying from 3.7 to 10.7, depending on conditions of employment and other factors in the separate branches of the economy. It is claimed that part of the receipts from this tax are earmarked for sickness and old age insurance.[13]

Why is commodity taxation the dominant method of extracting savings from the population in the Soviet Union? Conversely, why is little reliance placed upon income (direct) taxation, the form of levy preferred in the United States and in many other Western nations?[14] Soviet preference for commodity taxation is certainly not to be explained on ideological grounds. In fact, the predominance of the turnover tax among Soviet taxes has proved embarrassing to Soviet economists. Marxist writers consistently attacked indirect taxes as socially inequitable and regressive; bad associations also stem from the reliance of the tsars on highly regressive excise taxes (especially on alcoholic beverages) for the bulk of their revenue. That the Soviets rely on commodity taxation in spite of their "ideological" bias attests to its superiority for their purposes.[15]

Soviet preference for commodity taxation appears to rest primarily on three considerations. First, there is the "money illusion," which has it that workers are more conscious of the impact on their economic position of changes in wages than of the impact produced by changes in prices. A corollary to this is the hypothesis that workers are more sensitive to changes in direct taxes (and thus in take-home pay) than to changes in indirect taxes (reflected in commodity prices). The money illusion, therefore, would cause commodity and income taxes of equal size to have different impacts on work incentives. This is particularly important in the Soviet Union, where almost all income is earned income. Analytically, it is possible to separate the impact of taxes on incentives into at least two categories: the effect on the work-leisure ratio and the effect on differential wages as a factor in choosing between jobs. Most writers dealing with this subject concentrate on the work-leisure ratio, arguing that high taxes, and particularly high marginal rates of tax, reduce the incentive to work, and that indirect taxes, as a consequence of the illusion, minimize the disincentive effects of taxes. This line of reasoning ignores the income effect of taxation,[16] or at least assumes that the substitution effect between work and leisure is more important than the income effect. There is no empirical evidence, to my knowledge, to support this assumption, and, in fact, the income effect may actually be strong enough to induce Soviet workers to greater effort. If this were the case, it could not be argued that the Soviet choice of commodity taxation preserves work incentives.

It can be argued, without equivocation, that the Soviets took advantage of the money illusion effects of commodity taxation to preserve the effectiveness of their differential wage structure as an incentive mechanism for allocating labor. In order to attract workers, Soviet policy has been to pay higher wages to persons in jobs requiring greater skills, in expanding industries, and in jobs or areas where work conditions are undesirable. Up until the late 1920's or early 1930's this policy had not been implemented successfully, hampered to a considerable extent as it was by the hangovers of an earlier "equalitarian" philosophy regarding wage differentials.[17] An attempt was made to improve the situation; in 1931 Stalin intervened and, in a speech calling for greater wage differentials, set the new policy. He said: "In a number of our factories, wage scales are drawn up in such a way as to practically wipe out the difference between skilled labour and unskilled labour, between heavy work and light work. The consequence of wage equalization is that the unskilled worker lacks the incentive to become a skilled worker and is thus deprived of the prospect of advancement; . . . in order to get skilled workers we must give the unskilled worker a stimulus and prospect of advancement, of rising to a higher position. . . ."[18] Bergson's wage study indicates that wage differentials in the Soviet Union in 1934 were about as great as those in the United States at a comparable stage (1904) of economic development.[19]

In the late 1920's and early 1930's, at the same time that Soviet wage differentials were being increased for incentive reasons, taxes were also being increased. The average rate of taxation about doubled from 1926 to 1936, increasing by substantial amounts almost every year of the period;[20] by 1930 it amounted to about 50 per cent of household income.[21] Clearly, Soviet differential wage policy was in danger of being weakened by Soviet tax policy. Reliance upon income taxation under these circumstances would have had a much more adverse impact on the incentive-wage system than commodity taxation for at least two reasons. First, under the Soviet pay-as-you-earn system of income taxation, workers are as likely to base job decisions on differential take-home pay as on gross wage differentials. On the other hand, if no income tax were levied, gross wage differentials would probably retain much of their incentive effect, even with high levels of commodity taxation. Second, for political reasons income taxation would almost necessarily have to be progressive, or at least proportional, thereby reducing wage differentials relatively as well as absolutely; this would not necessarily be so for sales taxation, especially when the tax is hidden, and when it has a highly differentiated rate structure, as is the case in the Soviet Union.[22] This facet of the money illusion is undoubtedly an important reason for Soviet use of commodity taxation.

A second factor explaining Soviet reliance on commodity taxation is administrative in nature. The turnover tax, particularly in the early stages of its development, was levied on and collected from state industrial enterprises (procurement agencies in agriculture) and wholesale organizations. This provided the cheapest and least evadable method of collecting money taxes from the population since the number of industrial enterprises and wholesale organizations was not large and they maintained relatively good money accounts; it also provided a continuous source of funds—the larger enterprises made daily payments to the budget. These considerations were quite crucial in the late 1920's and the early 1930's, before the administrative apparatus of the state had achieved anything like its present-day efficiency. Reliance upon income taxation would have meant levying and collecting taxes from 30 to 40 million householders, many of whom were still illiterate. Furthermore, at that time a large segment of the peasant population still had not been herded into collective farms, where it could be reached without excessive costs by tax collectors.

A third consideration, and one which is stressed by Soviet economists, is the use of the turnover tax to facilitate price planning. The Soviets have attempted to maintain a market for consumer goods in which free choice prevails. Prices are not set freely by decentralized agents as is usually the case in Western nations; rather, prices are centrally administered and the state is responsible for adjusting relative prices. Maintenance of appropriate price flexibility is, for obvious reasons, facilitated by the existence of a large element of tax in the cost-price structure. In fact, without either a commodity tax or a subsidy (which can be considered a negative commodity tax in this case) it would not be possible to alter relative prices much faster than relative changes in productivity would permit[23] (i.e. prices would approximate long-run cost).

Income Taxation

In spite of the advantages and magnitude of Soviet commodity taxation, the population is also required to pay an income tax. The only significant function which this tax seems to serve is to discourage private practice by professionals[24] (e.g. doctors and lawyers) and other "nonworker" elements in the urban population. These groups pay a discriminatorily high tax, which reaches 55 and 65 per cent, respectively, on incomes in excess of 70,000 rubles; workers and salaried employees, who comprise 90 per cent or more of the non-agricultural labor force, pay according to a schedule which reaches a maximum rate of 13 per cent on all income over 12,000 rubles annually. While the "class policy" feature of the income tax may have been important twenty years ago, before the private sector of the economy had been thoroughly squelched, it can hardly be considered so any more. Moreover, the tax certainly has little fiscal importance.[25] It is difficult to understand why the Soviets continue to use direct levies on income when they could be replaced very easily by a small increase in commodity taxation. Perhaps they are continued through inertia, or because the Soviets wish to maintain intact the direct tax apparatus for possible future use.

Sales of Government Bonds

Sales of government bonds constitute, in effect, another form of direct levy on the Soviet population. Similarity of these bond sales to taxation rests on the following characteristics: considerable social pressure is brought to bear upon the population to subscribe from two to four weeks' wages a year; these amounts are deducted from workers' wages every month just as direct taxes are; most bonds are not redeemable until the full term has expired;[26] a series of conversions (1930, 1936, 1938) and the 1947 Currency Reform have together resulted in extended maturities, reduced interest rates, and a reduction by two-thirds, in 1947, of the value of all outstanding obligations; rapidly rising prices have steadily reduced the real value of these highly illiquid assets. The disadvantages of direct taxes, in general, seem to apply to sales of bonds also, although bond sales in the late 1920's may have been more "voluntary" in nature. To the extent that they were (are) voluntary, disincentive effects would, of course, have been (be) reduced.

Since the Currency Reform of 1947, consumer goods prices have declined steadily. If this trend should be continued, the usefulness of bonds as a form of taxation will have been substantially reduced. On the one hand, falling price levels will cause the real rate of interest on the bonds to exceed the nominal rate so that, in time, repayment may become a real burden on the current Soviet budget. Before 1947 the real rate of interest was undoubtedly negative due to continuous inflation—the burden of repayment was insignificant.[27] On the other hand, it seems doubtful that price levels will fall rapidly enough to increase voluntary savings, especially in the form of illiquid bonds, to the amount of the annual issue of bonds. Thus, as prices fall the disadvantage of larger "real" repayments would seem to more than offset the advantage of smaller disincentive effects as the bonds become a slightly less unattractive form of investment.

Retained Profits

Funds for investment are also available in the form of retained profits accumulated by both state enterprises and collective farms.[28] The annual plans usually call for a substantial part of the investment in the fixed and working capital of established state enterprises to come out of the retained profits of these enterprises. State enterprises also receive grants from the budget for the same purpose. It is difficult to understand what difference, if any, there is between these two methods of finance, and why the Soviets do not concentrate on either one or the other. It is frequently contended that managerial incentives are sharpened if managers are allowed to finance investment from retained profits rather than by budget subsidy. There is the implication in the case of retained profits that, if the manager is more (less) efficient, he may have more (less) funds to invest because profits will be larger (smaller). This implication does not square with the usual conception of an enterprise's fulfilling its investment plan from retained profits and then automatically transferring the remainder, after deductions into the Directors' Fund, into the budget.[29] Part of the Directors' Fund is, of course, used for extra-plan investment; but the incentive to increase profits by reducing costs and increasing output exists regardless of whether the enterprise has its own profits to begin with or receives a budget subsidy.[30] Soviet preference for budget-financed investment probably lies in the greater administrative flexibility which this method *may* confer; it is, undoubtedly, simpler to alter investment plans in the short run if funds are doled out from the budget than if they are accumulated by enterprises in which the investment is planned.

The collective farms (and other cooperatives) not nationalized and the property of the state (though under strict state control, of course) must meet the bulk of their investment requirements from their own resources. The farms are required by law to withhold from 12 to 20 per cent of their total net money income (after meeting costs of production, excluding payments to labor) in a so-called "indivisible fund" which is to be used for capital investment.[31] Most of the current money income of the collectives is, of course, distributed among the collective farmers in payment for their labor. Investment by the collective farms (except in kind) has never amounted to much because most of their machinery requirements (tractors, combines, etc.) are met, for a price, by the state-owned machine tractor stations (MTS). The MTS have been since 1938 included in the budget on a gross basis; all of their expenditures, including new investment, are financed by budget subsidy. Collective farms with insufficient funds to finance their investment requirements can borrow small sums from the Agricultural Bank.

Funds for Amortization

Most economic organizations which use capital equipment are required to consider depreciation a cost of production and to maintain depreciation reserves. Western economists generally consider that these reserves understate depreciation in view of the extensive Soviet cost inflation, because of the fact that original rather than replacement cost is used in computing depreciation, and because inexpert handling of equipment appears to be widespread and may have had the effect of reducing the physical life of much equipment. Originally, the reserves were devoted exclusively to replacing old, and constructing new, equipment. Since 1938, part of these funds have been made available for capital repair.

Minor Sources of Budget Receipts

The more important sources of budget revenue have already been noted: turnover tax, deductions from profits of state enterprises, the social insurance markup, direct taxes on the population, and sales of government bonds. The budget derives revenue from many other sources. Customs are, perhaps, the most important of these. In the prewar period they amounted to as much as 2 per cent of total budget receipts in some years. During the war, receipts from tariffs on regular imports were strongly supplemented by local currency resulting from lend-lease sales; since the war, regular receipts have been supplemented by reparations. Other sources are an inheritance tax which at present is simply a fee for the processing of legal documents, fees for commercial forestry and fishing, fines, licenses, the *gross* receipts of the machine tractor stations, and taxes on the profits of the collective farms and other cooperatives. Taken individually, these items do not generally provide much revenue; in the aggregate, however, their contribution is not insubstantial.

The State Bank: Changes in Currency in Circulation

A substantial share of the working capital requirements of the economy are financed by the State Bank (Gosbank) in the form of short-term loans. In the early 1930's, when the basis of the present Soviet banking system was established, the Bank was given authority to extend short-term credit to finance goods in transit, seasonal production processes and expenses, and other temporary working capital needs connected with the production and turnover of goods.[32] Permanent working capital was to be furnished to new enterprises needing it by the budget in the form of interest-free grants; additions to permanent working capital were to be financed either by the budget or out of the retained profits of the enterprises. If the working capital needs of enterprises had been seasonally stable, there would have been no necessity, in the original Soviet scheme of things, for the short-term credit operations of the State Bank. "The function of short-term credit in the Soviet economy . . . [was], broadly speaking, to level out fluctuation in the flow of materials and goods."[33] The functions of the State Bank were extended in the mid-1930's, however, when it was authorized to finance a large percentage of the *permanent* working capital requirements of trade organizations; and again in 1939 when it was assigned the task of regularly financing part of the *permanent* working capital needs of heavy industry. This deviation from the original principle which guided the granting of short-term credit was introduced with the purpose of giving the State Bank control over the activities of enterprises in these sectors.[34] Apparently, these enterprises "experienced little variation in working capital requirements, and thus were able to escape the control and supervisory functions of the Gosbank."[35] This is the situation at present; it should be noted, however, that during the war the Bank was authorized to advance large credits for the reconstruction of enterprises in liberated areas, to make payments to military personnel under certain special conditions, to facilitate the evacuation of industries eastward during the German advance, and to meet other extraordinary needs. Presumably, credit is no longer granted for these special purposes.

It is important to note that the State Bank is, in normal times, the *only* source of currency issue in the U.S.S.R. With the exception of the years 1941–1943—years of great internal disruption, when the budget ran deficits which were financed by currency issue—short-term loans to finance the above-noted working capital needs of enterprise have been the sole source of new currency in circulation. The extension of new short-term loans does not always, or usually, lead to a currency increment, however. New currency is issued to finance short-term loans only if no currency is returned by the population from other sources. Other sources of funds are excesses of budget receipts over budget expenditures, of retained profits over investment financed from retained profits, of depreciation reserves over expenditures from depreciation reserves, etc. These funds and others mentioned above are all reflected in the accounts of the State Bank either by direct deposit or indirectly through the deposit in the State Bank of the reserves of the special banks for long-term investment (see below). To the extent that currency receipts in the State Bank are greater than expenditures (including long-term loans) from these receipts, new short-term credit can be extended without the issuance of currency; in fact, if there should be a surplus of deposits over expenditures, including short-term loans, currency will be withdrawn from circulation. If, on the other hand, expenditures, including short-term loans, exceed receipts, new currency is circulated. If, therefore, we were interested in measuring the amount of Soviet nonconsumption expenditures (as we are below) from sources of finance, we would not include gross changes in the amount of short-term credit outstanding; this would involve a double count because bank loans are an expenditure item in the national financial accounts. We simply add (subtract) increases (decreases) in currency in circulation. To clarify this point, an estimate of Soviet financial accounts for 1936 is presented in Table 2.

TABLE 2

ESTIMATE OF SOVIET NATIONAL FINANCIAL ACCOUNTS, 1936

(billions of rubles)

Receipts		Expenditures	
1. Budget receipts (including bonds)	94.4	1. Budget expenditures	92.5[a]
2. Retained profits		2. Investment and other expenditures financed outside budget	
a. State enterprises	8.9	a. From retained profits	
b. Collective farms	1.5	i. State enterprises	8.9[b]
c. Others	?	ii. Others	2.6[c]
3. Depreciation reserves	4.9	b. Depreciation	?
		c. Net increase in short-term credit (State Bank)	8.1
		d. Long-term loans to collective farms and farmers	1.5[d]
Subtotal	109.7		
4. Currency issue	1.6	Subtotal	113.6
5. Discrepancy	2.3	3. Currency withdrawal	0
Total	113.6	Total	113.6

NOTE: Figures for which sources are not cited were taken from tables later in this chapter [which are not included in this volume].

[a]Same source as budget receipts.

[b]Planned investment in fixed capital from S. N. Prokopovich, *Biulleten'*, March, 1936, No. 127, p. 30. Planned investment in working capital from G. F. Grinko, *Financial Program of the U.S.S.R. for 1936* (Moscow: Foreign Languages Publishing House, 1936), p. 15.

[c]At least 2.6 billion rubles of other investment from profits can be estimated from A. Smilga, "Finansy sotsialisticheskogo gosudarstvo" ("Finances of Socialist State"), *Problemy ekonomiki* (*Problems of Economics*), 1937, No. 2, p. 115.

[d]K. Plotnikov, *Biudzhet sotsialisticheskogo gosudarstva* (*Budget of the Socialist States*), Moscow, p. 140.

It would hardly be necessary to discuss the special banks for long-term investment had they not been misnamed banks. Their primary function is to disburse and supervise the use of funds previously collected rather than to create new credit. The bulk of these funds are budgetary grants to enterprises in the national economy for investment in plant and equipment and working capital. Other funds held and disbursed by these banks are retained profits of state enterprises, the indivisible fund, retained profits of other cooperatives, and that part of the reserves for depreciation used to finance new investment.[36] Apparently, the special banks "lend" to both individuals and enterprises, but the amounts involved are not significant and will be ignored here except for long-term loans by the Agriculture Bank to collective farms. The special banks keep their excess funds on deposit with the State Bank; thus the State Bank is seen to be the custodian of excess investment funds for virtually the whole Soviet economy. Long-term loans of the special banks, like short-term loans, are expenditure, not receipt, items in Soviet financial accounts; they are reflected in "sources of finance" only insofar as they affect the amount of currency which has to be circulated by the State Bank to finance its short-term credit operations.

Taxation in Kind

No mention has been made so far of taxation in kind of agriculture because it does not *directly* provide the state with monetary reserves for financing nonconsumption expenditures; indirectly, however, it does. The tax in kind takes the form of compulsory deliveries of agricultural products by collective farms and peasant farmers to state and cooperative procurement agencies. While the farms and peasants are not uncompensated for their deliveries, the price paid by the state (called procurement price) is usually far from sufficient to cover costs of production; and, of course, it is only a fraction of the retail price (minus processing and distribution costs) at which the state resells these items to the population. The high retail price is achieved by superimposing a turnover tax on procurement price plus costs of processing and distribution. The portion of the turnover tax collected by virtue of the below-cost procurement price is the monetary equivalent of the tax in kind on that part of the compulsory deliveries sold to the household.[37] Delivered produce not sold back to the household (e.g. stockpiled or used in the production of final products not sold to the household) is not reflected in the budget and may be classified as "investment in kind" by the state.

This classification holds in all circumstances in which producing agents are directly paid less than cost of production or less than the value of their product (or not at all). A major case in point is, of course, that of unfree labor in the Soviet Union. The evidence indicates that workers in this category are remunerated at less than the free market wage for comparable performance.[38] To the extent that the products of unfree labor are sold to the population at high prices and add to the receipts of the turnover tax, the tax in kind on unfree labor (in the form of below-market wage payments) is reflected in budgetary receipts. To the extent that the services of these laborers are directed into nonconsumption activities such as gold mining, construction, irrigation projects, and the building of dams and roads (and these are the sorts of activities typically handled by the MVD), they may be classed as investment in kind by the state.

It should be noted that there is still another important source of investment in kind in the Soviet Union. We refer to that part of the income in kind of the agricultural sector of the economy which

is neither taxed away by the state nor consumed by peasant households, but which is devoted to the following years' production (e.g.
seed, feed, stockpiles, increasing livestock herds). Needless to say,
none of the above categories of investment in kind are readily susceptible to measurement; nor can we, for that matter, even say what part
of the turnover tax is a tax on the consumer and what part is a tax
on the agricultural producer.[39]

How is Soviet preference for taxation in kind of agriculture to be
explained? Basically, the difference between taxation of industrial
income and taxation of agricultural income stems from the fact that
industry and the output of industry are almost 100 per cent state-
owned, while agriculture consists primarily of collective farms, which
are not owned by the state, and of individual peasant farmers.[40] This
form of organization of agriculture, rather than state-owned farms
with the farmers receiving wages, creates two serious problems for
the state. First, the state must secure by some means a substantial
share of the output of the agricultural sector to be transferred to the
city for personal and industrial consumption and for export. Taxation
of the money incomes of agricultural producers would not necessarily
secure this result: if the amount of the tax were calculated on the
basis of actual money income, the peasants could reduce their money
income, hence tax payments, by cutting down sales of agricultural
output; even if taxable income were based on production, the
peasants could, by cutting back on their consumption of industrial
consumer goods, still avoid the necessity of having to sell as much
agricultural output as the state needed to meet its requirements.
These are not idle possibilities in a country where adequately feeding
the population has been—and will continue to be, barring unforeseen
developments—a very serious economic problem. By means of money
taxation, alone, it might prove impossible to reduce the food consumption of the peasants below a level consistent with the needs of
the nation as a whole for food. Second, as we have seen, for incentive
and other reasons the state collects most of its budget receipts in the
form of indirect taxes. Since the bulk of the turnover tax, the major
indirect tax, is collected in the form of a markup on agricultural
products (because food is the principal item of personal consumption
in the Soviet Union), the incidence of the turnover tax on the agricultural population considered as consumers is relatively small because a large part of its income takes the form of consumption of
home-produced food. Another form of tax on the peasantry must be
substituted for indirect money taxation if a high rate of saving for
the economy as a whole is to be maintained. The tax in kind solves
these two problems at once for the state: it insures state procurement
of the required amount of agricultural produce, and it forces a high
level of savings upon the agricultural population.

NOTES TO SELECTION 4

[1] Before 1930 the transportation and communications systems were included in the budget on a gross basis; this was true of almost all state enterprises during War Communism (1918–1921).

[2] Money continues to flow, of course, but the possessor of money has so little notion as to its use that the role of money in the transaction must be considered trivial.

[3] And not only for ideological reasons. Remember that Western investors took a heavy loss when the Bolsheviks refused to honor the very large foreign debts of the Russian imperial government.

[4] Amounting to as much as 3 to 4 per cent of total budget receipts.

[5] Demand deposits pay only 3 per cent.

[6] Cf. F. D. Holzman, "The Burden of Soviet Taxation," *American Economic Review*, September, 1953, Table 1.

[7] Since the currency reform, consumer goods prices have declined steadily; this may eventually have a positive effect on the incentive to save. From 1928 to 1947, consumer goods prices increased, on the average, about twentyfold. Cf. Naum Jasny, *The Soviet Price System* (Stanford University Press, 1951), Chap. 2.

[8] Perhaps it should also be noted that the Soviet rural population appears to have the usual peasant distrust of banks and prefers to hold a large part of its savings in the form of cash.

[9] The Soviet state budget is a consolidated budget consisting of the all-Union, republican, and local budgets. It is equivalent to the sum of the federal, state, and local budgets in the United States.

[10] Looked upon as a markup over cost, as is customary in the West, the tax rates are much higher, of course. A 50 per cent tax becomes one of 100 per cent; a 90 per cent tax becomes one of 900 per cent.

[11] Although for convenience it will be referred to as a profits tax.

[12] For incentive reasons from 1 to 5 per cent of planned profits and 15 to 45 per cent of overplan profits are deducted into the Directors' Fund. These amounts are disbursed as bonuses to workers and managers, for workers' housing, for cultural projects, and for extra-plan investment in the enterprises.

[13] We might also have included in the category of taxes which enter the commodity price structure the incomes of economic organizations which are allocated "to the trade unions and special funds for workers' training and education." Cf. Abram Bergson, "Soviet National Income and Product," *Quarterly Journal of Economics*, May, 1950, p. 288.

[14] The Soviet income tax on the urban population does not differ substantially from the income taxes in other countries except that different social and economic classes pay according to different rate schedules in application of Soviet "class policy." Thus workers, artists, professionals with private practices (e.g. lawyers and doctors), and private shopkeepers pay at rapidly ascending rates (on identical money incomes) from left to right. The rural population pays a very different sort of tax (called the agricultural tax) because the bulk of peasant income is in kind. This necessitates, among other things, fairly cumbersome methods of assessing personal income and estimating the amount of tax to be paid. The agricultural tax discriminates in favor of the collective farmer and against the private peasant.

[15] In fact, for about twenty years they have not referred to it as a tax on the population, but rather as "accumulation of socialized industry," implying that the amounts returned to the budget are a result solely of great increases in productivity.

[16] That persons having their incomes reduced by taxes would tend to work harder.

[17]Cf. Abram Bergson, *The Structure of Soviet Wages* (Harvard University Press, 1946), Chaps. 13 and 14.

[18]Joseph Stalin, *Problems of Leninism* (Moscow: Foreign Languages Publishing House, 1940), pp. 371–73.

[19]Bergson, *The Structure of Soviet Wages.*

[20]Cf. Holzman, "The Burden of Soviet Taxation," Table 3.

[21]*Ibid.,* Table 3.

[22]The Soviet turnover tax appears to have had a somewhat regressive rate structure in the prewar period; the postwar structure seems to be considerably less regressive and may be roughly proportional. The rate structure is much too complex, and the information on income-expenditure patterns much too limited, for us to come to any but the most tentative conclusions on this matter, however. Cf. F. D. Holzman, *Soviet Taxation: The Fiscal and Monetary Problems of a Planned Economy* (Harvard University Press, 1955), Chap. 6.

[23]This is especially true since the Soviets have virtually no explicit rent payments but include them implicitly in the turnover tax.

[24]Also perhaps to extract the "economic rent" from such practices.

[25]What we have said of the urban income tax applies also to the agricultural tax. The agricultural tax discriminates against the private farmer and in favor of the collective farmer.

[26]Lottery winners have their bonds redeemed at the same time they receive their lottery prizes. At present, one-third of the subscribers to a bond issue eventually win lottery prizes.

[27]Of course, very few bonds were ever actually paid off: the conversions put off repayments in the 1930's and the currency reform of 1947 eliminated the need for repayment on two-thirds of all outstanding obligations. However, even if there had been no conversions, the real value of ten-year bonds at maturity could hardly ever have amounted to more than about one-quarter of original value, so rapid was the rise in consumer goods prices in the pre-1948 period. Cf. Naum Jasny, *The Soviet Economy during the Plan Era* (Stanford University Press, 1951), p. 58.

[28]This is also true of the consumer and producer cooperatives, but the amounts have never been significant.

[29]More often than not, the retained profit of a group of enterprises has been redistributed among them for investment purposes by the administrative head of the group (or *glavk,* translated "chief administration"). Recently, the power of the *glavk* to do this was reduced. Cf. *New York Times,* August 14, 1952, article by Harry Schwartz.

[30]This is because the bulk of the deduction into the Directors' Fund is based on overplan profits, and a firm which reduced planned losses by a certain amount would be considered to have exceeded the plan in the same direction as one which increased positive profits.

[31]Receipts from sale of surplus property or livestock are also deposited in the "indivisible fund." Initially, this fund is based on the value of the property and money payments of the collective farmers to the collective farm at the time the farm is organized.

[32]Cf. Alexander Baykov, *The Development of the Soviet Economic System* (London: Cambridge University Press, 1946), p. 404.

[33]L. E. Hubbard, *Soviet Money and Finance* (London: Macmillan, 1936), p. 228.

[34]This refers to the well-known "control by the ruble." That is to say, by making state enterprises dependent upon the State Bank for funds, the Bank is placed in a position in which it can supervise and check the progress of enterprises, and put pressure on enterprises which are not operating satisfactorily or according to plan.

[35]Gregory Grossman, "The Union of Soviet Socialist Republics," *Comparative Banking Systems,* ed. B. H. Beckhart (Columbia University Press, 1954), pp. 733–68.

[36]The part used for capital repair is deposited in the State Bank.

[37]If the procurement price of a bushel of grain which cost 40 rubles to produce were only 20 rubles and the state resold the grain (as bread) for 100 rubles, the turnover tax on a bushel would be 80 rubles, of which it could be said that 20 rubles (40 minus 20) was paid by the producer and 60 (100 minus 40) by the consumer.

[38]Bergson, in his famous study of Soviet wages, demonstrated that relative wages in the Soviet Union appear to reflect relative differences in productivity (cf. Bergson, *The Structure of Soviet Wages*, pp. 207–9). On this basis one can take the free-market wage for a particular job as a rough measure of the value of the job performance to the state.

[39]This separation is attempted for grains, on the basis of heroic assumptions, in Holzman, *Soviet Taxation*, Chap. 7.

[40]The *sovkhozy*, or state farms, are owned by the state but produce a very small percentage of total agricultural output.

Part II

Comparative Fiscal Systems

EVEN a casual observer is immediately struck by the substantial differences both in level and in structure between the fiscal systems of rich and of poor nations. The article by Alison Martin and W. A. Lewis, both then of Manchester University, was one of the earliest attempts to examine and draw generalizations from these patterns of public revenues and expenditures. Their efforts illustrate both the possible dangers and some of the rewards of such intercountry comparisons and are today still well worth a careful reading.

Like a number of others who have examined fiscal data, Martin and Lewis concentrate on the gap between the rich and the poor and say little about the considerable differences among the fiscal systems of the poorer nations themselves. The second selection in this section, an extract from a recent report of the United Nations Economic Commission for Asia and the Far East, indicates the range of this diversity even in underdeveloped countries with similar economic structures. A number of perceptive and useful observations on tax policy are also made in this selection, as in the preceding one.

Finally, the more legally oriented survey of Latin American tax systems by Joseph Crockett brings out the similarities and differences within what is perhaps the most homogeneous of the less-developed regions. Both the ECAFE extract and Crockett's paper provide some idea of the complexities of comparative tax analysis.

89

5

Patterns of Public
Revenue and Expenditure

*by Alison Martin and W. Arthur Lewis**

I. Introduction

THIS article[1] compares the revenues and expenditures of sixteen
countries at different levels of economic development. Its main purpose is to see how patterns of expenditure and sources of revenue
vary with economic development, in the hope of discovering in this
process what patterns are appropriate to different levels of development.

The basic statistics are set out in six tables at the end of the
article, which are described more fully in the Statistical Appendix
[not included here]. Except in the case of Colombia, the material is
for a year overlapping with 1953 or 1954. The figures have been
classified according to the categories of expenditure and the sources
of revenue. They are all shown as proportions of Gross National
Product at factor cost.[2] Current expenditure is distinguished from
capital expenditure, but no distinction is made between transfer
expenditures and expenditures on goods and services. The figures
are consolidated for all public authorities (central state, and local
authorities), except in Tables 8, 9, 13, 14, and 15, which relate to
state and local finance exclusively.

Comparisons of this kind are subject to several criticisms. First,
different countries classify the same expenditure in different ways.
We have tried to meet this by going through the budgets and classifying expenditures according to a common pattern; hence the figures
for each country appear according to our classification, which is not
necessarily the same as that used in the country's budget.

Secondly, expenditures which appear in the budgets of some countries are left to other agencies in other countries. For example the

Manchester School of Economic and Social Studies, XXIV (September, 1956),
203–32. This article is reprinted here with the kind permission of the Krause Re-
print Corporation, New York; only Tables 1–9 have been included in this volume.

expense of medical care falls mainly upon the government in the United Kingdom, but is left to private individuals in the United States of America. The figures are not intended to show how much a *country* spends on a service, but only how much its *governments* spend. Public undertakings and nationalised industries are the most difficult case. We are concerned with these only in so far as they affect the budgets of the public authorities. For example, if their profits are paid into the Treasury, or their losses met by the Treasury, they (i.e. the surpluses or deficits only) are included in our accounts; but if their surpluses or deficits are not in the government's accounts they are excluded. Similarly, if the government has to find capital for them, this will appear in our figures of capital expenditure; but if they borrow in the capital market or finance capital expenditure out of their own profits, these sums are not shown in our figures.

Thirdly, comparisons of the Gross National Product of different countries are always shaky. We escape most of the usual problems, since our tables do not require G.N.P.'s to be compared directly. Nevertheless the structure of G.N.P.'s differs, especially in the respective proportions of monetary and of subsistence income, and also in the different ways in which subsistence income is valued, and these differences need to be taken into account in making comparisons. Despite the difficulties inherent in using G.N.P. as a base, we have preferred to use it instead of using "Total Expenditure" or "Total Revenue," because we find it more illuminating. For example, general administration as a proportion of current expenditure is 13 per cent in Sweden and 35 per cent in India. We find it more illuminating to note that general administration costs 3.07 per cent of G.N.P. in Sweden and 3.09 per cent in India, but any reader who prefers to convert our tables into proportions of total revenue and expenditure can do so for himself.

Section II of the article deals with expenditure, distinguishing current and capital expenditure. Section III is concerned with the sources of revenue, excluding loans. Section IV is a brief note on the finances of "local" authorities, using this term to include not only municipal and rural authorities, but also states, provinces and other units in federal structures.

II. Expenditure

When we began this investigation we expected to find that public expenditure rises relatively to national income as income grows. This is very broadly true, as far as total expenditure goes. Table 1 shows current expenditure of the sixteen countries, in order of G.N.P. per head. Column *A* shows total current expenditure, while Column *B* shows the total excluding expenditure on social insurance, food or agricultural subsidies, defence and public debt.

TABLE 1

CURRENT EXPENDITURE AS % OF G.N.P.

	A	B		A	B
Tanganyika	11.91	10.68	Colombia	11.80	8.42
Uganda	12.26	10.78	Italy	24.58	12.79
India	8.84	6.15	Trinidad	15.54	12.42
Nigeria	4.98	4.34	France	25.76	10.79
Ceylon	14.42	11.59	U.K.	34.00	11.52
Gold Coast	12.20	10.43	New Zealand	30.12	13.77
Jamaica	13.08	10.38	Sweden	23.49	13.26
British Guiana	14.29	11.44	U.S.A.	27.43	7.24

It will be seen from Column A that there is a rough relationship between total expenditure and G.N.P. per head. The mean of the first four figures is 9.50 per cent, the mean of the second four 13.50 per cent, the mean of the third four 19.42 per cent, and the mean of the last four 28.76 per cent.

This relationship does not, however, extend so clearly to Column B. The great differences between the richer and the poorer countries are in the amounts spent on defence, on the public debt (which reflects past defence expenditure), on social insurance schemes, and on food or agricultural subsidies. Expenditure in these four categories is excluded from Column B, so that what is left—the civilian administrative services, health and education—comprises the major expenditures of the poorer countries, suitable for comparison with similar expenditure in the richer countries.

"Basic" Expenditure

Let us begin by comparing only this "basic" expenditure, which is common to countries at all levels of development. The figures in Column B show only a slight correlation with income per head. The mean of the first four is 7.99 per cent; of the second four 10.96 per cent; of the third four 11.11 per cent; and of the last four 11.45 per cent. The coefficient of rank correlation is only 0.46.

If we confine ourselves for the moment to the services included in "basic" current expenditure, it is appropriate to ask why anyone should expect the proportion of G.N.P. spent on these services to be a function of G.N.P. per head. There are three reasons for expecting the proportion to grow with G.N.P., and one reason for expecting it to fall.

The first reason for expecting the proportion to grow turns out to be fallacious: it is that the proportion has in fact grown in Europe and in North America during the past hundred years, during which G.N.P. per head has also grown. This is the fallacy of *post hoc propter hoc*. The main reason why these countries now spend relatively more on their public services than they did a hundred years ago is not that they are richer, but that they have a different conception of the duties of the state. The citizens did not take it for granted a hundred years ago that public authorities must pay for schooling for every child, that they must pave and light the streets of every village with a thousand inhabitants, or that they must maintain those public services which have brought the infant mortality rate down from 250 to 30 per thousand. But this change in ideas is not confined to the richer countries, and is not proportional to income per head. It has affected the poorer countries just as much, and it shows up in just as great an increase in the ratio of public expenditure in poor countries as in rich countries.

A second reason why we might expect the proportion spent on public services to rise is the relatively slow growth of productivity in this sector of the economy. This is best illustrated by making the extreme assumptions. Suppose that the number of policemen required varies directly with the output of commodities. Suppose also that while the total population, the number producing commodities, and the productivity of policemen remain constant, the productivity of those making commodities doubles, and so therefore does the output of commodities. It will follow that the number of policemen required will double. And if a policeman is paid the same as a producer of commodities it will also follow that the percentage share of commodities received by policemen will double. It is hard to measure the productivity of services. Thanks to the typewriter, the telephone, the mechanical computer and other inventions, it has undoubtedly increased. But it is generally believed to have increased less than productivity in manufacturing or in agriculture, and to this extent the share of national income spent on public services would rise if these services were a function of output.

This brings us to the third point. Is the need for public services a function of output? To revert to our previous example, if the number of policemen needed is a function not of the output of commodities but of the number of men making commodities, and if the number of men is constant, and if policemen are paid the same as others, then the percentage share of policemen in commodity output will be constant whatever may happen to productivities, absolutely or relatively. Similarly if teachers are paid the same as other people, and if the ratios of teachers to children and of children to adults are constant, then the percentage share of teachers in the national income will be constant whatever may happen to productivity. Actually the ratio of children to adults is greater in poor countries, so if other things were equal the proportion of the national income spent on education would fall as productivity increased.

Assuming for the moment that public servants are paid on the average the same as other people, we can cut through this tangle by asking our question in the form: does the proportion of the population required in the public services vary with output per head? Different answers may be given for different services. As far as justice, police, and administration (narrowly defined) are concerned, there is no obvious reason why the proportion of men required should vary significantly with output per head, though there is possibly less voluntary public service in the richer communities, and correspondingly more people on the public payroll. (Cf. the amount of administration and of judical work done by the "squire" in eighteenth century England.) There is also greater expenditure on foreign missions, and on other representation in foreign countries—though the cost of this may be as much a function of size and of status as it is of income. As for the economic services, the proportion of men required should on balance grow with income per head. The proportion required as agricultural extension workers should diminish as the farmers become more educated (and decline relatively in numbers); but the proportion engaged in maintaining roads, or water supplies or public works may be expected to increase. In the social services, the proportion required in education and in health is primarily a matter of policy. In one sense backward countries need relatively more spent on health and education because of the leeway to be made up, but in practice the numbers engaged in these services are relatively larger in rich than in poor countries.

It follows that we should expect the proportion of the population engaged in the basic public services to increase with income per head. Column *B* in Table 1, however, shows that the difference in the proportion of national income spent on these services is relatively insignificant. Probably the main explanation of this paradox is the fact that a public servant usually costs more in relation to average income per head in poor than in rich countries. In Britain or the U.S.A., government employees receive an average income not very different from the average in the country. This is not so in the poorer countries. It is not merely that the higher civil servants and scientists cost relatively more, especially when these are imported from richer countries. There is also the mass of clerks, nurses, teachers and other subordinate grades. An elementary school teacher in Britain earns a salary about equal to that of an industrial worker, but an elementary school teacher in most poor countries (India is a notable exception) earns two or three times as much as the average farmer. As output grows and education spreads, the skills commanded by public servants become relatively less scarce, and their share of the national income would decline sharply but for the factors already mentioned which bring about a relative increase in numbers.

The importance of these factors comes out more clearly when we split "basic" expenditure into sub-groups, as is done in Table 2. The exact meaning of the terms used can be found by reference to Table 10 and to the Appendix. Broadly speaking, "Administration" excludes the economic departments—Agriculture, Commerce, Labour, etc.— which are included with public works and roads in "Economic."

TABLE 2

"BASIC" CURRENT EXPENDITURE AS % OF G.N.P.

	Adminis-tration[a]	Economic[b]	Education	Health	Total
Tanganyika	3.87	3.83	1.70	.28	10.68
Uganda	3.17	4.16	2.39	1.06	10.78
India	3.09	1.85	.77	.44	6.15
Nigeria	1.42	1.61	.78	.53	4.34
Ceylon	2.77	3.81	2.94	2.07	11.59
Gold Coast	2.56	3.58	3.06	1.23	10.43
Jamaica	2.89	3.44	1.99	2.06	10.38
British Guiana	3.24	4.08	2.19	1.93	11.44
Colombia	3.26	2.64	1.68	.84	8.42
Italy	3.76	3.96	2.99	2.08	12.79
Trinidad	3.23	4.49	2.24	2.46	12.42
France	3.32	3.88	1.97	1.62	10.79
U.K.	2.36	2.41	3.47	3.28	11.52
New Zealand	2.92	4.75	2.68	3.42	13.77
Sweden	3.07	3.35	4.27	2.57	13.26
U.S.A.	2.40	1.52	2.40	.92	7.24

[a]Row 1 in Table 10.
[b]Rows 4 to 16 in Table 10.

Table 2 shows that the proportions spent on administration and on economic services are relatively constant, while the proportions spent on education and on health vary considerably.

In the sub-group "Administration," 10 out of the 16 countries spend between 2.77 and 3.32 per cent of G.N.P. The four which spend less than this include two poor ones (Nigeria and Gold Coast) and two rich ones (U.K. and U.S.A.) ; and the two which spend more are also widely separated (Tanganyika and Italy).

In both Nigeria and the Gold Coast much administration is done by chiefs, whose major source of income is from trade or farming or other payments which do not enter into the public accounts, so the figures do not fully measure the real resources used in administration.

On the other hand, considerable expenditures on colonial development are hidden in the French figure for administration, which would otherwise be nearer to those of other countries at the richer end of the table.

In the economic sub-group, nine out of the sixteen countries spend between 3.35 and 4.16. New Zealand and Trinidad spend even more, in both cases because of much more than average expenditure on roads. On the other hand, in the cases of India, Nigeria, the U.K. and the U.S.A. some part of the relatively low figure is due to expenditure on ports, railways and other works either being done by private companies, or else appearing in separate budgets which are not incorporated in the general budget.

It is notable that, apart from housing subsidies (which are included in "Economic") the U.K. and the U.S.A. spend almost exactly the same proportions of G.N.P. on administration (2.36, 2.40) and on economic services (1.73, 1.52). The great differences between these two nations are to be found in their social services and in the categories excluded from Table 2. Also, one must remember that the Federal Government finds it easier to finance some essentially civilian expenditures on the defence vote (e.g. research) so "basic" civil expenditure is rather larger than these figures show.

The fact that the Colombian figures are for 1947 should be borne in mind, since this was before the governments of underdeveloped countries got into the swing of their post-war development programmes. Unfortunately we have not had access to later Colombian figures, which are probably much higher, and which would be more fully comparable with the other figures in this article.

The expenditure on health varies most widely. Four countries spend less than 1.0, five spend between 1.0 and 2.0, five between 2.0 and 3.0, and two over 3.0. In general it is the richest countries which spend the most, but the fact that the U.S. spends less than 1.0 while Ceylon spends more than 2.0 emphasises that in this field policy is as important as income per head. The doctrine that it is the duty of the state to provide an adequate health service for all the citizens is very recent, and different countries have responded to it in widely differing degrees.

The duty to provide education is of much older recognition, and this expenditure varies less than health, though more than administrative or economic expenditure. The ten countries which spend more than 2.00 include six of the seven richest, as well as British Guiana, Gold Coast, Ceylon and Uganda. India's expenditure is specially low because the average income of teachers is much closer to average national income in India than it is in other poor countries, but even with this allowance the figure is a reminder that India's large output of university graduates rests on a rather narrow base of primary and secondary education.

In all these figures India and Nigeria stand out for the poverty of their public services. Their expenditures are so small when compared with those of poorer countries (Tanganyika, Uganda) or of countries not so very much richer (Ceylon, Gold Coast) that they cannot possibly be explained in terms of national income per head. These low figures are due to large portions of these two countries having been governed until fairly recently by rulers who had low standards of public service. What they have in common is that they have both been ruled through native princes, who were left to decide for themselves what public services were required, and who remained steeped in mediæval notions of the functions of government. Outside the Indian States and the Nigerian Emirates the British Raj busied itself creating a modern framework of government, but in these two great areas the initiative was left to native rulers. The resulting figures for India and for Nigeria are the clearest proof that the proportion of national income spent on public services is a function not mainly of national income per head but of how "backward" or "progressive" are the rulers of the state.

Other Current Expenditure

The four items we have so far excluded are far more important in the budgets of the richer than of the poorer countries. These items are defence, public debt, social insurance and agricultural subsidies. If we exclude New Zealand, the U.S.A. and the countries of Europe, the total of these four items averages only 2.26 per cent of G.N.P. in the remaining ten countries, whereas in New Zealand it is 10.23 per cent, and in the rest it ranges up to 22.48 per cent, which is twice as much as "basic" current expenditure.

There is least variation between countries in the cost of the public debt. It is less than 1.0 per cent of G.N.P. in the African countries, in India and in Sweden (thanks to absence of wars). At the other extreme there is a big gap between the largest figure, the U.K.'s 4.77, and the next largest, New Zealand's 2.76. The U.S.A. has not fought such long wars as has the U.K., and is not so socialistically inclined as New Zealand; she escapes with 2.16 per cent. Italy and France have fought lengthy wars, but with less care to prevent inflation, so their debt costs only 1.97 per cent of G.N.P. in each case.

One important conclusion is that several of the poorer countries have such small debt burdens that they could afford to finance much development by borrowing. Much the same conclusion was reached by Dr. Finch, who approached the matter via the balance of payments.[3]

The leading country in the field of social insurance is New Zealand, which spends 7.98 per cent of G.N.P. in this way. The U.K. and Sweden spend significantly less, respectively 5.84 and 5.59 per cent. Italy comes next with 4.33 per cent, followed by France 3.51 and the U.S.A. 3.49 per cent. Clearly, policy is as important as degree of industrialisation in determining how much is spent in this way.

Finally, defence. This is an insignificant item in the British colonies and in Ceylon (0.50 per cent of G.N.P. or less). It absorbs 1.43 per cent in Colombia, 1.91 per cent in India, 3.74 per cent in New Zealand and also in Sweden, 5.33 per cent in Italy, 9.49 per cent in France, 9.89 per cent in the U.K., and 13.90 per cent in the U.S.A. Probably the U.S.A. figure for defence includes some civilian expenditures which the administration finds it convenient to classify under this head for political reasons.

Comparison between the U.S.A. and the U.K. will interest those U.K. taxpayers who are groaning under the burden of current expenditure totalling 34 per cent of G.N.P. The U.K. spends roughly the same as the U.S.A. on administration and on economic services (apart from housing subsidies) and 4.0 per cent of G.N.P. less on defence. It spends 1.1 per cent more on education, 1.3 per cent more on food or agricultural subsidies, 2.4 per cent more on health, 2.4 per cent more on social insurance, and 2.6 per cent more on public debt. Significant cuts in these expenditures are unlikely outside the fields of food subsidies and and defence.

Capital Expenditure

Capital expenditure is less easy to compare than is "basic" current expenditure, because the extent to which governments provide for capital formation through the budget varies more widely. In Table 3 the expenditure is grouped under four sub-heads. "Departmental" in this table covers a wider range than "Administration" in Table 2; it includes education, health and social insurance, and also economic departments, with the exception of those otherwise specified. "Transport" includes roads, and the whole of public works. "Finance" includes agriculture, water, industry and housing, which are the services where there is greatest variation in the extent to which finance is privately or publicly supplied.

It is at once apparent from Table 3 how wide is the range of capital expenditures by governments—from 2.3 per cent of G.N.P. in India to 14.0 per cent in Sweden. The figures are misleading because they exclude the expenditures of those public agencies which do not appear in the budget, and these vary from country to country. For example, the capital expenditures of publicly owned railways, harbours or electric power stations are included in some cases and excluded in

TABLE 3

CAPITAL EXPENDITURE AS % OF G.N.P.

	Departmental[a]	Transport[b]	Finance[c]	Defence	Total
Tanganyika	1.27	1.24	1.45	.02	3.98
Uganda	2.37	2.17	2.17	.10	6.81
India	.21	.59	1.40	.10	2.30
Nigeria	.62	1.19	.49	.10	2.40
Ceylon	.98	1.91	4.30	.26	7.45
Gold Coast	1.80	4.03	2.28	.13	8.24
Jamaica	.60	1.48	1.96	—	4.04
British Guiana	1.62	1.58	2.76	—	5.96
Colombia	d	2.66	.55	—	3.21
Italy	.67	1.62	3.26	—	5.55
Trinidad	1.06	2.03	2.42	—	5.51
France	1.01	1.90	4.02	1.18	8.11
U.K.	1.24	.68	2.99	.46	5.37
New Zealand	1.56	2.40	4.31	—	8.27
Sweden	2.64	4.69	3.76	2.90	13.99
U.S.A.	1.18	.99	.71	1.38	4.26

[a]Rows 1, 2, 3, 13, 14, 15 and 17 in Table 11.
[b]Rows 4, 5 and 6 in Table 11.
[c]Rows 7, 8, 9, 10, 11, 12 and 16 in Table 11.
[d]Included in Transport, which also includes some items of Finance.

others, so the figures do not accurately state the total spending of public agencies. What they do state is the total spending for which the Minister of Finance holds himself responsible, in so far as his decision to include these figures in the budget indicates that he regards the financing of their expenditures as a part of his responsibility. They are therefore a good measure of the extent of the fiscal problem as he sees it.

The smallness of the "Departmental" and "Transport" expenditures is remarkable. The expenditures listed under "Administration," "Health" and "Education" in Table 2 account for about 70 per cent of basic current expenditures. Yet these three together are slightly narrower than the category listed as "Departmental" in Table 3, which takes typically much less than 2 per cent of G.N.P. Basic current expenditures are mainly on administration, education, and health, but it is economic services which make the large drafts on capital expenditure.

The smallness of the capital expenditures on education and on health is particularly remarkable. The mean capital expenditure on education (the mean of row 2 in Table 11) is 0.5 per cent of G.N.P. while the mean current expenditure (the mean of row 2 in Table 10) is 2.3 per cent of G.N.P. Similarly the mean capital expenditure on health is 0.3 per cent, whereas the mean current expenditure is 1.7 per cent. The capital expenditure may be understated, since some budgets hide expenditure on schools and health buildings under "public works," but this is probably not very significant. In making public expenditure programmes one of the maxims is that it is not safe to plan only in terms of capital expenditure because some of the items which look attractive because of their small capital requirements are in fact very expensive because of the heavy commitment of current expenditures which they carry. The figures in Table 3 cannot be used to prove this by comparison with Table 2, since Table 3 shows only gross additions to capital, while Table 2 shows current expenditures associated with all existing capital. But the maxim is undoubtedly relevant to education and to health.

Expenditure on roads is also remarkably small. The mean capital expenditure is 0.73 per cent of G.N.P., and the mean current expenditure is 0.71 per cent. The largest combined expenditure is 2.69 per cent, which occurs in Sweden.

It is therefore clear that the extent of government capital expenditures depends mainly on how far the "productive" sectors of the economy—agriculture, transport, and industry—lean on the government for finance (and also on how much government finance goes into housing). This is not primarily a question of the extent to which these sectors are publicly owned, since publicly owned industries may raise their own finance privately in the capital market, while privately owned industries may be financed by loans from government sources.

The idea that the government should be a source of saving is relatively new. It follows from three policy objectives. First, the amount of private saving in under-developed countries is relatively small, and so also is the amount available through international investment. Hence, if a large investment programme is to be financed it must be through forced saving, and this is more equitably achieved through taxation than through inflation. Secondly, some developed countries have exactly the same problem of a tendency for investment to exceed saving, and the prescription of a budget surplus to counter inflation in these circumstances is exactly the same solution reached by a different road. Thirdly, socialistic governments are anxious that new capital be created on public rather than private account, and since all capital is created out of saving the only way to prevent private fortunes from growing *pari passu* with capital formation is to finance capital out of public rather than private saving. Public ownership is not the antithesis of private wealth if, through dependence on private saving, all increase in publicly owned capital is matched by an increase in privately held government bonds.

The extent of public saving can be deduced by subtracting the total of current expenditures shown in Table 10 (row 21) from the total of current revenue shown in Table 12 (row 12). This yields the results in Table 4.

TABLE 4
PUBLIC SAVING AS % OF G.N.P.

Tanganyika	.32	Colombia	1.07
Uganda	4.88	Italy	−1.05
India	−.56	Trinidad	.19
Nigeria	3.43	France	3.14
Ceylon	4.93	U.K.	3.09
Gold Coast	10.00	New Zealand	3.06
Jamaica	.20	Sweden	9.82
British Guiana	3.38	U.S.A.	1.88

The figures in Table 4 indicate the extent to which a country is "socialistic" in the sense of believing in public *ownership* (rather than in the sense of believing in public *control,* or in *equality* of income or of opportunity) since they show how much new capital is being created in the community without a corresponding increase of private wealth. On the other hand they somewhat understate the amount of public saving because they omit sinking fund contributions (which are in any case a small percentage of G.N.P.), investment by publicly owned enterprises financed out of their own savings, and, in the case of the African territories, grants from the statutory Marketing Boards for general development purposes (which are substantial).

Here again the range is remarkable. Even in 1953 there were two governments not raising enough revenue to cover even their current expenditures. The Gold Coast and Sweden stand out as the most "socialistic governments" with Ceylon, Uganda, Nigeria, British Guiana, France, U.K., and New Zealand following a long way behind.

A Frame of Reference?

Does this analysis help to answer the question: what is the appropriate level and distribution of public expenditure in under-developed countries? The question cries out for an answer, if not in rigid quantitative terms, but at least in terms of some principles which may be used in judging government programmes. Throughout the world Ministers and officials are busily engaged in working out five-year plans for public expenditure, and they look anxiously to economists and to others for guidance as to what is appropriate. Neither is there any lack of advice offered. The United Nations International Bank has sent out a succession of missions which have produced reports tendering such advice. Also many economists have sat on fiscal or other commissions reviewing public expenditure, and they seem usually to have been able to decide what levels were appropriate. But in none of the mass of published reports can one discover how the authors have decided what level or pattern of public expenditure was appropriate. Judgments in this sphere of public finance boil down to little more than personal assertions.

This analysis can make only one small contribution to the present situation—that of providing material with which to make comparisons. Such material does not enable the planner directly to answer the question: "Is my pattern right?," but it does enable him to answer the question: "How does my pattern differ?," and thereby sets him to seek the reasons for difference.

This contribution is most usefully summarised in a table showing the median and upper quartile expenditures of our sixteen governments in each category of expenditure. As we have already seen, the basic current expenditure of governments does not vary significantly with national income per head, so the median expenditures can be used as an indication of "standard" practice by a government seeking to achieve no more than "average" performance. Upper quartile expenditures indicate a more than average performance, though not the best (or most extravagant). However, since no government wishes to show more than average performance in every sphere of activity, the sum of the upper quartiles (13.18 current and 8.23 capital in Table 5) exceeds the upper quartiles of total expenditure (12.01 current and 7.78 capital), and only Sweden and New Zealand surpass the upper quartile totals of spending.

TABLE 5
COMBINED EXPENDITURE AS % OF G.N.P.

	Median			Upper Quartile		
	Current	Capital	Total	Current	Capital	Total
Administration	3.08	.42	3.50	3.25	.57	3.82
Education	2.32	.50	2.82	2.97	.73	3.70
Health	1.78	.27	2.05	2.27	.42	2.69
Water supplies	.16	.31	.47	.29	.75	1.04
Public works	.65	.39	1.04	.82	.45	1.27
Roads	.73	.68	1.41	.90	1.00	1.90
Transport	.64	.53	1.17	.85	1.03	1.88
Agriculture[a]	.98	.49	1.47	1.21	1.10	2.31
Industry[b]	.29	.31	.60	.44	.73	1.17
Housing	.11	.72	.83	.18	1.45	1.63
	10.74	4.62	15.36	13.18	8.23	21.41
Social insurance			1.29			
Defence			1.09			
Public debt			1.10			
			18.84			

[a] Rows 7, 8, 10 and 11 in Table 10 and corresponding rows in Table 11. Irrigation is included but agricultural subsidies are excluded.
[b] Rows 12, 13, 14 and 15 in Table 10 and corresponding rows in Table 11.

Let us reiterate that Table 5 does not claim to show how any particular country must distribute its expenditure. For example, the appropriate expenditure on roads is probably relatively larger in a sparsely settled than in a densely settled country. The table is intended merely to stimulate enquiry into differences.

Table 5 shows that average performance takes 15.4 per cent of G.N.P. for basic and capital expenditure, plus 3.5 per cent for social insurance, defence and public debt, making a total of roughly 19 per cent of G.N.P. Among the under-developed countries analysed here, this level of expenditure is attained by Uganda (19.1), British Guiana (19.8), Gold Coast (20.0), Trinidad (20.3) and Ceylon (21.8).[4] It seems not unreasonable to conclude that the governments of countries making a special development effort will find themselves spending between 19 and 22 per cent of G.N.P.

As a by-product of this analysis, we can compare the expenditures proposed under India's Second Five-Year Plan with the figures in Table 5. To do this we have to deduct development expenditure under the First Five-Year plan from the figures we have been using, and to add development expenditure under the Second Five-Year plan. The distribution of development expenditure in the year 1953–54 is given in the *Five-Year Plan Progress Report for* 1953–54, page 300. We have deducted this, and have added one-fifth of the proposed expenditure under the Second Five-Year Plan, as set out on page 35 of the *Draft Outline of the Second Five-Year Plan.*[5] The result gives the average public expenditure (ordinary plus development) contemplated under the Second Five-Year Plan. This is shown in Table 6 as a percentage of the 1953/4 G.N.P. and compared with the Median expenditure taken from Table 5.

TABLE 6

INDIA'S SECOND FIVE-YEAR PLAN AND MEDIAN COMPARED

	India	Median	Difference
Administration	3.34	3.50	− .16
Education	1.35	2.82	−1.47
Health and water	.94	2.52	−1.58
Agriculture and irrigation	2.30	1.47	+ .83
Industry	2.80	.60	+2.20
Roads, works and transport	3.19	3.62	− .43
Housing	.18	.83	− .65
	14.10	15.36	−1.26

Two comments can be made on this comparison. First, there is furious debate in India on the question whether the total expenditure envisaged under the Plan is not too large. The answer to this question is "Obviously not." The proposed expenditure will merely bring India into line with such countries as Tanganyika and Jamaica, and will leave her still far behind other progressive governments in Asia, in Africa and in the Caribbean. If it is contended that the expenditure is too large for the revenue-raising capacity of the Indian governments, the answer is simply that it is ridiculous for a government in the middle of the twentieth century to be raising less than 10 per cent of G.N.P. in taxation, or to be claiming that it would be an intolerable burden or an insuperable task for the fiscal administration to raise as much as 15 per cent. But elaboration of this answer must wait for Section III of this paper.

The second feature which the comparison throws up is the great difference between the proportions in the Median and in the Indian proposals. India proposes to spend very much less on the "social" services, education, health and housing, and very much more on agriculture and industry. The proposed expenditure on industry is large only in the sense that in the countries included in our survey a larger part of the financing of industry is usually left to private enterprise. But the total capital investment in industry by public and private sources is not remarkable. The figures given in the draft outline amount to about 2.6 per cent of G.N.P. for large scale industry (excluding power), to which one might add another 1.0 per cent per annum for cottage industry. Comparable gross investment in the U.K. is consistently above 4 per cent of G.N.P. Apart from industry, agriculture and the railways receive substantial provision, but the proposed expenditure on roads is almost incredibly small.

India's small expenditures on health and education distinguish her sharply from other progressive governments, and especially from the programmes of the new nationalist governments in Ceylon, in the Gold Coast, and in Nigeria.[6] In reply to the contention that economic expenditures should precede social service expenditures, politicians in these countries reply both that health and education expenditures are necessary for increasing the output of commodities, and also that it is just as important to get rid of illiteracy and of disease as it is to provide more steel or cloth. Some West African politicians explain the difference mainly in terms of political structure. India, they say, is ruled by her upper classes, in a situation where caste and class differences are pronounced. Her rulers do what they think is best for the masses of her people, but they do not have to take much account of what the masses themselves think they want. West African society, on the other hand, is nearly classless. The masses have great political influence, and they make it clear that they value expenditures on health and education more than any other kind of government expenditure. In the final analysis there is no "model" which can show what government expenditure ought to be, without taking account of differing political pressures.

III. Revenue

We have seen that the government of an under-developed country needs to be able to raise revenue of about 17 to 19 per cent of G.N.P., according to the extent of its defence burden, in order to give a not better than average standard of service. How it can be done, and is done, is the subject of this section.

Table 7 summarises the information in Table 12 by classifying the sources of revenue in three groups only. "Direct taxes" consists of income tax, poll tax, social insurance tax, land tax, rates and death duties. "Taxes on foreign trade" are shown separately, because it is much easier to raise large sums by way of import and export duties in countries where exports account for as much as 40 per cent of G.N.P. than it is in those, such as India, where exports account for less than 10 per cent of G.N.P. The remaining category consists of excise taxes, motor licences, earnings of government departments, interest and miscellaneous fees. Grants-in-aid and loans are not included in the table.

Direct Taxes

Much the most important direct tax is the income tax, with a yield ranging from 1.61 per cent of G.N.P. in India to 13.52 in the U.K., 15.86 in the U.S.A. and 16.75 in Sweden. (That the U.S. figure is

TABLE 7
REVENUE AS % OF G.N.P.

	Direct Taxes	Taxes on Foreign Trade	Other Revenue	Total
Tanganyika	6.11	2.81	3.31	12.23
Uganda	3.71	10.36	3.07	17.14
India	2.51	1.53	4.24	8.28
Nigeria	1.94	4.51	1.96	8.41
Ceylon	5.49	10.80	3.06	19.35
Gold Coast	3.47	14.72	4.01	22.20
Jamaica	4.31	4.39	4.58	13.28
British Guiana	7.56	6.19	3.92	17.67
Colombia	4.22	1.99	6.66	12.87
Italy	7.09	1.27	15.17	23.53
Trinidad	6.87	3.60	5.26	15.73
France	9.47	1.99	17.44	28.90
U.K.	20.99	6.92	9.18	37.09
New Zealand	20.12	2.44	10.62	33.18
Sweden	19.63	1.68	12.00	33.31
U.S.A.	21.82	.18	7.31	29.31

larger than the U.K. is worth noting. Personal income tax rates are higher in the U.K., but taxes on profits, not set off against personal income tax, are much higher in the U.S.A. Paradoxically, in any debate on the alleged greater enterprise of business men in the U.S.A. most business men or economists offer the explanation that it is due to higher taxation of profits in the U.K.—a piece of inaccuracy which merely underlines how little we know about the effect of taxation on incentives.)

Compared with the richer countries, the fundamental reason for the difficulty the poorer countries have in raising public revenue is their reluctance to levy adequate sums through the income tax. This reluctance is based on certain misconceptions.

First, it is sometimes believed that a poor country would have to tax relatively more people in order to raise the same proportion of the national income, but this is true only if the distribution of income is more equal in the poorer country. Income is probably more evenly distributed in West Africa than in Western Europe, because in West Africa the farmers all have access to land free of rent, or at negligible rents. On the other hand, in the overcrowded parts of Asia a handful of landlords takes up to 50 per cent of the farmers' output in rents, and the distribution of income is as uneven or more uneven than in Europe. The top 10 per cent of the population receives as much or more of the national income, so an income tax falling on the top 10 per cent should be capable of yielding just as large a percentage of the national income if comparable rates were charged.

Income tax yields much less because comparable rates are not charged, especially in the middle ranges of the income scale. The rates in the upper ranges are often quite high—for example in India, where nevertheless the income tax (including agricultural income tax) brings in only 1.61 per cent of G.N.P. Taxes on profits may also be very high—for example, the standard rate is as high in British West Africa as in the U.K. The general practice in the poorer countries is to have high exemption limits for personal incomes with generous allowances, so that even if the sum payable at £10,000 a year may be very substantial, the sum payable at £1,000 a year is usually only a token amount, compared with what would be paid in the U.K. The man earning £200 a year usually escapes altogether.

Now, in a country like India or Nigeria, a man earning £200 a year is extremely well off in comparison with the average income of the population, which is only about £60 a year per person gainfully occupied. Even the £100 a year man is definitely "middle-class," and a cut above his neighbours. The effect of present policies is to exempt practically the whole of the "middle-class" from paying income tax, and so the yield of the tax is bound to be small. In the U.K. the number of people paying income tax is equal to just over 30 per cent of the population. In the U.S.A., where the allowances are greater, and where the gainfully occupied are relatively fewer, the number paying income tax equals 25 per cent of the population. The percentage in Jamaica is 2.1, in Trinidad 1.8, in British Guiana 1.4, and in Ceylon 0.6.

Present policies also have the effect that the middle-class pays proportionally less of its income in taxation than the poorer classes, on whom the incidence of indirect taxation is relatively heavier. The Colwyn Committee showed that this was happening in the U.K. in 1925, when U.K. allowances were similarly generous.[7] According to Dr. Das-Gupta, this was also the situation in Ceylon in 1942, though the difference is not now so pronounced.[8] There is also evidence that it is the situation in urban areas in India.[9] Such a policy is particularly inequitable in under-developed countries since in these countries the £100 to £500 a year man benefits more from public expenditure than the rest of the population. It is his children who get educated in the state schools, and his family that uses the hospitals. Most of the poorer people in the countryside are outside the reach of these services, and most of the richer use private schools, private nurses and private doctors. It is therefore quite unjustifiable morally to exempt this class from paying direct taxation.

Objection is sometimes made on the ground that it is costly to collect small sums from large numbers of persons, but the importance of this is grossly exaggerated. It is traditional in Asia and Africa to levy a direct tax upon nearly every adult—the land tax in Asia and the poll tax in Africa—and the cost of collection has been small. The average sum paid by each taxpayer is smaller than in Europe, but so also is the average salary of the tax collector. It is not differences in the cost of collection that explain why only 0.6 per cent of the population pays income tax in Ceylon, compared with 25 per cent in the U.S.A.

Apart from the income tax, the yield of other direct taxes is bound to be small in under-developed countries, though it might be larger than it is. Death duties are bound to be small because the ratio of capital to income is low. Assuming that the country's capital (including land) is worth 1.5 times its G.N.P., the amount becoming liable for death duties in any year (which depends on the death rate) would be only 3 or 4 per cent of G.N.P., so even rates of duty comparable to those of the U.K. would not yield much more than 0.8 per cent of G.N.P. The case for higher death duties in these countries must rest on political and equity considerations rather than on the prospect of raising revenue. The land tax used to raise 1.25 per cent of G.N.P. in India before the war, but now raises only 0.66 per cent, inflation having proceeded faster than re-assessment. If it were politically acceptable to classify all rural land into four or five rough grades of potential fertility, the process of assessment would be greatly simplified and accelerated, without grave injustice. But such a simple reform is contrary to a tradition of making a lengthy, detailed, and expert assessment of every acre. Finally, there is the social insurance tax, which yields as much as 6.4 per cent of G.N.P. in New Zealand. However, since social insurance payments usually grow faster than the yield of this tax, it does not contribute towards the cost of "basic" services in any of our sixteen countries. Unless the income tax rates are sharply increased in the middle income ranges, the poorer countries will have to continue to rely mainly on indirect taxation.

Taxes on Foreign Trade

Taxes on foreign trade are popular with governments because of the ease with which they can be collected, and because they are a means of levying taxation even upon the poorest citizens. Their protectionist function, which is considered important in developed countries, is seldom significant in the less developed.

Import duties raise on the average 3.59 per cent of G.N.P. in the nine poorest countries in our survey. The lowest figure is 1.14 per cent in India, where imports are only 5.7 per cent of G.N.P., and the highest is 5.77 per cent in the Gold Coast, where imports are 35.6 per cent of G.N.P. The average rate of the tax is therefore 20 per cent in India, and 16 per cent in the Gold Coast.

Heavy taxation of exports is entirely a post-war phenomenon, and is confined to Ceylon, Uganda and the Gold Coast, where export duties raise respectively 5.78, 7.02, and 8.95 per cent of G.N.P. (not including the profits and reserves of statutory marketing agencies). In the remaining six of the nine poorest countries the average is only 0.55 per cent of G.N.P. The purpose of levying these high duties has been to take advantage of some extraordinary increases of prices. For example, in the Gold Coast before the war a price of £30 per ton for cocoa was considered good. Allowing for the average trebling of commodity prices, a post-war price of £100 a ton would have been considered good. Actually the post-war price soared for a time as high as £500 per ton, and even now, when it is thought to be low, it exceeds £200 per ton. Essentially the governments' object has been to siphon off some of these windfall profits into the public purse.

This policy has been criticised on the ground that it is unfair to pick on a small section of the farming community for such heavy taxation; but it is equally arguable that the man most able to bear taxation is he who has received a sudden windfall increase in his profits. It is also objected that this high taxation has diminished private saving. This is true, but it has also much more than correspondingly increased public saving. Much money which the farmers would otherwise have spent on Cadillacs and on other forms of conspicuous consumption has gone instead into water supplies, electric power stations, and schools.

More serious is the possible long-term effect of such high taxation of a few commodities. It would be foolish to keep the net price to the farmer so low that he finds other crops more profitable—the Gold Coast has avoided this error, but Uganda has not. In the long run one may expect the prices of these commodities in the world market to come into line with the prices of other commodities, so that there is no longer a windfall margin to be taxed. It is a sensible policy to tax away part of the windfall while it lasts, but the governments in this favoured position ought to be preparing to cultivate other sources of taxation, since it is improbable that they will for long be able to rely on such substantial contributions from a few favoured exports.

One permanent legacy of these interludes is that they have shown the value of basing export duties upon a sliding scale varying with the commodity's price. The value of this system does not lie mainly in its contribution to the public revenue, since it makes export duties a very unstable source of revenue, and since what is gained in the boom may well be lost in the slump. Its value lies rather in that it helps to stabilise the economy internally. In the absence of such arrangements the internal price levels of these countries are dragged up and down in the wake of external prices, which may move 50 per cent in either direction within twelve months, and the strain of pushing up wages and trying to get them down again does considerable unnecessary harm to industrial relations.

Other Revenue

The only other large source of revenue is excise duties, raising an average of 1.94 per cent of G.N.P. in the nine poorest countries, and an average of 6.28 per cent in the seven richest, with France achieving the peak of 12.09 per cent. The main reason for this big difference is the adoption of sales and purchase taxes in many of the richer countries, a form of taxation which is now spreading into the under-developed countries.

If an under-developed country needs to raise some 15 to 20 per cent of G.N.P. in revenue, and cannot rely on a large yield from taxing foreign trade, the adoption of some form of sales tax is inevitable. A general sales tax is not as difficult to collect as one might think. One begins by registering all the people who have to pay it—manufacturers, wholesalers, and retailers. The larger units have in any case to submit their accounts for income tax purposes, so it costs little to extract the sales tax from them. One draws a line below which small traders are not assessed individually—say a turnover of £1,000 a year—and levies instead on these traders a lump sum tax of say £5 a year if the sales tax is one-half of one per cent.

If a commodity passes through several hands before reaching the final consumer, a sales tax levied each time it changes hands must encourage vertical integration. Such a tax is known as a multi-point sales tax, whereas a tax which is paid only once is known as a single-point sales tax. A multi-point sales tax is attractive because the opportunities of evading it are less than the opportunities of evading a single-point sales tax, since the single-point sales tax has to distinguish between sales which are taxed and sales which are not taxed, and this opens up loopholes for evasion. On the other hand, a multi-point sales tax would be a pronounced encouragement to vertical integration unless it were small, so in effect a multi-point sales tax can hardly be more than 0.5 per cent. This in turn means that it cannot yield much revenue. If one needs to raise 4 or 5 per cent of G.N.P. through a sales tax, as India will have to do, one must choose instead a single-point sales tax of around 10 per cent. The problem is then to prevent evasion. The system works by keeping a register of all those who are liable to pay the tax, and by taxing all their sales except sales to other people on the register. Some sellers then produce false receipts purporting to be from other people on the register, and some fraudulent evasion is inevitable, however busy the tax inspectors may be. But, in a country which has little foreign trade, what is the alternative to taxing domestic trade? The answer implicit in India's *Draft Outline of the Second Five-Year Plan* is: "Inflation." But most economists would agree that a proper exploitation of available sources of taxation should have priority.

A Frame of Reference?

When we were dealing with expenditure it was easy to construct a tentative frame of reference for under-developed countries by taking the medians and upper quartiles, since the differences between countries at different levels of development were not large. This cannot be done on the revenue side since the difference here is tremendous owing to differences in the burden of defence.

The frame of reference for expenditure gives some indication of the revenue required. Assuming median levels of expenditure, it is 18 to 20 per cent of G.N.P., according to the burden of defence. Some of the capital formation can be financed by borrowing, but having regard to the low availability of international loans; and to the fact that private domestic saving is itself inadequate to finance an appropriate level of private investment; and to the fact that the private sector leans on government agencies for some finance, especially for agriculture, for factories and for housing; the minimum target of the government of an under-developed country should be to save enough to finance its own capital expenditures. Of course, if these governments receive substantial grants-in-aid from other countries their fiscal task will be lightened, but the immediate prospect for substantial international aid is not bright.

Assuming that a government needs to raise 20 per cent of G.N.P., and is not able to rely on taxing windfalls in export trade, the following "model" is tentatively suggested:

Income tax	8.0
Land tax, rates	1.5
Death duties	0.5
Export duties	1.0
Import duties, excise, sales tax	7.0
Earnings, fees, interest	2.0
	20.0

This division is based on one of Mr. Gladstone's canons of finance: that the revenue should come about equally from direct and from indirect taxes. Our goal for consumption taxes, 7.0 per cent of G.N.P., is not far removed from current practice, since the mean sum raised by the nine poorest countries in import duties and excise taxes is already 5.53 per cent. In fact this goal is already nearly reached by Ceylon (6.12), by Colombia (6.18), and by Trinidad (6.84), and is passed by the Gold Coast (7.29), by Jamaica (7.46) and by British Guiana (7.55). The big increase in our "model" is in the income tax, since our goal of 8.0 per cent compares with a mean of 3.59 per cent raised by the nine poorest countries. The three under-developed countries nearest to this goal are Tanganyika (5.21), Trinidad (6.08) and British Guiana (6.97).

IV. LOCAL GOVERNMENT FINANCE

The people of under-developed countries will not willingly pay higher taxes unless they can see the fruit in additions to those categories of public service which they value, which are more especially roads, water supplies, medical services, schools and electric power. They will also pay more willingly if they can play a part in planning the services of their own locality, instead of depending on plans made in a distant capital city. Hence it is important to have the right balance of central and local expenditures, and also of central and local taxation. In another context the difficulties produced by an inappropriate balance can be seen in acute form in India, where the initiative to step up the expenditure programmes comes from the centre, but where the three taxes which could add most to the revenue

(the agricultural income tax, the sales tax and the land revenue)
are controlled by the states, who are reluctant to increase taxation.

Expenditure

Table 8 summarises the information given in Tables 13 and 14.
Current and capital expenditure are combined in this table. The
categories are the same as in Table 2, except that an additional
column "Other" is added for expenditure on social insurance, defence,
and public debt. The expenditure of the regions in Nigeria and of
the states in India and in the U.S.A. is included.

TABLE 8
LOCAL GOVERNMENT EXPENDITURE AS % OF G.N.P.

	Adminis-tration	Economic	Education	Health	Other	Total
Tanganyika	1.18	.20	.31	.31	—	2.00
Uganda	.71	1.01	.45	.12	.03	2.32
India	2.59	2.93	.72	.42	.38	7.04
Nigeria	.73	1.42	.74	.55	.31	3.75
Ceylon	.40	.37	—	.07	.04	.88
Gold Coast	.77	.49	.36	.40	.03	2.05
Jamaica	.33	.46	—	.27	.56	1.62
British Guiana	.30	.95	—	.20	.10	1.55
Colombia	1.65	1.70	1.09	.41	1.23	6.08
Italy	1.54	2.14	.51	1.13	1.06	6.38
Trinidad	.27	.67	—	.44	—	1.38
France	1.49	2.66	.36	1.02	.75	6.28
U.K.	1.16	4.24	3.38	.38	.93	10.09
New Zealand	1.11	2.66	—	.22	.30	4.29
Sweden	3.06	5.53	3.60	2.68	1.17	16.04
U.S.A.	1.44	2.16	2.83	.96	1.59	8.98

NOTE: The figures must be treated with reserve. It is not possible
to be certain that one has got hold of the figures of each of several
thousands of local authorities, and in several cases expenditures on
capital account have not been obtainable (whether because there
are no such expenditures, or because they are included in the current
accounts or because we could not find a source). Errors here make
little difference to the aggregates in Tables 2 and 3, but they are of
course of greater significance for Table 8.

The main conclusion, however, is not obscured by the shakiness
of some of the figures. This is: that the weakness of local government
in relation to central government is one of the most striking phe-
nomena of under-developed countries. In Ceylon, in Africa and in
the West Indies the central government directly controls the major

part of the public service. This weakness of local government is particularly marked in relation to education. Only in the U.K., Sweden, and the U.S.A. do local authorities play a significant role in the education system; in five countries they play no role at all. On the other hand, except in Nigeria (where the powers of the regional governments were substantially increased in 1953 under a new federal constitution) the countries where the local governments spend less than 6 per cent of G.N.P. are all small, and the fact that New Zealand is included among them suggests that the absence of strong subordinate authorities may be due to their size rather than to their state of development. Nevertheless one retains the impression that the size of some of these countries, especially in Africa, would justify greater regional devolution, and it is interesting to note that this has become a major political issue in some of them.

Revenue

To construct Table 9 we have first arranged countries in order of the percentage of G.N.P. accruing as revenue to subordinate authorities (including grants), and we have then averaged the receipts of the first four, the second four, and so on. For example, the first four (i.e. those receiving least) are Ceylon, Trinidad, Jamaica and British Guiana. They receive in land tax and rates respectively 0.32, 0.27, 0.78 and 0.43 of G.N.P. The average of these figures, 0.45, is entered in row one, column one of Table 9.

TABLE 9
SOURCES OF LOCAL REVENUE AS % OF G.N.P.

	First Four	Second Four	Third Four	Fourth Four
Land tax, rates	.45	.70	.52	2.07
Income and poll tax	.19	.47	.63	1.75
Excise duties	—	.10	1.55	.91
Grants from centre	.33	.61	1.11	1.79
Other revenue	.43	.62	.66	2.73
Total	1.40	2.50	4.47	9.25

A tax on land or houses is the most popular source of local revenue; it is the only tax which is levied at the local level by all the sixteen countries in our survey. It is usually also the largest single source of revenue. Next in popularity (with governments if not with taxpayers) is a local income tax, levied by nine of our countries. Local excise duties do not normally bring in a substantial revenue. Grants from the central government usually account for between 20 and 25 per cent of the revenues of subordinate authorities.

NOTES TO SELECTION 5

[1]Some of the material of this paper was used for the Sidney Ball Lecture delivered at the University of Oxford by Professor W. A. Lewis on May 4, 1956.

[2]Except in two cases, where we have had to use other national income concepts. See Statistical Appendix [not included here].

[3]D. Finch, "Investment Service of Under-developed Countries," *International Monetary Fund Staff Papers,* September, 1951.

[4]These totals exclude agricultural subsidies.

[5]In classifying the expenditure shown on page 35 of the *Draft Outline* it is assumed that half the expenditure on the Backward Classes and on Rehabilitation should be credited to Education. The other half is credited to Agriculture in the first case, and to Industry in the second case. But in making deductions from the 1953–54 figures it is assumed that the half which is here credited to Education was originally credited to Administration in the source from which we took the figures. Power is included in Industry.

[6]The Nigerian figures in these tables are for 1952/53. The constitutional changes of 1953 have resulted in a very large increase of public expenditures, especially on health and on education.

[7]*Report of the Committee on National Debt and Taxation, Cmd.* 2800, 1927, p. 96.

[8]*Report of the Taxation Commission* (Colombo, 1956), p. 52. This Report quotes Dr. Das Gupta's conclusion.

[9]*Report of the Taxation Enquiry Commission* (New Delhi, 1955), I, 69.

6

Government Revenue Systems in Asian Countries

by the United Nations Economic Commission for Asia and the Far East*

THE revenue systems in most countries are built up haphazard. In ECAFE countries, they show the influence of historical accidents, emulation of the tax systems of metropolitan or other advanced countries, and the *ad hoc* responses to the specific situations encountered. However, the criteria by which they were supposed to be judged—such as the Smithian canons of taxation—have themselves undergone a drastic change in the last twenty or thirty years. Many countries have effected considerable changes in their revenue systems to make them more serviceable for the tasks of fiscal policy outlined in Chapter 4 [not included here]. They have attempted to use them to increase the long-term ratio of national non-consumption to income, to influence the balance of payments, to channel resources into the public sector so as to give greater control over their utilization, to counteract short-term fluctuations in economic activity and to reduce the large—and may be growing—inequalities of income and wealth. This chapter reviews the salient characteristics of the existing revenue systems in the ECAFE countries, assesses their merits and limitations, and explores the means of enhancing their effectiveness in realizing these objectives. The impact of revenue policies, however, should be evaluated not in isolation, but in conjunction with the expenditure policies reviewed in Chapter 5 [not included here].

THE VOLUME OF GOVERNMENT REVENUE

Undoubtedly, government revenue in the countries of the region grew in volume between 1951 and 1958. The only exception has

*United Nations, Economic Commission for Asia and the Far East, *Economic Survey of Asia and the Far East 1960* (Bangkok, 1961), Chap. 6 pp. 84–103. Reprinted with the kind permission of the United Nations Publishing Service.

been Indonesia, where internal disturbances have seriously affected revenue collection by the government; revenue appears to have fallen in real terms. The growth of revenue elsewhere has, in a majority of cases, been smaller than that in expenditure. Among the few cases where revenue has grown in the same or greater measure than expenditure, the latter continues to be in excess of revenue.

Only a few countries, such as Burma, Ceylon, China (mainland and Taiwan), the Federation of Malaya and Japan obtain one-sixth or more of their national product in revenue (see Table 1). The

TABLE 1

ECAFE COUNTRIES: GOVERNMENT REVENUE, 1950–1958

(Per Cent of Gross National Product)

Country	1950	1951	1952	1953	1954	1955	1956	1957	1958
Burma	17	15	17	17	22	23	15	20	19
Cambodia[a]		11	14	11	14	13	12	12	. . .
Ceylon	15	19	21	20	21	21	25	24	23
China: mainland[b,d]	15	26	29	31	36	35	32	33	33
Taiwan	. . .	18	20	17	19	19	20	20	22
Federation of Malaya[c]	12	14	16	15	. . .	17	18	17	. . .
India[d]	8	9	8	8	9	10	10	11	11
Indonesia	. . .	16	15	16	12	12	13	12	13
Japan	23	22	22	22	22	20	21	22	22
Korea, southern				7	9	8	8	11	13
Pakistan[d]	11	13	11	10	8	9	9	10	11
Philippines	8	10	11	10	11	11	10	11	11
Thailand	9	10	11	12	13	11	12	12	12

SOURCE: See the explanatory note, page 63 [not included here].

[a]Revised estimate for 1952 and budget estimates for 1953–57.

[b]The concept of national income differs in mainland China from the one commonly used in private enterprise economies. It refers to material production only, and excludes economic activities not contributing directly to material production such as public administration and defence and personal and professional services. The estimates refer to net national income or product; they have been obtained indirectly by applying indices for the period 1950–57 given on page 20 in the *Ten Great Years* (issued by the State Statistical Bureau and published by the Foreign Language Press, Peking, 1960) to the official figures given by Li Fu-chun, chairman of the State Planning Commission, on page 37 of the October 10, 1959, issue of the *Red Flag* (in Chinese).

[c]Including Singapore up to 1953.

[d]Net national product.

proportion is relatively smaller for Japan than for the advanced industrial countries of North America or western Europe. There is considerable disparity even among the poor and newly developing countries. Whereas mainland China raises one-third, and Burma, Ceylon, China: Taiwan and the Federation of Malaya between one-sixth and a quarter of national income in revenue, the proportion for the rest remains between only 11 and 13 per cent of the national income. Of course, each country has its own specific advantages and problems; even so, countries with similar types of economy such as Burma and Thailand or Ceylon and the Federation of Malaya show considerable disparity in the revenue they raise. Despite India's progress in other directions, its fiscal system has remained under-developed to the extent that the country ranks among the lowest in terms of the percentage of revenue collected to its national income.

The percentage of national product obtained by governments as revenue has, on the whole, increased, although the increase in per-centage is much less striking than the increase in the volume of revenues. However, both in magnitude and in growth, the results of the efforts made by governments to transfer to themselves resources to defray their commitments have lagged behind the increase in these commitments. This is not to maintain that revenue ought to strike a balance with expenditure. If government revenue does not rise *pari passu* with government expenditure, the difference has to be made up by a correspondingly greater rise in private saving than in private investment. Such a rise was obtained, in fact, through "forced" saving as is reflected in the rise in levels of prices and cost of living for all countries except the Philippines, as shown in Table 21 [not included here]. The relative impact of government deficits on domestic price levels, and the measures through which the rise in them was sought to be contained, will be discussed more fully in Chapter 7[1] [not included here].

In Japan, the share of government revenue to total national income has remained remarkably stable. This development is the outcome of two offsetting influences. On the one hand, the Japanese Government has pursued a policy of containment of the public sector from direct participation in the functioning of the national economy. On the other hand, for various reasons, it has not succeeded in curbing expenditure, which has been claiming an increased share of the na-tional product.[2] In the field of revenue, however, the Government has been periodically lowering taxes on personal incomes and corporate profits as inducements to the private sector to increase investment and exports. Despite these measures, revenue has risen with the con-tinued prosperity of the Japanese economy; some of the commodity taxes on consumption goods have brought in significant amounts.

The sharpest rise in government revenue in relation to the na-tional product took place in mainland China. For a time, consider-able revenues were obtained by the new Government from confiscation of domestic and foreign private assets, collection of back taxes and imposition of fines for tax evasion. But, as time went on, the socializa-tion of private industrial and commercial enterprises, reviewed in Chapter 5, became the more important element. Between 1951 and 1959, total revenue grew more than fourfold, whereas, according to official indices, "prices" remained stable; the share of profits from state enterprises in total revenue increased from 24 to 61 per cent. While the volume of agricultural taxes and industrial and commercial taxes has grown, their share has fallen. These taxes are also payable by state enterprises and by the communes. The payments made by state enterprises for taxes, together with the profits transferred to revenue, raised the total contribution of these enterprises from 49 per cent of government revenue in 1951 to 92 per cent in 1959.[3] Obviously, the state derives most of the revenues required directly from its control over the productive apparatus; it has to raise revenue from "other sources" to the tune of only about 8 per cent of non-consumption or non-saleable output, or 4 per cent of consumption or saleable output. No wonder that despite the sharp increase in non-consumption output, the price level in mainland China has remained stable since 1951; however, the stability is unimportant from an economic standpoint. The question of price stability is quite different in a centrally planned economy; prices are so administered as to equate money incomes with consumption or saleable output. Price stability becomes a problem only if saleable output is to be reduced. If, however, total output is increasing, an ever-larger slice of the increase can be taken out as non-saleable output without causing undue concern as to the consequences of monetary demand on the price level.

While, on the one hand, Japan has sought to contain the expansion of the public sector and, on the other hand, mainland China has gone all the way in the opposite direction, the rest of the countries of the region—all of them private enterprise economies in varying stages of under-development—have grappled in the middle ground with the problems of raising the percentage of national income collected for government revenue. Indonesia has not succeeded. The progress in many other countries has remained unimpressive. There has been some increase in the percentage of revenue to national income, but the figures in Table 1 give a picture of relative stagnation after initial spurts rather than one of a continuing growth.

This stagnation gives some cause for concern. How is it that the newly developing private enterprise economies of Asia find it difficult to obtain progressively larger slices of their increased incomes for non-consumption, even assuming that voluntary private saving has risen *pari passu* with government revenue? Mainland China has tackled the problem through physical control over the entire productive process. Can the private enterprise economies, within the political range of possibilities open to them, adapt their fiscal systems and monetary institutions in such a way as to improve the present proportion of non-consumption to national income? Even with their built-in flexibility and progression, existing income taxes have not contributed to any material extent to raising the proportion of na-

TABLE 2

MAINLAND CHINA: GOVERNMENT REVENUE AND ITS COMPOSITION, 1950-1959

Year	Total Revenue	Wholesale Prices	Composition of Government Revenue (Per Cent of Total Revenue)				
	Indices: 1950 = 100		Industrial and Commercial Taxes	Agricultural Tax	Other Taxes	Profit of State Enterprises and Services	Other
1950	100	100.0	. . .	29	. . .	13	12
1951	199	117.9	. . .	. . .	. . .	24	14
1952	269	118.1	35	15	5	33	12
1953	334	116.6	38	12	5	35	10
1954	402	117.1	34	12	4	38	12
1955	417	117.8	32	11	4	41	12
1956	441	117.2	35	10	4	47	4
1957	476	118.3	36	10	4	46	4
1958	642	118.3	34	8	3	52	3
1959	831	. . .	29	6	3	61	1

SOURCES: *Ten Great Years* (Peking, 1960). *Tung Chi Kung Tso (Statistical Bulletin)*, June 29, 1957. *Tsai Cheng (Public Finance)*, August 5, 1957. Li Hsien-nien (Finance Minister), "Report on the Final State Accounts for 1958 and the Draft State Budget for 1959," *Peking Review*, April 29, 1959; "Report on the Final State Accounts for 1959 and the Draft State Budget for 1960," *Peking Review*, April 5, 1960; "China's Great Financial Achievements During the Past Ten Years," *Peking Review*, November 24, 1959. Shen Ping, "Industrial and Commercial Taxation in Recent Ten Years" and Li Shu-teh, "Agricultural Taxation in Recent Ten Years," both in *Great Financial Achievements of the People's Republic of China in the Past Ten Years* (Peking, 1959). *State Statistical Bureau's Communiqué on the Fulfilment of the 1955 Economic Development Plan* (Peking: Statistical Press, 1956). Shang Ping, "Prices and People's Living Standard in China," *Ta Kung Pao*, Hong Kong, October 1, 1958.

tional income taken in revenue. How can the fiscal systems be adapted to make them more progressive in relation to national income? Any attempt to answer the question immediately raises the query as to how the rise in national income gets distributed. Information on the subject is meagre and inadequate. India has begun a fresh search for sources of additional tax revenue by launching an inquiry to ascertain who benefited from the growth in national income during its first two five-year plans and the spending and saving patterns of the beneficiaries. Pending the availability of more dependable information, an attempt is made in the following pages to review, in the light of easily accessible material, the revenue structure of the ECAFE countries, not only in respect of its past and present functioning but also of its potentialities for adaptation to the prime task which the governments of the countries have set for it, viz. that of raising the ratio of non-consumption in order to secure a high rate of economic growth under conditions of long-term stability.

TAXES ON FOREIGN TRADE

With the exception of Japan and the "free" ports of Hong Kong and Singapore,[4] almost all countries of the region depend to a substantial extent for their revenue on taxation of imports, exports or foreign exchange and on profits of export monopolies or monopolistic distribution of imported items. Foreign trade is the predominant provider, accounting for about two-fifths of total revenue or more in Afghanistan, Brunei,[5] Burma, Ceylon, the Federation of Malaya, Indonesia, Iran, Laos, North Borneo, Sarawak and Thailand. Although, generally, total revenue is growing, the share of revenue from taxes on foreign trade and payments is falling in several countries.

The attempt by the governments of the countries of the region to restrict the use of foreign exchange only to essential needs has resulted in the curtailing of all imports except those of consumer necessities and of producer goods; both these items are admitted either duty free or with low duty. Imports of all other items are restricted either through import controls or by steep taxes in countries relying on fiscal methods to cut imports. Protective tariffs also restrict imports of goods competing with domestic production. In fact, in many newly developing countries of the region, economic growth is based on a policy of import substitution of consumer goods, causing restrictions to be placed on the imports of several revenue-yielding items such as textiles.

Quite apart from saving foreign exchange and protecting domestic industries, tax rates on relatively less essential consumer imports went up as part of the general attempt to restrict consumer spending and to introduce the principle of progression in the field of indirect taxes. Either the consumer, particularly the rich consumer, stopped spending money on imported amenities or luxuries altogether or else he paid high taxes to the government. However, since the demand for many of these goods, except perhaps for motor-cars,[6] is highly price sensitive, the revenues either fell or increased only slightly; restrictive effects were more substantial; to that extent, the government was helped in its attempt to improve the balance of payments position. The outlet of import spending having been plugged, problems arose elsewhere. The incomes which would have been spent on paying for imports and for taxes on imports were left in the hands of consumers for spending on domestically produced goods or for saving. The marginal propensity to save, however, has remained small; the reduction of spending on imports only intensified the bidding for the domestic supply of goods and services. In other words, while the balance of payments position improved, domestic inflationary forces were strengthened.

TABLE 3

ECAFE COUNTRIES: THE COMPONENTS OF GOVERNMENT REVENUE

(Per Cent of Total Revenue)

Country	Year	Taxes on Foreign Trade			Taxes on Internal Transactions			Taxes on Income and Wealth			Profits of Government Enterprises	Other Revenue[b]
		Import Taxes	Export Taxes	Other Taxes[a]	Excise and Sales Taxes	Fiscal Monopolies	Other Taxes	Taxes on Persons	Taxes on Companies	Land		
Afghanistan	1951	—39—			11	—21—		—18—		12	10	[c]
	1956	—39—				2		—16—		3	3	26
Brunei	1951	3	1	35					58		1	3
	1958	3		30					46			20
Burma	1950	22	3	33	11		2	—10—		2	1	17
	1958	28	3	10	18		3	—23—		2		12
Cambodia	1952[d]	—41[e]—			18		10	—9—		3		19
	1958[f]	24	2	4	29		20	—6—		1		14
Ceylon	1950	31	27		7		4	13	7		1	11
	1958	25	28		8		5	14	9			10
China: Taiwan	1951	17		[g]	5	8	30	8	7	1	15	9
	1958	14		[g]	9	16	30	4	6		10	11
Federation of Malaya	1950	33	34		3		6	—11—			1	12
	1958	36	17		3		7	—16—			4	17
Hong Kong	1950				30		8	10	17		7	29
	1958				23		7	15	21		5	29
India	1950	16	10		27		3	17	5	6	5	12
	1958	8	2		40		3	14	4	7	5	17
Indonesia	1951	14	13	40	12		3	9	6		1	2
	1958	8	1	34	23		2	12	10		1	9
Iran	1949[f]	—21—		12	34			—15—			—18—	
	1958[d]	—23—		53	7			—10—			5	2

Country	Year	1	2	3	4	5	6	7	8	9	10	11
Japan	1950	—	—	—	20	17	2	35	13	—	—	13
	1958	4	—	—	31	10	1	22	25	—	—	13
Korea, southern	1949	6	—	—	17	18	1	8	14	28	—	8
	1958	12	—	7	21	10	4	9	7	10	—	16
Laos	1951[f]	68	—	—	6	—	7	15	—	—	—	4
	1958[f]	53	7	—	28	—	3	9	—	—	—	16
Nepal	1952[f]	31	—	—	2	—	5	—	—	1	—	4
	1958[d]	37	—	—	8	—	6	—	—	42	—	2
North Borneo	1950	40	27	—	—	—	3	1	4	24	—	14
	1958	35	18	—	1	—	4	1	9	—	—	11
Pakistan	1950	48	—	—	14	—	7	6	1	3	—	17
	1957	20	—	—	22	—	2	10	3	9	—	30
Philippines	1950	16	—	—	51	—	2	19	—	—	—	19
	1958	26	—	—	33	—	3	8	10	—	—	29
Sarawak	1950	26	50	—	2	—	5	8	—	—	—	11
	1958	30	16	—	2	—	6	—	22	—	—	20
Singapore	1950	—	—	—	46	—	6	26	—	—	8	17
	1958	—	—	—	42	—	8	28	—	—	7	24
Thailand	1950	27	8	7	13	12	9	7	—	—	11[h,i]	14
	1958	29	5	15	21	7	7	7	—	—	4[i]	15
Viet-Nam, southern	1952[f]	55	2	—	22	—	3	7	—	1	3	17
	1958[f]	23	—	—	50	—	7	7	—	2	8	17

SOURCE: See the explanatory note, page 63 [not included here].

a Brunei: royalties from oil; Burma: contributions from the state-managed boards; Cambodia: fees on entries and exits; Indonesia: taxes on foreign exchange; Iran: 1949/50: oil revenue; 1958/59: oil revenue and monopoly profits; southern Korea: taxes on foreign exchange; Thailand: rice premium and profits of the Rice Bureau.

b Charges and fees for services, royalties and rents and other income from property, income from land sales, interest received, etc.

c Included under taxes on internal transactions.

d Revised estimates or provisional results.

e Including some receipts from excise and turnover taxes.

f Budget estimates.

g Included under "other" taxes on internal transactions and profits of government enterprises.

h Including gross receipts of railways.

i Including gross receipts of posts and telegraphs and electricity departments.

Several countries of the region also attempted to explore the revenue potentialities of the export trade in primary products. This they have done by means of export duties, by penalty exchange rates on export commodities, or by a government monopoly of export marketing. On an average, taking good and bad years together, revenue collected from all types of taxes on exports formed roughly over a half of the total revenue in Iran, over a third in Indonesia, between a third and a quarter in Burma, Ceylon, the Federation of Malaya and Sarawak, and about a fifth in North Boreno and Thailand. The proportions, although lower, were still of some significance in China: Taiwan, India and Pakistan.

The revenue from exports is a function of the trade in the primary products of the region, which reveals two special features in the period since the end of the Korean war. First, on the whole, the demand grew only slowly; petroleum is the only notable exception. The supply situation was also far from satisfactory. War damage, unsettled conditions and growing internal demand for food and for raw materials slowed down the increase in export availabilities. The second special feature of the export trade in primary products of the ECAFE countries was its tendency to experience sharp fluctuations in volume and prices. The fluctuations were caused on the supply side by domestic factors, and on the demand side by booms or recessions in the primary importing industrial countries.[7]

The revenue from exports, therefore, has been subject to large fluctuations. In fact, the secondary effects of a change in export conditions influence revenues from other sources as well. Thus, for instance, when the demand for exports is strong, increased export earnings lead to larger imports. Even import controls tend to be relaxed during an export boom, leading to a more than proportionate rise in revenue from import taxes. Export prosperity is also reflected, in course of time, in increased revenue from income taxes and excise and sales taxes.

As a consequence, the revenue system, on the whole, has shown a high and progressive correlation with the movements of foreign trade. And this is a possible explanation for the lack of progressivity of the revenue system in relation to national income. It is predominantly dependent on taxation of foreign trade, and reflects, in large measure, the weakness of the region's primary export trade in world markets since the end of the Korean war.

Export taxes have, however, achieved considerable importance as anti-inflationary devices. During the period when export demand for their primary products was extraordinarily strong, the governments of several countries of the region raised the tax rates in order to siphon off excess purchasing power to themselves rather than allow it to go to the private sector and set up an additional demand for locally produced goods and services or imports. The countries used both sliding-scale duties or specific taxes the rates of which were changed by administrative action from time to time. The variation in rates permitted the duties to be lowered when export markets were sluggish. However, as anti-deflationary devices, export taxes are not equally suitable. The taxes when lowered still act as a drag on exports; at the most, they could be abolished. Very few countries went further and granted export subsidies. The rare instances are the price support measures for jute and cotton in Pakistan, and for copra, sugar and other "weak" commodities in Indonesia.

Several methods, other than straightforward taxation, were tried by countries of the region, which had the effect of taxing (or subsidizing) imports, exports or exchange transactions. Most of the measures were devised to serve several purposes, among which conserving the balance of payments and preserving domestic stability were the principal ones. Considerations of increasing revenue were often of minor relevance in the initiation and implementation of these measures.

An important device for insulating the economy from export fluctuations was the export marketing mechanism adopted in Burma and Thailand in respect of rice, in China: Taiwan in respect of sugar, and in Indonesia in respect of copra. Since these items, in the countries concerned, are of importance to the community as food items in the consumer budget and as sources of producer incomes, the governments sought to maintain domestic price stability by establishing monopoly procurement and insulating the economy from the sharp fluctuations in their prices in export markets. The experiment with rice marketing secured substantial revenues to the Governments of Burma and Thailand, since world prices of rice remained well above the domestic prices paid to the rice growers.

The revenue collected from exports in Burma reached its peak between 1952/53 and 1954/55 when it provided about half of the total revenue. The State Agricultural Marketing Board in Burma (SAMB), which has a monopoly of rice exports, made a direct purchase of paddy from the producers, or rice from the mills, at a price which remained unchanged from 1948 to 1955/56. As the export price of rice went on rising, the profits of the SAMB rose from about 28 per cent of the export price of rice in 1947/48 to 47 per cent in 1952/53. Since then, it has fallen, resulting in lower profits for the SAMB per ton of rice exported. The SAMB pays income taxes on its profits and makes an additional direct contribution to government revenue from the balance.

The rice marketing monopoly in Thailand was less strict than in Burma. Thailand, unlike Burma, used a combination of multiple exchange rates, flexible export duties, and exports on government account. The procurement operations of the Government's Rice Bureau were not as effective as in Burma; in order to induce deliveries, the Government began giving up the monopoly; it allowed a certain proportion of private exports of rice if the exporter delivered the balance to the Rice Bureau. The private exporter was also allowed to retain and sell on the free market the foreign exchange earned on his export volume to the extent that the prices received by him were higher than the government-to-government contract prices. On the other hand, a charge—the so-called premium—was made when the private exporter obtained his export license. In other words, the system contained government procurement and sale at profit, private exporter procurement and sale at two rates of profit—one consisting of the difference between his cost and the government-to-government contract price converted in baht at official exchange rates, and the other of the difference between his sale price and the government-to-government contract price converted at free market exchange rates—and a system of export duties on private exports. The Government relinquished its rice monopoly in 1955, and the trade was turned over entirely to private merchants under a system of export licensing. The domestic price of rice has since risen; government revenues have fallen.

Similarly the copra monopoly of Indonesia fell through on grounds of procurement difficulties. Unlike the rice monopolies, the Copra Fund of Indonesia operated at a loss during periods, such as 1948–49, when world copra prices fell below the prices paid to domestic producers. It appears that the Fund encountered difficulties at both ends. When the export prices were above domestic prices, the Fund could not procure supplies; when export prices were below the Fund's prices, it incurred large losses. The Fund was replaced by a purely marketing co-operative in 1957.

The sugar marketing monopoly of China: Taiwan was caught in the problem of maintaining a parity between sugar and rice prices, which put it in a financial squeeze, during 1952–53 prior to the establishment of the International Sugar Agreement in 1954.

The cotton and jute price support schemes in Pakistan during the post-Korean-war slump were purely anti-deflationary measures. Faced with an adverse export situation which led to a fall in domestic prices below an established "floor" price, government agencies offered to buy up unlimited quantities at the "floor" prices in an effort to safeguard growers and traders against further declines.[8] The operation of these schemes posed problems of financial losses and surplus disposals to the Cotton and Jute Boards of Pakistan. The scheme was first converted into a direct export subsidy scheme, by the Government offering not to buy up but only to make good the difference between the price received by the private exporter and the government floor price. Price supports were finally abolished in August, 1952.

The governments of the region have also practised exchange rate manipulation, primarily in order to improve their balance of payments position although they have earned profits in the process. The most important among the countries obtaining revenue from taxes on foreign exchange have been Indonesia and the Philippines. The Philippines, from 1951 to 1956, had a straightforward 25 per cent tax on foreign exchange supplied by the Government. It was, in fact, an import tax, going beyond the taxation of merchandise imports to cover "invisibles." The multiple exchange rates of Indonesia, Thailand and China: Taiwan formed a system of taxes and subsidies and covered both imports and exports.

The system of multiple exchange rates in Indonesia is fairly complicated and has gone through many changes. During the two years from March 1950 to February 1952, when the exchange certificates system was in operation, the effective rupiah value of a unit of foreign exchange earned from export, say the United States dollar, was kept at about one-third of the rupiah value of the dollar provided for imports. With the decline in traditional exports, the rupiah value of the export dollar was effectively raised to correspond to the value of the import dollar; a series of new export duties was imposed, with differential rates on "medium-strong" and "strong" exports, in addition to the "basic" export duties in force at the time. Several other devices, all rather ineffective,[9] were tried between 1953 and 1956. In mid-1957, the export promotion certificates system was introduced, again setting up a sharp disparity between the rupiah values of the dollar in export and import trade. Under the export certificates system, all foreign exchange surrendered was made subject to an exchange tax of 20 per cent, and, on the exchange provided, the requirements were classified into six categories with progressively increasing surcharges. According to the 1959 changes, a dollar turned over to the Government fetched 36 rupiahs (that is, Rp 45, the official rate, *minus* 20 per cent exchange tax). The rate charged by the Government for providing the dollar varied from 45 to 135 rupiahs (that is, the official rate *plus* surcharges up to 200 per cent) depending upon the purpose for which the foreign exchange purchase was made.[10] The taxation of foreign exchange has provided Indonesia with its major source of revenue; in 1958, it yielded 34 per cent of total revenue, in addition to the contribution made by import and export duties.

The profits made from foreign exchange in Thailand, during the period 1947–54, when the official exchange rate applied to rice exports was about 40 per cent less than the free market rate, were credited to an exchange stabilization fund in the Bank of Thailand, and not to government revenue. The latter received only the profits of the Rice Bureau and export premiums on private rice exports. Since only a part of the exchange earned for rubber and tin exports had to be surrendered, the effective rate on these commodities was less unfavourable than that on rice exports. During the period 1950–54, the profits accruing to the Bank of Thailand from foreign exchange transactions were of a magnitude of about 15 per cent of total government receipts, whereas government revenues from export taxation came to only 8 per cent of the total. As the markets for Thailand's export products turned soft, the multiple exchange rates were abolished in 1955 in favour of export duties which were adjusted to yield increased revenues.

In China: Taiwan, the profits from foreign exchange transactions also went to the Bank of Taiwan, although these profits were brought over to government revenue. The profits accrued from the disparity between the official rate at which the exchange earned from sugar and rice exports was purchased by the Bank and the rate it charged in providing foreign exchange for imports. The brunt was, however, borne by the Government's sugar monopoly which had to turn over all foreign exchange earned by it to the Bank of Taiwan at the official rates. The sugar monopoly, unlike the rice monopolies of Burma and Thailand, ran into financial difficulties.

Oil exploitation and exports, on the other hand, have provided high and sustained revenues to Iran (except for the period of its dispute over the nationalization of the British-owned petroleum company), Indonesia and Brunei. The latter two derive their revenue from oil in the form of royalties on crude oil and a tax on the profits of the oil companies. Indonesia also levies export taxes on oil. The system in Iran is more complicated. According to the agreement reached in 1954 between the Iranian Government, the National Iranian Oil Company (NIOC) and a group of international oil companies known as the Consortium, the latter pay to the Government and the National Iranian Oil Company one-half of the difference between the posted price of the oil taken by the Consortium and the cost of production of crude oil. The payment is made to the oil company in the form of crude oil, or its value at posted prices, up to about one-eighth of the payment due; the balance is paid to the Government as income tax. The NIOC also receives one-third, and the Government two-thirds, of the tax on refinery operations. The NIOC in its own turn has to turn over to the Government any surplus left from its share after meeting expenses which are subject to government scrutiny. In the period since 1955 oil revenues have come to well over one-half of the total receipts of the Iranian Treasury.

How does taxation on foreign trade stand with respect to providing growth of revenue? Undoubtedly, as disincentives to dissipation of foreign exchange or as counter-measures to cyclical fluctuations, the various measures described here have indeed been helpful. Their significance is more limited for the long-term problem of increasing government revenue. Given a policy of economic development, the high-revenue-yielding imports of amenities and luxuries will continue to be curtailed drastically; permitted imports of basic necessities and producer goods could be highly taxed but, in general, it may not be desirable to do so. Export markets have, in the long run, turned soft; the revenue potential from export taxation is not high. In 1960, even crude oil prices had come down.[11] The rice producers who did well for nearly a decade after the war have been, for some time, finding difficulties in selling rice; an increased volume is disposed of only at lower prices. Other commodities are in a still more vulnerable position. In any case, exports will remain, to a large extent, subject to demand conditions beyond the control of the exporting countries; revenue from this source can be counted upon to be neither growing nor dependable. Export monopolies and multiple exchange rates have also lost their steam; only in Burma and Indonesia do they remain of some consequence.

Even apart from the question of yields, taxation of exports is rather indiscriminate in its impact on producers—the small in relation to the large and the efficient in relation to the inefficient. It is, of course, administratively convenient, which is a great merit; it has, on the other hand, drawbacks as regards incentives and equity. In the long run, the problem of finding a solution which will make the revenue system more progressive in relation to national income— one which will increase the incremental output-revenue ratio—will have to be tackled by reducing the present preponderant dependence of the fiscal system on foreign trade and by giving it a re-orientation.

TAXES ON INTERNAL TRANSACTIONS

Internal taxation of commodities and services, in the postwar period, was increased in several countries of the region to serve three main purposes: raising of revenue, curtailment of consumption (especially of luxuries), and saving on imports. The general principle in commodity or service taxes for raising revenue is that they should be levied on commodities or services with a low price-elasticity and high income-elasticity of demand. The low price-elasticity would secure a more than proportionate increase in revenues when prices are raised; the high income-elasticity would do so as incomes increase. The attempt to increase revenue from taxation of commodities, to some extent, caused price rises on a broad general front, but the main objective has been the withdrawal of spending power from the private sector in an effort to control inflationary pressures. If the increase in government expenditure was not in its turn induced by increased revenues, the transfer from the private sector to the government would at first raise the prices of goods taxed but would prevent the initial rise from spinning into a spiral of spending, higher incomes and more spending.

The possibility of practising differential taxation makes commodity taxation secure both a restriction of consumption of inessential items and a diversion of productive resources from taxed goods to other goods. The generally practised methods of taxing luxuries and exempting capital goods are attempts in this direction. The success in this field depends again on the elasticities of demand and supply. A greater elasticity in both would secure a more effective restriction of consumption and a diversion of production from the commodity taxed. It would follow, therefore, that the items which are big revenue yielders are not the ones which would effectively restrict consumption; on the other hand, the items which are responsive in this direction would not be revenue-yielding.

The third purpose, viz., that of restriction of imports, is attained directly through import taxes. Here again, if the duties are really successful, revenue yields are small. Some of the import taxes, in countries where there is some domestic production of items similar to imports, are collected as excise taxes. If the imported items alone are taxed, or are taxed more highly than domestically produced goods, they have a protective effect, and they assist in improving the balance of payments position.

Subject to these considerations, the attempt to increase revenue has led to a steepening of the tax rates on the traditional favourites of finance ministers—tobacco, liquor, gasolene, motor-cars and entertainments. Revenue from taxes on liquor, and that from the extremely steep tax rates on narcotics, is being sacrificed in several countries in an attempt to prohibit their consumption altogether. Tobacco, being price-inelastic, is a good revenue yielder; income-elasticity is introduced by differential taxation of the different brands. For example, the indigenous *bidi* of the Indian or Pakistani worker is taxed more lightly than the western-type cigarette. China: Taiwan, Japan and Thailand collect tobacco revenue not as excise duties but through fiscal monopolies. Gasolene also satisfies the criteria of low price-elasticity and high income-elasticity to some extent; however, since the poor cannot afford cars and the import of cars for the rich is being restricted in order to improve the balance of payments, revenues have not risen to high levels.

The revenue from excise taxes has increased, however, not so much from increased consumption or increased rates of duty (although both these factors account for some part of it) on the traditional items, as from getting a wide range of items in the tax net. In India, for instance, the items which were not subject to excise taxes in 1948/49 yielded 24 per cent, and the items which were not taxed in 1938/39 yielded 71 per cent of the total revenue from excise taxes in 1953/54.[12]

The attempt directly to curtail general spending as distinct from spending on individual commodities, has given an increasing importance to general sales taxes or turnover taxes. The general sales taxes levied by the governments of ECAFE countries are not quite *general;* they are, in fact, an expanded version of excise taxes. Food and basic necessities are usually exempted from sales taxes; differential rates are charged on other items—depending on whether they are amenities or luxuries.

The curtailment of spending is brought about by sales taxes in two ways. The ability to spend is curtailed by taking spending power away from the consumers; the incentive to spend is weakened, since the consumer is given the choice to reduce his tax liability. The sales taxes, in this respect, have an advantage over income taxes in that they can catch persons who are able to avoid or evade income taxes. They would also catch spending out of accumulated wealth. The real motive for the sales taxes in the newly developing economies of Asia lies in its catching not the rich, but the poor and middle income groups, who pay no income tax at all or very little, if any, and who, in their spending, are more price-sensitive.[13]

Sales taxes tend to be levied at various stages, the choice being a matter of administrative convenience. In general, a one-stage tax at a relatively higher rate is to be preferred to a tax with multiple stages and low rates. Burma, Indonesia and Pakistan have adopted single-stage taxes—the former two after experimenting with turnover taxes on successive transactions from the first dealer to the final customer. The taxes are levied on imports at the import stage and on domestic products for internal consumption at the manufacturing or wholesale stage as is done in Pakistan. Basic food items are exempt; other necessities are treated leniently and taxed at around 5 per cent; luxury goods are taxed more severely—at 10 per cent in Indonesia, 12.5 per cent in Pakistan and 15 per cent in Burma. India is also attempting to streamline its sales tax system, which being a state subject, varies from state to state. The state of Madras has a "general" sales tax with a multi-point system and several exemptions and differential rates including one-point taxation on some items. The state of Bombay has modified its multi-point sales tax (introduced in 1953/54) to a two-point tax. The states of West Bengal and Bihar, on the other hand, have preferred the single-point sales tax. Japan has a combination of excise and sales taxes. Manufacturers pay a tax when goods are moved out of warehouses and retailers also pay a tax on 70 items listed in the commodity tax law.

TAXES ON INCOME AND WEALTH

It is evident from Table 3 that all the newly developing countries of the region rely to a greater extent on the taxes on commodities and services—the so-called "indirect taxes"—than on taxes on incomes and wealth. Only in Japan, do the latter add up to nearly half of the total revenue.[14] Even so, the proportion in Japan is lower than in several other economically advanced countries of the world. Even if we consider land taxes as gross income taxes, as is done in Table 3, the proportion of "direct" taxes to the total comes to around one-third in Hong Kong, between 20 and 30 per cent in Ceylon, India, Indonesia, southern Korea, Nepal, Pakistan, Sarawak and Singapore, and lower fractions in the other countries of the region.[15]

Among the "direct" taxes, those on incomes of persons, including juridical persons, are the most important. Taxes on wealth or property, on the other hand, collect a very low amount of revenue. Even where they are levied, their application has remained limited and their rates have been low.

The Present Status of Income Taxes

The income tax was already in existence before the war in Burma, Ceylon, mainland China, India, Indonesia, Japan, Pakistan and the Philippines. In Burma-India-Pakistan, it has been in continuous existence since 1886. The Philippine income tax dates back to 1913. In territories such as Brunei, China: Taiwan, the Federation of Malaya, Hong Kong, southern Korea, Nepal, North Borneo, Sarawak, Singapore and Thailand, it is a postwar innovation. The tax in Nepal is the youngest; it was introduced in the 1959/60 Budget.

Income taxes in most countries are levied on global incomes—that is, on incomes earned by residents as well as non-residents within their geographic jurisdictions and those of residents earned abroad. In Burma, India and Pakistan, income from agriculture is exempt from the income tax administered by the central government; it is supposed to be covered by land taxes levied by state governments. However, in an attempt to obtain more revenue and to introduce progressivity in the operation of the land tax, several of the state governments have also introduced agricultural income taxes. The income tax systems of these three countries have several other special features.[16]

Since 1947, the Japanese income tax system is based on estimated taxation and self-assessment. This is distinct from the present Burma-Ceylon-India-Pakistan system or the Japanese system before 1947, when income tax was assessed by the government income-tax department on the actual income of the previous year. Under the self-assessment system, the taxpayer estimates his income in the taxable year, computes his tax liability, files a return and pays the estimated tax. Final adjustments are made on the basis of actual results. The tax on wages, interest and dividends and on certain types of business income is withheld at source. The Japanese system of taxation on personal incomes, and that of Ceylon, the Philippines and several other countries, have graduated rates rising in smooth progression all the way from the lowest to the highest income bracket on which the tax is due; this is less complicated than the two-tier system of personal income- and supertaxes in Burma, India and Pakistan prior to 1960. Under the Japanese system of exemptions from taxable personal income, a basic exemption is given for the taxpayer himself, and additional exemptions in declining amounts are given for his dependents. Ceylon operates the quotient system in this regard; a bachelor has one-and-a-half quotient, a married couple two, and additional quotients at the rate of half a quotient for each child up to a maximum of four children, bringing the maximum of quotients to four per family. Taxable income is divided according to the number of quotients; each quotient is assessed at the rates applicable. In this way, marginal rates are reduced for persons with larger family responsibilities. India recently made some small adjustments to favour persons with dependents. As in Burma, and in India and Pakistan until recently, Japanese shareholders, in the assessment of their tax liabilities on personal incomes, are given credit in respect of a part of the taxes paid by the companies.

The income tax systems in other countries combine most of the general features of the income-tax system—tax exemption limits, allowances, exemptions or tax credits for dependents, progressive rates, and differential treatment of individuals and companies. The tax in Brunei and Sarawak is only applicable to companies. The large revenue from the profits of the oil company in Brunei has made taxes on personal income unnecessary. The Hong Kong tax is composed of taxes on four schedules: property, salaries and annuities, profits, and interest; the new tax in Nepal covers only salaries and business profits. Both these systems fall short of a full income tax. In southern Korea, many other refinements in income taxation are sacrificed in order to tax income at the time it is earned, or as soon as possible after it is earned.

With its advantages of flexibility and progression not only between different taxpayers but between successive changes in the volume of incomes potentially subject to taxation, income taxes appear to provide the most suitable weapon for implementing broad fiscal policies,[17] including the provision of incentives to save and to invest. That these advantages have been generally recognized can be seen from the fact that most of the countries which did not have income taxes before the war have introduced them in the postwar period. However, the share of revenue from such taxes, on the whole, has remained less than one-third except in Hong Kong and Japan.[18] Nor is it, in any sense of the term, a mass tax in the newly developing countries as it is in Japan and in other advanced countries of the world. In India, for instance, the income tax in 1957/58 covered only 570,000 individuals who were assessed on their personal incomes, 55,000 Hindu undivided families, and about 49,000 business partnerships and companies. If we assume an average number of five persons effectively covered per assessee, the tax was effective in relation to less than 1 per cent of the total population of the country. The national income in the year was estimated at Rs 117 billion; the taxable potential income would be higher than the national income, since taxable transfer incomes are not included in national income. Total taxable potential would therefore be in the range of Rs 130–140 billion. The income assessed to income tax, including those of partnerships and companies, came only to Rs 10 billion and tax collected to only Rs 2.2 billion. Thus, 99 per cent of the population and about 93 per cent of the potentially taxable income in the country remained outside the purview of the income tax system.

Personal Income Taxes

Coverage

One of the reasons for this low coverage is that the minimum exemption limits laid down exclude almost all but a fringe at the top of the social pyramid. A married couple with three children remains untouched by the income tax system in Ceylon, the Federation of Malaya and India until the family income is 9 to 12 times, and in Burma and the Philippines over 15 times, the average national per capita income. The corresponding coverage begins at less than twice the national per capita income in Australia, Canada, Mexico, the United Kingdom and the United States (see Table 4). Such an underdevelopment of the income tax system in the newly developing countries of Asia is accounted for by the smallness in absolute terms of the majority of incomes to be taxed and on the assumption that this majority is already adequately covered for taxation purposes through various "indirect" taxes. In any case, it is considered that the administrative machinery required for covering the masses through the income tax systems would be large in relation to revenue yield; a more thorough investigation of the tax returns of upper income groups would be more productive of revenue per unit of administrative expense.

Various aspects of the problem have to be considered here. First, any effort in a poor country to raise savings at the expense of consumption will have to obtain these from the poor; the standard of

TABLE 4

ECAFE REGION AND THE REST OF THE WORLD: THE BURDEN OF TAXES
ON INCOME FOR A MARRIED COUPLE WITH THREE CHILDREN IN RELATION TO
PER CAPITA NATIONAL INCOME IN SELECTED COUNTRIES

Countries ranked in order of the approximate size of per capital national product	The level of income up to which no tax is paid (Stated as a multiple of per capita income)	Income taxes paid on earned income at various upper income levels. (Taxes paid as a percentage of earned income assuming earned income to be:			
		10	20	50	100
			times the per capita national income)		
United States of America	1.3	23	35	54	69
Canada	1.9	19	32	45	55
Australia	.7	30	43	55	59
United Kingdom	1.9	28	44	67	78
France	2.1	13	23	35	45
Germany, Federal Republic of	2.2	20	28	39	46
Argentina	7.7	3	16	34	43
Japan	3.4	11	19	31	39
Mexico	1.9	2	4	9	17
Federation of Malaya	9.8	neg.	4	12	21
Philippines	15.6	—	1	10	19
Ceylon	12.5	—	2	9	23
India	11.5	—	2	8	21
Burma	19.0	—	neg.	4	11

SOURCE: Compiled in the United Nations by the Fiscal and Financial Branch of the Economic and Social Affairs Department from United Nations and national publications.

NOTE: Reference years are: for per capita national income—1955/56 for Burma, 1957 for the Federation of Malaya, 1958 for Canada, France, Argentina, Mexico, Philippines, 1959 for the Federal Republic of Germany, Japan and India and 1959/60 for Australia; for tax laws—1955/56 for Burma, 1959 for France, Mexico, Japan, the Federation of Malaya and the Philippines, 1959/60 for Australia, United Kingdom, Ceylon and India, and 1960 for the United States, Canada, the Federal Republic of Germany and Argentina.

minimum taxable capacity might have to be placed at a lower level. As for there being no taxable capacity in the low-income groups owing to the incidence of indirect taxation, there is no clear evidence. In India, for instance, the incidence survey carried out by the Indian Taxation Enquiry Commission gave the following results:

TABLE 5

INDIA: INCIDENCE OF TAXATION BY EXPENDITURE LEVELS

(*Tax as Per Cent of Total Expenditure*)

Monthly Household Expenditure Level	Rs. 1–50	Rs. 51–100	Rs. 101–150	Rs. 151–300	Above Rs. 300	All Expenditure Levels
Rural	2.2	2.3	2.7	2.8	4.4	2.9
Urban	3.3	4.4	5.1	5.1	8.3	5.9
Rural and urban combined	2.4	2.7	3.1	3.3	5.6	3.6

SOURCE: Government of India, *Report of the Taxation Enquiry Commission*, I, 69.

The national income in 1953/54, the year of the inquiry, was Rs 280 per head and the average size of the household in the survey was 5 persons; monthly income of the national average family was, therefore, around Rs 120 per month. On this reckoning, only the first two groups constituted sub-average income-groups. On them the burden of indirect taxation was less than 3 per cent; if the redistributive effects of government expenditure are taken into account, they paid practically no net taxation and, insofar as persons in these groups were on "subsistence" levels, rightly so. On the other hand, the question arises if it is possible to raise more taxes from the average or above-average groups, either by lowering the income-tax exemption limits or by selecting for indirect taxation items important in their consumption pattern. The lower taxation in the rural areas is perhaps compensated by land taxes, the incidence of which in the present circumstances is on the poorer sections of the rural community. It is the urban community which seems to permit some, although not much, scope for raising the proportion of taxes levied. There is some point in the contention of tax administrators that administrative difficulties are involved in such a move; we shall refer to them later.[19] There is, on the other hand, a distinct advantage in lowering the tax exemption limit. If the tax exemption limit remains, say at Rs 6,000 as is the case at present in Pakistan, incomes between Rs 6,000 and 7,500 earned by small and medium traders may escape taxation altogether, since it is difficult to be definite about the income-tax liability of any such person. If, however, the limits were down to Rs 2,000, such persons would have been forced to report some income and thus pay taxes which they are at present able to evade. Of course, the transition will have to come about gradually; the exemption limits will have to be lowered and administrative machinery built up over a number of years in a step-by-step process.

Tax Rates

While most of the income tax systems of the under-developed countries show very high (and only partially effective) personal income tax rates at the top, the average rate of tax applicable to the incomes of persons taxed is much smaller than in the advanced countries. The married couple with three children, mentioned above, in Ceylon, the Federation of Malaya, India and the Philippines pays only 8–12 per cent, and in Burma only 4 per cent, of the assessed income in taxes when the family income is more than fifty times the national per capita income. On the other hand, a similar family unit with only ten times the national per capita income in the Federal Republic of Germany, the United States, Australia and the United

Kingdom pays from 20 to 30 per cent, of its assessed income in income and wealth taxes (see Table 4). In India, in 1957/58 the "harsh" taxes—taxes taking away more than half of the assessed personal incomes—affected only about 7,000 assessees, or about 35,000 persons,—that is, less than one person in ten thousand. There is little doubt that this apex had already exploited the available avenues for avoidance and evasion, reducing the "harshness" in relation to their total incomes as distinguished from "taxable incomes." The minimum disclosed taxable income of this group was about two hundred times the national per capita income; those with incomes above the exemption limits but below the 200-time level paid on an average only 9 per cent of their assessed incomes in personal income taxes. Taking into account, therefore, the national average level of living in the country and the incidence of existing indirect taxes—that is, an additional 6 per cent according to Table 5—it cannot be said that either the tax coverage is extensive or the rates, in their practical application, are harsh.

Tax Base

Of course, the tax systems show rather high rates for the upper brackets of assessed income. Even when they have recently been brought down, the highest marginal rates on earned incomes of persons in India remain at 77 per cent, in Pakistan at 75 per cent and in Ceylon at 60 per cent. Nevertheless, the income tax systems are only superficially progressive;[20] in practice, the rich are able to *avoid* the tax through legal "loopholes" and in most countries, to *evade* it through administrative deficiencies. The "loopholes" on personal (and company) income taxation generally lie in the definition of the tax base, namely "taxable income." Profits on the sale of capital assets— capital gains as they are called—were not taxable until recently in most countries; even so, they pay lower rates. As capital assets appreciate particularly in inflationary periods, profits are realized on their sale. Under the British system, these profits are not taxed on the principle that it is the fruit of the tree, and not the tree itself, which should be subject to tax. However, from an economic standpoint, or from that of the property owners, there is no distinction between income from property (which is ordinarily taxable) and income from the sale of this property (which is not, or which is subject to a lower tax), except to the extent that the capital gain is ascribable to genuine currency depreciation over the holding period of the asset. Other "loopholes" include the escape from personal income tax liability through undistributed profits in closely held companies or trusts. The share values go up as reserves are piled up; in the event of sale at appreciated values, the profits realized can be passed off as capital gains. A third "loophole" is the system of perquisites such as office-provided cars, living accommodation, travel, or expense accounts in general, which are charged off to business expenses, but which may not truly be "expenses that are wholly, exclusively and unavoidably incurred in earning the profits of the year."[21] Death duties are also avoided by gifts to beneficiaries made during the lifetime of the giver.[22] All these loopholes have been so universally exploited that there is a considerable amount of truth in the popular aphorism that taxable income is the only luxury the rich cannot afford.

To plug several of these loopholes, as well as to evolve a tax system which would encourage saving and investment but discourage consumption, the Governments of Ceylon and India took a series of measures containing an adjustment of the rates of taxes on personal income, and new taxes on capital gains, on net wealth, on personal expenditure and on gifts. These are to be assessed as a single operation on the basis of a single comprehensive return provided by the taxpayer. In adopting these measures, the Ceylon Government did not bring down the higher rates of income tax to 45 per cent—the level recommended as the maximum.[23] This made the burden on the upper income levels considerably higher than was necessary to secure revenue without severely impinging on incentives or putting a strain on honesty. India, too, did not lower the income tax rates to the extent recommended; on the other hand, the new measures were much milder than the original proposals.[24] The integration and the interdependence of the scheme as a whole were vitiated. This was due, to some extent, to the not altogether unjustified apprehension that the unavoidable initial administrative difficulties would prevent the new taxes from making up the revenue loss which would result from an abandonment of the well-established top income-tax rates.

Not only is the tax being legally avoided. There is widespread evasion. The actual extent of this malpractice is a matter of speculation in several countries. In India, however, an attempt was made to put a value to it. According to one estimate,[25] the tax annually evaded was on income totalling Rs 5.8 billion, or about three-quarters of the income assessed to tax in 1955/56, and that the magnitude of the revenue lost through evasion was of the order of Rs 2–3 billion, as compared with Rs 1.8 billion collected from all classes of assessees in that year. The Central Board of Revenue of India estimated the income evading tax assessment at about 40 per cent of the first estimate. Even the lower estimate suggests that income evading income tax was about 30 per cent of the income assessed to tax, and that revenue lost might be well over one-half.[26]

Company Income Taxes

In advanced countries, a considerable proportion of economic activity is organized in the form of limited liability companies; company profits provide a major source of revenue. The importance of this sector in the newly developing countries is rather small, although it is growing. Two ideas permeate the subject of company taxation. The first is that a company is nothing but "an aggregate of a number of shareholders banded together for the achievement of some common purpose under limited liability; it is sufficient to impose the (personal) income tax upon the shareholder . . . and needless to impose the tax upon corporate income,"[27] The second view is that since "the general law of the land entitles a corporation with a personality of its own and regards it as an entity distinct from the shareholders who are its members, a corporation owes a duty to pay the corporation tax on its income apart from the income tax on the shareholders' income."[27] The two-tier system of company taxation in Burma and Japan, and in India and Pakistan until recently, pursues both these ideas. The two tiers consist of an "income" tax and a "super" or "corporation" tax; while the former is refunded as a tax credit on the personal income taxes of shareholders in respect of the dividends received by them, the "corporation tax" is not so refundable. With effect from 1960/61, India and Pakistan have abolished the tax rebate; the two taxes—income tax and supertax—for practical purposes, will be operated as if there was only one non-refundable corporation tax.

Corporate taxes are generally levied at a flat rate on all companies. Several countries, however, levy a slightly lower rate on companies earning smaller amounts. The rates vary. In general, they are not as high as the United States (52 per cent). Where a rebate is given to shareholders on their personal income tax, their real incidence is even smaller than what the rates suggest. The rates in Indonesia rise from 40 to 52.5 per cent. India and Pakistan charge a flat 45 per cent (with the abolition of the tax rebate); North Borneo a flat 40 per cent; Brunei and Sarawak a flat 30 per cent; Japan two rates of 33 and 38 per cent and southern Korea of 17 and 22 per cent.

The administration of corporate income taxes is being tightened up in many countries by a more vigilant scrutiny of "deductible expenses." The more technical problems, however, in this field of taxation relate to the treatment of inter-company distribution of ownership and dividends, assessment of depreciation and valuation of fixed assets and inventories, particularly in a period of changing prices, and the treatment of business losses during the life time and at the time of winding up of companies.

While the governments have been in general enthusiastic in taxing company profits in the private sector, they have not been equally vigilant or successful in increasing or taxing the profits of their expanding public enterprises. Most of the profits in the column under government enterprises in Table 3 are from some variant of fiscal monopolies; the strictly commercial enterprises are generally making losses on their operations. As we saw in Chapter 5, the enterprises come under pressure from the workers for uneconomically high wages from their "model" employer—the state—and for uneconomically low prices from the consumers. An example of such tendencies is provided by Ceylon in recent years. If the governments were to continue their policies of fostering public undertakings, there is an obvious need for changing the present price and wage policies in such a way as would enable undertakings to earn profits, unless doing otherwise is a matter of state policy. There is also a need to tighten up administrative expenses.[28]

Incentives for the Private Sector

In respect of tax levels, the question of their implications for incentives is often presented in the general form that high taxes put a damper on output. This simple assertion needs closer examination. Of course, businessmen have always complained about the adverse effects of the income tax throughout the history of its operation, irrespective of whether it was a penny or a shilling in the pound; every rise in it would, it was forecast, bring down economic doom. And still, most of the developed economies have come to accept the fairly high rates of income (and company) taxes as quite normal; once these rates are accepted as such, they stop being disincentives. It is not the general level of taxation, therefore, that is injurious to economic productivity; it is rather the sharp steepening of the rates, or the absence of tax discrimination between those who play the game according to the rules and those who do not. A generally low level of taxation may increase some saving and some investment; it may also increase consumption and speculation. And, by reducing government revenue it may have the net effect of lowering the national rate of saving and investment. It would indeed seem a wiser policy to adopt in general a high average level of taxation and give discriminatory relief, in ample measure, to those who save and invest according to the priorities set in the national plans or programmes of economic development. Of course, a generally high level of taxation on incomes should not be mistaken for punitively high rates on the top income brackets; these, as we saw, would only encourage tax evasion.

The most potent instruments for encouraging personal saving are really the taxes on spending, such as sales taxes, various commodity taxes and the expenditure tax. These provide the negative incentives to save, since tax liability can be avoided by refraining from spending. Among the positive measures of incentive provision in personal income taxation are the deductions allowed, up to a specified limit, for contributions to life insurance premiums and to certain other savings schemes. Interest received from postal deposits or government bonds is also tax-exempt in several countries.

It is taxation of business incomes, however, which has, as its special feature, the system of incentives that are woven into it in order to encourage non-distribution of income as dividends and its reinvestment. In respect of the former, however, the governments have to find a practical compromise between two opposite aims; non-distribution is desirable as a mode of saving in an inflationary situation; given high rates of personal income taxation in the upper income brackets, it may be used for income tax avoidance. As result, the legislation in several countries enforces an upper limit to non-redistribution at the same time as it penalizes the distribution of dividends. A distinction is also made between closely held companies, which have a greater incentive to practise non-distribution of dividends in order to avoid personal income taxes, and loosely held companies, where the shareholder is not a partner in any real sense but only the owner of "a piece of paper with a market value." In Asia, at present, not many of the companies can be strictly described as loosely held.

Among the specific incentives to invest may be mentioned the provision for a tax holiday for a specified number of years for desired types of investment. The applicability of the tax holiday provision is confined to "new and necessary" industries in the Philippines, or "approved industrial" projects in Ceylon, India, and Pakistan. Pakistan also makes the further stipulation that the industries concerned should be those "using wholly or mainly raw materials produced in Pakistan." The laws in Ceylon and India provide the statutory tax holiday, for a period of five years. In Pakistan the tax holiday is for four years in the developed areas of West Pakistan and six years in East Pakistan and in the less developed areas of West Pakistan. The tax holiday in Afghanistan and in Japan is for three years, in Burma also for three years with a possible partial exemption for an additional period. In some countries, for example, in the Federation of Malaya, the period varies with the amount of capital invested. The Philippine law (originally approved in 1946), however, granted the concession only for a period of four years. The law was amended in 1953 making the concessions valid as follows: complete tax holiday up to the end of 1958, and progressive increases in tax liability through 10 per cent in 1959, 25 per cent in 1960, 50 per cent in 1961, 90 per cent in 1962 to full tax liability in 1963 and thereafter. However, no assessee was to enjoy any proportion of tax exemption for a period exceeding six years. Ceylon and India put an upper limit to the income that could claim tax holiday; tax exemption applies to profits of "approved" industrial undertakings in Ceylon only up to 5 per cent, and in India up to 6 per cent of the capital employed in the undertaking. The Philippine law exempts the "new and necessary" industries from liability in respect of all taxes during the holiday period; Ceylon, India and Pakistan exempt them only in respect of direct taxes.

To provide concessions to investors whose savings are to be attracted to useful enterprises, Ceylon, the Federation of Malaya and India also exempt dividends paid out of exempt profits from liability in respect of personal income tax.

Another incentive provision in the tax systems of the countries of the region is the allowance of higher and accelerated depreciation for fixed investment in approved channels. This incentive receives added weight from the fact that an enterprise which follows a policy of continuing investment will indefinitely retain this benefit, whereas its effect for enterprises not doing so, although still substantial, will be limited to a postponement of tax liability tantamount to an interest-free loan to the undertaking equal to the amount of the tax differential in the initial period. The concession enables the companies to write off the assets earlier than would otherwise be possible. However, the total tax paid over a number of years is the same, since the tax liability of the undertaking will be higher in later years as the depreciation allowance is reduced. In some countries, for example, the Federation of Malaya which provides for both types of incentives, the law permits the postponement in the use of these special investment concessions until after the tax holiday period so as to protect the former from being absorbed by the latter.

In Ceylon and India, the accelerated depreciation allowance was replaced by a system of development rebates, under which depreciation allowance is granted in excess of the original cost of fixed assets. In Ceylon, an outright development rebate equal to 20 per cent of the cost is granted for all new plant and machinery installed in a business undertaking in any year; the rate of concession is 40 per cent where the enterprise is considered essential for the economic progress of the country. In India the rate is 25 per cent; in Japan it is as high as 50 per cent. The development rebate is in addition to the normal depreciation allowances available for these assets. While the accelerated depreciation allowances have the effect of only postponing the tax liability, the development rebate is a direct tax relief to the enterprise and does not reduce the written down value of the asset on which depreciation is later allowed.

Recognizing the importance of stimulating the self-financing of industrial expansion, some countries provide tax incentives for the reinvestment of profits. Thus, in Burma, profits reinvested within one year are exempt from income tax. In Pakistan, the tax exemption is subject to the condition that profits be reinvested within one year of their accrual and that not more than 40 per cent of them be distributed.

Because of its special importance to the economy, the promotion of exports is given special tax concessions in Japan. Amounts transferred to reserves to provide for export losses are deductible as business expenses in computing the taxable income of companies. Special deductions were also in vogue during some periods when a small fraction of the value of export contracts could be set apart as a tax-free allowance.

Although concessions to provide incentives to save and to invest have been built into the tax systems of most countries, it is questionable if they have made much difference either way. To some extent this is due to the fact that legal concessions lose their meaning if the effective tax levels are low or if easier avenues permit tax avoidance or evasion. A more important factor, however, is that tax incentives are rather a delicate instrument of economic policy, they can be effective only if the general climate is favourable to private investment. Tax liability is only one of several factors taken into account in arriving at investment decisions; although it is an important consideration, it is not necessarily the most important one. If the concessions are to be effective, they have to be co-ordinated with other factors having a bearing on private investment. The most powerful incentive for private investment in the postwar period has perhaps been provided by the aggregative effect of fiscal policy on the level of effective demand in the economy and by the assurance that the demand will continue to expand and that competing products from abroad will be shut off by protective tariffs. It is factors such as these which are more pertinent in influencing private decisions than the specific concessions mentioned above. However, it must not be overlooked that these concessions have advantages when superimposed on other measures enabling the revenue system to service more efficiently the requirements of economic growth.

Social Security Taxes

Another means of tapping revenue from the growing organized sector of the community is provided by social security taxes. While company taxes would tax company income as a whole, and personal income taxes affect the incomes of salaried company officials, directors and shareholders, a large part of increasing worker incomes are likely to remain outside the purview of these taxes, even if the exemption limits were lowered. On the other hand, the state is likely to be called upon, as noted in the previous chapter, to enlarge the scope of its social services not only to cover the traditional fields of education and public health but also to offer benefits covering unemployment, sickness and retirement. Assuming that these expenditures will have to be met, there is a strong case for getting some revenue from the workers in the form of social security contributions when they are in employment. Several countries have already made a beginning with social security or similar taxation in recent years; the system appears to be well developed only in Japan and in Ceylon where the annual contributions from the private sector come to around 3 and 1 per cent respectively of the national income.[29] Ceylon is also experimenting with crop insurance, which may be described as an application of social security principles to the rural area. Like income taxes, social security taxes have a built-in flexibility; in periods of prosperity or inflation net receipts tend to go up; in times of unemployment, there are net payments. This would assist in maintaining short term stability. With the growth in the coverage of the organized sector, the revenues are also likely to grow.

Land Taxes

Agriculture is the source of livelihood for a large majority of the population of the under-developed countries of the ECAFE region. In an attempt to reach this group for revenue, farming has been subject to a variety of taxes. Agricultural incomes are taxed under the central income tax in Ceylon, Indonesia, the Philippines and Thailand, and under the state income tax in Pakistan and in several states in India. However, a more common form of agricultural taxation in the ECAFE region, as well as in the Middle East, is the tax on farm output. It is primarily a tax on the staple crop, but that is often extended to include livestock, fruit trees, vegetable gardens, etc.

There are two main types of taxation of farm output according to the method of its assessment and collection. The older one of the two is that of crop-sharing between the cultivator and the state. The tax is assessed on the basis of actual harvest and collected in kind or in cash. Such an actual output tax is in operation at present in China (mainland and Taiwan) and Korea (northern and southern). The second method common to Burma, India, Nepal and Pakistan is a combination of output and property taxes. The annual output is taxed, however, not according to current yields but according to the long-term charges fixed in cadastral assessments made periodically— every 20 or 30 years—with the tax base of gross or net output in one single year, or an average of several years preceding the year in which the assessment was made. As a tax on incomes, the land tax is a highly regressive tax; the burden is smaller for higher incomes, and varies inversely with the changes in income over the relatively long period during which a given settlement remains valid. In certain parts of India and Pakistan, land settlement was made in perpetuity at the end of the eighteenth century. The tax burden in these "permanent settlement" areas has become meaningless over this length of time; with successive transfers of ownership, it has already got capitalized in land values.

Both Thailand and the Philippines tax land on its capital value. While income to be derived from property is an important element of its value, the difference between this property tax and the traditional land tax of India and Pakistan is in the tax base. Since capital value is the base of the former tax, values arising from factors other than agricultural yields are taken into account, including actual prices paid for land. The taxes also apply to urban areas where land is used for housing. The land tax in India and Pakistan is generally confined to agricultural output; property characteristics such as irrigation facilities and quality of soil are taken into consideration only as indicators of output.

As it stands, land tax, among the fiscal systems of the countries of the region, is of importance only in Nepal. In 1950, it accounted for more than half of the country's total revenue; by 1958, the tax had given pride of place to customs duties. The tax in the plains in the south—the *Tarai* areas—is the ordinary land tax assessed and payable in cash, whereas in the hills it is assessed in kind but collected in cash, at prices which are a fraction of market prices, since the assessment prices have not been revised for about half a century. To increase revenue, the Government of Nepal, in its 1959/60 Budget, introduced surcharges on the land tax and abolished the *Birta* system, which was a system of tax free gifts by the state to individuals who had the right in perpetuity to collect land taxes from the landowners, but who had no corresponding obligation to pay anything to the Government for the privilege enjoyed. Both these measures were designed to arrest the fall in revenue from land taxes; in the present context of economic development of the country, land tax alone offers the most promising field of augmenting national saving.

The cadastral land taxes have the great demerit of being inflexible. Their share in total revenue has fallen; in the combined revenues of India and Pakistan, for instance, it fell from 13 per cent in 1938/39 to 7 per cent in 1957/58. In fact, agricultural taxation, which is the oldest form of taxation in the history of public finance, has provided low potentials of growth, unless agriculture was of a type where it had to be carried on in large units such as plantations or its products had to pass through the customs shed prior to export. Taxation of small "subsistence" or largely non-marketed outputs of a large number of peasant cultivators—practised for centuries—has given rise to complexities in tenurial systems and property rights, and to extortionate and iniquitous taxation of the small tenant cultivator, not so much for the benefit of the state as of the intermediaries between him and the state. Any attempt to alter the basis of land taxation, therefore, gives rise to serious problems of administration, equity and incidence. No one is in favour of taxing the subsistence farmer if he is really that; on the other hand, both the wartime rise in real prices, and postwar increase in output resulting from investments in agriculture—largely at public expense—have brought about a rise in agricultural incomes in real terms, which has not been tapped for revenue except in the export-orientated economies.

The question of what can be done to tax this increase in agricultural incomes revolves around the difficulty of ascertaining the beneficiaries of the rise. As far as export trade is concerned, governments have been able to tap the increment through export taxes, marketing boards, discriminatory exchange rates and other similar measures. But in the case of cultivation for domestic consumption, there is a presumption, but no accurate information, that the benefits have accrued to producers, who have increased their own consumption and who have received higher prices on what they have chosen to sell. There is again a difference of opinion here as to the extent to which the gain has gone to the subsistence farmer or to the landowner or moneylender.

This question of tapping the increase in agricultural incomes for revenue received the attention of the inquiries into taxation by a Commission in India and by a Committee in Pakistan. The Indian Commission also made the attempt noted above[30] to study the difference in incidence of all taxation as between urban and rural population and as between the several income groups. Its findings were that, on incomes below the income tax exemption limits, the level of tax incidence in urban areas was higher than in rural areas, although the difference between the two was "not quite as great as is often believed." On the other hand, the disparity was large in respect of incomes subject to the central income tax. The Commission therefore concluded: "there appears to be greater room for increased taxation of higher rural incomes, if the country is to have a more satisfactory picture of incidence."[31]

In the context of rising output and increasing price levels, one way of taxing agricultural incomes would be by price-fixing of agricultural produce, letting real prices but not the real incomes of producers fall. This has, in fact, been done in Burma and Thailand, where governments have been able to keep domestic prices of rice below export prices in order to secure revenue. The price-fixing of agricultural produce intended for domestic consumption will not be revenue-yielding; but it will serve one of the major objectives of fiscal policy, namely, the maintenance of long-term stability. The prices could be pegged at fairly stable levels by controls over transportation and sale, physical procurement of supplies and maintenance of buffer stocks, as have been tried in India and in other countries of the region. If these methods are successful, stabilization is secured directly rather than through a fiscal intervention.

This is not to deny the considerable scope which the present land tax system permits for its rationalization to yield more revenue. India and Pakistan have made attempts to expand the purview of their taxation on incomes to include agricultural incomes. But, since the exemption limits exempt all but a minor group and since the rates have been relatively low, yields have remained small. Apart from revenue considerations, agricultural income taxes are intended to introduce progressivity in land taxes; another method by which this is sought to be done is progressive surcharges on the land tax. A second source of revenue is provided by betterment taxes levied on property benefiting directly from development projects such as irrigation works.[32] If, however, land values rise from general economic development or from inflationary conditions or speculative demand, capital gains taxes could be used to catch the increment in land values. Private investment and utilization of land could also be stimulated by taxes on unimproved or unutilized land. However, none of these taxes is likely to bridge the large gap between the rise in agricultural incomes and the trend of revenues from land taxes.

RATIONALIZATION OF REVENUE SYSTEM
AND ADMINISTRATION

To sum up, contrary to what has often been generally believed, taxable limits—whatever they are—have not been reached in the newly developing countries which indeed possess a revenue potential sizably greater than what they have so far exploited. On the whole, they succeeded well in taxing transactions in foreign trade, although this source, as we saw above, is not likely to provide growing revenues. The tax systems, on the other hand, were not as effective in improving the balance of payments; considerations of revenue have been in conflict with those of saving foreign exchange. The balance of payments problem was more effectively tackled by direct controls.

In respect of counteracting short-term disturbances to stability, the relative under-development and the time-lag between the earning of income and its assessment have made taxation of incomes less effective than what could be expected from it in view of its built-in flexibility for this purpose. The governments had greater success with export taxes as an anti-inflationary device in times of export boom; they counteracted deflationary situations through an expansion of expenditure rather than through tax reduction. Nor was the income tax system fully effective in promoting investment or channeling it in desired directions; the promotional incentives lost their attractiveness and the deterrents their punch owing to the restricted scope of the tax system in general and the wide-open possibilities for tax avoidance and evasion.

For the prime task of raising national rates of savings, taxes on internal transactions in commodities and services and on domestic incomes and wealth provide the most suitable fields for further exploitation. In the process, the question of tax incidence and discrimination between the poor and the well-off has to be seen from new angles. It is not possible to give a categorical answer to the query if the poor in the newly developing economies of Asia provide further tax potentials, until a basis is prepared giving factual information on whether and what the poor have gained from the rise in national income, and the incidence of existing taxes on their incomes and spending.

However, we may clarify some points. There is one real problem. The pre-occupation with questions of incidence, when carried to the extreme and applied to every individual tax, is likely to lead the tax system eventually into losing revenue and making it regressive in relation to national income if the bulk of the rise in the national income goes to increase, although by a little, the small incomes of the poor. In such circumstances, seeking progressivity may lead to a regressive tax system. Indeed, it is not the incidence of an individual tax but that of the tax-and-expenditure system as a whole which should matter in this regard. Taxing a few necessities, or lowering income-tax exemption limits, or devising schemes of rural taxation will make the tax system more progressive in relation to the national income; it will raise incremental income—"non-consumption" ratio for the economy as a whole. If the poor have little choice between paying taxes and remaining in "disguised unemployment" or suffering inflation, they will be better off paying the taxes.

There is also the question of definition as to who precisely constitute the "poor" and what constitutes "poverty" in the context of Asia. One way of defining poverty would be to reckon as poor all the family units with less per capita income than the national average. Those above the average could then be distinguished as middle income groups or the rich on the basis of a certain multiple, say ten times, of the per capita national income. Thus, if the average family size is reckoned to be five persons in all income groups, persons earning less than five times the national per capita income could be described as the poor; those earning from five up to fifty times as the middle classes; and those earning more than that as the well-off. If then, the poor, on this definition, remain still on the "subsistence" level, they should not be taxed. Any taxation of persons at subsistence levels would impinge on human capital and would be highly injurious to economic growth. If, on the other hand, the taxpayer has crossed the Rubicon, even if his income be still below the average levels, there is a case for touching him for some portion of his income, and a strong case for tapping an increased portion of his incremental income.

As for the well-off, they need to be dealt with, but a little more carefully. To the extent that they are, in effect, lightly taxed, despite the high rates on top brackets of "taxable income," there is ample scope for getting more out of them. This can be done by redefining "taxable income," by taxing wealth and spending, by plugging all the legal loopholes and by taking more effective measures aimed at catching tax evasion, like those taken in Pakistan when the new Government came into power. On the other hand, the tendency to overtax should be avoided for two reasons. First, it will only encourage tax evasion. At the top levels of income, when the marginal tax burden is 90 per cent, a tax avoidance or evasion worth one unit of currency has for the taxpayer a value equal to earning ten units. Secondly,— and this is rather important—such taxation may be injurious to saving. In India, for instance, more than half of the tax revenues from personal income taxes in 1957/58 was collected from only 7,000 individuals, each of whom was assessed as having a minimum of two hundred times the national per capita income. Even assuming that there was no tax avoidance or evasion and that the income reported was their only income, these people would still be left with enough wealth, if not enough income, after paying their taxes, to permit luxury consumption. Income taxation and even commodity taxation does not seriously affect the consumption levels of the truly rich. So the net result would hardly be a reduction in consumption. Direct controls, rather than fiscal measures, may perhaps be more effective. The taxes do not increase the national total of savings; they merely transfer the savings of the rich to the government. Such transfer is often advocated on the argument that it would curb speculative investment; but, if the rates are really high, the speculators might as well take their chances on cheating the tax collector. Compulsory, punitive and unrequited transfers of *bona fide* savings to the government, on the other hand, would have adverse effects on incentives to earn, save and invest in the private sector. It may well be that the governments are motivated by considerations of national priorities in investment and by a belief that in view of these priorities the targets of investment in the public sector need to be filled even at the expense of investment in the private sector. It would, however, be regrettable if the availability of revenues were only to encourage the governments to indulge in extravagant consumption or give-away redistribution at the expense of private saving and investment.

The expansion in the scope of the revenue system, advocated above, requires a strengthening of the revenue assessment and collection machinery. In Burma, India and Pakistan, the stagnant land tax absorbs administrative resources out of proportion to its yield; income and excise or sales taxes, on the other hand, are only inadequately enforced. A great deal of the administrative burden could be reduced by simplifying the tax structure. Thus, if capital gains were treated as ordinary income, there would be no need to verify whether an income was a capital gain or not. If an accessions tax on beneficiaries was introduced, it would obviate the need to have both the inheritance taxes and gift taxes. There is also a great merit in built-in cross-checking in the Kaldor proposal of a comprehensive return, filed once a year by the taxpayer, on his wealth, income and spending. Strengthening of the cadre, and mechanization in the offices, would go a long way to avoid delays in assessment and collection. If it is desired to extend the scope of income taxes to cover lower income groups, tax forms and assessment methods could be simplified. The taxes could be collected from employees by having them withheld at the source. Small traders or businessmen could be assessed on their gross income. Self-assessment under oath could be made the general rule for non-wage incomes, and tax tables for ready reckoning distributed as is done in Japan; presumptive assessments could be levied on defaulters by tax officers unless the assessees were to prove their lower liabilities for tax by producing accounts and books. Some simplified accounting system could be evolved, and standard forms incorporating such a system could be distributed to educate taxpayers in bookkeeping.

These administrative improvements are relevant not only in the field of low-income taxation; they have ramifications over the entire range of fiscal administration in under-developed countries. Illiteracy is, of course, an important problem, but not the big bugbear it is made out to be. The land tax, in operation for centuries in several countries of the region, has, in fact, involved the taxation of illiterate rural masses; whole revenue cadres have been built up in the course of its administration. Unfortunately, the land tax is inflexible and regressive from the point of view of fiscal development; if need be, it could be abolished altogether, and the administrative resources released could be redirected to administer a simplified, more rational and flexible system of income, property and commodity taxes on the lines reviewed on these pages. Of course, there would still be tax evaders, but cases of tax evasion discovered could be punished more severely to deter others from practising fraud. At the moment, the discoveries of evasion are so infrequent, and the penalties on the evasion discovered so lenient, that the taxpayers, particularly self-employed professionals like doctors or lawyers and businessmen, can easily take a chance on not being caught at all or being let off lightly if caught. Special tax courts, instead of the ordinary legal machinery for civil suits, may be instituted and the legal processes tailored to deal expeditiously with the specific problems of tax evasion. A stricter supervision of the lucrative profession of company accountants and tax advisers or consultants might also bring to light the deficiencies of tax legislation and its practical application and administration.

NOTES TO SELECTION 6

[1]It may be noted that, owing to the Korean war, the base year 1950 was itself a year of high prices in several of the countries listed in Table 21 [not included in this volume].

[2]See United Nations, *Economic Bulletin For Asia and the Far East*, September, 1960, p. 29.

[3]Po I-po (the then Finance Minister of the Central People's Government), "Report on the 1953 Budget," *Ta Kung Pao* (Hong Kong), February 18, 1953; Li Hsien-nien (the present Finance Minister), "Report on 1959 State Accounts and 1960 State Budget," *Peking Review*, April 5, 1960.

[4]The ports are really not "free" for all commodities; excise taxes on gasolene, liquor and tobacco, for instance, are collected at the customs shed.

[5]See footnote 14.

[6]The demand for motor-cars appears to be less price elastic than one would tend to think; possession of a car has become a status symbol. For the higher priced cars, imports of which have been restricted in several countries, fantastically high prices are reported to have been offered for the few that are available.

[7]See United Nations, *Economic Survey of Asia and the Far East 1959*, Chap. 4.

[8]This is quite similar to the government purchases of raw cotton in the United States.

[9]Except, perhaps the import pre-payments and the tax on importers.

[10]In 1960, the exchange tax was abolished. The value of the export dollar thus rose from 36 to 45 rupiahs. The sixfold classification of imports was reduced to only two categories—"essentials" and "less essentials." The first category was divided into three groups with no surcharge, with 25 per cent surcharge and with 60 per cent surcharge. The "less essentials" were subject to a special rate of exchange, initially fixed at 200 rupiahs to a dollar. Tariffs, on exports as well as imports, were also revised.

[11]It is still too early to predict whether this means that the role of petroleum as a source of increasing revenues is a thing of the past.

[12]Government of India, *Report of the Taxation Enquiry Commission* (New Delhi, 1955), II, 259.

[13]The popularity of the sales tax in advanced countries, on the other hand, has been, to some extent, due to a feeling that any further steepening of income taxes would have disincentive effects.

[14]The significant proportion in Brunei under this head in Table 3 reflects mainly taxation of profits of the oil company, which was already taken note of in the earlier section on taxes on foreign trade (see text at footnote 5 above).

[15]The sharp rise in Burma reflects mainly a change in accounting; from 1953/54 the state marketing boards were required to pay income taxes on their profits. As a result, the share of income taxes in total revenue went up and that of "other taxes on foreign trade" went down. Similar changes have also affected the structural classification in Table 3 in respect of several other countries.

[16]Except for some recent changes, the system, as it operated through most of the postwar period, was a two-tier system of income and supertaxes in respect of both individuals and companies. Secondly, the Hindu undivided family, a unit of considerable significance in the business organization of the Hindu community, received special treatment. There was no tax allowance for family size; there was differentiation between earned and unearned income; and, finally, insofar as company incomes were distributed to individuals as dividends, a tax rebate was given on personal income tax liabilities of the shareholders in consideration of a part of the tax—the "income tax" but not the "supertax"—paid by the companies.

[17]As distinguished from specific policies which are best implemented by special excises and differential rates of customs duties on particular commodities.

[18]See footnote 14.

[19]See final section of this discussion.

[20]Henry Simons, before the war, called this a "subtle kind of moral and intellectual dishonesty . . . a grand scheme of deception whereby enormous surtaxes are voted in exchange for promises that they will not be made effective. Thus the politicians may point with pride to the rates, while quietly reminding their wealthy constituents of the loopholes." *Personal Income Taxation* (Chicago, 1938), p. 219, quoted by Nicholas Kaldor: *Indian Tax Reform*, p. 11. In Asia, there is perhaps less of deception than a genuine misunderstanding on the part of the politicians.

[21]Kaldor, *Indian Tax Reform*, p. 66.

[22]While top marginal rates of income tax could well be lowered, there is a case for steepening the inheritance taxes; and since progressivity should affect not the dead but the living, the beneficiaries could be taxed progressively on the basis of amount received over the years, irrespective of whether that was an inheritance or a gift.

[23]Nicholas Kaldor, *Suggestions for a Comprehensive Reform of Direct Taxation* (Government of Ceylon, 1960), p. 7.

[24]Kaldor, *Indian Tax Reform*, p. 2.

[25]*Ibid.*, pp. 103–6.

[26]In Pakistan also, the voluntary disclosures, in response to the two-month amnesty granted in November, 1959, indicated that the tax evaded each year exceeded half of the income tax collected.

[27]Government of Japan, *Outline of National Tax in Japan, 1957*, p. 18.

[28]The "perks" for officials in public undertakings often match those in the private sector; the former, in addition, enjoy the security of tenure and easy transferability in the event of things going wrong, neither of which is available to the same extent to their counterparts in private enterprise.

[29]Social security taxes are also well developed in Latin America; Chile collects 4.5 per cent, and Brazil, Costa Rica and Dominican Republic about 1 per cent, of national income as contributions from the private sector. The operations are generally organized under separate agencies, with semi-independent powers of taxation, investment of funds and disbursements of benefits. In Latin America, the investments have generally been made in real estate; similar investments in Asia may relieve the government of the load of providing housing facilities for lower income groups, although there is scope for re-orienting investment from real estate to industrial projects.

[30]See Table 5.

[31]*Report of the Taxation Enquiry Commission*, I, 78.

[32]India is experiencing some resistance in the East Punjab state in collecting betterment levies on lands benefiting from the Nangal project.

7

Tax Pattern in Latin America

by Joseph P. Crockett*

CONSIDERABLE public attention has been focused of late on taxation in Latin American republics as a result of the approval by representatives of the Organization of American States of programs for social improvement and economic development. These programs, evolved in a series of meetings, are incorporated in the Act of Bogotà. (Doc. CECE/III. 70; approved by Council of OAS, Oct. 11, 1960), and tax reform is assigned an especially high priority on the agenda of surveys and studies to be undertaken and of objectives to be achieved. In furtherance of the purpose of this Act governments of the member states have created and capitalized the Inter-American Development Bank, and it is anticipated that the Bank's promotion of development will be supplemented by increased investment and activity of United States enterprises in lands south of the border.

Apart from specialists and the tax or accounting departments of enterprises already operating in Latin America, there is little knowledge in the United States about taxation in the southern republics. In fact, a general provincialism on the subject of foreign taxes prevails here, as in other countries. This is often manifest in references to "income," as if the concept were internationally uniform, and to "rate scales" as if the progression were a fair index for a comparison of tax burdens. A brief description of a Latin American tax system, concepts and practices may serve to correct common erroneous assumptions and to point up some fundamental differences which exist between United States tax patterns and those of Latin America.

In an approach to this subject it is pertinent to stress that there are twenty Latin American republics, and while viewed in the aggre-

*National Tax Journal, XV (March, 1962), 93–104. Mr. Crockett, a member of the Bar of the District of Columbia, was formerly technical advisor in the foreign tax field to the Internal Revenue Service. He has served with technical assistance missions as consultant to the Finance Ministries of five Latin American Republics, and at present is consultant on taxation to the Pan American Union, the Secretariat of the Organization of American States. This article is reprinted here with the kind permission of the publisher.

gate, they have some general characteristics in common, differences in detail, including tax detail, are very great among them. A separate description of twenty tax systems or of twenty income tax structures obviously could not be compressed within the confines of an article. The full picture, moreover, is complicated by the evolving nature of Latin American taxes, often without the intervening or transitional administrative experience which leads to or develops precise definitions and concepts. Of necessity a composite picture would not reflect taxation in any country, and hence the system of one must be used for basic illustration; for this purpose the system of the largest and most populous of the republics, Brazil, has been chosen.

After independence the Latin American government relied overwhelmingly on indirect taxes, the principal ones being import duties, taxes on sales, consumption and production; it also imposed taxes on legal documents and official acts, usually collected by the use of stamps or stamped paper, and taxes on land for which the taxable base was sometimes not the land's fair market value, but more often a theoretical annual rental value imputed to it. It remains true today unfortunately that a major part of public revenues in many Latin American countries is derived from the custom house while indirect taxes falling on consumer goods provide a large share of the remainder. This condition, however, is slowly changing. All the republics now have some form of income or profits taxes, and while in many the yield of these constitutes less than 15 per cent of the tax revenue and administration could often be improved, there is manifest a marked tendency to develop this type of tax, and in the larger countries it provides from 30 per cent to 35 per cent of the revenues of the national government;—in Colombia, over 50 per cent.

The taxes of Brazil are fairly typical in most respects of the Latin American systems, and serve well to illustrate the differences between those systems and the patterns prevailing in the United States. Brazil is divided politically into twenty-one states, five territories and a federal district, and these are subdivided into about three thousand townships or municipios. Taxes are imposed and collected by the federal, state and municipal governments. In 1960 revenues of the Federal Government, which constituted 45 per cent of all public revenues, aggregated nearly 180 billion cruzeiros, of which 95 per cent represented tax receipts. For 1961 total revenues of 225 billion are anticipated. Of tax receipts about 40 per cent was derived from consumption taxes; 35.5 per cent from income taxes, 13.3 per cent from stamps and other internal taxes, and exceptionally for Latin America, only 11.1 from duties on imports. State governments which receive 44 per cent of total public revenues, derived 77 per cent from taxes, the principal ones being on sales (about 70 per cent of total). Others are on suburban and rural land, on transfers of land, on inheritances; there are also stamp taxes. The remaining 11 per cent of public revenues is the share of municipal governments. Their chief taxes are those on urban real estate and rents. They also impose taxes on business and professional activities, admissions to shows and some stamp taxes. Substantial variation exists in local tax patterns, both state and local.

In general it can be said that the taxes of Brazil apply to goods produced, imported or sold in the country; to transactions and activities carried out within its territory, and to land and other property situated therein; with one exception to be noted taxation ends at the frontier. This principle, initially dominant and exclusive, still permeates Latin American thinking on tax proprieties. To be taxable property should be physically in reach; activities should be locally conducted, and income should be of domestic source. The approach is very practical, and represents a marked difference in respect of the income tax from that of the United States, which taxes on the basis of citizenship and residence as well as of source.

In Latin America, income and profits taxes, in the modern sense, are of recent adoption; in some of the republics such taxes were introduced only after the beginning of World War II. Fantastic as it may now seem, only a few short years ago tax havens were scattered all over the map. Initially and for many years after adoption, income and profits taxes applied only to income and profits of national source. This limitation was not expressed in any law; it was implicitly assumed, being conformant with the Latin American approach to all taxation. Today, however, a substantial number of the republics assert the right to tax foreign source income—at least to some extent; it is not believed, however, that this assertion is based on any deep-rooted convictions or that it is productive of any substantial amount of revenue. It would appear to be more in the nature of a retaliatory measure adopted in response to the long reach of the Internal Revenue Bureau of the United States, or as one Latin American official put it, "necessary for prestige." Only two Latin American countries grant by law a foreign tax credit, and only one (Honduras) is party to a tax treaty (with the United States). Hence any effective enforcement of the tax on foreign-source income would result in extremely burdensome double taxation.

Psychologically, furthermore, the Latin American still imputes an ethical stigma to the taxation of foreign-source income. As recently as 1953 the Cuban delegate proposed to the Fiscal Commission of the United Nations a resolution that capital-exporting countries refrain from taxing income arising outside their territory, and a number of recent resolutions adopted by bodies of the Organization of American States are to the effect that the member states restrict their taxation to income having a domestic source as a stimulus to the free flow of investment capital. But whatever may be the majority ideal, at present the laws of some Latin American republics subject to tax income derived from any source in the world by their citizens, residents and companies—for example, Mexico. Some subject all income of resident individuals to tax, but only the domestic income of companies and other enterprises—for example, Brazil. In others only income of domestic source is taxable—for example, Argentina. Thus, each of the three largest republics has a different pattern.

But if the three republics differ in the treatment of foreign-source income, the kinship of the general structure of their income taxes is obvious. The systems of the three are schedular, and require complicated classification of elements of income in contrast to the Internal Revenue Code, which segregates only capital gains for special treatment. This structural pattern is of historical significance and practical consequences. In the United States, as in British countries, we are accustomed to think of "the taxpayer" as an individual or a corporation subject to tax on his collective income and profits of all kinds and from all sources except those elements which have been specifically exempted by statute. The amount of the tax due is computed on the one taxable base by reference to a graduated table for individuals or flat rates for corporations. No distinctions are made according to class of income with the single exception of the special treatment of capital gains,—which the Latin American does not regard as income.

The Latin American derived his initial ideas of the income tax from France, where formerly there was no lumping of income into a common taxable mass. Categories or schedules were singled out for computation of bases under special rules applicable to each, and special rates or rate tables were prescribed for each schedule. More important still, to be taxable, income had to fall within the definition of a particular schedule. If it did not, then it was not subject to tax.

An individual, of course, may receive types of income falling within several schedules, all of which are taxable, but surprisingly enough, perhaps not to him as the "taxpayer." The "taxpayer" may be the individual's wholly owned enterprise. It is convenient but usually erroneous to refer to the corporation profits tax of many Latin American republics. The corporation's profits are, of course, subject to tax, but that is because the corporation conducts an enterprise engaged in an activity defined by the Commercial Code of the country as "commercial." Likewise taxable are the profits of any such enterprise, be it conducted by a partnership or one of the several other forms of business organization recognized by Civil Law or simply by an individual proprietor. Commercial profits, it is pertinent to add, normally comprise any gains to which the English term, business profits, would apply.

Initially the Latin American income taxes were imposed only on one or more types of income, and that is still true in some republics—for example, Guatemala and Ecuador. Profits of enterprises registered under the Commercial Code were always the type or among the types initially taxed. The Code for long years past had already required the keeping of specified books of account, which books, and each page thereof, had to be duly registered and stamped by an official, usually the Judge of Commerce, and as the enterprise was normally required to be a member of the local Chamber of Commerce, a semi-official organ in Latin America, the government had ready to hand a register of taxpayers and records all set for the enforcement of a tax on profits.

The Code, in fact, imposed penalties for incorrect books, and legal redress and the validity of transactions were dependent upon their proper entry of record in these books. The mere entries were and still are indeed vested with a certain evidentiary value of the facts that they purport to show. So obviously the government needed only to require the registered merchants to compute a tax on the profits shown by their books. In at least one republic the Tax Department even now does not require the filing of a return. The taxpayer enterprise simply writes the Tax Director that its books show a specified amount of net profit for the preceding year, and encloses a copy of its balance sheet and an abbreviated transcript of its profit and loss account. A revenue agent calls to examine the books, making adjustments by eliminating expenditures that are not deductible, such as the profits taxes paid, personal and family expenses of the owners if any such appear, salaries exceeding deductible limits set by law, and the like. The tax on the commercial profits of an enterprise is usually computed by a progressive rate table. This progression, which sets a penalty on size, often leads to the division of an enterprise into two or more units for tax saving.

Other types of income which were subjected early to schedular taxes by some Latin American republics were salaries for personal services performed for an employer established in the country, professional fees and income from specified loans and investments. Some countries still tax only a few schedules, and taxed profits, when distributed to the shareholder or other participant, are received free of any further tax. But in other countries, those most developed, the types of income comprised within the several schedules are so broadly defined as to result in a tax on all income except capital gains, which are usually completely free of tax. The shareholder, partner or individual proprietor of an enterprise, itself fully taxed, moreover is required to include his individual share of profits in his personal income subject to tax. The result in such cases is that the United States policy of taxing profits to the corporation and then taxing the dividend paid from those taxed profits to the shareholder is extended to the profits of all enterprises and their owners, and except in the case of corporate profits, the owner pays tax on the total of the profits (less the tax paid by the enterprise) whether or not withdrawn by him.

A good illustration of the schedular income tax structure is the tax of Brazil. The individual resident of Brazil must segregate his income for tax purposes into eight possible categories or schedules, to each of which specified deductions apply. Briefly described, these schedules and the applicable schedular tax are:

SCHEDULE A: interest from Brazilian Government bonds, 3 per cent; if bonds are in bearer form, 6 per cent.

SCHEDULE B: other interest, 10 per cent; from bonds in bearer form, 21 per cent.

SCHEDULE C: salaries and wages, 1 per cent.

SCHEDULE D: professional fees, 2 per cent.

SCHEDULE E: rentals of land and buildings, 3 per cent.

SCHEDULE F: dividends and profits of all enterprises taxed, and all foreign source income (nil.) Bearer dividends, 28 per cent.

SCHEDULE G: profits of farming, livestock raising and the producer's processing of his products, nil.

SCHEDULE H: all other types of income, 5 per cent, specifically including rents for use of patents and trade marks, rents of subleases.

Having computed the schedular net incomes and taxes, the individual resident then adds together the net incomes (except that from bearer shares or bonds) deducts from the total the amount of interest and life insurance premiums paid by him; losses from fire, storm, shipwreck or other natural calamity, charitable contributions, fees for medical care, his personal exemption and exemptions for his dependents. On the basis of this net amount he computes a complementary tax according to a graduated table, ranging from 2 per cent to 50 per cent of net income exceeding $4,500,000.[1] The individual's total income tax is the sum of the schedular taxes and this complementary tax. If he is a man over 25 and unmarried, he must add 15 per cent of the tax to the amount payable; if married but without children, 10 per cent; if over 45 with only one child, 5 per cent. If his tax exceeds Cr.$20,000, he must buy Brazilian development bonds of a face value equal to 15 per cent of the tax; if his tax exceeds Cr.$250,000, he must invest 20 per cent of the tax in the bonds, and if the tax exceeds Cr.$1,000,000, 25 per cent. There is a separate tax on the transfer of real estate situate in Brazil, measured by the capital gain.

It will be noted that a resident individual who receives dividends or as owner or partner is entitled to the whole or a share of the profits of an enterprise must report those profits as an element of his income on which the complementary tax is computed. But the enterprise itself, regardless of the form of its organization, must pay a tax on its net profits of Brazilian source: 18 per cent of the first Cr.$500,000, and 23 per cent of the profits in excess of that amount.

In addition the enterprise may have to pay an excess profits tax on the part of its profits which exceed 30 per cent of its capital for the year, i.e. paid-in capital plus undistributed profits. At the taxpayer's election, however, taxable excess profits may be computed as the excess over double the average profits for the period 1947–8–9, or as a percentage of gross income—6 per cent of the first Cr.$3,500,000; 5 per cent of the next Cr.$1,500,000, and 4 per cent of the amount above Cr.$5,000,000. The tax on excess profits ranges from 20 per cent to 50 per cent. The enterprise must also buy development bonds in an amount equal to 15 per cent of its tax and 4 per cent of its reserves. If the undistributed profits of a corporation exceed the amount of its paid-in capital, a 30 per cent tax is imposed on the excess.

It is here pertinent to add that the Brazilian subsidiary corporation of a foreign corporation is taxed as a national company, and on paying a dividend to its parent must withhold the 25 per cent tax which is generally imposed on income passing to a nonresident. If the foreign corporation operates through a branch in Brazil, the branch pays the profits tax on its profits of Brazilian source, and must also withhold the 25 per cent tax on profits sent the foreign owner. And in each case an amount equal to 15 per cent of the tax withheld must be also withheld and invested in the development bonds. Such then is the picture of a highly developed Latin American income tax.

In the course of this description I have referred to residence, deductions, net income, foreign and domestic source and other concepts which have a fixed meaning within the framework of English terminology. But just as the physicist had to revise his ideas of the absolute in the light of the quanta theory, so concepts must be divorced from the comfort of the absolute in the foreign tax field. Residence, for instance, is normally defined by the Latin American, for tax purposes at least, by reference to physical presence in the country. In Brazil a twelve-month stay makes a resident. In other republics the period is only six months, without prejudice to an immediate residence if the former nonresident accepts employment, opens a regular business, buys a home or otherwise manifests an intent to remain indefinitely. An examination of a number of Latin American Civil Codes furthermore indicates that domicile and residence are synonymous. Certainly there is no indication of the nice distinction between the two recognized by Anglo-Saxon law.

Relative vagueness is a characteristic of Latin American tax legislation. One longs for voluminous regulations and the Internal Revenue Bulletin, but he longs in vain. The income tax of many of the republics must be sought in a vast mass of laws, decrees, decree-laws, proclamations, ministerial decrees and other forms of legislation which are usually brief in scope, and create new taxes, or amend, modify or repeal all or parts of prior legislation which often is not cited. There is a lack of precision and detail in legislation and regulations with the result that much must often be inferred. For example, deductible business expenses may be defined as those required for the production of the income under recognized accounting principles. Then follow limitations on the principles, such for example as a ceiling on the amount that may be deducted as salaries paid to managers or the disallowance of all expenses incurred abroad.

This lack of detail, it would seem, is a heritage from the accounting requirements of the ancient Commercial Codes. By these every enterprise was (and is) required to maintain prescribed books and to register them in the city of its operations. Anciently, and sometimes now, the entries reflect business transactions that are all local. The owner or his bookkeeper evolved an accounting system that satisfied him; these schemes differ greatly, and Latin American revenue agents complain that it is very difficult to interpret the records. Still, such were the existing and required records when the income tax was adopted, and wisely the government thought best not to disturb established custom, which at all events offered a clue to the tax base. Consequently such rules as appear in the laws are likely to be merely exceptional changes, or very new accounting ideas for the country, such as a depreciation allowance.

The foregoing observations do not apply universally, and it is, of course, true that highly competent accountants have practiced in Latin America for many, many years. Price Waterhouse and Haskins and Sells are well represented there. But their services naturally are rendered to the larger firms, while numerically the small enterprises of the local citizens are those which reflect the broad picture. And that picture is simply an evolution of the application of the Commercial Code. Perhaps the owner of an enterprise had branch establishments in other cities. Originally each branch was an "enterprise," and when the income tax was enacted, became a "taxpayer" all on its own. This is evident from Brazil's legislation in which it is meticulously specified that the income of all branches must be shown on the profits tax return of the head office. Analogously, a republic which taxes the profits of a "resident foreign enterprise" from whatever source derived does not mean the head office and its world-wide branches. The "resident enterprise" is the local branch, no more. And if that branch enters on its books income or transactions from foreign sources, it will likely be taxed on that income although the expenses incurred abroad may not be recognized as proper deductions.

The rates of the Latin American income and profits taxes are usually lower than the 52 per cent which the federal government imposes on profits of United States corporations, or even the 38 per cent (in effect) imposed on profits of the Western Hemisphere Trade Corporation. But a lower rate does not necessarily mean a lower tax. The Internal Revenue Bureau and the Latin American Tax Administration may compute a branch's net profits as two entirely different figures. The following hypothetical illustration, somewhat extreme perhaps but quite possible, will point up the reasons for the discrepancies: Suppose that the branch of a United States commercial corporation in the Republic of C realizes net profits of $150,000 as computed by the Internal Revenue Bureau. In this computation deductions included $25,000 representing the salary and office expense of an agent, resident in New York, who acted solely as a buyer of goods for the branch and attended to the proper packing and shipping of the goods. $10,000 was paid in New York for advertising posters, insurance on stocks of the branch and interest on a loan used wholly for business of the branch. Salaries of $60,000 in the aggregate were paid to the three branch managers in the Republic C; a deduction of $20,000 was allowed on account of the depreciation of fixed assets of the branch, and $10,000 was allowed as a deduction for a fair share of the head-office expenses.

There was no dispute about the amount of the receipts and expenditures, but the tax administrator of the Republic of C, acting correctly under its tax laws, disallowed the $25,000 and $10,000 expenses because expenses incurred abroad are not deductible. He disallowed $20,000 of the $60,000 paid as salaries to the branch managers because the ceiling was $40,000, that being a percentage of gross sales. He reduced the depreciation deduction to $15,000, that being the amount deductible computed at the rate fixed by law. He disallowed the $10,000 share of head-office expense, that deduction being expressly forbidden by a special decree. As a result of all these adjustments, he determined net profits of $220,000 or $70,000 more than the amount computed by the Internal Revenue Bureau.

The method of computing income has as great a bearing on the amount of tax as the rate itself, and is very often largely conditioned by source rules. Despite the importance of determining source, however, only three Latin American republics have legislative definitions of source, and tax administrators of other countries consulted seemed unaware of the problems involved in a determination of source, seeming to regard source as simply obvious. Probably this complacency results from the facile acceptance of the accounting used in the required books. An examination is made of the entries, and adjustments required by law follow. Thus personal expenditures are added back to income; expenses incurred abroad are not accepted as deductible—in short, effect is given to the bans of statute. In checking gross profits, the agent compares the book entries with invoices and Custom House documents; perhaps with advices from the Central Bank on sales in foreign currency. The Latin American agent is not interested in ascertaining "where the sale occurred," a legalistic question which plagues the US Internal Revenue agent. And he has little or no powers to require banks and others probably having knowledge of the income of a taxpayer under examination, to cooperate with him.

It seems that what grew up under the record requirements of the Commercial Codes, as varied as it was in accounting, can be likened to the Anglo-American common law. There were no precise rules of accounting, just trends and tendencies, yet withal a general pattern, never nicely exact, evolved. But no Lord Coke arose to bring order into the mass of customs; no Law Institute to pick and choose and give a Restatement. Then again as in the case of the common law, after these accounting methods were accepted for income tax purposes, the common practices were specifically changed, confirmed or amended by statutes. For that reason perhaps Latin American income tax laws seem fragmentary; they merely modify an existing body of accounting concepts which evolved without statutory enactment.

In the absence of statutory provisions, it is pertinent to inquire: What are some Latin American source rules? For instance, what is the source of compensation paid by a nonresident employer to a nonresident employee for services performed in Republic C. Very probably: foreign source and not taxable. Of course, if the nonresident employee overstayed his six months, then he would be resident, and probably taxed if caught. What is the source of compensation for personal services rendered abroad by a resident of Republic C for an employer of Republic C? National source and taxable. The answer might be the same even if the employee were a nonresident of C. It might be added also that if the salary were not taxed to the recipient, it would probably not be allowed as a deduction to the employer, being expense incurred abroad. In some countries there is also manifest a tendency to tax that part of salary earned abroad which is brought into the country.

The approach indicated above is very common in the discussion of payments for technical services furnished by the foreign parent or head office to its Latin American subsidiary or branch. In a few republics these payments are allowed as deductions, and the right has been rather flagrantly abused in some instances with the result that in the drafting of income tax legislation, this subject frequently arouses considerable acrimony. There are alternative solutions which the Latin American usually finds acceptable and which rather well illustrate his reasoning on foreign source deductions and domestic source income. The solutions are these: 1) the payment for technical services performed abroad is not deductible by the subsidiary or branch and is not taxable to the parent or head-office, or 2) it is deductible and is taxable to the recipient. The latter solution was adopted in the recent legislation of Chile. Of a somewhat different nature is the deduction by a subsidiary or branch of a share of general administrative expenses of the head-office. Usually no such deduction is allowed in Latin America, and often such a deduction is singled out for express prohibition in a law. Chile, however, authorizes it, and in the tax treaty with the United States, Honduras agreed to do so.

The common Latin American view of profit computation on goods locally produced and sold abroad, or vice versa, excludes any division of profit between the country of production and that of sale. The U.S. Internal Revenue Code, it will be recalled, requires such a division. But again the harshness of the view (of which few tax administrators south of the border seem conscious before being consulted about it) is mitigated by what has been and still is acceptable practice under the Commercial Codes. The local producer-exporter will likely enter on his books the wholesale world price, if the product is coffee, cacao, sugar or some such commodity, and the revenue agent will not be concerned about where the sale occurred or if a sale has occurred or what was the price received. Incidentally income is sometimes expressly defined as arising from the export of goods. There are circumstances, however, in which the actual selling price must be recorded on the books. In the event of currency controls it may happen that the dollars representing the actual proceeds of a sale must be deposited to the credit of the government of the producer country in a New York bank, and the exporter receives from the central bank of his government an amount in local currency which is computed at some official rate and is treated as the equivalent of the dollars. Analogously the foreign manufacturer which exports its goods to Latin America for sale through a local branch or subsidiary corporation will invoice them at a wholesale value, which of course, exceeds their cost, and the invoice value, entered on the books of the branch then serves as basis for computation of the gross sale profit realized by the branch.

Other commonly accepted but unlegislated rules are: that interest in general has its source at the residence or principal place of business of the debtor, and if the debtor is a branch of a foreign enterprise, the "branch" would be the debtor if it contracted the loan and entered it on its books. An exception to this general rule is that interest derived from a loan secured by real estate is always treated as having its source in the country in which the real estate is situated. The source of a dividend is usually the country in which the payer corporation was organized. Royalties for the use of trade marks, copyrights, patents and the like and rentals of movable property are usually considered as originating in the country in which they are utilized, but in actual practice they would likely be taxed where the payer enters them on its books, and not elsewhere.

While not within the proper ambit of source rules, it is pertinent to add here that a high percentage of Latin American income tax assessments are based on arbitrary determinations of income. Such determinations are authorized when required books are not kept and displayed, or those displayed fail to inspire the revenue agent with confidence.

So much for general impressions of the unwritten law of source rules. A few words are in order concerning the rules of two countries which have devoted considerable legislative attention to the subject: Argentina and Mexico. Income of Argentine source is first generally defined as that derived from capital, property rights situate in the country or economically utilized in the country; from activities in the country or work performed there, and from activities occasionally carried out abroad by persons resident in the Argentine. This definition would obviously cover the compensation for personal services rendered abroad and the gains from casual transactions. Interest paid by a resident or company organized in the Argentine or on a loan secured by Argentine real estate is defined to be of Argentine source. And very interesting rules relate to the source of profits from trafficking in imported or exported goods, to-wit: income derived from the export of goods produced, manufactured, processed or *purchased* in the country is wholly of Argentine source. No reference is even made to the country of sale. The net profit, however, is computed somewhat artificially, being wholesale price at destination less freight, insurance, commissions and other expenses *incurred in the Argentine*. Furthermore, if the wholesale price on the invoice or record is less than wholesale value, collusion will be presumed between buyer and seller, and the wholesale value substituted. The presumption may be rebutted, however. As the same rule in reverse is made expressly applicable to consignments or sale made by a foreign firm to its Argentine branch or subsidiary, the effect seems to be that a foreign manufacturer's production profit escapes the Argentine tax. This rule closely parallels the United States rule.

Mexico, one of the few Latin American countries which taxes the world-wide income of citizens, residents and companies, as we do, and grants a foreign tax credit, has enacted rather extreme views of what constitutes income of Mexican source. By the general definition, income of Mexican source results from any transaction in which an enterprise or resident of Mexico contracts with another or undertakes to perform a service. Under a very literal construction of this definition a nonresident's participation in any transaction or operation with a resident or enterprise of Mexico would put the Mexican source label on any income or profit that might result. But in practice, it is understood, that the definition is not given such a wide sweep. A resident of Mexico can buy in Detroit an automobile without (theoretically) subjecting the manufacturer's profit to Mexican tax. If he pays salary to an employee for work in Detroit or to a lawyer there for services, the salary and fee would be taxable. Conversely the compensation of an employee working in Mexico for a nonresident employer would be taxed as of Mexican source. Even a casual act of commerce, e.g., a sale, barter, lease, involving property, real or personal, situated in Mexico stamps the profits as of Mexican source and a tax of 20 per cent of it is due. If the acts are numerous, the party to them, although a nonresident without office or agency in Mexico, may be held engaged in business there, and hence subject to the graduated profits tax.

The rental from leased property used in Mexico, e.g., railway rolling stock, is of Mexican source; so are payments received for construction work done in the country. The Mexicans profess pride in their "economic" or "realistic" approach to taxation as contrasted with an approach based on legalistic tests such as the country in which passage of title passed, as marking the source of sales profits. Certainly an approach on such a wide front nets more taxable fish, and offers little chance for avoidance by artificial arrangements. But it also causes more double taxation, for the U. S. foreign tax credit is available only against U. S. tax on income which is recognized under Internal Revenue rules as having its source within the taxing country, and the United States does not have overlapping rules in this respect.

A problem indissolubly linked with taxing the profit inherent in so many types of payments made to the nonresident is the computation of the amount that represents profit. For example, the Mexican branch or subsidiary of a foreign firm is entitled to deduct payments made by it for technical services furnished by the foreign head-office or parent. But what part of the payment is profit to the head-office or parent? That is fixed by agreement between taxpayer and tax authority. The tax authority may even permit *by agreement* the deduction of a share of head-office general expenses. Such arrangements illustrate the delegation of an administrative power of discretion which is much broader in Latin America than in the United States.

NOTES TO SELECTION 7

[1]For 1962 and succeeding years the rate table for the complementary tax will be geared to multiples of the minimum wage as fixed by the Federal Government. Thus net income equal to 24 times the minimum wage will be tax-exempt; the part in excess of 24 times but less than 30 times the wage will be taxed at 1 per cent; the part in excess of 30 times but less than 45 times the wage will be taxed 3 per cent, and so on progressively to the part exceeding 800 times the wage, which will be taxed at 60 per cent.

Part III

Income Taxes

Despite the definitely less important role that income taxation now plays in developing countries, as pointed out in the articles reproduced in Part II, a good deal of the literature still emphasizes this form of taxation. This is no doubt due, in part, to the backgrounds of the authors. In large part, however, this emphasis exists because of the important role income taxes must play both in improving the yield of the tax system and in fulfilling widespread demands that the tax system also serve the ends of equity and social justice. The first selection by Richard Goode, now with the Brookings Institution in Washington, was written in 1951 and is a classic statement of the argument against heavy reliance on income taxes in underdeveloped countries.

The next three selections form a group. The first, from the Report of the Commission to Study the Fiscal System of Venezuela, led by Carl Shoup of Columbia University, treats the basic structural issue of a schedular versus a global income tax system. It is followed by a brief critical comment from a review of the Report by Francesco Forte, a noted Italian fiscal expert. The second excerpt from the Shoup Mission report is a careful discussion of the taxation of corporations as an element in a general system of income taxation. This is perhaps the single most complex technical question in income taxation, and one with extremely important economic consequences.

The extract from the United Nations report which follows this rather technical discussion takes a broader view and considers some different ways in which poorer countries, given their special problems of administration and economic structure, might tax corporations. The brief suggestion in this extract on the taxation of remittances abroad is almost the only discussion in the present volume on the highly significant and complicated question of the taxation of foreign-source income.

Nicholas Kaldor of Cambridge University has become well known in recent years for his striking and provocative ideas in the field of tax policy. The excerpt included here, from his 1956 report to the Indian Government, concerns the taxation of business profits.

Another complex question—the taxation of capital gains—is surveyed in a critical fashion in the extract from a report to the Colombian Ministry of Finance by four American lawyers. Finally, a brief note by Milton C. Taylor on some problems of the tax exemption program in Puerto Rico concludes this section. This interesting look at the most successful use of income-tax incentives to promote development is the only item dealing with the subject included here: it has been thoroughly surveyed in the recent Harvard Law School International Program in Taxation publication by Jack Heller and Kenneth Kauffman that is cited in the bibliography at the end of this volume.

8

Reconstruction of
Foreign Tax Systems

*by Richard Goode**

THE mission or individual expert who conscientiously undertakes
to prepare a plan for reconstruction of a foreign tax system faces a
difficult task. Even to understand how the existing tax system actually
operates requires considerable knowledge of the local social organization, legal institutions, administrative practices, and economic system.
Most of us find it hard to say what results can be expected from a
new tax law or administrative reorganization in our own country
and will find it still harder to do so in an unfamiliar setting.

The outside expert, nevertheless, does enjoy some advantages. He
is more likely to subject to critical examination local preconceptions
with respect to economic and social consequences of taxation and to
question accepted procedures. He brings with him some acquaintance
with other, and presumably more advanced, revenue systems.

Ordinarily the country to be studied is economically underdeveloped with a relatively low income per head. Agriculture or extractive
industries will usually account for a large fraction of total production.
Often there is a large group of virtually self-sufficient farmers and at
the other extreme a section of the economy heavily dependent on export of a few crops, forest products, or minerals. The export industries and complementary activity will be subject to wide fluctuations
originating in the outside world, whereas the subsistence farmers may
participate only indirectly in these movements. Usually the government's budget will represent a larger share of national income than
it did in industrialized countries at a similar stage in their development, because of public investment programs, modern ideas about the
welfare state, and military expenditures. In many countries unbal-

*National Tax Association, *Proceedings of the Forty-Fourth Annual Conference
on Taxation* [held in Dallas, Texas, 1951] (Sacramento, 1952), pp. 212–22. At the
time of the writing of this paper, Dr. Goode was with the International Monetary
Fund; naturally, the opinions expressed in the paper are the author's and do not
necessarily reflect the official views of the Fund. This article is reprinted with the
kind permission of the publisher.

anced budgets have been partly responsible for an inflation that has also been fed from other internal and external sources.

The following remarks are addressed mainly to the fiscal problems of an underdeveloped primary-producing country of the type just described. My only experience in a tax survey in such a country was acquired in Bolivia as a member of a United Nations mission which visited that country in 1950. I shall draw liberally on that experience but shall not attempt a detailed analysis of Bolivian problems. I shall touch on four principal subjects: (1) the role of income taxes; (2) export taxes; (3) consumption taxes; and (4) real estate taxes.

ROLE OF INCOME TAXES

Most of us are inclined to look first to income taxes as the most desirable means of increasing total revenue or replacing harmful or ineffective taxes. This faith in income taxation is shared by a good many intellectuals and politicians in the underdeveloped areas, and a few of the countries have fairly elaborate income tax statutes. In most underdeveloped countries, nevertheless, net income taxes are a relatively minor source of revenue, and the income taxes on the books are erratic or discriminatory in application.

Conditions for Successful Use

When the visiting expert tries to determine the cause for the unsatisfactory status of income taxes and to recommend changes, he is forced, perhaps for the first time, to give systematic thought to the prerequisites of successful use of income taxation as a major revenue source. The following paragraphs mention some of the factors that seem to me most significant.

1. The first condition is the existence of a predominantly money economy. The subsistence farmer cannot be satisfactorily reached by an income tax, not so much because he does not have money to pay —that may mean that he cannot pay a tax of any kind—as because the greater part of his real income cannot be satisfactorily assessed. Even highly skilled administrators have made little progress toward including the value of home-produced and -consumed foods in the taxable income of farmers. In many underdeveloped countries these products and others obtained by barter make up a major fraction of the total real income of large segments of the population. Admittedly these groups are usually the poorest in the society, and failure to subject them to direct taxation may not be seriously objectionable from the equity point of view. It does, however, encourage use of other taxes.

2. Another condition that may not be strictly necessary but is very helpful is a high standard of literacy among taxpayers. In many underdeveloped countries the majority of the population is illiterate. For example, among the eleven Latin American republics for which data are readily available, seven have illiteracy ratios higher than 50 per cent.[1] In many regions of Asia and Africa the figure is higher, as it probably also is for several Latin American countries for which data are not available. Illiteracy, like exclusion from the money economy, is most characteristic of the poorest farmers, but often wage earners, independent craftsmen, and small shopkeepers cannot read and write well enough to fill out the simplest income tax return with the guidance of printed instructions. Wage earners may be covered by withholding, but in any refined system they must be able to file claims for exemptions and refunds.

3. Prevalance of accounting records honestly and reliably maintained is another prosaic but important condition for satisfactory income taxation. In most underdeveloped countries many businessmen keep no books at all; others maintain two or more sets. Vigorous tax administration can do much to improve accounting standards if combined with an educational campaign, but more trained personnel and office equipment are essential.

4. A fourth requirement for satisfactory income taxation is a large degree of voluntary compliance on the part of taxpayers. The best administrative organization cannot satisfactorily collect income taxes from the self-employed when, as in many countries, evasion is generally attempted and incurs little or no moral disapproval from the public. The roots of a tradition of voluntary compliance with tax laws are not easy to trace, but it is fairly clear that such a spirit does not grow up overnight. Although something can be done in the short run, a long period of popular education and efficient and equitable administration of those taxes that can actually be enforced seems necessary to establish firmly the habit of general voluntary acceptance of the fiscal responsibilities of citizenship. Adoption of elaborate measures that will not be uniformly applied delays improvement in taxpayer morale.

5. The political conditions for development of income taxes into a major revenue source, like the spirit of voluntary compliance, are intangible and hard to explain. The environment most favorable to progressive taxation seems to be one of free political democracy. In many underdeveloped countries wealthy groups have enough political power to block tax measures that they consider threats to their position. Until the popular will is stronger and more united or until the rich are ready to accept the ability-to-pay principle—whether from altruism or a sense of guilt or fear—steeply progressive taxes will not be collected.

6. Honest and efficient administration is needed for any tax, but minimum acceptable standards appear to be higher for income taxes than for many other levies. Difficult as the task of establishing a satisfactory administration may be, it is probably the condition for successful income taxation that can be met most quickly. The expert, nevertheless, must guard against the assumption that a tidy organization chart and nonpolitical staffing assure good administration. Nor can he be confident that the best obtainable administration will eliminate obstacles to heavy reliance on income taxes.

Progressivity in a Capital-Poor Country

A basic economic issue concerns the wisdom of progressive taxation in a capital-poor country. Income taxes, of course, need not be highly progressive, but they are virtually always somewhat so, and their heavy use opens the way for steep progressivity. Critics of progressive taxation warn that it will absorb private savings, dull initiative and enterprise, and perhaps stimulate capital flight. They assert also that high income taxes will discourage foreign investment. They argue that the industrialized countries built up their capital stock and acquired a great comparative advantage at a time when the income tax was low or nonexistent. The suggested conclusion is that the underdeveloped countries should wait until they have accumulated more capital and passed through at least the first stages of industrialization before attempting heavy income taxation.

These objections call for fuller examination than they can be given here, but I do want to raise some opposing considerations. In the first place, the picture of a frugal class of wealthy persons who invest their savings in capital equipment is more appropriate for an expanding capitalist system than for most underdeveloped countries. Lavish consumption appears to be more characteristic in many of these societies. Savings when made often go into land holdings and construction of elaborate residences. Lack of capital markets and savings institutions impedes the flow of savings from both the wealthy and the middle classes into productive domestic investment.

High tax rates, to be sure, may discourage enterprise; but, again, the more serious difficulty is usually the absence of a spirit of enterprise and a low social evaluation of business as compared with the liberal professions and gentlemanly agriculture.

Capital flight seems to be motivated more often by fear of political instability, expropriation, or currency devaluation and by lack of suitable local financial institutions than by tax avoidance. In the long run the problem can be resolved only by elimination of its causes. Short of a basic solution, exchange controls may be fairly effective in checking undesirable capital movements.

The foreign capitalist will undoubtedly look at income tax rates, along with many other factors, in deciding whether to invest in a country. High tax rates in his home country, however, may prepare him for considerably more severe income taxation than exists in many underdeveloped countries. United States investors in particular may find that, by virtue of the U.S. foreign tax credit, their total liabilities on profits and dividends withdrawn from a foreign business are unaffected by an increase in foreign tax rates.[2]

Perhaps the most significant point is that most underdeveloped countries have long refrained from heavy income taxation and still have not realized in large measure the benefits attributed to this policy. Other factors must be retarding economic progress.

These considerations weaken the argument that higher income taxes are incompatible with economic development. But I do not believe that they wholly destroy the case. The country that succeeds in moving toward a higher level of development must somehow greatly increase the flow of domestic savings into productive investment. One approach is to try to encourage private savings and investment. Avoidance of high and progressive income taxes will not in itself assure success, but the outside expert should not be too critical of a government that deliberately adopts a policy of moderate income taxation along with other more positive measures to stimulate private capital formation. The alternative is for the state itself to mobilize the resources. This course may sometimes be appropriate, but the wise planning and skillful administration necessary for its success call for a level of competence on the part of the civil service that is extremely difficult to achieve in any country.

Taxation of Business Profits

Taxation of business profits presents special problems in all fiscal systems. Many underdeveloped countries tax the unincorporated firm as a unit, separate from its owners. This practice is dictated partly by administrative convenience and seems also to reflect a preference for schedular income taxes which many countries took over from France. The results often seem rather arbitrary, especially when the business income tax is at graduated rates and is not integrated with the global personal income tax.

The corporation income tax, of course, also raises the issue of the desirability of integration with the individual income tax. The corporate tax, however, often is in good part a levy on large-scale foreign-owned enterprises. Since the local government does not have jurisdiction over foreign shareholders, it cannot reach them by an individual income tax. This consideration and the administrative complications of a refined integration plan are arguments in favor of an independent corporation income tax. On the other hand, caution is advisable in order not to discourage adoption of an efficient form of business organization.

The excess-profits-tax principle has considerable appeal in the underdeveloped, as in the developed, countries. But the problem of establishing a reasonable base is usually even graver in the under-developed countries because of lack of adequate accounting and statistical records and trained personnel. Where inflation is more or less chronic, both the invested-capital and the base-period-earnings methods may yield harsh results. The visiting expert and local officials will be well advised to be cautious in recommending an excess-profits-tax. If the principle is adopted, they should bear in mind that special risks and the capital shortage justify profit rates that may seem very high in comparison with those prevailing in industrialized countries.

Appraisal

Most underdeveloped countries are not ready for major reliance on income taxes. Under existing circumstances, these taxes may lack the distinctive advantages that we usually associate with them. There are, undoubtedly, a good many countries in which substantially increased income tax yields are feasible and desirable. Greatly improved administration and compliance, however, are essential in most instances to prepare the way for the larger role that income taxes may appropriately fill at a later stage of development.

Export Taxes

Export taxes, being barred by the U.S. Constitution (Art. I, secs. 9 and 10), have received little attention in this country. These duties are important sources of revenue in certain mining countries and are used to a somewhat lesser extent by agricultural countries. Since the mineral-producing countries consume only a negligible part of their own output, their export taxes are roughly equivalent to production or severance taxes. They take the form of export duties mainly because the border is a convenient control point.

Often the economic equivalent of an export tax is obtained through foreign exchange controls. Exporters are required to surrender all or part of their foreign exchange receipts to the government and are compensated in local currency at a rate that overvalues the local currency. The difference between the true value to the exporter of the local currency and the compulsory delivery rate is, in effect, a tax on gross proceeds from exports. The following discussion draws no distinction between this type of arrangement and an outright export tax.

The popularity of export duties on minerals is partly attributable to the almost universal feeling that the area in which mineral deposits are found should share in the gains from exploiting these wasting resources. The largest mining companies are often foreign-owned, and the export duties are an easy way of taxing these businesses. Sometimes the taxes are partly at the expense of foreign consumers. Another attraction of export taxes, especially when they are specific rather than ad valorem, is that they are comparatively simple to administer.

Economic Effects

In order to analyze the economic effects of export duties, let us first consider a country whose exports of a taxed mineral are only a small part of the world total. Domestic producers will be faced by a world price determined largely by external demand and supply. They can sell their whole output at the world price but cannot obtain a higher price. The export duty may be viewed either as a reduction in net proceeds from exports or as an additional cost of exporting. With any given price and cost conditions the duty makes it unprofitable to mine some ore that would otherwise yield a net return above costs, and production will fall. To some extent this contraction will be brought about by closing marginal mines, and may occur slowly. But for many types of minerals a prompt first adjustment will be made by changing the grade of ore extracted in almost all mines. Suppose, for example, that the price of the mineral is $1 a pound at the mill and the cost of extracting and milling a (short) ton of ore is $60. The pay limit will then be an ore of 3 per cent fine metal content. It will be profitable to extract all ore of 3 per cent or higher grade, but no firm will deliberately mine a lower grade. Now suppose that an export tax of 25 cents per pound of fine metal is imposed. Costs and the world price will remain approximately the same, but the pay limit will be raised to ore with 4 per cent metallic content. This shift may forfeit a large fraction of economically available deposits. When selective mining processes are used, low-grade ores may be permanently lost unless drastic price increases or cost reductions occur at a later date. The foregoing is a highly simplified but broadly accurate description of the operation of Bolivia's taxes on tin exports.

The export tax is likely both to hasten the day of exhaustion of the country's mineral resources and to reduce current exports. The available supply of foreign exchange will decline, and imports of both consumer and capital goods must be curtailed. Sometimes it is argued that the immediate decline in output is desirable because the life of the industry is prolonged. Presumably this contention is based on the assumption that export taxes will be reduced in the future or cost-price relations will improve. One objection to this argument has already been stated: The low-grade deposits left by selective mining can usually be recovered only at costs higher than would have been incurred had they been extracted along with the high-grade ores. Another consideration is the fact that an underdeveloped country has a high time preference for imports and can reasonably subject prospective future receipts to a substantial discount. Finally, postponement of extraction incurs the risk that substitutes will be introduced.

The situation will be less dark when the taxing country accounts for a large fraction of the world supply. In this case, contraction of its output will raise the world price, and part of the tax will be passed on to foreign consumers. Nevertheless, the higher price will encourage development of substitutes and economy in use of the taxed commodity. The history of the Chilean nitrate industry is instructive. Chile has the only commercial deposits of natural nitrates, and prior to World War I the government and the industry took advantage of this situation to levy a high export tax and to establish a cartel and price-maintenance arrangement. During World War I, however, a synthetic nitrate industry was established in Europe and America. The synthetic industry has grown until at the present time natural nitrates account for only a minor fraction of world consumption. Since 1930, Chilean production has remained below the 1910–13 level. Of course, we cannot assume that Chile could have prevented the rise of synthetics, but it does seem reasonable to suppose that the new industry would have developed much less rapidly had the Chilean government and nitrate industry followed tax and production policies that allowed lower prices for natural nitrates.

Alternatives

It appears that a policy of high export taxes may be shortsighted. Yet the fiscal expert must recognize the force of the sentiment in favor of special taxation of the extractive industries and also the difficulty of finding substitute revenue sources. It seems to me that a special tax on net profits of the mining industry, supplemented perhaps by a modest royalty on production or gross receipts, is the best compromise. The profits tax will not change the pay limit or affect production with existing plant and equipment. To be sure, it may discourage investment and thus over time curtail production. But the injurious effects are much less immediate and direct and probably smaller in the long run.

The foregoing argument is much abbreviated, but it is, I think, a useful example of a type of problem that will be encountered in many underdeveloped countries.

CONSUMPTION TAXES

Consumption taxes are the backbone of the revenue system in many underdeveloped countries. They raise the familiar issues of equity and possible unintended distortion of production patterns. Where a large fraction of the population is desperately poor, heavy taxes on necessities and on so-called luxuries of mass consumption will impose a cruel burden and may also impair health and productive efficiency.

But government is a necessity and must be supported. Hardly any underdeveloped country is in a position to forego substantial consumption taxes. Considerable revenue can often be obtained from taxes on commodities consumed mainly by middle- and high-income groups. It may be possible to select many excises that are mildly progressive over a fairly wide income range in a society where there is a sharp distinction between consumption habits of rich and poor. Much nonessential consumption is in the form of imported goods, and the taxes can often be most simply collected as customs duties with supplementary excises on any domestic production.

As a means of raising the remainder of consumption tax revenue, much can be said for a tax of broad coverage and comparatively low uniform rate in preference to a large number of special excises that usually reflect no clear social or economic policy. The general tax will be less discriminatory among consumers and producers and will often be simpler to administer. The tax can usually be collected more effectively at the point of importation or from wholesalers or manufacturers than from retailers in countries where retail trade is largely carried on by small shopkeepers and itinerant vendors. A good economic case can be made for exempting capital equipment. Administrative expediency may suggest exempting much handicraft production. Caution is advisable, however, to avoid uneconomic discrimination against larger and more mechanized producers.

The broad consumption tax will undoubtedly be regressive. Where the poorest section of the population is composed of largely self-sufficient farmers, however, regressivity will be less pronounced than in a country in which a larger fraction of output passes through the money economy. Furthermore, the alternative to the consumption tax is often greater inflation, which is even more regressive in impact.

Real Estate Taxes

To the North American expert, taxes on land and buildings will appear to be an obvious revenue source in a predominantly agricultural community. Throughout most of Latin America, however, extremely low rates and assessment ratios make the true property tax almost miniscule.

Intensive use of the property tax is blocked in most Latin American countries by a small but politically powerful group of large landowners. Even the low property tax rates in existence are rendered almost meaningless by original undervaluation, omitted properties, obsolete assessments, and widespread delinquency. Assessments twenty to twenty-five years old are common, even in countries that have experienced many years of inflation. New construction is often not added to the rolls, and when it is the unfortunate owner usually finds his assessment ratio far out of line with that of his neighbors.

In Bolivia in 1950, for example, real estate was subject to nominal tax rates of 0.4 per cent in rural districts and 0.2 to 0.8 per cent in cities. Conservative estimates indicate that the average assessment did not exceed 20 to 30 per cent of current values. The average true rate on taxed rural property therefore appears to have been on the order of 0.1 per cent and on urban property nowhere to have exceeded 0.25 per cent. Much real estate completely escaped taxation.

Real estate taxes are not merely a promising source of revenue. They have positive economic advantages. A grave social and economic problem in many Latin American countries is the practice of holding large tracts of good farm land completely idle for speculative or prestige reasons or of using the land as pasture. A property tax based on a realistic assessment of the land's value in its most productive use would put a carrying charge on idle or underutilized land and would tend to break up large holdings or force them into higher and more economic uses. In the cities, another problem arises from the popularity of real estate as a hedge against inflation. Substantial taxes on urban land and buildings would help drive capital into socially more productive uses than construction of luxury residences, hotels, and office buildings. These taxes would also put a charge on a favorite form of conspicuous consumption.

Formidable political and administrative obstacles stand in the way of effective property taxation in the underdeveloped countries. Improvement of real estate taxes, nevertheless, seems to me to be one of the key problems on which the visiting fiscal expert and the local government should concentrate their energies.

Conclusion

A useful tax survey is much more than a listing of Adam Smith's four canons or some modern variant of them, an outline of the existing revenue system, and a facile prescription for rewriting the tax laws and reorganizing the administrative machinery. If the standard textbooks and treatises are not already available in the country seeking advice, they can be sent at far less expense than a foreign mission. The visiting expert must make a real effort to understand the local situation, to appraise the economic effects of the tax system, and to foresee the consequences of his recommendations. The kind of skill that is required is a scarce commodity even in the most advanced countries, but fortunately the supply does not diminish by being shared with others. In carefully studying a foreign system the expert will gain by being forced to re-examine some of his own ideas. It is often easier to concentrate on economic and administrative essentials in a new environment.

NOTES TO SELECTION 8

[1] United Nations, *Statistical Yearbook, 1949–50,* pp. 486–94. The figures are for various dates between 1930 and 1945 and refer to the population 7–10 years of age and over.

[2] Section 131 of the Internal Revenue Code provides, in effect, that foreign income and profits taxes may be credited against U.S. income and excess-profits taxes to the extent that the foreign tax rate does not exceed the U.S. rate.

9

Schedular and Global Income Taxes

by the Commission to Study the
Fiscal System of Venezuela*

The present system of schedular taxation [in Venezuela] is a source of considerable complexity in the income tax. Initially, all income must be classified among the nine schedules. Since the rules for determination of net income in the various schedules are different, and also since the rates vary, even though the variations are minor, problems of definition and classification arise. Thus, the gain on the sale of real property bears a 3% rate if classified in schedule 8 but a $2\frac{1}{2}$% rate if classified in schedule 3, a variation which presents a difficult definitional problem. Further, it is not clear whether rental income from personal property falls in schedule 2 with a 3% rate or schedule 3 with a $2\frac{1}{2}$% rate; moreover, under schedule 2 none of the expenses incurred in the rental of the property would be allowed, although all such expenses may be deducted under schedule 3. It seems obvious that such problems of classification and definition should be eliminated as far as possible in an income tax. These legal problems could perhaps be tolerated if important consequences were to follow from the classification. In fact, however, the rate differences among the schedules are so minor that they cannot justify the resulting legal difficulties.

The division of a taxpayer's income among schedules tends to produce differences in technical rules that are not justified. Thus, only the cash method of accounting may be used in schedules 1, 2, 6, 7, and 9 but only the accrual method may be used in schedules 3, 4, 5, and 8. Taxpayers engaged in activities under schedules 3, 4, or 5 may use fiscal years, but other taxpayers must use only calendar years. Expenses allowed under one schedule are not allowed under

*The Fiscal System of Venezuela: A Report (Baltimore: The Johns Hopkins Press, 1959), pp. 101–6. Carl S. Shoup was the director of the Commission to study the Fiscal System of Venezuela; the other members were John F. Due, Lyle C. Fitch, Sir Donald MacDougall, Oliver Oldman, and Stanley S. Surrey. The article is reprinted here with the permission of the publisher.

another, though in both situations the expense is incurred in the production of income. Thus, depreciation is not allowed in computing rental income from real property under schedule 1 or from personal property under schedule 2, but depreciation is allowed in computing business income in schedule 3. Expenses such as interest and taxes that may be incurred in producing interest income under schedule 2 are not deductible, though such expenses are deductible in computing rental income under schedule 1. The inequities resulting from these disparities, apart from the problems of classification mentioned earlier, could be tolerated if they involved only the $\frac{1}{2}\%$ to 1% variations among the schedules involved. But these rules for computing schedular income also govern the computation of income for the complementary tax, where the rates do go higher. The resulting inequities can thus be considerably more serious. But the very existence of the schedules and their low rates tends to conceal the importance of these technical rules and their significance for the complementary tax.

In addition to these aspects of classification, definition, and equity, the existence of nine schedules makes for a complicated declaration form and for a complicated tax computation. Separate taxes must be computed for each schedule in which the taxpayer has income. While most declarations involve income in only one schedule, principally schedule 7 relating to salaries and wages, a large number of declarations show income in several schedules. Thus, the total number of schedules showing taxable income in the declarations for 1957, for the Caracas Office, was 108,125, while the declarations involved were only about 75,000. For declarations having incomes under Bs.200,000, the tax computation is made by the Tax Administration on a machine. The schedular system requires that a separate card be punched and tax computed for each schedule, so that the computation of tax for a single taxpayer can involve a number of cards for the schedules and then another card for the complementary tax, and then the addition of the amounts on each card. Similar steps are involved in the hand computations for the returns over Bs.200,000. A later administrative recommendation suggests that the computation of tax be performed as far as possible by the taxpayers themselves. It will be simple to achieve this result if only the computation of a single tax is involved; and in fact the feasibility of the suggestion may depend on the change to a single tax.

Most important of all, perhaps, is the fact that the existence of a number of schedular taxes and a complementary tax makes it difficult to think clearly about the structure of the income tax, its impact upon taxpayers, and the burdens it involves. It is necessary to keep in mind several sets of exemptions for the various schedular taxes and a different set for the complementary tax. Moreover, the schedular exemptions do not take account of family status, while the complementary tax exemptions do vary with family status. Further, one must remember the different rates under the schedular taxes and the complementary tax. It becomes very difficult to grasp the cumulative effect of these taxes on any particular taxpayer or class of taxpayers, in order to perceive readily and clearly just what their tax burdens may be. Thus, one tends to think of the complementary tax as involving the heavier burden because its rates are progressive and rise to 26%. But for many taxpayers the schedular taxes are more important, since the schedular exemptions are lower and the rates higher. Thus, for a single person engaged in business, the tax under schedule 3 is higher than the complementary tax until the income rises somewhat above Bs.100,000; for a married person with two children the schedular tax continues to be higher even at Bs.200,000. But this is not so under schedule 7 relating to salaries. Here, for a single person the complementary tax is heavier until Bs.19,200; at Bs.19,201 the schedular tax is heavier; above Bs.30,000 the complementary tax again becomes the heavier. For a married person with two children the schedular tax is heavier until about Bs.50,000. As respects corporations in business, the complementary tax is heavier until Bs.19,200; at Bs.19,201 the schedular tax becomes the heavier; at about Bs.70,000 the complementary tax again becomes the heavier.

These differing impacts of the various taxes make it impossible clearly to visualize the Venezuelan tax system. The existence of these various taxes also makes it difficult to present statistical tax data in ways in which they can readily be grasped, for much the same reasons.

The only argument that appears to be advanced in favor of the present system is that it permits variations in the burden among the different types of incomes. This view, of course, assumes at the outset that meaningful qualitative distinctions exist between the various income sources, distinctions which can be quantitatively reflected in different tax rates. But it is not at all clear just why rents should be taxed less heavily than interest, or why patent royalties received by an inventor should be taxed less heavily than either. Moreover, excluding salaries and wages, the range in the schedular tax rates does not exceed 1%. As respects rents, interest, business income, and capital gains, the range is only 1/2%. Similarly, as respects professional income and business income, the variation is only 1/2%. Certainly, if significant qualitative differences exist, they are not adequately reflected in these quantitative figures. Put another way, the qualitative differences surely cannot be analyzed so finely as to justify or warrant 1/2% differentials. Put still another way, if the qualitative differences only warrant 1/2% differentials, or are to be accorded only 1/2% differentials, those qualitative differences are not worth worrying about. On the other hand, the adoption of large rate variations among the schedules would involve serious distortions in the economy. The result would be a hodgepodge of incentives and burdens that could materially affect the economic life of the country. For this reason the schedular variations must be confined to almost meaningless differences. So confined, they become hindrances to an effective tax system for the reasons earlier advanced.

The most significant variations in the present schedules involve the income of employees and agricultural income. As respects salaries and wages, the schedular rate is 1%. If variations are to exist among income sources, then the classification of income between earned and unearned income probably is the most defensible classification. It is this differential that is most strongly stressed in explanation of the present system. While a differential in favor of earned income necessarily involves technical complexity, there are many who think the equity factor outweighs that complexity, at least in the lower brackets and in the absence of a separate tax on wealth. It is not necessary at this point, however, to decide this policy issue. For if differentiation in favor of earned income is desired, it can readily be supplied without resort to a schedular system. Given a unitary tax rate structure applicable to all income, the differentiation can be supplied either by the exclusion of a percentage of earned income, or an absolute amount of earned income, or a percentage of earned income up to a ceiling amount. Thus (to illustrate the method and not as an indication of the actual figures), if one supposes a first bracket of Bs.5,000 taxed at an 8% rate, and if it were desired to tax earned income in this bracket at three-quarters of the rate on unearned income, then 25% of earned income could be exempted from gross income up to a total exemption of Bs.1,250. (This could also be expressed as a special deduction from gross income.) Or an earned income credit *against tax* could be used, under which there could be credited against the tax 2% of earned income up to a total credit of Bs.100. The figures, of course, depend on the actual rates of tax and on the differentiation desired. Necessarily, the amounts stated in the formula under the method that uses an earned income credit against tax are less than under the earned income exclusion or deduction method, for a given general level of earned income relief. The significant difference in the methods is that the deduction or exclusion method applies the benefit of the earned income differentiation at the taxpayer's top bracket rate of tax, while the credit-against-tax method applies the benefit at the initial bracket rates.

If an earned income differential is to be adopted, it should be restricted to salaries, wages and other compensation. The extension of the differential to professional income would in turn probably necessitate its further extension to all self-employed activity, including individually owned and operated business. But all income from self-employment arises, in varying degree, from both the taxpayer's capital and his labor, so that a division of the income between earned and unearned income is then required. This can only be done on some arbitrary rule-of-thumb basis which would hardly be supportable case by case, or by an attempted analysis of each case separately, which would be impossible from an administrative point of view. Moreover, under the present system, all business income is grouped together at a 2½% rate under schedule 3, and this is only ½% more than the schedule 6 professional rate. Thus, despite some claims by professional people and other self-employed for an earned income differential, it would be best to limit the differential to employment income.

As respects agricultural income, the differential exists partly in the rate, which under schedule 5 is 2% as compared with 2½% for business generally, and in the Bs.30,000 schedular exemption vanishing at Bs.50,000 as compared with the Bs.12,000 exemption vanishing at Bs.19,200 under the other schedules. Presumably this differential exists as an intended tax subsidy to those engaged in agricultural enterprises; it does not extend to agricultural labor. It is difficult to defend this differentiation in favor of agricultural activities and against other business. The tax system is basically not a suitable vehicle to provide a subsidy; grants and direct subsidies are preferable. Incidentally, the operation under the present system of this agricultural differential alongside the earned income differential is somewhat bizarre. A salary or wage earner pays more tax than a farmer up to Bs.50,001. Up to this figure, then, the agricultural subsidy argument outweighs the earned income argument; above this point, the earned income argument outweighs the agricultural subsidy argument.

Again, this matter of tax policy need not force a schedular tax system. If a tax subsidy is desired for agriculture, it likewise can be granted in the form of a special agricultural exclusion or deduction or credit against tax, as in the case of earned income. A possible, and simple, solution would be to treat agricultural income as earned income, and thus grant it any differential that may be accorded to earned income.

If the schedular taxes are to be eliminated, two steps are necessary. First, the schedular rates must be combined with the complementary rates to provide one unitary progressive rate structure. The shape of this structure, and the exemptions, tax rates and brackets used, depend of course on the revenue yield desired.

10

Comment on Schedular
and Global Income Taxes

by Francesco Forte*

The two comments of the Commission about the weakness of the
system of taxation of income, which arise respectively from the in-
sufficiency of the taxation of companies and from the inadequacy of
the assessment of earnings on shares, appear quite persuasive [see next
selection]. The case of Venezuela only confirms what (only too well)
emerges from the experience of Italian tax policy. Considerable per-
plexity arises, on the other hand, from the other comment of the
Commission: that is, that the qualitative discrimination of classes
of taxable income is one of the principle causes of the weakness of
the direct taxation of Venezuela. The observation that the countries
where the taxation of the income is most robust and achieves the
best results generally are precisely those which do not resort to
qualitative discrimination hits the mark. But it remains to establish
whether the nexus of cause and effect between qualitative discrimination and low efficiency of the taxation of income does not operate
in a direction inverse to that suggested by the Commission. Qualitative discrimination, that is, could be an effect (rather than the cause)
of the stunted development of the direct taxes. It is well known that
when the fiscal apparatus is weak and incapable of analytical assessments of actual income, the criterion of levying a lower rate on income from work and going to higher rates on professional income,
enterprise income, and income of pure capital can be a substitute,
crude perhaps, but not certainly to be disparaged, for progressivity
according to income. This can explain why the countries where the
direct taxation is weakest are those which make a qualitative discrimination of classes of taxable income and which most tenaciously
defend it. Think of the glaring inequalities which, for example, would
be created in Italy at present if every discrimination of rate between
wages and salaries on one hand and other income on the other were

*Rivista di diritto finanziario e scienza delle finanze, 1961, I, 126–27. Translated
by C. K. Cobb, Jr., of the Harvard Law School International Program in Taxation.
Reprinted here with the kind permission of the author.

abolished at a stroke and all income were subjected to the same rates of a single progressive tax!

Qualitative discrimination of classes of income, again, as various Italian economists have shown (from Einaudi, to Fasiani, to Griziotti), has also a justification independent of that as a substitute for quantitative discrimination. At any rate the observations of the Shoup Commission on the administrative difficulties and on the psychological disadvantages of a too minute discrimination furnish interesting matter for reflection. We limit ourselves here to posing some questions. Is it preferable to insist on making such a qualitative discrimination by varying the rates on classes of income, or is it advisable to achieve it with the adoption of a tax[1] on wealth (*patrimonio*)? Could this stand by itself, or should it be accompanied by some simple discrimination of classes of income (for example distinguished into two classes only: from work as an employee and "others")? What proportion would have to be achieved between the variation in the rates as a function of the different nature of the various classes of income and the variation as a function of the size of the total income? And finally, is qualitative discrimination more advisable in a system of direct taxation which, as a whole, exerts a low pressure on national income (but in which personal progressive taxes function with difficulty) or in a system of direct taxation which exerts a substantial pressure on national income (and in which, therefore, certain refinements in the discrimination of the rates give more justification for the considerable administrative work which they require)?

NOTES TO SELECTION 11

[1]The Italian text uses "*impresa*," which means "enterprise" and is apparently a misprint.

11

Taxation of
Corporations and Dividends

by the Commission to Study the
Fiscal System of Venezuela*

TAXATION OF CORPORATIONS

UNDER the present tax structure [in Venezuela], individuals and corporations are subject to the same rates of tax as respects both the schedular taxes and the complementary tax. The only variation arises under the complementary tax, since here an individual obtains a basic Bs.12,000 exemption plus family allowances. Dividends are not included in the taxable income of the shareholder.

Need for Separate Corporate Rate Structure

The present system would be understandable perhaps in an economic society in which corporations were family-owned and family-managed. Consequently, under such circumstances an individual would, speaking generally, be taxed the same whether his wealth was in the corporate form or in individual ownership. But even this support for the present system would fall when individuals started to diversify their activities and to receive income from different sources. At this point the failure to tax dividends leads to the splitting of an individual's activities between himself and his corporation, and then in turn between himself and a number of corporations. This consequence of the present structure is already an aspect of Venezuelan economic organization, for knowledgeable taxpayers today engage in such splitting of income when the tax savings outweigh the factors making for unitary organization (such as stamp taxes and local *patente* taxes on gross receipts when intercompany transactions are

The Fiscal System of Venezuela: A Report (Baltimore: The Johns Hopkins Press, 1959), pp. 111–25. Reprinted here with the kind permission of the publisher. (See the editorial note at the beginning of selection 9 in this volume.)

involved, the corporate registration fee of Bs.1 per mil capital, and additional bookkeeping and administrative costs). This splitting of activities among various corporate enterprises and the individual himself through salaries and activities in his name is quite feasible when the various corporations are closely held.

The support for the present structure earlier indicated also falls, as corporations change from closely held, family-owned and family-managed affairs to large organizations in which management and ownership are separated and ownership is no longer closely held. This change has already occurred in Venezuela, as respects most of the larger and medium-sized corporations. The trend in the corporate area is steadily in the direction of the non-family corporation. As a consequence, on the whole, there is now probably little relationship between the tax brackets of the various shareholders and those of the corporate enterprise.

Thus, whatever the support that could originally have been advanced for the existing tax treatment of corporations, it is no longer available in the light of changed economic and business conditions. In addition, the present structure presents serious obstacles to any change in the revenue yield of the income tax. An increase in personal income tax revenues might require a lowering of exemptions or a rise in lower bracket rates. These changes, in turn, would, for equity reasons, require the top rates to rise. But as far as corporations are concerned, the factor governing their level would appear to be the treatment of the major oil companies. Any substantial increase in those rates, as long as the present annual 16–2/3% royalty (hydrocarbon production tax) is retained, would raise the Government's share of oil profits almost point for point above the 50–50 line. This being so, it is possible that the top corporate rates might not (for this reason alone) be increased substantially. It might also be thought inadvisable to increase these rates at this stage of economic development in Venezuela, wholly apart from the effect on the oil companies. Accordingly, the top corporate rates would have to be separated from the top individual rates, if the latter rose. At the other end of the scale, in the lower brackets, it is not appropriate to have the corporate rates determined automatically by the individual rates. Necessarily the individual rates, even under demands of increased revenues, will start at figures probably not higher than 5% to 8%. Such rates are inappropriate for corporations representing the collective ownership of shareholders in many different brackets. Further, if corporations are regarded as independent sources of tax revenue, wholly apart from their shareholders, rates as low as 5% or 10% are inappropriate. Also, while considerable progression is desirable within the individual rate scale, with a fairly large number of brackets, considerable progression and many brackets are not appropriate for corporate taxation, even when the corporations are regarded as taxable entities, for the fact that they are aggregates of shareholders cannot be disregarded too far.

In any case, much more flexibility in formulating tax policy is possible, if the corporate rate structure is not bound tightly to the individual rate structure.

For these reasons, it is desirable at this stage of Venezuelan economic growth to separate the tax-rate structure applicable to corporations from that applicable to individuals. Indeed, such separation will be a necessity if increased revenues are required from the income tax. This being so, it is imperative that dividends be included in the taxable income of the shareholders. This latter step is called for, wholly apart from any change in the corporate rates, because of the widespread splitting of income among family-owned enterprises.

As respects the corporate rate structure, it would be desirable to have at least two rate brackets, and probably three. Thus, the tax on corporations with incomes up to Bs.50,000 or Bs.100,000 could be 10%; the tax on the amount of income above this level and up to, say, Bs.10,000,000 could be 20%; the amount of income above Bs.10,000,000 would be taxed at the top rate, whatever it might be. Presumably this rate would be fixed so that it would at least maintain the present taxes obtained from the oil companies. The combined schedular and complementary top tax rate today is 28–1/2%. The first-bracket corporate rate should be fixed in relation to the individual initial bracket rates, but at a somewhat higher level. Such a three-bracket corporate rate structure might invite a minor amount of corporate splitting at the first-bracket level, but this would not be serious. It is unlikely that there would be much splitting at the Bs.10,000,000 level. If it did prove serious, it could be counteracted by requiring consolidation of the income of subsidiary corporations with that of the parent corporation, if the splitting took this form, or even with that of corporations owned by the same individual shareholder group, if the splitting took this latter form. Under this rate structure, as at present, there would be no exemption for corporations.

The present reductions in rates at the top three brackets for invested earnings should not be continued. As respects corporations at these levels, presumably the annual retained earnings are always sufficient to permit full utilization of the lower rates applicable to income that is reinvested. Consequently, the result is simply a somewhat lower rate structure expressed in this indirect fashion and always operative. This being so, the tax rates desired should be set forth directly as the actual rates, and the investment rate reductions should be discontinued.

Taxation of Dividends

As stated above, under the present treatment of corporations, and certainly under any separate rate structure for corporations, it is necessary to include dividends in the taxable income of shareholders. Without this step, it becomes impossible to maintain equitable taxation under the income tax. Dividends when received represent income to the shareholder and should be taxable to him. The matter of "double taxation" of corporate income will be discussed later.

The taxation of dividends as income will involve some technical and administrative rules, a few of which are here mentioned:

a) *Definition*. A dividend could be defined in terms of the corporate law, and presumably would cover distributions to shareholders out of corporate earnings and profits. Distributions from corporate earnings accumulated prior to these new rules would be considered as taxable dividends. Stock dividends would not be subject to tax, but their distribution would not capitalize the earnings for tax purposes, nor provide the shareholder with a tax cost for the stock dividend shares. Instead, the cost of his old shares would be pro-rated among those shares and the stock dividend shares.

b) *Taxation of Shareholder*. The Tax Administration would have to meet the problem of insuring full shareholder reporting of dividends. It may be desirable to require corporations to withhold some tax on dividends distributed, so that collection on the small shareholders would be assured, and also so that information would be available on the dividends received by the larger shareholders. (This aspect is considered in detail, below, in the discussion of "double taxation.") Splitting of stock among the family in order to escape tax should not be a serious problem in view of the rules of family taxation discussed earlier. If the stock were given to a wife or minor child, the husband would still be taxable. Outright gifts to adult children or other members of the family could reduce the tax if the donees were in lower brackets, but this is proper if the gifts are in good faith. Moreover, an effective gift tax would insure that some tax price was paid for any reduction in income tax so achieved. Treatment of foreign shareholders is discussed later.

c) *Bearer Shares*. Bearer shares would be a problem, but several solutions are possible. As respects publicly held corporations, the Stock Exchange rules could prohibit the listing of bearer shares. Perhaps the issuance of such shares could even be prohibited under corporate law. Another alternative would be the adoption of some device making the creation of bearer shares quite onerous, as through a very high stamp tax. The present inheritance tax has somewhat this effect, since it requires the corporation to pay an inheritance tax on the issuance of bearer shares if the shares constitute 50% or more of the shareholder's assets. Also, corporations could be required to withhold tax on dividends on bearer shares at a fairly high rate. At present bearer shares are not a prominent aspect of the corporate scene, though they do exist to a minor extent. Hence any effective steps taken to eliminate their use, in order to protect the taxation of dividends, would not injure corporate activity.

d) Retention of Corporate Earnings to Avoid Tax. If dividends are included in shareholder income, the shareholders of a closely held corporation may decide to retain the earnings in the corporation in order to reduce their taxes. This is not necessarily undesirable if the earnings are reinvested in actual operations. It is not desirable if they are simply invested in liquid assets. If capital gains on the sale of the shares are taxed in full, as is largely the case at present, the tax savings obtained are only those of postponement of tax. For these reasons, this aspect is not likely to be a serious problem. However, the corporate tax rates should be sufficiently high, in relation to individual rates, so that there is not a great inducement to retention of corporate earnings simply to reduce the tax on the shareholders. This preventive step is necessary to avoid too much temptation to the stockholder to fail to report his sales of corporate shares, and the capital gains, if any.

The Issue of "Double Taxation" of Corporate Income

Under the present structure, the so-called "double taxation" problem involved in having both a tax on corporations and the inclusion of dividends in shareholder income is not raised, since dividends are not taxed. Under the above proposal for a separate corporate tax and the taxation of dividends, the problem is created. There are several facets to this problem.

The first is that of the desirability or undesirability of taxing both corporations and dividends. Tax systems are divided on this point. There is, however, an increasing trend toward regarding the corporation as a separate entity from whom income tax may be obtained in addition to the tax on shareholders' dividends. The relative ease of collection of corporate taxes, the dominant role of corporations in business life, the separation of management from shareholders, are all factors in this trend. Thus, some may conclude that double taxation is either permissible or desirable. They would therefore be content to let the tax structure stand as above proposed. Others, however, who prefer to regard the corporation as an aggregate of shareholders and not as an ultimate tax entity would take the opposite point of view.

They would therefore seek mechanisms to eliminate or reduce the double taxation. In this latter view, the question becomes that of the desirable mechanism, and also of the extent to which the double taxation should be reduced.

It is not necessary to elaborate on the various alternative mechanisms, since they are well known. One is not to tax the corporation at all, but instead to treat it like a partnership and to tax each shareholder on his share of corporate earnings whether or not distributed. While this method gives full recognition to the aggregate concept of a corporation, it presents probably insuperable difficulties in administration. This is certainly so for large corporations. As respects small corporations, present law treats the limited liability company as a partnership, and this treatment could be continued so that those desiring this result could use this form of organization. Another method, offering only a partial offset, is to credit a portion of the dividends received against the shareholder's tax. Thus, the shareholder would include the dividend received in his income and then credit against his total tax 5%, 10%, or more of the dividend. This method has the virtue of simplicity, but not much else. It is inequitable as between small and large taxpayers, since it does not "gross up" the dividend, though a credit for part of the corporate tax is granted, and also since the corporate tax may be larger in relation to the small shareholder's own rate than the credit allowed, but smaller in relation to the larger shareholder's rate.

The two most defensible methods are that of a deduction from income to the corporation for dividends which it distributes, or that of a credit against tax, allowed to a shareholder, of the amount of corporate tax on his dividend, with inclusion in his income of the dividend received, "grossed up," however, by that corporate tax. The latter method simply regards the corporate tax as a withheld tax, the same as the tax withheld by an employer on an employee. Thus, if a shareholder receives a Bs.100 dividend and the corporate rate of tax is 30%, then the dividend is increased, i.e. "grossed up" to an amount obtained by dividing the Bs.100 by 7/10, or Bs.142.86. The shareholder would include Bs.142.86 in his income, and receive a credit of 30% of that figure or Bs.42.86. Both mechanisms reach the same result (assuming that the corporate tax is borne by the shareholders as a matter of tax incidence, and is not passed on to consumers or back to employees). Hereafter in the discussion, the first method, that of a deduction to the distributing corporation, is referred to as the dividend deduction or deduction-to-corporation method. The second method, that of the credit against tax allowed to a shareholder, is referred to as the credit-to-shareholder method. The latter should be distinguished from the credit method earlier discussed which does not "gross up" the dividend but merely grants a credit against tax.

Both the credit-to-shareholder method and the dividend deduction method reach the same net tax result to the shareholders and corporation considered together. Both plans assume that the corporate tax is borne, or largely borne, by the shareholders as a matter of tax incidence, and is not passed on to consumers or back to employees. Under each plan, the tax benefit involved—deduction to the corporation or credit for the shareholder—becomes available only on the distribution of corporate profits to shareholders. These plans may therefore encourage management to distribute more corporate earnings than if there were full "double taxation" of corporate earnings. Whether or not this encouragement is so strong as to be undesirable is a difficult question. The possibility of encouragement becomes more likely as the degree of relief from "double taxation" increases. It also is probably more likely under the dividend deduction approach, especially if corporate managers look on the mechanism simply as one that imposes a tax higher on retained than on distributed corporate earnings. The credit plan may have a somewhat greater tendency to encourage investment in corporations, since superficially the shareholders may regard the tax on dividend income as being lighter than that on other income because of the credit. However, any possible differences between the two plans in these respects are not readily susceptible of evaluation, since they rest essentially on the attitudes and impressions of corporate managers and shareholders.

The deduction-to-corporation method involves a greater dependence, in comparison with the credit-to-shareholder method, on collecting to the full the amount due from the shareholders under the personal income tax, since the deduction method lessens the revenue importance of the corporate tax. The credit-to-shareholder method, on the other hand, safeguards the revenue if the shareholder does not report the dividend, as long as the shareholder's rate of tax is not greater than the credit allowed. Consequently, if the dividend deduction method is used, it would be very desirable to accompany it with a withholding tax on dividends similar to that described in Chapter V [not included in this volume] for wages and salaries.

This withholding tax would insure collection at least from shareholders in the low tax brackets. An actual withholding tax is not needed under the credit-to-shareholder method, since the corporate tax itself, to the extent credit is allowed to the shareholder, is in effect being regarded as a tax withheld from the shareholder. Moreover, if either method is used, it may be desirable to use it only to a partial extent, and not to permit complete elimination of the corporate tax in either case, until more experience is obtained respecting the taxation of dividends to shareholders. Thus, under the credit-to-shareholder method, many taxpayers with rates higher than the credit may not report their dividends, while those with rates below the credit would do so and thereby obtain a refund. This would equally be so under the dividend deduction method, since shareholders with rates above the withholding tax rate may not report their dividends while the shareholders with rates below the withholding rate would do so in order to get a refund.

As respects administration, the allowance of a dividend deduction to the corporation is simpler of administration, considered alone, since the mechanics—the allowance of the deduction—take place at the corporate level. Under the credit-to-shareholder method, the mechanics—the "grossing up" of the dividend and the taking of the credit—occur at the shareholder level. Moreover, corporations would probably have to provide shareholders with information as to dividends to be included and credits taken. The credit method also involves refunds to those shareholders whose tax rate is less than the portion of corporate tax rate to be credited, whereas refunds are not involved under the deduction-to-corporation method. But these administrative advantages of the deduction method disappear if there is coupled with it, as is suggested above is almost necessary, an actual withholding tax on dividends. In this event the mechanics under the two methods are virtually the same at the shareholder level, with the individual shareholder required to "gross up" the dividend received, include it in income, and then take his credit. The difference is simply in the amount of credit. Under the withholding tax the credit is the rate of that tax; under the credit-to-shareholder method the credit is the portion of the corporate tax to be allowed as the credit. It may be that the two rates would turn out to be the same though their function is different. (The withholding tax is a compliance measure attached to the deduction-to-corporation method, the latter being the method to reduce "double taxation"; the credit-to-shareholder for the portion of the corporate tax is a method to reduce "double taxation.")

The above discussion of administration relates to the effect on individual shareholders. Where corporate shareholders are involved, the problems are different. Here presumably the desire is not to subject the dividend to any greater tax as a consequence of its passing through intermediate corporations before it reaches the individual shareholders. Under the credit-to-shareholder approach this can be done simply. Intercorporate dividends, i.e., dividends received by corporations, would not be included in income and the receiving corporation would not be allowed any credit because of the dividend received. When the receiving corporation distributed a dividend in turn to its individual shareholders, then they would include the dividend ("grossed up") in income and receive the credit. This arrangement leaves the operating company fully subject to tax, leaves the corporation receiving dividends free of tax on the dividends, and gives the credit to the individual shareholders.

It is somewhat more complicated, however, to properly treat inter-corporate dividends under the deduction-to-corporation method. Essentially, it is necessary to allow the deduction to the corporation first paying the dividend, then to tax the corporation receiving the dividend in an amount equal to the tax saved by the first corporation, and then to grant a deduction to the second corporation when it distributes a dividend, thereby relieving the latter corporation from that tax. This method thus leaves the operating corporation with the proper tax respecting operating profits, places a tax on the receiving corporation as long as it retains the dividend (so that parent-subsidiary corporations do not receive an advantage merely because a subsidiary pays a dividend to the parent), but then removes the latter tax if the receiving corporation later distributes the dividend (thus not subjecting parent-subsidiary corporations to any greater burden than single operating corporations as respects dividends paid to individual shareholders).[1] As a consequence of the differing treatments of intercorporate dividends, the credit-to-shareholder method may be somewhat simpler of administration.

As an overall administrative matter, the credit-to-shareholder method probably involves less compliance and avoidance risk for the government than the dividend deduction method, even when the latter is accompanied by a withholding tax. Under the credit-to-shareholder method the full corporate tax has been obtained and the relief from double taxation depends on shareholder initiative. Under the dividend deduction method, a lower corporate tax has been obtained and the relief from double taxation has been granted, so that the initiative of achieving the proper end result rests in this sense on the Tax Administration. In this light, the opportunities for avoidance and technical manipulation would seem somewhat greater under the dividend deduction method. Further, if the corporate rate schedule involves several brackets, the technical problems under the dividend deduction method are probably more troublesome than under the credit-to-shareholder method, assuming the credit is no higher than the lowest corporate rate.

The double taxation aspect of the corporate tax is thus a difficult problem, and does not yield readily to a satisfactory solution in Venezuela or elsewhere. It must, however, be remembered that the taxation of dividends to shareholders will be a distinct innovation in Venezuela. This being so, it may be appropriate to cushion the change through some offset against double taxation. At the same time, however, the concept that a corporation has a separate taxable capacity is not completely foreign to Venezuelan tax practice. This is shown by the fact that Venezuela does at present tax corporations at rates that in many situations are obviously higher than those that apply in fact to the corporation's shareholders, as in the case of publicly held corporations.

On balance, it is suggested that a mechanism to reduce double taxation be adopted, but that it not attempt fully to eliminate the effect of the corporate tax. If the mechanism utilized is that of affording the corporation a deduction from income for dividends distributed, the amount of the deduction should be in the range of $33\frac{1}{3}\%$ to 50% of the dividends distributed.[2] This method should be accompanied by a withholding tax on dividends for compliance purposes. If the mechanism utilized is that of affording the shareholder a credit against tax, after "grossing up" the dividend, the amount of the credit should be in the range of $33\frac{1}{3}\%$ to 50% of the corporate tax rate (the dividend would be "grossed up" by dividing the dividend by 1 minus the credit percentage). This would provide the same tax effect as the deduction method.[3] However, the credit-against-tax method which does *not* involve "grossing up" the dividend would not be an appropriate method, and must be carefully distinguished from the credit-to-shareholder method here regarded as proper.

On balance, the credit-to-shareholder method may be somewhat simpler of administration than the dividend deduction, as indicated above, and could be preferred for this reason. But if it is thought desirable to use the dividend deduction method, it would be an appropriate method and could be administered.[4]

As respects foreign shareholders, if the credit-to-shareholder method is chosen, the foreign individual shareholder would receive the credit. As indicated in Chapter IV [not included in this volume], such a non-resident shareholder should incur tax liability at the regular progressive rates. In Chapter IV a withholding tax is recommended generally for income going to non-residents and this withholding tax would equally apply to dividends. The result as to the non-resident individual shareholder would be that in effect there would be two withholdings, one the actual withholding tax on non-residents and the other the withholding implicit in the credit-to-shareholders method. Since non-resident individual shareholders of Venezuelan corporations are likely to be in the relatively higher brackets this combined withholding may be appropriate. At any event, by adjusting the rate of the actual withholding tax in the light of the amount of the credit, since the actual withholding rate need not necessarily be the same as the rate applied to salaries, wages, etc., going to non-residents, the desired combined rate can be obtained. If the foreign shareholder is itself a corporation, it would be proper to apply to it only the withholding tax and not to allow any credit against tax. Since intercorporate dividends are not taxed, it would not be proper to tax the foreign corporation as such. But since its income will ultimately go to individual shareholders who should be taxed (i. e., the non-taxation of intercorporate dividends assumes that the taxable recipients are the shareholders of the intermediate corporation, and hence the individual shareholders are regarded as receiving dividends from a Venezuelan source) it is proper to reach them by taxing the foreign corporation at some composite or average rate. The withholding tax, coupled with a denial of the credit, achieves this result. If the foreign corporation does business in Venezuela as a branch, then, as discussed in Chapter IV, the branch would pay the regular corporate tax. The question remains whether an additional tax, corresponding to the withholding tax applied to the dividend paid by the Venezuelan subsidiary to its foreign parent, should be applicable to the profits of the branch. Unless this tax is applied there would be a lesser Venezuelan tax burden on the operation in branch form of a business owned by a foreign corporate investor than where the business is operated through a Venezuelan subsidiary. It might be said that this difference is a reflection of the existence of both a corporation tax and a shareholder tax. A somewhat similar difference would exist in this sense between businesses operated by Venezuelans in proprietorship form and in corporate form. But the Venezuelan proprietor does pay tax at the individual progressive rates, whereas the foreign corporation owning a Venezuelan branch would pay a tax only at the corporate tax rate. If the individual progressive rates are higher than the corporate tax rate, it can be said that some additional tax should be imposed on the shareholders of the foreign corporation as the ultimate owners of the profits of the branch. To the extent that the dividends they receive from their corporation are from those branch profits, the shareholders can be regarded as receiving income from a Venezuelan source. Hence it would be appropriate to apply the withholding tax (at the rate applicable to dividends paid to non-resident shareholders) to the branch profits when distributed to the home office (or when used for a purpose other than investment in the branch operation), and thus in effect regard those profits as equivalent to the dividends paid by a Venezuelan subsidiary to its parent. It must be recognized, however, that the application of such a tax to branch profits is more difficult in administration than in the case of dividends. Unless the lack of such a withholding tax on branch profits would contribute to avoidance situations in closely held corporations, it therefore may not be necessary to apply that tax to branch profits.

If the method chosen is that of a deduction to the corporation distributing a dividend, this deduction would be applicable whether the dividend is distributed to a foreign individual shareholder or to a foreign corporate shareholder. The dividend would be taxed to the foreign corporation as would an intercorporate dividend distributed to a Venezuelan corporation. While a Venezuelan corporation would in turn receive a deduction for dividend distributions to its shareholders, this latter deduction would not be allowed to the foreign corporation since the shareholders of the foreign corporation would not be taxed by Venezuela. If a withholding tax is applied to dividends in general in connection with this method, it would apply equally to dividends to foreign shareholders. In this event, it would not be necessary to apply to those dividends any withholding tax applicable to payments to non-residents generally except to the extent, if any, that the latter rate exceeded the withholding tax rate on dividends. As respects such withholding taxes, a foreign corporation receiving a dividend would not get any credit against its tax. The discussion above respecting branches is also pertinent here; if an additional tax is to be applied to branch profits, it would be at the rate of any withholding tax on dividends plus any additional withholding rate on non-residents.

NOTES TO SELECTION 11

[1][Footnote giving details of the treatment suggested in the text omitted.]

[2]This does not mean, for example, that the result is relief of 1/3 or 1/2 of the "double taxation." Thus, if the corporate rate is 40%, and the deduction allowed is 50% of the dividend paid, then if a corporation earned a Bs.100 profit and distributed a Bs.75 dividend, it would receive a deduction of Bs.37.50 so that its tax would be Bs.25 instead of Bs.40. This is a corporate tax saving of 37½%. Thus the "double taxation" impact has been relieved to the extent of 37½% of the corporate tax otherwise applicable.

[3]Thus, if the corporate rate is 40%, and a credit of 20% is allowed (i.e., 50% of 40%), the result as far as relief from "double taxation" is concerned is the same as in the case of the allowance of a deduction of 50% of the dividend paid. If the corporation earned a Bs.100 profit, it would pay a tax of Bs.40 and could distribute a dividend of Bs.60. The shareholder would gross up the dividend to Bs.75. (i.e., $\frac{Bs.60}{1 - .20}$ and receive a credit against his tax of Bs.15 (i.e., 20% of Bs.75). The relief from "double taxation" is thus Bs.15, which is the amount of the reduction in corporate tax obtained under the dividend deduction method (see footnote 2, *supra*).

[4]The above discussion assumes that the entire income of the corporations involved comes from a Venezuelan source and is thus taxable; it also assumes that there is no exempt corporate income involved. For situations in which these assumptions are not met, so that the corporation has non-taxable foreign source income or has exempt income, appropriate technical rules would have to be devised so that the credit to shareholders or the dividend deduction is granted only with respect to dividends regarded as derived (on a pro rata basis) from taxable corporate earnings.

12

Special Features of Corporate Taxation in Under-developed Countries

by the United Nations Fiscal Commission*

SPECIAL PROBLEMS OF UNDER-DEVELOPED COUNTRIES

THE extreme diversity of economic conditions from one country to another and the multiplicity of economic levels attained in the process of economic development render the making of broad statements of general applicability to under-developed countries rather difficult. In a previous chapter a distinction was made between the two stages of economic development. The first consists of extractive and export industries developed by foreign corporations, and of basic industries, like transportation, communications, power, developed partly as aid to export also by foreign corporations. The second, a higher stage of development, includes not only basic and extractive industries but also processing industries like textiles, and shows a trend towards gradual or rapid replacement of the preponderance of foreign corporations by domestic corporations. Today in all the countries which are at either of these stages of development or at intermediate stages, the process of industrialization has in fact started, but in each of these countries there is a difference in the need for further development, a difference of degree in the diversification of activities, and a difference in the relative importance of various industrial activities and the relative importance and further need of foreign and domestic capital. These differences find their expression also in the tax treatment of corporate profits and dividends as may be seen by a comparison of the country studies on Argentina and India published in the Addenda.

The recent orientation in the under-developed countries towards planning of economic development, has made the governments of these countries more conscious of the direct role that they can play in national capital formation; public investment by the government

*Corporate Tax Problems (E/CN.8/66, November 25, 1952), Chap. 6, pp. 57–75 (mimeographed). Reprinted here with the kind permission of the United Nations Publishing Service.

has been a very significant feature of the economic development plans. This in turn has created the problems of mobilizing the financial resources. In the search for revenues to meet the ever expanding government expenditures, taxation of corporations has been looked upon as an important source for further revenues. Generally speaking, an economically advanced country has sufficient alternative means so that corporate taxation need not be decisive for the government's part of the development programme; nor is as much reliance required on government activity where domestic corporations are able and eager to engage in development activities on their own initiative.

While increasing tax revenues have been sought, the taxation system has to be so adjusted and modified as to serve the respective governmental evaluations and policies regarding the need for foreign exchange, for foreign capital, for private investment, for the reinvestment of corporate profits, for dividend distribution, for protection to domestic corporations, etc. These factors should tend to make the tax systems very elaborate. However, the tax structure has been forced to be less complex due to the lack of adequate accounting and discipline of the taxpayers on the one hand, and a lack of administrative organization, experience and qualified personnel in the governments, on the other.

The present chapter will analyze the economic effects of a number of the most important taxes levied on corporations in under-developed countries. An attempt will then be made in the next chapter to integrate the facts and considerations here developed so as to present, not a ready manual for tax reform, but a guide to its preliminary stages. This guide should lead to the facts and policies which must be determined before the actual tax measures through which these policies may be effectively implemented can be devised.

Gross Income and Production Taxes

As we saw previously, the rudimentary character of income taxation in some countries has induced governments to apply essentially taxation *ad rem*. This is true especially in countries which are at their first stage of economic development and where foreign financed companies exploit natural resources of international importance.

When determination of prices on the international market cannot be influenced by enterprises established in the country, the taxes fall on gross income and their aggravation may lead to an uneconomic exploitation of natural resources. Thus, the Technical Assistance Mission of the United Nations to Bolivia has underlined the fact that *ad valorem* customs duties on exports of refined tin induce the mining companies not to extract low grade ore,[1] which is one of the most important natural reserves of the country. Therefore, the government has an interest in not destroying the profitability of low grade ore exploitation through levying high export duties. The profit ability of low ore production may go hand in hand with high duties when international prices are high, but must take into account marginal enterprises which have heavier costs. The reverse is true in the case of a slump in the international market: maintaining high duties may prejudice the production potentiality of the country.

In respect of gross income or production taxes, the tax administration is in a better position to bargain with foreign investors when natural resources in the country are of strategic importance, than when the same resources can readily be found in other countries. For example, oil exploitation may be in a better position to pay taxes than cultivation of sugar cane and fruits. In practice, however, several other factors which are specific to the corporation to be taxed may intervene: importance of investments and fixed capital and possibility of replacing or relocating them.

A major factor in evaluating gross income and production taxes is that they provide the government with a source of foreign exchange. This may overshadow in importance any direct effects that may be traced to the taxes themselves.

There are also a series of special cases where corporations located in the country are in a position to influence prices on the international market because of the relative importance of their production and their relations with other corporations influencing the market.

Thus, in the case of oil, the relations which may exist between the main exploiting companies in the world are decisive with respect to the shifting of taxes to the consumer. The recent agreement between the government of Saudi Arabia and the Arabian Oil Company may have profound influence in the world market of oil. When the production of an under-developed country represents an important percentage of the world production, it is of interest to the government to know the exact position of corporations in producers' cartels, in order to know to what extent production can be taxed without harm.

In a period of high activity and sustained demand, the disadvantages of production taxation are reduced since corporations may include in prices a part of the taxes they have to pay.

When enterprises founded with local capital participate in production, these enterprises are generally small and cannot offset the lower profitability of exploitation in the particular country by greater profitability of enterprises in other countries, and they cannot spread their production costs over a longer period of time covering years of high activity and years of depression. In other words, taxation on gross income which hits enterprises blindly without taking into consideration the spread of production costs, may weigh more heavily on domestic enterprise and make exploitation possible only for foreign enterprises.

A government sometimes finds it advisable to levy a production tax on a mining company because the tax can be obtained from the company, even when the company makes no profits. This argument of conditioning the extraction of exhaustible resources on an adequate contribution to public revenue may be decisive when taxes on production are levied merely on huge corporations, domestic or foreign. On the contrary, the tax hits small companies which represent local industry in the course of development and which may not have resources apart from their net current income. The possible economic consequences of excise and sales taxes on the flow of international trade and investment are similar. In both cases the tax imposes a sort of penalty on output or sales. It may become worthwhile to attempt to raise the price somewhat even at the expense of some output or sales. To the extent to which excise taxes cannot be shifted entirely some of the immediate burden will remain on the shareholders and the long-term flow of investment funds may be curtailed.

IMPORT TAXES

In countries which are at their first stage of economic development, customs duties represent the major part of tax receipts. Historically, import taxes have been the main field in which the need of selectivity was felt at an earlier stage.

Import taxes have been used in two different ways to stimulate national economic development. In the one case, there is protective taxation, which is aimed at prohibiting the imports of commodities into the country. While doing so, the tax helps domestic "infant" industries which may try to supply the needs which might otherwise have been filled by the imported goods. Protective tariffs are generally the products of political pressures from domestic producers. The extreme "protective" tariff would be prohibitive; it would stop the import of the goods in question. In practice, many import taxes serve both "protective" and "revenue" ends—they do prevent some goods from coming in but they also yield revenue on the remainder.

The other direction has been the concessions given to enterprises which contribute to the economic development of the country. In countries at the first stage of development with the initiative of foreign enterprises, tax legislation gives franchises for building material and industrial equipment imported by the enterprises in order to expand their plants and pursue their activities. The countries having oil fields have legislated in favour of providing import facilities to oil exploiting corporations. Both foreign and domestic enterprises receive a favourable consideration in respect of imports of material equipment used for economic development in other under-developed countries in Latin America, the Middle and the Far East.

TAXATION OF CORPORATE NET INCOME

In the majority of under-developed countries the taxation of corporate net income is an integral part of the tax structure. This tax may be of general application, or may be specifically designed for particular companies.

As we have seen in the first part of this study, laws relating to income taxation in under-developed countries often provide for special treatment of certain taxpayers through decrees granted by the government. These special laws are of particular interest to large foreign corporations which initiate or extend activities in the country through branch establishments or subsidiaries, and to the new domestic enterprises.

In both the general and special cases, the taxation of corporations does not seem to raise any special problems in under-developed countries, as far as the determination of taxable income is concerned. No matter what the country in which the taxation takes place, it is necessary to obtain a determination of true net income.

In addition to the tax exemption of depreciation and depletion allowances, fiscal benefits granted to new enterprises are, however, of great importance in under-developed countries. These benefits do not have the sole purpose of alleviating difficulties which are inherent in the initial stage of an enterprise. They tend also to attract new enterprise to the country. Therefore, most cases of income tax exemptions during the first years of activity, as well as the carry-over of losses, may be found in under-developed countries. These exemptions constitute a loss in revenue for the government which may be offset by the stimulating effect obtained in the field of foreign and also of domestic investments.

Aside from these deliberate benefits, tax laws of under-developed countries often contain technical provisions of a rudimentary character which may lead to favourable treatment of corporations. Thus, in Haiti, under the law of September 8, 1948, relating to income tax, enterprises are allowed to put aside every year 10 per cent of the taxable income against possible losses; this means, in effect, a 10 per cent reduction of net taxable income of all enterprises in any circumstances.[2]

The non-inclusion of capital gains in the taxable income may influence the direction of foreign as well as domestic capital. In Colombia, where there is a large flow of investments, tax exemption of capital gains may be considered as a premium for speculative investments which increase the inflationary pressure of capital values instead of being of benefit to the economy of the country.[3] On the other hand, in India various British concerns have expressed willingness to start new industries, if concessions could be granted on the taxation and transfer of capital gains.

As for the tax rate, the methods prevailing in Colombia, Haiti, Iraq, El Salvador, according to which corporations are subject to the same progressive rates as individual taxpayers, deserve some remarks. When rates vary within narrow limits and when the maximum is obtained for an income which is not very high, the rate which is progressive for individuals is practically proportional for corporations, the income of the smaller ones falling in the same category as high individual incomes. The maximum rate of the individual income tax happens, therefore, to be the normal rate of the tax on corporate profits, because of the difference between the average of the incomes of a corporation and the average of incomes received by an individual. As a result, when one wishes to tax individuals severely, taxation becomes prohibitive to corporations. Applying the same rate schedule to individuals and corporations is possible, therefore, only as long as the tax burden is very low. If one wishes to increase this burden, a differentiation between the treatment of corporations and individuals becomes necessary. In Iraq, the income tax introduced in 1939 applied to both individuals and corporations, and its rate varied from 6 per cent on the part of income up to 150 dinars to 15 per cent on that part of the income exceeding 1,200 dinars, as previously mentioned. When the tax burden was increased in 1943 and a surtax added to the normal income tax, separate rates were provided for individuals and corporations subject to this tax. While progressive rates applying to individuals reach a maximum rate of 45 per cent for income exceeding 8,000 dinars, rates on corporations reach a maximum rate of 25 per cent for income exceeding 3,000 dinars.[4]

If it happens that the scale of rates is largely open, progressivity may also apply to corporations; these are more or less heavily taxed according to their size. This result represents a double disadvantage.

On the one hand, it hampers the development of small corporations created with local capital. These corporations can be stopped in their development through taxation before they have reached their optimal size, or they may be split up in various distinct entities which fall under smaller brackets. Such a tendency towards splitting up in order to avoid the higher rates is prevented by special provisions in the more elaborate tax legislations which subject corporations to progressive taxes. In under-developed countries this tendency may not be hampered by law or administration and may rule out the economic advantages of industrial integration at the expense of the economic and commercial progress of the country.

On the other hand, to subject all corporations to the same progressive schedule of rates may discourage certain investments which usually are made by large corporations falling under the higher rates. This may impede the exploitation of raw materials by discouraging the launching of important programmes requiring large investments and large enterprises. It may happen that large enterprises achieve such a return on their capital that the maximum rate as applied to them does not have any deterrent effect on investment: however, there may be a change in the schedule of rates which would be motivated by an increase of the government's need for revenue or by the desire to revise the tax treatment of personal income. In Colombia, the basic income tax rate and the 1946 surcharge apply equally to corporations and to individuals, but the special surcharge of 1948 which ranges from 5 to 16 per cent applies to physical persons only.[5]

Therefore, as a country progresses in its programme of economic development, corporate taxation should become distinct from personal taxation.

TAXATION OF PROFITS AND DIVIDENDS SENT ABROAD

A single tax on corporate income, to the extent to which it means a lighter tax burden than there would be if the taxation of dividends was added to the taxation of profits, makes the corporate form more attractive for growing domestic enterprises. It, however, results in a loss of government revenue.

We have previously dealt with discrimination in favour of undistributed profits by way of a differential tax treatment. The matter is especially important in view of the economic advantage which reinvestment of profits made by foreign and domestic investors brings to the under-developed country. A differential tax treatment implies that dividends are subject to the personal income tax.

But the provisions for credits (in advanced countries) against foreign taxation suggest that dividend taxation does not encourage foreign investors to reinvest in the country.

When dividends distributed by a foreign subsidiary are repatriated to the capital exporting country, the law of that country may provide for a credit on account of foreign taxes paid by residents. In this respect, Section 131 of the United States Internal Revenue Code is interesting, which grants this credit for foreign taxes on dividends paid to United States residents and nationals within certain limits and providing in addition that the tax paid abroad by a foreign corporation in which a resident corporation holds stock is considered as paid *pro tanto* by the resident corporation.[6]

The United Kingdom provides also for some credit on account of taxes paid abroad to an extent which depends on whether the taxes paid are paid within the Commonwealth or to foreign countries.[7] On the European continent, the credit practice is not commonly used but reciprocal exemptions are resorted to by applying strictly the principle of territoriality (France) or by allowing tax rebate (Netherlands) without having actually to take into account the amount of taxes paid abroad or by considering these foreign taxes as deductible costs.

Aside from its general interest on the level of international tax relations, the credit system used by capital exporting countries for taxes paid abroad is of great importance for under-developed countries. The tax levied on dividends by the capital importing country does not affect the foreign investors insofar as such tax does not exceed the maximum credit granted by the capital exporting country.[8]

If the government of an under-developed country decides to tax dividends or to increase the existing tax on this kind of income in order to make reinvestment of profits attractive taxwise, the direction taken by the exported dividends must be considered. The same increase in dividend taxation may for instance:

 a) not change anything for a corporation which distributes dividends to shareholders in the United States, where the tax increase will only amount to a revenue loss for the United States government without adding to the total tax liability of the shareholders.

 b) bring the expected result and increase the reinvestments of a corporation which sends its dividends to the United Kingdom where the allowed credit absorbs only part of the tax and let the tax increase have an impact on the whole tax liability of the shareholders.

 c) drastically affect the activity of a corporation which distributes its dividends to Swiss shareholders, the Swiss legislation not providing for any deduction and the total tax liability being increased by the full amount of the tax increase in the under-developed country.

Thus it appears, that increasing dividend taxation to foster reinvestment may be a difficult method—may even be an impossible method—depending upon the distribution by country of origin of the foreign investments in the country. The possibilities are different when all large corporations export their dividends to the same foreign country which grants credits for foreign taxes and when the imported capital comes from various countries which do not treat dividends paid abroad in the same way.

On the other hand, from the revenue side, it is interesting to note that when capital exporting countries allow credits, the under-developed countries enjoy an additional margin to increase their taxes without impairing the profit possibilities offered to foreign investors.

A possibility remains, however, that foreign investors will protest against an increase of the taxes levied by the government of the country where they carry on their activity although this increase is absorbed by the credit granted in their country. That may occur when these capital exporters are hoping to obtain from their own government outright tax exemptions for the dividends they repatriate.

All this does not only concern dividends but more generally the incomes transferred abroad which cannot be taxed as such by resorting only to dividend taxation. Indeed, besides dividend remittances to the capital exporting countries, there are cases where branches of foreign corporations send home their income in the form of profits.

As a rule, when the tax laws of capital exporting countries take into account the close relationship between a parent corporation and its subsidiaries and when the incorporation is possible under good conditions under the laws of the capital importing countries, foreign investments in the latter countries are more likely to establish subsidiaries rather than branches.

The organization of a subsidiary brings about the payment of the fees provided by the local laws for incorporating businesses; similarly with the issuance of shares. Despite these, limitation on liability enjoyed by an incorporated business makes it preferable to a branch, the activities of which affects the foreign corporation's entire establishment.

Taxwise, the organization of the business as a subsidiary is preferable to carrying on the activity through a branch because the parent corporation in the capital exporting country must show every year in its taxable income the profits made during the year through its permanent establishments abroad, while profits made through a subsidiary are subject to tax only when repatriated. The activity abroad through subsidiaries thus offers corporations of developed countries larger possibilities to postpone income taxation.

On the other hand, if the capital importing country taxes dividends after taxing profits but does not apply any special treatment for remittances abroad as such, the business activity through a branch may be preferable to an incorporation in the country where the business activity is carried on since exporting the income as profits rather than as dividends permits the avoidance of dividend taxation in the under-developed country.

This is of particular importance in the European capital exporting countries where income tax exemptions prevail for business profits made through a permanent establishment abroad. Thus a Swiss corporation will be exempt from the Swiss tax on its profits derived through foreign branches, provided that these profits are taken into account in computing the rate applicable to the taxable income. On the other hand, this taxable income must include dividends paid by foreign subsidiaries after foreign taxation.

In countries which grant credits for taxes paid to other governments, the taxpayer may not see any reason to avoid double taxation in the foreign country where he invested his money. Since tax rates in under-developed countries are usually lower than the rates in force in capital exporting countries, the credit allowed generally absorbs both the tax on the profits and the tax on the dividends levied by the under-developed country.

From the point of view of the tax authorities in under-developed countries which tax dividends but not repatriated profits, foreign corporations which carry on their activity in the country through branches (for whatever reason it may be) contribute less to government revenue than they would if they were carrying on their activity through subsidiaries. That is often an additional reason why certain under-developed countries provide that foreign corporations operating on their territory will have to incorporate according to domestic legislation.

Thus, with respect to the tax treatment of foreign investment income, dividend taxation may be replaced in an under-developed country by a tax on all remittances abroad which fulfills the same objectives and does not exclude remittances which are not dividends but the profits of branches. Besides the revenue it yields, such a tax may be a tool of fiscal policy in order to foster reinvestment in the country of the income earned by foreign investments. The burden of such a tax must be carefully devised according to the availability or non-availability of credit devices in the various capital exporting countries.

Withholding at source in dividend taxation is only a technical device when the amount withheld is credited to the shareholder on his tax liability. But when the shareholder is not a resident of the same country as the distributing corporation, withholding at source on dividends constitutes an autonomous levy, without any possible connexion with the ability to pay of the individual shareholder whose total tax liability will be affected by this withholding. Consequently, dividend taxation within the structure of personal income taxation is possible in an under-developed country only to the extent to which dividends do not leave the country.

A distinction may, however, be made between countries which are still at the first stage of their economic development, raw material exporting countries where the economic activity is practically limited to the activity of foreign corporations and the countries which are more advanced and where there is some domestic capital invested in business enterprise, in addition to foreign capital.

The significance of the problem of dividend taxation is greater than that of taxation of remittances of dividends in proportion to the importance of the role of domestic capital in the national economy of the under-developed country. The profitability of enterprises must be gauged more and more by reference to the domestic market, and the problem of the integration of corporate profits taxation and dividend taxation arises alongside the problem of co-ordinating the competing national laws.

When dividends do not leave the country, their tax treatment may be integrated into the tax treatment of personal incomes. The administrative difficulties which have already been discussed concerning developed countries may prevent this integration and let dividend taxation remain distinct from the treatment of other personal income. That is the case because of the problem of bearer shares versus registered shares. The proceeds of the latter may easily be taxed within the hands of the owner, according to his ability to pay. On the contrary, bearer shares, the use of which cannot always be discouraged, are difficult to trace in order to tax the dividends as well as to tax the shares themselves eventually. Withholding at the source may then remain the only way of levying a tax.

An interesting case in this respect is the case of Argentina which is no longer a country where most of the dividends are sent abroad. Under the law which has just been modified, the tax levied on corporations was credited to the shareholders on their personal income tax (the global rate of which reached 28 per cent) but when the shareholder did not return the amount of dividends received to the tax administration, a tax of 12 per cent was added to the tax of 18 per cent on the corporate profits by withholding at the source. In the new system, as mentioned before, dividends are only subject to a withholding tax of 6 per cent and are not included thereafter in the personal taxable income. To what extent this real taxation is justified by the administrative difficulty of following dividends distributed on bearer shares to the ultimate beneficiaries is not certain. On the other hand, the United Nations Mission to Bolivia recommended that withholding tax on bearer shares be levied at the top personal income tax rate of 50 per cent.

There is another problem which concerns all under-developed countries irrespective of their degree of development: the struggle against emigration of domestic capital which prefers the more attractive investment possibilities available on the markets of highly industrialized countries while their contribution to the domestic economic development would be very much needed. This struggle coincides with the efforts made to attract foreign investors and encourage them to reinvest their profits within the country. Their success depends upon the situation on the political level as well as on the economic level in general, aside from the role of taxation.

The study of tax measures against capital flight is not within the scope of this study. But it is interesting to note how important the repatriation of the profits made abroad by its residents can be for an under-developed country. This may lead to tax provisions penalizing corporations which keep their profits abroad. The Indian law taxes income from foreign sources in the year when it is made and again in the year when it is repatriated. That may induce taxpayers to repatriate profits made abroad within the limits of the fiscal year in which they have been made. For the same reason, under-developed countries, which are eager to avoid double taxation of foreign investors, have no interest in protecting their own nationals or residents against double taxation of income drawn from their investments outside the country.

CORPORATE TAXATION AND PRIVATE INVESTMENT

Countries Beyond the First Stage of Economic Development

When it is necessary to develop the economy, the tax authorities must first of all be cognizant of the extent to which foreign exchange is needed. Attempts to promote investment are futile if imported capital goods and supplies are required and foreign funds are lacking. Once the necessary foreign exchange is ensured the government may wish to apply a differential tax treatment against distributed profits. But in some cases, such a tax policy is not the only one or the best one which can be resorted to.

Indeed, the non-distribution of profits does not ensure their reinvestment. Undistributed profits may go to increase the idle reserves of corporations thus decreasing the available means for financing in the economy. This setting aside is the main purpose of a fiscal policy which tends to avoid inflation and to neutralize capital. On the contrary, within a programme of development, it is important to invest the capital.

When a corporation reinvests those of its profits which it does not distribute, the question still exists whether these reinvestments are wisely made and whether the investments made out of undistributed profits are as useful for the national economy as the investments made out of new capital obtained on the market. According to some writers, corporate management would tend to use undistributed profits with less care than they would with capital otherwise obtained and some evidence can be found for a lower productivity of a unit of reinvested profits as against a unit of other capital.[9] It may also happen that the expansion of existing corporations is not the most desirable form of investment for the nation's economic development. Instead of discouraging distribution of profits it would then be better to channel investments through the capital market; or if public investments are thought more appropriate, corporations and shareholders will contribute to them through an increase in government revenue from taxes on distributed as well as on undistributed profits.

The examples found in the national legislation of countries which have already reached a certain degree of economic development confirm somewhat this judgment on tax policies favouring reinvestment in a development programme. To the extent to which the reasons which motivated a discrimination through distributed profits taxation can be ascertained, it does not seem that a relative overburdening of dividends taxation was resorted to as a main tool for development.

In other countries more advanced in economic development and industrialization, laws provide incentives for self-financing. These incentives are selective and concern a given sector which is of special interest in terms of economic activity. Examples are the New Zealand law which assesses mining corporations on half of the dividends distributed and the French law exempting from income tax the reinvested profits of corporations engaged in oil research. In the Canadian law there was no discrimination between distributed and undistributed profits so far as income taxation was concerned up to 1950; in June, 1950, undistributed profits were made subject to special measures[10] but this served only to prevent personal income tax avoidance through the use of closely held corporations.

The absence of general tax incentives for reinvestment in a country like Canada which is still in the process of economic development and which still has large unexploited natural resources shows that tax discrimination in favour of undistributed profits is not necessarily an element of a development programme for a country which is not at the first stage of its economic development. Exception must be made, however, when the capital market is so depressed that new capital cannot be found to satisfy the requirements of the economy. Canada may neglect to foster reinvestments through special tax measures since capital needs may be satisfied on an active capital market which the Government helps develop.[11] But in many European countries which are in the category of developed countries, corporations have difficulty finding the money they need on the capital market and self-financing is the only possibility open to them to expand their activities. Thus, in those countries self-financing of enterprises plays a more important role than money obtained from the stock market and the banks aside from public investment.[12]

Countries at the First Stage of Economic Development

On the other hand, in some under-developed countries there is no private capital available in the economy while there are natural resources, the exploitation of which requires large investments. This is the case where the bulk of the economic activity is carried on by foreign corporations producing raw materials and basic agricultural products.

In some of these under-developed countries an income tax may be difficult to administer. However, when income is taxed, a discrimination in favour of undistributed profits through a differential tax treatment may appear as the only fiscal means to get corporate profits reinvested and retained in the economy which produced them and where they are needed.

The importance of reinvestments for corporations exploiting natural resources in under-developed countries results essentially from the fact that these corporations (most of them foreign corporations) are mainly interested in repatriating their profits to the home country. In countries which have already reached a sufficient degree of economic development, the bulk of distributed dividends remains in the economy. This does not necessarily exclude corporations financed by foreign capital; the corresponding dividends may not leave and may be invested in other corporations of the country which, being industrialized, offers many alternative opportunities, and to the extent to which dividends are sent abroad such a flow may be offset by a flow in the reverse direction.

In a less developed economy, dividends distributed by corporations exploiting the country's natural resources are sent abroad because the bulk of these corporations are foreign. The shareholders may want the return on their capital to be sent to them for consumption or investment purposes at home. If they want to reinvest on the spot the dividends which have been distributed to them, they do not have the opportunity to do so since there is no capital market to which they can bring their money.

In the rather rare cases where the important corporations which dominate the activity of the country are financed by domestic investors, the latter may suffer like foreign investors because of the lack of investment possibilities—on-the-spot possibilities which do exist in developed countries where industrialization is no longer at an early stage. Indeed, to the extent to which these domestic shareholders are more powerful than numerous, they may use their capital to undertake the development of another sector of the national economy. It is doubtful, however, that they will do so since activities other than mining or large-scale agriculture though urgently needed will not appear worthwhile in terms of profits in the near future.

They will not then reinvest their profits in the corporation and since consumption possibilities are also limited in the economy it may often happen that domestic investors send their profits abroad to invest or spend them in a developed economy which seems to offer more interesting possibilities as well as better economic and legal guarantees.

Taking into account the urgent need of revenue of most of the governments in under-developed countries, tax discrimination in favour of undistributed profits will be achieved through an increase in dividend taxation rather than by an alleviation of undistributed profits taxation. The report made by the United Nations Mission of Technical Assistance to Bolivia includes proposals for adding a 10 per cent tax on dividends in order to encourage reinvestments.[13] In a given country the optimum burden on dividends depends upon the tendency to send profits abroad and on the extent to which this tendency may be actually counteracted. The incentives for reinvestment may induce foreign corporations which play a dominant role in the country's economy to improve efficiency and the standard of living of their workers and employees. Supposing the marginal utility of investments in the business is already very low, it may happen that the corporation, induced to use its profits within the country, will undertake new activity, which will contribute to the development of another sector of the economy. But it may also happen that after an increase of the tax on the dividends which they distribute, corporations adopt a policy contrary to the government's purposes. First are the cases where undistributed profits instead of being reinvested become idle reserves and are lost to the economy at least temporarily, without adequate possibilities for the tax administration to ascertain whether the reserves are or are not justified. Second, foreign corporations may be willing to repatriate the same net amount of dividends whatever tax treatment is devised to discourage distribution. The government then gets increased tax receipts but reinvestments decrease instead of increase.

NOTES TO SELECTION 12

[1]See *Report of the United Nations Mission of Technical Assistance to Bolivia* [U.N. Pub., Sales No.: 1951. II. B. 5, p. 32].

[2]The new Haitian Income Tax Law of September 12, 1951, provides that, after three years, if the 10 per cent reserve has not been used up to make up for losses or for additional investment in agriculture or industry, what remains will be added to the profits of the fourth year. See article 12 of the law.

[3]See International Bank for Reconstruction and Development, *The Basis of a Development Programme for Colombia* (Washington, D.C., 1950), p. 265.

[4]See United Nations document E/CN.8/46/Add.4.

[5]See I.R.B.D., *The Basis of a Development Programme for Colombia*, p. 257.

[6]See *Addendum 8* [not included here].

[7]See *Addendum 8* [not included here.]

[8]Except to the extent to which the overall effective rate for the domestic income will be increased by the addition of the foreign income, which will, of course, not occur in the case of corporations whose tax rates are substantially non-progressive.

[9]See J. Ellwood Amos, *The Economics of Corporate Savings* (Urbana: University of Illinois, 1937).

[10]See *Income Tax Act,* Section 73.

[11]See the special treatment of the so-called 4K (new Section 64) companies in *Addendum 3* [not included here].

[12]For France, for instance, see *Quatrième rapport de la Commission des Investissements,* Chap. I, Sec. II.

[13]See the *Report of the United Nations Mission of Technical Assistance to Bolivia,* p. 36.

13

The Taxation of Business Profits

by Nicholas Kaldor*

THE NATURE OF THE PROBLEM

111. According to both British and Indian laws, taxable income is arrived at by allowing certain expenses to be set off against a person's receipts during a period, but the expenses that are allowed as a deduction are defined differently for different kinds of income. Whereas in the case of (a) an office, employment or pension, the deductible expenses are defined as those which are "wholly, exclusively and necessarily incurred in the performance of the duties of" the office or employment, in the case of (b) a business, profession or vocation, the expenses deductible are defined as those which are "wholly or exclusively laid out or expended for the purpose of" the business, etc.[1]

112. This difference in wording denotes an important difference in treatment—a difference caused not solely, or even mainly, by the word "necessarily" which figures in the one case and not in the other, but by the fact that in the case of category (a) incomes the expenses must be incurred "in the performance of the duties of" and not simply "for the purpose of" the office or employment. The basic principle governing the deductibility of expenses is thus quite different. Indeed, it would be no exaggeration to say that whereas in the case of profits the expenses allowed comprise everything which has been "laid out or expended" for the purpose of maintaining or improving the earnings prospect of a business, and therefore of the person or persons owning that business, in the case of an office or employment, the individual *qua* individual gets no expenses allowed at all for any form of expenditure incurred for maintaining or improving his own status or earning capacity as a person. Any allowance for expenses proceeds from the explicit or implied obligations assumed in a particular contract, not from the need or desire to maintain the earning capacity of the individual who enters into the contract. If the definition

Indian Tax Reform: Report of a Survey (New Delhi: Government of India, Ministry of Finance, Department of Economic Affairs, 1956), Chap. 7, pp. 63–84. Reprinted here with the kind permission of the author.

215

adopted for (*a*) were applied to (*b*), a business could only claim such expenses as could be shown to have been demonstrably and inevitably involved in the fulfilment of a particular contract, and not those which arise from the desire to maintain or improve upon the general profitability of the business as a continuing entity.

113. This sharp difference in conception is the cause of a serious injustice in tax treatment as between those who make their living as employees and those who work on their own account or live on property. The inequity of treatment takes the form of (*i*) the allowance for capital wastage which is recognised in the one case and entirely ignored in the other, and (*ii*) the allowance for a whole range of miscellaneous expenditure which, while not expenditure of a capital nature (i.e., which does not result in the acquisition of a physical asset), relates to the general improvement or maintenance of the earning capacity of a business, rather than to the fulfilment of a particular contract. Thus, in the case of persons who are taxed on the salary, etc., received, no allowance is made for the wastage of earning capacity due to the limited span of working life, or for the capital expenditure incurred in acquiring the skill, knowledge or the qualifications required for a particular employment. No allowance is made for expenses incurred wholly and exclusively for either the maintenance or the improvement of the status of a particular employee (as distinct from the expenses necessarily incurred in fulfilling his particular contract) —e.g., advertisement in a paper for a job, entertainments to present or to prospective employers or persons with professional connections; expenditure on clothing in order to make oneself more acceptable to present or prospective employers, etc., etc.

114. In Britain (and I have little doubt that the situation is the same in India), the inequality of treatment only becomes fully apparent in those particular cases where a man pursuing some peculiar trade or vocation may be alternatively assessed as a salary recipient or treated as a person who makes a profit from a profession. Thus a Medical Officer of Health employed by a public authority is denied any allowance for his subscription to medical journals or his membership fee to the Medical Association, though an ordinary doctor would be allowed these things without question. An actor on a permanent contract and paid at a regular monthly rate would get no allowance for make-up, clothing, entertainment, etc., while an actor who contracts for individual shows separately would get all such expenses allowed quite irrespective of their amount, even if his services are habitually employed by the same firm. But perhaps the most important difference arises out of the fact that no depreciation allowance is given for the outlay incurred in acquiring personal qualifications, as distinct from the outlay on material assets, though both represent capital expenditure of an essentially identical character.

115. In some countries (particularly, I believe, in some of the Scandinavian countries), an attempt has been made to widen the range of expenses allowed for an employee so as to embrace expenses incurred for the general maintenance of earning capacity.[2] The Majority of the British Royal Commission on the Taxation of Profits and Income, in an attempt to narrow the difference in treatment between the two types of income, recommended that the expenses rule of employees should be relaxed so as to cover "all expenses *reasonably* incurred for the *appropriate* performance of the duties," instead of "wholly, exclusively and *necessarily* incurred *in* the performance of the duties."[3] This relaxation does not really meet the problem of the inequality caused by the basic difference in principle between expenses incurred "in the performance of the duties"—i.e., in the fulfilment of a particular contract, and expenses incurred "for the purpose of," i.e., for the general maintenance or improvement of earning capacity. The Minority strongly opposed this recommendation on the grounds that it would make it difficult to draw a clear line of distinction between business expenses and personal expenses; that the standard of "reasonably incurred" expenses would be steadily raised in the course of years; and finally, that all the difficulties and ambiguities which now beset the assessment of profits would be reproduced in the case of wages and salaries, with little, if any, compensating gain in equity as between one employee and another.

116. In the remainder of this chapter we shall consider this problem from three particular aspects:—the general question of allowable expenses, the problem of capital allowances and finally, the treatment of losses.

THE GENERAL RULE OF EXPENSES

The Proposed Rule

117. It seems to me beyond dispute that, whether we consider the problem from the point of view of administrative efficiency or of equity between the tax-payers,[4] the appropriate principle for arriving at chargeable "income" for tax purposes is the principle underlying the expenses rule for category (*a*) incomes rather than that for category (*b*). It is true, of course, that the actual wording of the former rule could only be applied to contractual employments, and not to profits derived from trading. However, it would not be impossible or even very difficult to invent a form of words which applied substantially the same basic conception to profits as is actually applied to contractual incomes. A simple definition that immediately suggests itself is that of *"expenses that are wholly, exclusively and unavoidably incurred in earning the profits of the year."* The insertion of the

term "unavoidably" would fulfil the same functions for (b) as the word "necessarily" fulfils in the case of (a), whilst the restriction of expenses to those incurred in "earning the profits of the year" would be a proper equivalent in the case of (b) of the restriction "in the performance of the duties" applied to (a).

118. There can be little doubt that the original notion of "income" for tax purposes—the conception which underlay the original income tax legislation in the time of the Napoleonic wars—was intended to confine deductible expenses to direct and unavoidable outlays of this character. The extent to which the present conception of "income" departs from it is a measure of the erosion caused by over a 100 years of relentless pressure exerted by vested interests.

119. The introduction of a more strictly defined expenses rule for the purpose of calculating the amount of taxable profits would have important advantages not only from the point of view of equity as between tax-payers, but also because of its repercussions on the efficiency with which the resources of the community are allocated between different uses. The kind of definition suggested above minimises the extent to which the amount of the taxable gain is dependent on the free choice of the tax-payer. The generous and elastic provisions for deductible expenses currently given in the case of profits put a trader in a privileged position in comparison with other tax-payers not only because he is taxed on a narrower conception of "income" than the others, but also because he is put in a favourable position to benefit from opportunities to evade taxation by dressing up personal expenses as business expenses.

120. The second of the two considerations, the need to avoid distortions in normal economic behaviour, is equally important as the first, the need to secure impartial treatment to different sections of the community. If expenses are allowed which are not a necessary or an inevitable concomitant of producing the receipts against which they are set off, the Government, in effect, is subsidizing such expenditures through the instrument of taxation. In the case of outlays on unavoidable items no such subsidy is involved precisely because the trading receipts are directly dependent on them. The outlay on wages, fuel, materials, etc., per unit of production, is virtually unaffected by the tax provisions. But if general expenses of all kinds—the scale of which is variable within wide limits relative to the scale of activity of a business—are made deductible, the very exemption is the equivalent of a direct subsidy from the Treasury, the rate of subsidy being the same as the marginal rate of taxation. When the marginal rate is as high as 90 per cent the deductibility of avoidable or unnecessary expenses implies that 9/10th of such expenses is financed by the Government and only 1/10th by the tax-payer himself.

121. There is, of course, no general reason why private outlay should not be subsidised by the Government; nor is income tax the only instrument through which such subsidies are habitually given. It is important to recognise, however, that the tax exemption to such categories is but a variant of granting subsidies, and it, therefore, requires to be justified not on the principles of equity, but by the criteria of social utility. The avoidable and voluntary expenses which are outside the narrow definition suggested above comprise such varied categories as the acquisition of capital assets of all kinds, expenditure on research whether of a recurring or non-recurring nature, payments made to research and other scientific institutions, advertising and sales promotional expenses of all kinds, entertainments, and travelling expenses. (This list is not intended to be exhaustive.) Clearly, not all such expenses are equally deserving of a subsidy by the test of social utility. The important point is to recognise that the tax-exemptions accorded to all such outlays find their ultimate justification not in equity, but in economic or social expediency.

122. The ideal solution, therefore, appears to me to adopt a strict definition of expenses on the lines suggested in paragraph 117 and to allow any other kind of expenses only to the extent to which this appears justified in the social interest. Expenditure on scientific research, whether of a recurring or a non-recurring character, clearly deserves to be subsidised. But it is open to the Government to examine whether all research expenses should automatically be treated as deductible, or whether certain kinds of expenditure should be disallowed or only partially allowed. Equally, it is a matter for individual examination whether expenditure on such items as advertising, entertaining etc., should be disallowed altogether, or whether it should qualify as a deductible expense only up to a certain proportion of the turnover or up to a certain fraction of the expenses actually incurred.[5] (The relevance of these considerations to the question of allowances for capital expenditure generally will be discussed below.)

123. I realise that this approach runs counter to the prevailing trend, which shows a constant widening in the range of deductible expenses in most countries. Thus the recent Committees of Inquiry both in Britain and India appear to have conceded the claim that profits for purposes of taxation should be assimilated to profits computed on "sound accountancy principles," however incongruous such an assimilation may be in the light of its consequences on equity. The Committee on the Taxation of Trading Profits in the U.K., acknowledged the claim of businessmen that "the income tax system should give relief in respect of the wastage of all assets that are used up or consumed in the course of carrying on a business," without any recognition of the fact that assets are built up and not only consumed, in the course of a business (in the form of goodwill, for example),

and to allow capital wastage to be deducted without bringing capital accretion into charge is completely at variance with the basic principles of equality of treatment. The assimilation of the concept of profit for tax purposes with the accounting concept is neither justifiable on grounds of equity, nor is it supportable from the point of view of administrative efficiency or economic expediency. In fact, almost all authorities on public finance who examined this question during the past 50 years or so have come to the conclusion that the concept of "income" that is most appropriate for tax purposes need have no particular relationship to the concept of income appropriate for accounting, or to the economist's concept of "income" as the individual counterpart of the "national income."

124. The Minority of the British Royal Commission following the above reasoning concluded that a tax on trading receipts less unavoidable expenses only (which comes broadly to the same thing as a tax on the "value added" as defined for the Census of Manufacturers less outlay on wages, salaries, interest, and rent) would be fairer and less arbitrary in its incidence than the present type of tax on profits; and that it would be a far simpler tax to administer; also since the tax base would be so much broader, it would make it possible to effect a reduction in the rates of taxation. Nevertheless, they felt that it would be futile to advocate for immediate adoption such a radical departure from existing practice so long as the taxation of profits in other countries remained on the present basis. For the traders engaged in overseas trade might be put at a competitive disadvantage if they were not allowed to treat as deductible expenses, selling and promotional outlays of various kinds which qualify for tax deduction in the case of their overseas trade competitors. They accordingly recommended that the U.K. should press through the United Nations or other international bodies for the adoption of binding international conventions concerning the principles to be followed in the taxation of trading profits which would make it possible to proceed towards a more rational, effective, and equitable system of profits taxation than any one country would be able to adopt acting in isolation. In the meantime as a second best they recommended that the difference in the treatment between the two categories of income should be compensated for in a broad manner through a differentiation in the rates of taxation applicable to each. This, they thought, could be most conveniently done through a change in the rules governing earned income relief.

Role of Earned Income Relief

125. The original purpose of earned income relief was to introduce a differentiation in favour of incomes from work as against incomes

from property. The Select Committee of the British Parliament appointed to examine this question in 1906 was troubled by the problem of how to treat the profits which were in the nature of a joint return of the work of the trader and of the capital which he employed in the business. They concluded that the only practicable solution was to treat profits below a certain amount as if they were predominantly the reward of work and profits above that amount as if they were predominantly the return on capital. On this reasoning, they thought that rough justice would be done if the earned income relief were extended to all "earned" incomes (including the trading profits of individuals and partnerships) when incomes were below £2,000, but not if they were above that figure.[6] There was never any justification for imposing such a limitation on income derived entirely or predominantly from work, i.e., salaries and the earnings of a profession or vocation. In the circumstances of 1906 this inconsistency did not trouble the legislators, since neither salaries nor professional earnings were met with in the over £2,000 range, except in a few very exceptional cases.

126. The Minority of the recent British Royal Commission came to the conclusion that the earned income relief could be made to serve the purpose of compensating for the difference in the expenses rule for salary incomes and profits if (a) the relief were extended in the case of salaries to all incomes, without any upper limit; (b) in the case of professional or vocational earnings, it is equally so extended, but only given to those tax-payers who at their own option are willing to be assessed under the strict expenses rule applicable to incomes from offices and employment; and (c) in the case of business profits, the relief should be subject to an upper limit as it is at present, but only extended to those traders who at their own option are willing to be assessed under the strict expenses rule.

127. I described the current position in the U.K. and its historical origin in some detail because the Indian rules concerning earned income relief have obviously been taken over from the U.K. rules, and it is important therefore that Indians should be aware on what justification (or lack of justification) the existing delineation of that relief to certain categories of income, and its limitation to a certain maximum of income, rests. The Indian provisions concerning earned income relief until recently corresponded exactly with the U.K. provisions; recently, however, on the recommendation of the Taxation Enquiry Commission, a further provision was introduced in India whereby the relief, limited to the first Rs.20,000 of taxable income, is progressively withdrawn when incomes exceeded Rs.25,000, so that for incomes of Rs.45,000 or above, no relief is given at all.[7] (I confess, I cannot understand how the Taxation Enquiry Commission has arrived at this particular recommendation. If one considers the

variety of ways in which incomes from work are discriminated against by the present tax system through the more generous expenses rule applicable to profits, through the tax-exemption to capital gains, through the fact that the taxable capacity inherent in the owner-ship of wealth as such is unrecognised and that spending out of capi-tal is tax-free, not to speak of all the evasion possibilities inherent in the one and absent in the other, this additional whittling-down of an already inadequate concession appears singularly inappropriate.[8] The Taxation Enquiry Commission concedes that of all the arguments in favour of the earned income relief the one which suggested that "the taxable capacity of those who receive unearned income is greater since they have also a fund of capital in addition to the income which arises from it" appears to them to be the most important. In the light of this remark their recommendation introduced immedi-ately afterwards, and not supported by any argument, that "there should be a limit in terms of income beyond which the allowance should not be available"[9] is rather difficult to reconcile.)

128. If India were to adopt an annual tax on wealth and would reintroduce the taxation of capital gains, the arguments in favour of earned income relief would come to rest entirely on the difference in the treatment of expenses as between salary incomes and profit in-comes. This is not meant to suggest that the case for the relief would no longer be a strong one—for the discrimination caused by the two different rules for expenses is a very powerful one indeed. But it would clearly imply that the relief should be confined to those who suffer from this discrimination, i.e., to the salary recipient; and it should be given to them without any upper limit—i.e., what comes to the same thing, a sur-charge be imposed on all incomes from a business, profession or vocation, excepting only those of the profes-sional and vocational category who at their own option are willing to be assessed under the strict expenses rule outlined in para 117 above. The extension of the relief to all salaries without an upper limit coupled with its withdrawal in the case of income from other sources would (on the basis of the assessments in 1954–55) yield a small net gain in revenue.

The Case for a Strict Rule

129. I should like to emphasise, however, that a solution along the above lines is definitely a second best and is neither so satisfactory from an equity point of view nor does it secure the other important advantages that would follow from the adoption of a more strict expenses rule for profits. While the Minority of the British Royal Commission shied away from recommending such a radical change in the face of the opposition that its introduction would have en-

countered, I feel that the situation in India is a rather different one from that of the U.K. The argument of export promotion through entertainment and advertising is relatively far less important; the need of Indian industry for identity of tax treatment with foreign industry is far smaller, since Indian industry can be, and is, protected by tariffs from foreign competition (quite apart from the fact that the whole argument is a spurious one, since differences in the breadth of the tax base can be compensated for by differences in the rates of taxation), whilst the advantages from the point of view of administrative effectiveness of an income definition which is less ambiguous and less capable of manipulation by the tax-payers are considerably greater. By simplifying the concept of profit which is subjected to taxation—by reducing the range of items which qualify for deduction—the task of checking the accuracy of the remaining items by the tax officers is greatly simplified. The standards of administration are bound to be all the lower the more complicated are the taxes which the tax officers are asked to administer.

130. For all these reasons, I would strongly urge the re-definition of deductible expenses on the lines recommended in paragraph 117 above in preference to all other solutions. This would mean, in effect, that only the outlays on wages, material, fuel, as well as the outlays specifically mentioned in clauses (i), (iii), (iv), (v) and (x) of Section 10 of the Income Tax Act would be automatically covered. With regard to the other items (including capital expenditure discussed below), the case for deduction would depend on considerations of economic expediency, and would thus be capable of adjustment and variation from time to time and from case to case.

131. There are no statistics in India to show the effects on tax revenue of either the allowance for indirect expenses or of the allowances for capital expenditure. I made an attempt, however, to estimate the possible magnitude of the items on the assumption that the relationship of the cost of materials and fuel on the one hand, and of "other costs" on the other hand, is the same in India as in the U.K. On that assumption (in the sector of manufacturing industry covered in Table 2 [not included here]), "other costs" amounted to 5 per cent of the material and fuel costs, to three times the amount of depreciation, to about 11 per cent of "value added" and to about 26 per cent the net profit. If this relationship held for India, not only in manufacturing industry but in trade etc., as well, the additional amount of profits assessable as a result of disallowing all other but "direct" expenses and personnel costs (apart from allowances for capital expenditure) would come to about Rs. 150 crores. Not all of this would become taxable under the definition offered in para 117; some items (those mentioned in paragraph 130) would continue to be allowed. Hence, the excluded expenditure may be put

at the order of one-half of this sum, or Rs. 80 crores. This is not offered as an "estimate" but merely as an indication of the possible order of magnitude involved.

132. The suggestion for widening the concept of taxable profits by disallowing all but direct and unavoidable expenses is bound to arouse fierce opposition. The antagonists of this suggestion will employ every specious argument they can think of, to show that the proposed reform would have fatal economic effects. This opposition would lose a great deal of its force, however, if the proposal were combined with a simultaneous reduction of the rates of taxation; the advantage of charging tax at a lower rate on a broader base as against a high rate on a narrow and uncertain base, should be apparent to everybody.

ALLOWANCE FOR CAPITAL EXPENDITURE

133. On the original conception of the income tax, the money invested in a fixed asset was regarded as capital and the depreciation of fixed assets a form of wastage of capital. The exclusion of any allowances for capital wastage was the logical counterpart of the exclusion of capital gains or capital appreciation from the scope of taxable income. This explains why for more than a generation after the re-imposition of income tax in England in 1843, no relief of any kind was given for the depreciation or wear-and-tear of fixed assets of any kind; and even after they were introduced during the economic depression of the 1880's, their scope was severely restricted to particular types of assets until 1944. In accordance with the findings of the Royal Commission of 1920, no allowance was given for the depreciation of any asset (1) which "was not created by the expenditure of capital" (mineral depletion is an example of this) ; and (2) whose useful life was 35 years or longer (hence all buildings were excluded).[10]

134. Looking at the matter from the point of view of equity alone, it is clear that an allowance for capital wastage without a corresponding charge being imposed on capital appreciation is quite indefensible. Even with a system of taxation on realized capital gains, capital wastage ought only to be taken into account in the form of a corresponding allowance for capital losses, which means that the allowance should be given as and when the capital loss resulting from wear-and-tear and wastage is actually realized. To hold the balance evenly between the charge on capital gains and the allowances for capital losses, wear-and-tear etc., should only be allowed for tax purposes at the *end* of the useful life of an asset, when it is sold for scrap or otherwise disposed of. The current methods of allowing the write-off of capital expenditure by means of annual depreciation

allowances are far more favourable than this, even if one ignored the various forms of accelerated depreciation allowances (or the straight-forward subsidy to capital expenditure given in the form of the development rebate) now in vogue.

135. It follows that the depreciation allowances given for capital expenditure cannot be justified on grounds of equity, irrespective of whether capital gains are taxed or whether they are exempt from taxation. If capital gains are exempt, no allowance for capital expenditure can be so justified; if capital gains were taxed, the corresponding allowances should be given as and when capital losses are realized, and not earlier.[11]

136. The real justification for capital allowances is, therefore, not one of equity but expediency. It is in the social interest that capital expenditure should be encouraged; a system of income taxation, through the double taxation of savings and through its discriminatory effect on risk bearing, does the opposite—it tends severely to discourage it. Hence, the allowances given to capital expenditure are necessary to neutralise some of the worst disincentive effects of income taxation on the economy.

137. Once this is recognised it should be immediately apparent that the present form of these allowances are both unnecessarily complicated and unnecessarily costly in terms of revenue to the State. If neatly calculated annual wear-and-tear allowances (based on the probable lifetime of assets) are not part and parcel of an equitable definition of "income" for tax purpose, it is open to the State to select a form of allowances which is simplest to administer, and which is most effective for attaining the objectives aimed at per unit of cost to the State.

138. At the present time allowances are given at varying annual rates for different assets, the system generally followed being that of the so-called "reducing-balance" method, which implies the writing-off of an equal percentage of the outstanding amount of capital expenditure in each successive year. Table 1 exhibits the effects of this method in the case of various types of capital expenditure. Thus in the most common case of plant and machinery of various kinds, where the annual allowance is 10 per cent, the method implies that 90 per cent of the original cost is only written off in 22 years. In the case of first-class buildings, where 2½ per cent is allowed, 90 per cent of the original cost is only written off in a period of 91 years, and so on. From the point of view of a tax-payer who can freely borrow at the ruling interest rate, these allowances are thus the equivalent of the immediate remission of tax on an amount equal to the discounted value of the annual allowances. Thus, assuming a rate of interest of 5 per cent, an annual allowance of 2 per cent on the whole capital expenditure is equivalent (as shown in column 2 of Table 1) to an

immediate remission of tax on 35 per cent of the total cost. In the case of machinery and plant where the annual allowance is 10 per cent the annual depreciation allowance granted on the whole cost is the equivalent of an immediate remission on 67 per cent of the cost; and so on.

139. Most businesses do not, however, have an unlimited borrowing power or an unlimited command over liquid resources; and to them a system which allows the discounted value of the depreciation allowances immediately is far more valuable than one which allows them to write off 100 per cent of the cost, spread over a large number of years. For a man who builds up a successful business, the possible rate of expansion of the business is normally limited by its accumulated savings and borrowing power; and in these circumstances the immediate remission of taxation on capital expenditure is far more attractive, since it is the equivalent of an enlargement of his borrowing power. The latter, therefore, is necessarily a more powerful lever for increasing capital expenditure than the former.

140. It follows that the ideal method of making allowances for capital expenditure is to allow the expenditure at the time when it is incurred in the same way as in the case of current expenditure; but unlike the latter, to allow only a proportion of the cost, a proportion that should vary with the probable life of the capital asset, as well as other factors such as the need to encourage the use of particular kinds of equipment, or to subsidise investment in certain industries.[12] Thus, for instance, if instead of an annual allowance of 10 per cent an immediate allowance of 66⅔ per cent is given on expenditure on machinery and plant; instead of an annual allowance of 2½ per cent an immediate allowance of 33⅓ per cent on first-class buildings; and instead of an annual allowance of 5 per cent an immediate allowance of 50 per cent on the cost of second-class buildings, the value of the allowance to the trader is at least as great or greater, whilst the cost to the State (in the long run, at any rate) is appreciably less.[13] At the same time, on account of the fact that the allowances are given simultaneously with the expenditure and not afterwards, there can be no complaints on account of the difference between historical and replacement cost of the assets in times of rising prices; the allowance is always given in terms of currency of the same purchasing power as the one in which the expenditure is incurred.

141. The only objection that can be brought against this proposal is that the benefit to the trader is dependent on his ability to absorb the allowances (i.e., to set them off against current profits) in the year in which the expenditure is incurred. To the extent that there are not sufficient profits to absorb the allowance in the same business,[14] the benefit of making the allowances immediately available is correspondingly reduced. However, this difficulty can be perfectly

TABLE 1

PRESENT VALUE OF CAPITAL ALLOWANCES IN INDIA

Type of Asset	Basic Annual Rate Per Cent	Case I		Case IIa		Case IIb	
		Period in Years	Present Discounted Value Rs. Lakhs	Period in Years	Present Discounted Value Rs. Lakhs	Period in Years	Present Discounted Value Rs. Lakhs
1	2	3	4	5	6	7	8
First-class buildings and hydro-electric installations	2.5	91	34.97	86	38.50	58	46.53
Second-class buildings, overhead cables, steamers and vessels	5.0	45	51.87	40	55.69	26	62.12
Machinery and plant (general rate)	7.0	32	59.90	27	88.39	18	96.47
Furniture and mills, etc.	9.0	25	65.31	19	93.91	13	102.77
Machinery and plant (normal rate)	10.0	22	67.22	17	95.31	11	105.78
Salt works, excavators, etc.	15.0	15	74.64	9	101.31	5	106.01
Batteries, x-ray, photographic recording and projecting equipment	20.0	11	78.46	5	108.36	4	115.55
Aerial photographic apparatus, and portable underground machinery	25.0	9	81.52	4	115.55	3	120.63

Case IIa—Normal depreciation and an equal amount of additional depreciation for the first five years only are allowed; 25 per cent of the original cost is given at the beginning of the first year as development rebate for all types of assets except the first two types of assets.

Case IIb—Normal depreciation, an equal amount of additional depreciation for the first five years only, and half the normal allowances for double shift are given throughout; also 25 per cent of the original cost is given as development rebate for all but the first two types of assets.

SOURCE: Appendix (iii) to C.B.R.'s "Income Tax for the Layman," 1955, for basic annual rates.

NOTES:
1. It is assumed that the reducing balance method is followed for 90 per cent of the original cost and that the residual 10 per cent is allowed in the year following the year when the written down value is reduced to 10 per cent or under. The "period" of depreciation is calculated under this assumption.

2. Present value is calculated by discounting the allowances given subsequent to the year of installation at a rate of 5 per cent interest.

3. Case I—Normal depreciation alone at the basic annual rates shown in column 2 is allowed.

adequately dealt with by a further provision, according to which any *unabsorbed* capital allowance carried forward to a future year earns a corresponding rate of interest. Thus, assuming a 5 per cent rate of interest, if a trader incurs an expenditure of one lakh in a particular year, two-thirds of which are allowed, and there are only Rs. 20,000 of taxable profits to set off against the expenditure, the amount carried forward to the following year would be the unabsorbed allowance of Rs. 46,668 plus 5 per cent interest, i.e., Rs. 49,000 altogether, and so on.

142. In India at the present time in addition to the "normal" depreciation allowance, additional depreciation allowances are given which double or more than double the normal rate for the first five years after installation, and then a development rebate of 25 per cent is given on the whole amount of the capital expenditure which is additional to the depreciation allowances.[15] As Table 1 shows, the effect of these various concessions is that in many cases the discounted value of the various allowances exceeds the total expenditure. This is the case for plant and machinery, etc., with double shift working, when the basic annual allowance is 9 per cent or more and double shift allowance is given; with single shift working, when the basic allowance is 15 per cent or more. The result of these extra concessions is that for businesses which do not suffer from a shortage of cash and/or a limitation of borrowing power the incentives for tax evasion are reversed—instead of there being a temptation to dress up capital expenditure as current expenditure, there exists the opposite temptation of dressing up current expenditure as capital expenditure.

143. It is a matter for consideration whether the current extent of these allowances are not unduly generous (even within the present framework of the tax system), and whether some of the extra concessions ought not to be dispensed with. (The case for this would, of course, become much stronger if the marginal rate of taxation on profits were reduced in accordance with the suggestions made earlier.) It is unfortunately not possible to find out how much these concessions cost in terms of revenue, as the amount of capital allowances granted against chargeable income are not computed for statistical purpose.

144. I am quite certain, however, that these allowances are greatly excessive in relation to the alternative system proposed. If depreciation allowances were altogether scrapped, and the whole of the capital allowance were given in the form of an initial allowance or development rebate (whichever term is preferred), with an accelerator clause for unabsorbed allowances, the actual amount of the allowances ought to be considerably reduced. Subject to an annual addition of 5 per cent for unabsorbed allowances, the amount should not exceed, say, 90 per cent of the cost for equipment carrying a basic annual rate of 20 per cent or more; 66.66 per cent of the cost where the present

basic annual rate is between 10 and 20 per cent; 50 per cent of the cost when it is between 5 and 10 per cent; and 33.3 per cent of the cost where the annual rate is 2 per cent. These figures are not intended to be precise and are put forward mainly for illustrative purposes. The change-over to the new system may cause a temporary loss of revenue which, however, will be more than made good in future years through the saving in depreciation allowances.[16] Since on account of the present development rebate and the doubling or more of the normal depreciation for the first five years, a large part of these allowances are in any case given immediately (amounting at present to 45 per cent of the total expenditure for equipment carrying a 10 per cent basic annual rate and operated at a single shift, and to 50 per cent of such expenditure in the case of double-shift operation), this temporary revenue loss is not likely to be appreciable.

145. The question still to be dealt with is how balancing charges and allowances are to be reckoned under the new system. If the taxation of capital gains were re-introduced, the amount of the balancing charge would in any case not be limited to the original cost, but would extend to the whole of the difference between the price at which an asset is sold and its written down value. Under the system I am recommending here, the written down value would be equal to the original cost less the allowances granted (including any additional allowance representing interest on unabsorbed allowances), and the balancing charges and allowances would be calculated on the difference between the sales-proceeds of an asset and the written down value.

THE TREATMENT OF LOSSES

General Considerations

146. The original conception of the income tax as a tax on the recurrent yield from particular sources was no more consistent with the idea of granting relief for business losses than with the granting of allowances for capital expenditure. As the Majority of the British Royal Commission stated,[17] "if the idea of a loss of income involves that more money has been spent than has been received on income account during the period, the balance has in some sense been found out of capital, and to set the loss against taxable income, current or future, is to allow the depletion of capital to be made good at the expense of taxable income." Indeed, the very notion that the net yield from a positive source of income can be a negative one is questionable. No one is forced to carry on a business, and so long as the net worth of the business is positive the owner is always free to cut his losses (either by selling the business as a going concern or by liquidating it and selling the tangible assets separately) when the sale-proceeds

from the realisation would put him in a position to earn a positive income corresponding to the interest on the value realised. Hence no one can really be said to derive a negative income from the ownership of any asset or a group of assets with a positive value (as distinct from a negative income from a negative source, such as interest paid on a debt), and if a man elects to keep on owning assets or to maintain a trading activity even though it brings him continued losses, there is no reason why the tax system should treat that as charge on his general income.[18] At the same time, as the Majority of the Royal Commission pointed out, "the ascertainment of business profits at fixed intervals of 12 months is so arbitrary a process, considering the continuous nature of business operations, that [to allow] the carry-forward of losses is an obvious concession to common sense."[19]

147. However, the Majority of the British Royal Commission did not, in my view, draw the right conclusion from this reasoning, in that they supported the existing provisions which permit a loss from any one source to be set off against any other income in the same year or in the following year as well as to be carried forward indefinitely against future income from the same source. They even recommended that unabsorbed capital allowances should qualify for a set-off against future income of any kind (and not only against future income from the same source).[20]

148. The question of the proper tax treatment of losses ought to be examined, like other questions, from the aspects of equity, economic effects, and administrative efficiency. From the point of view of equity, if capital gains are not brought into charge there is no case for recognising losses for tax purposes in any manner except perhaps as a means of averaging income over time; the latter consideration would only justify a carry-forward of losses against future income from the same source, and not as a set-off against income from other businesses or against non-business income.[21] If capital gains were taxed, the notion of allowing losses as a deduction from taxable income would no longer be anomalous. But the present definition of a trading loss by no means corresponds with the definition of a capital loss which should be adopted for the purposes of a capital gains tax; nor is it consistent with the notion of income as a person's "increment of economic power." A trading loss is a loss on current (not capital) account. But since expenditures of a capital nature have come to be treated as deductions from current receipts, a trading loss on current account may result when certain capital outlays in a period exceed net current receipts, or even when certain capital outlays of a past period exceed net current receipts.[22]

149. The correct procedure from the point of view of equity—assuming that capital gains are brought into charge on the lines

recommended in Chapter 3—would be to allow only current losses in the strict sense (i.e., the excess of current unavoidable outlays over current receipts) as an offset against other income and to permit "losses" which represent unabsorbed capital allowances, etc., only to be carried forward against future income from the same source. If there is insufficient future income to absorb the allowances, the difference would be automatically allowed for when the assets are disposed of, either individually or upon the liquidation of the business, when the resultant capital loss can be off-set against any current or subsequent capital gain.[23]

150. From the point of view of economic effects, to allow a loss from one source to be set off against income from another source has the effect of encouraging the continuance of moribund or unproductive businesses at the expense of the Revenue and ultimately of taxpayers in general. A business which is not moribund will be able to absorb its own losses incurred in a bad trading year against the profits of future years. Hence, even under the conditions described in paragraph 149, where strict equity considerations would justify an off-set against other income, considerations of expediency suggest that it is better to limit the allowance to future income from the same source.

151. From the point of view of administrative efficiency, the main consideration is to prevent the abuse of the provisions through the creation of manufactured losses of various kinds, which take the form either of fictitious transactions between different taxpayers who are differently situated with regard to their overall tax position; or of the acquisition of concerns with accumulated past losses or current losses (in the sense of an excess of tax-free allowances over net receipts) for the purpose of tax avoidance. A general provision whereby a loss from any source can only be carried forward against future income from the same source, while it does not eliminate completely the possibilities of such manipulation—it would still be possible for a man to purchase a business with an accumulated loss and transfer to it profitable business which he would otherwise have carried on through another business—reduces its scope considerably.[24]

152. For all the above reasons, therefore, it appears that the ideal method is to treat income from each source as part of a separate "running account" between the taxpayer and the Revenue, and in consequence to allow a loss from any particular business to be carried forward against future income from the same business but not to allow it to be set-off against income from other sources, either in the same year or in subsequent years. The one respect in which some relaxation of this general rule may be permitted is in allowing a strict trading loss (i.e., an excess of unavoidable current outlays against current receipts) to be off-set against other business income in the same year.

The Current Position in India

153. Under the existing Indian provisions (*a*) a loss from any source may be off-set against any other income of the taxpayer in the same year; (*b*) in the case of a business (but not in the case of other kinds of income) a loss which is not absorbed in the first year can be carried forward indefinitely against future business income from any source, provided the business to which the loss originally related has not changed hands or identity, or has not ceased to exist in the interval; (*c*) the so-called "speculative losses" cannot be off-set against other income and can only be carried forward against future speculative gains.[25]

154. It seems to me that the most urgent requirement would be to make the recently introduced proviso[26] concerning the business remaining in the same hands quite general in its application. The Taxation Enquiry Commission recommended that an analogous provision should be introduced in the case of companies, as well as in the case of individuals by providing that a carry-forward should only be allowed if the shareholders in the year of off-set are substantially the same as those in which the loss had occurred.[27] In addition, the restriction should be applied to unabsorbed capital allowances as well as to trading losses in the narrower sense. At present the income tax law treats unabsorbed capital losses more liberally than unabsorbed trading losses. The off-set of unabsorbed capital allowances is permissible against any income in any future year, whereas unabsorbed trading losses can be set off only against business income. For reasons explained in paragraphs 148 and 149 above, unabsorbed capital allowances ought to be treated more strictly than trading losses and not more liberally. Even if capital gains are charged to income tax and realized capital losses can be carried forward indefinitely against future capital gains,[28] the allowances for capital expenditure—the normal wear-and-tear allowances or the additional allowance in the form of extra depreciation or development rebate—should only be allowed to be carried forward against future income from the business to which these allowances relate, with the further proviso that off-set will be admissible only if the business in question continued to remain in the same ownership. If a business changes hands unabsorbed capital allowances would automatically be taken into account either in the direct form of balancing charges or allowances on the individual assets or indirectly in the resulting capital loss or gain on the sale-proceeds of the business as a whole. There is a strong case for limiting the off-set of losses from any one source against income from any other source (whether in the same year or in the following year) to a trading loss in the restricted sense representing an excess of unavoidable current outlays over current receipts, and to dis-allow the

recognition of a loss for the purpose of any such off-set in all those cases where a profit and not a loss would have been shown, if development expenditures of all kinds had been excluded in the calculation of the trading profit.

NOTES TO SELECTION 13

[1] In the British Income Tax Act these words appear as a qualification to the enumeration of a list of items, the deduction of which is prohibited. The first item of the list mentions "any disbursement or expenses *not* being money wholly or exclusively laid out or expended for the purposes of the trade," etc. The Indian Income Tax Act proceeds exactly the other way round. It mentions the list of items which are allowed as deductions from the receipts, and ends up (in clause (XV) of sub-section 2 of Section 10) with a general sweeping up clause which asserts positively that "any expenditure . . . laid out or expended wholly or exclusively for the purposes of such business," etc., qualifies as a permissible deduction. The difference in the manner in which the definition is introduced in the British and Indian Acts is revealing. It shows that the definition was originally intended to strengthen the hands of Revenue in disallowing deductions. By the time the law was applied in India, it has come to serve the opposite purpose of ensuring that no type of expenditure which comes within the scope of this definition should fail to qualify.

[2] Recent Indian legislation also tended in this direction, i.e., in the provision to allow the cost of books up to a certain amount, and for the cost of maintenance of conveyances (cars, etc.).

[3] Cf., par. 140, page 47 of the Final Report (Cmd. 9474). The Indian Taxation Enquiry Commission ignored this problem altogether.

[4] These two aspect are not of course independent of one another. Provisions which cannot be effectively administered are themselves the cause of inequities.

[5] In the autumn budget of 1947, Dr. Dalton as Chancellor of the Exchequer proposed that only 50 per cent of expenditure on advertising and entertainment should qualify as deductible expense for tax purposes. As Dr. Dalton resigned from the Chancellorship immediately afterwards, and his successor did not press the proposals, they never got on the Statute Book.

[6] This rule was later amended, on the recommendation of the Royal Commission on Income Tax of 1920, so that the relief was made available to *all* earned incomes, whatever their amount, but only on the first £2,000 of taxable income.

[7] This means, in effect, a return to the system originally in force in the U.K. prior to the recommendation of the 1920 Royal Commission.

[8] It also has the incidental consequence that in the income range of Rs. 25,000–45,000, the progressive withdrawal of the relief is tantamount to a further increase in the marginal rate of taxation, which in these ranges is thus appreciably higher than for unearned incomes.

[9] Cf. T.E.C. Report, Vol. II, Chap. IX, par. 23. As indicated earlier in this chapter the Commission makes no mention of the inequities caused by the difference in the expenses rule applicable to salaries and profits.

[10] These principles were abandoned piecemeal in the U.K. after 1944, when the original reasoning behind the restrictions was long forgotten. The Report of the 1920 Royal Commission made it clear that the claim for capital allowances rests on expediency rather than equity.

[11] The tax system contains several "asymmetrical" provisions of this kind which put the man who is taxed on the profits of business in an anomalous position *vis-à-vis* other taxpayers. One of these consists in the permission given to traders to bring anticipated losses into account through the writing down of stocks below

cost if market value is less than cost—without a corresponding obligation to bring into account unrealized gains (i.e., to write up stocks when market value is above cost).

[12]If the Government wished, in accordance with the general aims of its economic plan, to encourage investment in particular industries and not in others, the ideal instrument is to vary the rate of these allowances accordingly; though from an administrative point of view the differentiation should not be based on the industrial classification of the user, but on the type of equipment purchased (e.g., engineering equipment, machine tools, power looms, etc.).

[13]The State (unlike private business) does not suffer from limited borrowing power.

[14]The question of allowances for losses will be examined below.

[15]The development rebates are also ignored for the purpose of calculating the balancing charges or allowances.

[16]It would, of course, be necessary to continue to allow depreciation in regard to capital expenditure incurred prior to the introduction of the new system, so that the depreciation allowances would taper off gradually.

[17]Par. 486, p. 147 of the Final Report.

[18]This is the reason why the United Kingdom law has never recognized the possibility of a negative loss being incurred in connection with the ownership of property. If the maintenance and repair expenditure on property exceeds the income, the difference is not recognised for tax purposes except that for the purpose of calculating the income from property the taxpayer is permitted to substitute the average of the maintenance and repair expenditure of the last five years against the actual expenditure of the previous year, and to deduct such expenditure from the receipts of the year up to the limit of such receipts. Income from property therefore can be zero but cannot be negative. Under the Indian law, on the other hand, a loss on property is recognised for tax purposes in much the same way as a loss incurred from business activity.

[19]They added that "theoretically, a carry back against the taxed profits of past years would be equally reasonable, but the practical arguments against refunds of tax paid are sufficient to lead us to reject any extension on these lines."

[20]A concession which is already in force in India as a result of the wording of clause (b) of sub-section (vi) of Section 10(2).

[21]Though of the two methods of allowing an off-set of losses—against other income in the same year or against income from the same source in any future year—only the latter can be made consistent with the English conception of taxable income, historically it was the former, not the latter, which was the first to be introduced. The right to off-set was introduced in England in 1890 whereas the right to carry-forward a loss (originally for 6 years, now indefinitely) against any subsequent profits of the same business was only introduced in 1926. This explains why the justification of the right to setoff is rarely questioned, and the carry-forward is commonly treated as a marginal provision to be made use of only when, and to the extent to which, there is insufficient "other income" to absorb the losses in the same year.

[22]Whenever developmental expenditure—either capital expenditure or expenditure on research, advertising, etc.—enters into the calculation of a current trading "loss," the effect of allowing such a loss to be off-set against income from other sources is that a taxpayer is able to build up a business at the direct expense of the revenue. In other words, capital for the development of a man's business 'B' is provided by the tax abatement on his income from source 'A.' Part of the current tax bill is transformed into capital. Such an arrangement goes beyond the notion of subsidising certain types of investment to the extent of allowing expenditure upon them to be deducted from the receipts of the business concerned. In the latter case, if the developmental expenditure exceeds net current receipts the business

must find the whole of the capital out of which to make the excess expenditure. In the former case the excess expenditure may be largely paid for by the Revenue. The situation in which a man is risking not his own capital but part of his tax bill in respect of income from other sources, in investing in a business a sum greater than his current receipts from that business, provides an incentive to take un-economic risks together with wide opportunities for deliberate tax avoidance.

[23]From a strict equity point of view, net realised capital losses should qualify as an off-set against other income in so far as they cannot be off-set against realized capital gains—though the case for this is much less strong when income and capital gains (above a certain limit) are charged at a proportionate rate than when they are charged at a progressive rate. However, for reasons analysed in the Minority Report of the British Royal Commission (par. 65–67, pp. 375–76) and duly recognized in the tax codes of all the countries which tax capital gains, it would be very unwise to allow this since it might lead to wide abuse. If capital losses qualify as an off-set only against future capital gains, it is possible that the taxpayer will not have sufficient capital gains during his life-time to absorb them; and I think that in such cases it would be equitable to allow the tax claim on an unabsorbed capital loss to be credited against the liability to estate duty (or gift tax) at death.

[24]This loop-hole could be completely closed if, as suggested below, the provision recently introduced in India on the recommendation of the T.E.C. that the recognition of past losses should be disallowed when a business changes hands, would be made perfectly general (i.e., made applicable to companies as well as individuals, and to unabsorbed capital allowances as well as to accumulated trading losses in the strict sense).

[25]A speculative transaction is defined by Statute as one in which "a contract for purchase and sale of any commodity including stocks and shares is periodically or ultimately settled otherwise than by the actual delivery or transfer of the commodity or scrips," provided that it is not a hedging transaction or one incurred by a dealer or jobber in the ordinary course of his business. The effect of the restriction on speculative losses must obviously be very limited.

[26]Clause (ii) of sub-section (2) of Section 24 of Income Tax Act.

[27]I presume that this recommendation can only be made effective in the case of private companies and not public companies—at least the interpretation of the meaning of "shareholders remaining substantially the same" would be very difficult in the case of any company which has a large number of shareholders none of whom exercises any direct control over the business.

[28]With a proviso also for unabsorbed capital losses mentioned in the footnote to paragraph 149 above.

14

Capital Gains Taxation

by a Harvard Law School Group*

THE PROBLEM

THE development of the proper tax treatment for capital gains and losses has been a vexing problem in most countries. We should emphasize at the outset that the problem is an exceedingly complex one which has been the subject of numerous books and studies. Of necessity, therefore, this brief report can only deal with the most fundamental and general considerations. Moreover, we have been supplied with no statistics concerning the incidence and revenue effects of a capital gains tax in Colombia. We have been unofficially informed that, unlike the United States, where the primary application of the capital gains tax is to securities transactions, in Colombia the problem is thought to center principally upon real estate dealings. Accordingly the problem must be considered in the abstract, without the requisite financial data.

The precise definition of "capital gains" and the further question whether such gains are truly "income" are questions which have intrigued economists for centuries. Obviously, we cannot go into them here. Suffice it to say that there are no compelling reasons from a theoretical point of view why capital gains should be treated any differently than other forms of income. Although there may be certain distinguishing characteristics between the most typical kinds of capital gains and the most typical kinds of other income, this fact, in itself, does not necessarily warrant different tax treatment—and least of all complete exemption—for capital gains. As one writer has recently pointed out, a unit of capital gain commands precisely the same economic power for a consumer as a unit of any other type of income. We shall, therefore, concern ourselves with the more immediate and practical problems which are said to stand in the way of taxing capital gains. It should be noted in this connection that many years ago the

*Analysis of Draft Law No. 462 and Evaluation of Comments on Income Tax Reform: A Report to the Minister of Finance of the Republic of Colombia, prepared under the direction of William S. Barnes, by J. Nelson Young, Frank E. A. Sander, and William Dobrovir (Cambridge, Mass.: Harvard Law School International Program in Taxation, 1959), pp. I-38–I-51 (mimeographed).

236

Kemmerer Mission [to Colombia] pointed out the theoretical desirability of taxing capital gain, but felt that the administrative problems involved were too complex and required further study. Two recent United Nations missions have also reached the conclusion that capital gains should be taxed.

Generally speaking, capital gains are said to arise upon the sale, exchange, or other disposition of property, such as the sale of an automobile or a house which had been purchased earlier by the taxpayer at a lower cost. One characteristic of many of these so-called capital transactions is that they are irregular, as opposed to the more recurring forms of income, such as salaries, and business income. Of course, there are persons who regularly deal in capital assets, such as real estate salesmen or stock brokers, and the income of such persons is not substantially more irregular than that of many wage earners (such as, for example, prize fighters). Hence, in one sense, the question comes down to whether occasional income should be treated any differently than recurring income. In another sense, the question corresponds somewhat to distinguishing between business and non-business income. However, it is part of the elusive nature of the problem that none of these distinctions are ironclad. There are many borderline cases involving situations which fit almost equally well into one or the other category.

Two practical arguments are generally advanced against the taxation of capital gains as ordinary income. The first relates to the matter of bunching. This results from the fact that under most tax systems, including that of Colombia, income is only taxed when it is realized. Yet, since the amount realized upon the sale of property frequently represents the appreciation in value of the property over a substantial number of years, the gain which is thus realized in one year is really attributable to several years. Without some special provision, the gain will all be taxed in the year of receipt, and because of the progressive nature of the tax structure, the gain will thus be taxable at a higher rate rather than if it had been taxed each year as it accrued. In other words, if, as has been suggested, a man were taxable on his unrealized appreciation of his capital assets at the end of each year, rather than on all the appreciation in the year of sale, then much of the difficulty of taxing capital gains would vanish, although, of course, such a proposal would introduce its own new complexities and problems. And so it is said by advocates of a preferential lower rate for capital gains that unless such a lesser rate is introduced or capital gains are exempted altogether from tax, an inequity will be created, since taxpayers with capital gains will be taxed more severely than those with more regularly occurring income.

There are several answers to this argument. To begin with, the problem of irregular income is a general one, not restricted to the recipients of capital gains. Authors, for example, frequently receive large sums in the year in which they initially publish a book, but then receive little or no income for a long period of years. The problem is simply one aspect of the difficulties inherent in an annual system of accounting. Moreover, the "bunching" often suffered by persons realizing capital gains is frequently offset by the choice which such persons have with respect to the time at which they wish to realize their gains or loss. Thus, if a taxpayer anticipates a gain upon the sale of property, he can often wait to realize it in a year when he has less taxable income or when the general tax rate will be lower, and he will thus have an advantage not enjoyed by other taxpayers. Also, it is worth noting that to the extent that taxation of capital gains pertains to the distinction between capital and labor, Colombia expressly favors the latter. Finally, and most significantly, the proper remedy for this admitted evil is not the complete exemption of capital gains, or their subjection to a lower tax rate, but a more limited cure adapted to the disease—that is, some sort of averaging for capital gains to eliminate significant lumping.

A second principal argument against the taxation of capital gains as ordinary income—one not entirely unrelated to the first argument —is the effect of the tax on the economy. To use securities as an illustration of the argument, if a shareholder holds appreciated stocks and he knows that a significant portion of his gain will be taxed upon sale, so that his reinvested property and the income therefrom will be reduced accordingly, it is said that he will be reluctant to sell. And this, in turn, means an unnatural damper on the free transferability of assets as well as an undesirable inhibition on investors who wish to shift their capital into more venturesome or efficiently operated enterprises. And, by thus drying up the supply of securities it is said that a tax on capital gains creates inflationary tendencies.

The difficulty with this argument is that not enough is known on this complex subject of the economic effects of various tax provisions. Such studies as there are have tended to show that the relationship between a capital gains tax and capital mobility is not a simple and direct one. The inhibiting effect of a capital gains tax in any particular case obviously depends on the effective rate of tax. In Colombia, if the gain were averaged over a period of years and subjected to its relatively low average rate of 20 per cent the deterrent to sale should not be substantial. Moreover, there are many other factors which affect a taxpayer's decision to sell, such as, in the case of stock, the position of the market and the relative merits of the old and new security. Also, a vital question is what the presently unwilling seller would put his money into if he sold. If he simply kept the cash, the effect might well be to put downward pressure on prices. But if he sought to purchase other property, as many people are prone to do, the net effect on the supply-demand curve might be fairly insignificant. Finally, a crucial factor is the related question of what treatment is given to property which is given away during the owner's lifetime or at his death. If, as in the United States, appreciated property given away at a taxpayer's death takes on the higher value which it has at the time of death, without either the decedent or the heir being taxable on the gain accrued up to death, then such a provision is at least as much of an incentive to retain ownership as is any capital gains tax in the first place. For, naturally, if a taxpayer can avoid paying any gain on the property by holding on to it until death, he will very likely do so.

As against these two arguments, there are the immense potential complexities attendant on special treatment of capital gains. This is particularly true where, as in the United States, there is a very substantial gap between the highest ordinary income bracket rate (91 per cent) and the optional maximum capital gains rate (25 per cent). Naturally, under such circumstances, taxpayers will go to immense lengths to channel their transactions into such forms that they will qualify for the favorable capital gains treatment, even though, in substance, they may be no different from other transactions taxable as ordinary income. Concomitantly, pressure will be put on Congress by powerful groups to include their special interests in the favored capital gains category even though there may be little or no logical basis for doing so. The end result is a tax law which is complex, illogical, and inequitable.

POSSIBLE SOLUTIONS

The obvious alternatives are to exempt capital gains from income tax altogether or to tax them in precisely the same way as all other income is taxed. Although there is some authority for either solution, neither of these extremes seems sound. Complete exemption is the solution which, largely for historical reasons, has been adopted by many of the British Commonwealth countries, as well as the United Kingdom. As already pointed out, this solution does not appear to be justified in theory. Moreover, since there must still be a characterization of the types of assets which are not to be taxed at all, most of the administrative difficulties are not avoided. Indeed, if the normal tax rates are fairly high, there is, as already indicated, great pressure on the part of taxpayers towards handling transactions in such a way as to bring them into the exempt class. Conversely, the government will insist on a very restricted application of the favorable treatment. Such counterpressures tend not only to obscure any logical distinction between capital and noncapital transactions but also can have all kinds of other ramifications. To cite merely one example, the capital gains tax has an obvious relation to the corporate tax; for, unless the gain on the sale of stock is taxable, a corporation can accumulate its earnings, and the shareholder can effectively realize his share of these earnings upon sale of his stock without paying any tax thereon. Naturally, this will constitute a ready avoidance of the dividend tax.

The other solution—complete taxation without special treatment of any kind—is arguably inequitable in that it does penalize a person realizing capital gains by subjecting him to an effectively higher tax rate as a result of the bunching of his gain. For this and other reasons, the 1958 special mission to Venezuela (which presently gives no special treatment to capital gains as such) recommended the addition of an optional 3 to 5 year spread-back of the gain.

Such a spread-back provision would seem to be the simplest and fairest solution to the only really special problem presented by capital gains, i.e., the bunching effect. And it is a solution which directly addresses itself to the problem rather than one that demolishes the entire structure in order to meet a specific defect.

There are, of course, some other solutions which have been suggested. For example, it has been pointed out that if all taxpayers were required to inventory their property each year, then the capital gain which had accrued during that year could be readily taxed, thereby avoiding all problems of bunching. This solution, though perhaps theoretically sound, usually has been rejected for practical reasons. However, in Colombia all individuals already are required to value their property at the end of each year for the net wealth tax; thus, much of the practical objection to this approach is eliminated. Nevertheless, it should be recognized that the inventory method of taxing capital gains differs from the more conventional capital gains tax in that it taxes unrealized as well as realized appreciation. Though avoiding the bunching inequity, it may impose another kind of financial hardship on the taxpayers.

The inventory method of taxing capital gains suggests an obvious relationship between the capital gains tax and the net wealth tax. However, there also are important differences between the two taxes, aside from the possible question of realization already alluded to. The net wealth tax imposes a relatively small, recurring tax on a taxpayer's entire capital; the capital gains tax encompasses only the increase in value, but taxes this at a relatively high rate. For this reason, there may be some question of whether or not the net wealth valuations will be precise enough for purposes of the capital gains tax. Finally, it should be noted that, unlike most capital gains taxes, the aggregate net wealth tax, with respect to any one asset, increases with the length for which the asset is held.

Another proposal designed to avoid the difficulties inherent in taxing large accruals of bunched income is the "roll-over." Under this proposal, if a taxpayer sold property, and within a specified period reinvested his proceeds, he would not be taxed and his old cost would carry over to the new property. Only when he ultimately disposed of the property, and wanted to realize the cash, would a tax be imposed. The United States presently utilizes a modified form of this device with respect to the sale and repurchase of a taxpayer's residence. But this proposal, when applied on a broad scale, also has its weaknesses. It would tax a person at the very time when he may be most in need of cash; for, presumably, that is the primary reason why he might decide not to avail himself of the law's benefits through reinvestment of his proceeds. And it only postpones rather than solves the basic difficulty.

Finally, it has been suggested that the tax law should contain a general averaging provision, allowing all taxpayers whose income is fluctuating to average his income over a period of years. Such a proposal, of course, would solve not only the capital gains problem but also the problem of other taxpayers, such as authors, etc., who have irregular and fluctuating incomes. However, here again, there is a gap between theoretical desirability and practical feasibility.

In addition to complete exemption or full taxation, various countries the world over have adopted differing solutions to the capital gains problem. In Sweden, for example, a varying proportion of the gain is recognized, depending upon the time for which the property has been held. Thus, if real property is held for more than 10 years or personal property for more than 5 years, the gain is not taxed at all. If, on the other hand, real estate has been held less than 7 years or personal property has been held less than 2 years, the gain is fully taxable. Between these extremes a sliding scale is established. The entire treatment, of course, applies only to property not held in the ordinary course of business.

The United States originally had a somewhat similar system but now recognizes only two kinds of gains—those where the property was held for less than 6 months and those where it was held for more than 6 months. The former receive no special treatment; the latter receive very favorable treatment. Again, in theory, this treatment applies only to property not held in the ordinary course of business, but, as pointed out above, in view of the great disparity between the ordinary income and the capital gains rates, the preferential capital gains treatment has been illogically and inequitably extended to many other kinds of transactions. Germany, also, has a somewhat similar system in that gains on business property are fully taxable and gains on nonbusiness property are either completely exempt or fully taxable depending upon whether the holding period is greater or less than two years in the case of real estate and three months in the case of personal property.

As pointed out before, a separate but necessarily related problem is the treatment which will be given to gifts or bequests of capital assets. There are three possibilities: a carry-over to the donee of the donor's cost, with the donee being taxed on the gain which accrued while the donor held the property at the time the donee ultimately sells it; constructive realization of the accrued gain at the time of gift or bequest; forgiveness of the gain accrued while the donor held the property, with the donee consequently taking on as cost the value of the property at the time he receives it. The second solution is perhaps the most logical; however, it may impose a severe financial hardship on the donee who no longer has the property. And in the case of a decedent, it can impose an even greater hardship since this tax will come on top of the estate tax, unless some sort of credit is allowed. The first solution would appear to be a ready alternative; however, it may involve serious administrative problems in that if the gift is from a decedent, the heir may have considerable difficulty in discovering the original cost. Perhaps, for these reasons, some countries, for example the United States, have resorted to the third alternative—at least in the case of testamentary as opposed to *inter vivos* gifts. However, such a solution is a rather illogical bonus to the taxpayer, and, as pointed out above, entails its own difficulties in creating a damper on the sale of property.

Another separate problem which must be faced up to is the treatment of capital losses. If capital gains are to be given any kind of favored treatment, the question arises whether losses should be similarly treated. In addition, if losses exceed gains in any particular year, the additional question arises whether such losses will be deductible against ordinary income or whether they can only be deducted against past or future capital gains. From the point of view of fairness, the more gains are treated like ordinary income, the more losses should be allowed to be taken against ordinary income. Even if gains are given some preferential treatment to compensate for bunching, net losses should probably be fully allowable if this is fiscally feasible. The United States has an intermediary solution in generally allowing capital losses to be taken only against capital gains. However, the excess of losses, to the extent there are any, may be taken against ordinary income up to $1,000 per taxpayer per year. Any remainder must be carried forward to the next five years.

CONCLUSIONS

The immediate question is whether the treatment of capital gains in Article 23 of the draft law is proper. There has been objection to the fact that the draft recognizes the taxability of capital gains, but postpones their taxability until such time as a special law governing the manner of their taxation is enacted. Unless capital gains are to be either completely exempted from tax or taxed precisely like all other income—and we have indicated above our opposition to these extremes—there is sound reason for recognizing now the basic principle that capital gains should be taxed but deferring the actual imposition of tax until such time as the manner of imposing the tax has been given appropriate study and specific legislation has been drafted.

Capital assets are defined in Article 23 essentially as follows: all property, real or personal, other than property which a person normally buys or acquires, extracts, grows, produces or transforms and sells, exchanges, contributes or alienates by any means in the ordinary course of a business, commercial activity or industry. This definition is adequate as far as it goes. However, several points should be clarified. A taxpayer often has property which he does not normally sell or deal in, but which is a part of his business assets, such as an automobile or a machine. It should be made clear that such assets—and indeed all depreciable assets—are not capital assets, and hence the gain on their sale is taxable as ordinary income. Such a definition would correspond to Article 35 (3) of the draft, which requires a taxpayer who sells a depreciable asset to include in his income the depreciation taken by him on such asset. The treatment of some common items such as patents, copyrights and accounts receivable also might be specified. Probably such items should be excluded from the capital asset concept, so that in essence the only capital assets would be personal property and real estate not related to the taxpayer's business. Consideration might also be given to a simple affirmative definition of capital assets (such as "all securities and real estate not related to the taxpayer's business") in lieu of the present negative definition. Finally, it should be made clear whether the capital gains tax has any application to entities (see Articles 27 and 28). Presumably if the definition is narrow enough, it would not.

A decision will have to be made eventually concerning the manner of taxing capital gains. We would suggest that at least on a trial basis, such gains be taxed at ordinary income rates, but that taxpayers have the choice with respect to such assets to spread back the gain realized on a sale over the years during which the asset was held. A maximum spread-back of three years might be established for administrative simplicity. It has been shown that such a period would substantially eliminate most bunching. Of course, the prior year's returns would not be reopened; the taxpayer would merely compute his tax for the years affected to determine the additional tax for each year. His current tax would then be the sum of all these additional taxes, unless he would have a lesser tax by taking the entire gain into the current year's income.

As an alternative to the spread-back, consideration might be given to granting the taxpayer an option with respect to his capital assets to include his unrealized gain in income each year. The cost of the asset would then be adjusted accordingly, and all problems of bunching would be avoided. At the same time, this would create an incentive for the taxpayer to report his full gain each year, and the capital gains tax might thus be turned into a useful enforcement aid to the net wealth tax.

If it were felt desirable to have a special tax rate for capital gains, an optional flat rate might be established for all capital assets held more than one or two years in lieu of the averaging provision just mentioned. In order to avoid excessive pressure on the capital asset concept, such a rate should be approximately at the midpoint of the ordinary rate table (20 per cent in Colombia). Under this type of provision, gain on the sale of assets held less than the one or two year period would result in ordinary income. With respect to gain on the sale of assets held longer than the requisite period, the taxpayer could either report the gain as ordinary income or could pay a flat tax of 20 per cent.

As indicated above, the law which will ultimately implement Article 23 of the present draft will have to make specific provision for such questions as the treatment for capital gains tax purposes of transfers by gift or bequest and capital losses. Concerning the former, a carryover of the cost from donor to donee with respect to both *inter vivos* and testamentary gifts would appear to be best. As regards the deductibility of losses, if income is to be fully taxable as ordinary income, net losses should be fully deductible.

As pointed out initially, the whole subject of capital gains taxation is a highly complex one. What is a satisfactory solution in one country may not be appropriate elsewhere. It is therefore essential to proceed tentatively and keep the entire problem under continuous study, so as to be alert for developing inequities, undesirable economic consequences or administratively unworkable provisions. Only in this way can a sound and constructive tax law be developed.

15

What Happens When Exemptions End: Retrospect and Prospect in Puerto Rico

by Milton C. Taylor*

THERE is a consensus that most of the new industrial firms which have been established in Puerto Rico by mainland United States investors have been attracted more by tax exemption than by any other inducement. Effectiveness of this fiscal device is attributable to the fact that each eligible firm under the Puerto Rican statute may obtain immunity from virtually all major United States and Puerto Rican taxes for as much as 10 years. The time is now approaching, however, when some of the early grants of tax exemption will expire. This development creates the issue of whether an appreciable number of firms will leave Puerto Rico upon the expiration of their tax exemption grants. Related to this problem is whether the Commonwealth government will extend exemption to grantees beyond the present terminal dates of their grants in order to forestall the possible movement of firms away from the island.

It is the contention of this paper that Puerto Rico will not lose an appreciable number of firms upon the expiration of their grants, and that the government will not amend the tax exemption statute in order to provide more than 10 years of exemption. Before stating the reasons justifying these convictions, however, it is first desirable to review some of the circumstances which formed the backdrop for the present industrial development on the island and to consider the particular role that has been played by tax exemption.[1]

THE BACKGROUND OF TAX EXEMPTION

Economic development is a tenuous thing, so impalpable that the exact causes are not easy to determine. Be that as it may, there is little

*Taxation and Operations Abroad (Princeton: Tax Institute, Inc., 1960), pp. 170–86; also Milton C. Taylor, "What Happens When Exemptions End: Retrospect and Prospect in Puerto Rico," Tax Policy, XXVI (November–December, 1959), Nos. 11–12. Reprinted here with the kind permission of the publisher.

question that development in Puerto Rico has been assisted by some unique circumstances. Unique, first of all, is Puerto Rico's political relationship with the United States, which gives the island self-determination in domestic affairs but makes the Commonwealth subject to United States jurisdiction and eligible for many federal services. Unusual, too, is the political stability, the geographical location at the crossroads between North and South America, and the general similarity of commercial laws and court procedures between Puerto Rico and the mainland United States. Principal among the economic advantages is that Puerto Rico is not subject to the internal revenue laws of the United States and there is an absence of any barriers to the free movement of people, goods, and money between the island and the mainland United States. There is also an abundant labor supply which can be employed at approximately one-half corresponding wage levels on the continent. Moreover, the productivity of Puerto Rican workers compares favorably with mainland standards except in areas requiring professional skills and executive ability.

At the same time, many of the conventional risks and liabilities of investing in a foreign country are absent. There are no import restrictions or exchange controls, and no regulations with respect to the repatriation of earnings. There is no more fear of expropriation than there would be in any of the 50 states of the Union. Subversive activities or threats of revolution are nonexistent. Government operations are unusually efficient and progressive, with public administrators having an exceptional degree of economic literacy and unqualified sympathy with the conception of free enterprise held by United States businessmen. It is quite unlikely that the combination of all of these circumstances could be duplicated in any other underdeveloped or partly developed area in the world.[2]

While the foregoing circumstances set the stage for industrialization, it was tax exemption, more than any other inducement, which provided the thrust forward. And again it was a unique combination of circumstances which made this device effective. Virtually complete tax avoidance of all major taxes was possible for both mainland and Puerto Rican firms because of an interaction of three conditions: (1) Puerto Rican individuals and firms were not subject to federal excises and to income taxes on income from sources *within* Puerto Rico; (2) the Puerto Rican exemption statute provided exclusion from all major taxes on the business level, as well as exemption of distributed corporate earnings from the individual income tax; and (3) mainland investors could avail themselves of several relief provisions of the Internal Revenue Code.[3] As a result of these circumstances, Puerto Rico became the only area of the world where it was possible to obtain a virtually complete tax holiday from both United

States and Puerto Rican taxes and yet remain within the tariff area of the mainland United States.

There is little doubt that tax exemption was strategic in encouraging most of the new firms to extend their operations to Puerto Rico. Certainly, there is no question that the officials responsible for the administration of the industrial development program are convinced that tax exemption has been the most important inducement that Puerto Rico has been able to offer mainland business.[4] This conviction is supported by a survey of 44 new operating tax-exempt firms in which it was found that the new investors themselves consider tax exemption to be the most important factor in selecting the island as a location for investment.[5] Without tax exemption, Puerto Rico possibly would have obtained only about one-quarter of the present number of new firms, and these investors probably would have been the type which are excessively labor-oriented.

The anecdote is related in Puerto Rico that Governor Muñoz Marín was once asked during the earlier days of the industrial development program for his conception of the type of manufacturing firm which was most needed by the island. He replied, it is reported, that there was no such thing as a bad factory. The Governor may have been misquoted, but his answer, nevertheless, reflects the attitude of the public administrators responsible for the development program during its earlier years. There was a tendency to construe any applicant as being worthy of assistance, even though some of the firms had appearances of being impermanent, unstable, and excessively labor-oriented. In other words, Puerto Rico threw off the yoke of *laissez faire* and threw it off with a vengeance.

This attitude of uninhibited economic determinism also manifested itself with respect to tax exemption. Because tax exemption was so effective, there was a tendency to look on the device as an unqualified blessing. It was publicized more than any other inducement with catchwords and phrases like the "taxpayers' holiday." Because investors reacted so spontaneously and with such enthusiasm, a feeling was generated on the island that exemption was the *sine qua non* which would guarantee an industrial future. Also, as the developmental functions of government rose in ascendancy, there was a tendency for regulatory responsibilities to be overshadowed. In particular, there was a tendency to construe the necessary regulation and enforcement of grantees of tax exemption as unduly restrictive.[6]

THE CHANGING GOVERNMENTAL ATTITUDE
TOWARD EXEMPTION

About five or six years ago the success of the industrialization program was assured. Any doubts as to its long-run viability were removed both by the number of new firms and by the promotion of more heavily capitalized factories. The early years of the industrial development program resulted in the development of a few dozen new firms each year, most of which represented a minimum investment and appeared to be frankly attracted by low-cost labor and tax avoidance. By 1954, however, newly established firms reached the level of about 100 each year, and they included firms with larger investments such as oil refineries and large electrical, textile, and cigar manufacturers.

Success of the industrialization program also brought with it a change in the government's outlook toward development. Now that Puerto Rico was "over the hump," there was less desperation to obtain one more new firm. Applicants for assistance were reviewed with respect to their long-run contribution to the economy, and some were even denied assistance. More attention was given to providing the necessary foundation for development, or to reducing the cost of non-labor inputs, without which profits could not be realized and tax exemption would be an empty gesture. This change in the industrialization program was also manifested in a changing outlook with respect to tax exemption. It is precisely because tax exemption is viewed in a somewhat different light on the island today that it is considered unlikely that the government will extend tax exemption grants beyond their present 10-year limits unless there is unusual pressure to do so.[7]

It became apparent, first, that there were certain burdens or indirect costs involved in the use of tax exemption. Conspicuous among these unseen costs was that exemption in various ways lacked selectivity, or the provision of an inducement in such a way that a minimum of resources was expended in order to attain a desired objective. Remission of all taxes for periods up to 11 years was often more assistance than was needed;[8] exemption of existing domestic firms in particular designated industries resulted in little new investment; certain exceptionally profitable labor-intensive firms received undue subsidization; while with some firms there was little relationship between the amount of tax relief received and the amount of resulting investment and employment.

True, it can be argued that Puerto Rico lost nothing even if the tax exemption program was unduly generous because most of the firms would not have invested on the island without tax exemption. Or again, it can be argued that the industrial development program had broadened other tax bases so that tax collections continued to rise even in the face of tax exemption. This contention is apparently true, for income tax collections are expected to total $60 million during the present fiscal year as compared to $49 million in fiscal year 1958. Despite these arguments, however, undue liberality of the exemption program became an issue because of a conflict with another prerequisite for development. Granting more exemption than was necessary meant that governmental revenues were not being maximized during a period of time in which there were very urgent and unsatisfied demands for direct developmental expenditures. In this sense, tax exemption could not be viewed as a costless subsidy. Not unexpectedly, the Secretary of the Treasury, who was charged with raising higher revenues for direct developmental expenditures, was conspicuous among those who saw in tax exemption a tendency to ignore the importance of tax revenues.

It also became evident (at least to some public administrators on the island) that a philosophically rational and equitable system of taxing business and individuals could not coexist in complete harmony under circumstances in which relatively large segments of important tax bases were excluded from taxation. Specifically, it became apparent that there was a direct conflict between the tax policy goals of providing incentives for private economic activity and the allocation of the tax load in a fair and equitable manner. This conclusion is based on the following logic: The basic requirement for a good tax system in Puerto Rico is a gradual secular de-emphasis of taxes based on consumption and indirect taxes on business and a commensurate increase in emphasis on direct taxes, principally the individual and corporate income taxes and the real property tax. Tax exemption, however, weakens the direct tax system, which in turn prevents a shift in emphasis from indirect to direct taxes.

Another burden or indirect cost was the administration of the tax exemption program. In the earlier days of exemption, it was assumed mistakenly that there would be no particular problems with compliance and enforcement when businessmen were exempt from the payment of taxes. In time it became apparent, however, that a basic characteristic of any exemption is the opportunity it provides businessmen to construe taxable operations as exempt. These illegal extensions of the scope of exemption occurred in two areas: extending the scope of a manufacturing exemption to include retail sales, and the use of tax exemption in Puerto Rico to evade tax liabilities in other political jurisdictions by illegal profit-shifting.

Another liability of the tax exemption program was the restiveness which it created among other taxpaying groups. Since the time that the tax exemption program was adopted in Puerto Rico, there has been a continuous procession of proposals and bills to extend tax exemption to other groups. This development has been encouraged by some government administrators who believe that exemption can work the same wonders in other areas as it has in the industrial sphere. Fortunately, the government for the most part has resisted this spread of exemption in order to maintain tax revenues, but there is little doubt that the taxpaying morale of some groups has been affected adversely because they have not become beneficiaries of tax relief.

Evidence that the government has become increasingly aware of these burdens and indirect costs of tax exemption is the legislative and administrative action which has been taken during recent years. A new exemption act became effective in 1954 which reduced some of the liberality of the previous statute.[9] While each new eligible firm was granted 10 years of exemption from the income tax and municipal license fees, dividends were given exemption from the individual income tax for only 7 years,[10] and real property, machinery, and equipment were given exemption from the property tax for periods of from 5 to 10 years depending on the amount of investment. Both of these dividend and property tax exemptions were more restrictive than under the earlier statute.

Compliance and enforcement of tax exemption grants was strengthened by the establishment of an enforcement unit in the Department of the Treasury in 1954. Although the establishment of this unit was prompted by a few conspicuous instances of evasion, the creation of a new regulatory agency was also indicative of an awareness on the part of the government that there were potential dangers involved in unrestricted private capital. With the establishment of the new enforcement unit, tax-exempt firms were audited, and some firms were prosecuted for illegal extensions of their grants.

Still another indication of Puerto Rico's awareness of the shortcomings of tax exemption is the interest which has been given to the evolution of a fair and equitable tax system for the long run, which would at the same time provide maximum incentives for economic development. Comprehensive research studies have been initiated and consulting advice has been obtained. Each report has concluded that there is a need for a greater degree of tax fairness and that tax exemption frustrates the attainment of this objective. Each report has also advised that the achievement of a desirable tax system requires the eventual abandonment of tax exemption.

In summary, as the industrialization program has emerged from a struggling and uncertain adolescence to maturity, there has also been a shift in the Commonwealth government's attitude towards tax exemption. That is not to say that the government has become disenchanted with the device. On the contrary, there is a realization, and it is well founded, that tax exemption remains strategic in order to continue building the base for a sound economy. At the same time, there is a pronounced tendency on the island at the present time to weigh the assets and liabilities of tax exemption and conclude that it is a short-run price to be paid for a more important long-run gain. There is a realization on the island that tax exemption is a means to an end in order to achieve industrialization, but industrialization, on the other hand, should not be based on relief from taxation.

This reaction on the part of the government is to be expected. Puerto Rico has experienced 10 years of very accelerated development. The advantages of this economic growth are obvious and are not to be questioned, but development has been accompanied by certain social costs in the form of unusually high profits and the exploitation of labor.[11] As these social costs have become evident, there has been a natural counteraction in terms of removing some of the excrescences of development. The present challenge facing Puerto Rico is to remove these excrescences without at the same time slowing down the rate of economic progress.

REACTION ON THE PART OF INVESTORS

Up to this point, the thesis has been developed that there are several reasons for believing that the Puerto Rican government is disinclined at the present time to extend the terms of tax exemption grants. But even if the validity of this thesis is accepted, is it possible that Puerto Rico will lose so many firms at the expiration of their tax exemption grants that the government will be forced to extend tax relief in order to stave off an exodus of firms? Several reasons may be advanced in support of the belief that relatively few firms will leave the island when their present grants terminate.

At the expiration of tax exemption grants, what else is Puerto Rico able to offer mainland investors? One set of advantages is an absence of those conventional "nonbusiness" risks which are faced by United States businessmen contemplating foreign investment. The more important of these hazards are expropriation, problems involved in the repatriation of profits, the possibility of military action, trade barriers, and discriminatory taxation practices. Although these risks cannot be quantified, their importance is such that they account in the aggregate for the general reluctance on the part of American businessmen to invest in foreign countries. Therefore, the fact that these risks of investment are not existent in Puerto Rico (or at least not to a greater degree than on the mainland) gives the island an immediate competitive advantage to obtain and to hold United States investment, for expected and realized Puerto Rican profits do not have to be discounted by a sizable risk factor.

In addition to an absence of these conventional liabilities of foreign investment, there are several positive advantages for investors in Puerto Rico. Some of these are characteristic of partly developed economies but others are unique. Low-cost labor is typical of partly developed areas but Puerto Rico has the distinctly unique competitive advantages of corporate tax rates which are relatively low; legal institutions which are similar to those on the mainland United States; a location which is strategic for export trade to the adjacent areas of Latin America; and inclusion within the tariff area of the United States. Puerto Rico has also supplemented these inducements with several cost-reducing aids and services. Low-cost credit is available through the Government Development Bank and the Puerto Rico Industrial Development Company. Factories are made available under liberal terms for purchase, lease, or lease with option to buy. Technical services available include the installation of machinery and equipment and assistance with management-labor relations and the control of quality.

On the debit side, there are certain obstacles to investment in Puerto Rico which are characteristic of most underdeveloped areas. These result primarily from narrow markets, lack of raw materials and supplies for manufacturing, scarcity of skilled labor, and lack of social overhead capital. But even these deterrents to profitable investment have been reduced during the past 10 years of accelerated economic development. The overcoming of these obstacles to industrialization has run the gamut of higher domestic living standards, increased productivity of labor, improvement in utilities and transportation, and more certain and intelligent public administration. As these nontax deterrents have been improved, it follows that there has been a commensurate reduction in the importance of tax incentives for investors.

Special mention should be made of the advantage of low-cost labor. Tax exemption may be the most efficacious and spectacular inducement, but it is low-cost labor which primarily determines the relative profitability of Puerto Rican as compared to mainland operations. This was the conclusion arrived at from research undertaken during 1952 and 1953. It was found at this time that the tax-exempt firms would have been as well off bearing double the prevailing income tax burden in Puerto Rico as incurring a 50 per cent increase in labor costs.[12] Since this period of time, labor costs have risen in Puerto Rico, but they have also risen on the mainland United States. The net effect is that Puerto Rico's relative labor cost advantage with the mainland has been substantially maintained, although absolute wage levels in both areas have risen. Moreover, there is a continuous supply of unskilled and semiskilled labor available in Puerto Rico, while periodically there are tight labor markets on the mainland.

At the same time, while low-cost labor remains an important attraction for many firms, there is also a trend for an increasing number of factories to be more heavily capitalized. From 1953 to 1957, investment per worker in factories established under the industrialization program rose from $4,600 to $8,300. Typical of the newer firms are Textron Inc., Sylvania Electric Products, United States Rubber, St.

Regis Paper, Mead Corporation, Consolidated Cigar, and two large oil refineries. Another wave of investment in sight for the future is petro-chemicals, with still higher investment levels. It appears unrealistic to assume that firms of this type have invested in Puerto Rico with the intention of leaving the island in 10 years at the expiration of their tax exemption grants.

Evidence that the net advantages derived from investing in Puerto are very substantial is found in the over-all profitable experiences of the tax-exempt firms. Not unexpectedly, it is characteristic of most firms to experience losses during the first few years of operations. This is illustrated by statistics for calendar year 1957, which show that there were 376 profitable and 142 unprofitable firms out of the total number of 518 exempt firms. But losses are small and transitory. Total profits reported for the group of 376 profitable businesses in 1957 were $48,183,000, while losses were only $3,484,000.[13] Moreover, the net return on equity for the profitable firms was at least double the same return on the mainland. For example, the ratio of net profit to equity for firms with assets below $250,000 was 9 per cent on the mainland United States and 31 per cent in Puerto Rico, while for firms with assets of $250,000 to $999,000 the net return was 16 per cent on the mainland and 32 per cent in Puerto Rico.

Finally, even if these firms become taxable, a substantial tax-saving advantage would exist on the island for these businesses as compared to the tax burdens which would be borne on similar mainland operations. This tax advantage arises from a combination of two circumstances: corporate tax rates in the Commonwealth are lower than the dual burden of state and federal mainland taxes; and profits derived from carrying on a trade or a business in a United States possession and not received within the United States are exempt from federal taxes.

This tax incentive is substantial because Puerto Rican corporate tax rates vary from an effective rate of 21 per cent to 36.75 per cent depending on the amount of net income.[14] Approximately 75 per cent of the tax-exempt firms presently fall within net income classes which would make them taxable at an effective rate of not more than 25 per cent, and about 67 per cent would not be taxable at more than 23 per cent. Although there is a plethora of considerations involved in any comparison for an individual firm between tax liabilities on the mainland and in Puerto Rico, it is possible to say that the corporate tax burden in Puerto Rico for most firms would be approximately one-half to two-thirds the similar burden on the mainland provided that the greater proportion of earnings is retained in Puerto Rico.[15]

The objection may be made that retained earnings must be paid out eventually, and then Puerto Rican profits will be subject to about the same rate of taxation as mainland earnings. Experience shows, however, that substantial repatriation of earnings is not likely to be practiced by most firms. It is a general characteristic of foreign subsidiaries of United States corporations to retain indefinitely the larger part of their profits for expansion and investment purposes outside of the United States. This tendency has also been evident in Puerto Rico, for it is estimated that approximately 80 per cent of total corporate earnings of tax-exempt firms has been retained on the island. It may be argued that these earnings are being retained in order to repatriate them eventually at capital gains rates through a liquidation or sale of the subsidiary. As long as profitable opportunities to invest continue to exist in Puerto Rico, however, there would appear to be a presumption established against the majority of firms either remitting most of their earnings or returning to the mainland, where in either case their tax liabilities would be increased.

But even if particular firms are compelled to remit earnings currently which are excessive for Puerto Rican investment, and these earnings become taxable at a rate of 52 per cent on the mainland, this eventuality still would not prove the undesirability of continuing their Puerto Rican operations. As long as the rate of return on invested capital remains higher in the Commonwealth than on the mainland, which has been the case in general during the past 10 years, firms are obviously better off operating in Puerto Rico and paying a 52 per cent tax on remitted dividends than in returning to the mainland to pay a 52 per cent tax on lower earnings. Moreover, because of the mechanics of the United States credit for taxes paid to other jurisdictions on income originating abroad, income from sources in Puerto Rico remitted to the United States is, in some cases, taxed at effective rates considerably below 52 per cent.

Conclusion

Evidence has been presented which supports the position that the government of Puerto Rico is not disposed to extend tax exemption privileges to present grantees unless faced with considerable pressure to do so. On the other hand, this pressure seems unlikely to arise, because it appears that most investors will be able to realize attractive profits even if operating under a taxable status. In other words, most of the new firms have been attracted to Puerto Rico by tax exemption, but they are not dependent on tax differentials to keep their operations more profitable than on the mainland.

That is not to say, however, that the transition period when tax exemption grants expire in considerable volume will not present some problems. As wage rates rise (absolutely if not relatively with the mainland), labor-oriented firms may find that they are in a competitive disadvantage with lower wage areas like Japan and the Philippines. The loss of tax exemption may be the marginal inducement which may cause these firms to leave Puerto Rico. But this development is a necessary concomitant of industrial progress. Just as there was an inexorable shift of investment from the mainland United States to Puerto Rico in order, in part, to exploit low-cost labor, it is inevitable that there will be the same movement away from Puerto Rico as per capita incomes and wage rates rise. Also, the loss of these less profitable firms involves the least sacrifice.

More serious would be the threatened closing of a few particularly valuable firms, which could arise from any number of unique reasons. But even this problem could be overcome. Tax exemption is not the only inducement which the Economic Development Administration may make available to industrial firms. There is a precedent for using direct subsidies rather extensively in order to attract "core" industries. These direct subsidies have taken the form of a year's free rent, the payment of either the purchase price or the transportation cost of machinery, and the underwriting of supervisory salaries. If Puerto Rico were faced with the loss of a few particularly strategic firms, direct subsidies could be used in order to retain such firms on the island without resorting to a general extension of tax exemption.

There is one final reason why industrial development is likely to continue even if tax exemption grants are not extended. Perhaps the most important lesson to be learned from the Puerto Rican industrialization program is that economic development comes to those who are capable of exerting the right effort rather than to those with the right contrivance. Only 10 years ago, most observers assessed Puerto Rico's future with varying degrees of pessimism. Their fatal mistake was to underestimate the intangibles—the capacity of the Puerto Rican people to resolve their own problems through imagination, vigor, and intelligence. Puerto Rico has learned to meet fortune three-fourths of the way. Considering the obstacles that have been overcome in the past, and the flexibility and ingenuity which have been demonstrated up to the present time, it seems unrealistic to assume that continuing economic advances must depend only on the extension of tax exemption grants.

NOTES TO SELECTION 15

[1]It should be observed at the outset that interpreting the likely course of events in Puerto Rico must, of necessity, be in the realm of conjecture, and should be interpreted in that light. No finite data can be presented to prove with certainty what will happen when tax exemption grants expire. All that can be done is to postulate certain premises and follow these to their logical conclusions. Moreover, in following this procedure, all interpretations are entirely personal and are not meant to reflect in any way the policy conclusions of other individuals or of governmental agencies.

[2]For an account of the earlier years of the industrialization program, see Harvey S. Perloff, *Puerto Rico's Economic Future—A Study in Planned Development*

(Chicago: University of Chicago Press, 1950). For a review of later periods, see Milton C. Taylor, "Puerto Rico: Recovery or Relapse?" *The American Journal of Economics and Sociology,* XIV (April, 1955), 225–39; and William H. Stead, *Fomento—The Economic Development of Puerto Rico* (Washington: National Planning Association, 1958).

[3]The definitive article on these tax-saving aspects of the exemption program is by Harry J. Rudick and George S. Allan, "Tax Aspects of Operations Under the Puerto Rican Exemption Program," *Tax Law Review,* VII (May, 1952), 403–37.

[4]See the article by Teodoro Moscoso, the Administrator of the Economic Development Administration, "Industrial Development in Puerto Rico," *The Annals of the American Academy of Political and Social Sciences,* CCLXXXV (January, 1953), 68–69.

[5]Milton C. Taylor, "Tax Exemption as Compared to Other Factors in Operating and Locating New Industrial Firms in Puerto Rico," *Social and Economic Studies,* IV (June, 1955), 121–32.

[6]These conclusions are derived from research undertaken while the author served as a consultant to the Secretary of the Treasury of Puerto Rico during 1952 and 1953. Empirical evidence supporting the interpretations may be obtained from *Industrial Tax-Exemption in Puerto Rico* (Madison: University of Wisconsin Press, 1957). This research was summarized in an article by the same title appearing in the *National Tax Journal,* VII (December, 1954), 359–71.

[7]Some of these conclusions and others which follow are supported by the trend of legislative and administrative action, and documentation will be offered whenever possible. Other observations are based on personal impressions of the ways in which the Puerto Rican government is reacting to its problems. These impressions were formed as a result of consulting activities with the Secretary of the Treasury of Puerto Rico during 1957 and 1958.

[8]Under Act 184 of 1948, grantees were given full exemption until 1959 followed by three years of partial exemption. While this made it possible for early grantees to obtain more than 10 years of exemption, it also meant that later grantees would receive shorter periods of exemption as their applications were processed closer to the terminal date of the exemption statute.

[9]Act No. 105, approved December 15, 1953.

[10]The Act provides that dividends paid out of the earnings of an exempt operation during its first 7 years of operations may be distributed free of taxes to resident individuals and corporations, but such distributions may be made within the period of 15 years counted from the commencement of operations of the exempt business.

[11]The caveat should be made that the term "exploitation of labor" is being used in a relative and not absolute sense. For example, in the 30 months following January, 1956, industrial hourly wages rose by more than 40 per cent.

[12]*Industrial Tax-Exemption in Puerto Rico,* p. 117.

[13]These statistics for 1957 may be compared to total profits of $31.6 million in 1955 and $39.4 million in 1956, and total losses of $2.5 million in 1955 and $3.3 million in 1956.

[14]Sample effective rates of the tax are: 24.9 per cent on net income of $100,000; 31.5 per cent on net income of $250,000; 34.1 per cent on net income of $500,000; and 35.4 per cent on net income of $1,000,000.

[15]Another feature of the Puerto Rican law is flexible depreciation which permits eligible firms in construction, manufacturing, and agricultural industries to recover their investment in all depreciable property acquired after December 31, 1954, at whatever annual rate of depreciation they wish.

Part IV

Sales and Expenditure Taxes

ALTHOUGH taxes on income receive most of the attention in the literature, taxes on consumption account for most of the revenue. The first article in this section, again by Richard Goode, while paying particular attention to capital formation, ably discusses a number of the issues relevant in developing countries to the choice, if any, among consumption taxes. An extract from the recent book by a young Indian economist, Raja Chelliah, discusses some of the same issues in the context of India.

In the field of consumption taxation, Nicholas Kaldor has caused a considerable stir in recent years with his fervent advocacy of a progressive tax on personal expenditures. The extract from his report to the Government of India outlines his comprehensive scheme for personal taxation, followed by a detailed description of his expenditure tax proposal. The Indian Government, did in fact, introduce a version of the expenditure tax in 1957, only to remove it in 1962. As the following selection reveals, Kaldor was not pleased with the form his idea had taken by the time it emerged from the legislative process. He nevertheless recommended substantially the same system for Ceylon, which also enacted his proposals in modified form and subsequently retracted most of them. These experiences were not conclusive, however, and there is little doubt that more will be heard of the expenditure tax in the future.*

The final item in this section is one of the few selections in the present volume not dealing for the most part explicitly with the problems of developing countries. It is included because it so neatly portrays the major theoretical and technical issues to be considered in selecting the appropriate form of a general sales tax, when one is to be levied.

*The Times of India, March 1, 1964, pp. 5–7, states that the 1964–65 general budget, presented to the Lok Sabha (parliament) by Finance Minister Mr. T. T. Krishnamachari, proposes the reintroduction of the expenditure tax in India at rates lower than previously and with fewer and lower exemptions.

16

Taxation of Savings and Consumption in Underdeveloped Countries

by Richard Goode*

AN INCREASE in the saving-investment rate is one of the conditions of economic progress in the less developed countries. Most of these countries have accepted the goal of a mixed economy and are seeking means of increasing saving and capital formation in both the public and private sectors. Even in a country which assigns to the state the major share of investment, private saving may be an important source of finance for public investment. The U.S.S.R., for example, has not been oblivious of the advantages of promoting private saving and the sale of government bonds.

Tax revenues are the principal source of government saving, and taxation influences private saving because it affects incentives and capacity to save. Owing to the heavy responsibilities that governments are assuming, not only for capital formation, but also for the provision of current services, the underdeveloped countries cannot promote saving merely by maintaining low taxes. Most underdeveloped countries need to raise more revenue, many of them, much more. Tax policy has the delicate responsibility of obtaining large amounts of revenue without unduly impairing private saving or, if feasible, by means that will stimulate private saving.

This paper considers the question whether the underdeveloped countries can devise and administer tax systems that will raise adequate amounts of revenue in socially and politically acceptable ways and at the same time allow or encourage desired increases in private saving. The paper examines some of the economic issues and problems of tax design that are met in efforts to draw up such a revenue system.

*National Tax Journal, XIV (December, 1961), 305–21. The author is a member of the staff of the Brookings Institution, Washington, D.C. Opinions and interpretations are his own and do not necessarily reflect the views of officers or other staff members of the Brookings Institution. The article is reprinted here with the kind permission of the publisher.

By concentrating on taxation I do not intend to imply that it is the most important influence on private saving or that variations of the tax system are the most efficient means of modifying the saving-income ratio. But, even if other policies are more significant, it does not follow that taxes exert only a trivial influence on saving.

ALTERNATIVE APPROACHES AND THEIR RATIONALE

Programs for fostering private saving by means of the tax system range from broad prescriptions regarding the distribution of the tax load through detailed schemes of tax incentives and penalties. A general admonition that is heard from time to time is that progressive taxes should be minimized or wholly avoided in underdeveloped countries. A positive recommendation, which is usually thought to be practically identical with this advice although theoretically distinguishable, is that major reliance be placed on indirect taxes. Lately there has been considerable discussion of proposals for partial or complete exemption of saving under the income tax and for the imposition of a direct tax on personal consumption expenditures.

These programs are intended to concentrate taxation on consumption and to leave private saving either free of taxation or subject to lower rates of tax. It is usually taken for granted that this policy will promote private saving, but the basis of the belief is not obvious and is worthy of attention. There is no ground for supposing that even full tax immunity of saved income would eliminate the influence of taxation on the amount saved. Savers would make their decisions in the light of their position after allowance for consumption taxes and other taxes, and it would be surprising if these taxes did not affect both saving and consumption. Preferential taxation of saving by reliance on consumption taxes or other means may encourage saving for two reasons. First, the possible reward for saving will be higher than under a different tax system. Second, the capacity to save will be greater in the sense that potential savers will have more resources at their disposal.

Progressive taxation of income will cut more deeply into the return on saving than will proportional or regressive taxation, if interest and profits receipts are a rising fraction of income as size of income increases. This is true in capitalistic countries but is less clearly so in preindustrial societies, where landowners are often the richest members of the community.

The terms of exchange between present and future consumption are more favorable to the latter under a system of consumption taxation than under a general income tax, and in this sense the reward for saving is greater under a consumption tax. Consider the alternatives open to a person subject to a 50 per cent income tax or a 100 per cent consumption tax. If in year 1 he receives 100 of income he will be liable for 50 of tax under the income tax. He can either consume the remaining 50 immediately or save and invest it and, at a market rate of interest of 5 per cent, realize a net return of 1.25 in one year (2.50 gross return minus 1.25 of income tax). Thus, by giving up 50 of present consumption he can enjoy 51.25 of consumption one year later. Under the consumption tax he can save and invest 100 in year 1 and have available 105 a year later, which will allow him to consume 52.50 at that time. In this case he exchanges 50 of present consumption for 52.50 of future consumption. The advantage to the saver under the consumption tax is due to the fact that postponement of consumption also postpones tax payment and allows the saver to receive interest on the postponed tax.[1]

It is by no means certain, however, that an increase in the net rate of return obtainable on savings will stimulate additional saving. The effect is not clearly indicated by either economic theory or statistical observation.[2] Whereas some individuals might be induced to save more, others might save less because a smaller capital sum would satisfy their demands for retirement income, family security, and dowries. Many might not respond at all. Total personal saving might increase, decrease, or remain unchanged.

The uncertainty of the influence of the rate of return on the volume of saving may justify the neglect of the possibility of stimulating saving by preferential taxation of interest and profit income. The absence of proposals of this nature, however, is probably due more to broad political considerations than to doubts about their effectiveness. The prevailing opinion throughout the world seems to be that justice demands that any differentiation in tax rates should run in favor of earned income rather than property income. Selective tax exemption of interest and profits from strategic sources is more acceptable on political grounds and is widely practiced. It is fairly certain that these schemes influence the allocation of savings among alternative uses, but it is not clear that they affect the total amount saved. Plans of this kind are not discussed in the present paper.

The capacity-to-save argument holds that aggregate saving can be increased by transferring taxation from those who are most inclined to save to those who are least inclined to do so; the capacity to save is increased where the inclination to save is strongest. It is not necessary that anyone change his attitude toward present and future consumption or accumulation. The community's saving ratio can be raised without altering the saving ratio of any individual, provided high savers are given command over a larger fraction of the resources available to the private sector.

This reasoning suggests that a tax on consumption will be more favorable to private saving than an equal-yield tax on income because the consumption tax will leave a larger proportion of real disposable income in the hands of those with higher-than-average saving rates. The argument, although plausible, is not conclusive. Differences in individuals' liabilities for the consumption tax and the income tax depend on the ratio of their total taxable consumption to their total taxable income, whereas the impact on saving is governed by the use to which individuals will put comparatively small changes in their real disposable income. In short, the marginal propensity to save rather than the average propensity is the relevant characteristic.

Persons with high average propensities to save may also have high marginal propensities to save. The assumption that this is true implies only a certain continuity of behavior, after any initial lags associated with a change in disposable income have been overcome. No doubt, however, there are individuals who save a large fraction of their income at a certain time who would save little if any of an increment to income. They may have been accumulating for a specific purpose which has been satisfied, or they may have been paying off a mortgage or other long-term debt (a form of saving) and feel free to consume more after getting out of debt or meeting contractual installments. On the other hand, some families who have consumed all of their income may save a large part of an increase in income. But such sharp changes in behavior seem exceptional. Average saving ratios reflect age and family composition, tastes, habits, opportunities, and other factors which change slowly, and presumably these influences also determine marginal saving ratios.

It is easy to form an exaggerated impression of what can be accomplished by reallocating taxes between high and low savers. Differences between the impacts of alternative tax formulas will not be as great as differences between the marginal propensities to consume of high and low savers, provided that the choice of tax formula does not itself influence individual propensities to save. This is true because all feasible measures impose taxes on both high and low savers; hence the effect on saving is a weighted average of high and low marginal propensities to save, with the weights depending on the amounts of tax paid. To illustrate, consider A and B, who have equal incomes but different saving behavior. Assume that A's marginal propensity to save is 0 and that B's is 20 per cent. If A is taxed while B goes free, private saving is unaffected; if B is taxed and A is not, saving is curtailed by 20 per cent of the revenue. There is, however, no feasible and socially acceptable means of taxing A while exempting B, unless they differ in characteristics other than saving behavior. The realistic alternatives are to tax both A and B on income, total consumption, selected items of consumption, or property. Under a general income tax A and B will pay equal amounts, and private saving will be reduced by 10 per cent of the revenue. If A and B

are taxed in proportion to their total consumption, A will pay 5/9 of the aggregate tax and B 4/9; private saving will be reduced by approximately 8.9 per cent of the revenue.[3] By selective consumption taxes, it may be possible to allocate a still larger share of taxes to A and other low savers; but B and other frugal people will have to bear part of the load.

The argument that regressive taxation (measured with respect to income) is more favorable to private saving than is progressive taxation may be viewed as an alternative approach to allocation of taxes between high and low savers. The assumption is that the marginal propensity to save rises with income size. This hypothesis has been supported by three kinds of evidence: (1) the common-sense belief that saving is hard for the poor but easy for the rich; (2) data from family budget studies conducted mostly in high-income, industrialized countries; and (3) the observation that national saving ratios tend to vary directly with income per head.

To a middle-class observer from North America or Western Europe it often seems that the poor in many underdeveloped countries live at the subsistence level and could not save if they wished to do so, whereas the rich must save inasmuch as there is positive private saving in most countries. This impression may be misleading. Social convention is probably more important than physiological necessity as a limitation on the saving capacity of a large majority of the population. Anthropologists tell us that in virtually all societies appreciable amounts of resources are used for ceremonial and other purposes that cannot be classified as physical necessities. These outlays often place heavy demands on the rich as well as the poor.[4] The extravagant standards of personal consumption and hospitality of the rich in preindustrial societies are notorious. In these conditions it seems naive to suppose that saving habits are predictably related to size of income. Heavy saving may reflect deviant behavior rather than a large income; or, as the classical economists usually assumed, saving may be done almost exclusively by receivers of profits and interest.[5]

It is doubtful whether the findings of family budget studies in high-income countries have much value as an indication of saving behavior in the underdeveloped countries. Few scientifically designed sample surveys of this kind have been carried out in underdeveloped countries. Studies in Puerto Rico and Delhi, India, it is true, agree with American and British surveys in indicating negative saving ratios in the lowest income classes and increasing saving ratios in higher income classes.[6] These data, however, measure average saving ratios rather than marginal propensities to save. They are not necessarily inconsistent with the existence of a uniform marginal propensity to save in the range where most income is found.[7] It has been cogently argued, moreover, that the cross-section data provided by the single-year budget studies which are available give a misleading impression of the normal relationship between income and saving, exaggerating the difference between low and high incomes.[8] Although important differences of opinion exist, there seems to be agreement among research workers in the field that, in the United States and Great Britain, the marginal propensity to save differs less between income classes than was formerly assumed on the basis of family budget surveys.[9]

The fact that the ratio of aggregate household saving to aggregate disposable income tends to be considerably higher in countries with high income per head than in low-income countries[10] is consistent with the hypothesis that the marginal propensity to save within countries varies directly with size of income. The correlation between national saving ratios and income per head is by no means perfect, however. Differences among countries may be due, not only to the level of income per head, but also to differences in the industrial composition of production, the factor distribution of income, social values, customs, and the security of property. The statistics, moreover, may exaggerate differences in saving ratios because of a tendency to understate saving in the underdeveloped countries in the form of precious metals (bullion, coin, and ornaments) and in the non-monetized sector.

Even if we conclude that the weight of evidence—or intuition—indicates that the marginal propensity to save rises with size of income in all countries, we should recognize the existence of differences in saving patterns of families in the same income class. "The" saving ratio for an income class is an average derived from a distribution including some families with lower ratios and some with higher ratios. The distributions for adjacent income classes—and perhaps also for widely separated classes—overlap. In the United States, the Survey of Consumer Finances indicates that in 1950 consumer units making up the highest one-fifth of income recipients had an average net saving ratio twice the national average; nevertheless, 38 per cent of these units had saving ratios below the national average, and 22 per cent of them were negative savers. About 23 per cent of consumer units in income classes below the top fifth had net saving ratios equal to or higher than the average ratio for the top income group.[11] Size of income is at best a rough method of classifying individuals according to saving propensities. A decrease in tax progressivity will augment the disposable income of rich spendthrifts as well as high savers.

None of the approaches, it seems, can confidently be expected to bring about a significant increase in private saving. All rest on questionable assumptions. Proposals for concentrating taxes on consumption and exempting saving or taxing it lightly are perhaps more firmly based than suggestions for preferential taxation of interest and profits and the avoidance of progressivity. The former, moreover, clash less openly with political values that have been spread around the world by the same social currents that have awakened the desire for progress and brought about the adoption of development programs. The remainder of this paper will be devoted to direct and indirect taxes on consumption and plans for exempting saving from income taxes. Although the extent of the influence on private saving of these measures is uncertain, they can be presumed to have some favorable effect, and they would at least leave the way open for an increase in private saving due to other policies and to social and economic change.

Objections to Efforts to Promote Saving by Tax Means

Before proceeding to a more detailed examination of means of taxing consumption with the objective of promoting saving, let us consider some possible limitations and objections of a general nature.

The argument that urgent revenue needs prevent tax concessions to saving has little merit. Inasmuch as private consumption represents a large proportion of total income at the disposal of the private sector in the underdeveloped countries, the tax base would not be greatly narrowed even if all private saving were exempt from taxation. Particular schemes for encouraging saving, of course, may jeopardize revenue yields, but this need not be true of all plans.

The objection that the taxation of consumption will retard development because it will narrow the market is also unconvincing. This objection implies that the underdeveloped countries can curb private consumption only at the risk of stagnation. One of the platitudes of the literature of economic development is that countries trying to speed progress nearly always face inflationary dangers due to excessive demand; the absence of such pressures has come to be taken as proof that the development plan is too modest. However, sectional difficulties are possible even when aggregate demand is ample or excessive. High excise taxes on certain items may discourage industries that could play a strategic role in economic progress. Hirschman has stressed the importance of certain industries in stimulating other industries that supply materials to them as that use or distribute their products ("backward and forward linkages").[12] If brewing, for example, is such an industry, as it seems to have been in several Latin American countries, a degree of restraint in taxing beer may contribute to development at certain stages. The argument cannot be generalized; it must be confined to strategic products and industries. An increase in saving, brought about by taxation or other means, must restrict demand for consumer goods and hence must damage the market for many products.

The promotion of private saving, as already indicated, does not necessarily mean that private investment will be enlarged relative to government investment. Decisions with respect to the allocation of investment are separable, in principle at least, from policies regarding saving. The government can borrow if private saving exceeds the amount of investment that the authorities wish to allow the private sector to undertake. Some methods of stimulating saving, to be sure, involve the encouragement of private investment as well.

A more substantive objection relates to the distribution of income and wealth. Even if a country does not eschew progressivity, a tax system designed to promote private saving may well be less progressive than a system worked out with little regard to that objective. An increase in private saving, moreover, necessarily implies the accumulation of private wealth and the rise of interest and profit income, which involve not only inequalities in consumption power but also, in most societies, distinctions in status that may be odious to egalitarians. A high rate of private saving, however, does not necessarily result in a cumulative rise in the share of income received by an identical top group or in greater inequality than now exists in the poor countries. Economic growth is accompanied by many changes in the composition of output and employment and in relative income and wealth of different groups.[13]

Perhaps the most important limitations on a policy of taxing consumption arise from possible discouragement of participation in the market economy and the curtailment of expenditures which, although classified as consumption, contribute to productive capacity. Certain items are so attractive that, if they are available at reasonable prices, farmers and villagers may be induced to increase output and bring more produce to market in order to earn money to buy the goods. Possible examples of such incentive goods in Asia and Africa are kerosene and bicycles. Marshall recognized the importance of what may be called "productive consumption" when he wrote, ". . . a great part of the wages of the working classes is invested in the physical health and strength of their children. The older economists took too little account of the fact that human faculties are as important a means of production as any other kind of capital. . . ."[14]

General Comments on Methods of
Taxing Consumption

Methods of taxing consumption that will be further examined in this paper are (1) an income tax with saving partially or wholly exempt; (2) a personal expenditure tax or spendings tax; and (3) indirect taxes in the form of excises, sales or turnover taxes, and customs duties. A policy of attempting to foster private saving involves not only reliance on taxes on consumption but also avoidance of taxes that are especially destructive of saving. Inasmuch as the latter taxes often do not yield large sums, especially in the less developed countries, the fact that a government raises a large proportion of its revenue from consumption taxes is not necessarily proof that it offers favorable treatment to private saving.

The indirect taxes on consumption are well known. Exemption of saving from the income tax is not so familiar, but the general import of this proposal is easily visualized. The personal expenditure tax is a direct tax on consumption expenditure; like the income tax it can incorporate personal exemptions, allowances for dependents, and graduated rates. Irving Fisher was a well-known advocate of such a tax, although he insisted on calling it an income tax since he defined personal income as equal to consumption.[15] The U.S. Treasury recommended a graduated spendings tax on personal consumption during World War II,[16] but the recommendation was rejected by Congress. More recently, Kaldor revived interest in the idea through a book published in 1955 and reports to the governments of India and Ceylon.[17] These two countries adopted expenditure taxes of limited scope, India in 1957 and Ceylon in 1959.[18]

A personal expenditure tax and an income tax with saving exempt are similar in that both are direct taxes falling on consumption. As explained in a later section, the two taxes would be assessed in much the same way. In practice, however, there are likely to be differences in coverage and rate structures.

Inasmuch as indirect taxes are traditional in most underdeveloped countries, the question may be raised how the policy under discussion differs from existing practice. Although this method of attempting to foster saving would be less novel than the other two, its consistent application would involve revision of the tax systems of most countries. Indirect taxes are now often imposed on capital goods as well as consumption goods. This is particularly true of import duties and not solely or even mainly for protectionist reasons. Taxes are often low and sometimes are not imposed at all on important kinds of consumption goods and services. A number of countries which obtain most of their revenue from indirect taxes nevertheless impose high rates of taxation on income, profits, and certain business enterprises.

In the following paragraphs the three methods are compared regarding coverage and selectivity and progressivity. Problems of tax design and application are examined in a later section.

Coverage and Selectivity

The expenditure tax, in pure form, distinguishes only between consumption and saving and, when graduated, amounts of personal consumption; it does not differentiate between kinds of consumption and forms of saving. The same tax rates apply to spending for imports and home goods, goods that are plentiful and those that are in short supply, items whose production competes directly with the development program and other items. Expenditures for education and cultural activities are taxed in the same way as spending for automobiles and fashionable clothes. The expenditure tax exempts all nonconsumption uses of income and wealth including hoarding, real estate purchases, capital flight, and other activities that the authorities may wish to discourage rather than stimulate.

A system that exempts all saving from income tax is as unselective as the expenditure tax. In practice, however, exemption is likely to be granted only for forms of savings that are considered desirable or innocuous. For example, a tax remission may be allowed for purchases of government securities or shares in approved industries and for bank deposits but denied for saving embodied in currency hoards, gold, and foreign securities.[19] Desirable forms of consumption can be favored by allowing the taxpayer to deduct specified personal expenses when he computes his taxable income, but this method of differentiation has limited flexibility. It can be applied only to items for which reasonably accurate information on individual expenditures is available; furthermore expenses are usually deductible in full or not at all and hence are subject either to the regular income tax rate or a zero rate.

The pure expenditure tax, of course, may be modified to exempt certain consumption outlays, but, like the income tax, it lacks flexibility as a means of differential taxation of consumption. Distinctions between forms of saving are less likely under the expenditure tax than under the modified income tax since the expenditure tax focuses on consumption as the tax base rather than on the concession offered to saving.

A difference in coverage of the expenditure tax and an income tax with saving exempt is that the expenditure tax base includes consumption financed by disposal of wealth as well as that supported from current income whereas the modified income tax may not reach this part of consumption. The importance of this difference depends largely on the length of the period for which tax is assessed. Dissaving is much more likely to occur in a short period than in a long period. It may reflect fluctuations in income or irregularities in spending. In Western societies different rates of saving and consumption are characteristic of different phases of family life; saving tends to be concentrated in the middle years with dissaving occurring in earlier and later years. As will be brought out more fully in a later section, a degree of averaging to eliminate year-to-year fluctuations would be highly desirable under either an expenditure tax or a modified income tax. The longer the averaging period, the less the difference in coverage of the two taxes. With lifetime averaging, the principal difference would be that the expenditure tax would strike consumption financed by using up inherited wealth whereas the income tax with saving exempt would not. Another difference in coverage, which may be more significant, is that the expenditure tax will reach consumption financed from capital gains, gifts, and other receipts which are not included in taxable income. In India, the possibilities of broader coverage of the expenditure tax have not been fully exploited. The tax does not apply to persons who, together with their dependents, receive from all sources an annual income of less than Rs. 36,000 after deduction of Indian income taxes.[20] Thus the expenditure tax does not reach certain extreme forms of dissaving or consumption financed from gifts but presumably does apply to consumption paid for out of tax-exempt income.

Indirect taxes are necessarily selective or discriminatory regarding forms of consumption and nonselective regarding means of finance. They apply unequally to different items of consumption but equally to expenditures financed from capital and those made out of income. Indirect taxes may also apply to capital goods and to certain forms of financial saving. Special taxes on security transactions are common, and in the Federal Republic of Germany the general turnover tax applies to gold transactions.[21]

Selectivity with respect to both items of consumption and forms of saving can be attained by combining indirect taxes with exemptions for enumerated forms of saving under the income tax.

Selectivity of taxation is not universally approved. According to one view, selectivity or discrimination should be avoided because it distorts the allocation of resources through the market. Formally stated, the argument identified selectivity as the source of an "excess burden" attributable to taxes that alter relative prices. Economic planning, however, is a process of selection even when not comprehensive or highly detailed. Few officials or legislators will be much impressed by a general argument against selectivity. They will be concerned with the political acceptability and efficiency of selective measures.

Progressivity

Much of the appeal of the expenditure tax and of the income tax with certain forms of saving exempt is due to the fact that these taxes can incorporate personal exemptions and graduated rates. The taxes are progressive with respect to consumption and are likely to be progressive also with respect to income. Whether they are more or less progressive with respect to income than an ordinary income tax depends on the rate structures and the relation between income and consumption expenditures over the relevant range of the income distribution. There seems to be a fair presumption that the maximum nominal rates of an expenditure tax would exceed the top rate of the modified income tax. Income tax rates are limited by a strong aversion to rates in excess of 100 per cent, but this tradition does not exist for the expenditure tax and rates above 100 per cent presumably would be less objectionable in an expenditure tax than in an income tax.

Most indirect taxes of large yield are commonly believed to be regressive, and there is statistical evidence to support this evaluation for some of the principal indirect taxes in certain of the richer countries. In the underdeveloped countries there is a strong presumption that the traditional levies on salt and sugar are decidedly regressive (except possibly where these items are extensively produced in the nonmonetized sector). Taxes on articles such as common cloth, matches, tobacco, and beer are probably also regressive over middle and upper income ranges but may not be regressive at the lower end of the income distribution, especially in countries where a considerable part of the population is employed mainly in subsistence agriculture or village economies with only limited participation in the monetized sector. Consumption of items such as automobiles, radios and other electrical appliances, the better grades of textiles, most cosmetics, and distilled spirits is still confined mainly to a fairly small and prosperous class in many underdeveloped countries. Taxes on such items may be progressive up to a rather high income level in these countries.

A judgment that the whole system of indirect taxes is regressive need not depend on the assumption that the marginal propensity to consume declines as income rises. Indirect taxes are usually low or nonexistent on many items that are important in the consumption patterns of upper income groups in the underdeveloped countries, including, for example, personal services of household servants and others, luxury foods of local origin, and foreign travel.

Although it may not be feasible to impose taxes on many services, it may be possible to devise indirect tax systems which are not highly regressive. On the basis of survey data, estimates have been made indicating that the system of indirect taxes in India is mildly progressive with respect to total consumption expenditures of both rural and urban households.[22] This finding can support an inference about progressivity in the conventional sense, that is with respect to income, only on the basis of further assumptions or evidence concerning the relation between total consumption and income. An earlier study indicated that the consumption taxes of El Salvador were somewhat progressive with respect to income up to a fairly high level.[23]

TAX DESIGN AND ADMINISTRATION

Difficult problems are encountered in the design of direct-tax provisions to favor saving. Less serious but still genuine problems are involved in the refinement of indirect taxes to help advance the social and economic objectives of the underdeveloped countries. The challenge is to design measures that are as consistent and logical as possible in allocating taxes in a manner calculated to achieve the objectives and which are within the administrative and compliance capabilities of the country. This includes the devising of return forms and information reports and the drawing up of detailed rules of tax assessment as well as the clarification of grand policy issues and the explanation of proposals to political leaders and the general public. Lack of attention to tax design may result in inaction or the adoption of measures that fail to produce the desired results and that have harmful side effects on economic progress, respect for law, and political maturity.

General economists have displayed great interest in tax policy but have usually left questions of tax design to the specialists. Tax administrators and technicians, like specialists in many other fields, tend to resist innovations. Neither the general economists nor the technicians have given enough thought to the irksome details that determine the practicability of fundamental revisions of the tax system.

Kaldor is a conspicuous exception to the statement that economists have not worked out the details of measures to put into effect their broad tax proposals. His reports on India and Ceylon display great ingenuity in this respect. These reports, together with Kaldor's earlier book on the expenditure tax, have stimulated a lively interest in ideas that had long been considered attractive but impracticable. Kaldor may have given too little weight to administrative and compliance problems, but he cannot be accused of ignoring them.

More space is given in the following pages to questions of tax design that would arise in any country setting out to give preferential tax treatment to saving than to the special problems of the underdeveloped countries. I have not stressed the environmental conditions that severely limit the successful application of direct taxes in most underdeveloped countries.[24] The omission involves a loss of realism but has the advantage of allowing us to concentrate on problems that have received less notice than the general deficiencies of tax administration and compliance in the underdeveloped countries.

Exemption of Saving under the Income Tax

The suggestion that saving be exempt from income tax or taxed at lower rates than other income may appear to be simple but on closer examination will be seen to entail complications. It would not be easy to define and measure saving, to prevent tax evasion, and to assure equitable treatment of persons who save in some years and dissave in other years.

Let us consider first a broad scheme providing tax exemption or preferential rates for the part of current income that is saved, regardless of the form in which the savings are held. If taxable income were measured, as recommended by Haig, Simons, and other students, as the algebraic sum of consumption and changes in net worth,[25] no special difficulty would be involved in putting into effect this scheme. The general practice, however, is to define taxable income by enumeration of includable receipts and allowable deductions. The assessment of income does not produce a figure for saving. Therefore, the authorities and taxpayers would have to go through all of the steps that are now required for the determination of taxable income and the additional steps necessary to measure saving.

In principle, saving could be measured as the difference between current income and consumption outlays or by the identification of increases in various forms of asset during the year. Few families, however, keep records of their consumption expenditures and even when available such accounts could not easily be verified. There is general agreement that the subtraction method is not practicable and that saving would have to be measured by the increase in assets. The authorities would have to require taxpayers to present evidence on all holdings of securities, real property, direct investment in business enterprises, cash balances, gold bullion, and perhaps other assets.

It would not be sufficient merely to ascertain new purchases of assets or increases in bank balances during the year. The scheme would be defeated if taxpayers could gain tax exemption by converting assets, that is, by selling one kind of asset and buying another or by borrowing and purchasing an asset. A measure of the net increase in all assets would be needed. This might be obtained from a full list of all capital transactions—purchases and sales of assets, gifts received and given, debts contracted and repaid, increases and decreases in cash balances, and certain other items. A better method, and indeed the only way of making sure that no changes were omitted, would be to examine complete balance sheets of each taxpayer for the beginning and end of the year. Comparative balance sheets would be highly useful also for the determination of net income and would be helpful in the assessment of an ordinary income tax. However, the authorities have not considered it feasible to require balance sheets of individual taxpayers who are not engaged in trade or business even in the countries with the most advanced tax administrations.

It would be especially important to obtain accurate balance sheets at the time the new plan went into effect. Taxpayers would have an incentive to conceal cash and other liquid assets because by converting these assets over a period of years they could appear to be accumulating new savings and could thus qualify for tax benefits. In addition, many persons would be reluctant to divulge their true assets because of fear of revealing past tax evasion and of exposing themselves to exchange controls and expropriation.

In countries that do not tax capital gains, information on capital transactions is not generally required for assessment of income tax. For these countries the introduction of an exemption for saving would greatly increase the scope of reporting and verification. Countries which now tax capital gains would not have to undertake a completely new activity, but they would face enforcement problems. One of the most difficult points would be the ascertainment of changes in cash balances (including bullion and, in some societies, ornaments), not required for assessment of capital gains tax but essential for the measurement of net saving.[26] The exemption of saving from the income tax would increase incentives for omitting transactions in which gains occurred and for understating gains. Taxpayers who did so would not only escape capital gains tax but would also acquire funds that could be used to purchase other assets or increase cash balances and thus to serve as evidence of "saving" that would entail a reduction in regular income tax liability. Of course, some moderation would have to be exercised in taking advantage of this means of evasion. Alert tax officials would become suspicious of persons who reported a high rate of saving if their living habits were obviously inconsistent with the indicated scale of consumption.

The saving and consumption elements cannot be readily distinguished in some transactions. Examples are purchases of jewelry and other durable consumer goods, purchases and maintenance of dwellings, payments of life insurance premiums, and expenditures for education. More or less arbitrary rules already apply to several of these items under the income tax, and similar conventions would have to be worked out to separate consumption and saving elements. An acceptable treatment would complicate administration but would not present unique or insuperable difficulties.[27]

Administration could be simplified by limiting the tax exemption to savings invested in a few kinds of assets, say government bonds, shares and bonds or debentures of approved private enterprises, and savings accounts in banks and similar institutions. It would be possible to require that all eligible securities be in registered form rather than bearer form in order to facilitate verification of claimed changes in holdings. This scheme would not provide tax exemption for net saving as such but for the acquisition of the designated assets. There would be nothing to prevent the taxpayer from acquiring the eligible assets by converting other assets.

Underdeveloped countries are concerned with the form in which savings are held as well as with the rate of total saving. As already noted, a degree of selectivity in tax concessions for saving would no doubt be regarded as an advantage by most governments. Too narrow and rigid a provision governing eligibility for special treatment, however, would sacrifice much of the advantage of private saving and investment compared with direct state investment, while retaining the conditions making for economic and social inequality. On the other hand, extension of the list of eligible assets would lead toward the problems associated with a general exemption.

A serious difficulty that is often overlooked relates to the length of the assessment period.[28] The purpose of a tax concession for saving is to encourage a permanent—or at least a long-term—increase in savings or in holdings of certain assets. This purpose would not be served by acts of saving which were soon reversed or offset by dissaving. Some means would have to be found to prevent a taxpayer from qualifying for an exemption say every second year by alternately building up and drawing down his savings. Opportunities of this kind would be limited by the desire to avoid violent fluctuations in consumption, but many possibilities of illegal evasion and legal avoidance would suggest themselves to imaginative taxpayers, for example, the use of personal loans or open accounts not revealed to the tax assessor to finance consumption in the years of nominally high saving and the scheduling of vacation trips and other postponable expenditures in alternate years.

Three means suggest themselves for dealing with ascertainable dissaving that follows a year in which an exemption has been granted for saving. The return of the earlier year could be reopened and tax reassessed, the dissaving could be added to taxable income in the year in which it occurred, or income tax could be assessed on the basis of a cumulative averaging plan covering several years or perhaps the taxpayer's whole life. Reopening of returns is troublesome, and most tax administrators like to minimize the extent to which it is necessary. The addition of dissaving to current taxable income seems preferable but, with progressive rates, could result in hardships for taxpayers or opportunities for manipulation. Cumulative averaging is an attractive idea even in an undifferentiated income tax; however, most countries have considered it too complex.

Expenditure Tax

The expenditure tax would be administered in almost the same way as an income tax with all saving exempt. The assessment procedure recommended by Kaldor is as follows: (1) all receipts from current net income, sale of assets, borrowing, gifts, inheritances, and other sources would be aggregated; (2) deductions would be allowed for gross saving in the form of additions to cash balances, investment outlays, and debt repayment; (3) deductions would also be allowed for any consumption expenditures exempt from tax and for certain direct tax payments; and (4) tax would be assessed on the balance, representing taxable consumption expenditures. As under the income tax with saving exempt, problems would arise in obtaining complete and accurate balance sheets (or comprehensive statements of capital transactions), in identifying the consumption and saving elements of certain transactions, and in fairly assessing tax on fluctuating levels of consumption.

The point of departure for a successful expenditure tax would be an accurate determination of net income. The addition of balance sheet data, essential for the expenditure tax, would facilitate the determination of income. On the other hand, the imposition of a steeply graduated expenditure tax or the addition of the expenditure tax to an income tax would increase incentives to classify personal consumption items as business expenses in the form of entertainment, travel expenses, and the like—an especially troublesome form of income tax evasion.

Sentiment could be expected for tax exemption for meritorious or unusual items of consumption such as medical expenses, educational expenses, election expenses, legal expenses, funeral expenses, marriage and birth expenses, and expenditures for religious purposes. Several of these items are exempt from expenditure tax in India and Ceylon. Such exemptions introduce an element of selectivity which may be desirable but also may open the way for the erosion of the expenditure tax base just as deductions and exclusions have narrowed the income tax base in many countries.[29]

Provision for spreading outlays for consumer durables over a period of years, by means of averaging or capitalization and taxation of the annual imputed service value, would be necessary for equity under a graduated expenditure tax.

Kaldor's reports on India and Ceylon and public discussions in these countries laid great stress on the advantages of an interlocking system of taxes and reports covering income, capital gains, wealth, and consumption expenditures. Space is not available here for a description of the tax systems of India and Ceylon or for a critical examination of the contention that they constitute "self-checking" systems.[30] It can be said that the combination of a wealth tax with an expenditure tax would discourage evasion of the expenditure tax through over-statement of saving because a person would thus subject himself to additional wealth tax. The force of this deterrent would depend on the rates of the two taxes, the time preferences or rates of discount applied by taxpayers to future liabilities, and the care with which the authorities integrated assessments of the two taxes. The addition of a wealth tax would not prevent concealment of income, expenditures, and assets or other forms of outright fraud.

Indirect Taxes on Consumption

The effective use of indirect taxation as an instrument of economic policy in the underdeveloped countries depends on the remedying of the defects already mentioned. Some of these are easily righted; others are much more difficult to deal with. Taxes on capital goods, for example, can be largely eliminated although they cannot well be entirely abolished because some items, such as passenger automobiles and sewing machines, are both consumer goods and capital goods.

Luxuries cannot be clearly distinguished from essentials. To a considerable extent, luxurious consumption consists in the liberal use of items such as food, clothing, and housing which are plainly essentials in some amounts. Differentiation on the basis of price or quality seems advisable even though it complicates administration. The experience of the United Kingdom with "utility goods" under the purchase tax during and after World War II may be instructive in this connection. Identification of luxury consumption is perhaps somewhat easier in the underdeveloped countries than in the economically more advanced countries because the consumption patterns of the rich and the poor differ more sharply in the underdeveloped countries. Often the higher income groups tend to prefer imported goods, and some differentiation is possible through customs duties. Care is advisable, however, to avoid setting up such high protective barriers that inefficient local production of nonessentials is unduly stimulated. Such industries have sometimes been brought into existence by import controls and exchange restrictions.

Ad valorem rates are usually preferable to specific excises because they impose heavier taxes on expensive items which are usually preferred by the well-to-do. A more important advantage of ad valorem taxes is that they respond automatically to price increases. Although more complicated than specific taxes, ad valorem taxes are within the competence of moderately effective administrative organizations. Certainly, ad valorem excises and customs duties are much simpler than any net income tax or expenditure tax. In countries imposing exchange controls, information on the value of imports is available to the exchange authorities and can be exploited by customs officials.

It does not seem feasible to impose excises on many kinds of personal services or foreign travel. Omission of these items limits the possible progressivity of indirect taxation. Perhaps contemporary experts should consider the practicability of supplementing the excises with direct taxes on a few services and other items of luxury consumption, similar to levies formerly imposed in Europe and to a lesser extent in the United States. In the eighteenth and nineteenth centuries, Great Britain, for example, levied direct taxes on carriages, men-servants, dogs, armorial ensigns, plate, horses, guns, and other indicia of high social status or luxurious consumption. Such taxes were the basis of Pitt's "triple assessment" which was the immediate ancestor of the modern income tax.[31] Dwellings appear to offer possibilities as a base for discriminating taxation of consumption.

CONCLUSION

Governments that wish to foster private saving may consider it advisable to concentrate taxes on consumption and to tax saving lightly. Economists can agree that this policy is likely to work in the desired direction, but, in the present state of knowledge, they have little basis for advising the authorities regarding the extent of the results to be expected.

As a means of taxing consumption in the less developed countries, excises and customs duties seem more practical than an income tax with saving exempt or an expenditure tax. Although the modified income tax and the expenditure tax are attractive in certain respects, their successful use would depend on the solution of serious problems of tax design and the existence of high standards of administration and compliance. These taxes are far more complex than an ordinary income tax, a measure which has had only limited success in most underdeveloped countries. At the present time ingenuity and energy can be more fruitfully employed in the improvement of indirect taxes and other conventional sources of revenue than in the introduction of an expenditure tax or a broad exemption for saving in the income tax.

The promotion of private saving is a proper objective of tax policy in underdeveloped countries but should be seen in perspective. Private saving is only part of total saving, and increased saving alone will not assure economic progress. Taxation is only one of the factors that determine the rate of private saving, and its relative importance is uncertain. Taxes also affect the economy through their influence on incentives to work and invest, industrial structure, and relative prices. Noneconomic considerations, moreover, are important for the social acceptability of a tax system.

NOTES TO SELECTION 16

[1] A 100 per cent consumption tax will yield less revenue than a 50 per cent income tax, if there is positive saving; but it can be shown that adjustment of rates to make the yields of the two taxes equal will not eliminate the advantage enjoyed by savers under the consumption tax. See A. R. Prest, "The Expenditure Tax and Saving," *Economic Journal*, LXIX (September, 1959), 483–90.

[2]There seems to be a growing tendency toward skepticism. Mill, Marshall, and Taussig conceded that individual reactions may differ but argued that on balance the total volume of saving is positively correlated with the interest rate. Wicksell, Knight, Keynes, and Joan Robinson stress the complexity and uncertainty of the relationship between thriftiness and interest rates. See John Stuart Mill, *Principles of Political Economy*, Book I, Chap. XI and Book IV, Chap. IV, sec. 3, ed. W. J. Ashley (London: Longsmans, Green, 1929), pp. 163–75, 729; Alfred Marshall, *Principles of Economics* (8th ed.; London: Macmillan, 1938), pp. 230–36; F. W. Taussig, *Principles of Economics* (3rd rev. ed.; New York: Macmillan, 1923), II, 20–33; Knut Wicksell, *Lectures on Political Economy*, trans. by E. Cassen (London: Routledge, 1934), I, 207–18; Frank H. Knight, *The Economic Organization* (New York: Augustus M. Kelley, 1951), p. 115; John Maynard Keynes, *The General Theory of Employment, Interest, and Money* (New York: Harcourt, Brace, 1936), pp. 93–94; Joan Robinson, *The Accumulation of Capital* (Homewood, Ill.: Irwin, 1956), p. 252.

[3]Let y = income tax rate, c = consumption tax rate, 100 = income of A = income of B. The yield of the income tax will be $100y + 100y = 200y$; saving will be reduced by $[0(100y) = .20(100y)] = 20y$; $20y/200y = .10$. Under the consumption tax A will pay $100c$ and B will pay $(1-0.2)100c = 80c$; the total yield will be $180c$. The reduction in saving will be $[0(100c) + .20(80c)] = 16c$; $16c/180c = .0888+$. Note that $.10$ and $.0888+$ are weighted averages of 0 and $.20$, with weights varying with the proportion of the total tax yield paid by A and B.

[4]Melville J. Herskovits, *Cultural Anthropology* (New York: Knopf, 1955), pp. 160–64; *Economic Anthropology* (New York: Knopf, 1952).

[5]W. Arthur Lewis takes the classical view. He asserts, "the ratio of savings to national income is a function not just of inequality, but more precisely, of the ratio of profits to national income." In his opinion landed aristocrats, peasants, and members of the wage and salary earning classes do not save much, except possibly in situations in which there is a "capitalist example to imitate." *The Theory of Economic Growth* (London: Allen & Unwin, 1957), pp. 227–28.

[6]Commonwealth of Puerto Rico, Department of Labor, Bureau of Labor Statistics, *Ingresos y Gastos de las Familias, Puerto Rico, 1953* (San Juan, 1960); Eleanor E. Maccoby and Frances Fielder, *Saving Among Upper-Income Families in Puerto Rico* (University of Puerto Rico Press, 1953); National Council of Applied Economic Research, *Delhi Saving Survey* (Bombay: Asia Publishing House, 1960); P. S. Lokanathan, "A Study of Saving in India," American Statistical Association, *1959 Proceedings of Business and Economics Section*, pp. 236–241L. The Delhi survey indicated that, if household income is measured as a multiple of mean income and net investment in consumer durables is classified as saving, saving ratios in that Indian city in 1959 were as high as ratios for comparable incomes in the United States in 1950 and higher than in the United Kingdom in 1951–52 (*Delhi Saving Survey*, pp. 23, 24).

[7]If saving is a linear function of income and the intercept of the saving curve is negative (indicating dissaving at zero income), saving will be a larger fraction of high incomes than of low incomes, but the marginal propensity to save will be the same for all income levels. Under these conditions the degree of tax progressivity will not affect the amount of private saving.

[8]William Vickrey, "Resource Distribution Patterns and the Classification of Families," in Conference on Research in Income and Wealth, *Studies in Income and Wealth* (New York: National Bureau of Economic Research, 1947), X, 272–74, 287–95; Milton Friedman, *A Theory of the Consumption Function* (Princeton: Princeton University Press, 1957); Franco Modigliani and Richard Brumberg, "Utility Analysis and the Consumption Function: An Interpretation of Cross-Section Data," *Post-Keynesian Economics*, ed. Kenneth K. Kurihara (New Brunswick, N.J.: Rutgers University Press, 1954), pp. 383–436.

[9]An extensive literature has grown up in recent years. Several valuable papers have appeared in the *Bulletin of the Oxford University Institute of Statistics, 1956–60,* and in *Consumption and Saving,* ed. Irwin Friend and Robert Jones (Philadelphia: University of Pennsylvania, 1960).

[10]Simon Kuznets, "Quantitative Aspects of the Economic Growth of Nations: V. Capital Formation Proportions: International Comparisons for Recent Years," *Economic Development and Cultural Change,* VIII (July, 1960, Pt. II), 74, 95–96.

[11]Derived from "1951 Survey of Consumer Finances," *Federal Reserve Bulletin,* August, 1951; September, 1951.

[12]Albert O. Hirschman, *The Strategy of Economic Development* (New Haven: Yale University Press, 1958).

[13]Simon Kuznets, "International Differences in Capital Formation and Financing," in *Capital Formation and Economic Growth,* Conference of the Universities-National Bureau Committee for Economic Research (Princeton: Princeton University Press, 1955), pp. 82–98.

[14]Alfred Marshall, *Principles of Economics* (8th ed.; London: Macmillan, 1938), p. 229.

[15]Irving Fisher, "Income Theory and Income Taxation in Practice," *Econometrica,* V (January, 1937), 1–55; Irving Fisher and Herbert W. Fisher, *Constructive Income Taxation* (New York: Harper & Brothers, 1942). The book contains a bibliography at pp. 249–60.

[16]*Annual Report of the Secretary of the Treasury,* 1943, pp. 410–20.

[17]Nicholas Kaldor, *An Expenditure Tax* (London: Allen and Unwin, 1955); *Indian Tax Reform, Report of a Survey* (New Delhi: Ministry of Finance, Government of India, 1956); *Suggestions for a Comprehensive Reform of Direct Taxation* (in Ceylon), Sessional Paper IV, 1960 (Colombo: Government Press, Ceylon, 1960).

[18]Harvard Law School, International Program in Taxation, World Tax Series, *Taxation in India* (Boston: Little, Brown & Co., 1960), pp. 421–34; Richard Goode, "New System of Direct Taxation in Ceylon," *National Tax Journal,* XIII (December, 1960), 329–40.

[19]See the suggestions of Raja J. Chelliah, *Fiscal Policy in Underdeveloped Countries* (London: Allen & Unwin, 1960), pp. 67–75.

[20]*Taxation in India,* p. 425. Rs. 36,000 is more than 100 times the national income per head (*International Financial Statistics,* July, 1961, p. 150; United Nations, *Monthly Bulletin of Statistics,* June, 1961, p. 2).

[21]International Monetary Fund, *Annual Report,* 1959, p. 157.

[22]Government of India, *Report of the Taxation Enquiry Commission, 1953–54* (New Delhi, 1955), Vol. 1, p. 69.

[23]Henry C. Wallich and John H. Adler, *Public Finance in a Developing Country* (Cambridge, Mass.: Harvard University Press, 1951), pp. 132–34.

[24]For a brief summary, see my paper, "Reconstruction of Foreign Tax Systems," *Proceedings of the National Tax Association,* 1951, pp. 213–15.

[25]Robert Murray Haig, "The Concept of Income—Economic and Legal Aspects," in *The Federal Income Tax,* ed. Haig (New York: Columbia University Press, 1921), pp. 1–28, reprinted in American Economic Association, *Readings in the Economics of Taxation* (Homewood, Ill.: Irwin, 1959), pp. 54–76; Henry C. Simons, *Personal Income Taxation* (Chicago: University of Chicago Press, 1938).

[26]In my opinion William Vickrey overstates the case when he asserts that, for high-income persons, there is "very little difference" between the administrative complications of an expenditure tax and an income tax including capital gains and losses ("Expenditure, Capital Gains and the Basis of Progressive Taxation," *Manchester School of Economic and Social Studies,* XXV [January, 1957], 18–20).

[27]See William Vickrey (*Agenda for Progressive Taxation* [New York: Ronald Press, 1947]) for a discussion of such items under the income tax and the expenditure tax.

[28]Chelliah, *Fiscal Policy in Underdeveloped Countries,* pp. 72–73, recognizes the existence of these problems but does not examine them in detail.

[29]Kaldor is critical of the exemptions under the Indian expenditure tax (*Economic Weekly Annual* [Bombay], January, 1959, pp. 195–98).

[30]See my paper on Ceylon, "New System of Direct Taxation in Ceylon," and references cited in it.

[31]C. F. Bastable, *Public Finance* (3rd ed.; London: Macmillan, 1903), pp. 497–501; Edwin R. A. Seligman, *The Income Tax* (2d ed.; New York: Macmillan, 1921), pp. 59–72.

17

Taxation of Consumption Expenditures, with Special Reference to India

by Raja J. Chelliah*

IT IS common knowledge that indirect taxes play a very important role in the finances of underdeveloped countries. The structure of indirect taxation in these countries has to be fashioned with the same objectives as direct taxation. It must be such as to raise the rate of capital formation in the economy while providing revenue for public consumption and investment. Here again we must ask not simply how to raise more revenue for the government, but rather how to raise the rate of investment and at the same time get more revenue for the government. It is necessary to consider also the effects on the incremental saving ratio.

One justification for the taxation of articles that are widely consumed is that it is necessary to raise enough revenue to finance at least the essential governmental services. In underdeveloped countries it becomes necessary to raise the greater part of tax revenue through commodity taxation. Looked at this way, commodity taxation is a contribution to meet the costs of common benefits and must be levied in as "equitable" a way as possible. High rates on luxuries and low rates on articles of common consumption are widely accepted rules. Such differentiation in rates introduces a broad element of progression.

When we look upon commodity taxation as a weapon for promoting economic growth, its justification lies in the fact that it has a tendency to restrain consumption. However, it should be used more for checking potential increase of consumption than for curtailing the actual consumption of the masses. It is easy to justify taxation that it is intended to curtail the consumption of luxuries and other commodities not essential for health and efficiency. But the taxation of goods consumed by the general population in a poor underdeveloped country may seem to go contrary to our principle of

*Raja J. Chelliah, *Fiscal Policy in Underdeveloped Countries with Special Reference to India* (London: George Allen & Unwin Ltd., 1960), pp. 85–90, 145–49. Reprinted here with the kind permission of the publisher.

laying the axe only on the element of surplus. The question may therefore be raised whether taxation of mass consumption has any role at all to play in developmental financing. Since there is scarcely an element of surplus in the incomes of the masses of the people, it would be clearly undesirable as well as unjustifiable to force them to contribute to economic development out of their meagre incomes. To argue that such taxation is necessary for the maintenance of essential governmental services is one thing; but to say that we must augment tax revenue from this source to raise the current rate of investment is an entirely different thing. As will be shown later, such a policy may not even be successful.

From the point of view of functional finance put forward in this book, the role of *mass* commodity taxation is not to raise the rate of investment at any given moment; it is to prevent consumption from rising as much as income rises as a result of past investment. It is for this reason that mass commodity taxation becomes essential in underdeveloped countries even from the point of view of economic development.

Raising the incremental saving ratio is one of the most difficult problems in underdeveloped countries. It must be remembered that it is not enough to persuade or cajole the richer classes alone to save and invest. In so far as a substantial part of the increase in incomes accrues to the poorer sections of the population, they are in a position to consume more than before. Their marginal propensity to consume being very near unity, their consumption will tend to rise almost as much as their incomes. If this is allowed to materialize, the increases in productivity will be almost fully absorbed by increased consumption. Increased commodity taxation could be used at this juncture to restrain increases in consumption and thus release some factors for purposes of investment.

The same holds good in respect of agriculture. When agricultural productivity increases, the peasants have a tendency to increase their consumption of farm products, especially of food. Again, when part of the under-employed labour force is drawn into industrial employment from the rural sector, those who remain on the farms may increase their consumption. On the other hand a continuing expansion in industrial employment requires an increase in the marketable surplus of agricultural products. Therefore, taxation might have to be used to transfer a part of the growing surplus from the rural to the urban sector.

It is not suggested, of course, that there should be no increase in the output of consumption goods; only that increases in productivity should not be fully absorbed in the consumption-goods sector. Indeed a rapid increase in the supply of some types of consumer goods is highly desirable in the context of disguised unemployment—even apart from humanitarian or political reasons. This will become clear when we examine the meaning in real terms of "increasing the incremental saving ratio."

For purpose of this analysis, let us classify consumer goods under three heads: (a) necessaries: required by all but the only goods available to those who are on the margin of subsistence; (b) nonnecessaries: these can be and are being consumed by a fairly large number of people who are above the subsistence level in varying degrees; and (c) luxuries: these are consumed mainly by the well-to-do.

Suppose that the population remains constant and that there is no disguised unemployment. Net investment will increase the real income of the population. This means that people will have higher money incomes at about the same level of prices, or about the same money incomes at a lower level of prices. When an individual's real income rises, he attempts to move in the scale of consumption from necessaries to luxuries. If this movement is restricted, we can have increased production of investment goods, instead of an increased production of non-necessaries and luxuries. The level of living remains constant or rises only a little, but the ratio of investment to income rises.

Suppose now that there is disguised unemployment in the economy and that it is desired to reduce it in course of time. The transfer of the under-employed to industrial employment creates the well-known "wage-goods gap." That is to say, though these people were consuming a certain amount of goods in their previous state of under-employment, the total demand for wage-goods in the economy rises when they are given industrial employment. This happens for two reasons: (a) they have to be paid a rate of real wages greater than their average consumption in partial idleness; and (b) those on the farms who are rid of their dependents tend to increase their consumption. In these circumstances, the volume of disguised unemployment cannot be reduced unless there is some increase in the output of wage-goods. In other words, the output of necessaries and some non-necessaries typically consumed by workers must increase, if we are to reduce the volume of disguised unemployment.

Suppose now that population is increasing, as it actually is in underdeveloped countries. When it is remembered that large sections of the population in these countries live on the margin of subsistence, it is clear that there must be a rapid increase in the output of necessaries and even some non-necessaries. So the role of indirect taxation is not to reduce the output of necessaries but to raise the incremental saving ratio. For this purpose, it has to be used in two different ways. First, it has to be used to restrain a rapid expansion in the output (or even curtail the output) of many non-necessaries and luxuries. Second, it has to be used to transfer part of the increased output of wage-goods to the investment and/or industrial sector. This, ultimately, is the *rationale* of the taxation of mass consumption from the point of view of economic development.

It must be remembered that the curtailment or restraint of consumption applies only to luxuries and non-necessaries. In the case of necessaries, what is required is only that a part of the *increase* in their output must be made available to the investment sector. To achieve this latter purpose it is clearly not necessary to tax necessaries themselves. Take, for instance, the question of increasing the marketable surplus of food. Taxation of the basic articles consumed by the masses will in no way help in inducing or forcing the farmers to part with a greater volume of farm output. More of farm output can be got in exchange for a given volume of non-farm output by turning the terms of exchange against the farmers, that is, by raising through taxation the prices of non-necessaries which farmers would wish to consume in increasing quantities with a rise in their incomes. Nor is it necessary, by tax measures, to restrain the consumption of necessaries by other sections of the population, in favour of those who are given employment in the investment sector; for the wages paid to the latter will automatically enable them to claim a part of the available supply of wage-goods in the economy.

Writers on the subject of fiscal policy in underdeveloped countries generally deplore the need to require the masses to contribute to economic development through higher taxation; but they often conclude that such taxation is inevitable. Now what exactly does one mean when one talks of forcing the masses to contribute to economic development through higher taxation? At any given time, the supply of wage-goods is fixed and is available for consumption. Higher taxation cannot immediately reduce actual consumption. Substantial reduction in consumption will come about only when taxation begins to curtail the output of consumer goods. But this will not be allowed to happen in the case of all consumer goods. The composition of future output will depend upon the pattern of present investment. Most investment plans currently under operation allow for a considerable increase in the output of wage-goods. Indeed as developmental plans get under way, the output of many different types of consumer goods will increase. How fast consumption output increases, and what kinds of goods will be produced in increasing quantities will depend, as pointed out above, on the pattern of investment. For instance, the more investment is keyed to deepening the capital structure of the country, the less rapid will be the rise in consumption output. Since some capital deepening is involved in all development, the pattern of investment will not, in all probability, allow for a rapid increase in the output of non-necessaries and luxuries. This policy will require the masses only to put up with a rather slow rise in the level of living, and not reduce their consumption of necessaries.

From the above analysis it is clear that the main role of mass commodity taxation is to check a rapid rise in mass consumption. This conclusion has some important implications for policy. First, there is no case for taxing necessaries. Second, non-necessaries and mass luxuries can be taxed at fairly low rates to begin with. The rates on articles of mass consumption should be raised only when there is a clear indication that *per capita* output of such articles is rising. It may be pointed out also that, in so far as the pattern of investment is determined by the planning authority, taxation merely serves to bring the pattern of future consumption in line with the pattern of investment. To tax necessaries, and at the same time increase their output through government investment and subsidy, is a clearly contradictory policy.

The TEC [Taxation Enquiry Commission] put forward a recommendation that goes contrary to our conclusion above. Discussing the most suitable structure of commodity taxation for India, it makes the statement: "Additional taxation of a wide range of luxury or semi-luxury products, at fairly substantial rates, accompanied by broad-based taxation of articles of mass consumption at comparatively low rates, is, therefore, indicated."[1] This is a statement to which no exception can be taken. But it goes on to say:

> For any substantial receipts from commodity taxation and appreciable restraint on consumption in the economy as a whole, it will be necessary to extend excise and sales taxation to the consumption of lower-income groups and of goods which are commonly classed as necessaries, including several goods which are included in the Essential Goods Act under Article 286 of the Constitution.
>
> . . . An extension of the taxation of necessaries appears unavoidable, if significant results by way of diversion of resources for financing public investment, are to be secured.

Some of the goods included in the Essential Goods Act are not essentials in the strict sense of being necessaries of life for the lowest-income groups. But as regards the necessaries of living, the Commission's recommendation is not acceptable at all. It is based on a purely "revenue approach" to the question of developmental financing and misconstrues the nature of diversions to be achieved.

If it is true that large sections of the population are living on the margin of subsistence, it is not clear how any policy designed to curtail the output of necessaries can be justified. On the contrary, it has been shown above that both the fact of population increase and the need to reduce disguised unemployment call for a rapid increase in the output of at least the basic necessities. The First and the Second

Five-Year Plans have provided for substantial increases in the output of these necessities. Therefore, the statement of the Commission that "an extension of the *taxation of necessaries* appears unavoidable, *if significant results by way of diversion of resources for financing public investment* are to be secured," goes directly contrary to the intentions of the planners themselves as well as to conclusions from economic analysis. (Emphasis added.)

* * * * *

AN EXAMINATION OF EXCISE AND SALES TAXATION IN INDIA

In our discussion of indirect taxation contained in Chapter III [relevant parts printed above], it was suggested that the structure of indirect taxation must be so fashioned as to achieve certain important objectives. These are: to raise revenue, especially from those who cannot be reached through direct taxes; to curtail the consumption of luxuries; and to restrain a rapid increase in mass consumption of non-necessaries. In order to achieve these objectives, it would be helpful to have in the tax system both excises and sales taxes. As mentioned above, "the sales tax can take cognizance of the varying degrees of specialization and differentiation which occur in goods as they leave the stages of production and primary processing." Further, under a federal structure, the introduction of sales taxation becomes necessary as a substantial source of revenue for the State governments. The production and manufacture of commodities considered suitable for excise taxation may be concentrated in a few States. It will then be best to leave excise taxation to the Central government. Central excise taxation will insure uniformity of taxation on the production or manufacture of a particular commodity throughout the Union. It is then left to the States concerned to determine the burden of taxation to be borne by the consumers living within their respective borders.

The General Sales Tax. The general sales tax is a suitable device for restraining increases in general consumption. It can help the government to increase the incremental saving ratio, because it makes the tax system more income-elastic. The tax system of an underdeveloped country, therefore, should contain the general sales tax. The type of tax needed is a multi-point system which would cover all consumer goods except necessaries. The tax should be levied at a flat rate applicable to all taxable sales, but luxury items should be subject to an additional tax at one stage in the series of transactions. Capital goods must be exempt from the purview of sales taxation. The general sales taxes in India satisfy the requirement of generality and of differential rates. But not all the States exempt necessaries like food grains and cheap cloth. Indeed, in Madras the items which yield the largest revenue are paddy and rice, articles sold in provision stores, and mill cloth.[2] In defence of its policy, the Madras government has pointed out that the rural consumers do not have to pay the tax on food grains because the cultivator consumes for the most part what he grows in his own field. If the rural consumers "escape" the tax on many necessaries, there is no reason why the poorer section in urban areas alone should be subject to the tax. As we have argued earlier, there is no case for taxing necessaries in a poor country like India. The TEC was of the opinion that the small dealers in semi-urban and rural areas would be unable to maintain complicated and separate accounts. Therefore it suggested that there should be few exemptions or none at all from the multi-point levy.[3] But in another connection the TEC itself recommended that for dealers who could not maintain elementary accounts, "there should be a scheme of composition under which the liability to tax is assessed on the basis of the purchases made."[4] Even now some States have this scheme. Since the inability of the small dealers to keep accounts can be got around in this manner, this reason for not providing for exemptions is not of much importance. Besides, under a recent agreement (December, 1957) between the Union and State governments, the Union government is levying additional excise duties on sugar, textiles and tobacco in lieu of the sales taxes. This means that these items have to be exempted from the general sales tax of all the States. If exemptions are going to be introduced at all, separate accounts must be kept of exempt and non-exempt items and the addition of a few more exemptions will not make much difference.

The TEC suggested that the single-point levy on "luxury" items must be at the retail stage and the exemption level of turnover must be much higher than for the multi-point levy. This would insure that only dealers with a fairly large turnover capable of maintaining fairly complicated accounts would be subject to the tax. We agree with this suggestion.

Union Excise Duties. The levy of excise duties, in addition to the sales taxes, is necessary, first of all, to insure sufficient revenue for the Union government. Under the Indian Constitution, the yield from taxes on personal income is divided between the Union and the State governments and the entire net proceeds from the estate duty are assigned to the States. It is therefore necessary that taxes on commodities also be shared between the Union and the States. Besides, whereas the general sales tax is a useful device for checking increases in general consumption, particular excises are more suitable for causing inter-industry diversions of resources. It is considered, therefore, that the existing arrangement, under which the Union levies excises and the States levy sales taxes, is essentially satisfactory.

It is inevitable that with the decline of customs the relative importance of excises in the scheme of Union finances should increase. While it is legitimate for the government to increase its revenue from excises, it is important that the commodities to be taxed be selected in accordance with some definite principles. It is preferable, in general, to confine excises to commodities that satisfy one or more of the following characteristics: (a) low price-elasticity of demand; (b) high income-elasticity of demand; (c) absorbing scarce factors needed in the public sector; and (d) in the nature of luxuries consumed only by the well-to-do. The bulk of the excise revenue must be derived from a few widely-consumed "mass luxuries," which are likely to satisfy the first two characteristics. Good examples are tea, coffee, tobacco, and superior varieties of cloth. Taxation of these goods insures that sufficient revenue can be expected to be raised, because of low price-elasticity and high income-elasticity. Outside of the types of goods mentioned above, certain selected commodities can be taxed with the diversionary effect in view. Luxuries and scarce "bottleneck" factors needed in the public sector are examples of this type of commodities.

As we have indicated earlier, there is no case for taxing necessaries. Nor is there a case for indefinitely extending the scope of excises. While it is true that the bulk of the excise revenue is derived from the taxation of certain non-necessaries like tea, tobacco, and superior varieties of cloth, the Union government taxes also certain necessaries like cheap cloth and sugar. Even if it is maintained that refined sugar is in the nature of a "luxury," because the poor use mostly unrefined sugar or *gur,* and that therefore refined sugar can be justifiably taxed, there is no case for the taxation of cheap cloth. Nor is it justifiable to tax kerosene at the high rates prevailing now.

Equally questionable is the policy of steadily extending excises to cover all industries that have grown up under protection. The TEC, unfortunately we think, lent its sanction to this policy. It noted: "The principles underlying the extension of excises from time to time are that indigenous industries which have developed under a protective tariff wall should be called upon to replace the loss of customs revenue on imports and that the country's tax structure can be made stable only by broadbasing the excises."[5] And when it looked around for new industries to be taxed, it mentioned the paper industry, among others, and said: "The industry has developed as a result of tariff protection, and this provides justification for the levy of an excise duty on paper."[6] The same argument was used in the case of some other goods selected for new taxation.[7]

While it is true that excises as a whole have to replace to some extent the loss in customs revenue, why should the grant of protection be considered a sufficient justification for taxation? Protection is (or should be) granted in the national interest. It is intended that the protected industries should grow. It could hardly be maintained, moreover, that the consumers of protected products have benefited directly from the policy of protection. On the contrary, they have been forced to pay higher prices because of protection. And they continue to pay the higher prices as long as the domestic price is higher than the price of the imported product exclusive of the import duty. It is far from reasonable then to ask these same consumers to bear the extra burden of the excise duty except perhaps in those cases where the domestic cost of production has been brought down so low as to have made possible the removal of the protective tariff. Indeed it could be argued with greater validity that while the consumers of the protected industries are bearing the brunt of protection, the consumers of the non-protected industries should be required to bear the burden of excises. Actually, however, protection and non-protection cannot be important considerations in selecting commodities for excise taxation. It is submitted that the principles we have put forward earlier must be applied in every case before taxation is decided upon.

One reason why the Union government has been forced to extend the coverage of excise taxation is that the revenue from excises has been very inelastic with respect to price and money income changes. This is due to the fact that excise duties are mostly specific. While prices have been rising almost steadily since 1938, the revenue from excises existing at any given time has lagged behind, so that the government has been forced to increase the rates of existing taxes and add continually to the list of goods taxed. For example, in the case of articles subject to duty between 1938–39 and 1953–54, it was found that, in spite of rate increases, the rates of duty as percentages of the prices of the articles taxed declined substantially during these years, with a consequent reduction in the average tax burden on these articles. The extension of coverage was more significant than the rate increases in bringing more revenue. "Thus, in 1953–54, only 29 per cent of the revenue from excise duties was raised from articles which were subject to duty also in 1938–39 and 76 per cent from articles which were taxed in 1948–49."[8]

It is suggested that it might be a better policy to convert as many of the duties as possible into *ad valorem* duties than to extend the excise to such goods as dry and storage batteries, tyres, and varnishes. Apart from other reasons, the continual extension of coverage makes the whole excise administration complex and unwieldy.

In closing, we may mention two other cases in which excise duties can be used. The first is the case of petrol, which is taxed in all countries on the basis of "benefit principle." The second is the case of goods whose export can be promoted to earn more foreign exchange by discouraging domestic consumption. This policy is fruitful, however, only when the elasticity of the foreign demand for the product concerned is greater than unity, for if it were less than unity, the fall in the price due to increased exports would lead to a shrinkage in the foreign exchange earned. In India it may be possible to promote the export of superior varieties of cloth by such a policy.

NOTES TO SELECTION 17

[1] *TEC Report,* I, 149.
[2] *TEC Report,* II, 36.
[3] *Ibid.,* p. 63.
[4] *Ibid.,* p. 64.
[5] *TEC Report,* II, 257–58.
[6] *Ibid.,* p. 315.
[7] *Ibid.,* pp. 315–17.
[8] *TEC Report,* II, 259.

18

The Expenditure Tax in a System
of Personal Taxation

by Nicholas Kaldor*

THE CASE FOR A COMPREHENSIVE REFORM
OF PERSONAL TAXATION

Introduction

THE purpose of personal (or "direct") taxation is to provide equity
and fairness in the distribution of the tax burden in the community.
Looking at the problem from the revenue aspect alone, it might be
administratively simpler to collect any given total of revenue by taxes
on transactions such as sales taxes, excise duties, etc.—or *ad rem* taxes
of various kinds—rather than by taxes levied on persons assessed according to some overall criterion (or criteria) of "ability to pay," on
a graduated scale. But in a developing economy, where privately
owned wealth grows rapidly and unevenly, a situation in which the
burden imposed on the broad masses of population is not comple-
mented by an efficient system of progressive taxation on the minority
of wealth-owners would become socially intolerable. The question of
the necessity of reforms in the scope, comprehensiveness, and efficiency
of administration of personal taxation should not be judged, therefore, from a narrow revenue point of view alone. Certain reforms may
be essential even if the immediate revenue prospect is small, if they
can be shown to be a necessary pre-condition for imposing higher
burdens on the community at large, in a manner consistent with the
prevailing sense of justice and equity of the community.

This problem is a particularly important one for India which is
on the threshold of a period of accelerated economic development,

*Nicholas Kaldor, *Indian Tax Reform: Report of a Survey* (New Delhi: Government of India, Ministry of Finance, Department of Economic Affairs, 1956),
Chap. 1, pp. 7–16, and Chap. 5, pp. 39–47. Reprinted with the kind permission of
the author.

and whose people desire to strike a "middle road" between Western capitalism and Eastern Socialism. In India the great bulk of the national wealth is, and will continue to be, privately owned—industries or landed property that may be taken over by the State will not fundamentally alter this state of affairs if due compensation is paid to the owners, so that the growth in public property will be offset by the growth in public indebtedness[1]—it appears inevitable, therefore, that both the amount of privately owned wealth, and (in the absence of effective tax measures) the skewness of the distribution of ownership of that wealth should increase *pari passu* with economic growth. Owing to the fact that the savings of the community are more unevenly distributed than income, there is an inevitable tendency, unless effectively counteracted by the tax system or other instruments of public policy, for the wealth of the largest property owners to grow at a faster rate than wealth in general. The more income and wealth grow, therefore, the more the inequality of wealth between individuals increases.

All politically "advanced" democracies possess some form of progressive personal taxation, generally based on "income." But with the possible exception of Sweden, none have succeeded in bringing about the degree of re-distribution of wealth and income the attainment of which has been the avowed objective of their taxation policies. Thus in the United Kingdom, though the combined income and surtax rates for the last 15 years have exceeded 90% in the top brackets, and estate duties reached a maximum of 80%, vast new fortunes are still being made, and the degree of concentration in the ownership of wealth—as measured, e.g., by the percentage of persons owning one-third of the national wealth, etc.—has not been reduced. The same is true, I believe, of the United States and other Western countries. The reasons are to be sought in the fact that owing to the numerous loopholes of one sort or another that are tolerated (and in some cases deliberately nurtured) by the legislatures, as well as the failure of the tax administration to force a full disclosure of income or wealth, the true burden of taxation on the owners of property is far below that indicated by the nominal rates of taxation on "income." On incomes derived from office, employment, or pension on the other hand, i.e., on salaries and wages, the comprehensive reporting systems introduced during and after the war ensure practically 100% coverage; nor does the definition of "taxable income" permit the same kind of manipulation here as with the profits of business or of income derived from the ownership of capital. The only important loopholes in the case of salary-incomes are expense allowances and benefits in kind provided by the employer; and these can be, and are being, plugged by means of special legislative provisions such as those recently introduced in the United Kingdom, India, and some other countries. Public employees, like judges or high civil servants, who do not receive such "perks" from their employer, and have no tax loopholes to fall back on, are exposed to the full blast of punitive rates that are only nominally applicable to the other sectors of the community.

So far from attaining its avowed objectives of mitigating economic and social inequality, progressive taxation in most Western countries has thus served to create new inequities by imposing an altogether disproportionate burden on the professional classes, on intellectuals and administrators, and in particular, on leading public servants of all kinds. The strongest disincentive effects have been on the quality of entrants in the public service, and on the level of ability of the administrative personnel of public enterprises of all kinds. There is no need to stress the disadvantages and dangers of this in a society which will be increasingly dependent on the quality and initiative of its public service.

In my view, the main factors responsible for the failure of progressive taxation to attain its objectives are the following (the relative importance of these factors varies, of course, for different countries):

a) Absence of a clear and comprehensive notion of what constitutes "income" for tax purposes; and the consequent exclusion of numerous kinds of beneficial receipts (of which capital gains and capital profits of all kinds are the most important) ; and the consequent impossibility of preventing manipulations of innumerable kinds which aim at making the accrual of benefits from the ownership of property or business activity appear as non-taxable capital profits or gains rather than as taxable receipts.

b) Failure to recognise that the ownership of disposable assets confers a benefit on the owner over and above the income which the property yields; and the failure to supplement taxes on income with taxes on net worth.

c) The elastic definition of expenses as permissible deductions to be set against receipts in the calculation of trading profits, together with over-generous recognition of the notion of, and over-generous provision for the relief of, "losses," which bring it about that a trader can manufacture "losses" for tax purposes and thereby build up assets at the cost of the revenue, without his consequent gains being brought into charge.

d) Failure to secure the true aggregation of a man's (or a family's) total property or income for tax purposes, due (in part) to defective provisions concerning the compulsory aggregation of family income, and to provisions concerning the transfer of income or property into trusts and settlements, etc. (quite apart from any illegal concealment of income).

e) Failure to secure the full reporting of income, or of property, due (*i*) to the absence of any automatic reporting system for property income and property transactions, analogous to that existing for incomes from employment; (*ii*) to the failure to make the return required of the tax payer comprehensive enough to ensure that it is self-checking in character; (*iii*) to the facilities afforded in common law for the concealment of income and property through the registration of property in bogus names (*benami* holdings) or through anonymous holdings (like bearer bonds, or the system of blank transfers in the case of shares).

Points (*a*) to (*d*) above provide the sources of (legal) tax avoidance, while (*e*) the facilities for (illegal) tax evasion. The difference between the situation in India and majority of Western countries is only that in the case of India (*e*) is probably more prominent, and in consequence (*a*) to (*d*) relatively less important, than for the countries of the West.

I am convinced that it would be technically feasible so to reform the tax system as to eliminate altogether, or at least greatly to diminish, both the legal avenues for tax avoidance and the scope for large-scale tax evasion. For reasons explained below, the administrative feasibility of doing so is far more promising in the case of a comprehensive reform than in the case of the adoption of partial or piecemeal remedial measures. Neither in the case of countries like the United Kingdom or the United States of America, nor in the case of India, is large-scale tax avoidance and evasion an ineluctable consequence of human or administrative imperfections or folly, or of the private enterprise system, or any other ineradicable feature of society. The factor which has so far prevented the establishment of an effective system of taxation on profits and capital in the Western democracies or in India is the opposition of vested interests, not the "technical" impossibility of devising an equitable and foolproof system.

The Three Major Considerations

The three prime considerations that should be taken into account in framing an effective tax system are equity, economic effects, and administrative efficiency.

From the point of view of equity, the most important consideration is that the tax system should not contain a systematic bias in favour of particular groups of tax-payers and against others. For reasons which I analysed in some detail in my book[2] and which it is unnecessary to repeat here, equity in taxation between income from work and income from property cannot be secured unless (*i*) the concept of "income" is made sufficiently comprehensive to embrace *all* beneficial receipts which increase the tax-payers' spending power, and not merely the conventional forms of income; (*ii*) the tax on income is supplemented by an annual tax on capital wealth in recognition of the fact that taxable capacity cannot be adequately measured either by income alone, or by capital wealth alone, but can be approximated through a mixture of both; (*iii*) in the calculations of taxable income, profit or gain, permissible deductions should proceed on uniform and non-discriminatory principles as between different kinds and forms of income. This means, in effect, that only such expenses should be chargeable against the receipts as can be shown to have been necessarily involved in producing the receipts of the year in question.

From the point of view of the economic effects of taxation the major consideration is to prevent the tax system from becoming too much of a disincentive on effort, initiative or enterprise. Taxes on income make it less attractive to undertake work or to risk capital in productive enterprise; and through the factor of "double taxation" of savings, penalise savings and put a premium on spending. The importance of all these effects depends on the marginal rates of taxation. I am strongly of the view that the developments of the last 15–20 years which imposed (nominally) fantastically high marginal rates of tax, while permitting the continuance of wide loopholes for tax avoidance, are highly pernicious in character. As Henry Simons said before the War[3] the whole procedure smacks of a "subtle kind of moral and intellectual dishonesty." "One senses here a grand scheme of deception whereby enormous surtaxes are voted in exchange for promises that they will not be made effective. Thus the politicians may point with pride to the rates, while quietly reminding their wealthy constituents of the loopholes."

These high marginal rates, amounting to 80 to 90% (in the U.K. at one stage they amounted to 97.5%) could never have been imposed had they really been what they pretended to be, a tax on the genuine accrual of wealth. As is it, these confiscatory tax rates truly apply only to a small minority of people who cannot avoid their incidence, and their long-run effect is bound to be wholly pernicious, both in penalising the prospects of certain careers which are vital from the national point of view, and in undermining public morality.[4]

Assuming a comprehensive tax-base, the marginal rate of income tax ought never to exceed, in my view, something of the order of 40–50% for income that is both earned and saved. (For spent income, the effective rate could, of course, be made considerably higher, if income tax were supplemented by a progressive spendings tax, in replacement of the higher brackets of super tax.) For unearned income (income from business or property) a differential tax should be imposed in the form of an annual tax on wealth (in addition to the tax on income) which has not the same disincentive effects on the productive employment of capital (i.e. on the assumption of risks) as a tax on income. This tax, however, has a similarly discouraging effect on savings as income tax, and for that reason, an annual tax on wealth, conceived as a progressive tax, ought not to exceed a top marginal rate of $1-1\frac{1}{2}\%$ per annum.

From the point of view of administrative efficiency the main requirements are:—

i) *Simplicity.*—The taxes should be based on simple definitions, avoiding, as far as possible, exemptions of various kinds or the special treatment of special categories, since all such complications lend themselves to manipulations (e.g., the existing difference in tax treatment between different kinds of companies, or as between companies and individuals, or as between the "profits" of business and "capital profits").

ii) *Comprehensiveness.*—Taxes on income should embrace all forms of beneficial receipts, taxes on capital wealth all forms of property. Exceptions to this should only be made on strictly administrative grounds (e.g., exemption limits for the sake of limiting the number of cases to be dealt with).

iii) *A single, comprehensive return; a self-checking system of taxation; and an automatic reporting system.*—These, I consider, are the most important requirements from the point of view of administrative efficiency:

a) A Comprehensive Return

At the moment the taxpayer is only asked to return his income; and since the question whether a particular receipt falls into the category of "income" or not, is often a highly doubtful matter, the taxpayer is left, in effect, to decide for himself whether particular receipts are returnable or not. The Revenue authorities have power to ask for a return of capital assets and other details, but these powers are sparingly used—as it is indeed not possible to compel taxpayers to supply information on matters that are not directly relevant to the assessment of their tax liabilities. If a complete set of accounts is to be furnished i.e., a statement of total wealth at the beginning of the year, all accruals during the year—by way of gifts, bequests, winnings, etc., as well as all forms of taxable income and gains; the application of these to personal expenses and investments—as well as the resulting asset-position at the end of the year, the concealment of particular items of income or property, or the falsification of accounts, would obviously become far more difficult. (This is not to suggest that it is impossible to keep a complete duplicate set of books or to make out a "phoney" set of comprehensive accounts. But it is obviously a more difficult thing to do than to conceal receipts when only a partial return is called for.)

b) A Self-checking System of Taxation

The present system of taxation already contains, of course, some self-checking elements. But owing to gaps in the legislation, the vagueness of the distinction between taxable and not-taxable receipts, and other factors, the efficiency of this is limited and it only works in certain directions. Assuming, however, that in addition to the present taxes on income, all realized capital gains are brought into charge (the transfer of assets by way of gifts, bequest and legacy counting as "realization" in the same way as transfer by way of sale), a gift tax is imposed along side of (and ultimately in replacement of) estate duties, and finally a personal expenditure tax is introduced, the system becomes completely self-checking in the sense that A's attempt to ensure that he is not over-assessed with regard to his own tax liabilities automatically brings to light the receipts and gains made by B, and so on. If the present taxes on income were extended to capital gains and other receipts of a capital nature, and were supplemented by an annual tax on wealth and a gift tax, if a super tax were levied on an expenditure-base, (see below), and if all these taxes were assessed at the same time, by the same authority, and on the basis of a single comprehensive account submitted by the tax-payer (containing all receipts in the year, all tax-exempt outlays, a record of all capital transactions, and a full statement of all property owned) evasion and concealment would become more difficult, not only on account of the difficulty of the individual tax-payer to conceal consistently particular receipts or items of property but owing to the fact that the evidence furnished by one tax-payer (in the interests of minimising his own liability) directly serves as a check on the return furnished by others. Thus in computing A's liability for a personal expenditure tax all "exempt outlays" must be returned, and such exempt outlays represent taxable receipts of one kind or another (i.e., profit, capital gain, gift, etc.) to B. Similarly, since under this system all gains or losses on capital transactions are brought into the account, there is an automatic check on all new purchases of capital assets through the record of sales, and it is in the interest of the purchaser not to allow an under-statement of the price at which an asset was acquired since this enhances his future liability for a capital gains tax, as well as his liability to the personal expenditure tax.

c) An Automatic Reporting System Extending to All Property

A system extending to all property transactions and all cash payments over a certain sum is outlined in Chapter 6 [not included in this volume]. As indicated there, by means of a system of code numbers and tax vouchers, it would be relatively simple (administratively) to introduce an automatic reporting system for all property transactions requiring registration and attracting stamp duty. As suggested, the system can be extended to various other types of transactions if taxes were levied on personal expenditure, as well as on income.

Outline of Main Proposals

An effective system on the above lines requires taxes on (*a*) income; (*b*) capital gains; (*c*) net wealth; (*d*) personal expenditure; and (*e*) gifts. All these can be assessed as a single operation, and on the basis of a single comprehensive return provided by the tax-payer.

a) Income Tax

In place of the present income tax and super tax there should be a single income tax which, for individuals and partnerships etc., is progressive up to an annual income of Rs. 25,000 and at a flat rate of 7 annas in the rupee for all income above that level. The top marginal rate on income, therefore, becomes 43½% (or, say, 45% including the sur-charge) above that level. Companies should not be required to pay income tax but should pay a non-refundable tax of 7 annas in the rupee on their whole income (in place of the present income and corporation taxes). Income tax should be deducted at the maximum of 7 annas in the case of all interest and dividend payments as a matter of collection at source and credited to the recipients' income tax account.

b) Capital Gains Tax

All capital gains on realization and all casual gains and capital receipts not chargeable at present (such as the sale of terminable rights, premium on leases, etc.) should be charged to income tax which means a flat rate charge of 7 annas in the rupee once the combined income (including capital gains) exceeds Rs. 25,000. Capital gains of companies should be chargeable to tax in the same way as trading profits.

This means that all beneficial receipts (whether trading or capital profits, other kinds of income, individual or company income, or the income of public or of private companies) are charged at a single uniform rate of 7 annas in the rupee (in the place of the present multiplicity of rates and exemptions), except that individuals are charged at reduced rates when their aggregate beneficial receipts are less than Rs. 25,000. The tremendous advantage of this, both as regards administrative simplicity and the prevention of evasion and manipulation of all kinds, cannot be over-emphasized.

c) Annual Tax on Wealth

Payable by individuals, HUF's, partnerships, etc. Suggested scale, ⅓% p.a. on personal net worth of, say, Rs. 1,00,000-4,00,000; ½% p.a.

on 4,00,001-7,00,000; ¾% p.a. on 7,00,001-10,00,000; 1% on capital value of Rs. 10,00,001-15,00,000 and 1½% in excess of Rs. 15 lakhs (tax liability to be calculated on the slab system).

d) Personal Expenditure Tax

Payable on a per head basis, on personal outlay in excess of Rs. 10,000 p.a. per adult (infants counting as one half adult for the purpose) on a progressive scale, calculated on the slab system, rising from 25% for expenditure between Rs. 10,000-12,500 to 300% on expenditure in excess of Rs. 50,000 p.a. per adult. (Example: A family of four, father, mother, 2 children, incurs an expenditure of Rs. 40,000 a year. As the family consists of 3 adult units, the expenditure is Rs. 13,333 per adult, and the tax liability is three times the tax on the first Rs. 3,333 of taxable expenditure.) [5]

e) General Gift Tax

Payable on gifts in excess of Rs. 10,000 for any single recipient of gifts (the donee) and taxed at a rate depending on the total net worth of the recipient (as ascertained for annual wealth tax) at the rate of 10% if the net worth is below Rs. 1,00,000 and at double the current corresponding estate duty rates for correspondingly higher amounts of net worth, i.e., at the rate of 15 to 80%, depending on the net worth of the recipient. (Examples: (*i*) A receives a gift of Rs. 50,000 from his parent; possesses no property; his tax liability is Rs. 4,000. (*ii*) B receives a bequest of Rs. 50,000 and possesses net worth (before the bequest) valued at Rs. 2,50,000; B's liability is 25% on 40,000, i.e., Rs. 10,000. (*iii*) C inherits from his father Rs. 2,00,000; has no other property; his liability is Rs. 26,500. (*iv*) D owns property valued at Rs. 5,00,000; receives a gift of Rs. 50,000; his liability is 40% of Rs. 40,000 i.e., Rs. 16,000.) It is suggested that once the annual wealth tax is in operation, and adequate returns are obtained on annual net worth, the above gift tax should replace the present estate duty altogether. The latter is based on an antiquated conception. The true incidence of inheritance taxes falls on the recipients of the inheritance, and not on the deceased. Also, there is no justification in equity for a difference in treatment as between gifts *inter vivos* and the receipt of legacies or bequests. Hence a single progressive tax on gifts should take the place of the estate duty, as well as serving as a tax on all other gratuitous or quasi-gratuitous property transfers.[6] (The exemption of Rs. 10,000 should apply, of course, only to the initial gift received by a particular donee.)

*   *   *   *   *

A Personal Expenditure Tax

In Chapter 1 [see above in this volume] it was proposed that a progressive tax on personal expenditure (with a relatively high exemption limit) should be imposed along with other suggested reforms, and the maximum rate of income tax should, at the same time, be lowered to 7 annas in the rupee (or 45% including sur-charge). The effect of these proposals would thus be the replacement of the higher ranges of super tax on personal income with a super tax on personal expenditure. The purpose of this chapter is to explain these proposals in more detail, and at the same time to deal with some of the objections that have been raised against the introduction of a personal expenditure tax in India.

General Considerations

In my book,[7] I argued the case in favour of a personal expenditure tax on grounds of both equity and economic expediency in some detail and, therefore, do not wish to repeat the general arguments here. The main arguments which have been put forward against the proposals made in my book, in the particular context of India, may be listed as follows:—

a) It would not be practicable to impose an expenditure tax on top of the present taxes on income, since this would make taxation altogether too severe.

b) Taxation of expenditure in replacement of taxation of income means the exemption of savings; this would greatly stimulate accumulation by the wealthier classes and would lead to an even greater concentration of property ownership. If property taxes were imposed to counter the tendency to concentration of property, this, in turn, would cancel the advantages of the expenditure tax in regard to the incentive to save.

c) The expenditure tax would be administratively more difficult to handle than the income tax.

d) As expenditure met out of agricultural income would have to be exempted from taxation, it would encourage people to debit the maximum part of their expenditure against their agricultural income.

I think it ought to be made clear that while an expenditure tax is superior to income tax, both because "expenditure" is more strictly definable than "income" as the basis of taxation and because "expenditure" is a better index of taxable capacity than "income," there is nothing inherently wrong in having both a tax on expenditure and a tax on income side by side. Even if it could be argued that the present taxation of income at the high rates of income and super taxes is being applied effectively, one could still justify the introduction of an expenditure tax if economic considerations require a restriction of personal spending and if that restriction could not be attained by a further increase in income and property taxes. If income and property are taxed too severely, while expenditure out of accumulated wealth is not taxed or restricted, the effect would merely be to encourage the capitalists to dissipate their wealth rather than to reduce their living standards.[8] I argued in earlier chapters that the present high marginal rates of taxation on income would have far more deleterious effects on the behaviour of wealth-owners (i.e., on their incentives to save or to invest) if these taxes were applied effectively. The fact that these effects are largely avoided because the tax system contains large enough loop-holes to permit the owners of risk capital to make tax-free gains and to accumulate capital out of tax-free savings, is an argument against the present system of taxation, and not against the expenditure tax. For if these loop-holes were closed (i.e. all capital gains, etc., were brought into charge in the same way as other income) it would soon become evident that these high marginal rates on income could not be maintained. Hence progressive taxation, if it is to be both effective and impartial, cannot be levied beyond a certain point on an income-base, but only on an expenditure-base.

It would also be incorrect to say that imposition of taxes on property (whether in the form of an annual tax on wealth, estate duties, or the general gift tax) would cancel the advantages of an expenditure tax in restricting spending. On the contrary, the imposition of a personal expenditure tax would counter the disincentive effects of these property taxes on the spending and saving habits of the rich. A progressive expenditure tax taken by itself would effectively reduce the standard of living of the upper classes, though it might augment the rate of accumulation of large fortunes. Property taxes cut down the rate of accumulation but encourage spending. A combination of the two types of taxes, therefore, far from cancelling the good effects of either, makes it possible to restrict effectively the living standards of the rich without sacrificing the long-run egalitarian objective of a more even distribution of property.

While an expenditure tax would be administratively more difficult to handle than the present income tax, it is not more difficult to handle than a comprehensive and effective system of income taxation. On the contrary, the incorporation of an expenditure tax in a system of personal taxation which includes both taxes on income (including capital gains) and on property would ease considerably the prevention of evasion—partly because it would introduce an opposition of interests between the different parties as regards the concealment of particular transactions (whereas under the present system both parties to a transaction may have an identical interest in concealing altogether or in understating the value of a particular transaction), and partly also because the necessity to account for the amounts spent on personal purposes over a particular period together with the obligation to produce a balance-sheet of personal net wealth at the beginning and at the end of the period forces the taxpayer into a full disclosure of receipts; just as the need to make a full return of current receipts and expenditure forces the taxpayer into a full disclosure of capital assets.

It should also be remembered that the problem of personal expenses being met out of business expenditure accounts or benefits given in kind rather than in cash already arises under an income tax. The obligation of a taxpayer to return his personal expenditure as well as his income would make it easier to detect such cases of income tax evasion since they would automatically be reflected in an unduly low figure being returned for personal expenditure. The plain fact is that the incorporation of an expenditure tax would make the administration of the income tax a great deal more effective as well. It is possible for a man to conceal some part of his expenditure effectively by concealing a corresponding part of his receipts, or by getting some part of his own expenses paid by someone else (his business employer or some friend or relation in a lower tax bracket), but the important point is that such concealments could not be carried to the point at which the taxpayer's own returned figure for his expenditure becomes apparently inconsistent with his mode of living. I think the experience of income tax officers would confirm that while it is not possible to estimate from external criteria a man's expenditure with any great precision, it is certainly possible to do so with a fair margin of approximation.[9] A man who keeps several houses, a large number of servants, and several cars and entertains frequently, might well manage to understate his true expenditure by a few thousand rupees a year, but he could not possibly return a figure of, say, Rs. 10,000 when in fact he spent Rs. 50,000 or Rs. 1,00,000. Yet under the present system, there is no limit to the extent to which he could understate his income through fraudulent concealments or the extent to which he can economise on having a taxable income by converting income into capital gains or economise on super tax by transferring property into trusts and settlements.

With regard to the point concerning agricultural income, the constitutional position seems to be rather in favour of the expenditure tax. The Constitution does not assign specifically a tax on expenditure either to the Centre or to the States, nor does it state anywhere that expenditure out of agricultural income (as distinct from the agricultural income itself) should not be taxable by the Centre. I believe, therefore, that a tax on personal expenditure would be constitutional irrespective of the sources from which the expenditure was drawn; and the revenue from it could be taken as belonging exclusively to the Centre under item 97 of List I of the 7th Schedule to the Constitution.

The one contention which no one has called into question is that a progressive personal tax on expenditure is a most potent weapon for inducing economies in personal spending among the well-to-do classes. It is also beyond dispute that an accelerated rate of economic growth requires a higher proportion (and not merely a higher amount) of investment expenditure to total expenditure—i.e., a higher proportion of savings in the national income. Resources for such additional savings can only come from a reduction in consumption in relation to current income. As the consumption standards of the masses of the population in India are so near to the bare minimum level, the reduction in the propensity to consume of the well-to-do classes appears to me as an indispensable requirement for sustaining a higher rate of economic growth. Luxury consumption is in fact the only part of the national expenditure that could be compressed for the sake of releasing resources for a higher rate of capital accumulation; and a graduated progressive tax on personal consumption is undoubtedly the ideal instrument for attaining this end.

Definition of Expenditure and Mode of Assessment and Graduation

The Real Basis of the Charge

Although, as explained further below, the taxpayer would not normally be required to give any detailed account of his outlays on consumption (but only a statement of his total outlay as part of a comprehensive return showing all his receipts, investments, etc., and all the items for which he claims exemption) the legal basis of the charge ought to be a reasonable every day conception of personal consumption (or expenditure), including not only items met by expenditure out of the taxpayer's own spending but also consumption out of benefits and gifts received in kind, expenses met by the employer, friend or relation, subject to an annual exemption limit of, say, Rs. 2,000 a year per head for such gifts or benefits received. If the charge is based on personal consumption thus defined, attempts to avoid tax by making gifts to persons of low spending power, etc., (in return for such persons meeting part of the taxpayer's expenses) or by getting employers or businesses to meet one's personal bills would all be unavailable. The taxpayers would, in fact, be chargeable on the value of all goods and services received for personal consumption irrespective of how and by whom these were financed.

Definition of Personal Consumption

Personal consumption excludes outlays on the following items:
a) Business expenses in the strictest sense; the question of adequacy of the present legal definition of such expenses as expenses

"wholly or exclusively incurred for the purposes of a trade or business" will be further discussed in Chapter 7 [not included in this volume].

b) All investment outlays i.e., sums devoted to the purchase of income yielding property (like land, stocks and shares, securities of all kinds) or non-income yielding "stores of wealth" (like bank deposits, bar gold, current deposits, bank notes and coins);[10] loans of all kind and sums devoted to the repayment of past indebtedness.

c) Capital expenditures for personal use, only the annual benefits from which, and not the outlay itself, enters into "consumption." The purchase of a dwelling house for owner-occupation, works of art, jewellery and ornaments above a certain value (say, Rs. 10,000) fall into this category.

d) Gifts made to other persons above a certain amount (say, Rs. 2,000) including settlements made on children, dowries,[11] etc.

Claims for exemption under items (a) to (d) would have to be supported by duly certified tax vouchers as described in Chapter 6 [not included in this volume] but whilst outlays under items (a), (b) and (d) carry complete exemption, outlays under (c) would carry a notional addition to personal consumption in the year of purchase and subsequent years (until the items are sold), based on, say, 5% of the purchase price.[12]

Chargeable and Exempt Consumption Expenditure

Outlays not falling within categories (a) to (d) above may be defined as personal expenditure but not all such expenditure would be charged to tax. Certain categories of necessitous items should be exempted and the range of such items would vary with the particular customs and modes of living. Items which I would regard as falling reasonably within the "necessitous" categories and deserving exemption in addition to all personal taxes paid are: (i) funeral and birth expenses; (ii) medical expenses up to a certain amount per head; (iii) any additional expenses incurred as a result of severe physical disabilities up to a certain amount per year; (iv) fines, etc., imposed by courts; and (v) expenses incurred as a result of fire, burglary, theft, flood, damage, etc. (Since all such outlays represent insurable risks, it would be administratively convenient to restrict such exemptions to payments received under the insurance policies rather than to the outlays themselves.)

Treatment of Chargeable Consumption Expenditure

The residual left after deduction of exempted items constitutes chargeable consumption expenditure; not all of which, however, is fully chargeable in the year of purchase. Expenditure on durable goods of all kinds like furniture, motor-cars, house repairs etc., or on unusual outlays like weddings, can be spread at the taxpayer's option over, say, a five-year or possibly a ten-year period. Since under a progressive system any tax relief obtained on account of such unusual expenditure would automatically swell the taxpayer's chargeable expenditure in the following and subsequent years, spreading would be against the taxpayers' interest except in so far as it genuinely assisted to even out his rate of expenditure over time. There would be no need, therefore, in these categories to require the same kind of proof to be furnished as would be necessary for claiming exemption under categories (a) to (d) under "Definition of Personal Consumption" above.[13]

Mode of Assessment and Graduation

Since the purpose of the tax is to discourage high level spending by steeply rising marginal rates on expenditure, it is far more neces- sary in the case of this tax than in the case of income tax to take into account differences in needs arising out of differences in the size of the family which the taxpayer has to support. Hence unlike the income tax (where only a very small difference is introduced in the tax liability through a variation of the amount of initial exemption), the rates of taxation in the case of expenditure tax ought to vary with the scale of expenditure per head rather than the total expenditure of the whole family unit. This means the adoption of the so-called quotient system, which is already applied in France for income tax purposes, according to which the income (or expenditure) of all mem- bers of the family is first aggregated and then divided into a number of parts, depending on the number of persons in each family, and the tax is charged separately on each part. Children may count as one-half unit each (though the fraction could be varied with their age and number).[14] Apart from wife and children it may be permitted to add other family members living in a joint household to the con- ception of the "family," provided only that their receipts, income and property, are effectively aggregated with the family for tax purposes. It would be reasonable, however, to count such additional members in the same way as children as a fractional rather than full unit each. This is because the aggregate family expenditure, assuming a given living standard, rises less than in proportion to the increase in the numbers in the household. I would therefore suggest that additional family members should be converted to adult units on a tapering-off scale so that a family of say 4 members would count as three adult units, a family of 7 members as four adult units and that five should be the maximum number of adult units for a family. That means that the minimum liability to tax in case of a large family is as on the total family expenditure divided by five, this liability being multiplied five times.

The pre-condition of this method of charging, as already stated, is the effective aggregation of all receipts, income and property of the family members. Although, in principle, such aggregation could be adopted for purposes of the expenditure tax only without being applied for income and property taxes, from an administrative point of view, it would clearly be far more convenient if the rules of aggregation applied equally to all types of personal taxation. In India, unlike in England, the income of husband and wife is not automatically aggregated for tax purposes, though there are special anti-avoidance provisions which enforce aggregation in case of partnership shares, etc., and cause income and property transfers between family members to be ignored for tax purposes. It would, however, be far more equitable as between different taxpayers if a general rule of aggregation were adopted for purposes of income and property taxes as well as for purposes of expenditure tax as between husband and wife and minor children (excepting in the case of a legal separation). In the case of other family members aggregation for income and property tax purposes would be optional but a necessary pre-condition for aggregation for expenditure tax purposes.

Suggested Schedule of Rates

In Chapter 1 [see above in this volume], it was suggested that there should be an exemption limit of Rs. 10,000 per adult and expenditure in excess of this amount should be charged according to the slab system of graduation, starting from 25% on the lowest slab (i.e., on the expenditure between Rs. 10,000 and Rs. 12,500) and rising gradually up to a maximum of 300% on expenditures in excess of Rs. 50,000 per head. An exemption limit and schedule of rates of this character seem to me appropriate for replacing the present super-tax on personal incomes on the slabs above –/7/– annas in the rupee— i.e., in excess of gross income of Rs. 40,000 and a net family income, after income tax, of Rs. 30,000. Since the typical family may be assumed to comprise at least three adult units, a net expenditure of Rs. 10,000 per head corresponds to a net family expenditure of Rs. 30,000. Assuming that personal expenditure corresponds to net income after tax, the substitution of an expenditure tax on this scale for the higher brackets of super tax would not change appreciably the total burden of taxation. There would, of course, be a considerable shift in the tax burden as between relatively high spending and relatively high saving tax-payers.

It could be argued, however, that in the present conditions of India a stronger deterrent to spending and a stronger stimulus to personal saving would be justified, and therefore, the exemption limits ought to be put lower and the scale of graduation made stiffer than the scale which is the nearest equivalent to the present super tax. If the exemption limit were put at Rs. 6,000 per head and the maximum slab of 300% were imposed on expenditures in excess of Rs. 30,000 per head the liability to tax would extend to a considerably larger segment of the population and it would have a more powerful effect in restraining spending. It might, therefore, be more appropriate in the present situation of India even though it would probably imply considerable increase of the present tax burden of a typical family in the higher income groups.

There are unfortunately no statistics available in India, even on a sample survey basis, of the consumption expenditure of the top income groups. Some of the cases investigated by the Taxation Investigation Commission, I understand, suggest that personal expenditure might be rather low in relation to true income. In these particular cases, however, the amount of concealed income was probably very large in relation to declared income and it is quite possible that such concealed income is saved to a far greater extent than declared income precisely because the spending of concealed income would cause suspicion and might lead to detection. There might be a large number of cases where the level of expenditure is greatly in excess of the taxable income and where the difference is financed not out of concealed income, but out of capital gains that are exempted from taxation or simply out of accumulated wealth. Some observers put the expenditure of the upper classes in India at over Rs. 500 crores a year—an amount which is considerably in excess of the total of net incomes after tax of all income recipients with incomes of over Rs. 10,000. It is possible, therefore, that total yield of the tax would prove to be very much greater than the present yield of that part of the present super tax which it replaces. It is, however, impossible in this case to make even a rough guess of the magnitude of the probable yield.

Administration

The tax would be administered in much the same way as the present super tax on the basis of individual assessments relating to the previous year and paid around 18 months in arrear. The mode of administration of the tax could perhaps best be illustrated by showing in a simplified form the type of comprehensive return which, it has been suggested should replace the present tax return and which would provide the material for assessment for the other proposed taxes, the annual wealth tax, the capital gains tax and the gift tax, as well as the expenditure tax.

It will be evident from the sample comprehensive return reproduced in Appendix 'A' to this Report [not included in this volume]
that the tax-payer would not be asked to give a direct account of his
personal expenses, the amount chargeable for the expenditure tax
being arrived at as a residual after deduction of various items from
the receipts. The need to make the various items and parts of this
return consistent with one another, together with the requirement
that a duly certified voucher should be submitted in support of each
particular claim for exemption, provides the check on the accuracy
of the computed figure of expenditure. The tax-payer would, however,
also be required to make a formal declaration that to the best of his
knowledge and belief the computed expenditure tallied with his true
personal expenditure for the period in question. The Revenue would,
of course, have the power to ask for details concerning particular
items of expenditure (such as the amount paid for electricity or other
public utility services, the rents paid for the year, the amounts spent
on the children's education, etc.), as well as details concerning his
mode of living (e.g., the number of servants kept, the number of
rooms, furniture and fittings, motor-cars and travels made during the
year) which would enable the tax officer to check the accuracy of the
computed figure and the consistency of the whole return.

NOTES TO SELECTION 18

[1]Deficit financing or public loan-expenditure equally imply, of course, a corresponding increase in privately owned wealth.

[2]*An Expenditure Tax* (London: Allen & Unwin, 1955) Chap. I, pp. 25–42.

[3]*Personal Income Taxation* (Chicago, 1938), pp. 219.

[4]I feel bound to say that I regard the current proposals in India for a "ceiling"
on income as carrying these trends to their ultimate logical absurdity. The authors
behind these proposals never stop to inquire just what is the meaning and definition of the term "income" which they so light-heartedly wish to be subject to
an absolute upper limit; and how such proposals could serve to reduce social
inequality so long as wealth continues to be privately owned. In the sense in
which (in the U.K.), for instance, the marginal tax on income had already reached
97.5% in 1946–51, this marginal tax could clearly be raised to 100% without making
any radical difference. But can anyone seriously believe that this instrument
could be made to serve the elimination of anything but desirable social incentives?
The extremes of wealth and poverty will not be eliminated thereby—for the simple
reason that as far as capitalists are concerned, the benefits accruing from capital
will not be lost, merely that they will take on some other form than "income."
(As it is said in England, heavy taxation makes taxable income into a luxury which
"the rich can no longer afford to have.")

This is not meant to suggest that the current agitation for a "ceiling on income"
proceeds from any but the highest moral and social motives; and I am sure that
their authors meant them to apply to the true benefits derived from the ownership
of property just as much as incomes derived from work. They were wrong,
however, in thinking that a ceiling on "income" was an appropriate instrument
for giving effect to these aspirations—unless the notion of "income" were broadened
considerably in relation to the current legal definition of this term and the "ceiling"
were meant to comprise a ceiling on the ownership of wealth, and not only on an-

nual accruals. Interpreted in this comprehensive sense, however, the proposal is not one which a country like India could adopt, without seriously compromising her prospects of growth and improvement or even the maintenance of existing standards. Soviet Russia discovered to her cost that economic incentives cannot be eliminated without perilous consequences—except perhaps at a stage of economic well-being which is far above that of even the richest nation (like the U.S.A.), let alone India.

There is, no doubt, a strong case in India for reducing the prevailing degree of economic inequality. But the way to do this is by making the tax system comprehensive and administratively effective, not by introducing absolute "ceilings." (There may be a case for a ceiling on land holdings, but in my view this provides no analogy for ceilings on income and capital. Since the effective size of farms in India is relatively small, land ownership above a certain amount serves no economic purpose and is merely a method of exploiting the peasantry, and often a positive impediment to improvements in productivity on the land. This is certainly not true of the high incomes earned through a successful business or professional career, or of the accumulation of fortunes through successful enterprise.)

I am fairly confident that the proposals for an "income ceiling" will not eventuate either in the introduction of 100% marginal tax rates or in any legal prohibition for the payment of income above a certain maximum. Yet the agitation will have done considerable harm if it led to low top-salary scales being paid to the top executive personnel in the newly established State enterprises. I think it is essential to the success of India's current approach to her future development—"the Socialist pattern of society"—that the important enterprises in the public sector should be able to attract the best available talent; and this means that they should be able to pay remuneration on a scale that is fully competitive with that offered by private industry. I do feel, therefore, that it would serve important national interests if public pronouncements on this subject could, as early as possible, be veered round towards the objective of a reduction in the inequalities of wealth through comprehensive and effective taxes on wealth, instead of the spectacular but meaningless (and indirectly harmful) notion of an "income-ceiling."

[5] These suggested scales for the expenditure tax were so chosen as to cause the tax to come into operation only when the net expenditure of a typical family unit exceeds the net income remaining on a taxable income of Rs. 40,000 a year—the level at which the present combined income and super tax rate begins to exceed the marginal rate of 7 annas in the rupee at present—so that the tax becomes a substitute for the loss of the present super tax on slabs above 3 annas in the rupee. It would be possible, of course, to fix lower exemption limits that would be more consonant with the standards of living and the expenditure scales of the top income groups of India.

[6] The level of rates and the degree of progression needs, of course, to be higher than with the estate duty, since the rates vary with the size of the individual gift or bequest, and not the size of the total estate of the donor; hence the suggestion that the rates should be double the current estate duty rates.

[7] An Expenditure Tax.

[8] Moreover, such dissipatory spending, by increasing profits, would offset the effect of high taxation in reducing the income and the savings of the capitalist classes; if the community's investment expenditure is given, the true incidence of taxes on income and property can only fall on the capitalist classes to the extent that their propensity to spend is reduced in consequence. By encouraging spending, the tax system thus unwittingly causes the burden of taxes to be shifted from the profit-earning classes (taken as a whole) to other sections of the community.

[9] In fact, obvious inconsistencies between a man's disclosure of income and the mode of living are already being used in India and in other countries as a means of detecting income tax evasion.

[10]The latter require to be deposited with the banks or other institutions to qualify for exemption.

[11]These gifts may be subject to gift tax in the hands of the recipient.

[12]It is thus proposed that the purchase of works of art, jewellery and ornaments should be treated as capital expenditure and thus exempted from the personal expenditure tax but an annual charge should be imposed in all cases where the taxpayers claim exemption under this head. It is not proposed, however, that such a notional charge should be made with respect to any existing possessions of jewellery, ornaments or works of art.

[13]An alternative method would be to permit the spreading of all expenditure for tax purposes and to calculate the tax on a moving average of the expenditure of the last five years rather than the actual expenditure in a particular year.

[14]This means that two adults comprising a family would pay twice the tax of a single person with half that expenditure, a married couple with two children would pay three times the tax payable by a single person with one-third of the joint family expenditure and so on.

19

Tax Reform in India

*by Nicholas Kaldor**

An effective system of progressive direct taxation is vital to the survival of democratic institutions in India. The need for this arises not merely on financial grounds—to raise adequate resources for purposes of accelerated economic development—but in order to bring about the degree of social cohesion and co-operation that is essential for the successful functioning of a democratic system. In a community where there is such a wide gap between the position of a privileged minority of well-to-do and the vast majority who live in dire poverty, social cohesion can only be achieved if economic inequality is effectively lessened and the tendency towards increasing concentration of wealth is effectively counteracted. This can only be done through the instrument of taxation. It is in any case inevitable that heavy burdens should be laid on the broad masses of the population if India is to attain a satisfactory rate of development in the coming decades. It will not be possible to carry through the programme successfully with the consent and co-operation of the people if the privileged minority of the well-to-do are not made to bear a fair share of this burden. Moreover in matters of taxation, like in the administration of the law, it is not enough that justice should be done—it must also be seen to be done. If owing to defects in the tax law, or in their administration, highly progressive taxes on wealth or income have no visible effect on the prevailing economic inequality, or in the standards of living of the rich, the mere enactment of advanced tax legislation will prove fruitless.

A Fair Start

In the last few years India has made a fair start towards creating an effective system of progressive taxation with the introduction of

*Economic Weekly (Annual) (Bombay), XV (January, 1959), 195–98. Substance of an address given to the informal consultative committee of the Parliament in New Delhi on December 16, 1958. Reprinted here with the kind permission of the publisher.

the new taxes on capital gains, on wealth, on personal expenditure, and on gifts. It has thus laid the basis for a system which may serve as a model to other democracies, both developed and underdeveloped. But it is no use blinking the fact that the reforms so far introduced are, at best, a beginning; that the legislation of some of the new taxes is seriously defective whilst the measures for their effective administration have not yet been provided; and that other and equally important reforms in the field of business and company taxation have not been tackled at all. Unless some of the recent legislation is amended in important respects, and unless it is supplemented by legislation in other fields and by far-reaching reforms in the administrative field, there is a serious risk that this noble attempt at creating an egalitarian democracy will end in failure.

Whether the political or social urges which led to the recent reforms continue to prevail or not, I am convinced that the Indian tax system could not be frozen still at the point which it has now reached. If an effective tax structure is to be created, reform will have to be carried a great deal further; if on the other hand political forces were to become dominant which would effectively bar this development, there would be little point in preserving such a complicated system of taxation.

Among the new taxes the expenditure tax and the gift tax are so heavily riddled with loopholes and exemptions that they bear only a superficial resemblance to the taxes whose introduction I originally recommended. Though the new capital gains tax represents a considerable advance on the form in which it was originally enacted in India, it still suffers from serious shortcomings which undermine the basic purpose of personal income taxation of securing equality of treatment between different taxpayers. The wealth tax alone was enacted in a form that is comparatively free from loopholes, though this too contains features that could justifiably be criticised.

Defects of Expenditure-Tax

The most serious defect of the Expenditure-tax Act is that it ties the liability to this tax to a minimum income limit which opens the door to endless manipulations and is bound to make the tax largely ineffective in practice. Expenditure represents an alternative base to income for measuring spending power or ability to pay. The difference is only that the latter taxes savings and exempts dis-savings, whereas the former exempts savings and brings dis-savings into charge. There is much to be said (for administrative and other reasons) for making use of both principles of taxation, and levying some of the taxation on an income base, and some on an expenditure base. But it is essential, in this case, that the liability to the one should not be made dependent on the extent of the liability to the other. By making the liability to the expenditure tax dependent on the size of income, a concession is made to savings without making a corresponding charge on dis-saving.

This is far more serious than it may appear at first sight since it is always open to any taxpayer to make his income smaller than it could be (even though he may not always be in the position to make it larger). This provision thus makes it possible to a taxpayer to telescope his income into particular years in which his spendings are kept low, and to telescope his spending into those years in which his income is kept low enough to entitle him to exemption from the expenditure tax. It is therefore bound to have a highly destructive effect—one is almost tempted to say that this particular provision alone makes the tax a little more than a show-piece.

In addition, the Expenditure-tax Act contains a long series of exemptions of various kinds—such as expenditure on marriages, on medical expenses election expenses, the purchase of cottage industry products, etc.—which have no counterpart in the income tax laws and which will make it very difficult to administer it effectively. I do not wish to argue the moral or economic justification for exempting any particular form of personal expenditure from taxation—any one of these exemptions may have something to be said for it, either on grounds of fairness or expediency. But it is surely inequitable to exempt particular categories of personal outlay from expenditure taxation if these are not also exempted from income taxation.

For the great majority of people income provides the sole source of expenditure; their ability to spend is confined by income taxation just as effectively as by expenditure taxation. If it is not justified to reduce a man's liability to income-tax on account of his having exceptional expenses to bear on illness or on wedding for example, why is it justified to reduce his liability to expenditure tax? Why should people whose source of spending is capital as well as income be more leniently treated than people whose only source of spending is the income which they earn? And (bearing in mind the high exemption limit to expenditure tax and the low exemption limit to income tax) why should the necessitous expenditures of large spenders be so carefully looked after when the necessitous expenditures of small and moderate spenders are not? From the point of view of equality of treatment whatever concessions are made on grounds of necessitous expenditure for the one tax ought to have their counterpart in the other tax.

GIFT TAX EQUALLY DEFECTIVE

Analogous criticisms can be made against the Gift-tax Act, which in its final legislative form is only a pale shadow of what it was originally intended to be. The purpose of a gift tax, like that of the estate duty, is to restrict the freedom of individuals to pass on their property rights to others. As the American economist Henry Simons once said, the whole of private property, and the income derived from it, is a gift from the community. It is only by the will of the community that particular individuals can enjoy the privileges of ownership protected by law and administration; and the constantly evolving property laws define the actual nature of the rights which these privileges confer. Inheritance taxes are, in effect, a form of limitation on the privileges conferred by ownership: they allow an individual (subject to various limits circumscribed by law) the unfettered enjoyment of his own property, but they do not allow him to pass on his property unhindered to the next generation. But if this limitation is held to be justified, on what basis can one differentiate between inter-vivos gifts and gifts by deed or will?

There is a long list of exemptions in the present Gift-tax Act which has no counter-part in the Estate-duty Act; and the provisions of that Act are so framed as to make it possible for an owner through the mere process of spreading the gifts over time to reduce the incidence of the gift tax to a small fraction of that of the estate duty, or even to avoid the tax altogether. As is well known, it was the introduction of the estate duty which led to the wholesale passing on of property by means of inter-vivos gifts so as to avoid that duty—hence the need for a gift tax. But the present tax, by failing to integrate gifts over successive years for tax purposes, and by giving a series of exemption to gifts of particular kinds (including a large annual exemption) entirely fails in this purpose.

These loopholes in the expenditure and the gift tax legislation are bound to reduce the yield of these taxes to a small fraction of what they should have been—which in turn is bound to create agitation for their complete removal. Opponents of these taxes are certain to ask, if such complicated taxes yield so little, what is the point of having them at all?—ignoring the fact that the low yield will be the very consequence of the loopholes and exemptions on the introduction of which they have insisted. In the absence of loopholes, the gift tax and the estate duty taken together at the current rate schedule, could be expected to yield some 20–30 crores of rupees annually. As it is, the combined yield will amount to less than one-fifth of this sum. The expenditure tax, properly administered, and in the absence of the present loopholes, should yield at least 15–20 crores of rupees at the current schedule of rates. In its present form it will hardly yield one-tenth of this sum.

INCENTIVE TO CONVERT INCOME INTO CAPITAL GAINS

With regard to capital gains the new legislation has the great advantage over the old one in that capital gains are now integrated with other forms of income for income tax purposes. But they are not liable to Super-tax, which means that they are only liable to a maximum rate of tax of 27.5 per cent, whilst other kinds of unearned income are liable to a maximum rate of 84 per cent.[1] There is therefore still a very considerable incentive for converting income into capital gains, and thereby reduce the effective taxation of those who are in a position to benefit from it to well below the rates applicable to other taxpayers. Moreover, while the new law disallows certain of the exemptions provided in the original Act, the important loophole of exempting transfers of property through inter-vivos gifts and through inheritance remains open, which means (if American experience is any guide) that only about one-third of the capital gains made by each generation come effectively within the tax net.

The effective rate of taxation of capital gains, even in the absence of any evasion, will thus not be $27\frac{1}{2}$ per cent, but something more like 10 per cent.

There is undoubtedly some force in the contention that a high rate of tax on capital gains (such as the combined maximum rate of income tax and super-tax at present) might have highly undesirable economic effects. But this provides an argument not in favour of a discriminatory treatment of capital gains, but in favour of reducing the rates of taxation on ordinary income. There is no real justification for continuing the discrimination between income which takes the form of capital gains and other income; they both generate the same spending power, and both represent the same taxable capacity. The maintenance of the high marginal rates of income-tax thus serves neither the interests of equity nor of revenue if it provides the justification for the continuance of the differential treatment of capital gains or for the maintenance of other equally serious loopholes in income-tax legislation.

ELASTIC DEFINITION OF EXPENSES

Of the latter the wide and elastic definition of deductible expenses in the case of business profits is undoubtedly the most important. So long as the owners, directors and managers of businesses are able to pass off so much of their living expenses as business expenditure the incidence of taxation is bound to remain highly arbitrary, and the effective rate of taxation on the business community will remain much below the apparent rate. In my report I suggested that the range of deductible expenses should be confined to "expenses wholly, exclusively and unavoidably incurred in earning the profits of the year" (as against the present rule which permits the deduction of all such expenses which are "wholly and exclusively laid out or expended for the purpose of trade"). This would undoubtedly strengthen the hands of the Revenue in disallowing expenses of various kinds, though the extent to which it will succeed in bringing the treatment of business incomes fully into line with that of contractual incomes will depend on the interpretation given to it by the Courts. It is a matter for consideration therefore whether, in addition to a stricter general rule for deductible expenses, the deduction of particular types of expenses (such as the so-called "expense accounts," entertainment outlays, private cars, etc.) should not be explicitly prohibited.

A further source of loopholes arises from the non-integration, or incomplete integration, of total family wealth and income. To close this it would be necessary to aggregate minor's income and property with that of the parents, and to include agricultural income and property within the scope of the Union income tax, wealth tax and capital gains tax. This latter reform may require a constitutional amendment which, however, might well be carried with the support of the States, if the revenue resulting from the extension of these taxes to agriculture is earmarked to the States.

Tax Evasion

Even if these loopholes were plugged, the administration of the system will not become effective until far-reaching reforms are introduced for checking tax evasion. The compulsory disclosure of Benami holdings, the abolition of the system of blank transfers of shares and of bearer shares are essential ingredients of this. The introduction of a comprehensive reporting system on capital transactions and of a single comprehensive return for direct taxation are other necessary ingredients. These are matters within the purview of the Direct Taxes Administration Enquiry Committee recently set up and it is very much to be hoped that their recommendations will pay due regard to these basic requirements of the efficient administration of an integrated tax structure.

In closing I should like to refer to two particular matters on which the Government of India has frequently been criticised for its failure to follow my original recommendations. One relates to the failure to reduce income-tax to the maximum rate of 45 per cent and the other to the extension of the wealth tax to companies.

45 Per Cent Income Tax

I fully maintain the view that with a system of direct taxation of the kind I suggested, the maximum of rate of income-tax should not exceed 45 per cent. It should be evident, however, that this system has by no means been fully adopted; nothing has been done to tighten up business taxation, while the new taxes, owing to the truncated form in which they have been adopted, will only produce a fraction of yield which they would have produced otherwise. In their present form, and with the present administrative techniques, the new taxes will hardly yield 20 crores.

In the absence of these gaps in legislation and with an efficient system of administration, they should produce at least 50 crores more —quite apart from the gain in income tax revenue resulting from lower tax evasion, and the disallowance of certain classes of business expenses. As against that the loss of revenue resulting from the reduction of income tax to the ceiling rate of 45 per cent would only amount to 18 crores. I doubt whether the interests which agitate for the latter would willingly exchange the present high rates of surtax for these further legislative and administrative changes which would involve them in additional taxation amounting to several times this sum.

Wealth Tax on Companies

As regards the wealth-tax on companies, I would agree that this does not serve the same purpose of securing equity in the distribution of the burden of taxation as the wealth-tax on individuals. On the other hand it is no more inequitable than the taxation of the profits of companies as such—they both involve the taxation of legal entities over and above the taxation of individuals who own them, and on principles which are unrelated to the taxable capacity of the owners. But considered as an alternative to a higher rate of profits taxation on companies, it has this to be said in its favour that its economic effects are distinctly more favourable than that of the profits tax. For it penalises firms who earn a low rate of profit on the capital which they employ and favours those firms whose earning power is high. It thus rewards efficiency and penalises inefficiency, and in the present stage of India's development, it is well worth while to offer special inducements to companies who use the resources at their command efficiently.[2] For this reason I should favour putting more of the burden of taxation on companies in the form of a wealth tax, and less in the form of a profits tax,—i.e., of raising the wealth tax rate (which at $\frac{1}{2}$ per cent is very low) if the combined income-and-profits tax rate on companies were correspondingly reduced.

NOTES TO SELECTION 19

[1] I cannot, incidentally, see the advantage of maintaining the distinction between earned and unearned income once the wealth tax is introduced—it means using two separate instruments for the same purpose. It is true that the present wealth tax rates are very moderate. The effective rates are only one-third of the Swedish rates and yield only about two-thirds of the schedule of the rates which I recommended. But it is better in that case to increase the rates of the wealth tax than to maintain the sur-charge on unearned incomes.

[2] Many other features of the present company tax legislation, such as the excess dividend tax, run completely contrary to this and these ought to be abolished and the whole system of company taxation rationalised and simplified without delay.

20

Concepts of Sales Taxation

by Clara K. Sullivan*

This brief study on the concepts of sales taxation is designed to enable students and others to handle rationally the many problems encountered in the drafting and interpretation of sales tax legislation and in the day-to-day administration and enforcement of a sales tax. The first of the eight sections of this study describes the consumption and income types of sales taxation and relates them to three basic concepts of taxation: an indirect personal tax, an impersonal business tax, and a control device. The succeeding two sections deal respectively with taxable persons and taxable transactions, while the fourth section contains a comparison of three methods of applying and collecting the tax: the general turnover tax, the single-stage levy, and the value-added tax. The fifth section relates the consumption and income types of sales taxation to the three methods of collecting the tax, while section six discusses the range of rates of tax. The next section deals with the application of sales taxes to international transactions, under both the destination and the origin principles. Finally, the study stresses the need to evaluate sales tax concepts in terms of their effects, that is, in terms of the specific economic, social, and political environment in which the tax is to operate.

At present this study is being used experimentally, in conjunction with materials on sales taxation in particular countries, in the Harvard Law School's International Tax Research Tax Seminar. The attempt has been made to combine the economic and legal approaches to sales taxation, and, as revision and clarification will no doubt be required, the suggestions and comments of readers will be welcomed by the editors of this volume.

*Dr. Sullivan was a staff economist with the Harvard Law School International Program in Taxation during most of the time she worked on this paper, but she completed it while she was a member of the Columbia University International Economic Integration project, under the direction of Professor Carl S. Shoup. This article is here appearing in print for the first time.

319

PRINCIPLES OF SALES TAXATION

Introduction

Sales taxes may be defined as general taxes on sales of products, "general" meaning that the taxes apply to all, or a wide range, of goods and services. Thus they are distinguished from special excises or selective sales taxes, such as those on tobacco, liquor, and motor fuels,[1] most of which are rationalized either as taxes intended to discourage the production or consumption of particular items or as special benefit levies—such as motor fuel taxes used to finance road construction.[2] In the case of sales taxes, on the other hand, it has been conventional to assume a lack of rationale other than fiscal expediency, thus accounting for their being classified among the "transactions taxes."[3] However, this position is no longer justified because economic analysis has demonstrated that sales tax concepts are based on general principles of taxation.

In terms of general principles, sales tax concepts may be classified into three groups. The first group comprises those general levies which represent an indirect approach to personal taxation, that is, taxation of individual income-recipients. Actually, however, the special excises may, in effect, be personal taxes[4] and, in that case, they ought to be integrated with the sales taxes, unless the maintenance of separate levies is required for administrative reasons. The second group of sales taxes are those which are intended to operate as impersonal business taxes. Finally, there are those sales taxes which resemble the special excises and which are intended as a method of controlling production or consumption of certain goods rather than as a method of raising revenue.

Indirect Approach to Personal Taxation

As an indirect approach to personal taxation, a sales tax may be intended to approximate either an indirect spendings tax or an indirect income tax.[5] In most instances, the tax is probably thought by legislators and others to represent an indirect spendings tax, that is, a consumption tax.[6]

Consumption-Type Sales Taxes

An individual with an income of $1,000, who purchases during a given period consumer goods and services worth $800, may conceivably be assessed directly under the spendings tax on his $800 outlay.[7] Direct assessment means that the purchaser pays tax on his purchases to the tax collector at the end of the given period, in accordance with a tax declaration made by or for the purchaser. On the other hand, the purchaser may be taxed indirectly through increases in the prices of the consumption goods which he purchases. Rather than tax him, say $200, under a direct spendings tax, he may be reached through a 25% sales tax imposed on the business firms from which he purchases the consumer goods and which are expected to shift the tax forward to the ultimate consumer by raising their prices by 25%.[8] The overall tax base may be visualized as the community's aggregate consumption expenditures, for each consumer in the community is taxed on his total expenditures. In the event that capital investment in the community is taking place only to the extent necessary to offset depreciation, the tax base will equal community net income or product, customarily designated as national income or product in statistics of national income.

The indirect approach is essentially less refined than the direct procedure because of the greater difficulty under the former of adjusting the tax burden to the situation of individual taxpayers. Planned rate progression and personal allowances are not possible under the indirect procedure. Although progression has been attempted by exempting items comprising most of the consumption expenditures of low-income groups and by increasing the rates on items considered luxuries, such efforts have limited success because of the lack of correspondence between levels of income and types of items purchased. Although some thought has been given to the possibility of introducing rate progression and personal allowances by distributing coupons among individual consumers,[9] the administrative cumbersomeness of such schemes has thus far discouraged experimentation with their use. It is also possible to effect personal allowances through credits under the income tax system for sales taxes paid; in the course of introducing its 3% sales tax, the State of Wisconsin considered using an income tax credit of $15 per family member,[10] or the equivalent of the 3% tax on purchases amounting to $500.[11]

Given the validity of the premise that, for the average individual, consumption expenditures represent a declining proportion of his income as income rises,[12] the consumption type of sales tax must be regarded as a regressive tax, that is, the tax burden is inversely correlated with income level. Even if this is not the case, the indirect approach may well be regressive because of the usual exclusion from the tax base of items consumed by those at the higher income levels, especially products which take the form of services.[13]

In one sense, even the progressive direct expenditure tax may be considered regressive. To the extent that it allows individuals who abstain from consumption to avoid the tax, it is likely to bear more heavily on the lower and moderate income groups than on the higher ones, which can more easily afford to refrain from consumption. However, the tax can at least be designed to ensure that nontaxed funds be used productively by excluding from the definition of savings uses of funds not considered desirable in a given economy. Thus, the progressive direct expenditure tax is in principle a concept especially appropriate for underdeveloped economies, but its implementation unfortunately assumes the existence of a highly developed tax administration.[14] It is true that under the indirect approach, outlays considered nonproductive in a given situation can also be discouraged insofar as they are made through taxable business enterprises. However, certain types of expenditures, when made by individual consumers and organizations which are treated in a manner analogous to individual consumers, and which may at times be regarded as nonproductive, such as foreign land speculation, are not reached by sales taxes.

There are apparently two reasons why an indirect rather than a direct approach to personal taxation is employed. One is the comparative administrative difficulty of using the direct procedure in certain situations. The other reflects the view that a combination of the direct and indirect approaches may effect "a more nearly perfect, or less imperfect, system of taxes than could be obtained through the use of only one of them, and such a system, by exerting equal pressure over the whole area subject to taxation, assures not only a greater degree of equality in taxation, but also the highest possible revenue-yield."[15] Obviously, the combined use of both procedures assumes that the maximum effort has been made to effect an adequate assessment under each approach. Two measures full of loopholes will scarcely be an improvement over one adequately implemented approach.

Income-Type Sales Taxes

If, instead of approximating an indirect spendings tax, a sales tax is supposed to represent an indirect approach to income taxation, the tax is designated as an income-type tax. In this case, it must reach not only sales of items destined for ultimate consumption but sales of items destined for business investment. The taxation of investment goods, that is, those items customarily capitalized and depreciated rather than expensed, is the only way in which the indirect approach can attempt to reach individual savings and thereby approximate the allocation of tax burden effected under a direct income tax.

One version of the income-type concept would tax investment goods with no allowance for depreciation. In fact, the single-stage taxes imposed under the rule which limits the avoidance of multiple taxation to physical ingredients and analogous items may be considered a rough application of this concept. However, the taxation of investment goods under sales taxes has usually been explained in terms of fiscal or administrative expediency rather than as the application of some rationale.[16] Nevertheless, it is logical to classify a sales tax designed to reach items destined for final investment as well as for final consumption as a gross product or gross income type of tax. The expression "gross product type of tax" is to be used frequently throughout this paper to designate a sales tax so designed, because the aggregate tax base equals community gross product, customarily designated as gross national product in statistics of national income.

Such a tax is invariably condemned on the ground that it subjects business investment to a double tax, once when the investment goods are purchased and again when their depreciation enters into the price of the items which they help produce, while direct labor is taxed only once.[17] However, it may be properly contended that direct labor is likewise subjected to double tax to the extent that the wage and salary earner makes consumption outlays which are analogous to the raw materials, fuels, research, and other intermediate outlays of business firms (see discussion below).

In any event, current economic theory seems to insist upon the income-type concept which allows depreciation, on the assumption that such an allowance is needed for the maintenance of adequate rates of savings and investment. Under this concept, the tax is imposed on sales of investment goods, but the purchasing firm is permitted to reduce its taxable receipts by an allowance for depreciation of the investment goods it has used in turning out the taxable products,[18] the aggregate tax base being equal to community net income or product.

As in the case of an indirect spendings tax, the indirect approach to personal income taxation is necessarily less refined than the direct procedure. It is difficult to effect personal allowances and personal rate progression. It may be noted that the taxation of investment goods introduces a progressive element into the gross product type of tax although the rate pattern is probably indeterminable. Meanwhile, the income concept which allows depreciation may be considered a proportional levy. As in the case of the consumption type of sales tax, the indirect approach may be justified for income taxation either because of the excessive administrative difficulties under the direct approach or because a combined direct and indirect approach is thought to achieve a more adequate assessment of income.

A Note on Intermediate versus Final Product

The problem of distinguishing between individual outlays for ultimate consumption and business purchases of intermediate products,
that is, items representing only a step in the production of final goods,
is a delicate one which involves fundamental issues of economic,
social, and political philosophy. A related problem having the same
serious implications is that of distinguishing business outlays which
should be currently expensed from those which should be capitalized
and depreciated. These matters deserve much more attention than
they have received thus far, especially in view of their importance
for tax legislation.

In national income accounting, it is necessary to distinguish between
final and intermediate products in order to avoid double counting
and in order to decide which items should be included in the final
figures designating national income. The U.S. Department of Commerce has noted the difficulty of making this distinction and states
that it has been forced to rely on convention:

> . . . No precise line can be drawn between final and intermediate
> products from mere observation of the nature of the products or the
> uses to which they are put. It would be easy, for example, if all consumer
> purchases were made for goods like Sunday clothes and holiday dinners,
> which are obvious elements of the good life, and if all business pur-
> chases were raw materials for further processing, which are obvious
> intermediate goods. Between these two extremes, however, there is a
> wide range of purchases for which neither the motivation nor the use
> is so clear-cut and which must be placed in one category or the other
> by somewhat arbitrary rules.
>
> For this reason any measure of total production must be somewhat
> conventional. For instance, it must overlook the fact that the expendi-
> tures of individuals in their business capacity are influenced by their
> standards as consumers, and that expenditures of consumers are in-
> fluenced by their activities as producers. It must overlook also the fact
> that the conditions under which work is performed have an important
> bearing on the welfare of individuals. These conditions are affected by
> business expenditures on goods and services that are classified as inter-
> mediate just because there is no satisfactory way to take account of the
> benefits in a quantitative measure of final output.[19]

Under conventional accounting, the criterion for distinguishing
business from consumption expenditures is the motivation behind the
outlay. All outlays by business concerns are generally presumed to
have been made for purposes of increasing output rather than for
personal consumption; abuse of expense accounts has however led
to the disallowance of some business outlays under tax laws. Mean-

while, expenditures by individuals as such are assumed to represent consumption.

As the Department of Commerce indicates, however, consumers make purchases which may be classified as business outlays while business concerns may make expenditures akin to personal consumption outlays. A true definition of income would then require the expensing or capitalization and depreciation of consumer outlays intended to increase production and the nondeduction of outlays by business organizations which resemble personal consumption expenditures.

Individuals as such make many outlays which only arbitrary and artificial disinctions separate from those regarded as business expenses. Educational, medical, and recreational facilities or similar fringe benefits provided by a business firm for the benefit of its employees are classified as business outlays because intended to increase output. Individuals who prefer or who are obliged to purchase such services on their own account are assumed to make consumption expenditures despite the fact that the motivation may be the same as that of the business concern. The services of radio and television are treated as intermediate business outlays while entertainment in the form of books or attending the theater or symphony purchased by individuals is considered ultimate consumption regardless of the fact that the individual may be seeking relaxation in order to work better. A business concern may build a plant which rivals a czar's palace and no question is raised concerning the business nature of the expenditure. The outlay of an individual working in an industrialized community who purchases a home in the suburbs because he thinks this will enable him to do better work is however deemed final consumption.

Two other criteria for distinguishing business expenditures from ultimate consumption are the presence or absence of personal gratification and the effect on production.[20] The test of effect on production is especially suitable for modern policymakers who are concerned with the problems of maintaining or raising an area's standard of living or fighting inflation. The question is whether the use of a product could be discontinued without decreasing production; results rather than motivation are emphasized. Either motivation or productivity is superior to the criterion of personal gratification in a system emphasizing productivity, as the latter implies that time spent in gratifying work constitutes consumption.

However, it must be conceded that application of any of the criteria to both individuals and business concerns would be difficult. If such application were made, some of the outlays undertaken by individuals and usually regarded as ultimate consumption would be classified as business outlays while some business expenditures would be classified as ultimate consumption. On the whole, final product would probably be much less than under present definitions.

Professor Kuznets points out the nature of the problem when he states that wage and salary earners may be regarded as independent concerns:

> The meaning of the term enterprise is far from unique and specific. An economic enterprise in general, including such nonprofit organizations as governmental agencies, may be described as a unit set up for production processes that result in economic goods. What then prevents us from classifying each wage earner as a separate economic enterprise whose primary purpose is to render labor services at the highest possible price? If this were done, the net value of products turned out by a factory would have to exclude wages paid to wage earners, since such payments would represent the value of consumed products of other enterprises. Instead we would have to add the net value of products of the various enterprises called wage earners. This net value would equal not the full amount of wages received (the *gross* value of the product of these wage-earning enterprises), but wages minus the cost of products wage-earning enterprises buy from other enterprises and consume in the process of producing labor power (food, clothing, and other means of maintenance and reproduction). Consequently, this extension of the concept of enterprise would materially reduce both the net value of goods produced by the economic system and national income.[21]

Kuznets explains that the conventional definitions reflect a view of the economic system in which human beings are not regarded as "so many machines for performing labor, management, entrepreneurial, or capital-saving functions. It is this idea of economic goods existing for men, rather than men for economic goods, that gives point to the concept of ultimate consumption and special interest to national income as usually defined."[22] Furthermore, as he suggests, the concept of the wage and salary earner as a business concern implies that the employee performs the management functions and undertakes the risks of an entrepreneur. The extent to which this is true under the institutional arrangements of highly industrialized societies varies with the type of business concern and the calibre and interests of employees.

If the wage and salary earner were regarded as a business concern, he would be allowed to expense or, in the case of certain items, to capitalize and depreciate "business" outlays, defined as expenditures required for productivity. Such outlays would presumably include not only expenditures for food, clothing, and shelter, at least up to a certain amount and probably varying with localities, but also allowances for recreation and for entertainment necessary to elicit the good will of employees and others in one's own profession, insofar as similar allowances are granted to business organizations. Even more important are those expenditures by individuals which are akin to the capital outlays of business organizations, such as the expenses of training for a particular vocation. Likewise, in principle, deductions should be permitted for old-age reserves on the ground that human capital should be granted a depreciation allowance. Whether the cost of rearing children constitutes a business expense, personal consumption, or perhaps a social cost assumed by individuals is another important issue.

The view that certain expenditures classified as consumption are less essential to production than those made by business organizations merely revives the classical distinction between productive and unproductive expenditures. Actually, every human being is generally both a producer and consumer; and his production may be so closely interwoven with his consumption habits that to reduce one will reduce the other. Furthermore, even when some consumption seems superfluous, it may be a necessary incentive for production in any given society.

Naturally, some consumption is less essential than other, and to the extent that it can be eliminated without decreasing output, it may be considered "pure" consumption.[23] Pure consumption is likely to be most prevalent in the upper income groups where, if there is any possibility that changed consumption will increase output, it concerns the pattern, rather than the quantity, of consumption. "No doubt," writes Shoup, "some change in the pattern of consumer goods even in the wealthier areas of the United States would give rise to an increase in output; but the increase would perhaps be closer to 10 per cent than 50 per cent of the increase in consumer goods utilized."[24] Furthermore, even though the production of such groups may not respond to increases in the quantity of consumption, it may be sensitive to decreases.

Increased consumption may have no effect on production or may even cause a decline in a poverty-stricken community where natural resources are scarce and where the population pressure has created an enervating struggle for existence. Such a situation may be hopeless except for the relief provided by migration, preferably with outside assistance to facilitate the adjustment process. This is not to say that a region without natural resources is incapable of prospering; for there are areas in the world where skilled labor is the only important resource, the essential raw materials being imported for processing.

The question of the extent to which business outlays should be capitalized and depreciated rather than expensed, as well as the number of years for which they should be capitalized, raises issues similar to those created by the problem of separating final from intermediate purchases. When business outlays are capitalized, they are

in effect regarded as being destined for final use, at least until the cost
of depreciation enters into the price of the final product. Expensing
rather than capitalizing, or shortening the term of capitalization,
should presumably also depend upon the effect on productivity. However, in the case of income tax laws, which through accelerated depreciation and similar measures have been tending toward the expensing of investment outlays, the issue has been complicated by the
prevailing view that employment is most readily created through
stimulating investment by business organizations.

If a situation develops in which conventional definitions of business
outlays become inadequate, it is probably because the pressure of
population on natural resources, on plant and equipment, or on both
has become excessive. It may then become necessary to curb the wasteful use of resources by redirecting outlays through interventionist tax
policies which reflect a revised set of definitions and which in certain
circumstances may entail considerable economic planning.

Impersonal Business Taxation

The second group of sales tax concepts considers these taxes as
impersonal business taxes rather than as indirect personal taxes. Under
this concept, the tax may be regarded as a business privilege or benefit
tax.[25] Some versions of the concept regard the tax as a price paid for
governmental services rendered to business, the tax being considered
comparable to payments for raw materials or services from outside
firms or, alternatively, similar to payments for the services of a factor
of production, such as wages or rents.[26]

The older theories seemed to assume that the hypothesis of the
business benefit tax required the gross product type of sales tax
(defined above)[27] although Professor Colm suggested the possibility
of depreciation allowances.[28] However, recent theory seems to regard
the consumption-type tax as compatible with this rationale. For example, Professor Papke observes that either the expensing of capital
purchases or the alternative of taxing them and allowing depreciation
are appropriate methods of applying the business benefit hypothesis
which underlies the Michigan business activities tax.[29]

One variant of this concept seems to have been derived from the
work of Professor Roscoe Arant of Iowa State Teachers College, who
recommended adoption of the value-added form of sales tax by state
governments.[30] Arant thought that a value-added tax, applied to an
economy's total output and therefore to investment as well as consumption goods, would not be shifted forward. Instead, he assumed
that it would be allocated proportionately among the various factor
incomes, part resting on profits and the remainder being shifted backward to the rewards for other factor services—wages, rent, and profits.

Hence, he considered it a form of proportional personal income taxation.[31] Soon after, Professor H. G. Brown expounded a similar thesis while making clear that its validity required the assumption of perfect competition,[32] which of course does not exist in reality. After being ignored for many years, the thesis has been re-examined by Professor Earl R. Rolph, Dr. J. A. Stockfisch, and Professor Richard A. Musgrave.[33] Rolph and Stockfisch substantiate Brown's position although Stockfisch criticizes Brown for applying his thesis to a retail sales tax, which Stockfisch holds would not be imposed on most investment goods.[34] Actually, Brown seems to have assumed a gross product type of sales tax; and, at the time he wrote, retail sales taxes generally did apply to sales of investment goods for final business use. Meanwhile, Musgrave introduces a divergent position by maintaining that there is "equivalence between the general income tax and (1) a sales tax on consumer goods plus a tax on all interest income, or (2) a tax on wage income plus a sales tax on capital goods."[35]

In any event, it is difficult to see how personal taxation can be effected by a sales tax which is not shifted forward, given imperfect mobility of resources and other imperfections in the competitive system. (However, the view has recently been expressed that the value-added type of sales tax is "passed backward as an income tax."[36]) The application of a sales tax on the assumption that it will achieve some type of personal taxation despite the absence of forward shifting seems to tell business firms that they are being assessed so much tax under a sales tax and that they should distribute the burden imposed on them in whatever manner they are willing or able. Now it is obvious that if the tax burden is not to be distributed in an erratic fashion, this hypothesis must assume some system of administered prices which will permit business firms to effect a rational distribution of the burden; or, perhaps, as in the case of export taxes in underdeveloped economies, it is hoped that the tax will rest on business profits and thus constitute a sort of business income or even excess profits tax, less likely to be avoided than a tax based on accounting profits.[37]

Sales Taxes as Control Devices

Instead of being regarded as a method of allocating the general tax burden, sales taxes may be imposed for the purpose of selective fiscal control, that is, the discouragement of production or consumption of certain products.[38] Output in the taxed sectors is expected to be reduced or discontinued, with the released factors of production supposedly moving to the nontaxed areas. At times this philosophy has dominated the application of the British purchase tax to products, the production or consumption of which affects the balance-of-payments deficits.[39] Similarly, import taxes in the Latin American economies are often intended to discourage the importation of certain products for balance-of-payments reasons. Export taxes, also, may be applied as instruments of control, being used to conserve domestic resources or, like tariffs, to encourage the development of domestic activities.[40]

As previously noted, this type of taxation is similar to the system of special excises, attention being focused on particular products rather than on general outlays. Under this approach, sales taxes may be properly classified as transactions taxes.

TAXABLE PERSONS

Generally speaking, the legal taxpayers under sales taxes are the business firms which sell taxable products. However, except in the case of certain business-tax concepts, the business firms are merely regarded as collecting agents for taxes due from the ultimate consumers or users of the products. The sales taxes in the Canadian provinces are unusual in that the legal subject of the tax is the purchaser rather than the vendor, the vendor being legally established as the collecting agent for the provinces. In this way, the tax avoids the provisions of the British North America Act of 1867 which reserves the power to levy indirect taxes to the Dominion Government.

Sometimes the statutes require separate quotation of the tax, usually for the purpose of making the actual taxpayer aware of the amount of his liability, although sometimes for the additional reason that it facilitates forward shifting. In the case of the French value-added tax, separate quotation is an essential part of the technique of collecting the tax; when sales are made, the amount of tax must be quoted in order that the purchasing business may credit the taxes paid on its purchases against those due on its sales. Finally, some statutes contain provisions making forward shifting mandatory; such provisions are meaningless however because economic forces rather than legal requirements determine incidence.

The definition of "business firm" varies with individual statutes although in principle it should encompass all those enterprises which turn out the economy's final products. Among the broadest definitions is that used by the German general turnover tax under which the business firm, called the "entrepreneur," is defined as "one who exercises a business, professional or other activity independently, continuously or for the purpose of realizing receipts, although not necessarily profits."[41] However, the laws frequently encompass only vendors of tangible commodities, sometimes defined as those who purchase for resale.[42] Moreover, even under taxes of broad scope, such activities as farming, banking, insurance, rentals, governmental enterprises, non-profit institutions, and transportation are usually considered special situations which are excluded or exempt, sometimes being subjected to special levies. Likewise, small firms may be exempt for one reason or another, the most valid being the administrative difficulty of collecting the tax from them.

Whenever the sales tax is supposed to implement the principle of indirect personal taxation, the exemption of certain firms and industries should, as a general rule, be based on the treatment to be given the consumers or users of the products turned out by these firms and industries rather than on conditions existing in these firms and industries. It is true that because of the greater elasticity of demand for their products, some types of economic activity, and therefore some firms and industries, will be injured more than others, but this is the way the tax is supposed to work. The situation is essentially the same as under a direct income tax when the individual taxpayer whose income is reduced curbs his purchases of certain products more than of others.

On the other hand, the situation of the business firm rather than that of the ultimate purchaser would seem to be the relevant consideration when exemptions are granted under the business concepts of sales taxation. However, most sales taxes of any significance have implied use of the personal concept. In any event, the rationale of particular measures should be respected so as to avoid the kind of muddled situation in which an exemption is provided both on the ground that it favors purchasers and at the same time protects concerns which have difficulty in shifting the tax.[43]

TAXABLE TRANSACTIONS

Sales taxes intended as general measures should in the first instance, be conceived as applying to the total value of all final products created by the economic system during a given period of time. Therefore, they should encompass not only products which take the form of tangible commodities but also those which take the form of services. The taxes are not intended to apply to transactions which represent merely a transfer of capital assets or personal property. Hence, they are not applicable to the value of assets transferred on the stock market or commodity exchanges or to mere transfers of, as distingushed from new construction of, real estate. They would, however, apply to the services of agents and dealers carrying on such transactions. Also, they might conceivably apply to the mere transfer of secondhand goods to the extent that the nontaxability of such transactions constituted a method of avoiding the tax on new items.

Of course, the taxes should in principle apply to any value added to such items, including the services of dealers. Finally, the extent to which a sales tax will be applied to the casual transactions of persons not classified as taxable business firms presumably rests on administrative considerations and on the assumption that the amount involved over-all in such transactions is relatively insignificant in the economy.

Because the sales taxes are supposed to reach the total value of products, their application should in principle be extended through the retail stage. If limited to the earlier stages, the taxes discriminate in favor of products having a large part of their value added in later stages. Thus, a 20% tax at the manufacturing stage on a product which sells finally for $100 excluding tax would represent an effective rate of 15% when 75% of the value has been added at the manufacturing stage, but only 6% if the manufacturing stage accounts for 30% of the final value. Thus the tax burden varies on different commodities, unless variations in burden are offset by pyramiding, that is, a constant markup applied to cost including tax.[44] Furthermore, such discrimination allows the taxes to vary with distribution channels, thereby causing changes in business methods by transferring functions from the taxable stage to the nontaxed stage.[45]

Attempts on the part of the taxing authorities to equalize the burden may cause a considerable amount of constructive pricing, that is, estimation of taxable price. Firms in the taxable stage may make sales at prices which include values not taxed if added by independent distributors, thus requiring an adjustment through discounts applied to the sales price in order to reduce it to the level appropriate to the taxable stage. Secondly, an even more troublesome problem arises when functions are transferred from the taxable stage to nontaxable stages in order to avoid the tax, thus requiring an increase in taxable prices, the so-called "uplift." Similar difficulties arise from the exclusion of services from the taxable stage.

As in the case of exemptions for certain activities, removing the tax from transactions involving certain products should be based on considerations of the position of the ultimate purchaser under personal concepts of sales taxation. Sometimes product exemptions are allowed for items subject to special excises; but it is generally preferable for administrative simplicity to tax such items and reduce the special excises. In addition to activity and product exemptions, certain purchasers may be allowed to purchase free of taxes—for example, nonprofit institutions or governmental entities. Such concessions to nonprofit organizations have the effect of favoring group over individual consumption. The exemption of sales made to the government level imposing the tax is based on the valid contention that to tax such sales merely involves the transfer of money from one pocket to another. However, it is probably better to tax them for the sake of simplifying the task of administration and compliance by eliminating the need to segregate taxable from exempt transactions. The exemption of sales to government levels other than the one imposing the tax involves intergovernmental relations; while the exemption from tax will reduce the net revenues of the taxing governmental units, the imposition of tax will reduce the net revenues of the taxed governmental unit.

THREE METHODS OF COLLECTING SALES TAXES

General Comparison

Sales taxes are usually classified into three major groups: the general turnover tax, the single-stage tax, and the value-added tax. From one point of view, these different forms of tax may be regarded as alternative methods of collection.

The oldest and crudest form of sales tax is the general turnover tax, which is imposed whenever a product undergoes a market transfer. The fact that the tax base includes previously taxed transfers causes the burden on the value of the final product to vary with the number of previous transfers or, in other words, with the number of independent firms involved in adding value to the product. Thus the tax subsidizes integrated producers and, because of the variation in the effective rate on final products, discriminates among ultimate consumers. In the case of investment goods, it discriminates among ultimate business users, although on the whole the burden on investment goods is relatively light because such goods usually undergo a small number of taxable turnovers.[46]

The single-stage and value-added procedures have been devised in order to avoid the multiple taxation characteristic of the general turnover form. This is accomplished under the single-stage taxes by allowing business firms to sell intermediate products without paying tax, provided that the purchaser provides an exemption certificate indicating their destination. Thus the tax is "suspended" until the product reaches the final taxable stage or, given a tax intended to reach the total value of the product, the retail stage. The value-added procedure, on the other hand, imposes the tax on all business sales but limits the tax liability of each business firm to the value it adds to the final product.

The three different procedures can best be understood by comparing them through a simple numerical example. Let it be assumed that there are three business firms, one at the manufacturing stage, one at the wholesaling stage, and one at the retail stage; the manufacturer sells a product for $100 to the wholesaler who in turn sells it for $125 to the retailer who finally sells it to the ultimate consumer or user for $200. Then, given a 4% tax rate, the comparative situation under a general turnover tax, a single-stage tax, and a value-added tax may be visualized from Example I, below. It is obvious that the general turnover tax would result in a final effective rate equivalent to that under the noncumulative levies only if the three independent firms had been integrated into one enterprise.

EXAMPLE I

COMPARATIVE OPERATION OF GENERAL TURNOVER TAX, SINGLE-STAGE TAX, AND VALUE-ADDED TAX, WITH 4% RATE

| Economic Stages | Value of Product Excluding Tax | General Turnover-Tax[a] | Single-Stage Tax | Value-added Tax | |
				Value Added Excluding Tax	Value-Added Tax
Manufacturing	$100	$ 4.00	E.C.[b]	$100	$4.00
Wholesaling	125	5.00	E.C.	25	1.00
Retailing	200	8.00	$8.00	75	3.00
Final Value of Product	$200			$200	
Tax at 4% on Final Value of Product		$17.00	$8.00		$8.00

[a]The fact that in actual operation the general turnover tax is imposed on the tax collected at prior stages has been ignored to simplify the exposition. Had it not been, the tax at the wholesaling stage would have amounted to $5.16 and the tax at the retail stage to $8.37, with the total tax burden equaling $17.53.
[b]Exemption Certificate.

The application of any of these forms of taxes may be limited to a stage prior to the retail stage by restricting taxpayer registration to manufacturing or wholesaling enterprises. Then, under the general turnover tax, only registered firms are liable for tax; under the single-stage procedure, only registered firms are qualified to present their suppliers with exemption certificates; and, under the value-added method, only registered firms may credit taxes paid on their purchases. Firms whose operations are integrated with nontaxed stages require constructive pricing in all three of these procedures.

Methods of Applying the Value-Added Procedure

While the single-stage method of eliminating multiple taxation can be implemented through only one approach, namely, the imposition of the tax on sales at the final taxable stage, the value-added method may be applied in more than one way. In the first place, either a subtraction or addition procedure may be used.[47] Secondly, the subtraction procedure may in turn be effected either through the subtraction of previously taxed purchases from sales, sometimes called the "basis on basis" method[48] but herein designated as the cost-subtraction procedure, or through the crediting of taxes paid on purchases against the taxes due on sales, the tax-credit procedure.

Under the addition method, value added is computed through adding together the payments made to the various factors of production in the form of wages, rent, royalties, interest, and profits. Under the cost-subtraction approach, purchases of intermediate products are subtracted from sales to arrive at value added. The result will be identical if the definition of factor payments and intermediate products is the same under both procedures. It will not be if the addition procedure treats as a factor payment a component which the subtraction procedure regards as an intermediate product—as occurs, for example, if investment goods are capitalized under the addition approach but expensed under the subtraction procedure. With an identical base and the same tax rate, the amount of tax liability will, of course, be the same under both procedures.

As in Example I, assume that the total value of a finished product is $200 and that it consists of the payments made to the various factors of production. For simplification in presentation, assume that the payments to factors consist only of wages and profits. Then, the addition and cost-subtraction method of arriving at value added for the individual firm may be illustrated as in Example II below.

EXAMPLE II

ADDITION AND COST-SUBTRACTION PROCEDURES OF COMPUTING VALUE ADDED

Economic Stages and Components of Value	Value (excluding tax) of Product and its Components		Computation of Value Added through Addition Procedure	Computation of Value Added through Cost-Subtraction Procedure
Manufacturing				
Value of product	$100			$100
Intermediate product		$ 0		−0
Wages		60	$ 60	
Profits		40	40	
Value added by manufacturing			100	100

EXAMPLE II—*Continued*

Economic Stages and Components of Value	Value (excluding tax) of Product and its Components		Computation of Value Added through Addition Procedure	Computation of Value Added through Cost-Subtraction Procedure
Wholesaling				
Value of product	125			125
Intermediate product		100		−100
Wages		15	15	
Profits		10	10	
Value added by wholesaling			25	25
Retailing				
Value of product	200			200
Intermediate product		125		−125
Wages		50	50	
Profits		25	25	
Value added by retailing			75	75
Final value of product or total value added	$200		$200	$200

Example III below compares the tax-credit and cost-subtraction procedures under a general 4% rate and then under rate differentiation, first when a 10% rate is imposed at the manufacturing stage (with a 4% rate at previous stages). It is evident that the cost-subtraction procedure, and hence the addition procedure, give different results than the tax-credit method, in the absence of a uniform tax rate. Assuming the objective is imposition of a planned rate of tax on the total value of the final product or on the value of the product through some particular stage, the tax-credit procedure is the preferable method, for it gives the same result as a single-stage tax collected at the final taxable stage. The use of the cost-subtraction procedure might conceivably be justified under certain concepts of business taxation. Adams, for example, suggested that, aside from the problem presented by integrated businesses, turnover would be an appropriate measure for a business privilege tax;[49] and the cost subtraction method would eliminate the multiple counting which characterizes the aggregate turnover measure. Moreover, as discussed in the section below on the international aspects of sales taxes, the cost-subtraction procedure is being currently recommended as the appropriate one for the application of the jurisdictional principle which allocates the tax base to the area of origin.

EXAMPLE III

COMPARISON OF THE COST-SUBTRACTION PROCEDURE AND TAX-CREDIT PROCEDURE OF COMPUTING VALUE ADDED UNDER THREE SITUATIONS: A UNIFORM 4% TAX RATE, A 10% RATE AT THE MANUFACTURING STAGE WITH A 4% RATE AT OTHER STAGES, AND A 10% RATE AT THE RETAIL STAGE WITH A 4% RATE AT OTHER STAGES

Economic Stage	Value of Product at Each Stage	Value Added at Each Stage	Tax Paid at Each Stage Under the Cost-Subtraction Procedure			Tax Paid at Each Stage Under the Tax-Credit Procedure		
			Uniform 4% Rate	10% Rate at Manu-facturing Stage	10% Rate at Retailing Stage	Uniform 4% Rate	10% Rate at Manu-facturing Stage	10% Rate at Retailing Stage
Manufacturing	$100	$100	$4.00	$10.00	$ 4.00	$4 − 0 = $4	$10 − 0 = $10	$ 4 − 0 = $ 4
Wholesaling	125	25	1.00	1.00	1.00	5 − 4 = 1	5 − 10 = −5[a]	5 − 4 = 1
Retailing	200	75	3.00	3.00	7.50	8 − 5 = 3	8 − 5 = 3	20 − 5 = 15
Final value of product	$200	$200						
Tax on final value of product			$8.00	$14.00	$12.50	$8.00	$8.00	$20.00

[a] The negative tax of $5 means that a $5 reimbursement should be granted the wholesaling firm, which invoices a tax of only $5 on its sales to the retailer.

SALES TAX BASES

*Relationship to Tax Concepts and Methods
of Collecting Tax*

Two Alternative Bases

A sales tax base, that is, the amount to which the tax rate is applied, must be constructed in a manner appropriate to the concept
which the tax is supposed to implement. Whether a general sales tax
is intended to effect indirect personal taxation, on the one hand, or
impersonal business taxation, on the other, it should be levied upon
either a consumption- or income-type base. The general turnover
taxes which, at least among the Member States of the European Community, appear to be regarded as consumption taxes are irrational
in that they apply to sales of products destined for business resale or
final investment as well as to those destined for ultimate consumption. Business investment is spared only in the case of integrated
firms which manufacture the items for their own use.

The irrational tax pattern imposed by turnover taxes justifies their
classification as transactions taxes rather than as national-income
taxes.[50] Along with the personal income taxes, the latter group encompasses the income type and consumption type of value-added
sales taxes as well as the single-stage taxes, at any rate, the single-stage
retail sales tax.

Consumption-Type Base

The consumption-type base should comprise only those products
classified as consumption goods. In other words, on the assumption
that the tax is shifted forward, it would apply only to items destined
for the use of ultimate consumers.[51] Thus, investment goods are
supposed to be entirely exempt from tax, thereby actually treating
them as intermediate products rather than as finished ones.[52]

Under the single-stage form of sales tax, the exemption is effected
by allowing business firms to purchase in suspension of tax[53] by
presenting exemption certificates not only for items currently expensed
but also for items customarily capitalized and depreciated.

Under the value-added tax, the exemption would be effected in the
case of the cost-subtraction procedure by allowing business firms to
deduct from their taxable sales items purchased for business investment as well as items currently expensed. Under the tax-credit subtraction procedure, the taxes paid on all business purchases of taxable
goods and services would be credited against the taxes due on sales.
Under the addition procedure, the wages and profits in Example III

would represent the consumption-type concept if, generally speaking, the usual accounting profits exclusive of capital gains were on the one hand increased by the firm's depreciation allowances and on the other decreased by the purchase of capital assets.

The comparative situation under the subtraction procedures of computing the value-added taxes and the single-stage taxes may be most readily seen through the simple numerical example below in which firm A at the first stage not only processes shoe leather but also manufactures a machine used for making shoes. Both products are sold to firm B, the machine being sold for $40 and the leather for $35. Then B manufactures the shoes with the aid of the leather and machine. For simplicity in presentation, B is assumed to sell the shoes directly to ultimate consumers rather than through distributors and does so for $200.

It is evident from the above example that the tax burden on the finished product under the value-added approach is the same as it would have been if a single-stage tax had been imposed on the retail sales of the shoes. What has happened under the value-added procedure is that the manufacturer, A, has advanced part of the tax ultimately due on the aggregate final value of the shoes—a tax collected entirely from B under the single-stage procedure. Rate differentiation would create the same discrepancies under the cost-subtraction procedure as those noted in Example III, that is, the final burden would differ from that under the tax-credit procedure and a single-stage levy.

If the tax is not expected to be shifted forward, the situation is less clear. In the above example, A's machine is subjected to tax along with the sales of the intermediate products, but, on his sales to final consumers, B's tax base is reduced by all his purchases from A, including the machine. Such a tax might conceivably be rationalized as a business fee for services rendered by government. The cost of the services would be thought of as being allocated among business firms according to a consumption-type definition of value added, under which business profits or all factor earnings in the investment goods industries would be expected to shoulder part of the burden, albeit the precise allocation of the burden cannot be determined in the absence of administered prices. The situation would be similar under a single-stage levy not expected to be shifted forward.

The relationship between the subtraction and addition procedures of computing a consumption type of value added may be demonstrated through comparing the accounting formulas which might conceivably be used under each method of arriving at the base. It should be recalled that the addition procedure arrives at the same result as the cost-subtraction method but, given rate differentiation, does not arrive at the same result as the tax-credit subtraction method

EXAMPLE IV

COMPARISON OF SUBTRACTION PROCEDURES OF COMPUTING *Consumption* TYPE OF VALUE-ADDED TAX AND SINGLE-STAGE PROCEDURE WITH 10% TAX

Firms	Value of Product at Each Stage		Value Added	Value-Added Tax		Single-Stage Tax
				Cost-Subtraction	Tax Credit	
A	Machine	$ 40				
	Leather	35				
	Total	75	$ 75	$ 7.50	$ 7.50 − 0.00 = $ 7.50	E.C.[a]
B	Shoes	200	125	12.50	20.00 − 7.50 = 12.50	$20.00
		$200	$200	$20.00		$20.00
Final value of product	$200					
Tax on final value of product				$20.00		$20.00

[a]E.C. = Exemption Certificate.

or a single-stage tax. Table 1 below summarizes the formulas for computing the consumption-type tax base through the addition and subtraction procedures.

TABLE 1

FORMULAS FOR COMPUTING THE CONSUMPTION-TYPE
BASE OF THE INDIVIDUAL FIRM

Income Approach or *Addition Procedure*	*Sales Approach or* *Subtraction Procedure*
Wages and salaries Interest paid to individuals Income type of value-added profits, including subsidies[a] Depreciation Sales of a concern's own fixed assets *minus* capital outlays *minus* net additions to inventories	Receipts from sales of goods and services including rents, and from interest Owner's personal consumption of firm's products *minus* all purchases from other firms[b] *minus* excess of other indirect taxes over subsidies

[a]Profits should include estimated profits on the owner's personal consumption of the firm's products; but the imputation may be omitted for administrative reasons. Value-added profits must exclude dividends received from other firms, to prevent double counting. Capital gains and losses should also be excluded except that gains arising from sales of the concern's own fixed assets would be reached if it were necessary to tax its receipts from sales of such assets in order to avoid a tax loophole. State and local income taxes are included in taxable profits. However, it should be noted that the treatment of taxes in defining the base of a value-added tax as well as the treatment of the value-added tax under the direct personal taxes requires more serious study than has thus far been given to these issues. In brief, value-added profits approximate a concern's operating profits except that interest payments have been deducted while receipts from sales of its capital assets might be included.

[b]Some formulas would include rents and all interest payments in the tax base. In that event, they would not be allowed as deductions for purchases of intermediate products while interest and rent receipts would not be included in taxable sales. Under the addition procedure, rental payments and all interest payments would be treated as factor payments while profits would exclude interest and rent receipts.

The equivalence of the bases under the two methods is obvious. A business concern would deduct from its sales receipts all purchases of goods and services customarily expensed or added to inventories and all outlays for purchases of investment goods; and this residual would equal payments to current factors of production, plus depreciation, less purchases of items added to inventories and of capital goods. It should be noted that interest paid to other business firms is treated as an intermediate expense rather than as a factor payment to be included in the tax base. Rent is likewise treated as a purchase of an intermediate product although some formulas would treat it as a factor payment. Finally, indirect taxes are deducted while subsidies are added in arriving at the tax base, although it might be argued that the value added by a concern should be measured in terms of what consumers are willing to pay for the products, including taxes on such products.[54] However, such taxes are usually deducted on the ground that they do not represent income produced by business.

In order to visualize how the tax would be computed in the case of a particular concern, imagine a firm, the Bristol Boat Building Company, a corporation which manufactures small cabin cruisers which it sells to dealers and individual purchasers. To turn out its product, it must purchase certain materials and supplies from other concerns including lumber, paint, engines, machine tools, heat, and electrical energy as well as certain services, such as banking services and the advice of lawyers and marine architects. Also, it must have buildings in which to manufacture, display, and sell its boats. Then assume that in a given month the concern has taxable sales of $100,000. Aside from the value-added tax on these sales, there is a 10 per cent luxury excise of $10,000 which is included in the sales of $100,000. During the month, $5,000 in goods is added to its inventories, and it spends $40,000 on materials and supplies, $100 for interest on a bank loan, $500 for fees for advice of marine architects, $10,000 on wages to its own workers who construct a new building for its own use, and $3,000 for a new lathe. Its total payroll, including the amount spent on the workers who constructed the building, is $30,000. Also, it has a monthly depreciation charge on its existing capital of $4,000. It has operating profits during the month of $30,400, of which $2,000 is paid out to individual bondholders.

Addition Procedure		*Subtraction Procedure*		
Payroll	$30,000	Taxable sales		$100,000
Interest paid to		Deductible outlays		
individuals	2,000	Luxury		
Net profits	28,400	excise	$10,000	
Depreciation	4,000	Materials and		
Capital outlay	−13,000	supplies	40,000	
Inventories	− 5,000	Interest paid		
Value added	$46,400	to bank	100	
		Architects' fees	500	
		New lathe	3,000	
				−53,600
				$46,400

The addition approach summarizes the payroll, interest payments to individual bondholders, net profits, and depreciation while subtracting the $10,000 of wages for constructing the building, the $3,000 for purchasing the lathe, and the $5,000 inventory accumulation. Under the subtraction procedure, the $10,000 spent for the building is ignored. If outside contractors had been hired, the cost would have been deducted; in that event, the construction workers' wages would eventually have appeared in the contractor's taxable sales. As it is, the Bristol Boat Company is in effect regarded as selling the building to itself and subtracting the amount which it has spent on its construction. It may be noted that if one of the stockholders had obtained a boat free of charge for his own use, taxable receipts would have been increased by the amount of the value imputed to the boat.

The same tax base might have been reached through the suspensive method ordinarily utilized by single-stage sales taxes. This procedure merely reverses the subtraction method of computing value added. Instead of taxing all receipts from sales and deducting purchases of goods and services, the suspensive method uses tax exemptions in the case of items purchased from other business firms; the excise would of course still have to be deducted. Thus, the Bristol Boat Company would have purchased materials and services from suppliers who did not pay the tax due on their sales to the boat company. Instead, the collection of tax is postponed to the stage where a business firm sells the finished product to a nonbusiness purchaser or, if the tax does not extend through the retail stage, to the stage where a business firm sells the product to a business firm in the nontaxed stages. The tax is not collected from each firm as it adds value to the product but only from the firm which makes the final sale, and then the tax is due on the total value.

Income-Type Base

The difference between the consumption- and income-type bases under a sales tax which is supposed to be shifted forward is that the income-type bases are designed to reach purchases of investment goods for final investment as well as purchases for ultimate consumers. Thus, as contrasted with the situation under the consumption-type tax, the output of investment goods is treated as a final product rather than as an intermediate one; it is capitalized rather than expensed.

The taxation of investment goods is managed under single-stage taxes by disallowing purchases in suspension of tax when the purchases are made for final business use. Under the value-added procedure, the purchaser is not allowed to deduct his purchases of investment goods from his sales or, given the tax-credit procedure, is not allowed to credit the tax on his purchases of investment goods against the taxes due on his sales.

Using the same data as in Example IV and ignoring the question of a depreciation allowance, the situation under the subtraction procedures and single-stage method may be visualized through the example below.

In principle, the income-type base should include not only investment goods but inventory accumulation.[55] Inventory accumulation has never been reached in practice under an income-type base, probably because of the administrative complexities involved. The Japanese value-added tax proposal would have reached inventory accumulation under the option to compute value added through an addition procedure in which profits were to be taken from the firm's accounts for the national income tax.[56]

A tax on inventory accumulation is compatible with the single-stage as well as the value-added procedure. Under the single-stage approach and the addition method of computing value added, the purchasing firm would pay the entire tax on inventory accumulation. Under the subtraction methods of computing value added, the vendor would still advance the part of the tax relating to the items added to inventory by the purchasing firm, the purchasing firm merely receiving smaller deductions or tax credits than if it had not been taxed on its inventory accumulation. In other words, the purchasing firm should not be allowed tax credits on purchases entering into inventories. In addition, the tax should be imposed on the value of closing inventories less opening inventories.

The income-type concept which allows depreciation is invariably considered in terms of the value-added procedure. The concept might conceivably be implemented under the single-stage approach by granting the firm which makes an investment a tax reimbursement equal to the amount of a depreciation allowance times the tax rate; but this is a rather awkward arrangement. When the subtraction procedure of computing value added is referred to in the remainder of this discussion on the income-type base, the cost-subtraction method will be assumed in order to simplify the presentation. However, it should be borne in mind that, unlike the tax-credit procedure which would credit the amount of tax on depreciation allowances against the taxes due on sales, both the addition and cost-subtraction methods make it impossible to apply a planned tax rate to the final value of the product, given rate differentiation—an issue which is important in the case of the personal concepts of sales taxation but not necessarily for the business-tax concepts.

EXAMPLE V

COMPARISON OF THE SUBTRACTION PROCEDURES OF COMPUTING *Income* TYPE OF VALUE-ADDED TAX AND SINGLE-STAGE PROCEDURE WITH 10% TAX

Firms	Value of Product at Each Stage	Value-Added	Cost-Subtraction	Tax-Credit	Single-Stage Tax
A	Machine $ 40 Leather 35 ——— 75	$ 75	$ 7.50	$ 7.50 − 0.00 = $ 7.50	E.C.[c] + $ 4.00
B	Shoes 200	165[b]	16.50	20.00 − 3.50 = 16.50	20.00
Final value of product	$240[a]	$240	$24.00	$24.00	$24.00
Tax on final value of product					

[a] As the machine is now treated as a final product, the value of finished goods turned out by the two concerns has increased by $40.00.

[b] Firm B's value added has been increased by $40 because its purchase of the machine is no longer treated as an expensed intermediate product.

[c] E.C. = Exemption Certificate received from firm B for sales of leather. The $4.00 tax applies to the sale of the machine.

The addition and subtraction formulas for computing the income-type of value added which allows depreciation are presented in Table 2 below.

TABLE 2

FORMULAS FOR COMPUTING AN INCOME-TYPE BASE
OF THE INDIVIDUAL FIRM

Income Approach or Addition Procedure	Sales Approach or Subtraction Procedure
Wages and salaries Interest paid to individuals Value-added profits, including subsidies [a]	Receipts from sales of goods and services including rents and interest Investment on force account[b] Net addition to inventories Owner's personal consumption of firm's products *minus* current account purchases of goods and services from other firms[c] *minus* excess of other indirect taxes over subsidies *minus* depreciation

[a]Profits should include estimated profits on the owner's personal consumption of the firm's products; but the imputation may be omitted for administrative reasons.

[b]Investment through use of firm's own factors of production.

[c]Some formulas would include rents and all interest payments in the tax base. In that event, they would not be allowed as deductions for purchases of intermediate products while interest and rent receipts would not be included in taxable sales. Under the addition procedure, rental payments and all interest payments would be treated as factor payments while profits would exclude interest and rent receipts.

Given this income concept, the Bristol Boat Building Company described earlier would have a value added equal to $60,400, rather than the $46,400 under the consumption concept. Under the addition procedure, value added would include the payroll of $30,000, interest paid to individuals of $2,000, and profits of $28,400, reaching a total of $60,400. Under the subtraction procedure, the value of the building constructed by the firm's own labor force and inventory accumulation would be added to sales, giving a total of $115,000, while deductible outlays would amount to $54,600 ($10,000 for the excise, $40,600 for current expenses, and $4,000 for depreciation). No deduction would be allowed for purchase of the lathe. Thus, $115,000 — $54,600 = $60,400.

While in the period an investment is made, the income-type base is larger than the consumption-type base and thus results in a higher tax liability, over the life of an investment, the aggregate tax base is the same under both procedures. The gain to taxpayers from the consumption-type base over the income-type base is measured by the interest on the postponed tax payments. Thus, if the building and lathe of the Bristol Boat Company have an expected life of ten years, the tax base under the income-type concept is greater than under the consumption-type by $13,000 during the first year, but $1,300 less in each of the ten years following the one in which the investment is made. Similarily, the inventories included in the income-type base during the period of accumulation would result in deductions for withdrawals from inventories during later periods which would not be available under the consumption-type base. Finally, in the absence of net inventory accumulation and with the rate of investment no greater than the rate of depreciation, the income and consumption measures are equal.

The Definition of Taxable Price

The avoidance of competitive distortions requires that the tax base be defined in terms of a uniform taxable price. In the case of a tax extending through the retail stage and applied to products which take the form of services as well as commodities, the problem of doing so is not very troublesome. An allowance is invariably made for discounts, returned merchandise, and cancelled sales. Some controversy may arise over whether the tax should apply at the time the purchaser receives his goods or services or at the time or times the vendor receives payments and over whether there should be an allowance for bad debts. Also, if the tax is imposed on sales of investment goods destined for business use, there arises, among related concerns, the possibility of fictitious prices which require some constructive pricing by the administrative authorities. These and such problems as how to treat trading stamps and sales through vending machines are of less than major significance and, at least among the states of the United States, are not always solved in the same fashion.[57]

On the other hand, real difficulty can be created if the tax does not reach services, and especially if its application does not extend through the retail stage. The problem arises when the actual sales price of a firm includes values for services that it performs—such as transportation, financing, warranty, and advertising—which would not be taxed if rendered by an independent firm classified as a service enterprise. Thus, a decision has to be made as to the extent to which an allowance will be granted when the rendering of such services is integrated with the sale of commodities. Granting adequate allowances may involve a considerable amount of constructive pricing, thereby complicating compliance problems and creating increased opportunities for evasion. Also, if the exemption of services goes so far as to exempt commodity rentals, then it is necessary to take steps to ensure that taxable sales are not disguised as tax-free rental arrangements.

If the tax does not extend through the retail stage, attempts to ensure a uniform taxable price may, under certain circumstances, cause constructive pricing to become a dominant feature of the tax, as has been the case of the Canadian manufacturers sales tax and the British purchase tax, a wholesalers sales tax.[58] Under a manufacturers sales tax, a discount must be allowed when the manufacturer sells directly to ultimate consumers or to retailers at a price including distributive margins. On the other hand, an increase in actual sales price, an "uplift," may be required if some manufacturing functions have been transferred to retailers. Under a wholesalers sales tax, a discount is required on direct sales to ultimate consumers, while an uplift may be necessary on direct sales by manufacturers to retailers; Due maintains that the problem of uplift under the wholesalers tax may well create greater administrative problems than those under a manufacturers tax where a discount would probably constitute the prevalent adjustment.[59] Yet, among the countries using the wholesalers tax, only Great Britain has used an uplift, while Switzerland, New Zealand, and Australia have managed without one, presumably because their taxes have not been heavy enough to cause a transfer of functions to the retail level.[60] The French tax, which in principle is a wholesalers levy, has also avoided use of an uplift, despite heavy rates. This is the case perhaps because integrated retailers have to pay the value-added tax, albeit with a discount to allow for retail profit margins, but more probably because the option granted wholesalers to pay the local tax rather than the value-added tax makes it possible to limit the base of the value-added tax to the manufacturing level. Finally, it should be noted that the problem of fictitious pricing among related concerns is likely to be considerable in the case of taxes which exclude services or distributive sectors of activity.

RATES OF TAX

Rates of sales taxes may vary from the moderate or low rates used by various political subdivisions, such as the 3–5% general rates for the retail sales taxes in the states of the United States and in the Canadian provinces to the 25% general effective rate of the French value-added tax, which is limited to the wholesale or manufacturing level. The low nominal rates under the general turnover taxes understate the effective rates which may amount on the average to three or four times the stated rate, after taking into consideration the cumulative burden imposed by the tax. Rate differentiation is probably more characteristic of high-rate taxes although under the low-rate levies the differentiation may take the form of special excises.

On the assumption of equal tax bases, a high-rate tax is often said to be more difficult to administer than a low-rate one on the ground that the high rate stimulates evasion and avoidance.[61] On the other hand, a low rate resulting from a more extensive base, as under the general turnover taxes, would appear no less troublesome than a higher rate imposed on a commensurately narrower base, as when a single-stage or value-added base is substituted for the general turnover base. Also, the higher rates needed when taxes are limited to the manufacturers and wholesalers stage rather than extended through the retail level are offset by the narrower bases. Moreover, administration is facilitated by the reduced number of taxpayers involved in the manufacturers and wholesalers taxes. However, this advantage will be of little significance if constructive pricing characterizes the nonretail taxes, a situation which suggests that extension of the tax through the retail level is advisable.

INTERNATIONAL ASPECTS OF SALES TAX CONCEPTS[62]

Two Jurisdictional Principles

In the case of the purchase and sale of goods or services across international boundaries, sales taxes may be imposed under either the destination principle or the origin principle. The destination principle requires that all products having the same place of destination, that is, place of final consumption or use, be subjected to an equal tax burden regardless of their geographical origin, that is, where they were produced. The origin principle requires that all products originating in a given jurisdiction be subjected to the same amount of tax regardless of the destination. Presumably the principles also imply the allocation of the tax proceeds to the area having jurisdiction, although this issue has not yet been considered to any extent.[63]

Destination Principle

Under the destination principle, the country which imports the products has tax jurisdiction over the total value of the products and will tax the items at the same rate as similar domestic products, while exports are completely exempt from tax, not being within the tax jurisdiction of the exporting country. This principle is designed to implement the personal concepts of sales taxation; under these concepts, the final purchaser pays the tax on his purchases regardless of their origin. The forward shifting of the sales taxes to the final purchaser is, of course, assumed.

The destination principle can be applied with either the single-stage or value-added methods of collection. Countries using the general turnover taxes have also attempted to use this principle; in addition to exempting export transactions, these countries seek to reimburse exporters for taxes imposed on previous transfers, and to subject imported products to additional taxes to take account of the turnover taxes borne by the same kinds of goods produced domestically. In practice, however, the equalization aimed for cannot be satisfactorily effected because the number of previously taxed transfers is not known.

The destination principle is most adequately implemented by a tax applied through the retail stage, because the administrative task of exempting exports and imposing a compensatory tax on imports is complicated by the existence of international transactions occurring at stages subsequent to the taxing stage. With a single-stage retail sales tax, all exports can readily be exempted by extending the suspensive procedure to cover all vendors, including retailers, who sell directly abroad; imports made by anyone other than an ultimate consumer or user would likewise be exempt from tax. The value-added method operates in a similar manner if the tax-credit procedure is used. The export transaction is exempt and a reimbursement is granted for the tax credits which have arisen from taxes imposed at earlier stages. Under the cost-subtraction or the addition procedure of computing value added, it would be difficult to effect an adequate export exemption if differentiated rates had been imposed on parts of the value of the final export product in the course of its production. However, this is merely another instance of the fact that rate differentiation causes difficulty under these methods of determining the tax base. Also, imports would have to be taxed in order to reach value added abroad, while, under the tax-credit procedure, the absence of a tax credit would automatically provide for the inclusion of such value. Under all of the methods of collecting a sales tax, special provisions, called use-tax provisions in the United States for constitutional reasons, must be included in the sales tax law in order to impose tax on purchases by ultimate consumers or users made directly from abroad rather than through domestic business firms.

The major difficulty with the application of the destination principle is the administrative one that, given rates above a certain level, it becomes necessary to establish customs machinery or special collection arrangements with importers and exporters[64] in order to ensure that imports do not evade the tax. It is this problem which is being emphasized to support the recommendation by the Commission of the European Economic Community that the destination principle be abandoned with respect to sales among the Member States—although it would be retained with respect to transactions with third countries.[65] It should be noted, however, that the destination principle is also being opposed by those who believe that it favors a policy of obstructing imports and subsidizing exports.[66]

Origin Principle

As contrasted with the destination principle, which subjects the total value of a product to the tax of the importing country, the origin principle allocates the value of the product according to the area in which the value is deemed to have been created. Thus, on the assumption that the value has arisen entirely within the exporting country, the product is subjected to the tax of the exporting country and is exempt from tax by the importing country. On the other hand, if part of the value is assumed to have arisen in the importing country, then that part of the value will be subjected to the tax of the importing country and exempted by the exporting country.

Allocation of the value of the product will therefore require source rules similar to those which are found in the application of the origin or source principle of income taxation. This can be most readily visualized with the aid of a simple numerical example. Assume two countries, A and B, and a product shipped by an exporter in A to an importer in B for $100 with its price representing the following components of value:

> $60 wages and salaries
> 5 rent
> 5 interest
> 30 profit (including depreciation) [67]
> ———
> $100 Total value of product

In contrast to the destination principle which would allocate the entire $100 to B, the origin principle of sales taxation requires that the various components of value be allocated to the country where they were deemed to have originated according to source rules. As the components of value represent payments to factors of production which constitute taxable receipts under income taxation, the same source rules would presumably serve both taxes. An allocation formula might be used, but inter-country agreement on a particular formula may be difficult to attain, perhaps more difficult than agreement on refined source rules. Of course, use of the same source rules for income and sales taxes does not imply the same allocation of the tax burden, for incidence is not likely to be the same under the two types of taxes.

The above example might have been made more realistic by assuming that part of the value had been added by business firms in A

or even in a third country prior to the export of the product. In other words, only the value added by the exporter requires allocation; values added previously will already have been allocated, thus suggesting that the value-added method of collecting the sales tax is the appropriate one for the origin principle, although the single-stage method could conceivably be used. In any event, any value of the product deemed to have arisen in *B*, as, for example, part of the profits of the exporter in *A* or the value added by the exporter's selling establishment in *B*, would lie within *B*'s taxing jurisdiction, not *A*'s.

It seems to be generally assumed that the cost-subtraction procedure of computing value added would be used to apply the origin principle of sales taxation, and therefore the addition procedure would likewise be applicable. However, these procedures are satisfactory only on the assumption that there would be little domestic rate differentiation under the taxes.[68] Given the tax-credit procedure, tax credits would have to be transferred to the importing business firm in *B* if he were not to be taxed on the value added to the product in *A*, a system which implies *B*'s acceptance of *A*'s application of the source rules. If the rates differed between the two countries, *B*'s tax credit would have to be computed in terms of *B*'s rather than *A*'s tax rate, for otherwise a higher rate in *A* would make the tax burden on the value added in *B* too low, while a lower rate in *A* would make the tax burden in *B* too high. Thus the exporter in *A* would quote the tax which he has paid to *A*, say $10 under a 10% rate. The business firm in *B* would then know that value added in *A* amounted to $100 and that in terms of *B*'s tax rate, say 6%, the tax credits available in *B* equal $6.

Unlike the destination principle, the origin principle of sales taxation is not compatible with the concept of personal taxation, in the event that the tax rates differ significantly between the taxing jurisdictions, because it makes it impossible for a country to tax its residents on the total value of their purchases, the value having been divided among different jurisdictions. Rather, it seeks to implement an impersonal concept of taxation in which taxes are regarded as payments for the benefit of governmental services rendered to business firms and, in essence, treats tax systems as competing cost factors. Given more conventional philosophies of taxation, it is generally assumed that competition would make it impossible for countries to maintain much, if any, difference in sales tax rates under the origin principle,[69] in which case the only difference from the destination principle is in the allocation of the tax receipts. Whether a sales tax is shifted forward seems not to be a matter of major concern under the origin principle of sales taxation, applied with significant rate differentiation, as contrasted with the personal concepts under which forward shifting of the tax is considered essential.[70] Finally, it should be noted that, if the destination principle reflects a trade policy of favoring exports over imports, the origin principle does the reverse.

THE NEED FOR EVALUATION OF SALES TAX CONCEPTS IN TERMS OF THEIR EFFECTS

With the objective of raising a certain amount of revenue, the decision to adopt a sales tax rather than either another type of tax or deficit spending ought to be made in terms of anticipated effects. Similarly, anticipated effects must be considered in choosing a particular concept of sales taxation. If additional spending is being contemplated, an attempt should be made to appraise the effects of the expenditures as well as the methods of raising revenues. In any event, the concept of the sales tax as a price paid for governmental services implies that expenditures as well as revenues will be taken into consideration.

Sales taxes, like income taxes, as well as the expenditures financed by such levies, are virtually all-inclusive in scope and therefore require macroeconomic analysis. However, it should be borne in mind that the theoretical tools which have been devised for such analyses have been developed from economic models which involve a high degree of abstraction from actual situations. The underlying assumptions with regard to economic development, degree of competition, and mobility of resources are invariably so far removed from reality that at most this approach can serve only as a rough guide to policy. Furthermore, the macroeconomic approach must be supplemented by an attempt to visualize the effects of the taxes on the economic units, individuals, and business firms which in the final analysis are responsible for the life of an economic system.

Consequently, there is no escape from the arduous task of relating public finance proposals to the specific economic, social, and political environment in which they are to operate. For example, incidence assumptions appropriate to a highly developed, relatively self-sufficient economy may prove completely erroneous in an underdeveloped country whose national income has a large foreign-trade component. Other relevant factors may be the adequacy of the money and banking system and the degree of monopoly characterizing business organization.

Thus it is impossible to assume offhand that sales taxes are generally shifted forward. Similarly, macroeconomic concepts such as consumption, savings, and investment have significance only in terms of a particular context; and policies with respect to their taxation or non-taxation must be related to a specific economy. A policy of exemption of savings and investment, in the interest of solving productivity and employment problems, may in fact lead to disappointing results if the definitions of savings and investment encompass nonproductive employment of funds or if an allowance is not made for the rigidity of productive factors. Finally, it must be borne in mind that the questions of the extent to which taxes should continue to be viewed in the conventional manner as contributions to the cost of government by individuals or instead treated as impersonal business costs; of whether consumption- or income-type bases should be used; and of whether a direct or indirect approach should be adopted may involve fundamental issues of economic and therefore social and political philosophy.

NOTES TO SELECTION 20

[1] This distinction is customarily made. See, for example, John F. Due, *Sales Taxation* (Urbana, Illinois: University of Illinois Press, 1957), p. 3.

[2] Some special excises might conceivably be justified as compensation for certain social costs, that is, costs to the economy not included in the accounts of business firms, such as the cost of air or water pollution. However, in the absence of any serious attempts at social accounting, such rationalization can hardly be applied to existing taxes. The difficulties of its application are effectively illustrated in James E. Meade, *Problems of Economic Union* (Chicago: University of Chicago Press, 1953), pp. 24–26.

[3] See, for example, the classification used by the World Tax Series, Harvard Law School International Program in Taxation.

[4] See, for example, Due, *Sales Taxation*, pp. 149, 187, 267.

[5] Sales taxes are designated as taxes on the use of income, in the report of the Fiscal and Financial Committee of the European Economic Community. See Commission, Communauté Economique Européenn, *Rapport du Comité Fiscal et Financier* (1962), p. 25. However, in addition to sales taxes, strictly speaking, the Committee includes within this category special excises and customs.

[6] This is the concept which Due applies to sales taxes. See *Sales Taxation*, pp. 3–4.

[7] For a detailed analysis of the concept of direct expenditure taxation, see William Vickrey, *Agenda for Progressive Taxation* (New York: The Ronald Press Company, 1947), *passim*. A brief survey is given on pp. 4–6. Another comprehensive analysis is that undertaken by Nicholas Kaldor, *An Expenditure Tax* (London: Allen & Unwin, 1955).

[8] The 25% sales tax rate applies to price excluding tax and amounts to 20% of price including tax, just as the direct spendings tax amounts to 20% on income including tax and 25% on income excluding tax. Under the indirect tax, the individual will presumably spend $1,000 in order to purchase a quantity of goods and services which would be obtained for $800 in the absence of a sales tax.

[9] See study prepared by U.S. Treasury Department, Division of Tax Research, and submitted by Randolph E. Paul, General Counsel for the Treasury, "Considerations Respecting a Federal Retail Sales Tax," *Revenue Revision of 1943*, Hearings Before the Committee on Ways and Means, House of Representatives, 78th Congress, 1st Session (Washington: 1943), pp. 1167–81.

[10] *The Wall Street Journal*, September 28, 1960, p. 1, col. 5.

[11] "The General Sales Tax," *Report of the Governor's Minnesota Tax Study Committee* (Minneapolis: Colwell Press, Inc., 1956), p. 476, illustrates the extent to which progressivity would be introduced into the sales tax system by a $10 credit (allowed under Minnesota's 1953 personal income tax), for each single person and each family member, for a 2% sales tax reaching almost all consumption expenditures. However, the progression is not constant and, in fact, regression

persists in certain income brackets. For example, after credit, the sales tax would have amounted to .89% of the average gross incomes in the bracket $3,000 to $3,999, but only .81% in the bracket $4,000 to $4,999. It is about .97% of average incomes in the bracket $5,000 to $5,999, but only .94% in the bracket $6,000 to $7,499. Moreover, the analysis is limited to incomes under $10,000; all incomes of $10,000 and over are lumped together, thus concealing regressivity with respect to upper brackets.

[12]On the whole, this premise seems to conform with reality. For a survey of divergent positions, see Daniel C. Morgan, Jr., "Reappraisal of Sales Taxation: Some Recent Arguments," *National Tax Journal*, XVI (1963), 90–94.

[13]See, for example, Dr. Richard Goode's statement concerning the failure to tax certain items in underdeveloped countries, "Taxation of Saving and Consumption in Underdeveloped Countries," *National Tax Journal*, XIV (1961), 316 [see selection 16 in this volume]. Nevertheless, Goode is of the opinion that, "It may be possible to devise indirect tax systems which are not highly regressive."

[14]See, for example, the interesting analysis by Joseph Moscarella, "Aspects du développment économique de l'Amérique Centrale," *Revue de science financière*, XLIX (1957), 455 and especially p. 461. See also the excellent analysis by Richard M. Eigner, "Indian Income, Wealth and Expenditure Taxes: Integration and Administration," *National Tax Journal*, XII (1959), 151–62.

[15]Antonio de Viti de Marco, *First Principles of Public Finance*, trans. from Italian by Edith Pavlo Marget (New York: Harcourt Brace & Co., 1936), p. 135.

[16]See Due, *Sales Taxation*, p. 298 f., and Carl S. Shoup, "Theory and Background of the Value-Added Tax," *Proceedings of the Forty-Eighth Annual Conference of the National Tax Association* (1955), p. 8.

[17]See, for example, Due, *Sales Taxation*, p. 67; Charles Campet, *The Influence of Sales Taxes on Productivity*, The European Productivity Agency of the Organization for European Economic Co-operation, Project No. 315 (Paris, 1958), p. 37; Maurice Lauré, *La taxe sur la valeur ajoutée* (Paris: Recueil Sirey, 1952), p. 61.

[18]See the analysis of the concept in Shoup, "Theory and Background of the Value-Added Tax," pp. 9–11. The measure is also discussed in more detail below.

[19]U.S. Department of Commerce, *National Income 1954 Edition, A Supplement to the Survey of Current Business* (Washington, 1954), p. 38.

[20]Carl S. Shoup, *Principles of National Income Analysis* (Boston: Houghton Mifflin Company, 1947), pp. 147–54.

[21]Simon Kuznets, *National Income and its Composition, 1919–1938* (New York: National Bureau of Economic Research, 1941), p. 36.

[22]Kuznets, *National Income and its Composition, 1919–1938*, p. 37 f.

[23]Shoup, *Principles of National Income Analysis*, p. 149.

[24]*Ibid.*, p. 153.

[25]This philosophy underlies Professor Thomas S. Adams' view of business taxation. See T. S. Adams, "Fundamental Problems of Federal Income Taxation," *Quarterly Journal of Economics*, XXXV (1921), 551.

[26]See, for example, Paul Studenski, "Toward a Theory of Business Taxation," *Journal of Political Economy*, XLVIII (1940), 648 f. Also, see the rationalization of the Michigan "business activities tax" by James A. Papke, "Michigan's Value-Added Tax after Seven Years," *National Tax Journal*, XIII (1960), 251.

[27]See Adams, "Fundamental Problems of Federal Income Taxation," p. 553, and Studenski, "Toward a Theory of Business Taxation," p. 648.

[28]Gerhard Colm, "Methods of Financing Unemployment Compensation," *Social Research*, II (1935), 161.

[29]Papke, "Michigan's Value-Added Tax after Seven Years," p. 359.

[30]See Roscoe Arant, "The Place of Business Taxation in the Revenue Systems of the States," *Taxes, The Tax Magazine*, XV (1937), 191.

[31]Arant, "The Place of Business Taxation in the Revenue Systems of the States," p. 199.

[32]H. G. Brown, "The Incidence of a General Output or a General Sales Tax," *Journal of Political Economy,* XLVII (1939), 254–62; reprinted in The American Economic Association, Richard A. Musgrave and Carl S. Shoup, Selection Committee, *Readings in the Economics of Taxation* (Homewood, Illinois: Richard D. Irwin, Inc., 1959), pp. 330–39.

[33]See Earl R. Rolph, "A Proposed Revision of Excise Tax Theory," *Journal of Political Economy,* LX (1952), 102–17; J. A. Stockfisch, "The Capitalization and Investment Aspects of Excise Taxes under Competition," *The American Economic Review,* XLIV (1954), 287–330; Richard A. Musgrave, *The Theory of Public Finance* (New York: McGraw-Hill Book Co., Inc., 1959), Chap. 16.

[34]Stockfisch, "The Capitalization and Investment Aspects of Excise Taxes under Competition," p. 291.

[35]Musgrave, *Theory of Public Finance,* p. 379.

[36]See Charles P. Kindleberger, *International Economics* (3d ed., Homewood, Illinois: Richard D. Irwin, Inc., 1963), p. 428.

[37]See the analysis of the "new export taxes" intended to reach the incomes of foreign factors of production and of luxury importers in Jonathan V. Levin, *The Export Economies* (Cambridge, Mass.: Harvard University Press, 1960), especially pp. 263–67, 269–71. Dr. Levin explains (p. 271) that, "The most prevalent method of assuring that the burden of the new export taxes is not shifted back to domestic factors of production, then, has been direct government regulation."

[38]Designated as "demand-shifting excises" in the study by Albert G. Hart and E. Cary Brown, assisted by H. F. Rasmussen, *Financing Defense, Federal Tax and Expenditure Policies* (New York: The Twentieth Century Fund, 1951), pp. 48–56.

[39]Due, *Sales Taxation,* pp. 226–28.

[40]Levin, *The Export Economies,* p. 264.

[41]See Harvard Law School International Program in Taxation, *World Tax Series: Taxation in the Federal Republic of Germany* (prepared by Henry J. Gumpel and Carl Boettcher, correspondent) (Chicago: Commerce Clearing House, Inc., 1963), 16/2.1.

[42]As in the French sales taxes, see *Code Général des Impôts,* art. 256.

[43]See, for example, the explanation given for the rate concessions to farmers under the German turnover tax, in Due, *Sales Taxation,* p. 55.

[44]As explained by Due, *Sales Taxation,* p. 21.

[45]This problem has been thoroughly analyzed by Professor Due. See John F. Due, "Report of the Sales Tax Committee: One Year in Retrospect," *Canadian Tax Journal,* Vol. 5 (1957), p. 88, and Due, *Sales Taxation,* pp. 154–57, 210–16.

[46]See Lauré, *La taxe sur la valeur ajoutèe,* p. 107.

[47]The addition procedure is sometimes called the "direct" method, see Due, *Sales Taxation,* p. 66.

[48]See Commerce Clearing House, Inc., *Tax Harmonization in the Common Market,* a translation of the Neumark Report, Draft Directive on Turnover Taxes, Commission's Statement on Draft Directive; and a Comment by Hans von der Groeben on the Draft Directive (Chicago: Commerce Clearing House, Inc., April 1963) par. 3458.11, p. 47. This procedure is sometimes also called the "direct" method, see Dr. G. Schmölders, "Die Veredelung der Umsatzsteuer," *Public Finance,* IX (1954), 111–12, and Wissenschaftlicher Beirat beim Bundesministerium der Finanzen, *Organische Steuerreform, Bericht an den Herrn Bundesminister der Finanzen* (Bonn, 1953), p. 61. The term "purchases subtraction procedure" might also be used.

[49]Adams, "Fundamental Problems of Federal Income Taxation," p. 551 f.

[50]See Shoup, "Theory and Background of the Value-Added Tax," p. 8. Shoup also places the manufacturers sales tax and wholesalers sales tax in the category

of transactions taxes, presumably because of the economic disturbances which they may create with respect to varying channels of distribution. Moreover, he assumes that the retail sales tax is limited to sales destined for ultimate consumption if it is to belong to the national-income category.

[51]One version of the consumption-type base, which Professor Shoup calls the interest-exclusion variant, would tax purchases of investment goods as well as of consumption goods, but would allow a deduction from taxable sales for depreciation and interest earned on the investment. See "Theory and Background of the Value-Added Tax," p. 12.

[52]It should be noted that under all the methods of imposing the tax, the value of products destined for personal consumption by the owners of the business would have to be included in the tax base if a loophole is to be avoided.

[53]The term "suspension" implies that the tax liability exists even though payment is postponed to a later stage.

[54]See Shoup, *Principles of National Income Analysis*, p. 342 f.

[55]Shoup, "Theory and Background of the Value-Added Tax," pp. 14–15.

[56]Shoup Mission, *Second Report on Japanese Taxation* (Tokyo: Japan Tax Association, 1950), p. 17 f.

[57]A thorough discussion of these problems and a number of other administrative problems faced under the United States state retail sales taxes are discussed in John F. Due, *State Sales Tax Administration* (Chicago: Public Administration Service, 1963).

[58]See Due, *Sales Taxation*, pp. 154–55, 210–15.

[59]*Ibid.*, p. 364.

[60]Due notes that the problem has been solved under the Swiss tax through allowing retailers to register as taxpayers and subjecting them to a tax rate less than the general one, with the reduced rate reflecting average retailers' margins. However, the solution might not prove adequate if the Swiss rate rose much above 5.4%. The New Zealand and Australian taxes impose high general rates of 20% and 12½%, respectively; but, as Due points out, the legislation contains extensive exemptions. See Due, *Sales Taxation*, p. 364

[61]See *ibid.*, p. 353.

[62]The subject of this section is more fully analyzed in Clara K. Sullivan, *The Search for Tax Principles in the European Economic Community* (Cambridge, Mass.: Harvard Law School International Program in Taxation, 1963).

[63]Professor Cosciani once suggested that if the origin principle were adopted for consumption taxes in the European Economic Community, the country which consumes the taxed products should receive the proceeds of the tax. See Cesare Cosciani, "Aspects de la fiscalité dans la C.E.E.," *Revue de science financière*, LIII (1961), 562.

[64]Compare the so-called use taxes in the United States, which impose collection liability on out-of-state sellers shipping goods into the taxing state. See *Scripto, Inc. v. Carson*, 362 U.S. 307 (1960).

[65]See Commission, Communauté Economique Européenne, *Rapport du Comité Fiscal et Financier*, pp. 79, 81.

[66]See Ivar Galeen, "Outsider's Views on EEC Tax Problems," *European Taxation: A Fortnightly Review*, Vol. 2 (1962), pp. 120–31.

[67]Depreciation is included because it is part of actual sales price, and its possible deduction under certain concepts of sales taxation does not affect the issue being discussed here.

[68]See Commission, Communauté Economique Européenne, *Rapport du Comité Fiscal et Financier*, pp. 42, 80.

[69]*Ibid.*, pp. 78, 80 f.

[70]See, for example, the statement of Dr. G. Schmölders, "Die Ueberwalzung der Umsatzsteuer mit der en Gelingen ihr Charakter als Verbrauchsteuer steht und fällt. . . ." ("The forward shifting of the sales tax with whose success its character as a consumption tax stands or falls. . . ." [my trans.]), *Organische Steuerreform: Grundlagen, Vorarbeiten, Gesetzentwürfe* (Berlin und Frankfurt a.m.: Franz Vahlen, 1953), p. 128.

Part V

Local Finance and Real Property Taxes

THE opening selection, from the excellent book on Indonesian finance by Douglas Paauw, treats in detail the role of local finance in a developing country, a subject that has been all too often neglected in the rush toward ever more grandiose national development plans. While much of the detail in Paauw's work is of course peculiar to Indonesia, the issues are world-wide, as our second selection, by Joseph Froomkin, points out. Froomkin's article is especially notable for the emphasis placed on the different problems faced by urban areas of different size. The financial problems of rapidly growing urban areas in developing countries remain a subject needing much more study than it has received thus far.

The extract from the report on the financial problems of Jamaica by Professor J. R. Hicks and Mrs. U. K. Hicks of Oxford University contains an interesting proposal for improving the property tax systems of urban areas in poor countries. A similar idea is presented in a rural context in the extract from the World Bank report on Colombia; the next selection, taken from the recent book by Albert O. Hirschman, contains the detailed history of what happened subsequently. As noted in the introduction to the present volume of readings, Professor Hirschman's account is the most detailed study of the implementation of a tax reform proposal of which we are aware; it is worth careful reading even by those not interested in either Colombia or land taxes.

Finally, the paper prepared for the 1963 World Food Congress describes Japanese experience with land taxation at the end of the nineteenth century, and places in a specific context the important problem of the role of agricultural taxation in economic development. It is often noted that Japan's success in rapidly transforming its economy at the end of the nineteenth century might well be a model for other countries; the information in this last paper supports as well as argues against reliance on Japan's experience, at least with regard to agricultural taxation.

359

21

Local Finance in Indonesia

by Douglas S. Paauw*

OUR discussion up to this point has dealt mainly with the role of Central Government in financing Indonesian economic development. Given the political and social framework discussed in the Introduction, and the factors outlined at the end of the previous chapter, it is clear that the potential role of local finance should also receive serious consideration. Indeed, the success of domestic financing of economic development in Indonesia will depend in large measure upon taking full advantage of the resources that can be mobilized through local fiscal processes.

The contribution of local finance to Indonesian economic development has not received much attention. During the Dutch period, lack of concern for local finance was perhaps an inevitable consequence of colonial rule which had little concern for development of the economy as a whole. Investigations of local finance were chiefly concerned with the extent to which local taxes added to the burden which the colonial government imposed upon the indigenous population.[1] The scope and importance of local finance continued to grow, however, as the Netherlands East Indies government responded to Indonesian demands for greater local autonomy. In 1904 an ordinance which authorized the formation of local councils to levy taxes for the support of local development projects provided a great stimulus to the local financing of community-development investment activity (such as "water supplies, slaughter houses, markets, public baths, cemeteries, irrigation works, drains, sewers, drainage of waterlogged lands").[2] The ordinance applied primarily to Java and Madura; on the Outer Islands considerable autonomy already existed through the device of "Native States," which were given almost complete local autonomy in political and fiscal matters and were ruled by native princes loyal to the colonial government—although the colonial government collected certain of its indirect taxes. As a result, the total tax burden

*Reprinted with permission of The Free Press of Glencoe from *Financing Economic Development—The Indonesian Case* by Douglas S. Paauw. Copyright 1960 by The Massachusetts Institute of Technology. Reprinted here are pp. 268–307.

per capita in the Native States was found to be the lowest in Java, but it is suggested below that the Native States were capable of financing more local capital formation than the directly governed territories. The difference in the central tax burden between the two types of regions apparently was large enough to allow a lower total (central *and* local) tax burden in the autonomous regions even though their tax systems produced more local resources for financing local capital-formation projects.

The importance of that state of affairs for present Indonesian development planning lies in the fact that local fiscal autonomy led to a relatively high rate of locally financed investment. Furthermore, it paved the way for the evolution of attitudes toward central and local taxation which have greatly influenced the postwar realities in which economic development must be financed in Indonesia.

Data are not available to provide a satisfactory estimate of the significance of total local government investment during the last decade of colonial rule. Although investment expenditures of the Native States were reported, there are no reports for the directly governed territories. A comparison of investment in the Native States with colonial government investment, however, underlines the prewar importance of local finance. Such a comparison is made in Table 1.

TABLE 1
GOVERNMENT INVESTMENT, 1935–1938

(*Thousand NEI Guilders*)

Year	Central	Native States	Total	Native States as Per Cent of Total
1935	3,057	2,570	5,627	46
1936	4,628	3,680	8,308	44
1937	11,405	4,693	16,098	29
1938	9,282	5,507	14,789	37
Average				39

SOURCE: Data obtained from Ministry of Finance, Nederlandsch-Indië, *Het Tweede Tiental Begrootingen met den Volksraad* (The Second Decade of People's Councils' Budgets), Dept. van Financien, Batavia, 1938; and annual editions of Statistische Jaaroverzicht van Nederlandsch-Indië, published by the Dutch colonial government's Central Bureau of Statistics.

The data in Table 1 indicate that the Native States alone contributed a significant share of the total investment realized through government accounts—an average of almost 40 per cent of total colonial and Native States government investment during the period 1935–38. If the capital formation of nonautonomous local governments were added, the local government component would be somewhat higher.[3] It should be understood, however, that Indonesia shared the world depression of those years, and that the colonial government's ability and willingness to finance capital formation were considerably less than they had been a decade earlier, while this was not equally true for local governments. This suggests, incidentally, that local government investment expenditures were less sensitive to cyclical fluctuations. Investment expenditures of the Native States were ordinarily a substantially greater percentage of their total budgetary outlays than in those of the colonial government. In 1938, for example, capital formation accounted for 15 per cent of total Native States expenditures but only slightly more than 1 per cent of colonial government expenditures.[4] A related point of significance is that local government capital formation was necessarily financed by local government savings while colonial government investment was often financed by borrowing.

The ability of local governments to finance capital formation during the colonial period was facilitated by their access to compulsory labor services (*Heerendiensten*) for local public works. In 1938 the monetary equivalent of the compulsory labor services that were recruited by the Native States was 4,932,000 guilders; and investment was reported at 5,507,000 guilders.[5] In the same year compulsory labor services valued at 5,468,000 guilders were mobilized by the directly governed territories, suggesting that in these localities, too, considerable investment activity was taking place. Although the means through which labor services are mobilized have become less compulsory, this method of financing investment has continued to be of importance since independence.

Thus it may be stated that local governments in Indonesia have a history of a relatively great degree of fiscal autonomy involving responsibility for local developmental activities. It is also clear that these governments have a tradition of rather vigorous fiscal policy capable of supporting significant amounts of local capital formation.

Despite the lack of published information on postwar local finance in Indonesia and its contribution to Indonesian economic development,[6] there are unmistakable evidences that developmental investment has continued to be undertaken by local governments. Numerous observers have returned from localities throughout Indonesia impressed with local fervor for prosecuting both output-increasing and welfare-type investment. In the provinces outside Java there is a strong urge for local autonomy both in government functions generally and in the fiscal process in particular, an urge dramatically expressed in vigorous efforts to provide local improvements from resources available to the political subdivisions. Considerable attention has been given to the problem of delegating political and economic functions to local levels of government, but delay in introducing a workable division of authority has brought conflicting tendencies toward centralization and local autonomy. On Java, where Central

Government control has consistently been relatively firm, domination of local fiscal processes by Central Government has tended to stifle the local urge for development throughout the period since the transfer of sovereignty to Indonesia in late 1949. In the outlying provinces, where interest in local improvement is strong, attempts at Central Government domination of local functions continually produced friction, leading to increased independence from Central Government control until 1956, when several localities virtually established their independence from Central Government jurisdiction. Even during the years before the open break, local disaffection prevented coordination between central and local developmental activities and led to a lack of awareness in Djakarta of the contribution which local finance could make to effective planning for Indonesian economic development.

The operating assumption in Djakarta had been that local finance—both on the expenditure and on the revenue side—had been almost completely inoperative after the Dutch relinquished control over the archipelago. It was assumed that the local financial offices had not reclaimed their financial functions, pending the government's clarification of the distribution of revenue sources and proceeds between central and local authorities. Demarcation of these functions was implicitly called for in the Constitution of 1950, and it has been the subject of study by a continuing committee (the Nasrun Committee). The view that local levels of government were inactive in fiscal operations was unequivocally put forth in the Karakacheff report on the Indonesian budget system:

> It may be stated that the general budget of the Central Government includes practically all expenditures of the local authorities. Most of them have no receipts of their own. The few existing taxes in certain of them, such as entertainment tax or dog tax in Djakarta Raya, are rather insignificant. Thus the grants of Central Government cover almost the totality of expenditures of the local authorities.[7]

The 1953–54 *Report of the Bank Indonesia* expressed a similar view of local finance:

> Pending the issue of legal regulations governing the financial relationship between Central Government and *daerahs* [autonomous regions], in recent years practically all taxation has been incorporated in the budget of the Central Government.[8]

Gradually, Central Government has begun to show some awareness of local fiscal processes. The Dris report data on the income and expenditures of local governments, obtained from Central Government sources, are presented in Table 2.

TABLE 2

INCOME AND EXPENDITURES OF THE REGIONAL OR
LOCAL COMMUNITIES, 1952–1956

(Million Rp.)

Year	Expenditures	Gross Totals Local or Regional Resources	Grants From Central Government
1952	2,014.0	200.0[a]	1,887.0
1953	2,130.0	340.0	1,836.0
1954	2,733.0	377.7	2,355.0
1955	2,719.0[a]	429.0	1,775.0[b]
1956	?	?	3,120.0

[a] Estimated.
[b] Exclusive of capital expenditures.
SOURCE: M. D. Dris, "Taxation in Indonesia," *Ekonomi dan Keuangan Indonesia*, XI (August–September, 1958), 408.

The evidence presented in this chapter suggests that these estimates greatly underrate the extent to which local governments have actually succeeded in financing expenditures from local resources. Furthermore, it is our impression that the Dris report minimizes the extent to which the collection apparatus has been maintained and improved in the Outer Islands, and that it overrates the collection capacity of Central Government.[9]

During the transition years 1953–56 the Indonesia project of the Center for International Studies, Massachusetts Institute of Technology, conducted studies of local fiscal activities both on Java and in the outlying provinces. That research, as well as observation and discussions with other observers, indicated that the views accepted by Indonesian officials were at least partially wrong. Local governments not only continued to exist; in many areas they performed important financial and economic functions. It should be pointed out, however, that the effectiveness and scope of the financial offices in the areas nearest Djakarta (e.g., West Java) were the most limited. Here the influence of Central Government, which attempted to compress all fiscal and economic functions within its budget, was the greatest; and local governments became dependent upon Central Government resources. Proximity of these areas to the seat of Central Government has no doubt led to the currency of the mistaken views described above. In reality, the degree of local fiscal activity and local initiative in financing economic development has tended to vary almost directly with distance from Djakarta.

Intensive research conducted by the author on both Java and Sumatra provided a contrast between local governments whose finance was dominated by Central Government and those with some degree of fiscal autonomy. The results of these studies compare the pre-1956 situation in West Java with that in the province of Central Sumatra. The results given below are based on discussions with local financial officials in Bandung, the capital of the province of West Java, and in Bukkittingi and Padang, both sites of administrative offices for Central Sumatra. It was clear from this investigation that the structure of West Javanese local finance reflected the proximity of the Province to Djakarta, and that local finance in Central Sumatra and the attitudes of the province's officials reflected resistance to Djakarta's attempts at centralization, as well as a strong propensity for local independence in fiscal matters. The effects of this basic difference in orientation are shown in the patterns of local revenues and expenditures.

THE STRUCTURE OF LOCAL FINANCE PRIOR TO REBELLION

In the period before the breakdown of Central Government authority in the Outer Islands after 1956, local financial operations were carried on at three levels of administration—*desa* (village), *kabupaten* (district), and province—in both West Java and Central Sumatra.[10] Cities (*kota besar*) in each province formed separate fiscal administrative units similar to the *kabupaten* in level of jurisdiction. Legally, each level of local government was responsible for supervising fiscal administration of the level below it. However, supervision of village finance by the *kabupaten* was more meaningful in Central Sumatra than in West Java. In Central Sumatra, villages were in fact required to submit their budgets to the *kabupaten* above them for approval and forwarding to the province and to the Central Government. This system was in effective operation in 1954. In West Java, on the other hand, villages failed to draft budgets for transmission to the higher levels of government.

Desa Finance

Since village budgets are not published, satisfactory information on *desa* finance could not be obtained for West Java. It was apparent, however, that the village was responsible for the maintenance of some local capital facilities such as roads, bridges, and public buildings, which were financed in part by local recruitment of labor services, thus obviating the necessity for monetary tax collections. Yet financing of village expenditures was provided mainly by Central Government subsidies, which in 1954 and 1955 provided about Rp. 100,000 for each village on Java and Madura, totaling about Rp. 2 billion on these islands alone.[11]

In Central Sumatra village budgets (numbering 1,200) were regularly transmitted to the *kabupaten*. Their compilation, analysis, and approval were delayed as the province awaited Central Government action in confirming provincial and *kabupaten* jurisdiction over the budgets as well as underwriting the costs of printing and compiling them. Hence no aggregative statistics on village finance in Central Sumatra were available, although certain generalizations about village finance in this area were made on the basis of the submitted budgets. The budgets provided for the mobilization of both monetary and nonmonetary resources. Current expenditures requiring payment in monetary terms were estimated, and the estimates were used as a basis for allotting the head tax among the village inhabitants. Additional monetary income was frequently obtained from local levies such as the *pasar* (market) tax, the slaughter tax, taxes on forestry products and coastal fishing, and harbor fees, despite continual controversy between Central Government fiscal representatives and local authorities over the proceeds from such levies.

Investment and capital-maintenance projects which could be carried out with little more than labor resources, including construction of schools, irrigation works, and roads, were supported primarily by local mobilization of voluntary labor contributions. The capital equipment for such projects was ordinarily obtained from the province or Central Government as subsidy to the village. It was my impression that substantial net investment was taking place in such projects even at the village level in Central Sumatra, where there appeared to be considerably more drive for improvement than in West Java.

The leading item of expenditure in the village budget in Central Sumatra was for construction and maintenance of the primary schools (*sekolah rakja*), which was estimated to comprise about 60 per cent of the total. Local interest in providing educational facilities in Central Sumatra appeared to have reduced the cost of education as a provincial undertaking. Expenditures for education absorbed less than 40 per cent of the Central Sumatran provincial outlays while they absorbed at least 60 per cent of provincial outlays in West Java, where there was less interest in undertaking such expenditures at the village level.

Kabupaten Finance

On the *kabupaten* level of administration there were also significant differences in local finance between the two provinces surveyed. At this level, too, the greater dependence of local levels of government in West Java on Central Government support was apparent. In Central Sumatra, Central Government financial assistance was not used to finance current administrative expenditures; subsidies were received only for assistance in construction of roads, and were equal to approximately 20 per cent of total *kabupaten* income. In West Java, however, Central Government subsidies supported more than two-thirds of current expenditures. Here government subsidy comprised about three-fourths of the combined (current and capital) budget.

The assumption was easily made in West Java that Central Government was responsible for providing all the fiscal resources for supporting the capital budget of the *kabupaten* (as well as a substantial share of the current budget). Yet it was felt that this dependence on Central Government subsidy restricted *kabupaten* investment. This impression was confirmed by observation in Central Sumatra, where both the initiative for undertaking investment projects and the means to support them were sought locally. Here capital expenditures comprised a considerably larger share of the total budget than in West Java, and local officials were preoccupied with drafting new development plans and implementing them locally. Mobilization of resources to finance the projects appeared to place no great strain on the local economy. This suggests that resources out of which local investment projects may be financed lie near the local administrative level and can be effectively mobilized there. Sumatran fiscal authorities argued that strict adherence to Central Government policy would have greatly limited the scale of the *kabupaten* investment program; hence, they defied a Ministry of Interior dictum that all local investment projects should receive both Central Government approval and financing. In West Java, where this principle was taken seriously, the complaint was made that capital expenditures did not represent as large a share of the total budget as in the prewar era.[12] Local authorities doubted that net capital formation was being achieved, while in those areas on Java with less Central Government domination and in the Outer Islands there was unmistakable evidence of positive capital formation at the *kabupaten* level.

The proximity of the West Java provincial seat to Djakarta and the consequent close identification with Central Government finance may not be the only factors in the loss of fiscal autonomy in *kabupaten* finance and the relatively low rate of local capital formation. Several other factors should be weighed and investigated. First, there is evidence that per capita incomes in Sumatra are substantially above those on Java because of the more favorable resources-population ratio in Sumatra.[13] A second factor is the distribution of income. The evidence suggests that income is distributed more unequally in West Java than in Central Sumatra, particularly in the rural sector.

The preliminary results of a number of studies have indicated that the rural tenancy problem is more serious in West Java than in other areas of Indonesia. A strong landlord-rentier class has emerged since the end of World War II, and there has been a significant shift in the distribution of rural incomes in the direction of such upper-income groups. Our discussion in the preceding chapter suggests, further, that such shifts have not been followed by compensating changes in the tax structure. Rural taxation, as it has been enforced on Java, is particularly incapable of reaching increments in incomes accruing to these groups. Since local finance in Indonesia is in large part based on the rural sector, the changes in the composition and size of rural income may account for differences in local finance as well as for the presumption that there was greater capacity to finance local development expenditures in Central Sumatra than in West Java.

Kabupaten income in both West Java and Central Sumatra varied greatly by locality within the two provinces. Since Central Government failed to resolve the problem of fiscal interrelationship among the various levels of government, there were no accepted or formally authorized sources of *kabupaten* income. Fiscal authorities in Central Sumatra were making efforts to follow the postwar shifts in the size and distribution of incomes in their province. In West Java the structure of *kabupaten* levies, although extremely diverse and complex, remained quite similar to that during the Dutch colonial period, comprising a few traditionally local taxes, a large number of "retributions,"[14] and a limited amount of poaching on what Central Government regarded as its revenue sources.[15] In Central Sumatra, local fiscal authorities had by 1953 escaped the strait jacket of Dutch colonial tradition and had added new levies, while continuing to collect most of the traditional local taxes and retributions. New sources of revenue included *kabupaten* duty on rubber exports from the eastern part of the province to Singapore (the largest single revenue producer in that area), levies on incomes from mines, duties on forest products, and receipts from *kabupaten*-operated enterprises. Hence there was an effort in this area to exploit the new tax base produced by increased local incomes and greater exports. It should be pointed out, however, that this effort usually produced conflict with Central Government authorities since Central Government tax devices, rather than new methods, were adopted to reach the new sources of revenue.

Provincial Finance

In both Central Sumatra and West Java provincial expenditures were financed almost exclusively by Central Government subsidy before the conflicts of 1956–58.[16] The province of Central Sumatra had no legal revenue sources of its own although provincial officials were responsible for collecting certain types of taxes and remitting the proceeds to Central Government offices. In West Java a few insignificant revenue sources still belonged to the province: income from lease of public lands, resale of provincial stocks of goods, and surtaxes on two Central Government taxes (urban real estate tax and household tax). In 1953 locally collected revenues contributed only Rp. 4,500,000 to a total provincial budget of Rp. 225,000,000 (2 per cent).[17]

In 1954 capital expenditures comprised only 9 per cent of budgeted expenditures in West Java, while estimated investment expenditures comprised about 40 per cent of provincial outlays in Central Sumatra,[18] a result which shows the force of historical precedent on fiscal performance at the local level. Where the precedent of autonomy is great, as in Central Sumatra, the local fiscal processes tend to be more vigorous, both in financing investment and in supporting general local expenditures through local fiscal processes. Expenditures on education absorbed almost 60 per cent of provincial expenditures in West Java and only about 40 per cent in Central Sumatra, largely the result of greater fiscal autonomy at the subprovincial levels of government in Central Sumatra and greater interest in providing educational facilities at the lower levels of government. Local fiscal autonomy apparently resulted in more scope for expenditures on public health in Central Sumatra, where they were 17 per cent of the budget as against only 2 per cent in West Java. In Central Sumatra this expenditure consisted primarily of new medical installations—hospitals, clinics, and medical equipment—and as such represented predominantly investment expenditure.

Judging from newspaper reports, the seizure of fiscal autonomy by local units greatly spurred local expenditures for economic development. In Central Sumatra, for example, where fiscal autonomy was asserted in 1956 and continued throughout 1957, considerable progress was reported. According to the Djakarta daily, *Pedoman,* Colonel Husein, Chairman of the *Benteng* Council, reported that Central Sumatra expenditures increased from Rp. 196 million in 1956 (when Central Government subsidization of the provincial budget still existed) to Rp. 411 million in 1957.[19] Expenditures for "development activities" rose from Rp. 34 million in 1956 to Rp. 175 million in 1957. Another newspaper source reported that expenditures for construction (one item of capital formation) rose from Rp. 13 million in 1956 to Rp. 114 million in 1957.[20] The newspaper account emphasized that this progress should partially be ascribed to the increased amount of voluntary labor services mobilized through the *gotong rojong* (mutual assistance) system.

Similarly, in the North Celebes area, where virtual autonomy existed during 1957, an extensive new development program financed mainly by voluntary labor mobilization was reported in many newspaper accounts. One account described an extensive highway and construction program which yielded impressive results during 1957.[21] The point was made that the program was financed primarily by *gotong rojong* subscriptions of labor services, with some monetary allocations from local governments.

Such reports were representative of many which have come from areas where some degree of local autonomy was achieved as a result of the challenges to Central Government authority. A consistent strain of emphasis is placed upon the importance of freedom from central prerogative to approve or disapprove local projects if such undertakings are to flourish. A related point which is repeatedly made is that local sacrifice for development activities varies inversely with the degree of dependence upon Central Government subsidy for financing local projects. The issue at stake is whether or not local units wield the power of decision in choosing, financing, and prosecuting local development activities. Where this power clearly rests with local units, local governments are willing to provide financing. Where it is lacking, there is a strong tendency to acquiesce in Central Government prosecution of all aspects of capital formation, including its financing.

The Role of Central Government Fiscal Offices in Local Finance[22]

It is impossible to draw a complete picture of local finance without reference to the role of Central Government fiscal offices and their relationship to local fiscal systems. The tax impact of Central Government in areas outside larger cities was felt almost exclusively through those offices. Moreover, the problem of intergovernmental fiscal relationships arose mainly from the play of forces that shaped their role in localities. It is particularly important to review this role briefly since those offices represented Central Government's sole direct fiscal access to the rural sector, where we have discovered the greatest potential tax capacity from which tax resources for financing economic development may be mobilized.

Central Government fiscal offices outside Djakarta were the local representatives of the Ministry of Finance; as such they should be distinguished from the local fiscal operations described in the first part of this chapter. They collected a substantial part of Central Government revenues, since, although they did not collect customs duties, which are Indonesia's most important revenue producers, other taxes of major importance were assigned to their administration. The most important single revenue producer under their jurisdiction was the company tax, followed in the order of their importance by the income tax on individuals, the wages tax, and the sales tax. They were also responsible for collecting taxes of lesser importance, including the urban real estate tax, duties on property transfers, the stamp tax, the capital-assets tax, the vehicle tax, the reconstruction tax, and the tax on private property.

A general lack of clearly differentiated responsibility between the

Central Government fiscal offices and local government tax officials has been one of the major problems in the Indonesian tax system. Legally there are virtually no sources of tax income available to local governments. All tax collection, therefore, has been a Central Government prerogative during the period since independence. In practice, however, the government has found it necessary to rely on local officials to collect a part of its tax revenues. In general, this situation had resulted in a certain amount of division of labor in tax collection, and it has led the government fiscal offices to distinguish two collection functions under their jurisdiction: first, the function of assessing and collecting certain taxes directly, and, second, the function of supervising the collection by local officials of certain taxes delegated to them. These lines of responsibility are not consistently drawn throughout Indonesia, and the division of the tax collection function reflects both precedent and the capabilities of Central Government offices in particular tax districts.

In both Central Sumatra and West Java we found Central Government tax officials protesting that they were responsible for collecting an extremely complex and diverse series of taxes. The complexity of the tax structure under their administration had adverse effects upon both local acceptance of Central Government taxation and the efficiency of administration of the tax system as a whole. The attempt to collect the total tax levy through duties on a variety of economic functions not only promoted evasion but also bred the feeling that the local fiscal process had a nuisance rather than revenue-producing quality. The conclusion that Central Government taxation would become more generally accepted if the fiscal burden were limited to two or three direct levies was inescapable. Popular resistance interfered particularly with efficient collection of the reconstruction tax, a tax on the patrons of restaurants. Because of popular feeling against this postwar tax, it was ordinarily impossible for the restaurant owner to collect it from his patrons. Hence it came to be collected as an additional business tax on the restauranteur. Since no sales records were kept, collection was usually effected through a rather arbitrary process of assessing the owner's ability to pay. Thus a difficult and costly collection process was necessary, and the reconstruction tax produced relatively small yields in the provinces studied.

In both Central Sumatra and West Java it was apparent that the diversity of Central Government taxes interfered with effective administration of the important revenue producers. Each tax for which the Central Government tax offices were responsible had its own complicated array of regulations. Since the officials were responsible for collecting a large number of minor taxes as well as the important revenue producers, they were unable to concentrate on the assessment and collection of taxes which, with sufficient effort, could have contributed considerably greater revenues. Specialization of tax collections would have required reducing the number of taxes to the few important revenue producers; tax officials in both provinces contended that simplification of the tax structure would have doubled the tax yield.

A further collection problem—one which was found to be especially serious in the Outer Islands—was the inability of Central Government tax officials to supervise collection of taxes beyond the larger cities where the tax offices were located.[23] In Central Sumatra and other areas where communications are still rather primitive the provincial inspectorate's control over local tax officials was limited. As a result, local tax representatives often failed to remit tax proceeds to Central Government tax offices. It was also pointed out that local tax officials were frequently reluctant to assess and collect taxes strictly. To promote more effective enforcement, government tax officials in some areas made periodic visits to the more important tax districts. A visit by the tax inspector from the Padang office in Central Sumatra to one of the larger but more remote cities in the province revealed that laxity of the local tax collector had resulted in substantial leakages in revenues. By personally enforcing the regulations of the two major taxes, the tax inspector was able to triple the Central Government tax yield in this particular area. Even on Java the lack of transportation facilities was emphasized as a major deterrent to stricter enforcement of existing tax legislation. The local representatives were not provided with the transportation to supervise adequately collection of taxes within their districts. Both in Central Sumatra and in West Java tax officials suggested that enlarging the tax cadres and equipping them more adequately with means of transport would produce high returns in terms of greater tax yields.

Such problems go far toward explaining the inability of Central Government to enforce direct taxation in the rural sector of the economy. Even where the fiscal officials made a serious attempt to carry out the administration of the many taxes under their jurisdiction they failed to reach much beyond the cities in which their offices were located. It is for these same reasons that Central Government found it necessary to delegate all or a part of the assessment and collection of revenues outside urban centers to local officials.

The second major responsibility of the Central Government tax offices, therefore, was supervision of the collection of the taxes delegated to local government officials. Potentially most important is the *padjak ketjil* (rural income tax). Efforts to enforce this tax in the rural sector began after 1952 but results have been disappointing. In Central Sumatra the collection of this tax was delegated completely to the local government officials; in Java, Central Government tax officers penetrated into the villages to collect the tax on incomes above a specified minimum (which varied by locality). In Central Sumatra, the Central Government office exercised only indirect supervision over the collection process. A government official was given responsibility for a particular tax district, a division of the *kabupaten*. Responsibility for collection fell to the *kepala negeri*, the local village head corresponding to the *lurah* on Java. This official had little motivation for accurate assessment of incomes or upward revision of tax rates, in accordance with postindependence legislation, since there was no local benefit from the revenues he collected in behalf of Central Government. Even on Java, where collection was shared with Central Government authorities, there was a tendency toward laxity in collection and assessment of the rural income tax. In East Java the income line dividing local collection and Central Government collection was Rp. 3,400; in West Java the income line was Rp. 5,000. There was a natural tendency on the part of both the taxpayer and the local tax collector (*lurah*) to keep the assessment within the bounds of local collection, a tendency for underassessment of rural incomes which was aggravated by the fact that in many areas on Java the *lurah* was allowed to retain a percentage of the tax proceeds which he collected. This amount was retained by the *lurah* personally rather than being used for the *desa* treasury.

This division of responsibility for collection of the rural income tax has been one of the basic reasons for the inefficiency of Central Government tax enforcement. The tax system has attempted to reach too far down into the structure of Indonesian society, leading the Central Government collection efforts in areas where they were inevitably ineffective. Since Central Government tax officials have been incapable of reaching the greater part of this tax base directly, they have relied upon the cooperation of local officials who have no great interest in maximizing Central Government revenues. An almost inescapable conclusion follows. It would both relieve the problem of tax administration and reduce Central Government subsidization of local Governments if this particular tax were turned over to localities.

Local Finance and Economic Development

The most significant aspect of local finance for Indonesia's economic progress is the extent to which local levels of government employ their fiscal processes to undertake investment. Investigations in Central Sumatra, West Java, Jogjakarta, East Java, and Bali indicated that locally financed investment projects are of major importance to the Indonesian economy. The case for recognizing the scope of such investment activities, their nature, and their variation by area cannot be put too strongly. Effective development policy should be aimed at maximizing this type of local investment, first, to alleviate the heavy financial burden of central subsidies to local governments, and, secondly, through coordination of local efforts with the financing and execution of Central Government development efforts, to utilize local development activities for the prosecution of a program of genuinely national character.

In the period when nominal unification existed in Indonesia (1950–56), Central Government policy tended to stifle rather than promote local initiative in undertaking and financing small-scale development projects. *Kabupaten* and provincial governments were required to obtain approval for proposed local projects from the Ministry of Interior, with the Ministry pre-empting responsibility to arrange financing. Approval ordinarily involved extended delays, causing dwindling local interest in the projects and frequently their abandonment. Governments in the outlying provinces—particularly Central Sumatra and Sulawesi, where local autonomy was greatest—assumed initiative in financing and prosecuting developmental projects within their means without awaiting government approval; but integration of those projects with larger-scale planning and the opportunity to draw on the technical assistance and general support of Central Government would have speeded their completion. Djakarta's awareness of the problems and the potentialities of mobilizing local resources for capital formation is essential to sound planning for increasing the rate of investment accomplished by all levels of government. This issue has become so important in Indonesia that, and as a first prerequisite to carrying out a program of economic development, Central Government must resolve the problems of local autonomy and delineation of fiscal processes before it can reassert general control throughout Indonesia.

Part of the problem lies in the fact that Central Government has failed both to recognize the importance of granting local autonomy and to comprehend the contribution which local fiscal processes can make to financing development by mobilizing resources beyond its reach. In Indonesia, as in other underdeveloped countries, the fiscal capacity of Central Government has been overrated and that of local governments overlooked, perhaps because of lack of information. In this sense, planning the finance of development programs may be more hampered by the shortages of statistics than by shortages of financial experts. In most studies available to the Indonesian government the assumption has been made that local expenditures are undertaken only where Central Government provides subsidies to finance them. This assumption, for example, lies behind Neumark's methodology, resulting in understatement of the investment component of national income.[24]

Analysis of the summary of local budgets issued by the Ministry of Interior for 1953 (Table 3) reveals the extent to which local capital formation is underestimated by Neumark's estimate, which was based exclusively upon Central Government statistics. The Ministry of Interior budgets for local governments are drawn up on the assumption that local governments to which Central Government subsidies are made (province, *kabupaten,* and *kota*) have no resources of their own, hence that subsidized expenditures comprise their total outlays.

TABLE 3

MINISTRY OF INTERIOR SUMMARY OF TOTAL BUDGETS
OF LOCAL GOVERNMENTS, 1953

(Thousand Rp.)

	Province	Kabupaten	Kota	Total
Ordinary expenditures	1,116,922	369,788	120,325	1,607,035
Capital expenditures[a]	221,721	34,381	15,075	271,177
Subsidies to primary schools	18,086		4,288	22,374
TOTAL	1,356,729	404,169	139,688	1,900,586

[a]Comprising expenditures on roads, bridges, irrigation facilities, public buildings, new classrooms and equipment for primary schools, health facilities, agricultural and veterinary facilities, and expenditures for development of inland fishing.

In the case of provinces, the finance of which is closely associated with the Ministry of Interior budget, this estimate of gross capital formation may be roughly correct; but in the case of *kabupaten* and *kota,* which in many areas have independent budgets and independent fiscal resources, both total expenditures and capital formation are grossly underestimated. *Kabupaten* capital expenditures for all Indonesia were estimated at only Rp. 34,381,000. In Central Sumatra alone, capital expenditures in 1953 were reported to total approximately Rp. 40,000,000. The Ministry of Interior estimate included no recorded capital expenditures at the *kabupaten* level for this province or for North Sumatra, South Sumatra, Kalimantan (Borneo), and Sunda Ketjul; it included only small amounts for Sulawesi (Celebes) and the Moluccas. Yet in the provinces visited by our research teams investment activities were observed to be more vigorous on the *kabupaten* than on the provincial level. The Ministry of Interior (as did Neumark) also excluded any reference to capital projects undertaken at the *desa* level. In short, although investment at the local government level is one of the most important components of investment in the economy (perhaps approaching the size of Central Government investment), its significance has not been recognized by either Central Government or its observers.

For the years prior to the assumption of autonomy by the outlying provinces, a rough estimate of net investment performed by local governments of Rp. 1.5 billion annually appears to be conservative. The Ministry of Interior reported subsidies of Rp. 271 million for new investment projects (net investment) for the year 1953. On the basis of the limited data to which we had access, it seems realistic to estimate the value of investment projects completed by local governments without the support of the Ministry at roughly four times this amount. Moreover, it appears that the amount of local capital formation could have been doubled had fiscal functions been intelligently divided among the various levels of government and if tax enforcement had been tightened.

Our emphasis upon the importance of local government investment requires a description of the process as we found it. At the lowest level of government (the *desa*) the greater part of the mobilization of resources did not enter the sphere of monetary calculus, although even at the *desa* level the economy itself was highly monetized. Labor services for the local projects were mobilized directly through the village council, which drew upon the village labor supply according to the seasonal demands of primary occupations in a given area.[25] Hence the monetary sector of the economy was consciously side-stepped in the mobilization of resources to provide labor for investment projects. This suggests an awareness of seasonal underemployment of labor resources and an effort to mobilize them for combination with other factors of production provided by financing through the monetary sector. Thus the labor input (which was estimated by local authorities to represent 70 per cent of total "cost") was combined with material and equipment financed from monetary tax collections undertaken by the *desa* itself or, more usually, obtained from higher levels of government as subsidy. It was pointed out that skilled labor, technicians, and engineers represented the scarcest real factors. These factors, too, were economized by *kabupaten* and provincial governments, which shifted them among local projects according to demand. It was emphasized that the rate of local investment could be greatly accelerated if Central Government could provide an increased supply of these specialized factors to be allocated for investment activity by local governments. Foreign aid programs could contribute significantly to local investment by providing technical experts (engineers, surveyors) at provincial or *kabupaten* levels of government rather than assigning them exclusively to Djakarta.

At the *kabupaten* level the process of local investment varied greatly between Java and the more autonomous outlying provinces. On Java there was a tendency to rely on Central Government financing for development projects, while responsibility for both the financing and mobilization of the real factors was largely assumed by the *kabupaten* in the Outer Islands. This situation was reflected in the efforts of the local governments outside Java to capture a part of the increments in taxable capacity which have appeared to emerge since the end of colonialism. In Central Sumatra the provincial office for *kabupaten* administration assumed responsibility for the drafting of plans for local development projects; it advised on direct recruitment of the labor supply for their implementation; and it provided technical advice to local governmental units where there was initiative for undertaking new projects. Here, too, the financing was provided partly from monetary tax collections and Central Government subsidies and partly by employment of the idle labor resources recruited by the individual *kabupaten* itself. At this level, however, the nonmonetary "financing" of development projects was considerably less than at the village level.

Much of the investment activity taking place at the local level, particularly in the outlying provinces, was supported from genuinely local resources. Financing was partly in terms of monetary tax collections (which may or may not have interfered with enlarged Central Government tax collections) and partly in terms of nonmonetized resource mobilization (which presumably did not interfere with Central Government taxation).

CENTRALIZATION VS. DECENTRALIZATION IN FINANCING INDONESIAN ECONOMIC DEVELOPMENT

The foregoing review of the structure of local finance in Indonesia and its potential role in the development of the economy raises important questions concerning fiscal relations among the various levels of government. From the point of view of economic development, it is critical that intergovernmental relations allow each level of government to contribute the maximum in mobilizing resources from which development can be financed. It is also important that the supply of technical skills and administrative abilities available at the various levels of government be fully utilized in a program of economic development. In Indonesia, as in other underdeveloped countries, such skills and abilities are not found exclusively among Central Government officials. In fact, Indonesia possesses a vast reservoir of competent officials at the lower levels of governments,[26] a source of abilities and skills which could contribute significantly to economic progress both in mobilizing the fiscal resources to finance development plans and in the actual implementation of such plans. Realization of the potential contribution which might be made from local resources depends on the proper balance between local autonomy and Central Government coordination in relationships among the various levels of government.

Our empirical studies in Indonesia also indicate that the ultimate basis of economic development in a democratic society—individual and group initiative—is related to the degree of autonomy which localities have been able to achieve. The greatest amount of local participation in development programs was found where localities had been able to resist the attempts of Central Government to dominate their political and fiscal functions. In such areas individual and local initiative produced relatively high levels of local capital formation and rising levels of per capita income. Local autonomy preserves the link between individual sacrifice and benefit, providing the incentive for the release of new energies necessary to transform an economically stagnant society into a dynamic one.

The case for a sizable local ingredient in Indonesian economic development and its financing is a strong one. Yet local developmental activities alone cannot produce the structural changes needed to solve some of the basic economic problems of a newly independent country. A plethora of local irrigation works, transport facilities, and export processing plants cannot create an industrial structure adequate to free Indonesia from its present dependence on foreign trade for industrial imports; nor can it provide an effective take-off to cumulative economic growth. Undue emphasis on decentralized development of the type described here would not result in effective use of Indonesia's broad variety of economic resources through specialization and division of labor. The heavy investment requirements necessary to meet the more general objectives of Indonesian economic development are obviously beyond the capacities of local levels of government. Central Government alone possesses the fiscal power and financial capacity to undertake the broader type of social overhead investments which are essential to maximize the productivity of smaller-scale investments by localities and individuals.[27]

Conflicts between the central and local governments over the distribution of revenue sources, as well as in the specific role of financing economic development, became increasingly severe as the struggle for local autonomy became more general in the Outer Islands. Insecure Central Government control led to renewed efforts to centralize fiscal functions more completely. In the Outer Islands this state of affairs produced uneconomic duplication of expenditure functions, with considerable confusion as to who was responsible for financing current and developmental activities. Several levels of government participated in the support and construction of schools, hospitals, and road and irrigation facilities, while Central Government insisted on its prerogative to approve and finance such projects as far down as the *kabupaten* level. On Java the result was excessive central control over local governments, which has blurred the relationship between local benefit and local contribution. Local autonomy over functions providing exclusively local benefits is desirable, as suggested above, since such functions can be performed more efficiently at the local level and financing can be arranged more economically through use of local resources which cannot be mobilized through Central Government fiscal processes.

The situation which prevailed in the years before the outlying provinces declared their virtual independence of Djakarta was a particularly unsuccessful combination of centralization and decentralization in reaching revenue sources. The provinces had virtually no sources of income, while *kabupaten* and *desa* tended to exploit any sources of revenue within their purview, regardless of Central Government efforts to tax the same sources. The effects of the multiplicity of taxation had important implications for financing economic development:

1) Central Government fiscal offices engaged in the collection of taxes for which they were not administratively suited, i.e., taxes which could have been more effectively collected by local governments. (The rural income tax and the tax on private property are notable examples.) This effort made Central Government tax administration in the provinces a cumbersome and inefficient process and was a major factor generating hostility toward Central Government.

2) Central Government interference with tax bases structurally adapted to local collection deprived local units of natural revenue sources and caused them to seek a diversity of petty and uneconomic levies to finance their expenditures, which in turn produced a pattern of local revenues yielding small income relative to costs of collection.

3) The uneconomic distribution of taxable capacity necessitated large-scale Central Government subsidization of localities, representing a heavy drain on its budget and limiting its ability to undertake the financing of a development program.[28] Even so, in the provinces on Java it was felt that arbitrary decisions as to the size of government subsidies to provinces and *kabupaten* and uncertainty as to their amount limited the capacity of provincial and *kabupaten* governments to undertake capital formation of the scope called for by local need. In short, the haphazard system of distribution of revenue sources and subsidies which emerged after independence was inadequate to support necessary functions of local governments. Further, a broad subsidy program, which was an inevitable consequence of that system, by its very nature implied relatively great Central Government influence over local finance and consequent loss of local autonomy.

Paradoxically, in the first years after Indonesia's independence considerable thought was given to these problems, and a governmental committee undertook to study them.[29] The recommendations of this committee assigned a number of taxes to local levels of government[30] and provided for the division of other tax revenues between central and local governments. Taxes such as the rural income tax, which are potentially the most lucrative sources of local revenues, were to be collected under Central Government supervision and the proceeds divided according to a formula which provided no link between local sacrifice and local benefit. The Nasrun study did not deal with the role of local finance in economic development and it failed to delineate the expenditure function in detail among the various levels of political administration in Indonesia. After several years before Parliament, most of the Nasrun recommendations were enacted into law in late 1956, under pressure of threats of local rebellion. The 1956 legislation requires further Parliamentary action to put into effect the Nasrun proposals.

The existing relationship between Central Government and local units limits the financing and prosecution of economic development because Central Government has attempted to go beyond the reaches of its administrative capacity on both sides of the fiscal accounts. In this volume it has been suggested that revenues could be increased if taxes which could be more efficiently collected by local administrations were transferred to local units. It has also been suggested that the rate of capital formation could be accelerated by yielding jurisdiction over local investment projects to the appropriate level of local government. At the same time, local capital formation could be increased by Central Government provision of those technical skills and materials which are most scarce. All this would involve a degree of coordination and cooperation between Central Government and local development activities which has not existed in most areas of Indonesia.

Available evidence points to the conclusion that there is significant scope for local development projects in Indonesia's total program of economic planning. The present study suggests that there are margins of taxable capacity which can be reached only through taxation at the local level. It also suggests that idle resources which cannot be mobilized through the Central Government fiscal process could be brought into the development program by local investment projects. Moreover, the psychological urge for improvement could be activitated by the incentives provided by the link between sacrifice and opportunities for local benefit. Once this process was set in motion, the heavy burden of subsidies to support local current and investment functions could be gradually withdrawn from the Central Government budget, a move which would tend in itself to increase the government's capacity to finance its development plan.

Development activities which can be prosecuted from resources available to local levels of government could become an important component of Indonesia's development plan. Local investment projects could provide facilities to increase the output of food, improve local transport, and increase export earnings. In fact, the productivity of large-scale Central Government development projects—such as large-scale irrigation and power plants and national communications systems—can be maximized only if local facilities are supplied to complement such external economies. The optimum pattern of Indonesian economic development consists of a blend of centralization and decentralization in planning and execution which would fully exploit the fiscal and administrative capacities at each level of authority.

In the immediate future, restoration of national unity and prosecution of the Five Year Plan require that Central Government face and resolve the problem of its relationship with regional groups in the Outer Islands.[31] Some of those groups appear to have launched local development programs with renewed vigor, employing the revenues which formerly flowed to Djakarta for financing provincial development. Unless the pattern of national dissolution is soon reversed, Indonesian economic development over the long run will consist of a series of local plans, with Central Government planning restricted to the island of Java. This result would deprive Indonesia from realizing the most important potential gain of national economic development —regional division of labor and specialization between highly populated Java and the natural-resource-abundant Outer Islands. As economic regionalism proceeds, the possibility of establishing political unity and the feasibility of a national program designed to combine the advantages of a mixture of central and decentralized development will become more remote. Historical precedents showing the relationship between political fragmentation and the failure of plans for economic development are uncomfortably abundant. The Kuomintang government of Mainland China, for example, failed to achieve its development goals partly because it was unable to extend its fiscal and political powers beyond two or three provinces where its control was almost totalitarian.

We must emphasize, in conclusion, that solution to the problem of central-local fiscal relationships will require a broad settlement of the political problems which have plagued the Indonesian Republic since its formation. Throughout the years from 1950 to 1959 a formula to preserve both national unity and local autonomy has been sought. Understandably, Central Government has pressed for enough control at all levels of political organization to enable it to execute national decisions. The essence of the Indonesian problem, however, has been that Central Government control has been exerted by erecting a structure of government tentacles which function independently of, rather than *through,* existing (primarily traditional) local political institutions. We have seen evidence of this duality in the fiscal system; in fact, it is characteristic of all political functions. This duality has produced conflicts over a wide range of issues, making it increasingly difficult to move toward a settlement in terms of a blend of local autonomy and central authority. Prior to the breakdown of Central Government authority in the Outer Islands in 1956 and 1957, the government was able to rig control over what should constitutionally be local functions by resorting to escape clauses in the basic Territorial Government Law of 1948.[32] The unfortunate consequence of that breach of democratic intent is that it has hampered the realization of a basic settlement by arousing such fear and resentment among Indonesians in some areas that it has become difficult if not impossible to accept legitimate Central Government demands for effective unification. Contemporary Indonesian history teaches, once again, that voluntary popular support for a central government diminishes where traditional, perhaps even instinctive, local functions are arrogated by authority rather than yielded by consent. Yet voluntary and enthusiastic support for *national* goals is a *sine qua non* for successful prosecution of a development plan.

An attempt to solve the problem by legislation in 1956 failed because neither Central Government nor the local units would negotiate a basic settlement.[33] The new decentralization law which resulted from a series of conferences was hardly a compromise. Taxes to be transferred to local governments represented only 1 per cent of total Central Government tax receipts in 1956.[34] Recent events suggest that the road to national unity will be difficult;[35] it may be impossible to resolve the problem under the present republican form of Indonesian government. Nevertheless, constructive thinking about Indonesian development prospects requires emphasis upon the blending of central and local participation. The fact that a basic political settlement is prerequisite to a program of this nature does not invalidate the conclusions of this chapter. The writer believes that the poignant failures confronted during the short span of independence—of which political fragmentation is the greatest—may yet lead to a resurgence of national cooperation. If—as suggested here—a successful development program requires integration of the parts and the whole, economic development may become the cause around which political support for national unity can best be rallied.

NOTES TO SELECTION 21

[1]See J. W. Meyer-Ranneft and W. Huender, *Onderzoek naar den Belastingdruk op de Inlandsche Bevolking* (An Inquiry Concerning the Tax Burden upon the Native Population (Landsdrukkerij, Weltevreden, 1926).

[2]Department of Agriculture, Industry and Commerce, *1930 Handbook of the Netherlands East Indies* (Buitenzorg, Java, 1930), p. 97.

[3]Nonautonomous regions were directly governed by the central colonial government; they did, however, possess some fiscal functions of their own.

[4]Data are from annual editions of the *Statistiche Jaaroverzicht van Nederlandsch-Indië* (Statistical Abstract of the Netherlands Indies), published by the Netherlands Indies Central Bureau of Statistics.

[5]Labor services have been converted to monetary terms by using the money-payment equivalent required to redeem labor services into cash payments.

[6]In the past few years, however, Indonesian newspapers have carried accounts of local development activities. These reports reflects rising popular interest in the scope and importance of local governments in economic development.

[7]V. Karakacheff, "Notes on the Budget System of Indonesia" (mimeographed), p. 2.

[8]*Report of the Bank Indonesia, 1953–1954*, p. 54.

[9]M. D. Dris, "Taxation in Indonesia," *Ekonomi dan Keuangan Indonesia,* XI (August–September, 1958), 524–25.

[10][Footnote omitted.]

[11]These figures are from a statement by Indonesia's former Prime Minister, Ali Sastroamidjojo, published in American Indonesian Chamber of Commerce, Inc., *Information Bulletin,* No. 402 (March, 1955), p. 30.

[12]In fact, officials concerned with *kabupaten* finance pointed out that in the prewar period about 70 per cent *kabupaten* expenditures were capital-producing in nature; since independence this percentage has declined to about 40 per cent.

[13]A former Governor of the Bank Indonesia, for example, argues that this is true. See *Report of the Bank Indonesia, 1956–1957,* p. 17.

[14]Retributions are conceived of as payments for specific government services and, hence, are distinguished from taxes. In West Java they include levies on the construction of new buildings, on legal contracts, on reproductions of legal documents by the government, on inspection of meat and animals for slaughtering, on *pasars,* on trash removal, on public sales of sea produce, and on parking places for public vehicles.

[15]This same pattern appears to have existed in East Java. See John D. Legge, *Problems of Regional Autonomy in Contemporary Indonesia* (Modern Indonesia Project, Southeast Asia Program, Department of Far Eastern Studies; Ithaca: Cornell University, 1957), p. 41.

[16]The *Report of the Bank Indonesia, 1954–1955* (p. 18) quotes Ministry of Interior data showing that total *daerah* expenditures were Rp. 2,733 million, of which only Rp. 378 was financed from local resources, the remainder by Central Government subsidy. The same result is shown by evidence presented by Gerald S. Maryankov in *Decentralization in Indonesia: Legislative Aspects* (Modern Indonesia Project, Southeast Asia Program, Department of Far Eastern Studies, Ithaca, Cornell University, 1957), p. 53.

[17]A similar situation is reported for East Java. In 1956, provincial levies contributed only Rp. 7 million to an expenditure of Rp. 412 million. See Legge, *Problems of Regional Autonomy in Contemporary Indonesia,* p. 41.

[18]These data are from the budgets drafted by the provincial governments.

[19]*Pedoman,* January 4, 1958.

[20]*Mimbar Umum,* January 2, 1958, reprinting an article from *Haluan,* the Padang daily.

[21]*Pikiran Rakjat* (Menado), September 21, 1957.

[22]The organizational structure of this part of the tax service and the responsibilities of district offices are described in M. D. Dris, "Taxation in Indonesia," *Ekonomi dan Keuangan Indonesia,* XI (August–September, 1958), 430–35.

[23]The Dris report, published four years after our study was made, also emphasizes the significance of this problem: ". . . the [Central] Administration [of Inland Revenue] lacks two vital sections—a service responsible for inspecting the district offices at regular intervals and another responsible for collecting taxes."

> Senior officials in the technical division do in fact have authority to carry out certain tasks in the country as a whole; but the exigencies of their own office work prevent them from travelling more than occasionally and this means that

the central Administration has no direct or regular contact with its district offices; the latter merely send in extremely brief monthly statistical reports, no really effective control is exercised over the internal organization of these offices, the output of their staff or the regularity of their operations. . . . This short-coming is particularly serious in Indonesia in view of the size of the country and the widely varying economic and social conditions in different areas; it should at all costs be remedied at the earliest opportunity, and after thorough investigation, the national revenue service should propose drastic measures to clear the considerable backlog of assessments and prevent the recurrence of such a situation. (M. D. Dris, "Taxation in Indonesia," *Ekonomi dan Keuangan Indonesia,* XI [August–September, 1958], 430–31.)

[24]S. Daniel Neumark, "The National Income of Indonesia, 1951–1952," *Ekonomi dan Keuangan Indonesia,* VII (June, 1954), 357–58.

[25]*Gotong rojong.* This system of financing local projects has a long and successful history in Indonesia.

[26]The M.I.T. group of social scientists who completed the "Modjokuto" study in Central Java were impressed by the competence of local administrators. Dr. Clifford Geertz, returning from a field study in Bali in 1958, reported the same impression. He also found a tendency among traditional rulers to assume new economic roles, leading to a vigorous indigenous entrepreneurship. Utilizing this reserve of administrative capacity may well be Indonesia's most significant opportunity to rapidly raise its capacity to absorb as well as to mobilize capital for economic development.

[27]The ways in which the two reinforce each other are emphasized in William Lockwood's study of economic development in Japan, *The Economic Development of Japan, Growth and Structural Change, 1868–1938,* Princeton: Princeton University Press, 1954).

[28]For 1953 the Ministry of Interior reported subsidies to local governments amounting to Rp. 1.9 billion, approximately 16 per cent of total reported Central Government expenditures (Rp. 11.9 billion). By 1955 such subsidies were near Rp. 3 billion. The adverse effects of the subsidy system on financing economic development are presented in detail by the Governor of the Bank Indonesia in *Report of the Bank Indonesia, 1954–1955,* pp. 19–20.

[29]The Nasrun Committee was appointed to study the problems of financial relations between central and local governments. Its recommendations appeared in an Indonesian document and were also presented in Indonesian and Dutch by J. de Bruine in a series of articles in *Ekonomi dan Keuangan Indonesia.* The Nasrun Committee recommendations appear to have been the basis for 1956 legislation on the problem of central-local fiscal relationships.

[30]The *pasar* (market) tax, the amusement tax, and the bicycle tax are three local taxes now in effect to be retained by local units. The urban real estate tax, the vehicle tax, the tax on consumption in restaurants, and the household property tax are examples of taxes to be transferred from Central Government.

[31]For a general review of this issue see Maryankov, *Decentralization in Indonesia.*

[32]Legge, *Problems of Regional Autonomy in Contemporary Indonesia,* pp. 19–21.

[33]*Ibid.,* pp. 50–62.

[34]Hans O. Schmitt, "The Economics of Political Disintegration in Indonesia," Chap. 4, p. 32 (unpublished manuscript).

[35]Since the rebellion was put down in 1958, guerrilla warfare and local resistance to central authority continue to plague the government in Djakarta.

22

Fiscal Management of Municipalities and Economic Development

by Joseph Froomkin[*]

INTRODUCTION

Many countries have experienced a rapid concentration of population in urban settlements concurrently with economic development. The proportion of the population living in cities of 100,000 and over to the total population is roughly correlated with the proportion of the population engaged in industry and to levels of per capita incomes in most countries.[1] This growth of urban populations poses a serious problem for municipalities since they are faced with the need for additional services. In underdeveloped countries the need for these services is going to be quite acute, because during urbanization caused by economic development the largest city, usually the capital, does not grow as fast as other, hitherto smaller, cities. Since the smaller urban settlements in underdeveloped countries have maintained very low standards of services, the need for improvement in municipal functions is likely to be pressing. Furthermore, if the experience of the Soviet Union and Brazil can be relied upon as a guide, a number of urban settlements will probably spring up in places where no cities or towns existed before.[2]

The extent of municipal investment depends on the type of cities which an underdeveloped country can afford to build. Since economic development, and especially the growth of an industrial working force, is hindered by city slums, and since urbanization should be accompanied by increased access to health and educational facilities, it becomes obvious that the magnitude of planning and financing municipal services in an underdeveloped country is of very large proportions. Thus, the planning and the execution of programs of municipal invest-

*Reprinted with permission from *Economic Development and Cultural Change,* III (July, 1955) (Chicago: The University of Chicago Press, 1955), 309–20. Copyright 1955 by The University of Chicago.

ment and management must be organized within some system of priorities in a more general program of economic development.[3]

THE TASK OF URBAN DEVELOPMENT

The task of urban development in developing countries is greatly magnified by the difference in municipal services provided today in the leading cities and in the smaller urban settlements. For example, in Iraq only the three largest cities have any electric generating plants worthy of the name.[4] In Colombia, the per capita revenue and service expenditures of municipalities vary according to their population, i.e., the smaller municipalities spend very much less money per inhabitant than the large ones.[5] In general, in most underdeveloped countries the leading cities have been able, apparently because of the aid from the central government, to provide more complete social services than the smaller communities. Not only has the central government been readier to grant assistance to the larger towns, but it has also allowed them generally more taxing power than small municipalities. In underdeveloped countries, industrialization and the growth of smaller towns with less financial autonomy than large cities will pose problems out of proportion to those presented by the leading city or cities. Hence the situation with respect to municipal finance of the larger cities in underdeveloped countries is the reverse of that in the United States.[6]

Municipal programs have never received the emphasis in the development planning to which they are or should be entitled, and municipal development during the growth phase of an economy is likely to be neglected. Thus, in Mexico, a country which has industrialized at a rapid pace during the past 15 years, investment in municipal development was characterized by a group of experts as follows:

> Public buildings [amounted to] 2% of total investment for the entire 1939–1950 period. Compared with many other countries, these proportions are low. In the 1939–1950 period, Mexico . . . left for the future the main task of providing low-cost housing and health facilities for most of the population.[7]

The amount by which Mexican expenditures fell short of a desirable goal is illustrated by comparison with the recommendations of the International Bank for Reconstruction and Development for Colombia. The Bank mission there recommended that 10.5 per cent of the total investment in 1953 be spend on municipal facilities and power, 22.5 per cent on housing and 8.8 per cent on buildings.[8]

What is more, even in an underdeveloped country in which expenditures on government services are traditionally low, the cost of effective municipal services appears to be fairly high. For example, in Ceylon, which possesses a fairly competent health service, the cost of health expenditures per capita is 13 rupees (U.S. $2.75) [9] while an effective program of disease control in Brazil has cost the government approximately U.S. $2.50 per capita.[10] Since per capita budgets of municipalities are very low (e.g., in Nicaragua municipalities spend $3.00 per capita per year[11]), the planning and determination of the minimum acceptable level of services which a municipality can provide becomes a serious matter.

PLANNING MUNICIPAL EXPENDITURES

At present, the limited taxing power of municipalities in underdeveloped countries has hampered the smaller towns in assembling the necessary staffs to perform those functions which are relegated to them. At the same time, the absence of capable administrators has prevented them from benefiting from a number of facilities which are provided by the central government for the asking. The personnel of municipalities in underdeveloped countries must be built up in order to place them in a position to benefit from central government aid, and to prepare them to provide purely local services which central authorities are not willing to finance and administer. In most countries, present municipal administrations are weak and must be strengthened considerably before they can undertake increasing responsibilities.

The following description of conditions in Guatemala applies to some degree to most countries in South America:

> Guatemala shares in the Spanish tradition . . . of highly centralized public administration and almost negligible local self-government . . . Most regions and local communities outside of the capital city are economically too little developed to maintain an expensive system of provincial or local government . . . The existing system of highly centralized public administration has resulted in focusing disproportionate attention on the capital city to the comparative neglect of the needs of the rural departments.[12]

To judge from the World Bank report on Iraq, conditions are similar in the Middle East. An example of the inability of municipalities to take advantage of central government aid may be cited as an illustration of the confusion which can result from the absence of adequate local services:

> As an aid to town and city planning there has been created within the Department of Municipalities of the Ministry of the Interior a planning section to provide "technical advice with regard to municipal schemes

for the organization of planning of cities and towns in accordance with common principles." [Municipalities have retained the right to zone and plan specific developments] . . . [As a result of unclear allocation of responsibility] surveys, plans, and partial plans have been hastily drawn and with [no general regard for needs] . . . The various ministries concerned with the erection of schools, hospitals, public buildings and bridges generally locate their projects without reference to the overall plan and without consultation with each other.[13]

The best intentions, and the most attractive institutions for the financing of municipal development can scarcely overcome the incapacity of municipalities to plan for the necessary services. The resulting lack of municipal services in smaller municipalities in Colombia has already been mentioned. This low level of services has continued there despite the establishment of the *Fondo de Fomento Municipal* (Municipal Development Fund) and despite the fact that the policy of loans for water supplies, sewer systems and electric plants, favors small or poor municipalities. The same fund also provides money for the building of hospitals and schools. The Bank report on Colombia remarks that "the poorest municipalities may find it impossible to finance even 10 per cent (the amount required by the *Fondo* to be put up by municipalities) of an expensive project out of funds on hand."[14]

The chief requirement for municipalities in underdeveloped countries, in addition to the need for more revenue, is the necessity of creating administrative bodies which are able to plan and pass on the feasibility of projects to be undertaken. Only when such a nucleus is established can one consider an increase in the responsibility of municipalities.

The increased responsibility, as well as increased financial resources, is especially desirable during a period of economic development. During a period of growth, a municipality must have a planning staff to segregate current expenditure (to be covered by ordinary revenue) from capital outlays for which assistance from the central government can be requested. The distinction between current and capital expenditure is often tenuous. For example, the laying of a new or larger water pipe or the paving of a street can be either current or capital expenditure, depending on whether the old pipe is corroded or not, or whether the new street would have been paved or repaved in line with the normal growth of the town. It is crucial for municipal governments to be able to map out the needs of the town, and to determine those financial responsibilities which can be shouldered independently, and those which have to be shifted to other bodies.

Municipalities in underdeveloped countries must not only have qualified people to map out the needs of the city, but they must also have a staff who knows how and whom to ask for aid in the central government. In the smaller municipalities such a staff consists in the establishment of city councils. It is highly improbable that for long the smaller cities will be able to recruit civil servants of the same caliber as the larger towns. If a city is developing, the personnel to staff a relatively efficient city council may be found among the backers of the new industries. A city council concerned with city improvements and a minimum plan may prove to be the only practical answer in many underdeveloped countries.

At the same time, if central government aid is to be allocated realistically and efficiently, supervision by a government agency is necessary, especially since much of the cost of municipal development will have to be borne by the central government. If the central government desires to take a more active part in this development, it may guarantee certain revenues or taxing powers to municipalities on condition that certain standards of service are maintained by the local entity. The function of such an agency can be roughly defined by the generic title "city planning." This central authority should centralize research on low cost housing, planning for necessary urban services and the establishment of municipal utilities.

FINANCING MUNICIPAL DEVELOPMENT

The burden of financing municipal development will depend on the financial organization of the countries concerned. In most countries, local authorities, such as townships and counties, have considerably less financial autonomy and responsibility than similar government entities in the United States. In these countries a large number of current services and capital expenditures of local bodies are financed by the central government. On the surface the smaller the sphere of responsibility for services the fewer problems are likely to be encountered by municipalities in financing their own economic development. Municipal sources of revenue are not very income elastic, and reliance on central governments with larger resources seems to be much more promising. At the same time, this reliance may prove to be a handicap, since the demands by municipalities during a peak period of development (which is already straining the public treasury) are likely to fall on deaf ears. Furthermore, the larger municipalities are likely to get more attention from the central government irrespective of the relative need or urgency of their demands, because of their greater ability to present concrete proposals to the central authorities. In this way, smaller municipalities may find themselves with less money, rather than more, in a moment of great need. Unless a catalogue of needs and methods of financing is developed well in advance, urban blight, characteristic of growing towns during the European industrial revolution, is not an unlikely prospect.

In broad outline, there are three types of arrangement between municipalities and superior layers of government, one exemplified by British, another by French, and the third by a federal government such as the United States of America. Both the British and the French models are characterized by a close reliance of municipalities on central government subsidies for the operation of current services. The chief difference is the extent of subsidies. Municipalities in federal government systems, in contrast, get much smaller subsidies from the center.[15]

The pattern of allocation of responsibility for municipal services in underdeveloped countries has closely followed that of the developed country whose tax system was adopted. Thus, French influence is paramount in Latin America, while the British have left their mark in their former colonies in Asia.

In general, those underdeveloped countries which have been under the British influence have succeeded in building up their municipal services to a higher level. Although they follow, on the whole, the British model, national governments play an even more important role in accepting what are considered municipal functions in the United States. Adaptations of forms of federal government in some former British possessions (e.g., India) have resulted in subsidization of municipal activities by the states, rather than by national government. On the other hand, the national government still retains many responsibilities in such fields as health and education (e.g., Ceylon).

Despite the fact that central governments in Latin America have assumed more responsibility for municipal services, they have neglected these responsibilities more than governments which have been under British influence.

Reform of municipal structure in underdeveloped countries must take account of existing patterns of responsibility by local bodies and the normally limited revenues. Consequently, one cannot contemplate an expansion of municipal services to approximate the responsibilities borne by cities in the United States. The model in Table 1 sketches the distribution of responsibilities between municipalities and other government bodies in the United States, France, and Great Britain. It also outlines a model likely to fit the needs of underdeveloped countries. It will be noted that the scope of the services allocated to municipalities there is restricted compared to more highly developed countries. In addition to general administration, fire control, and sanitation—minimal services which are everywhere provided by municipalities—it is suggested that municipal government assume only a minor part of the expenditures on health and highways,[16] and provide two additional functions, those of libraries and recreation, whose aggregate cost will not be high in most underdeveloped countries.

TABLE 1[a]

FUNCTIONS AND RESPONSIBILITIES OF MUNICIPALITIES
IN VARIOUS COUNTRIES FOR CURRENT SERVICES

	17 U.S. Cities	England (London)	France (Paris)	Proposed Model for Under-developed Countries
General control	Municipality	Municipality	Municipality	Municipality
Police	Municipality	Shared	Shared	Other
Fire	Municipality	Municipality	Municipality	Municipality
Schools	Shared	Shared	Other	Other
Libraries	Municipality	Other	Other	Municipality
Recreation	Municipality	—	—	Municipality
Welfare	Shared	Shared	Shared	Other
Correction	Municipality	Other	—	Other
Health	Municipality	Shared	Other	Shared
Highways	Shared	Municipality	Shared	Shared
Sanitation	Municipality	Municipality	Municipality	Municipality
Hospitals	Municipality	Municipality	Shared	Shared

[a]Country data adapted from Haig and C. S. Shoup, *The Financial Problem of the City of New York*, Chap. II.

FINANCING MUNICIPAL SERVICES IN AN UNDERDEVELOPED COUNTRY

Most of the traditional methods of financing municipal capital expenditures, as well as municipal services, i.e., borrowing, matching grants, etc., are not available to most municipalities in underdeveloped countries. There is no capital market for municipal bonds, and in some countries the municipalities do not have recourse to central government borrowing facilities either. Matching grants offered by central governments cannot be taken advantage of because municipalities do not have sufficient funds available. There is also far too little experience with subsidies in underdeveloped countries.

As a rule, funds for municipal services (both current and capital), are marginal expenditures of the central government, and are often financed out of specially created and earmarked taxes. In many cases, the revenue from these taxes is insufficient to finance the object for which it is earmarked. This results in the deterioration of services. In other cases, too much money is earmarked and extravagance is encouraged. The confusion and the inconvenience to the administration which result from earmarking is illustrated by conditions in Nicaragua.[17]

In Nicaragua there are fifteen assigned taxes. Two of these are set aside to finance the school lunch fund, and another the construction of the National Stadium. In addition, a semi-postal stamp is sold to finance the same stadium. Several shared taxes supply financial resources for such activities as the welfare board and the national sports commission. Other taxes are earmarked for the construction of schools and sanitary facilities. Other taxes, e.g., one on insurance premiums, earmarked to finance public education, have been diverted from this purpose. In general, the yield of these assigned taxes has been meager, and well out of proportion to the confusion created in the fiscal administration. Though it is granted that central bank financing is notoriously inflationary, unless it is matched by a surplus on government account, new sources of revenue, or an increase in private savings, the practice of earmarking has even more deleterious effects since it has crippled the tax system of many Latin American governments, and has greatly contributed to the inefficiency of tax collection.

THE ROLE OF THE CENTRAL GOVERNMENT IN PROVIDING LOCAL SERVICES

By United States standards, central governments in underdeveloped countries provide a large number of services which are generally conceived to be the responsibility of municipalities. At the same time, because of the financial weakness of municipalities, it becomes imperative for some central government authority to supervise and disburse funds for capital investment of a municipality during the period of economic development.

In this context, the role of the central government during a period of economic development must be made clear. In the first place, as the smaller municipalities are growing and assume more importance in the economic life of the country, the central government must be prepared to spend more money on providing those current services for which it is responsible in order to bring them up to par with those available in the larger cities.

In the second place, investments necessitated by municipal growth must be made part of the general development plan. These expenditures must be financed by outright grants or subsidies. The shortcomings of matching grants in underdeveloped countries have already been mentioned. Subsidies must be administered more carefully than matching grants, since the municipalities have no financial responsibilities in connection with their disbursement. In order to derive maximum utility from these expenditures, rigid control must be exercised by the central government, while the detailed planning for the location and the extent of the projects must be worked out in conjunction with municipal planning bodies.

The receipts of municipal governments in most underdeveloped countries do not amount to more than ten per cent of the total tax bill, generally between one and two per cent of GNP. An increase in municipal revenue by half would be barely sufficient to finance the planning of central government services and the minimal extension of local services. This will not suffice for contributions to capital expenditures, especially during economic development.

Unless there is a drastic and extremely thoroughgoing reform of municipal taxation, it is improbable that the sources of revenue of municipalities will increase sufficiently, and the central government must continue to shoulder its present share of current municipal expenditure, and face the prospects of contributing to the capital fund.

Local Responsibility for Services

The existing financial resources of municipalities do not permit them to maintain an adequate standard of services even in the limited area reserved to them. Under these conditions, it is not realistic to recommend that functions now borne by the central government be shifted to the municipalities. For example, foreign experts in El Salvador have recommended that municipalities above a certain size administer their own schools. In view of the large gaps in services now available in urban areas, the direction of expansion of municipal governments should be in fields not provided by the central government, rather than take over responsibility from other levels of government.

The standards and level of a number of municipal services provided by the central government will have to increase more than proportionally to the growth of population. This is due not only to the lagging standard of services in the smaller towns which are likely to grow during a period of economic development, but also to the fact that the rate of expenditure for police protection increases faster than the population after the population of a town tops the 100,000 mark. Towns in which a greater proportion of the population is engaged in mining or heavy industry pose a bigger problem in law enforcement than those which specialize in commerce or light industry. Policing problems are larger in a fast growing town than in one growing slowly.

The recommendation of shifting most of the capital expenditures of municipalities to the central government, as well as the assumption of a number of quasi-municipal functions by the central authority, might have given the impression that a severe limitation of the rights of municipalities is advocated, yet in an economy short of skilled professional labor, standards of service will be higher and savings in manpower may be accomplished if certain functions are centralized. Furthermore, municipal governments are so weak today that it is inconceivable to burden them suddenly with additional functions. First, the standard of service of those functions which they actually do perform must be improved.

Later, as municipalities increase their resources, their activities should be directed to fields traditionally neglected by central authorities, such as provision for adult education, public parks and libraries. It might appear frivolous to suggest expenditures for recreation in a community which is struggling to provide minimum standards of health or education. Actually, this is not so. Many of the migrants to the city are of working age. This means that they do not have a chance to go to school. Recreation activities are the only channels through which they can be brought to practice the social cohesion necessary for life in cities and the *esprit de corps* necessary for a person's adaptation to the process of machine production.

Even in backwoods counties in the Southern United States, recreation programs utilizing the existing school buildings during the evenings contributed to organized social action in the communities. Such apparent frills as recreation programs, public libraries, and city-sponsored adult education programs play an important part in creating a labor force with higher qualifications. Unless economic development in a particular country is carried out chiefly by large companies, who may be induced to start their own educational and recreation projects, such functions rest with the municipalities themselves. Large income receivers there do not endow libraries, parks, or technical institutes. Should municipalities in underdeveloped countries restrict themselves to a number of ancillary activities, in addition to a few functions which, in terms of United States expenditure patterns, are purely local in character, the outlays of municipal bodies would correspond to activities which constitute 30 per cent of the current outlay in a large United States city. If we assume costs in underdeveloped countries to be half those in the United States, expenditures of $9.00 per capita would be required (see Table 2). In line with present expenditures, this would necessitate new taxing powers for municipalities.

CHANGES IN MUNICIPAL TAXING POWER

Unless the present tax base is changed, a small increase in the responsibility of municipalities must necessarily result either in the creation of special central government taxes to cover the new expendi-

TABLE 2

PER CAPITA FIGURES FOR EXPENDITURES IN U.S. $ FOR FUNCTIONS
TO BE ASSIGNED TO UNDERDEVELOPED MUNICIPALITIES[a]

	Median of 17 U.S. Cities
General Control	$ 4.65
Fire	3.67
Libraries	1.00[b]
Recreation	1.79
Health	.87
Highways[c]	1.66
Hospitals[c]	1.66
Sanitation	2.67
Total	$17.97
Total Exp. of 17 cities	60.27%
Share of proposed model to present spending in U.S.	30 %

[a]Haig and Shoup, *The Financial Problem of the City of New York*, p. 40, Table 9.
[b]Estimated.
[c]Shares 50–50 with others in proposed model.

tures or increased grants from state or provincial governments. The problems which must be decided by municipalities in developing countries are: (1) Who shall bear the cost of capital improvements? (2) Who shall bear the cost of new or expanding functions? (3) How will money be raised for these functions which the municipality has to pay for?

The answers to the first two questions have been given in the analysis presented above: the cost of municipal improvements and the more expensive outlays which have been borne hitherto by the central government must continue to be shouldered by them. Yet, even if the modest program for municipalities outlined in the preceding section is adopted, municipalities must find sources of additional revenue.

In a number of underdeveloped countries the fiscal powers of municipalities cannot be increased easily. For example, in Colombia an amendment of the constitution to delimit the taxing power of the national and other governments is long overdue. At present, Colombian municipalities have very little power to obtain new sources of revenue. Similarly, in Brazil the taxing power of municipalities, as well as other administrative bodies, is written into the constitution, and a change of these taxing powers necessitates constitutional amendment.

Nevertheless, even within this restrictive framework, much can be achieved through joint action by central, state, and municipal governments if an attempt to delineate their activities, the introduction of a system of grants, and the standardization of the system of municipal taxation (through extending to the smaller cities some of the powers of the larger towns) is used to bring the services of small towns up to par with those of the larger cities. Possibly a municipal equalization fund, of the type used in England, between different London boroughs, may be set up to finance the poorer municipalities.

The next step in the creation of effective municipal governments is the granting to municipalities of the right to levy more taxes. One of the more important criticisms which visiting foreign experts have made about tax systems in underdeveloped countries is that the central government levies more taxes than it can efficiently administer. A simplification of the central government tax system which must go hand in hand with development can be accompanied by an increase in the fiscal powers of municipalities, who would take up those taxes which are relinquished by the central government.

The most promising sources of revenue for municipal governments are: (1) local property taxes, (2) taxes on activities specifically concentrated in towns, such as amusements, and (3) licenses for specific activities. In a number of countries the scope of municipal taxation is restricted in all three of these categories by taxes already imposed by central or state governments. If these taxes were dropped by the central government, they could become important sources of revenues for municipalities.[18]

Even if these taxes are retained by the central government there is no severe onus to the double taxation of property, amusements, and licenses by both central government and municipal authorities. In most underdeveloped countries, property valuations are only a fraction of their actual market values, and the rates are well below one per cent of these low assessments. In comparison with rates of two, three, and four per cent, on the full market value of the property imposed in the United States, there seems to exist considerable taxable capacity for municipalities in underdeveloped countries in this area. The more promising prospects of municipalities in developing urban property as a base for taxation will materialize when the appraisal of property is turned over to them, and when real estate values are fixed more realistically. In a small municipality this task could be performed by a committee of selectmen rather than a professional staff which it could ill afford. Whenever amusements, which are luxuries available only to a few, are taxed by the central government there is little reason to object to double taxation so long as combined rates are not excessive. Considering the low level of taxation on businesses which generally prevails in underdeveloped countries, it may be considered feasible to impose surcharges on license fees as well, if these are not dropped from central government rolls. Furthermore, municipalities may come to an arrangement with the central government to have it act as a collector of municipal taxes in order to avoid duplication of staff and to reduce the cost of collection to the local bodies. The efficiency of collection by central governments is likely to be better than that of small municipalities.[19]

While there appears to be considerable promise in the double taxation of property or amusements, as well as in increasing revenue from the licensing of more activities than is actually undertaken by municipalities, the prospects for the introduction of a municipal sales or income tax in underdeveloped countries are not very promising. In a number of underdeveloped countries a fairly heavy sales tax has already been imposed either by the central or by a provincial government. Under these circumstances, an increase in these taxes would be inadvisable. When sales taxes are not imposed, their collection would require elaborate administrative machinery and is beyond the means of most municipalities. The administration of a municipal income tax is also much beyond the capabilities of local governments in underdeveloped countries.

The new taxing powers of municipalities should enable them to eliminate a number of nuisance taxes which have hampered the development of trade. In Bolivia and Brazil, for example, municipalities have levied special import and export taxes on products entering and leaving these cities. Recommendations to eliminate these taxes were made to the Government of Bolivia, and legislation to eliminate them has been passed in Brazil. Yet, since the municipalities have been unable to find offsetting revenues, the implementation of both the recommendations and the legislation has been delayed.

CONCLUSION

It has been shown that municipalities in developing countries are urgently in need of increased tax revenue to finance the general services on this level of government in order to make it possible for them to take part in the planning of improvements necessary to implement economic development. Short of the extension in the scope of municipal administration—and even in the light of the best intentioned efforts of central governments—the results are likely to fall short of their intended goals.

It has also been shown that municipal development falls short of desirable norms set by international experts for underdeveloped countries. Consequently more attention should be paid to the building up of municipal services in underdeveloped countries. The solutions recommended in this article are: (a) increased fiscal responsibility for the municipalities, and (b) a more careful allocation of municipal development costs as part of general economic development plans by the central governments themselves.

NOTES TO SELECTION 22

[1] A. J. Jaffe, "Summary of University Seminar on Urbanism," *Bureau of Applied Social Research* (New York, 1951) (mimeographed).

[2] Carl Hammer, "Rank Correlation of Cities and Refinement," *Bureau of Applied Social Research* (New York, 1951) (mimeographed).

[3] Municipal improvements are likely to reinforce the forces which foster development; yet building city streets and sewers and expanding health services and educational facilities have a lower priority than building feeder roads to the city or improving the transportation system in that part of the program labeled "social overhead." The existence of a modern municipality is not likely to result in the establishment of new industry. It may encourage the migration of wealthy persons from rural areas, and result in a boom of service and small-scale industries in the city and in the blight caused by absentee landlordism to the farming hinterland.

The improvement of municipal services should be planned after an initial impetus from the establishment of new industry swells the population of the city. The establishment of a cement plant, a smelter or a flour mill usually increases the population in a small town in an underdeveloped country in a few years. If this town is selected later as the site of additional industrial installations, and the location of the town is believed to be favorable for further industrial growth, then it might be worth while to gamble on investment in the improvement of municipal services.

Municipal governments may often be forced into undertaking certain activities (such as the building of houses), if it is more clearly understood that better living accommodations play a role in the shaping of worker attitudes. The recent emphasis on the adaptation of indigenous building materials and living patterns to housing units which satisfy minimum demands for hygiene, comfort, and sanitation indicates that such investments may prove to be advisable.

[4] A mission of the International Bank for Reconstruction and Development recommended the installation of plants with generating capacity of 10,000 kws., a really modest potential, in cities other than Baghdad, Basra, and Kirkuk. International Bank for Reconstruction and Development, *The Economic Development of Iraq* (Washington, 1952), p. 109.

[5] International Bank for Reconstruction and Development, *The Basis of a Development Program for Colombia,* Report of a Mission (Washington, 1950), p. 276, Table 97.

[6] Compare, e.g., *The Basis of a Development Program for Colombia,* pp. 270–82 with R. M. Haig and C. S. Shoup, *The Financial Problem of the City of New York,* General Summary Volume (New York, 1952), esp. Chaps. I–II.

[7] International Bank for Reconstruction and Development, "Report of the Combined Mexican Working Party," *The Economic Development of Mexico* (Baltimore, 1953), p. 17.

[8] I.B.R.D., *The Basis of a Development Program for Colombia,* p. 595.

[9] International Bank for Reconstruction and Development, *The Economic Development of Ceylon* (Baltimore, 1953), p. 712. Even then the health service there was unable to provide sufficient guidance for the enforcement of minimum hygiene needs and the combating of large epidemics. See *ibid.,* Chap. XVII.

[10] *New York Herald Tribune,* March 11, 1953.

[11]International Bank for Reconstruction and Development, *The Economic Development of Nicaragua* (Baltimore: Johns Hopkins Press, 1953), p. 81.

[12]International Bank for Reconstruction and Development, *The Economic Development of Guatemala* (Washington, 1951), p. 263.

[13]I.B.R.D., *The Economic Development of Iraq*, p. 56.

[14]I.B.R.D., *The Basis of a Development Program for Colombia*, p. 227.

[15]*The British System.*—Both in Britain and in the countries which are, or have been part of the British Empire, the general lines of the financial and managerial responsibility are divided as follows:

a) The task of policing urban settlements devolves to the national government, with the municipalities contributing about half the cost of the upkeep.

b) Welfare functions are borne by the national government at no expense to municipalities.

c) Fire protection (partially subsidized by the central government), highways, sewers, sanitation services, libraries, etc., are maintained by the municipalities themselves.

d) The municipalities administer public education and public housing expenditures, but are reimbursed for the major part of their outlay by the national government.

The property tax is sufficient to pay for the services maintained by municipalities.

The French System:—

a) Municipalities contribute about one-fourth of the cost of police protection which is provided by the central government.

b) The national government is responsible for most, but not all, public health functions.

c) Most social welfare expenditures are borne by the central government.

d) The municipalities are responsible for fire protection, maintenance of roads, sewers, sanitation standards, parks, etc.

e) Education is a national government function, with the exception of vocational training. The municipalities usually contribute one-half of the expenditure for fixed plant, and shoulder the cost of maintenance.

f) A large number of taxes, among them a tax on rentals (a modification of the real property tax), a sales tax, a tax on amusements, and a variety of other taxes are imposed by municipalities.

The slightly more extensive responsibilities of municipalities under the French system have forced the central government to grant to municipalities the power to impose a variety of taxes to finance these expenditures.

The Federal System.—The relationship between municipalities and the state and federal government is much more complicated under federal arrangements. In the United States municipalities receive grants from or through the intermediary of the States, some of which are financed by State taxes, and others of which originate with the federal government. Education, public welfare, and part of the cost of road construction are financed in that manner. In other countries with federal types of government, the ratio of revenues collected by the states to those collected by the federal government is greater than in the U.S.A., and the state revenues, in conjunction with federal grants, contribute more to the cost of operation of the municipalities.

[16]There is usually no allocation for hospitals to be built in cities in most underdeveloped countries. The paving of streets, which can often be financed by local special assessments, is usually only partially subsidized by the most generous central governments.

[17]I.B.R.D., *The Economic Development of Nicaragua*, pp. 350–52.

[18]In a number of South American countries hundreds of miscellaneous taxes yield four to five per cent of government revenue. Their yields are equivalent to 50 per cent of current receipts of municipalities.

[19]The cost of collection by the central government must be carefully taken into account. In Haiti the charge for collection of municipal taxes by the central government is 15 per cent of the tax receipts. A mission considered the charges to be too high for that service. United Nations Mission of Technical Assistance to Haiti, *Mission to Haiti* (New York, 1949), p. 318.

23

The Taxation of the
Unimproved Value of Land

by J. R. Hicks and U. K. Hicks*

THE first thing which we shall do in this chapter is to discuss the proposal for Unimproved Value Rating, which has won so much support in Jamaica. We shall then go on, as a result of this discussion, to make certain recommendations of our own. We believe that these recommendations, if put into action, would have nearly all of the beneficial results which are claimed for Unimproved Value Rating; that they would avoid some awkward results of that proposal, to which too little attention has been paid; and finally that they would be capable of being realised without it being necessary for valuers themselves to work upon new and unfamiliar lines, so that they could be put into force while the actual valuation lists were compiled, as they are being compiled at present, upon the basis which has become traditional.

It will be convenient, as a basis for this discussion, to quote from the only authoritative statement which has ever appeared on the island, as to what the proposal for Unimproved Value Rating really is. These are the words of the Bloomberg Commission (1943):

> The Commission recommends that the present system of land valuation be changed and that the unimproved value of land as defined below be taken as the basis for land taxation, for urban, sub-urban, and rural lands.

*J. R. Hicks and U. K. Hicks, *Report on Finance and Taxation in Jamaica* (Kingston: Government Printer, 1955), Chap. 10, pp. 133–43. Reprinted with the kind permission of the authors. While the decision to include the passage from the Jamaica report was due mainly to the attention it gives to specific proposals, Professor Hicks regards the passage as having been largely superseded by his paper delivered in January, 1957, to the Economics Society of Nairobi, Kenya, "Unimproved Value Rating—the Case of East Africa," reprinted in J. R. Hicks, *Essays in World Economics* (London: Oxford University Press, 1959), pp. 237–44 (see item 31 of the Selected Bibliography at end of this volume).

"Unimproved value" of any land means the sum which the owner's estate or interest therein, if unencumbered by any mortgage or other charges thereon, might be expected to realise at the time of valuation if offered for sale on such reasonable terms and conditions as a bona fide seller might be expected to impose, and if no improvements (as hereinafter defined) had been made on the said land.

"Improvements" on land means all work done or material used at any time on or for the benefit of the land by the expenditure of capital or labour by any owner or occupier thereof in so far as the effect of the work done or material used is to increase the value of the land, and the benefit thereof is unexhausted at the time of valuation; but does not include work done or material used on or for the benefit of the land by the Crown or by any statutory public body, except so far as the same has been paid for by the owner or occupier, either by way of direct contribution or by way of special rates on loans raised for the purpose of constructing within a parish any road, bridge, irrigation works, water-races, drainage works, or river protection works:

Provided that the value of improvements made out of loan-moneys raised for the purpose of constructing within a parish any road, bridge, irrigation works, water-races, drainage works, or river protection works as aforesaid shall not exceed the amount of principal estimated by the Valuation Commissioner to have been repaid by the owner in respect of any such loan by way of special rates.

It may be observed that the Commission supported their recommendation by very little argument or evidence. Two things were said in favour of the proposed system:

i) that experience in various countries has shown it to be practicable,
ii) that the taxation of improvements is a disencouragement to the making of improvements, so that the withdrawal of such taxation will be an encouragement.

Neither of these statements can be for a moment questioned; but they do no more than scratch the surface of the problems which are in fact involved in the introduction of such a system into Jamaica. A much closer examination is called for, before the way can be regarded as cleared for so considerable a change.

We would suggest that in order to get to closer grips the problem may be looked at in the following way. The change from "improved value" to "unimproved value" is usually thought of as incorporating two sorts of changes: one, which is the less important, is that sites which are "ripe for development" will be assessed at their potential value, as sites for development, rather than at their value in their existing use; the other, which is more important, is that the value of improvements (which largely, but not exclusively, means buildings) will be excluded from the assessed value of properties—in effect, buildings and other improvements will be derated. It is desirable to consider these two changes quite separately, beginning with the less important, in order to get that out of the way before proceeding to the larger issue.

The inclusion of development value. The expansion of a town, or of the business quarter of a town, is always attended by a rise in the value of surrounding properties. This rise in value takes place before the property in question is built on or rebuilt; it is due to the expectation that the property will be able to find a use in the future that will be worth more than the use to which it is put at present. Notoriously, as the "development" of a particular quarter comes into sight as a practical possibility—even though it may still lie some way ahead—speculators begin to acquire plots of land in the district, with the hope of making a speculative gain later on when the development materialises. Even those plots of land which are not sold to speculators may be retained by their existing owners *as a speculation*—that is to say, while the existing owner would otherwise have been willing to sell at a fairly low price, he retains his land in the expectation of selling it at a better price later on. During the interval, before the development (or new building) actually occurs, the land continues to be used in the old manner; persons who would be willing to develop it if it were obtainable at a price adapted to its existing use, will not be able to acquire it because speculators (some of whom may be the original owners) are holding it off the market.

It is often maintained that one of the advantages of unimproved (or site) value rating is that such speculators will have to pay a tax or rate which is proportional to the value they themselves set upon the land—including its "development value"—and not one proportional to the value of the land in its present (less valuable) use. A tax upon site value will accordingly act as a tax on speculation, so that it will tend to reduce the time for which speculators are willing to hold back land from development. Development will be much cheaper, and will proceed faster. This particular argument in favour of site value taxation has not been much emphasised in Jamaica, but it has undoubtedly exercised great influence in other countries, such as New Zealand, which have adopted the unimproved value system. It is important to consider how this part of the effect of an unimproved value rate would work out in Jamaica, because it has a considerable bearing on the whole issue, not least upon the financial aspects of the change we are considering.

In most countries, when the adoption of unimproved value rating has been considered, the alternative has been a rate on annual value. Now if the land which is the subject of speculation is taxed on its annual value (based upon the rent which any one would pay for its use for a single year), no attention will be paid to the way in which its capital value is going up as a result of the prospect of development; the annual value will not in any way reflect the speculative element, so that a tax based on annual value is no deterrent to speculation. But in Jamaica we start from a tax on capital values, not on annual values; if capital values are properly assessed, they should take the speculative element into consideration. Thus it would seem that one part of the advantage which is supposed to be got from unimproved value taxation is, at least in theory, got in Jamaica already.

We say "at least in theory"; for we would admit that in practice the development element in capital value has proved hard to catch. It is hardly possible, in practice, for an official to set a *higher* value upon a property than the amount which he can substantiate by un-impeachable evidence; if he attempts to do so, even on strong grounds, he can be almost certain that his decision will be set aside on appeal. Suppose that, in the case we have been discussing, a few pieces of land begin to pass at prices which are decidedly above their value in current use; what is he to do? He will, for the reasons explained in the pre-ceeding chapter, be reluctant to mark up the values of those pieces of land in a way which puts them quite out of line with other apparently similar pieces of land in their neighbourhood; the most he can really do, in consequence, is to mark up the speculators' land to some extent, but less than the full extent of its rise in value on the market. And even when it comes to a general revaluation, if the development has not yet occurred, the situation is still difficult. How is he to say how far the increased value due to development prospects extends? How far should he mark up the land in the vicinity of a new cinema, or new grocery store, when that land has not yet changed hands at enhanced prices? Yet, if he does not so mark up the land which has not been sold, it is difficult to take full account of the rise in value of that which has. Even on the existing Jamaican system the element of development value sets the valuer a pretty problem.

Evidently, still looking at this side of the general problem only, it would be possible to re-draft the existing Jamaican law so as to make more explicit the inclusion of development value in the capital value on which property is assessed; but this change in phraseology would make little substantial change in the existing situation. Valuers could in principle bring in more development than they do at present, even without any change in the law; but whatever change was made, they would still be confronted with the same difficulties as confront them at present. It should not be expected that very much would come of a purely legislative change in this matter.[1]

The de-rating of improvements. With the question of development value put, thus provisionally, out of the way, we can turn to the major question—the de-rating of improvements (chiefly buildings).

The advantage of such de-rating, in encouraging improvements, has been much emphasised, and is indeed obvious; there are, however, certain difficulties which have received much less attention, though (if the scheme is actually to materialise) they must be faced. The first of these concerns the financial aspect.

If, as has just been shown, there is very little to be gained in the way of revenue (which is not available already) from taxing development value, the de-rating of buildings must involve a net reduction—and a considerable net reduction—in the total value of the property on which tax is levied. If every piece of property contained land ("Unimproved land") and buildings in the same proportion, this would not really matter; though the value of the property was reduced from (say) £500 to £250, those of all other properties would be reduced in a similar proportion, and a tax rate of twice as high as before would bring in the same revenue, leaving everyone with the same amount of tax to pay. But in fact some pieces of property contain large and expensive buildings, whose value would probably have to be assessed at much more than half the total value of the property, while others contain next to nothing in the way of buildings, so that the de-rating of buildings would affect their valuation only little. Since the total value of the property assessed was being greatly reduced, the poundage which would have to be levied in order to produce the same revenue would have to be raised—quite sharply; and the owners of these latter properties, which did not contain much in the way of expensive buildings, would have to pay a considerably increased amount of tax.

Just how all this would work out in the distribution of the rate burden is not, in detail, easy to see, especially since there is undoubtedly some tendency (at least in an urban area) for the more expensive buildings to be put up on the more expensive sites. But even in an urban area (such as the urban—as opposed to the sub-urban and rural—part of Kingston), there is likely to be some tendency for the value of buildings, relatively to their sites, to be highest in the case of the wealthiest property-owners, so that a de-rating of buildings would reduce taxation on those who are more able, and raise it on those who are less able, to pay. In a less developed area (say the rural part of the Parish of Kingston and St. Andrew), this tendency must be expected to be still more marked. The de-rating of buildings would reduce the amount of tax to be paid by the owners of expensive villas; and though some of this tax would be made up by increased rates upon the gardens of those villas (so that they would really come back to the same place), some would undoubtedly fall to be paid by the cultivators of the poorer and less attractive lands in the vicinity. The effect of de-rating buildings on the distribution of the rate burden could hardly fail to be, on the whole, in the direction of laying less taxation on the rich and more on the poor.

Up to the present we have been assuming that the technical problem of valuation has been overcome—that a way has been found by which the value of buildings can be separated from the value of the land on which they are situated. It is round this technical point that most of the discussion on site value rating has hitherto turned. It has been pointed out, on the one side, that a site and the building on it cannot be sold separately unless the building is pulled down; and that a building will not be pulled down unless its value, as building, is next to nothing. Thus there can be no direct evidence about the separate values of site and building, and the indirect evidence provided by occasional vacant sites is not enough to go on. Against this it is observed that site value rating has been found to be practicable in several parts of the world, and that this must mean that valuers have found some way of making the split. Thus the discussion very easily gets bogged down. On it we would merely make the following comments.

Separate valuation of site and buildings is very much easier in a country where buildings are frequently pulled down and rebuilt, so that, at any particular time, most buildings are *new*. When a building is new, the cost of the building and that of the site are clearly separate; but once the building begins to have a history, the value of building and site are intermingled, since one cannot be sold without the other, until the building is pulled down. Thus active and continual rebuilding makes separate valuation much easier. No doubt site value rating does itself encourage such rebuilding, but it is by no means the only cause of the condition in question. The most striking examples of such a situation are to be found in communities which are already wealthy, and are still rapidly increasing in wealth; when population is very mobile, and building materials relatively cheap; all of which conditions are present in New Zealand. This is not to say that even in such conditions the separate valuation of land and buildings is easy; but it is easier than it is elsewhere. Excepting in such conditions no regular separation in value between land and buildings can in general be made; though it may appear to be made, closer examination would always reveal that it had only been done by the use of arbitrary rules, which cannot be relied upon to have the effects which a proper separation would have—at least in theory.

Positive proposals. We have been piling up objections to the plan for unimproved value rating; but we have not been aiming to show that in consequence the whole plan should be discarded. For in fact the arguments for, and the arguments against, the proposal do not quite meet. The argument for the proposal is the encouragement which is given to *new* building; the arguments against are concerned with the de-rating of *old* buildings, which has been shown to be both technically difficult and of very dubious equity in its financial consequences. Why then de-rate the old buildings? You cannot get more old buildings—or, in general, more past improvements—by de-rating them. It is the new buildings, the new and future improvements, to which the case for de-rating applies. And in the case of such buildings, as we have seen, the technical difficulties of separate valuation are at a minimum.

This is the line on which we believe that a solution should be found; but there is still some way to go between the discovery of the general principle of a solution, and its embodiment in a workable scheme. For it is clear, to begin with, that a simple scheme, whereby all improvements to be made in the future (after an appointed day) should be de-rated, would not be acceptable. As time goes on, new improvements become old improvements, new buildings become old buildings; we have only to look forward to (say) 1970, and think how people would feel with a system under which buildings put up before 1955 were fully taxed, while those put up after 1955 were not taxed, to see that this would not do. As time went on, the distinction between improvements which were taxed and those which were not taxed would become more and more arbitrary; it would have less and less relation to anything actual. The advantage which is given to new improvements must clearly be less than this, or rather it must extinguish itself with a limited period.

The proposal to which we seem to be led is therefore one for the de-rating of new improvements *for a limited number of years after they have been made*. The simplest way of putting this plan into practice would be to continue to *value* on the old basis (which makes things easier for the valuer) but to allow a deduction from the full value, thus assessed, equal to the amount by which the full valuation had been put up as a result of the improvement. This deduction should be allowed, however, for no more than a limited period, during which the rateable value of the property would be no higher than it would have been if the improvement had not been made. After that period the rateable value, on which tax would be paid, should rise, either at once or by steps, to the full value. Even though the deduction did not continue indefinitely it would give a real stimulus to the making of improvements; it would provide most of the stimulus which would be provided—less equitably and at far greater expense—by a complete system of unimproved value rating.

This, in general terms, is what we recommend. We think that a suitable period for the allowance of the full deduction would be three years, with a 50 per cent deduction for a further three years, so that six years would elapse before the full value of the improvement became taxable. From the point of view of the local authority, this would mean that there would be some delay in its acquisition of new rateable value from new development; but the delay would not be unreasonable. The interest of the parochial boards would itself require that the delay (the period over which the deduction was spread) was not too long.

There is still the question of the types of improvement which should qualify for the deduction. It would indeed be possible for it to be made universal; but it is very much of a question whether it would be wise to go so far as that. It does not seem necessary to give away revenue (and the parochial boards, it should now be clear, would be giving away revenue) in order to stimulate improvements of every kind, including new buildings of every kind, regardless of the purpose for which the building was to be used. It would seem wiser—it would certainly be cheaper—to regard the de-rating as a privilege, which could be given to such sorts of building as it was particularly desired to encourage, but could be withheld (either wholly or in part) from "improvements" that are in fact more of a luxury character. It is one of the advantages of the system which we propose that it can be applied selectively. It is very important (as in the case of profits taxation, discussed in Chapter VI above [not included in this issue]) that selectiveness should not mean arbitrariness; but some broad distinction between broad classes of improvements would seem to be justifiable. We would ourselves recommend a classification on the following lines.

i) *New industrial buildings, and improvements to them.* It would clearly be right, and consistent with the general policy of the Jamaican government, that these should be given the full concession, as defined in the preceding paragraph. The concession should not be confined to such industries as are scheduled as "pioneer"; it should be general over all "productive industry" (for which there is a suitable definition in the U.K. de-rating legislation of 1929). An explicit and regular concession of this sort in the field of local taxation should be a more effective encouragement to industry than a mere practice of undervaluation, which gives intending or expanding firms nothing on which to rely.

ii) *Commercial buildings, and improvements thereto.* Under this heading we include shops, offices, banks, cinemas and so on. There seems to be much less case for making a concession in favour of buildings of this character than there is in the case of those which fall under the first head. One distinction between the two classes is that expansion of the facilities for "productive industry" is much more likely to be accompanied by a significant expansion of employment; another is that "productive industry" is more likely to assist in exports, or to enable the island to economise on imports. Finally, expenditure on commercial buildings can more easily contain elements of a luxury character. We are accordingly of the opinion that the concession should not be given to commercial buildings; or, if that seems inequitable, that it should be given in a much reduced form. A fifty per cent deduction for three years only, without any period of full deduction, is the maximum which we should think to be justifiable.

iii) *Hotels.* If these are looked at as an export industry, they might perhaps claim the deduction on the same footing as industrial buildings; but if any weight at all is given to the luxury aspect, they most decidedly fall within the second class. They do accordingly present a very difficult case. It would probably be cheaper to encourage the expansion of the hotel industry by these methods than by those now employed, methods which we have discussed in Chapter VII above [not included here]. On the whole, we are prepared to recommend that new hotels, and improvements to existing hotels, should be allowed the full deduction (as for class (i)); but this recommendation is to be taken as governed by our other main recommendation in this field, that the hotels should be called on to finance their own publicity. If that major recommendation were not accepted, we feel that the balance of argument on this minor matter would swing the other way.

iv) *Private dwellings.* It is clearly desirable that *small* private dwellings should have the full advantage of the deduction, since it would tend to encourage improvements in the general standard of working-class housing in Jamaica; and anything which does that is to be welcomed. It is, however, much more doubtful whether it should be given to all private dwellings without distinction. Our proposals about Schedule A income tax (para. 24 of Chapter V above [not included in this volume]) will themselves do something to discourage the more luxurious forms of building; but there is no reason why these should be offset by special provisions on the side of the land tax. In particular, there is no reason why Kingston (to whose board this matter is evidently of the greatest importance) should be delayed in the securing of an important (and in itself quite unobjectionable) expansion in revenue from the expansion of its suburbs. We accordingly recommend that there should be a ceiling on the amount of the deduction from full (improved) value which should be given on private dwelling-houses during the first three years. In the case of a new house, £1,000 might be a suitable maximum; in the case of a minor improvement, the maximum might be fixed at some lower figure. During the second three years after construction or installation the deduction would of course be limited to one-half of this maximum. This provision would set a maximum value upon the allowance to be given in respect of any one house at any particular time.

v) *Agricultural improvements.*—These seem to fall into two classes. On the one hand, there is the question of "crops," the assessment of which to tax has, we understand, been in the past one of the main indictments against the present system. It is not easy to understand how ordinary annual crops could come to be assessed to land tax; perhaps it is not this which has happened. It is more intelligible that the case may have been one of trees, fruit trees and other plantations, which could more reasonably be regarded as "fixtures." Even so, we consider that it was a mistake to include such things as these in the assessed value in any case. We accordingly recommend that the object of assessment should be redefined so as to exclude them; in effect, they would be entirely de-rated, not merely temporarily, but permanently. Secondly there is the case of "land improvements," such as draining and irrigation—the things which figure so largely in the Development Plan. These, on the principles of the Bloomberg Commission itself, (see passage quoted in para. 2 above [not included in this volume]) should not be de-rated, in so far as the cost of installing them was paid for by government money. They do not need encouragement by this method, because they are being encouraged in another way. Improvements, on the other hand, which are made on the initiative of the landowner, without direct government assistance, should however qualify for the full deduction, like the industrial improvements in class (*i*) above.

We should like to insist, in summing-up, that the detailed provisions for distinction among various classes of improvement, which we have put forward in this last paragraph, are much less important than the principle of the temporary deduction for new buildings and improvements, which is our main recommendation. If it were to be decided that the temporary deduction should be applied without distinction, to all new buildings and improvements, that would be quite a sensible thing to do. But it would be expensive; a moderate degree of discrimination between classes of improvement, along the lines we have been describing, would make it possible for all of the main advantages of the scheme, and nearly all those which have been claimed for Unimproved Value Rating, to be secured at much less expense.

Some important remarks about the administration of the scheme must be made in conclusion. It must be insisted that it is based upon the assumption that there will be regular (and full) revaluations of all property at frequent intervals, and that these full values will stand on the books, ready for reference. It further assumes that all significant improvements will be valued as soon as they are made, and that the dates at which they are made will be carefully recorded. It will then be possible to state, on the demand note to each taxpayer who is entitled to a deduction, what is the full value of his property, what is the (temporary) deduction to which he is entitled, and what, in consequence, is the value on which, in the current year, he has to pay tax. There should also be stated the number of years for which the deduction has still to run, so that the taxpayer can tell what is the date at which he must expect to be taxed on the full value. Should the value of the whole property be substantially increased at a re-valuation falling within the six years, he would still be entitled to his deduction (based upon the old valuation) but he would know that he would ultimately be taxed upon the full enhanced value.

These provisions would be necessary if the proposals which we have made in this chapter were adopted, without any other steps being taken. Their relation to those which would be necessary if the further recommendations which we shall make in the following chapter were also adopted, will be discussed when those proposals have been set out.

NOTE TO SELECTION 23

[1]It should be emphasised that the position would be different if we were starting from a system of rating on annual values, and still more different if we were starting from the primitive system of rating buildings only, such as existed in Jamaica in the nineteenth century, and in other places still more recently. A change from that system to a system of unimproved value rating (such as lately occurred at Dar-es-Salaam) would be an unquestionable benefit; but so would a change from that system to the system in force in Jamaica from 1900 to the present.

24

A Graduated Land Tax

by the World Bank Mission to Colombia*

We feel that the most effective method of achieving maximum utilization of land is a system of taxation which would penalize poor use of good land. The special tax on unimproved land imposed in various countries and the mild penalty tax on unimproved and un-utilized urban land in Colombia itself are precedents in point.

The system might work somewhat as follows:

The first step is to revalue for tax purposes the best farm lands of Colombia to reflect the steady increase in land values. Most good land is grossly undervalued. Additional funds and facilities should be afforded the Instituto Geográfico Militar y Catastral to enable it to accelerate its revaluation of farm lands. First attention should be paid to the highland valleys of Cundinamarca and Boyacá, and next the lowland valleys of Valle, Cauca, Bolívar, Tolima, Huila, Magda-lena, Cundinamarca, Santander and Santander del Norte.

We do not suggest at this time that the existing basic tax rate of Ps.$4 per thousand be altered.[1] An increase in valuations would in itself provide a very substantial increase in yields for urgently needed local services. We suggest, however, that this basic rate be progres-sively increased as the net income from the land falls below a certain percentage return on the current market value of the land as deter-mined by the Instituto Geográfico. In general, the high valleys of Cundinamarca, Boyacá and certain sections of Nariño may be ex-pected to yield less than the valley lands of Valle, Tolima and so forth. It is probably desirable, therefore, to set as norms different rates of return for these different types of land. The actual rates and the degree of progression should be determined after careful study. How-ever, in view of the relatively high return to capital in general, it

*International Bank for Reconstruction and Development, *The Basis of a De-velopment Program for Colombia* (Washington, 1950; Baltimore: The Johns Hopkins Press, 2nd and 3rd printings, 1952, 1953), pp. 384–87. Reprinted with the permission of the publisher.

Professor Richard A. Musgrave, now of Princeton University, was the Mission's adviser on finance, money, and banking.

seems reasonable to assume that land in the savannas of Cundinamarca should, if properly farmed, yield a return of at least 10 per cent on market value. If land use produces the normal rate of return, the basic tax rate would apply. If uneconomic use of land brought lower returns, the tax rate should be progressively raised as indicated in Table 1. For lands in the lowland valleys, the standard rate of return might be taken as 14 per cent of market value and the whole rate schedule stepped up correspondingly. It might also be desirable to raise the lower limit at which the excess profits tax begins to apply in the case of property subject to this tax.

TABLE 1
ILLUSTRATIVE TAX RATES PER THOUSAND BY INCOME CLASSIFICATION

Income	Tax	Net Return	Equivalent Income Tax Rate (2) as Per Cent of (1)
(1)	(2)	(3)	(4)
Ps.$100	Ps.$ 4	Ps.$96	4.0
90	5	85	5.6
80	6	74	7.5
70	8	62	11.4
60	10	50	16.7
50	13	37	26.0
40	16	24	40.0
30	20	10	66.7
20	25	− 5	125.0
10	32	−22	320.0
0	40	−40	—

The progressive rate should probably not apply to land undergoing reforestation or planted in cacao or palm nut trees. Administration of the tax could be carried out by the National Government, but the receipts should go back to the country districts to improve health and education and to finance local services in accordance with established formulas and under standards laid down by the National Government.

It must be reemphasized that we are here concerned not so much with the details as with the principle of this proposal. The important thing is that these valuations be made and the rate of progression determined in such a way as to provide an immediate and positive incentive to correct the present misuse of the best lands of Colombia, which constitute much the largest part of the national patrimony.

In addition to providing a direct stimulus to more intensive farming, the proposal would also operate to depress inflated land values— i.e., those not justified by the productive capacity of the land in question—and so put better land within the reach of poorer farmers.

Moreover, it would tend to increase employment opportunities, since it has been the general experience that conversion of land from cattle grazing to intensive cultivation, even with machinery, creates an increased demand for agricultural labor and equipment operators. By expanding the productivity and incomes of agricultural workers generally, it should help to expand the market for manufactured products and thus lay the basis for more efficient and diversified industries in Colombia.

While our tax proposal will tend to make the acquisition of land easier for small proprietors, the land affected will still usually be beyond the means of most rural people. To satisfy their desire for more land, and to achieve the economic and social benefits of ownership of land by those who cultivate it, this proposal needs to be supplemented by other measures. The Government in recent years has inaugurated a farm purchase program through the Institute for Parcelization and Colonization of Land. This program is excellent in intention, but the cost is heavy and the progress has been slow. The Institute should make arrangements to take full advantage of the services, personnel and experience of such agencies as the Extension Section of the Ministry of Agriculture, the Caja Agraria, the Housing Institute, and perhaps others. In addition, we feel that this program should be enlarged and pushed forward more vigorously, but it must be supplemented by other more direct and immediately effective measures if tangible results are to be achieved within a five-year period.

NOTE TO SELECTION 24

[1]Established by Decree No. 2473 of 1948.

25

Land Taxes and
Land Reform in Colombia

by Albert O. Hirschman*

THE LAND TAX PROPOSAL OF THE WORLD
BANK MISSION OF 1949

THE idea of using taxation for bringing pressure on landowners to cultivate their holdings was briefly discussed in the early days of the first López administration,[1] nothing came of it, however, and no further mention of the tax instrument appears until the publication some fifteen years later of the International Bank's survey *The Basis of a Development Program for Colombia*.[2]

Clearly the mission, headed by Lauchlin Currie, felt that the way in which agricultural activities were carried on in Colombia was both absurd and unjust: ". . . land use follows an unusual pattern. As a rule, the fertile level valleys are used mostly for grazing, while the steep mountainside slopes are cultivated . . . the cattle fatten on the plains while the people often have to struggle for a bare existence in the hills."[3]

The sharpness of this indictment is a good example of both the advantages and the limitations of the "fresh look" at a problem by a foreign mission. The advantage lies in the very fact that the outsider is not familiar with nor used to the local situation, does not grasp it in its "historical necessity," and has therefore the ability to be surprised and shocked by what he sees to a greater extent than even the most determined local social reformer. The failings of the visiting expert, on the other hand, are his readiness to label as absurd any order that is unfamiliar to him, and, perhaps more important, his inability to perceive the processes of change already at work in the society which he attempts to comprehend. Thus the land use pattern of the central Colombian provinces lent itself well to the

*Albert O. Hirschman, *Journeys Toward Progress: Studies of Economic Policy-Making in Latin America* (New York: Twentieth Century Fund, 1963), pp. 117–38. Reprinted with the kind permission of the publisher.

striking generalization of the Currie report, but this was so because the picture drawn by the mission was taken at a very peculiar moment in a continuing process of change. The long-drawn-out occupation of the mountainous and hilly lands by settlers in the central parts of Colombia had been virtually completed and most large estates in these areas had been broken up; on the other hand, the process of introducing mechanized agriculture in the flatlands had not yet started in earnest. Had the mission looked at Colombian agriculture only twenty years earlier it would have found large estates on the mountain slopes as well; and if the tendencies of the last ten years are projected for another decade, the growing of food and industrial crops will have largely replaced cattle grazing on the most fertile plains within twenty years after the publication of the report.

The obvious conclusion to be drawn from so "uneconomic and paradoxical"[4] a land use pattern as was denounced in the Currie report is to effect a revolutionary switch: let the peasants laboring on the slopes take over the fertile lands of the valleys and drive the cattle to graze in the hills.

Naturally a report submitted by the International Bank can hardly propose an agrarian revolution to a member government; hence the therapy advocated by the Currie report was mild in comparison to the revolutionary potential of its diagnosis. It proposed a tax on land that would penalize underutilization. The existing land tax (*impuesto predial*) of 4 per thousand of assessed value would apply to lands bringing a "normal" return or more (10 and 14 per cent were given as illustrative normal yields for two varieties of fertile areas) ; if the return were subnormal the land tax was to be raised progressively until it would reach 4 per cent of assessed value in the case of zero return.[5] In addition to providing a direct stimulus to more intensive farming, the proposal was also made with the idea that the increased tax load would make absentee landlords more willing to sell out to small holders and that land prices would come down. Better land utilization and more widely distributed ownership were stated to be twin objectives.

The report's scathing comments on Colombia's agrarian structure combined with the seemingly paradoxical nature of the proposal—at given land values, taxes would *rise* as income fell below a certain level —made a considerable impact on public opinion. Since the report was believed to be the forerunner of large-scale financial aid from the International Bank, all of its proposals were at least given the benefit of the doubt. Nevertheless, in the case of the land tax proposal, the immediate reaction was angry criticism, not only on the part of the landowning interests,[6] but also on the part of domestic fiscal experts and administrators. It was easy to show that the proposal was an administrative nightmare: Different "normal" returns would have to be set for different types of land, all kinds of exceptions would have to be granted, e.g., for land undergoing reforestation. Moreover, according to the proposal, the tax should be assessed on the basis of the "current market value," but how this value was to be set remained unclear. The existing 4 per thousand real estate tax was assessed on the basis of cadastral surveys conducted by the Geographical Institute, but as usual the values resulting from these slow surveys were far below the real values of the properties, especially after a decade of wartime and postwar inflation. Moreover, many parts of the country are not reached by the surveys and here the values declared by the owners serve as the tax base.

Thus the proposal was wide open to the comment which so frequently greets the foreign expert's advice. "His ideas are excellent, but they are impractical, they wouldn't work in *our* milieu." While hidden chauvinism and xenophobia no doubt have something to do with this judgment, foreign advisers often seem to make an all-out effort to deserve it. One reason is that they are not aware of the political restraints under which policy-making operates in the country which they advise; another is that they wish to "épater" the native with the latest policy gadget. In this connection, we may note that engineers would never advocate the introduction in an underdeveloped country of a production process which has not been proven to be free of "bugs" in an industrially advanced country, but the exercise of such restraint is unusual on the part of advisers in economic or social policies.

From a somewhat Olympian point of view the penchant of foreign advisers for impractical measures is perhaps not altogether lamentable, for this foible makes it possible for the native policy-makers to modify the expert's proposal and to make it *their own* in the process. Such an attempt to carve a workable measure out of the land tax proposal of the Currie report marks the next stages of policy-making on land use in Colombia.

After the report was issued, the Colombian government, in agreement with the International Bank, set up a committee of its own to consider the recommendations of the report. This "Committee of Economic Development" consisted of six respected Colombian citizens (three Conservatives and three Liberals). Although the committee retained Currie as its adviser, it pronounced itself against any immediate application of the tax and advised instead that the Geographical Institute be strengthened and its cadastral survey work accelerated.[7] Actually Currie had submitted to the committee a considerably revised version of his original tax proposal.[8] He limited the scheme to the fertile level lands which would be designated as such by the Institute and cut by one-half the rate of progression envisaged in the Bank report. Furthermore, he now faced the problem of how to get a realistic appraisal of land values and proposed that assessments be based on the owners' own declaration; to ensure truthful declarations he stipulated that the state could purchase any property at 140 per cent of its declared value. But even though in general Currie's advice carried considerable weight with the committee, the whole idea was shelved for the time being and the committee recommended the usual mixed bag of *fomento agropecuario* (agricultural and livestock development) measures: land surveys, agricultural credit, technical assistance, storage and distribution as well as tax *incentives* for increased cultivation of level lands. Only as a last resort, if all of these programs were to fail, then "the government shall consider the possibility to establish a tax on under-utilized agricultural land."[9]

The Bank mission episode was thus finished. Should it stand condemned as one of the many instances of unsuccessful technical assistance, of expert advice that went unheeded precisely because it was impractical or because it ignored "the weakness, if not the complete absence, of social and political forces that could induce the necessary concessions on the part of the ruling coalition?"[10]

In the light of later evidence, such a verdict would be too harsh. The Bank report had various merits: (1) it kept alive the discussion of improvements in the agrarian structure and in land use under highly adverse political conditions; (2) it deflected attention from the purely legal approach that had long held undisputed sway, to the possibility of promoting change through financial incentives and penalties; and (3) by formulating a concrete proposal it led to an awareness of the principal practical difficulties facing an attempt to use the tax instrument for purposes of agrarian reform.

ATTEMPTS TO ACHIEVE REALISTIC LAND ASSESSMENT

Discussion of the tax proposal had made it clear that the principal stumbling block to the effective and equitable use of fiscal policy was the assessment problem. In Colombia land is subject to taxation not only through the previously mentioned real estate tax of 4 per thousand, whose proceeds are the mainstay of municipal finance; in addition, federal taxation provides for a patrimony (net worth) tax with a mild progression from 1.35 per thousand to 15 per thousand in the case of taxable property in excess of one million pesos so that many large landed properties are theoretically taxed at close to 2 per cent a year, a rate that should be sufficient to exert that pressure toward either utilization, lease or sale that was aimed at by the Currie proposal. Such was also the conclusion of two United Nations experts who surveyed the country's fiscal system in 1951:

. . . the Committee on Economic Development was asked to advocate a special land tax on under-cultivated land. The authors of the present

report feel that the Committee made a wise decision in not recommending such a very complicated tax which could not possibly be levied
without giving excessive discretionary powers to the Public Administration. Under normal circumstances the patrimony tax, if well enforced
and based on realistic valuations of land, provides sufficiently for incentives to proper cultivation of land and especially so in the case of
those wealthy landowners against whom the special land tax was intended
to operate.[11]

This recommendation reflects the rationality of the British and
Dutch authors of the United Nations report. But it ceases to appear
so rational once the difficulties besetting the realistic assessment of
land are realized.

First, the technical obstacles in cadastral survey work are huge in a
mountainous country with poor communications and capricious
weather: on account of irregular downpours even in the so-called dry
season roads are frequently and unpredictably impassable. While
aerial photography is a technical achievement of considerable value,
its usefulness has been restricted in Colombia because of the almost
permanent cloud cover over large and important areas of the country.
A further technical advance, infra-red photography from high altitudes, has partially overcome this difficulty as it enables the camera
to take ground pictures from the air even through haze and light
clouds. Technical assistance in mapping the country from the air has
been extended by the United States but only on a small scale, and
progress has been slow.

Good cadastral surveys have, of course, been carried out in some
countries even before the advent of aerial photography. But the task
of making such a survey and of estimating the fair market value of
every farm is a most difficult one for an underdeveloped country where
land is privately owned. It presupposes a large corps of well-trained
surveyors who are incorruptible and courageous and a legislature that
is willing to make adequate appropriations for this work. Moreover,
it requires either an absence of inflation or frequent revisions through
resurveys or escalator devices. Rapid economic development and
urbanization also affect land values profoundly and differentially.
Thus, in Colombia, a country with powerful landowners (including
not only the hacendados but the numerous and politically influential
owners of middle-sized and small coffee farms), weak local administration, considerable inflation and rapid economic development, the
establishment of realistic land values for the whole country through
cadastral surveys has long been unattainable.

This is a most serious conclusion for it appears to rule out the use
of taxation as a means of coaxing landowners into making full use
of their land and therewith the gradual, peaceful solution of the

problem of underutilized latifundios. This situation is behind T. Lynn Smith's remark that it is much easier to have a revolution in Latin America than a really effective land tax.[12]

Whether or not it is easier than reform, revolution is always *easier to visualize;* for revolution requires "only" the violent overthrow of certain ruling groups, a head-on clash, whereas reform requires a special combination of circumstances, a sequence of moves in the course of which the ruling groups acquiesce to, or even connive in, the nibbling away of their own privileges.

Viewed in this fashion, reform is a feat of contriving which has a chance of being accomplished only if liberal use is made of some of the more wily arts of bargaining—intimidation, threats, professed willingness to resort to violence, use of surprise and deception, etc. Some of these arts received abundant, if somewhat erratic, application in the next period of Colombia's history—the dictatorship of General Gustavo Rojas Pinilla.

The General came to power as a result of the increasing tendency of the ruling Conservative faction to establish a sectarian dictatorship of its own. It began to persecute not only Liberals but even certain dissident Conservative groups, and it was increasingly unable to deal with rural unrest: for example, the large tropical flatlands (Llanos) east of Bogotá came to be largely controlled by guerrilla forces. General Rojas Pinilla promised an end to party strife and political persecution and persuaded some, though not all, guerrilla forces to lay down their arms. After a brief honeymoon during which some previously suppressed liberties, particularly of the press, were restored, it became clear that the new regime was bent on perpetuating itself in power. It developed a vaguely populist, anti-oligarchic, pro-underdog ideology of the Perón type. It was clearly animated by considerable resentment against the traditionally privileged circles of Colombian society. While its policy-making was frequently inept, it did have a highly resourceful, if irresponsible, protagonist in the Minister of Finance, Carlos Villaveces, who soon became famous for the many surprise decrees he issued, ranging from serious assaults on the financial position of the propertied classes to minor pinpricks. Only too willing to impose a heavier tax burden on the landlords he brushed aside the U. N. recommendation that the cadastral survey be improved by enlarging the staff of the Geographical Institute. With typical impatience, and intent on finding shortcuts, he issued two decrees. First, in September 1953, he ordered the automatic upward valuation of all assessments in accordance with the rise in the cost of living from the date of the last assessment.[13] Before the storm of protest against this edict had died down, he virtually countermanded it by providing, early in 1954, that the values of landed properties were to be set from now on by declarations of the owners themselves to municipal cadastral committees (*juntas municipales de catastro*). The decree contained the threat that the value declared by the owner would be the basis for payment by the state should the property at any time come to be expropriated. Here was the shortcut sought by Villaveces. Why bother with the endless, frustrating work of surveying the whole country, piece by piece, if the owner himself can be intimidated into telling us about the real value of his land?

We noted earlier that Currie had advocated the same shortcut in 1951, but he proposed that the state would have the right to acquire properties at 140 per cent of the self-declared value. Villaveces radicalized this suggestion and decided that 100 per cent was good enough.

This idea of enforcing honesty through the threat of expropriation at the self-assessed value is ancient.[14] But, like the threat of future expropriation of Law 200, it did not work, in both cases because of what our atomic strategists call the lack of credibility of the threat. When, as had long been the rule in Colombia, the state has to pay cash for expropriated property, its ability to acquire large tracts of land even at bargain prices is strictly limited and it is naïve to suppose that the landowners do not know this. Moreover, the individual landowner is likely to rate as low the probability that the government will single *him* out—and, anyway, he has a good, well-connected lawyer friend in Bogotá—so why worry?

Nevertheless, opinion about the effect of Villaveces' measure is divided. Reportedly, in some areas it did have the desired effect of raising valuations to more realistic levels. On the whole, however, much damage was wrought by disrupting the work of the Geographical Institute and there is evidence that the largest latifundios were as undervalued at the end of the Rojas Pinilla regime as at its start. Thus, in spite of occasional talk about land reform and the threat implied in Villaveces' decrees, the landed "oligarchs" did not suffer during the General's tenure while the country's industrialists and investors in corporate assets were badly hit by the abrogation in 1953 of a cherished and lucrative privilege—the exclusion of dividend income from the income tax. This differential treatment was perhaps due to the fact that the Rojas Pinilla clique bore far greater resentment against the impenetrable and haughty world of Antioqueño industrial and banking wealth than against the old-fashioned hacendado. Moreover, many among this clique—originally members of the lower middle class—were themselves consumed by the ambition to become landowners, and, needless to say, this ambition was abundantly realized, most conspicuously in the case of Rojas Pinilla himself. That they went slow in imposing tax burdens on themselves is not too surprising.

The point is more than anecdotal, for it reveals a fundamental change that had taken place with the vigorous economic development Colombia experienced since the thirties: land ownership became a popular investment among the expanding middle class and the hacendado thus acquired important allies in the defense of his own interests. Land and cattle ownership, still prized for the prestige it gave and for the protection it promised against currency depreciation and against the saver's own propensity to engage in wasteful spending,[15] became attractive also on other more "modern" grounds. Just because effective taxation on land and on income from it had lagged behind the comparatively heavy and progressive taxation on industrial and commercial income, land ownership and cattle operations became newly attractive to investors. Losses could easily be claimed in cattle operations and could be used by persons with large taxable profits from nonfarm operations to reduce total tax liabilities. Thus the progressive industrialization and urbanization of the Colombian economy, while of course creating a need for higher agricultural productivity, led to types of individual action that interfered with the fulfillment of this need.[16]

This lag in productivity did not matter too much as long as the country had a large and steadily increasing foreign exchange income as a result of sharply rising coffee prices: the necessary foodstuffs and agricultural raw materials could easily enough be acquired abroad. But when the coffee market broke in 1954 and foreign exchange once again became a scarce commodity whose allocation was subject to sharp scrutiny, the question inevitably was asked: why is it not possible for Colombia to satisfy its own needs in such products as cotton, oil seeds, barley, cacao and even cattle? Why in 1956, for example, did it have to spend $100 million or one sixth of its total import bill on agricultural imports?[17]

DECREE 290 OF 1957 AND ITS ALLEGED FAILURE

It was this desire for an expansion in food production that led to the next major legislative step, Decree 290 of 1957, issued by the military junta which governed the country for over a year after the overthrow of Rojas Pinilla. The decree was principally the work of Jorge Mejía Salazar, Minister of Agriculture, who was assisted by an adviser loaned by the International Bank.

The approach followed by the decree was foreshadowed by a special report on Colombia's agriculture prepared by a new International Bank mission in 1956. This mission had been requested by General Rojas Pinilla's first Minister of Agriculture. Since the report was rendered when the Minister had long been replaced and at a time (1956) when the regime was disintegrating rapidly, its immediate impact was minimal. Confirming the Currie diagnosis, the report adjudged land use patterns to be "uneconomical and illogical"[18] although it noted some progress "in very recent years" in cultivating the good level lands both in the tropics (rice, cotton) and in the highlands (wheat, barley, potatoes).[19] As a remedial measure the report again principally proposed tax measures, and recommended that the responsibility for land assessments be returned to an invigorated Geographical Institute and that assessments be made on the basis of "optimal potential use which the quality and location of the land warrants, not on the land's current use."[20] It appears from this phrasing that the report aimed at a value different from current market value. The latter will reflect the potential use of the land if this potential use is well known and clearly established by similar nearby properties. But then, why not use the market value as a first approximation to "potential use value"? To get directly at the latter poses a virtually insoluble task for the land survey teams of an underdeveloped country—but then foreign missions seem to have a penchant for saddling the countries they advise with such tasks!

Another recommendation of the Bank report was more practical and represented a simplification as well as an improvement of the discredited Currie proposal. To encourage cultivation or the leasing or selling of idle lands, landowners were to include into their taxable income a notional income from their lands on the basis of a "presumptive return equal to 3–5% of the value of land, cattle and fixed farm capital."[21] Clearly the efficiency of such a measure would again depend on the reliability of the cadastral survey. But it would have the advantage over the Currie proposal of avoiding the need to ascertain separately the actual income from the land; it would make it impossible to claim losses in land or cattle operations which would serve to reduce taxable income from non-farm sources and, provided again that assessments were realistic, it would reduce the attractiveness of investment in land for the rich.

This proposal was to be placed under active consideration by the Lleras government in 1960, some four years after the Bank report was issued. Why, in 1957, the infinitely more complex scheme of Decree 290 was drawn up instead is a real mystery, the more so as several of the Bank's recommendations were followed. Thus the self-assessment decree of Villaveces was duly repealed and the Geographical Institute was given a more autonomous status. Also, the report's suggestion that incentives in the form of land tax exemptions for specified periods should be given to landowners carrying out irrigation and drainage works was fully incorporated into the decree. Finally, the Bank report had classified land into three qualities: Type I: good level land, suitable for mechanized intensive agriculture; Type II: hilly and rolling land suitable for certain types of labor-intensive agriculture, and for cattle grazing; Type III: land unsuitable for agriculture though widely used for this purpose at present, to be used for grazing or to revert to forest. This subdivision had been made only for purposes of analysis, but Decree 290 made it into law adding one more category to the three, namely, land that is potentially usable but requires large-scale investment in means of communication, clearing, irrigation or drainage. The heart of the decree was the requirement that certain minimum percentages of these lands were to be cultivated. In other words the decree took it upon itself to define precisely the "economic use of land" which had been made into the condition of ownership by Law 200 of 1936.[22] It laid down the rule (Art. 5 and 6) that at least 25 per cent of Type I land and 15 per cent of Type II land had to be under cultivation once a year.[23] Those who would be found to default on this obligation were to pay a supplemental real estate tax which increased from year to year. Starting with 2 per cent of the value of the property in 1958, this penalty tax was to reach 10 per cent after four years.

Application of Decree 290 thus required first a classification of all farmlands and farms into the four land categories and, secondly, a yearly inspection to ascertain whether the various percentage requirements of the decree were satisfied. The measure was obviously and utterly unworkable, far more so than the Currie proposal which had been extensively criticized for its lack of attention to the "ambiente." Clearly the occasional passing of unworkable laws is very much part and parcel of the ambiente, and perhaps the foreign expert only shows he is becoming assimilated when he takes part in the game!

Our task being to understand, we may suggest two reasons for the decree:

The military junta had appointed a Cabinet of technician caretakers as Ministers. For example, the Minister of Agriculture was a civil engineer, who had previously worked for petroleum and construction companies. After the restless, willful and often vexatious improvisations of Villaveces, the affairs of state were to be handled in a competent and technical fashion. It is possible that the highly complex arrangement of Decree 290 recommended itself to the policymakers because with its land classification, percentages and other intricacies it had an impressive air of engineering technocracy.

Another explanation is that the decree was cast in general terms but that it was really meant to be applied only to a few well-defined zones with fertile, level, inadequately utilized land, close to the centers of population, and owned in fairly large blocks. Since the decree could not be applied until lands were classified into the four types, and since the principal purpose of the law was to increase rapidly the production of certain foodstuffs and agricultural raw materials that were being imported or whose scarcity contributed to inflationary pressures, the zones with greatest immediate potential would clearly be the first to be surveyed. Moreover, a decree which is clearly utopian for the whole breadth of the national territory can conceivably be made to

work in strictly limited areas whose economic and property characteristics are already well known, and where the available qualified
personnel would be concentrated. This was indeed the direction
Minister Mejía took: he started pilot projects for the application of
the decree in four small areas (about 10,000 hectares) in each of the
four most notoriously fertile and underutilized flatland areas of the
country (Sabana of Bogotá, Cauca Valley, Tolima Llanos, and
Caribbean coast). The application of the decree never went beyond
this pilot stage; for after a new minister (Augusto Espinosa Valderrama) was appointed in 1958 to the first Cabinet of President Lleras
nothing further was done to bring it to life.

As a result it is possible to assert—as was of course widely done—
that Decree 290 represents one more spectacular failure in the history
of attempts at dealing with Colombia's land problems. But such an
assertion must be reconciled with the fact that considerable progress
was in fact made in the late fifties in achieving the principal objective
of the decree, namely, increased agricultural production in a variety
of important lines (cotton, rice, barley, sugar cane, oil seeds). Imports
of barley dwindled to a negligible figure and from a substantial importer of cotton Colombia became a net exporter. Increasingly, enterprising middle- or upper-class operators rented or acquired tracts of
good flat land in the Sabana of Bogotá, the Cauca Valley and the
Tolima plains close to the Magdalena River and sowed them to commercial cash crops.

These developments must in part be credited to Decree 290. It is
conceivable that even though unenforced the threat of penalties, coming as it did after the recommendations of the various foreign missions
which had received wide publicity, had some psychological effect on
the owners. But the decree also contained some fat financial incentives
to cultivation. Going considerably beyond the recommendations of
the International Bank, it made a wide variety of agricultural investments deductible for income tax purposes.[24] Moreover, it cut in half
income and patrimony tax liabilities for a wide variety of agricultural
activities, with the sole exception of beef cattle operations on level
lands.[25] The decree aimed particularly at promoting the formation
of partnerships or corporations that would lease lands from large
landowners and grow commercial crops on them.

These incentive provisions were of course immediately taken advantage of: to become effective they only needed to be invoked by
the taxpayers, who can always be relied upon in such matters.[26]

Agricultural entrepreneurs taking advantage of these incentives received further timely help by concurrent legislation aiming at channeling larger bank credit resources into commercialized agriculture. In
1957 commercial banks were directed to reserve 15 per cent of their
deposits for loans to agricultural activities[27] and while selective credit

regulations of this kind had frequently been of dubious effectiveness it appears that this measure played an important role in orienting investment activity toward the raising of cash crops.

The modernization of Colombia's agriculture along capitalistic lines thus made rapid advances in the late fifties. A number of basic economic forces were also at work, such as the growth of markets as a result of industrial expansion and urbanization. Price supports and technical assistance supplied by official agencies or directly by industry were of importance in the more spectacular cases of barley and cotton.

It would probably be premature to attribute these changes to a new capitalistic mentality of the landowners. Rather, it could be argued that the continuing widespread desire to hold land, for prestige reasons, as an inflation hedge, or as a tax avoidance device, was a factor in the development of production because it led to a rise in land prices. Frequently one hears it said by landowners that with their land having risen so much in value, they cannot "afford" any longer to leave it in cattle, even though land taxation has not caught up with the increase in land values. This statement implies that the landowner, instead of maximizing income, behaves in such a way as to maintain some "normal" relationship between income from the land and its value. In other words, the potential maximum income would actually be earned only if this is required to restore the ratio between earned income and land value to its "normal" level.[28] The reasons for such behavior could be several: a loss of face could be felt and a suspicion of being incompetent could be aroused if one failed to achieve a certain earnings ratio; it is also possible that landowners who lack knowledge about market conditions or who, as a result of experience, doubt the ability of the market to absorb large additional quantities at constant prices, take an increase in land values as a more reliable signal that demand for agricultural products has expanded than a rise in prices, which may be ephemeral. The very propensity to hoard land may thus have indirectly stimulated crop production.

Viewing the agricultural progress of the fifties, one observer of the Colombian scene, Lauchlin Currie, completely reversed his earlier stand about the scandalous underutilization of Colombia's best lands and spoke of an "agrarian revolution" that had taken place silently and generally unnoticed. And he even candidly avowed that the tax proposal of the International Bank mission he had headed "would not have been advanced if the mission had arrived a few years later."[29] Currie's renunciation of his earlier views went much too far, for the problem of the idle or underutilized latifundio was still a long way from being solved. But as a result of the advances which Currie noted, the agricultural problem which policy-makers had to deal with was changing its face once again: inadequate production and unnecessary agricultural imports came to be gradually superseded as a principal cause for concern by the continued low income, depressed social status and unrest of the large mass of Colombia's campesino population. Nevertheless, the next phase of policy-making, from 1958 to mid–1960, was marked by a somewhat hectic attempt to avoid facing this problem or dealing directly with it.

New Tax Proposals under the Lleras Administration

In mid–1958, after one year of caretaker government by the military junta, Colombia started a novel political experiment, in accordance with the Liberal-Conservative pact which had given the impulse to the overthrow of Rojas Pinilla's dictatorship. Liberal President Lleras, duly elected by both parties (the Presidency was to alternate between representatives of each during four terms of four years each), formed a strictly bi-partisan cabinet, while each party held one-half of the parliamentary seats. Clearly such a political arrangement was not ideally suited to forceful action. Yet President Lleras was aware that his government had to be something more than a continuous, skillful balancing act. High expectations of an all-round better life had been raised and popular energies and pressures would once again be felt frequently and openly, rather than sporadically and in the form of backland guerrilla strife as during the preceding decade of military and "strong man" government. President Lleras thus had a doubly difficult task: his government had to play to popular galleries and at the same time it was hamstrung in its actions by its own split personality and by the suddenly restored power and assertiveness of Congress. The moves of the next period are difficult to understand if one does not keep in mind the particular tensions under which the government operated.

As previously mentioned, Espinosa Valderrama, the new, young and enterprising Minister of Agriculture, was unwilling to become the administrator of Decree 290. However, while he criticized the decree for the complex land classification system it required, he proposed a bill that would maintain this system intact, and would merely increase the cultivation requirements as well as the penalties imposed for non-compliance. The bill never got over its first parliamentary hurdle, but its introduction had two consequences: (1) it definitely buried Decree 290 insofar as the application of its penalty features was concerned; and (2) it led to a veritable free-for-all of proposals and counterproposals in and out of Congress and to widespread public discussion. Some projects that were seriously introduced appear to have been specifically designed to confuse the debate; for example, a project of the Sociedad de Agricultores (the pressure group of the large landowners and cattlemen) proposed yet another variant of Decree 290 featuring simultaneously two land classification systems, one the fourfold system of Decree 290 itself and the other the eight-fold system used by the Geographical Institute!

With Decree 290 clearly no longer in operation, the whole attempt started by the Currie report to coax owners into cultivating their lands through monetary penalties had proven abortive. Yet it was to be expected that the collapse of this attempt would give an important opening to those who saw the only solution in the expropriation of the idle latifundios. For this reason and because of the impractical nature of Decree 290 (and of its proposed variants) a comparatively simple proposal was at last worked out in 1959 by a group of "pro-gressive capitalists" and was introduced into Congress. It provided for the levying of a so-called "territorial tax" of 2 per cent on all rural properties. This tax would replace (by multiplying it by five) the old land tax (*impuesto predial*) of 4 per thousand, but unlike the latter it was to entitle the payer to a tax credit against his tax on income from agricultural activities. As a result only those who did not earn a fairly good income from their landholdings would be hurt: the tax would in effect be levied on properties that failed to yield income. Here was a simple proposal which in this form had never been put forward by any foreign expert.

The proponents of this measure realized that it could be frustrated if lands were not assessed at realistic values. They fell back on Vi-llaveces' device of self-assessment combined with the threat of expropri-ation at the declared value.

In November 1959, President Lleras gave strong support to this pro-posal with an address to a "National Peasant Congress" held in Bogotá. After having castigated those who merely held land in the hope that public highway construction and other works, paid for by the taxpayer, would make millionaires out of them, he went on to say that there were two solutions to the land problem: "Either the forcible distribution of landed wealth with the natural violence that this method brings with it, or the patient, continuous and inflexible action of the state through taxation which converts the land into a means of production, whose ownership is justified by the income it produces. Faced with this alternative I am sure that Colombians shall not hesitate."[30]

They did! Congress apparently was in no mood to approve a tax that would really hurt, and within the government itself there was resistance. The National Planning Council, which, in principle, was to coordinate not only development planning but economic policy as well, criticized the proposal as insufficiently "technical" and pro-posed an alternative: to impute to landowners a "presumed income" of the order of 7 to 10 per cent of the value of their land and to tax them in accordance with the normal progression of the income tax.[31] This is indeed an attractive formula: with the territorial tax proposal the accumulation of idle land would not be without cost, but the cost would be far less irksome, in comparison to his other tax burdens, for a taxpayer in the higher brackets (the top bracket rate of the Colombian income tax is 51%) than for middle or low income groups. It will be recalled that this proposal had been advanced some four years earlier by the Bank mission.[32] Intellectually the most attractive of the many variants of the same basic idea that were being discussed, it was least effective in gaining political support; it was not even introduced into Parliament as a proposed bill. The member of the Planning Council who had espoused the "presumed income" scheme actually became Minister of Agriculture for a short period in mid–1960, but at that time an entirely new, major effort was already under-way to satisfy the craving for some action on the land problem.

The Handicaps of Land Tax Schemes

If we date the effort at using the taxing powers of the state to force idle lands into production from the original Currie proposal, we can look back on a ten-year period of intense intellectual activity, abun-dant legislative experimenting, . . . and rather complete futility, at least if one discounts the effect that continuous public discussion of the issue may have had on the incriminated landowners. Why did this ten-year effort have so little to show in the end?

The most obvious explanation is the one we are already familiar with: the ruling class is too short-sighted and egoistic to seriously undertake a program of self-taxation, even though such a measure may eventually reduce the probability of expropriation. However, in the light of this decade of experience, one cannot find this explanation wholly satisfying. Granting that the foreign experts who recommended the measures were naïve and oblivious to the realities of class interests, why would there have been so much tinkering with such measures? Were not the various Ministers of Finance or Agriculture who were proposing unacceptable measures or creating unenforceable ones aware that they were playing with fire, that the failure of these pro-posals toward which they seemed to conspire would lead to demands for far more drastic measures? Moreover, it is simply not true that inaction and failure were planned in advance by the participants in what admittedly turned out to be an elaborate non-decision-making process.

Alternative or additional hypotheses are therefore needed. Let us first look at the specific characteristics of the task: it is desired to establish monetary penalties for holding idle or underdeveloped agri-cultural land. One trouble with this task is that it allows too much play to intellectual creativity and ingenuity of a rather low order (therefore sometimes referred to as "gadgetry"). There are so many possible solutions (self-assessment, imposition of additional tax payments for under-utilization somehow defined, taxation of potential income or of presumed income, territorial tax, etc.) that decision-makers tend to countermand the decisions of their predecessors in favor of a more "technical," or less "anti-technical," solution or cannot make up their mind between two equally attractive proposals.[33]

A more important reason for the lack of decisive and consistent action was that everything depended in the end on the quality of the cadastral survey or of some other method of classifying and surveying land and land values. It is perhaps the feeling that a realistic survey is beyond hope that accounts for the byzantine discussions about schemes, all of which are worthless without good survey work. A typical vicious circle is faced here: land taxation is ineffective without realistic land values, yet the administrative effort needed to make a reliable survey will hardly be forthcoming unless the prospective yield of land taxation makes such an effort worthwhile for the national authorities. One way in which the vicious circle can be broken is by technical advances in survey work, such as aerial infrared photography at high altitudes which would materially shorten the time within which an accurate survey can be completed. As a result, the effort may suddenly seem worthwhile to policy-makers with a rather short time-horizon.

Perhaps the cardinal weakness of the tax approach lies in the very simple fact that additional taxation is usually found acceptable only when there is an imperious need for specific new expenditures. Taxes are meant to defray expenditures and the decisive political push for them comes from those who have an interest in making the expenditures, whether they be interest groups or the state itself (for example, in the case of war). In our case, the link between the proposed measures and the beneficiaries was indirect and unclear to the group directly involved: the landless peasant, for example, could not perceive that land taxation would tend to make landowners more willing to sell or rent land to him and might also depress land prices. As for the small farmers, they were openly hostile to the various tax projects. In spite of provisions exempting them, they feared additional taxation far more than they were seduced by the vague prospect that land might become easier and cheaper to buy or rent from the large landowners. The 1960 parliamentary elections confirmed the basic unpopularity of the proposals. The victory of the Ospina faction of the Conservative Party over the Laureano Gómez wing was widely attributed to a swing in the vote of owner-cultivators in the coffee-producing Departments out of apprehension—actively fanned by the candidates of the Ospina group—over the land tax proposals that were being proposed by the government whose Conservative members were at that time primarily identified with the Laureano wing.

An Exception: The Cauca Valley Corporation

The maxim that to push through a tax one must first have or invent a good reason for spending the tax proceeds is confirmed by a successful experience with land taxation carried out in Colombia during the fifties in the Cauca Valley. Here a regional development agency, the "CVC," was established in 1954, after having been enthusiastically promoted by a group of prominent citizen-businessmen of Cali who had brought in David Lilienthal as a consultant.[34] The corporation retained the services of three consulting engineering firms, two from the United States and one from Colombia, and an investment program consisting primarily of large-scale hydroelectric installations and irrigation and drainage works was proposed in the hope that financing would be forthcoming from the International Bank and the national government. In the course of 1955–56, however, the fledgling organization saw this hope founder: first, the Bank decided to suspend new lending to Colombia as it lost confidence in the Rojas Pinilla regime; secondly, that regime itself became increasingly hostile to the CVC, partly because it favored the poorer Eastern provinces of the country and partly because the administrators and directors of the CVC were known to be out of sympathy with the Rojas clique.

Faced with a financial vacuum, the corporation had to lower its sights from the originally planned large-scale projects to pilot flood control and irrigation schemes that would require far smaller outlays and whose cost could be recuperated rapidly by assessing the landowners who benefited. Even so, there was need for initial financing and the CVC decided that it would try to obtain authority for doubling the 4 per thousand tax on rural properties and for earmarking the proceeds for its own operations. Normal legislative procedures having been suspended, a decree of the central government was then all that was needed to enact the additional tax. The Rojas Pinilla government acceded to the request, partly because it felt that after having created the CVC with great fanfare it had to do something for it, partly because it enjoyed taxing the Valle "money-bags," and partly because it secretly hoped that through the tax the CVC and the Valle authorities would make themselves thoroughly unpopular with important circles. A determined battle was indeed fought over the tax, with the traditional landowners and cattlemen in strenuous opposition. But support was forthcoming not only from the progressive business circles (industrialists, sugar interests, contractors, etc.) who were the original promoters of the Authority, but also from the Church, labor groups and public opinion at large where the CVC idea had become popular. The tax was decreed in January 1956,[35] but the battle over it was vigorously renewed after the downfall of Rojas in 1957, since legislative approval was now required for the tax to remain on the books. The enemies of the tax now tried to present it as one more arbitrary act of the Rojas government. The CVC compromised to the extent of acquiescing to a reduction from the 4 per thousand rate to 3 per thousand and of changing the tax partially into a compulsory bond issue. In this form the measure was converted into law in 1959.[36]

As a result of the tax, the CVC had of course acquired a considerable interest in realistic land assessments and it entered into a special contract with the Geographical Institute designed to accelerate survey work in the Valle Department. It thus demonstrated that while a land tax can hardly become effective without realistic assessment, the latter may follow rather than precede the institution of the tax itself. However, the tax can hardly be expected to muster political support unless the public is aware of and sympathetic to the uses to which the money is going to be put. The idea that public funds are usually wasted is deeply ingrained in Latin America; this is also the principal reason for which taxes, and especially new taxes, are so frequently earmarked for special *fomento* purposes, in violation of the rules of orthodox budgetary doctrine.

The Colombian experience is by no means unique. Whatever redistributive effects progressive income taxation has had in the advanced industrial countries has been a by-product rather than the primary motive. The latter was supplied by some compelling need to increase revenue, usually during wartime. External war, or the threat of war, is thus frequently the condition for achieving a *peaceful* redistribution of income within the country. Without such an external threat and the consequent imperious need to increase *total* expenditures, redistribution is far more likely to take place directly, i.e., through the have-nots seizing the belongings of the haves, than indirectly through taxation of the rich.

The peculiar difficulty facing land taxation as a means of improving the pattern of land utilization and ownership is not so much that it is directed against the "ruling class"—legislation taking a good slap at the "oligarch" is by no means uncommon in Latin America. The weakness of land taxation is that while it arouses the opposition of the landed interests, it does not hold out an obvious appeal to any other important social group.

NOTES TO SELECTION 25

[1]"The existence of large unutilized properties which could be cultivated must be curtailed. To this end, in addition to short terms at the end of which property rights are forfeited, a progressive and differential tax should be imposed so as to tax idle lands more severely than cultivated lands." Statement on agrarian policy of April 11, 1935, in A. López, *La política oficial*, II, 60.

[2]International Bank for Reconstruction and Development (Washington, 1950), Chaps. 5 and 18.

[3]*Ibid.*, pp. 62–63.

[4]*Ibid.*, p. 383.

[5]*Ibid.*, p. 385.

[6]*Revista Nacional de Agricultura,* January, 1951, pp. 8 ff.

[7]Comité de Desarrollo Económico, *Informe final,* September, 1950–August, 1951 (Bogotá: Imprenta Banco de la República), pp. 114–16.

[8]Unpublished document supplied to the author by Lauchlin Currie.

[9]Comité, *Informe,* pp. 116–17.

[10]P. Baran, "On the Political Economy of Backwardness," *The Manchester School,* January, 1952, reprinted in A. N. Agarwala and S. P. Singh, eds., *The Economics of Underdevelopment* (Bombay: Oxford University Press, 1958), p. 89.

[11]"Report and Recommendations on the Tax System of Colombia with a Short Chapter on Budget Presentation and Procedure," *United Nations Technical Assistance Programme* (New York, 1952), p. 52.

[12]As reported by Solon Barraclough, in "Major Land Tenure Problems of Latin America," *Latin American USOM's Seminar on Agrarian Reform,* February, 21–24, 1961 (Washington: International Cooperation Administration), p. 41.

[13]Art. 20 of Decree 2317 of 1953.

[14]In a memorandum which was given to the writer by the director of Colombia's cadastral survey, Dr. Alberto Pardo Pardo, it is traced back to the Roman king Servius Tullius!

[15]Alejandro López, "El retorno a la tierra," *Revista Nacional de Agricultura,* August, 1939, pp. 524–25.

[16]The quantitative importance of these actions in the total picture of Colombian agriculture cannot be ascertained. There were strong market forces working in the direction of better utilization of land. However, the awareness was widespread that land was being acquired by the rising middle class and that land and cattle operations were engaged in by industrialists for purposes of tax avoidance; and this fact is of importance in our context.

[17]Ministerio de Agricultura, *Memoria al Congreso Nacional 1957–58* (Bogotá: Imprenta Banco de la República), I, 18.

[18]International Bank for Reconstruction and Development, *The Agricultural Development of Colombia* (Washington, D.C., 1956), p. 5.

[19]*Ibid.*, p. 56.

[20]*Ibid.*, pp. 66–67.

[21]*Ibid.*, p. 67.

[22]Ministerio de Agricultura, *Memoria,* I, 21.

[23]Artificial pastures were to be considered "cultivation" provided they were "technically cultivated" and used for "intensive livestock raising duly proved."

[24]Article 18.

[25]Article 19 and 20.

[26]The provisions of Decree 290 on tenancy contracts may also have been of help. To avoid the famous disputes about improvements, which had such a long and tortuous history and which made landowners reluctant to rent out their lands, the contracting parties were permitted to stipulate which crops were to be grown and to exclude the landowner's liability for any improvements unwanted by him (Art. 26). Decree 291, issued together with Decree 290, supplemented by simplifying the procedure for evicting tenants who violated tenancy contracts.

[27]Decree 198 of 1957, later confirmed by Law 26 of 1959.

[28]Such behavior would be a counterpart to the Pigou effect according to which the propensity to consume increases with larger asset holdings. Here it is the propensity to produce that would be so influenced.

[29]*Programa de desarrollo económico del Valle del Magdalena y Norte de Colombia* (Bogotá: Informe de una Misión dirigida por Lauchlin Currie, Edt. Agra, 1960), p. 32.

[30]*El Espectador* (Bogotá), November 27, 1959.

[31]This program was incorporated into the "Economic Platform" of the government by the Planning Council and officially adopted in February 1960. Cf. *Legislación Económica* (Bogotá), April 18, 1960, p. 102.

[32]See pp. 126–27.

[33]It is reported that a British commission, sitting early in this century, had agreed to adopt the decimal system, but that it could not reach an agreement on the question whether the pound was to be maintained at its existing value and was to be divided into 100 new pennies, or whether it was to be redefined as 100 old pennies. A psychologist may of course assert that the trouble with the members of the commission was that they really wanted to hold on to the British system. But the fact that two equivalent solutions were available is of some importance in that it permitted them to gratify this wish while pretending to themselves and to the world to be reform-minded.

[34]In Spanish, CVC stands for Cauca, Valle del Cauca, and Caldas, the three Departments over which the authority of the Corporation (its full name is *Corporación Regional Autónoma del Cauca*) was originally supposed to extend. Eventually, in large part because of opposition to the tax measures about to be discussed, both Cauca and Caldas withdrew from the agency so that its authority and activity have been almost wholly restricted to the Valle Department. This Department, however, contains by far the largest portion of the river valley which is to be benefited under the regional development scheme.

[35]Decree 160 of January 31, 1956.

[36]Law 25 of May 30, 1959. Several of these changes had already been made by the military junta (Decree 282 of October 31, 1957) and were merely confirmed by this law.

26

The Role of Agricultural Land
Taxes in Japanese Development

by the Food and Agriculture Organization
of the United Nations*

IN THE widest sense, the interest of the Japanese experience for the developing Asian countries lies in the fact that Japan was the first Asian country which succeeded in bringing about a striking transformation in the productivity of its agriculture—whether measured in terms of land or labor. Despite other differences, the point of commencement for Japan in this process was much the same as for other countries of the region—a traditional agriculture characterized by small-scale subsistence farming and dominated by social relationships of a hierarchical or feudal character. The level of productivity of Japanese agriculture prior to the Meiji restoration—as measured by yields per acre or per man—was probably not very different from, or at best only moderately higher than, levels of productivity which persist to this day in many parts of the region.[1]

In a more specific sense, however, what is of interest to other countries is not so much the fact of this transformation in agricultural productivity. It is rather that it took place within a traditional framework of small-scale farming. The average size of the Japanese farm was approximately 1.0 hectare in 1878 and 0.8 hectare in 1962. At the same time, the average yield per hectare, in rice farming for instance, rose from 1.8 metric tons per hectare in 1868–82 to 4.0 metric tons (husked rice) in 1956–60. This is in marked contrast to other countries which have undergone rapid economic development. There, the rise

*Food and Agriculture Organization of the United Nations, Economic and Social Commission, *Agricultural Development in Modern Japan,* Commission Papers WFC/63/CP/IIC/1 (February 15, 1963), pp. 1–5, 9–11, 18–21. This paper is part of a comprehensive survey of agricultural development in modern Japan and was printed separately for the World Food Congress, organized by FAO, and held at Washington, June, 1963. The full report is available from the World Food Congress and from the Japan FAO Association, Tokyo. Reprinted here with the kind permission of the Food and Agricultural Organization.

in agricultural productivity has been associated with fairly large farms, or with farms whose size was actively increased—whether by opening up new land for large-scale cultivation, enclosure movements, or by the introduction of collective or cooperative farming.

This aspect of the development of Japanese agriculture—the maintenance of small-scale farming—is of deep interest to the developing countries of Asia today. In these countries the prevailing system of agriculture is one in which a relatively large rural population subsists on small-scale units of production. There is a pressing need to raise the productivity of agriculture to meet the food needs of a rising population and also as an essential part of general economic development. At the same time, however, the tempo of population growth today is often so fast—faster than that experienced by Japan—and the problem of finding employment for the growing work force so great, that these countries can seldom countenance methods of raising agricultural productivity which involve a marked reduction in the size of the rural population. On the contrary it is probable that as a rule the numbers of people dependent on agriculture will increase for some decades to come.

Herein lies, perhaps, the major significance of Japanese agriculture to the countries of Asia. Japan was able to raise agricultural productivity without a significant reduction of the total agricultural workforce, and within the system of small-scale farming. Between 1878 and 1912 the total agricultural workforce in Japan changed only slightly from 15½ million to 14½ million persons. In other words, although the expansion in the non-agricultural sectors of the economy was exceptionally rapid, it sufficed only to absorb the increment to the total workforce brought about by population growth. It was not rapid enough to cause a significant reduction in the agricultural workforce. If Japan had had to face a population explosion without a rapid growth of non-farm occupations the rapid growth of agricultural productivity would not have been possible.

How Japan succeeded in increasing the productivity of agriculture on small farms with the existing workforce is, therefore, the central point of interest in the Japanese story. There are, however, other points of interest as well. The transformation of productivity, especially during the early period, did not for instance involve the adoption of capital intensive methods of production on any large scale. This made possible an economy of capital resources in the process of agricultural development—a point which is of natural interest to countries which are relatively short of capital.[2]

Moreover, the Japanese experience illustrates how agriculture was able to fulfil its traditional role in the strategy of overall development. Japanese agriculture, in the course of the transformation in productivity, was able to assume the role of an earner of foreign exchange, a provider of investment resources for other sectors, and a supplier of raw materials for industry, as well as meeting for some decades the rapidly growing urban demand for foodstuffs. That all this was possible within a system of small-scale farming is, once again, the point of special interest in the Japanese example.

Nonetheless, raising the productivity of agriculture involved a number of major changes. There was, in the first instance, the need for changes in technology, for the introduction of methods of production which made high yields compatible with small-scale cultivation. There was also the need to provide the farmer with the incentive to increase production; this involved far-reaching changes in the system of land tenure, in systems of land taxation, and in the impact of monetary forces. Above all, there was the need to develop and transmit the knowledge of technology to the farming population; the creation of an elaborate network of research institutions and of extension and educational programs is an intrinsic part of the development of Japanese agriculture. The sections that follow pursue also these elements in the Japanese story. They review the several phases of the historical experience of Japan from the beginnings of the agricultural transformation to the present, and attempt to analyse the significance of the numerous factors that played their part in this remarkable transformation of a traditional agriculture.

We have stressed that in many respects the Japanese experience was unique, for the economic, social and traditional background in every country differs in some essentials from that of every other country. The historical setting of the early stages of Japanese development also differed sharply from the setting in which newly developing countries are only now embarking on economic development. For example, Japan's first steps were taken at a time of rapidly growing agricultural trade when it was probably less difficult than today to increase earnings from agricultural exports. The concept of welfare had scarcely penetrated Asia in the nineteenth century and some measures used in Japan might today be considered politically impossible. As already mentioned, population grew not much faster in Japan than in European countries during their early years of development, never reaching the explosive level common in developing countries today. All these factors make relatively more difficult the task of countries only now setting out on economic development. Yet they have some counterbalancing advantage, notably in access to a much more advanced technology than existed in the nineteenth century. There is also an inflow of foreign aid and investment which may fall far short of their needs, but is certainly much larger than any that Japan enjoyed.

Another obvious difference is climate. Japan is a well-watered and temperate country, while most developing countries today are in arid or in wet tropical climates. It is difficult to assess the significance of this difference, but it is noteworthy that Japanese methods were successfully transplanted to the very different climate of Taiwan, though only after a fairly lengthy period of research. Japan probably had an advantage in that the main body of agricultural science is related to temperate conditions. But corresponding advantages e.g. faster growth and greater opportunities of double cropping in tropical climates, or better control of water in arid irrigated areas may ultimately compensate for the initial disadvantages of most developing countries today.

All these are evident differences between Japan and most developing countries today. Our object in noting them is not to attempt any assessment of advantages and disadvantages, which could only be fruitless. It is rather to stress that the Japanese experience can seldom be transferred to other countries without considerable adaptation. This, however, in no way lessens its significance for those countries who seek to learn from Japan's remarkable achievement.

Agriculture in Japan: The Historical Pattern of Development

Modern economic growth began in Japan sometime in the late 1860's—[over] one hundred years ago. A vital part of this development throughout the entire period was the growth of agriculture. Although agriculture grew, developed, and changed during this entire century, there were certain distinct phases in the growth process which can be identified. These phases permit the splitting of the long period into shorter sub-periods, and can lead to a clearer analysis and understanding of the historical events.

According to our examination of the data, and in keeping with the text prepared by the Japanese experts, the development of Japanese agriculture went through three phases:

1. A period of rapid growth lasting from approximately the Meiji Restoration (1868) until World War I;

2. A period of slower growth lasting from the end of World War I through World War II;

3. And finally, a renewed period of rapid growth, starting almost immediately after the end of World War II and continuing to the present time.

Let us now examine the major characteristics of these phases.

The Initial Phase of Rapid Growth

According to all the relevant indicators (shown in the statistical appendix) agriculture developed extremely rapidly during these years. The annual growth rate of agricultural net output averaged almost

2.3 per cent, and the expansion rate of food crops was high enough to outstrip the growth rate of population. Land productivity nearly doubled, while labor productivity more than doubled. While these events were in progress, the absolute number of people engaged in agriculture remained more or less constant. At the same time, of course, the non-agricultural sectors of the economy were beginning their rapid development. Growth in the non-agricultural sector is somewhat outside our immediate subject, but it must be pointed out that during this initial phase agriculture and non-agriculture developed in relative harmony. Both developed rapidly, and agriculture was not lagging behind the other sectors of the economy.

The impressive achievements in agriculture had very important consequences for the rest of the economy, then undergoing initial industrialization. Japanese agriculture was able, at this time, to feed a growing urban population, and to minimize the pressures of inflation stemming from possible food shortages. In short, demand and supply of food grew more or less in equilibrium—and this was due almost exclusively to the development of domestic resources. But this is not all. We must also take notice of the great increase in the export of agricultural products during this phase. Tea and silk registered great gains, and thereby provided the necessary foreign exchange with which Japan could purchase the tools of industrialization. Furthermore, at this time, the central government depended on agriculture for most of its revenue, and central government expenditures played a crucial role in modernizing the country. These last points are worthy of somewhat more extended examination.

Before the Meiji Restoration the fiscal structure of Japan was based on rice taxes paid in kind by the peasants to their feudal lords. It has been estimated that the peasants at that time turned over approximately 35 per cent of their rice crops to the feudal rulers, and this constituted the major revenue of the entire samurai class. In the early 1870's the new central government instituted a new land tax essentially designed to lay its hands on the part of the agricultural product which had previously gone to the feudal rulers. The new land tax was assessed in terms of money, and had to be paid by the landowners. It has been estimated that the rate of taxation remained at pre-Restoration levels, in other words at about 35 per cent of the rice crop. This new land tax siphoned off much of the "surplus"[3] generated within agriculture, and was the principal source of revenue for the government. It may seem, therefore, that the pre-and-post Restoration situation was more or less the same, but this would be a serious misunderstanding of the situation. In the first place, the new government was intent on starting industrialization, and thus the "surplus" was used productively. This had not been the case in feudal Japan. Secondly, agriculture in general was growing rapidly and the amount of potential "surplus" was getting larger all the time. The government took a relatively constant amount, allowing the landowners (as distinguished from the tenants) to accumulate more capital. Many of these private funds accumulated by the landowners eventually found their way into modern industries. Again, the situation in feudal Japan had been different, because agriculture had not been developing nearly as rapidly.

We have shown that agriculture in fact developed rapidly, and also that its development was very important for the rest of the economy. We come now to a more difficult question: what factors made these happenings possible?

Let us note, first of all, that the increases in output and productivity were based on the traditional patterns of production inherited, in the main, from the Tokugawa period. The small family farm, averaging about 1 hectare per household, the distribution of land between owner-cultivators and tenants paying high rents—all of these characteristics were maintained during the first phase. There was thus considerable stability in the organization of agriculture side-by-side with rapid progress in agricultural productivity.

What were the elements making for progress? These took two forms, and we may call one technical and the other institutional, although there is obviously a considerable amount of overlapping between the two. On the technical side, we must begin by noticing certain key improvements in Japanese agricultural practice in keeping with the small unit of production. Two stand out: land improvement (including better irrigation and drainage facilities and some land reclamation), and still more, superior seeds, better methods of crop cultivation, and increased input of manures and fertilizers. (See input index in Appendix I [not included in this volume].) One must notice especially that the second type of improvement involved some increases in working capital but only very small increases in fixed capital, and was therefore very much in keeping with Japan's factor endowments: much labor and little capital. It is most interesting to note that in the early years after the Restoration, there was some interest in borrowing European and American agricultural techniques. In general, they were not easily transplantable, either because much of the Japanese borrowing was inappropriate or because the conditions in Japan were so different. Whatever the case, as a result of the failures the Japanese were forced to rely mainly on their own knowledge and abilities. The technical advances at this time—the so called "Meiji Technology"—in reality became a combination of indigenous know-how and very selective borrowing from the West.

Why did these improvements come at this particular moment in history? In attempting to answer this question we realize immediately that agriculture cannot be treated in isolation. So far we have stressed the support which agriculture gave to the rest of the economy, and we must now stress the support which other sectors of the economy and society gave to agriculture. We may begin conveniently with institutional changes. First of all, the Meiji Restoration brought to power a central government dedicated to modern economic growth. This government *unified* the country for the first time—in *fact* as well as in name. This may require some amplification. Pre-modern Japan was divided into over 200 domains ruled by feudal barons. These barons were vassals of a central ruler, the Tokugawa shogun, who ruled in the name of the emperor, although he was in fact much more powerful than the emperor. At that time, the degree of centralization was extremely limited, especially in the economic sphere. There were trade and travel restrictions between the domains, and the domestic market was limited through these measures. The Restoration abolished these and other restrictions, and thereby considerably enlarged the scope of the domestic market and increased demand. But unification was important in another sense. At the time of Restoration or unification, Japan had advanced agricultural areas (e.g. Kinki) and backward areas (e.g. Tohoku), and it was one of the special virtues of the new government that it helped to apply the more advanced methods on a national basis. This was done in part through the improvement of communications and the abolishing of interdomain barriers. The process was furthered by an extensive education program, extension services, and the like. It was also helped by the further development and improvement of indigenous agricultural methods, now sometimes aided by modern (imported) science. The government was active in all of these areas. It is true that furthering industry may have been its primary objective at this time, but one does not get the impression that agriculture was neglected.

Agriculture was also fortunate in possessing an active and forward-looking entrepreneurial class—the owner—cultivators or landlords before they yielded to the temptations of absentee landownership. At the time of the Restoration the peasantry was given the land on a formal basis (informally they had been limited proprietors even in the Tokugawa Era), and most of them became owner-cultivators. Insofar as they had tenants—and this must have been true of quite a few owners—they were interested in raising and stabilizing yields. Since the land tax was a fixed amount, based on the value of their land, they were also interested in producing more as individuals. These desires were heightened by continual increases in the price of rice. Mention should also be made of the fact that among the owners there was a significant minority of educated "middle-class" people. This was an important leadership group, and also a vital funnel for government policy. That these people, at this time, lived on the land

and worked side-by-side with smaller owners and tenants must also have contributed to their effectiveness.

*   *   *   *   *

The mechanism for extracting a "surplus" from agriculture for economic development was provided, in large part, as indicated in other parts of this study, by the tenurial and other institutional changes introduced after the Meiji Restoration. The extraction of revenue by the government through the land tax and of rents and profits on marketing and credit operations by an emergent class of landlords were the principal instruments in forcing a "surplus" out of the small farmer. The resources mobilized in this way were undoubtedly great. As shown elsewhere the government was dependent on the land tax for the major part of its revenue during the initial phase of the Meiji Restoration. The qualitative aspects of the process were also of importance. Resources extracted by the government by way of land taxes were applied to economic development, including the provision of services and facilities to the agricultural sector. This stood in some contrast to the use of resources under the more feudal disposition of the pre-Meiji era. The productive investment of savings, however, was not confined to the government. The new landlord class itself was inclined towards the making of investments in agriculture and industry.

The Japanese example, dating from the later nineteenth and early twentieth century, may offer no exact parallel for countries in search of resources for development in the present day in a different political context. Yet there are some points about the Japanese case that need to be noted. The mechanism of extracting savings from small-scale agriculture operated in a background of rising productivity and applied essentially to the increment to incomes that took place in the process of growth. There is little to indicate that this mechanism resulted in a worsening of the low living standards of the small farmers, though it did mean that the improvement in rural consumption was less than the increase in productivity. Further, the land taxes and rents were of such a nature as not to impede too much the incentives to additional production. The land tax, and rents, were generally fixed in absolute terms.[4] This implied that they did not damage the incentives to increased production on the part of the cultivator. In periods of inflation and high food prices, in particular, the burden of the land tax and to some extent of rents was substantially reduced.

All this apart, there is the moral of the Japanese experience which remains of significance to many countries. Without external resources or surpluses from other sectors of the economy there is no alternative but that agriculture should provide the "surpluses" needed for the initial phase of economic development. This role of agriculture could, of course, progressively be modified during the later phases. In Japan itself at the present time the surpluses for investment accrue largely from the industrial and other sectors. Indeed it is doubtful whether postwar Japanese agriculture during the current period with price supports at a relatively high level is in fact a net contributor of savings to the economy as a whole.

It has been noted that Japan needed a rapid rate of expansion in the non-agricultural sectors of the economy merely to absorb the increment in the workforce resulting from population growth. A substantial reduction in the agricultural workforce was thus not possible until very recently, and this implied in turn that Japan could not consider radical departures from the small-scale system of farming. That Japan succeeded in raising the productivity of her agriculture within the system of small-scale farming is, as mentioned repeatedly, of particular interest to the countries of Asia.

The rate of population growth in Japan, ranging from 0.7 to 1.5 per cent annually, did not differ greatly from the rates that characterized European countries as they passed through their demographic transition. And yet a more rapid expansion of the non-agricultural sectors was needed in Japan to absorb the increment to the workforce resulting from population growth in the countryside. This was because the rate of absorption of labor from agriculture depends both on the rate of expansion of the non-agricultural sector and on the existing share or weight of non-agricultural employment in the total workforce. In the developing countries of Europe the non-agricultural sectors already weighed quite heavily in the total workforce so that a fairly moderate rate of growth of those sectors was sufficient to provide employment for large numbers of workers migrating from the countryside and to lead eventually to an absolute reduction of the farm workforce. But in Japan the agricultural population still bulked so large in the total that a much more rapid expansion of the non-farm sector was needed to prevent a further increase in an agricultural workforce which was already large relative to the cultivable land available.

In many of the countries of Asia today population is rising at a considerably faster rate than during the corresponding phase in Japan. And in most of these countries, as in Japan during the early years of Meiji, the agricultural workforce represents an extremely large share of the total. Hence in this respect these countries face an even more formidable problem than did Meiji Japan. Even if these countries were to attain a rate of expansion in the other sectors of the economy which corresponds to the pace of the Japanese performance, this would not suffice to absorb the increment to the working population or to prevent a continued increase in the size of the rural workforce.

The conclusion that emerges is apparent. The countries of Asia, given an accelerated pace of population growth, would require an even faster rate of expansion in the non-agricultural sectors of the economy in order to reproduce the conditions which governed the success of Japanese agriculture. Clearly, if such expansion could only be brought about through the medium of large-scale industries requiring heavy capital investments and located in the urban areas the problem facing these countries would be formidable indeed, if not actually hopeless. There is, however, another aspect of the Japanese experience that is of relevance in this connection.

One of the important elements which enabled the non-agricultural sector in Japan to absorb the increment to the workforce resulting from population growth relates to the pattern of development of this sector. It is a salient feature of Japanese economic development that the growth of the non-agricultural sector was also characterized by the application of relatively labour-intensive techniques of production. This is particularly true of the initial phase of expansion up to about the first decade of the present century, and although capital-intensive techniques and industries came into prominence later, labour-intensive techniques once again assumed (side by side with capital-intensive techniques) a new importance in the postwar burst of industrial expansion.

This factor is of special relevance to the problem of population growth and the rural workforce in two ways. First, the growth of labour-intensive techniques in the non-agricultural sector increased its absorptive power and helped to keep down the members of the rural workforce. This would clearly have been more difficult to achieve had growth in the non-agricultural sector been of a more capital intensive type. Second, and perhaps no less significant, some of the important industries in the non-agricultural sector were actually located in the rural areas. This is true not only of the industries depending on the materials of domestic agriculture—food processing, silk reeling and weaving etc. but extended to industries of a more varied character. This result was facilitated by the speedy development of transportation and communications, and above all by the revolution in power brought about by electricity.

*   *   *   *   *

Land Tenure

In the Tokugawa feudal society, the peasants were bound to the land they cultivated. They had no right to sell or mortgage the land. There were restrictions even on the kind of crops they might raise.

After the Restoration, all land was made freely cultivable in 1871. In 1872 it was declared to be freely transferable, and land titles were issued to all occupants affirming their private ownership. However, having done this, the matter was left to the mercy of an unrestrained operation of the money economy. In consequence the place of feudalism was taken up by a new landlordism.[5]

For the next fifty or more years, relations between the landlord and the tenant were governed by the *laissez-faire* concept of freedom of contract. The new landlordism got a flying start even as peasant proprietorship was being established. A certain amount of tenancy existed even in the Tokugawa period, but much of it enjoyed traditional privileges, particularly in the matter of security of tenure. In its anxiety to create clear ownership titles in land, government neglected many forms of privileged tenancy which then existed and in effect reduced nearly all tenants to the status of ordinary tenants. Consequently, even early in the Meiji Era, nearly one-third of the cultivable land is estimated to have been tenant-cultivated. Secondly, government equally neglected numerous communal rights in land and instead declared all communal land, or in fact all land to which private title could not be clearly established, to be the state property. State property was interpreted in the same manner as private property and subsequently government sold some of the former communal land to private persons with means and this too created conditions for landlordism.

After the feudal tithe and dues were abolished, government levied a new land tax in 1873. It was a tax payable in cash and was initially assessed at 3 per cent of the price of the land. It amounted to about one-third the product of the land and the burden was probably not much less than that of the feudal tithe and dues of the earlier period. As it was to be paid in cash, it had its lien on anything and everything which the farmer possessed including the land which he had newly come to own. The heavy burden of the land tax, the need to pay it in cash, the unrestricted rights of alienation granted and the concept of freedom of contract all combined to create conditions which forced many a small farmer to sell his land and accept tenancy under a landowner. The process was typical of what later happened in other Asian countries where private ownership and unrestricted rights of alienation were created and then exposed to the free operation of a *laissez-faire* money economy.

The process was accelerated by the early development of an inflationary situation. In its initial years the new government had to incur large expenditures, notably the pensions which were paid in compensation to a large number of feudal lords and their vassals, and large military expenditures to keep them under control. At the same time the government was pushing ahead with a large programme of industrial expansion. The inflationary conditions became acute during 1879–81, as a result of civil war and the lump-sum issue of state bonds for pension commutation, and commodity prices, particularly that of rice, rose steeply. Under these conditions, it became increasingly profitable to lease out the land with rents payable in rice, though the land tax was to be paid in cash. More and more of the larger landowners therefore began to lease out their lands.

Then the tide turned. From 1881 to 1885, government adopted a deliberate deflationary policy and commodity prices came down. Even so tenancy continued to expand. Farmers were hit hard and the smaller farmers found it difficult to pay the land tax. Many ran into debt and finally lost their lands to bigger landowners. The number of farm households declined from 4.3 million in 1882 to 3.8 million in 1886.

After the stabilization of the currency in 1885, there followed a period of prosperity and agricultural prices improved. They received a further impetus by another wave of inflationary finance caused by the outbreak of the Sino-Japanese War in 1894 and one which was kept up through 1904 until the Russo-Japanese War. This period of 20 or 25 years was one of agricultural prosperity and one in which the landowning classes, both as owner-cultivators and rent-receivers, consolidated their position. With rising prices it was again profitable to rent lands in kind and to pay the land tax in cash, and tenancy continued to expand. Tenant-cultivated land rose from about 36.8 per cent of the cultivated area in 1883–84, to 40.0 per cent in 1892 and to 45.4 per cent in 1908.

Nevertheless it is this period, roughly from 1872 to 1908, which is of the greatest interest in the history of Japanese agricultural development, for in it great agricultural progress was achieved within the traditional framework of small-scale cultivation and under a land tenure which had grown merely out of the operation of a *laissez-faire* economy. Japanese experience suggests that in agricultural conditions closely akin to those still prevailing in many Asian countries, there is considerable scope for improving the productivity of land by an improved technology which need not be highly capital-intensive and which does not necessitate any fundamental alterations of the production structure.

Nevertheless, one should bear in mind two important conditions which the Japanese economy satisfied during this period. One is that though the technology by itself may have been relatively less capital intensive, its promotion and acceptance by farmers required an efficient system of agricultural education, extension, marketing and finance which often needed a very considerable capital outlay and heavy recurrent expenditure. The Japanese economy was able to find the needed funds and was able to build the necessary institutions for the purpose. Secondly, during the entire period the agricultural population in Japan did not grow, so that the agrarian problem in terms of man-land ratio did not at any time become more acute than before. This was achieved by a rapid enough growth of industry and of the entire non-farm sector. This certainly needed large capital outlays. The Japanese economy was again able to find the funds needed for the purpose.

Probably the most relevant fact in the context of development of predominantly agricultural economies of the other Asian countries is that in the initial stages of Japanese development, the major part of the funds needed both for agricultural and industrial development were supplied by agriculture. The Japanese economy was able to mobilize such large resources out of agriculture without any fundamental alteration in the production structure of agriculture by a combination of a purposeful Imperial government and an enterprising class of landowners who were part and parcel of the ruling power. The government took away about one-third of the agricultural product on all land by way of the land tax. On the tenant-cultivated land, which had expanded to almost half of the total cultivated area, the landlords collected about half of the agricultural product by way of rent, from which they paid tax. Fortunately, many landlords used their net receipts to good purpose too, namely, to improve agricultural production, marketing and finance, and to set up numerous small-scale industries in the countryside, particularly for processing farm products.

The landlords received their rental receipts in rice and were therefore interested in improving the quality of the rice they received and in obtaining a better price for it in the market. They therefore began to engage themselves in marketing of rice, and in a movement designed to improve the quality of rice. Their work in both these fields was of fundamental importance to the subsequent agricultural development in the country.

A natural extension of the marketing activities of landlords was the construction and management of rice warehouses and finally issue of "rice securities"; these were warehouse certificates which began to circulate as bills in the money market. A further extension was the setting up of local banks which extended low-interest long-term loans against the security of immovable assets of the farmer, mainly land. In 1897, the Land Mortgage Bank of Japan was established with the same objectives. The loans from these banking institutions began to be used for land improvement and reclamation projects. Many such land-adjustment projects were initiated by large landowners and were often financed through their own banking institutions. These projects led to increasing irrigation and drainage facilities and to generally improving the productive capacity of the soil.

Landlords also invested in small-scale industries particularly for agricultural processing, such as oil, flour, and paper mills, breweries and also spinning and weaving mills. Apart from its contribution to the overall industrial growth of the economy, the small-scale industry which was scattered all over the countryside served an important purpose in bridging the gap between agriculture and industry. On the one hand, it offered supplementary employment and income to agricultural workers, thus easing the pressure on the land. On the other hand, because the industry was located in the midst of agrarian communities, it kept down the social costs of industrialization and hence made comparatively cheap labour available to industry. Finally, by bringing industrial techniques and technology closer home to agriculture, it made the promotion of improved technology in agriculture easier.

In most of the other Asian countries, though the productivity of agriculture is presently not much higher than that prevailing in Japan at the time of the Meiji Restoration in 1868, the ideas of economic justice and social welfare have gone too far ahead to invite a combination of a purposeful Imperial government and enterprising landowners. That is also certainly not necessary. The important lesson to learn from the Japanese experience in the early period of its development is firstly that in the initial stages of the development of a predominantly agricultural economy, agriculture must provide the major part of the funds needed for development, and secondly that each such economy must devise its own institutions and an organization of its agrarian structure which will enable a "surplus" to be discovered and mobilized for use for economic development.

NOTES TO SELECTION 26

[1]Cf. Part III Chap. 25 [not included here] for some comparisons of present-day yields per acre in rice farming in several Asian countries. It is interesting to note that yields are relatively high in Korea and Taïwan where Japanese techniques have been transplanted.

[2]The improvement in productivity was, of course, closely associated with the increased use of working capital in the form of fertilizers, etc.

[3]The term "surplus" is used in this and following sections to mean any output in excess of that required in agriculture for continued production and the feeding of farm families.

[4]Nominally the land tax was a percentage of the value of the land, but as only one valuation was undertaken it was in effect a fixed tax base. The percentage was changed more than once during the Meiji period, but was not changed in later periods.

[5]"Landlordism" is used here to signify a rural economy dominated by large landowners, though at the beginning of the Meiji period a great many in fact farmed their own land. Tenancy spread rapidly, however, and within a few decades accounted for nearly half the cultivated area.

Part VI

Taxes on Foreign Trade

IMPORT duties and export taxes are the most important sources of government revenue in many underdeveloped countries, especially in the countries which have been labeled "the export economies" by Jonathan Levin, who is now with the International Monetary Fund's new Department of Fiscal Affairs. The export economies are those which are devoted primarily to the production of raw materials for export. In the first selection in this section, Dr. Levin points out how taxes on foreign trade have been used in the last two decades as instruments of revolt against the virtual control of these economies by two dominant groups—"the foreign factors of production," those men and companies that send their income out of the export economy back to the countries of their origin, and "the luxury importers," those who receive high export industry incomes and consume them within the country but who form too small a market to allow profitable production for their needs within the country and are thus obliged to import almost everything they consume. This discussion provides a broad and enlightening socioeconomic background to a consideration of the role of taxation in these economies.

The remaining three selections in this section cover a variety of problems connected with establishing a policy with respect to taxing foreign trade for a developing country. The original statement from the World Bank report on Nigeria, the subsequent detailed criticism by P. T. Bauer, and the reply by John Adler, a member of the World Bank mission to Nigeria, provide a stimulating discussion of a number of important and often neglected issues.

451

27

The Role of Taxation
in the Export Economies

*by Jonathan Levin**

RATHER than expel the foreign factors or luxury importers operating in an export industry, many new domestic factor governments have adopted measures which, while allowing the old pattern of export *production* or *trade* to continue, channel a larger portion of the export proceeds to other domestic factors. Through these measures, either the government itself has absorbed more of the export proceeds, through various forms of overt or implicit taxation, or the returns to private domestic factors engaged in the export industry have been legislatively increased.

ABSORPTION BY GOVERNMENT

The modern reaction against the export pattern of the past has swelled the government's share of export proceeds to great proportions in many export economies. In part, this increased stress on government revenues reflects the broad welfare goals which are generating the modern revolt and are being assigned to governments as the principal agencies available to carry them out.[1] This section is concerned only with that part of a government's export income derived from the *taxation* of the export industry—as distinct from its return for the performance of an export industry function. Such tax income may be levied through direct export taxes, other taxes, multiple exchange rates, or through government export monopolies, each of which are discussed in turn.

Export Taxes

The export tax is an old device but the reaction of the domestic factor governments has bent it to a new purpose. Previously, export taxes served many goals: (1) the protection of domestic industries processing or fabricating raw material exports, as in the old taxes on exports of raw hides and skins levied in India and Italian Somalia to encourage local tanning, or the Canadian export tax on lumber to encourage local pulp mills;[2] (2) the protection of processing industries elsewhere within the empire through preferential export taxes, as in the prohibitive export tax on Malayan tin ore not destined for smelters in Singapore, Australia, or Great Britain,[3] and the Philippine preferential export duty on Manila hemp destined for the United States, in effect from 1902 to 1913;[4] (3) conservation of resources, such as the export taxation of cows and heifers needed to build up local herds; (4) improvement of the quality of exports through heavy taxation of low-grade products, as by the heavy Angola export tax on uncleaned coffee; (5) the provision of fiscal revenues through moderate or low-level export taxes, sometimes—as in the old French Indo-China tax on rice exports—in lieu of a land tax;[5] and (6) the exploitation of a national monopoly position by the levying of export taxes which it was expected the foreign consumers would bear, as was the case with the export tax on Chilean nitrates while they held a world monopoly.[6] It was on this last point, of the possible incidence of export taxation upon foreign consumers, that most of the traditional discussion of export taxes centered. The export tax was generally discussed in works on international trade and public finance as symmetrical to the import duty, presenting a parallel problem; i.e., what portion of the tax is borne by the producing country and what portion by the consuming country.[7]

The possibility of passing an export tax forward to the consumers, it is generally agreed, increases with the inelasticity of foreign demand and the elasticity of domestic supply. Thus, in the case of a country with an elastic supply, holding a world monopoly on a product with an inelastic demand, most of an export tax might be paid by the foreign consumer. The inelastic demand, however, may be but a temporary phenomenon which a high export tax might help bring to an end by encouraging the development of substitutes and alternate sources of supply, as so many monopoly countries have learned. For a country which is only one small producer among many, the demand for its export is elastic, since any increase in price may drive its customers to other suppliers selling more cheaply at the world price. In this case the export tax is borne by the producers or others in the export country. The traditional examination of export taxes, then, focused on the possibility of shifting the tax burden to the foreign consumers, and benefiting the exporting country at their expense. This was not the orientation, however, of the newer export taxes levied by the new domestic factor governments.

With the reaction against the old export economy pattern the export tax was taken from its widely utilized old task of a moderate general levy[8]—often substituted for a land tax on small holders and an income tax on mining industries[9]—to become the instrument of heavy government absorption of foreign factor and, to a somewhat lesser extent, luxury importer income. The export tax had sometimes been opposed by foreign factors in the past as unfairly taxing those who produced in a colony rather than taxing only those who consumed there, and the government revenue systems of some colonies were consequently characterized by a heavy dependence on import tariff and excise tax receipts.[10] In some territories, export taxes were designed to exempt the products of foreign factors, as in the pre-World War I export tax on "rubber, excepting that grown on plantations" in German Cameroon.[11] In the hands of the new domestic factor governments, on the other hand, export taxes have increasingly been directed primarily against those factors of production which produce within the country but consume abroad—the foreign factors of production—and to a lesser extent, also against the luxury importers.

This new emphasis on export taxation gained great impetus during the years of the Korean War, the first commodity boom period after many of the Southeast Asian countries gained their independence. With commodity prices skyrocketing, many governments saw their first opportunity to share heavily in the windfall profits of foreign factors and luxury importers. "The establishment or extension of export taxes probably was the most nearly universal action taken by governments in the export boom."[12] In the Far East, however, most of the governments were not quick enough in imposing their increased export taxes to gain a large share of the swollen profits. Export duties gained only 8 per cent of the increased export earnings in Malaya, 14 per cent in Indonesia, less than one-fifth in Pakistan jute and about one-fourth in Ceylon rubber, during the Korean War boom period.[13] Though the export taxes were subsequently reduced as commodity prices receded, they remained of increased importance in the revenue of these countries as compared with the pre-World War II period.[14] The move toward heavier export taxation undertaken during the period of high raw material prices was evident in other parts of the world too. In many of the coffee countries, in Latin America and Africa, the price increases of the early 1950's brought frequent upward adjustment of export tax rates. By the mid-1950's high export taxes had become a prominent feature in the fiscal arsenal of the new export economies reacting against the export economy pattern of the past.

Other Taxes

In the mineral export industries the new drive toward absorption of foreign factor income by the domestic factor governments combined the traditionally important export taxes with a new set of measures primarily of the income tax variety. In pre-1952 Bolivia, for example, the old export tax on tin was supplemented by a special tax on mining profits, a tax on presumptive income (assumed on the basis of gross income), and a special tax on mining company dividends, in addition to the various license fees and surface taxes and the taxes implicit in penalty exchange rates.

In the petroleum export economies, a pattern of export taxation originated by Venezuela in 1948 was thereafter widely adopted by the oil-producing countries of the Middle East. This was the so-called 50-50 system. In Venezuela the oil and mining companies first paid the regular federal, state, and municipal taxes. Then, whatever was left above 50 per cent of their net income within the country before taxes was taken by the government under the Additional Income Tax.[15] Subsequently, Saudi Arabia, Iraq, Kuwait, Qatar, and Bahrein all signed 50-50 profit-sharing agreements with the oil companies, some retaining the preliminary royalty payment while others eliminated it for a one-step 50 per cent tax.[16] In 1957 and 1958, however, the 50 per cent government share was exceeded in several contracts signed by the oil countries with newcomers to the international oil industry. A Japanese group agreed to pay Saudi Arabia 56 per cent of net profits not only on the value of the oil as it crossed the border but on operations down to the retail level.[17] In Iran the government obtained a 75 per cent share of net profits by forming separate joint operating companies successively with Italian and American interests. Under these joint operating company arrangements net profits after the regular 50 per cent tax to the government were to be divided equally between the foreign company and the government's National Iranian Oil Company.[18] In December 1958, the 50-50 pattern was altered at its source as the Venezuelan government raised its income tax rates to a level that, together with other taxes and payments to the government, would bring it 60 per cent and more of some of the oil companies' net profits.[19]

The royalty payment used frequently in oil and mineral export economies is not an export tax but is one of several taxes whose effects are similar to those of the export tax proper. However, collected as a specific charge per ton exported or as a percentage of the exports' value, the royalty might differ from an export tax in the varying rate applied to different export concession holders. In Venezuela, for example, oil and mineral royalty payments varied between 16⅔ and 33⅓ per cent, depending upon agreements reached in the negotiation of each individual concession.[20] Other taxes too have been used in place of the export tax. In 1917 Mexico, for example, the government faced a situation in which all customs receipts had been pledged for the payment of interest on the foreign debt. To obtain revenues for domestic purposes the government levied what it called a production tax on the foreign-operated petroleum industry. Petroleum destined for home consumption was exempt from paying the tax, which was collected at the customs house and was thus, in all but name, an export tax.[21] In many of the Caribbean sugar-producing countries, where most of the crop is exported, production taxes on sugar and molasses serve as equivalents to export taxation with the additional effect of a consumption tax on local consumption.[22]

Tax incidence.—Through all of these various taxes the new domestic factor governments have directed the taxation of their exports to a new purpose. Whereas the goal of the old monopoly export tax was to fix the incidence of the tax upon the foreign consumer, the goal of the many, newer export taxes has been to fix their incidence upon the foreign factors and luxury importers. This has raised new problems for the taxing governments. They are now concerned not with the shifting of the tax forward to foreign consumers—which, in the unlikely circumstances that it does occur, is disturbing only if it diminishes future returns—but in preventing any shift of export tax incidence backward, to the domestic factors.

The backward shifting of an export tax burden by foreign factors or luxury importers could take various forms, depending upon their role in the production and export process. Processors or export traders could attempt to shift the export tax backward by paying lower prices to domestic producers, such as peasant small holders, estate owners, or tenants, for example. To prevent this type of backward shifting and to fix incidence upon the foreign factors or luxury importers, some governments have fixed minimum prices which must be paid to producers and have even regulated the processors' profit margins. Such regulation is sometimes part of an extensive marketing control system in which the export tax is maintained as the means of providing revenue to the government. In Uganda, where export taxes—primarily on the peasant-grown cotton crop—yielded about 43 per cent of total tax revenues in 1953, the charges and profits of the predominantly Indian-owned cotton ginneries were fixed by the British colonial government.[23] At the same time, since the regulation of producer prices may serve to fix incidence of a tax, this type of arrangement may also be used to fix the incidence of part or all of the export tax upon the native producer. Thus, in the operation of Burma's Marketing Board, as noted, the setting of various rice and paddy prices served to levy a tax both on the cultivator and on those millers and traders at work in the export industry, whose earnings were considerably reduced.

Plantation or estate owners faced with an export tax would ordinarily attempt to shift it back to their laborers through a reduction in wages or the avoidance of an increase in wages. In plantation economies where wages respond closely to export prices, some of the export tax might be shifted onto labor, depending on the elasticity of supply of labor, and the relative bargaining position of the laborers and the plantation owners. While it may be difficult actually to reduce wages in an attempt to shift the export tax backward, plantation owners may be able to avoid or delay any increase in money wages during a period of rising export prices or domestic inflation. It is quite possible, therefore, for export taxes to be shifted backward by estate-owning foreign factors or luxury importers onto their wage-earning laborers. In some estate economies, however, the wages of plantation laborers are conventional, paternalistic, or even largely nonmonetary, and subject only with great difficulty to any upward or downward changes. The situation of coffee estate workers in Guatemala evidently approximated this pattern and it was the belief of some observers that none of the heavy coffee export tax burden was passed by estate owners back to their laborers.[24] Probably the most important deterrent to the shifting of export taxes backward to plantation laborers, however, has been the fixing of plantation labor wages by some governments. Thus Ceylon's export tax on tea during the Korean boom could not be shifted back to labor by the predominantly British tea estate owners because the wages of estate workers were fixed by the government.[25]

In mining too the shifting of export tax incidence back to labor is most often prevented through wage legislation. In the Chilean copper industry, any attempt to reduce wages so as to shift backward the heavy tax burden was blocked by extensive government wage legislation, which tended, in fact, to increase the returns to labor.[26] The most prevalent method of assuring that the burden of the new export taxes is not shifted back to domestic factors of production, then, has been direct government regulation.

Tax disincentives.—Even with assurance that the burden of export taxation is not shifted back to domestic factors, there are important problems of export taxation to which export economy governments must turn attention. In the modern raw material export economies, as in guano-age Peru, the maximization of a government's export industry revenue requires the maintenance of a tax—or sales, or profit-sharing—arrangement giving those who operate the export industry the greatest possible incentive to promote the government's interests. Only if the tax arrangements are so ordered that by promoting the government's interests the exporters promote also their own, can the government gain the maximum revenue from the export industry. Especially is this so in the absence of a corps of government inspectors who would enforce any special regulations the government might enact to protect its interests in the operation of the export industry. It is important, therefore, to consider also the disincentive effects of various forms of export taxation.

Thus, the levying of an export tax reduces the export enterprise's return on each unit produced and exported, and may make production of the higher-cost units no longer profitable. As a result, a mining company may decide to by-pass lower-grade ores, which could thus be permanently lost because of far higher costs involved in returning to work them later on. In this way a heavy export tax may cause a country to forfeit a fraction of its otherwise economic mineral reserves—and revenues—and hasten the exhaustion of its exploitable mineral resources. This is reported to have been the case in pre-1952 Bolivia.[27] An export tax or any equivalent device raising the cost or reducing the return of each unit may in this way lead to a contraction of both production and government revenues. The extent of this contraction will depend upon the producer's elasticity of supply and may tend to reduce production more in the long run, in which the producer has an opportunity to adjust, than in the short run.

A tax on gross operating income may have a similar effect in reducing the volume of production which is still profitable. A tax on net income, however, which allows for higher costs in the marginal units and takes only part of the profits, would ordinarily not alter the level of production at which it is most profitable to produce. Even a tax on net earnings may be faced with special problems, however, in the case of foreign export enterprises selling their products to parent companies or affiliates abroad. Manipulation of the sales price may allow a larger profit to accrue to the subsidiary or parent company abroad outside the tax jurisdiction of the export economy government. This problem arose in guano-age Peru, for example, when some contractors were accused of selling guano to associated enterprises at lower than market costs and of paying the Peruvian government its portion of the low return on these sales while they shared with their associates the profits of resale.[28] Similar complaints have been voiced in the modern petroleum industry, notably by Saudi-Arabian officials who feel the Arabian American Oil Company's price for oil sales to its subsidiaries is artificially low and consequently yields the government 50 per cent of too low a "net earning." The Saudi-Arabian solution—already adopted in its agreement with a Japanese group—calls for a split of the integrated Japanese company's net profits right down to the final sale to the retail consumer.[29]

The tax on net earnings does offer one significant attraction to export economies, however, in the taxation of foreign factors' earnings which are subject to taxation once more in the countries to which they are remitted. If the remittance-receiving country—as is the case in the United States, United Kingdom, and Germany, for example—taxes income earned abroad but permits payments on foreign income taxes (net but not gross) to be credited against the home country income tax, the export economy may find it possible to obtain revenues at the expense of another government's treasury rather than at the expense of the foreign factor itself.[30]

Difficulties of administering income taxes, however, have prompted the introduction of various formulas for the taxation of unit exports or of gross operating revenues without discouraging the expansion of production. Thus, in Chile in early 1955 a tax on gross operating revenue was agreed upon with the two large American copper mining companies—the Anaconda Copper Mining Company and the Kennecott Copper Corporation—providing for a 75 per cent rate, to be reduced by one-eighth of 1 per cent for each 1 per cent of increased production over the previous five years' average up to a 50 per cent increase, and a reduction of three-eighths of 1 per cent for each 1 per cent increase thereafter, until a 50 per cent rate is reached.[31]

While some cost-increasing taxes may reduce the point of profitable production more than taxes on net income or on profits, all additions to the foreign factors' tax burden present a common danger, arising from the nature of the foreign factors of production in many of the export industries. While a mobile domestic factor of production may avoid a tax on one industry by shifting to another, it may not, without ceasing to earn, avoid a tax applicable to income from all sources. When the burden of taxation reduces the profitability of operations in one export country, however, a foreign factor of production may possess the international mobility to shift to operation in another part of the world. While this international mobility is not a characteristic of all foreign factors of production (who need only, by our definition, remit earnings abroad to become foreign factors), it may characterize capital, entrepreneurship, and even labor in some export economies.

Thus, even in the short run a foreign enterprise may be able to increase production in those of its mines which are located in a lower tax country. While it may find it impossible to liquidate its holdings in the comparatively heavy-tax country without taking too heavy a loss, it may discontinue reinvestments there and in the longer run build up its productive capacity elsewhere. Insofar as the foreign factor either of entrepreneurship or of labor is internationally mobile, it may find open the much simpler possibility of migration to other countries, where its net return would be higher. To the extent, then, that taxation reduces the return to foreign factors below that obtainable elsewhere in the world, and to the extent that these foreign factors have the alternative of moving abroad without sustaining too large an initial loss, foreign factors will move out of a high tax country. In the exercise of their new instruments of export taxation, therefore, the new domestic factor governments face problems both as to the types of taxation and the total burden which they may apply.

Multiple Exchange Rates

The widespread adoption of multiple exchange rates among many of the raw material exporting countries did not come as part of the reaction against foreign factors and luxury importers but rather as a means of meeting balance of payments difficulties. Once established, however, multiple exchange rates have been used to serve many additional purposes, and the absorption of foreign factor and luxury importer incomes is among them.

There are certain features in the structure of many export economies which lend particular justification to their use of multiple exchange rates. The rationale for a single rate of exchange for all export transactions lies in the expectation that factors receiving lower returns will then shift to the more profitable areas of employment, that is, to those areas where they are most efficient. This shift toward optimum efficiency, however, depends upon a condition of domestic factor mobility under which factors respond to lower income by shifting to higher paying employment. In many of the export economies this condition of domestic mobility is not present. This may result from several causes. Groups of small-holder peasants who produce an export crop, with or without subsistence gardening on the side, may be unwilling to move to labor in a mine or on a plantation despite the inducement of higher returns. Or, on the other hand, firms in a large export industry may hold either a natural monopoly, due to the limits of a natural resource, such as oil or mineral ores, or an exclusive government concession, or perhaps an exclusive position due to vertical integration with transportation and marketing facilities abroad. This, or perhaps only huge capital requirements, may restrict entry into the highly efficient and profitable export industry. As a result of either unwillingness to move or restricted entry, therefore, there may exist a domestic immobility of factors which prevents shifting from the less profitable to the more profitable areas of employment. Under these circumstances a lower return to the inefficient producer will mean not a shift to more profitable employment but continued production at a lower level of income.

A government may decide to increase the efficiency of immobile factors in less productive employments by using noneconomic means to induce them to move. It may, on the other hand, decide for social and political reasons to preserve the position of the immobile inefficient factors, and may undertake to raise their income through subsidies. One form these subsidies may take is the sale of their produce abroad at a depreciated rate of exchange, so that they need earn less foreign currency to obtain a unit of domestic currency and may sell their products more cheaply to compete on the world market. This was the form chosen to subsidize exports by the Chilean wine industry, in which more than 100,000 persons were employed.[32] In somewhat different form the United States government has done the same thing in selling surplus wheat, rice, cotton, and other farm produce abroad under conditions of payment constituting a reduction to below the world price.

An exporting country may seek another solution to this problem by adopting a single, unified exchange rate which is depreciated enough to allow these less efficient domestic factors to produce and export to the foreign market. To prevent the large, efficient firms in the restricted-entry export industry from pocketing the profits of the new favorable rate, however, the government may tax them more heavily. If these are domestic factors of production, a simple export tax may have the effect of returning their earnings to the level at which they would have been with the less depreciated rate of exchange. An export tax may thus serve to introduce what is in effect a multiple exchange rate.

To the extent that an export tax may be used to tax the foreign consumer—when the exporting country is an important supplier and finds the demand for its product inelastic—a multiple exchange rate may be used to do the same thing. It may raise the price of one export product without taxing other products for which demand is elastic and without taxing or subsidizing imports. To the extent that an exporting country is not an important supplier facing an inelastic demand, the multiple exchange rate, like the export tax, may simply be a method of taxing the producer. Since this producer may often be a foreign factor or a luxury importer, the increasing effort to absorb his income results in increasing use of multiple exchange rates as well as of export taxes proper.

When the large, efficient export enterprise is in foreign hands, as is often the case, some exporting countries have adopted another form of taxation through multiple exchange rates. In many export economies, foreign enterprises are not required to convert into domestic currency all their foreign exchange earnings but only enough of it to meet their domestic costs—that is, the cost of employing domestic factors of production and paying taxes. If a depreciated exchange rate were to be used to allow the less efficient domestic factors to produce other products for export, the foreign enterprises—whose export prices in terms of foreign exchange would probably stay the same—would be able to purchase their domestic currency requirements with less foreign exchange than before, reducing proportionately their domestic costs. Unless production were thereby expanded or domestic costs increased more than proportionately, the return to domestic factors of production in terms of foreign exchange would be reduced. To prevent this cut in the return to domestic factors—and to the country—and to absorb the savings in foreign exchange the foreign enterprises would otherwise receive, many countries have applied a high, appreciated rate to the foreign firms' purchase of domestic currency needed to pay for domestic costs. Among the countries using such a system of penalty rate conversion for foreign enterprises' domestic costs have been Chile, Syria, Venezuela, Bolivia, Iran, and Lebanon. The spread between the otherwise effective exchange rate and the rate at which foreign firms must purchase their local currency may range from very small, as in the 7 per cent margin in the rate formerly applied to the oil companies in Venezuela, to quite large, as in the more than 400 per cent margin in the rate formerly applied to the large copper companies in Chile.[33]

This appreciated exchange rate for foreign enterprises' domestic costs is in effect a proportional export tax upon the product of domestic factors of production. Like the normal export tax, it will be borne by the consumer—in this case the foreign enterprise—only when his demand for the product is more inelastic than the supply, although the tax may lead, even under such conditions, to other economic effects which may influence the distribution of the burden. The shifting of this "export tax" backward to the domestic factors, however, is rendered quite difficult by the government fixing or supervision of wages which characterizes some export economies. The increased cost of domestic factors, on the other hand, may lead the foreign enterprise to bring in more foreign machinery and equipment to be substituted for domestic labor in a new, more capital-intensive combination of factors. The governments of some export economies have attempted to remove this inducement to substitute foreign factors for domestic by requiring the appreciated rate exchange conversion not of actual domestic costs, but of some designated "legal domestic costs." These specially fixed "domestic costs," independent of the actual use of domestic factors, may remove the inducement to substitute foreign factors for high-cost domestic factors. The forced conversion of foreign exchange for domestic currency above actual requirements may even act to induce increased use of domestic factors and their substitution for foreign factors.

In this penalty exchange rate conversion of foreign exchange for domestic costs the tax is levied upon the product of domestic factors at a tax rate equal to the difference between the appreciated rate and the "normal" rate. For that amount of foreign exchange the foreign firm must convert above its domestic needs, however, the tax burden may not be determinable. In some instances—as was probably the case in the Chilean copper and nitrate industries in the early 1950's— the tax implicit in the multiple exchange rate may be far heavier than the officially-designated tax burden. Since the tax arrangements of many large foreign-owned export enterprises are determined in agreements negotiated between these firms and the governments of the export economies, however, the tax implicit in the multiple exchange rate may most often be taken into consideration.

In the area of multiple exchange rate practices, then, the effort of domestic factor governments to absorb the income of foreign factors and luxury importers has been expressed in several ways. Domestic luxury importers may lose income to the government through the application of an appreciated exchange rate to their export proceeds, yielding them—as the application of an *ad valorem* export tax would —a proportionately smaller amount of domestic currency for the foreign exchange they are required to surrender. Reducing their luxury imports, though it does not in the same sense absorb their income, may be a depreciated rate applied to the importation of luxuries. For the foreign enterprise, on the other hand, the absorption of income has sometimes taken the form of an appreciated exchange rate applied to its purchase of domestic currency for actual or fictitious local costs. This, like an *ad valorem* export tax on the product of domestic factors, raises its costs and reduces the foreign enterprise's net income.

In recent years the use of complicated multiple exchange rate systems has diminished markedly, particularly in Latin America, where in the years immediately after World War II it had been practiced most extensively. The decline of multiple rate practices has been primarily due to the accretion of many conflicting interests and objectives—among them the heavy taxation of foreign factors and luxury importers—which converged upon the foreign exchange authorities. The progressive inclusion of more and more conflicting objectives into the jungle-like multiple exchange rate systems made them impossible to administer. One by one the fixed multiple rate systems of Latin America have been abandoned in favor of single, usually fluctuating, rates.[34] With this development, the taxation of foreign factors and luxury importers—together with other objectives which the multiple rate systems had been called upon to implement—has devolved back to its previous centers of government action, such as the regular tax authorities.

Government Export Monopolies

Government export monopolies have been established for a variety of reasons.[35] In some cases, their major purpose has been to absorb the income of foreign factors or of luxury importers while allowing them to continue their production and trading functions. Such export monopolies have often performed only tax administrative functions, or minimal trading functions at best. This was probably the case in the Chilean government's requirement that copper companies sell their output at a fixed low price to the central bank in 1951. The central bank resold this copper abroad—most of it to the fabricating subsidiaries of Anaconda and Kennecott, owners of the large Chilean mines—at about 45 per cent above the price it had paid the mines.[36] How much of the foreign factors' and luxury importers' trading function is taken over by a government export monopoly and how much of the monopoly's income is derived strictly as a tax will vary from case to case. In Burma, as has been seen, the Marketing Board took on a considerable portion of the trading function, but at the same time used its monopoly trading position to tax those foreign factors and luxury importers who continued to operate as processors and intermediaries in the trade. In Thailand, the export-monopoly Rice Office performed little more than a simple tax-collection function in some of its dealings, as when it received rice from the mills and resold it at a price increase of 20 per cent to private traders holding permits for commercial export shipments. In some cases, however, the taxation of foreign factors and luxury importers remaining in the export industry may play a minor role indeed in the operation of state marketing arrangements, whose principal purposes may lie in other directions.

NOTES TO SELECTION 27

[1] U. K. Hicks, "The Search for Revenue in Underdeveloped Countries," *Revue de Science et de Législation Financières* (Paris, January–March, 1952), pp. 6–40.

[2] Jacob Viner, "National Monopolies of Raw Materials," *Foreign Affairs*, 4:587–588 (July, 1926).

[3] Gorton James, "British Preferential Export Taxes," *American Economic Review*, 14:56–57 (March, 1924). United States Tariff Commission, *Colonial Tariff Policies* (Washington, 1922), pp. 336–44.

[4] Viner, "National Monopolies of Raw Materials," p. 588. It was these colonial preference policies, in part, which raised to international importance the question of equal access to raw materials.

[5] *Colonial Tariff Policies*, pp. 50–52, 167.

[6] League of Nations, Secretariat, Economic and Financial Section, *Export Duties* (Geneva, 1927), p. 4.

[7] A. P. Lerner, "The Symmetry Between Import and Export Taxes," *Economica*, N.S., 3:306–313 (August, 1936). A. C. Pigou, *A Study in Public Finance* (3rd rev. ed.; London, 1952), pp. 193–202.

[8] *Colonial Tariff Policies*, pp. 89, 124, 166, 183, 195, 208, 211, 217, 251, 254, 256, 258, 260, 263, 292, 297, 304, 313, 320, 325, 335, 388, 391, 418, 470, 524, 525, 526.

[9] *Ibid.*, p. 167.

[10] Sir Charles Bruce, *The Broad Stone of Empire* (London, 1910), II, 228–48. Also see Oliver Oldman and Jonathan Levin, "A Case Study in Import and Excise Taxation in British Guiana in 1911" (mimeographed) (Cambridge, Mass., November 23, 1955).

[11] *Colonial Tariff Policies*, p. 256.

[12] E. P. Reubens, "Commodity Trade, Export Taxes and Economic Development," *Political Science Quarterly*, 71:59 (March, 1956).

[13]*Ibid.*, pp. 59–60.

[14]United Nations, Fiscal Division, Department of Economic Affairs, "Some Aspects of the Tax Systems in Certain ECAFE Countries in Relation to Economic Development," October 11, 1954.

[15]United States Department of Commerce, *Investment in Venezuela, Conditions and Outlook for United States Investors* (Washington, 1953), p. 145.

[16]United Nations, Department of Economic Affairs, *Review of Economic Conditions in the Middle East, 1951–1952* (New York, 1953), pp. 60–61.

[17]*New York Times,* December 17, 1957, p. 5, col. 3.

[18]*New York Times,* May 18, 1958, p. F1, col. 1. *Manchester Guardian Weekly,* August 7, 1957. *The Economist,* May 3, 1958, p. 433.

[19]*Wall Street Journal,* December 22, 1958, p. 2, col. 3.

[20]United Nations, Department of Economic Affairs, *Public Finance Surveys: Venezuela* (New York, 1951), pp. 73–74.

[21]H. E. Davies, "Mexican Petroleum Taxes," *Hispanic American Historical Review,* 12:408–409 (November, 1932).

[22]Louis Shere, "Sugar Taxation in the Caribbean and Central American Countries" (mimeographed) (Washington, December, 1952), sec. C–5.

[23]United Nations, Committee on Information from Non-Self-Governing Territories, *The Structure of Tax Revenue in Non-Self-Governing Territories* (July 28, 1954), pp. 18, 35, 37; also K. M. Stahl, *The Metropolitan Organization of British Colonial Trade* (London, 1951), pp. 275–80.

[24]J. H. Adler, E. R. Schlesinger, and E. C. Olson, *Public Finance and Economic Development in Guatemala* (Stanford, 1952), p. 101.

[25]C. E. Staley, "Export Taxes, A Problem in International Trade and Economic Development" (unpublished thesis, Massachusetts Institute of Technology, 1956), pp. 86–217. "Labour Conditions in Ceylon," *International Labour Review,* 60:592–593 (December, 1949).

[26]United States Department of Commerce, Office of International Trade, *Factors Limiting U.S. Investment Abroad, Part I, Survey of Factors in Foreign Countries* (Washington, 1953), pp. 23–24.

[27]Richard Goode, "Reconstruction of Foreign Tax Systems," *Proceedings of the Forty-Fourth Annual Conference on Taxation, 1951* (Sacramento, Calif., 1952), pp. 218–19.

[28]See above, p. 71 [not included in this volume].

[29]*New York Times,* December 17, 1957, p. 5, col. 3.

[30]The problems involved in the foreign tax credit device, which are complicated indeed, are examined in S. S. Surrey, "The United States Taxation of Foreign Income," *Journal of Law and Economics,* 1:72 (October, 1958), and in United Nations, Department of Economic Affairs, *United States Income Taxation of Private United States Investment in Latin America* (New York, 1953).

[31]*New York Times,* February 7, 1955, p. 31, col. 5; May 4, 1955, p. 48, col. 1.

[23]International Monetary Fund, *Fifth Annual Report on Exchange Restrictions, 1954* (Washington, 1954), pp. 82–83. *Noticias* (February 15, 1955), p. 7.

[33]W. J. R. Woodley, "The Use of Special Exchange Rates for Transactions with Foreign Companies," *Staff Papers,* International Monetary Fund, 3:255 (October, 1953).

[34]F. H. Schott, *The Evolution of Latin American Exchange Rate Policy Since World War II* (Princeton, January, 1959), *passim.*

[35]W. Z. Hirsch, "The Economics of State Marketing Boards," *Current Economic Comment,* 17:10–22 (February, 1955).

[36]United Nations, Economic Commission for Latin America, *Economic Survey of Latin America, 1953* (New York, 1954), p. 186. *New York Times,* June 21, 1953, p. F1, col. 1. *Wall Street Journal,* June 24, 1953, p. 1, col. 6.

28

Taxes on Foreign Trade in Nigeria

*by the World Bank Mission to Nigeria**

MARKETING BOARDS

THE purchase in Nigeria and the sale abroad of the principal export crops, oil palm produce, cocoa, groundnuts and cotton,[1] are in the hands of four statutory marketing boards, autonomous bodies established between 1947 and 1949 to take the place of control schemes instituted during the war. At the beginning of each crop year the boards announce minimum prices at which the firms licensed as the boards' buying agents will purchase crops from producers during the year.

The principal tasks of the Marketing Boards are the stabilization of producer prices, the promotion of the economic development of the producing industries and areas of production, and the encouragement and financing of research.

During their comparatively short existence the Marketing Boards have become one of the most important factors in the economic life and the financial structure of Nigeria. Because world prices have risen more rapidly than prices paid to producers, their operations have shown very large surpluses which, after the allocation of £25 million for economic development and research, stood at about £75 million at the end of 1953.

At the 1954 Lagos Conference it was decided to replace the existing boards, each of which has countrywide jurisdiction over a particular product or group of products, by four regional boards,[2] each with jurisdiction over all controlled commodities produced within its territory. There will also be a Central Marketing Board which will set standards of quality and arrange for transportation and marketing overseas. Price and stabilization policy will be determined by the regional boards with the advice of the central board.

*International Bank for Reconstruction and Development, *The Economic Development of Nigeria* (Baltimore: The Johns Hopkins Press, 1955), pp. 85–89, 113–14. Reprinted with the permission of the publisher.

On the whole, the operations of the Marketing Boards have benefited the producers of the controlled crops and the Nigerian economy in general. We found that both the producers and the commercial community were satisfied with the working of the system.

Producer prices are set and maintained for an entire crop season. Thus the producer as well as the middleman and produce buyer is protected against day-to-day fluctuations, the possibility of speculation is eliminated and crops are promptly collected and moved.

The boards have successfully used their price-setting powers to bring about great improvements in the quality of export produce. The introduction of wide price margins between "special grade" (edible) and "grade I" (technical) oil by the Oil Palm Produce Marketing Board has resulted in a radically changed composition of the palm oil supply: in 1950, less than 1% of the board's purchases was classified as edible, with a free fatty acid content below 4.5%; by 1953 more than one-half of the oil purchased was edible. The demand outlook for edible oil being considerably better than that for the lower-grade technical oil, the long-run prospects for Nigerian palm oil have been greatly improved. Similarly, the price differential between grade I and grade II cocoa resulted in 95% of 1952–53 exports being grade I, compared with only 47% in 1947–48.

The Marketing Boards must also be credited with bringing more Nigerians into the trade in export produce. Before the war, virtually all of this trade was carried on by European firms. By the end of the 1952–53 buying season, the Cocoa Marketing Board had 17 Nigerian licensed buying agents compared with only 6 in 1949–50, while the number of expatriate buying agents decreased from 19 to 18. Similarly, as of November, 1953, of 26 licensed buying agents for palm oil, 10 were Nigerians, and for palm kernels 18 out of 40. There are, on the other hand, no Nigerian cotton buyers and only two Nigerian groundnut buyers. The share of Nigerian buyers in the volume of produce purchases is still small, however.

To be able to set prices for an entire crop season and to lessen the impact of year-to-year world price changes on the Nigerian producer, the boards had to accumulate large reserves. These were built up over a short period, thanks to the sterling devaluation, the raw materials boom caused by the Korean war and the continuing higher-than-normal world price level thereafter. Partly as a matter of conscious policy and partly in expectation of a price fall which did not materialize, the boards fixed producer prices at levels which regularly netted substantial additions to reserves.

This course of action has been criticized as resulting in a withholding from the producers of their equitable share of higher world prices. Although we agree that in some instances the boards' price policies have been unduly cautious, we do not think that the generality of the criticism is justified. In the first place, under any stabilization scheme a period of rising prices is the time for the formation of reserves. Secondly, the setting of relatively low producer prices greatly mitigated the severity of inflationary pressures, to the advantage of the country in general, the producers included, at a time when no other machinery for anti-inflationary action existed. Finally, the accumulated stabilization reserves are large enough not only to assure producers the direct benefit of reasonable and relatively stable prices for many years to come but also to enable the boards to lend large sums on a long-term basis to government for development purposes.

In our opinion the marketing board system is well suited to Nigerian conditions. The combination of guaranteed prices for an entire crop year to the smallholder producers, adequate compensation for the buying agents, and price policies designed to encourage quality improvements provides the inducements necessary for increased and improved production and for a regular and efficient flow of produce, and the joint selling arrangements[3] strengthen Nigeria's position in the world market.

We recommend, however, that henceforth the boards' functions be limited to setting quality standards, fixing producer prices and purchasing and marketing crops. The financing of economic development and agricultural research is a responsibility of government and the boards should not attempt to undertake it. Nor should the level of expenditure for these purposes be left to the discretion of the boards or be dependent on the results of their operations. While the present reserves of the boards can be an important source of development capital, we recommend that the boards' contribution be made through long-term loans to government out of that portion of their funds which need not be kept liquid, as discussed below.

We also recommend that in fixing producer prices, the boards should have no object other than mitigating price fluctuations and giving an incentive to improvement of quality. The deliberate use of the price-fixing function for other purposes, such as the promotion of development or to counteract inflationary or deflationary trends, cuts across the responsibility of government.

Present stabilization reserves are ample and the boards should not aim to increase them. They can afford to adopt a long-term stabilization and reserve policy which we believe will result in producer prices higher in relation to world market prices than has thus far been the case. While in fixing producer prices the boards should continue to take account of the expected trend of world market prices, the prices they set should as a rule vary no more than 10% from those set for the previous year. This principle should be applied after an initial readjustment of those purchase prices which are lower than is warranted by world market conditions. We have in mind particularly the price of cocoa. Details of our recommendations and the calculations on which they are based are set forth in Technical Report No. 4. Our calculations indicate that to carry out this stabilization policy the boards would not need to keep more than an estimated £25 million as liquid reserves and that, after allowing for working capital, some £40 million, constituting the second-line reserves, could be loaned on a long-term basis to government for development purposes (see Chapter 5 [not included in this volume] for specific recommendations regarding Marketing Board lending). The existing boards have already agreed to lend £14 million to the Government of Nigeria,[4] of which £2.7 million has been drawn to date.

We believe that the foregoing recommendations would achieve a more appropriate demarcation of the functions of the Marketing Boards and of government. We also believe that the recommended price and reserve policies would enable the boards to pay the producers fair prices while giving them adequate protection against foreseeable risks, and would at the same time permit funds already accumulated to be used to finance development.

*   *   *   *   *

Customs Duties and Excise Taxes

In recent years, approximately 60% of all customs and excise collections have come from import duties and excise taxes (the latter mainly on cigarettes and beer), and the remainder from export duties.

Import duties are in general low, ranging between 15% and 20% for most articles. Alcoholic beverages, tobacco and certain luxury imports pay higher rates, while machinery, tools, fertilizers and other agricultural or industrial producers' goods are duty-free. Except for duties on such essentials as salt and kerosene, the incidence of the tariff is on the whole progressive. There is considerable evidence that the lowest income groups purchase only small quantities of imports, while persons in the middle and higher income brackets, particularly in urban areas, buy a relatively large volume of imports, especially textiles.

We recommend that import duties be increased—not for the purpose of increasing the federal revenues but as a means of alleviating the financial problems of the regions. We propose further that the full amount realized from the recommended increase be distributed among the regions.

Specifically, we recommend that duties on all imports except food, tobacco, motor spirit and kerosene be increased so that revenue from this source will rise by 50%. We recommend further that certain of the inequitable or undesirable features of the existing tariff be eliminated at the same time: all imports of food except confectionery and alcoholic beverages should be exempt from duty and so should all building materials except (temporarily) cement. Exemption of construction materials is desirable in the interest of promoting building activity but it may be necessary to retain the present duty on cement to give initial protection to the proposed cement factory.[5] We realize that this increase would make the fiscal structure even more dependent on the flow of the country's international trade. We therefore believe that it should remain in effect only until the yield of taxation on income and property rises sufficiently to take its place.

Since it will take some time to put these tariff changes into effect, we have not counted on any increase in revenue from this source until 1957. On the basis of information supplied to us in Nigeria, we estimate that the recommended revision would yield a net of £15 million over the period 1957–60.

Export duties on the most important agricultural products are 10% ad valorem with progressive surcharges if export prices exceed a "normal" level.[6] Minor exports are taxed at relatively low specific rates. At the export prices anticipated during the next five years, cocoa would be the only major export subject to duty in excess of 10%. We do not recommend an increase in these duties. On the other hand, we do not believe that the export duty on cocoa should be reduced as suggested in sections of the Nigerian press, even though at presently prevailing prices it far exceeds that on other dutiable exports.[7] There is ample evidence that producers of cocoa are, as a group, substantially better off than other agricultural producers. Their tax burden may therefore equitably be higher, especially if the price which they receive from the Marketing Boards is increased in accordance with our recommendation as to the price policies of the board.

NOTES TO SELECTION 28

[1]And the minor crops of benniseed, soyabeans and sunflower seeds, which are under the jurisdiction of the Groundnut Marketing Board.

[2]One for each region and one for the Southern Cameroons.

[3]Through the Nigeria Produce Marketing Company, Ltd. in London, owned by the several Marketing Boards.

[4]Of which £2 million is to be reloaned to the Western and Eastern Regions.

[5]See Technical Report No. 13.

[6]The price per ton at which surcharges apply is: cocoa, £150; groundnuts, £65; palm kernels, £50; technical palm oil, £65; edible palm oil, £75; cotton, £325.

[7]At the June, 1954, price of cocoa, the duty was 45%.

29

Comments on the World Bank Proposals

by P. T. Bauer*

THE mission suggests higher import and excise duties as the principal source of additional revenue. "Specifically we recommend that duties on all imports except food, tobacco, motor spirit and kerosene, be increased so that revenue from this source will rise by 50%" (p. 113).[1] It is not stated by how much the duties have to be raised to achieve this. At present most of the duties are between 15 and 20 per cent of c.i.f. values, with higher rates on alcohol, tobacco, and certain other items. As the revenue from duties is to be increased by 50 per cent, while rates in certain categories are not to be raised, the increase in the others must be proportionately greater. This brings up the question of the elasticity of the demand for some of these commodities, but this is not mentioned, and it is not possible to gauge the changes in the duties envisaged by the mission or their assumptions about the response of revenue to changes in the rates of duty. Throughout the report it is generally assumed[2] that neither supply nor demand is at all influenced by price. Such a complete inelasticity may have been assumed in the response of demand to higher duties, which is plainly impossible, especially at high rates.

There is no discussion either in the general report or in the technical reports of the incidence of taxation or of its effects on output.[3] This neglect is crucial. When considering the effects of increased taxation and of government expenditure on economic development, the repercussions of the additional taxation on the private sector must be examined, as otherwise it is impossible either to assess the merits of taxation for development or, what is equally important, to appraise the merits of the different ways of raising the funds. The report, in fact, implies that the revenues and expenditure of the government represent simply net additions to resources for development, without stating that they are derived from the private sector.[4]

*P. T. Bauer, "The Economic Development of Nigeria," *Journal of Political Economy* (Chicago: The University of Chicago Press), LXIII (October, 1955), 399–408. Copyright 1955 by The University of Chicago. Reprinted with permission.

Proposals for increased indirect taxation, especially of inessentials, are familiar in contemporary literature on development. These proposals often seem tacitly to assume that the whole economy is already on an exchange basis or, at any rate, that changes in the prices of consumer goods do not affect the supply of effort to the exchange sector. This assumption is clearly invalid for Nigeria, as for many other underdeveloped countries, especially in Africa, where much of economic activity is still outside the money sector and where there is a large extensive margin of cultivation along which production for sale is not appreciably more advantageous than subsistence or near-subsistence production.

Higher prices (or reduced supply) of commodities to be purchased in the exchange sector diminish the attractiveness of work for that sector relative both to subsistence activity and to leisure.[5] The response if the supply of effort offered to the exchange sector (chiefly through the production of cash crops and the acceptance of wage-earning employment) depends on such factors as the structure of wants of the producers; the access of producers to the exchange sector (and on differences between producers in these respects) ; the technical conditions of production; the type of commodities available; the terms on which different commodities are obtainable; and, of course, the money incomes obtainable in the exchange sector. The usual proposals, including those of the bank mission, generally favor the additional taxation of so-called "inessentials"—textiles, apparel, alcohol, confectionery, bicycles, and the like—which are particularly likely to serve as inducement goods to production for the market. There may be very many producers who will not be induced to sacrifice leisure or subsistence output to obtain these commodities when the terms on which they are available deteriorate (a fortiori if they disappear altogether). In these circumstances the additional indirect taxation of these commodities may substantially affect the supply of effort to the money sector, especially by reducing the attractiveness of production for sale.[6] Unless this is recognized, the merits of the proposal cannot be rationally assessed, nor is it then possible to allocate taxation among various commodities so as to minimize the contraction of the supply of effort to the money sector.[7]

These problems are unrecognized in the report; the most nearly relevant remark is the statement that Nigeria is very lightly taxed and that government revenue accounts for only $7\frac{1}{2}$ per cent of the national income; even at the proposed higher rates, this would rise to only $12\frac{1}{2}$ per cent (a higher proportion is envisaged after 1960). But this is misleading. A large proportion of the national income is subsistence output or, more precisely, output outside the exchange or money sector; as a percentage of the income of the money sector, the percentage of tax revenue to total income is much higher. In fact, the comparatively low ratio of government revenue to total national income is one aspect of the large volume of subsistence activity, and it thus emphasizes the importance of correct assessment of the effects of taxation which might retard the spread of production for sale.

Moreover, within the exchange sector the burden is very heavily concentrated on the producers of export crops controlled by marketing boards. This is so even if export duties alone are considered, and it is much reinforced when the surpluses of the marketing boards are also taken into account. For instance, in 1953–54, the year of the mission's visit to Nigeria, the cocoa producers received only just over half the net sales proceeds, the balance was taken in export duty and the surplus of the Nigeria Cocoa Marketing Board. This was not exceptional, since the inception of statutory export monopoly in 1939 these producers have received, on the average, barely half the available proceeds, most of the balance went to the surpluses of the marketing organizations and more recently in export duty. In 1953–54 the duty averaged over a third of the f.o.b. value of cocoa. As a proportion of the price received by the producer the figure was much higher, about two-thirds; this is because the Cocoa Marketing Board also accumulated a surplus, and under these conditions an export duty at a given rate of f.o.b. values represents a higher percentage of the producer price than it would otherwise.[8]

The mission says explicitly that the high export duties on cocoa should not be reduced because cocoa producers are, on the average, better off than other agricultural producers. A survey conducted in 1951–52 under the auspices of the Nigeria Cocoa Marketing Board found that over half the cocoa farmers sold less than 7 cwt. of cocoa in that season. In recent years (through 1953–54) the highest producer price has been £170 a ton at railhead; 7 cwt. would yield proceeds of about £50–£60 ex farm. Thus, on this basis, at least half the cocoa producers had annual cash proceeds from the sale of cocoa of less than £50–£60. The surplus of the Marketing Board and the export duty together totaled £56 a ton in that year. On the other hand, people with annual incomes of £2,000 pay only about 10 per cent in income tax, and Africans outside Lagos (including businessmen, professional men, and officials with high incomes) are exempt.

The burden of export taxes and surpluses on producers of the other export crops controlled by marketing boards has been lower in recent years, though it has usually been heavy. But until quite recently, it was of the same order, or even heavier, on these producers, and their incomes (both cash incomes and total incomes) were much lower than those of cocoa producers.[9]

This exceedingly heavy burden reflects to some extent the ease with which these levies can be imposed on producers subject to statutory monopolies and also the much greater political effectiveness of the urban population. Quite clearly the references to a taxation of 7½ per cent of the national income and to the prosperity of the cocoa producers are seriously misleading.[10]

In estimating the response of the supply of effort to changes in the prices of consumer goods, the changes in rates of duties or in the prices of the commodities are not the only relevant factors. Even if the rates of import and export duty were the same on all commodities and represented the same percentage of pretax incomes of all producers affected, a given percentage change would still have different effects on output, because of such factors as the differences in access to alternatives and the other factors listed earlier.

The two other sources of funds suggested by the mission call for briefer comment only. The mission proposes that the regional governments should borrow substantial funds from the marketing boards. This implies that the accumulated reserves of the boards are not to be returned to producers until well into the 1960's, if they are to be returned at all. This means that the lack of correspondence between those at whose expense the surpluses were accumulated, and those to whom the reserves would be distributed would be virtually total.[11]

The mission also proposes that the Nigerian government should draw on its accumulated reserves in London to the extent of about half its balance. Some remarks on the wisdom of holding large sterling balances at a time of continuously rising prices would have been appropriate.

Section IV

The report treats of certain technical matters of wide interest to students of development and of underdeveloped economies. In considering this treatment, it should be noted that the personnel of the mission included a chief economist, an economist, an agricultural economist, an expert on money and banking, and a consultant on agricultural export commodities and that the report includes twenty-one technical reports.[12]

The influence of prices on quantities demanded, supplied, or produced is neglected practically throughout the report (with one irrelevant but interesting exception noted below). Demand and supply are seen as physical quantities, affected by various factors but not by price.[13] This is particularly striking in the discussion of the factors influencing agricultural production. To quote only one of the many passages which reflect this disregard of the effect of price on supply:

> Nigerian agriculture, which now produces virtually all of the food consumed in the country as well as 90% of the exports, is readily capable of expansion. Climatic conditions are favorable in much of the country,

many varieties of crops and some livestock are well adapted to their environment, and land is abundant. But expansion in the immediate future and over the long term will depend upon the degree to which Nigeria can succeed in overcoming or minimizing the effect of such limiting factors as soil deficiencies, inadequacy of water supply in certain areas, low-yielding plant varieties, prevalence of plant and livestock disease, and primitive cultivation methods. The priority needs in the agricultural sector are surveys and research to ascertain the precise nature of these factors, tests of possible remedies to determine their local applicability, and finally practical application and demonstration of tested findings, all with the object of expanding production of export crops and increasing the output and improving the quality of food for domestic consumption [pp. 36–37].

Thus the price is not mentioned among the factors influencing production or the establishment of capacity. Yet in Nigeria the functional relationship between price and supply, especially long-term supply, is particularly obvious. There is a large extensive margin of production in most areas; transport costs are often substantial and are generally heavy between the producers along the extensive margin and the central markets or ports of shipment; producers can shift readily between different crops and activities; and outside the extensive margin there are large areas of subsistence activity. In these circumstances expansion of capacity (and thus of long-term supply) is necessarily a function of price, since the establishment of capacity and production for the market are not profitable (and often not even possible) in outlying areas, unless the price after covering transport costs yields a return more attractive than could be obtained from other activities.[14] Indeed, they are possible only if the return is greater than zero; and the area over which it will be positive must depend on price. It might be thought that the mission did not discuss prices because it regarded them as a factor outside the control of government and thus a factor to be taken for granted. This, however, is not so, since the prices received by producers are greatly affected, and, indeed, are practically determined, by government action through the policies of the marketing boards, which prescribe producer prices; and these prices are also affected by export duties, produce sales taxes, and so on.

In these circumstances, neglect of the relationship between price and supply greatly reduces the value of a development program aimed primarily at raising agricultural production and envisaging a large measure of government action and substantial taxation for this purpose. And in Nigeria the production and distribution of agricultural produce are much the most important forms of economic activity.

The relation between agricultural production and agricultural prices brings us to the treatment of the marketing boards, the statutory monopolies which handle almost all agricultural exports of the country, a system usually termed "statutory marketing."[15]

This important subject is considered in one section of the main report and in a technical report. In the mission's opinion, "the operations of the marketing boards have benefited the producers of the controlled crops and the Nigerian economy in general" (p. 86), and "in our opinion the marketing board system is well suited to Nigerian conditions" (p. 87). In assessing these remarks, the following facts and considerations, none of them mentioned in the report, should be noted.

Since the inception of statutory marketing,[16] the cocoa producers have received barely more than half the proceeds of the sale of cocoa; the producers of the other crops have not fared much better;[17] the difference between the sales proceeds and the prices paid to producers went partly to the surpluses of the marketing boards and partly to export duties, chiefly to the former.[18] The proportion of proceeds withheld from producers is nowhere mentioned. On page 85, the report says: "because world prices have risen more rapidly than prices paid to producers, their [the marketing boards] operations have shown very large surpluses"; and on page 87: "Under any stabilization a period of rising prices is the time for the formation of reserves." This is most misleading. The cocoa producers, for instance, have been underpaid since 1939; and, from that date until 1946, producer prices were very low. Even in money terms they were well below the level of reasonably prosperous years in the middle 1930's; in real terms they were, of course, far lower. Much the same applied to producers of other crops over a number of years. Nor do the statements show the proportion of proceeds withheld from these producers; or the connection between the surpluses and the export duties; or the sales below market prices; or the fact that not only have producer prices been kept at very low levels but that there have also been very large discontinuous changes in producer prices from one year to the next. It is also incorrect to say that stabilization postulates the accumulation of reserves in a period of rising prices. This is a confusion between *rising* prices and a level *higher* than a normal or expected level, which bears on the ambiguities in the concept of stabilization mentioned briefly later.

As the proportion of proceeds withheld from producers is not discussed in the report, the effects of the system are not, and indeed cannot be, considered either. There is no mention of the effects of the underpayment of producers on output or on the maintenance or establishment of capacity or on capital formation in the private sector, or of its effects in retarding the spread of the exchange economy.[19] The effects of the system on industrialization are also ignored. As operated in West Africa, it has retarded industrialization in at least two ways. First, by withholding very large sums from producers, it has restricted internal demand and therefore the emergence of a local market for simple products of manufacturing industry.[20] Second, the processors of controlled crops are subject to severe restrictions and, indeed, can exist only at the sufferance of the marketing boards. In several instances in Nigeria the establishment of processing enterprises was either banned or discouraged by the boards.

While the mission stresses the suitability of the system to Nigeria, it examines neither its history nor the conceptual problems of the idea of stabilization. This may have been excusable in the 1940's, when the system was introduced, but it is hardly permissible in 1954, after the experience of more than ten years of statutory marketing. Unless defined, stabilization is a meaningless omnibus expression empty of content; and, because it is empty of content, it can be invoked to justify practically any policy. The report does not discuss the relation between the stabilized price and the market price,[21] the problem of maintaining contact with the trend of prices and the dangers of the loss of this contact; the problem of distinguishing a fluctuation from the beginning of a trend; the lack of correspondence between the payers and the beneficiaries if there is any long delay between the accumulation of reserves and drafts on them, the problem of the apparent inadequacy of a given level of reserves when both market and producer prices are rising (because the higher the prices, the larger the sums necessary to maintain them at a given level over a stated period); or the distinction between stabilization (however defined) of incomes and prices.[22] There are frequent references in the report to rising prices, high prices, and higher-than-normal prices, without any indication of the problem of defining them; they are obviously meaningless unless related to a base or trend. This again is fundamental to any idea of smoothing fluctuations. It is never possible to tell whether a particular price is high or low in relation to the future or to gauge whether a price movement is a fluctuation or the beginning of a trend. For these reasons any stabilization measure is either meaningless or fraught with danger, or both, unless it includes a clearly defined mechanism for retaining or regaining contact with the trend.

Unless every one of these issues is clearly and expressly considered, the whole idea of stabilization is meaningless. For instance, there is no great difficulty, but no merit either, in keeping prices constant at a small fraction of the market price. Again, there is the problem of the lack of correspondence between those producers who were taxed to accumulate reserves and those who benefit when or if they are disbursed. If a long time elapses between the period of accumulation and the disbursement of reserves, the beneficiaries are necessarily a wholly different group of persons from those who made the sacrifices, so that the procedure is not one of stabilization, but of taxing one group and subsidizing another. In fact, if there is a long-run rise in prices, this procedure destabilizes the prices and incomes received by producers. This is what has happened recently in Nigeria.[23]

The report suggests that the marketing boards should be retained and that their functions should be price stabilization and the improvement in the quality of export produce. The report rightly says that objectives such as taxation for development and disinflation (which have often been adduced as justification for the underpayment of producers) do not belong to the sphere of the marketing boards, but to that of general fiscal or monetary policy. Unfortunately, none of the essential problems of stabilization are discussed, while the treatment of the maintenance and improvement of quality is marred by confusion between technical and economic efficiency. The mission commends the Cocoa Marketing Board for having raised the proportion of grade 1 cocoa in total exports from 47 per cent in 1947–48 to 95 per cent in 1952–53 by the payment of large differentials between grade 1 and grade 2. Unfortunately, the mission does not realize that these grade differentials are wholly unrelated to the world market, in which they find no reflection, so that the alleged improvement in quality represents only misdirection of effort.[24] This, incidentally, seems to be the only instance in which the mission recognizes that producers respond to prices; it is unfortunate that the discussion should be vitiated by a failure to understand the difference between technical and economic efficiency, which leads the mission to consider as beneficial a procedure which is wasteful.[25]

Inflation is another topic of wide relevance the discussion of which is unsatisfactory. The term is used by the mission as an omnibus expression to refer to any price increase. For instance, the discussion overlooks the fact that a rise in money incomes and, to some extent, in prices and cost may merely represent the monetary counterpart of a rise in real income, resulting from an increased demand for a country's exports in conditions of a fixed rate of exchange. At one stage (p. 115) the mission refers to the inflationary pressure caused by large export surpluses. In the context of Nigeria this is incorrect. The export surpluses reflect the austere policies of the marketing boards and, to a much lesser extent, of the central government. By paying producers much less than the proceeds of the exports, these policies constricted the demand for imports and have brought about an export surplus, which, so far from being a cause of inflationary pressure, reflects the contraction of internal monetary demand.[26]

NOTES TO SELECTION 29

[1]Machinery, tools, fertilizers and other capital goods are duty-free, and this exemption is to be continued.

[2]With one exception, not relevant to this discussion, which is considered in Sec. IV.

[3]Two minor exceptions, both more apparent than real, are the remarks on p. 113 that the incidence of the import duties is, on the whole, progressive, and on p. 114, where it is suggested that the extremely high rates of export duty on cocoa should be retained because "there is ample evidence that producers of cocoa are, as a group, substantially better off than other agricultural producers." The former proposition is of very limited meaning and of doubtful validity if we contrast the cash income and expenditure of the poorer agricultural producers with those of the more prosperous sections of the town population. The validity and relevance of the second proposition are considered later.

[4]These remarks do not bear on the desirability of government expenditure generally or on the productivity of government expenditure on particular projects, and much less on government intervention in economic life. They emphasize the importance of understanding the sources of the expenditure and the repercussions of the process of securing it.

[5]We shall be concerned primarily with the response of the supply of effort to the exchange sector arising from changes in the relative attractiveness of that sector and subsistence activity rather than with that arising from changes in the relative attractiveness of work and leisure. The former is much the more relevant aspect for our purpose; moreover, for reasons indicated in n. 7, on p. 480, the conclusions are most unlikely to be affected by concentrating on this aspect of the problem. As far as it is susceptible to economic analysis, the other aspect can be analyzed by the familiar method of income and substitution effects.

[6]This implies even more to the taxation of producers through export duties and surpluses of marketing boards, which are discussed later, especially in Sec. IV.

[7]Three semitechnical points may be noted here. First, the discussion does not allow for the effects of the expenditure of the receipts of taxation, since it is concerned with the implications of the proposal and not with the incidence of the fiscal system as a whole. Second, the analysis stresses the substitution effect of a rise in the prices of the taxed commodities relative to the price of leisure and subsistence output. It is possible that higher prices of incentive goods may cause some people to work harder to earn the additional money income needed to maintain a desired level of consumption of these commodities. It is most unlikely that in the conditions of Nigeria or most other underdeveloped countries the income effect would outweigh, or even approach, the substitution effect. Production for the market generally involves transport costs and other costs as well, and the rise in the price of consumer goods therefore tends to have disproportionate effects on marginal reward. This will be reinforced by the fact that the taxation is intended to be particularly heavy on inessentials. The income effect is not likely to outweigh the substitution effect when the additional taxation affects marginal income more than total income. Third, the suggestion that production for the market will be less refers, of course, to a comparison of what it would have been in the absence of this measure and not to a comparison with an earlier period; that is, it stresses the functional, not the historical, relationship.

[8]The connection between export duties and the surpluses of the marketing board is examined further in Sec. IV. The producers of these crops also pay, of course, import and excise duties, as well as various local taxes.

[9]I calculated elsewhere (*West African Trade* [Cambridge: At the University Press, 1954], Chap. xxii) that in 1950–51 the cash proceeds of most groundnut producers from the sale of groundnuts were less than £5 a year; in the absence of

export duties and surpluses of the marketing boards they would have been around £10–12, so that these levies represented taxation at a rate of more than two-thirds of available proceeds.

[10] As Nigerian exports are a very small proportion of world exports (and a fortiori of world supplies) of vegetable oils, oilseeds, and cotton, the incidence of the levies on these products is clearly on the sellers. On the other hand the incidence of the taxation on cocoa (of which Nigeria produces about 12 per cent and the Gold Coast about one-third of the world output) between producers and consumers is more complex and raises interesting issues. Its examination involves such matters as the elasticity of demand for cocoa; the length of the period over which producers are taxed; the response of producers to changes in price and the lapse of time before their decision affects market supplies; the co-ordination of policies pursued locally in Nigeria and the Gold Coast; and the growth of outside production under the stimulus of high prices. These issues, which are not considered in the mission's report, are interesting and important but do not directly affect the argument in the text.

[11] This matter is considered further in Sec. IV.

[12] Moreover, the mission regards the report as a model for simliar documents in the future: "The report is to a certain extent illustrative of the kind of analysis such a staff [the proposed economic secretariat] would make" (p. 82).

[13] The influence of prices and the functional relationship between price and the quantities demanded and supplied are ignored, not rejected explicitly. Rejection of market prices as a system of directives for the allocation of resources and/or the distribution of wealth is a political judgment which raises quite different issues.

[14] This is particularly evident in northern Nigeria, where distances are great, transport is comparatively poorly developed, and the returns yielded by the production of groundnuts and cotton are very low. The influence of even small differences in the price on supply under these conditions used to be explicitly recognized; until a few years ago cotton was exempt from export duty, which was then very low, to encourage the production by securing to the producer a slightly higher price.

[15] As I have reviewed the operation of these organizations repeatedly elsewhere, the discussion is confined to issues bearing directly on the mission's report. Detailed discussion of the origins and operations of the marketing boards will be found in *West African Trade,* Part 5. The problems of smoothing the fluctuations in prices and incomes of primary producers are also considered in two articles by Professor F. W. Paish and me in the *Economic Journal* for December, 1952, and December, 1954.

[16] It was introduced for cocoa in 1939 and for other products in 1942; it was put on a permanent basis after the war.

[17] This applies to cocoa whether the starting point is taken as 1939, when export monopoly was introduced, or 1947, when the present board was instituted. The corresponding statistics are more difficult to present for the producers of the other major crops (groundnuts, palm kernels, palm oil and cotton) chiefly because for a number of years all the exportable supplies were sold by the marketing authorities to the British purchasing departments at prices far below market prices. Indeed, for a number of years no surpluses could be accumulated, as the crops were sold on a cost basis, that is, at the prices paid to producers plus transport costs to the United Kingdom; and these prices were far below those paid by the Ministry of Food for bulk supplies from other Empire sources. When this method of purchase was somewhat modified, large surpluses were accumulated on these products as well. Details are shown in *West African Trade,* Chap. xxii, and in an article in the *Journal of the Royal Statistical Society,* 1954, Part I.

[18] There is a close connection between the level of export duties and the surpluses of the marketing boards. When the boards have surpluses, increases in export

duties diminish only the surpluses without directly affecting the prices received by producers. This naturally encourages the authorities to raise revenue by this means. As a result, not only are duties much higher than they were before the boards began, but the rates are also much higher than the corresponding rates on the few nonmineral exports not controlled by the boards, such as rubber, hides and skins, and timber. For instance, at the prices prevailing in the middle of 1954, the cocoa export duty in Nigeria was about 45 per cent of the f.o.b. value, and this represented then about 140 per cent of the price paid to producers. On the other hand, the export duty on rubber, which is produced in the same area of southern Nigeria, was then only 7½ per cent of the f.o.b. value. Yet, as already stated, the mission explicitly suggests the maintenance of the high rate of export duty on cocoa. Another tax—the produce sales tax—is levied only on products controlled by marketing boards.

In the Gold Coast all proceeds over £180 per ton f.o.b. are now taken by the government in export duty. This is a direct result of statutory marketing, since without the huge surpluses of the Cocoa Marketing Board this measure would have been politically quite impossible.

[19]In cocoa, though not in other products, in recent years part of the incidence of the system has been on consumers because the prolonged (over fifteen years) underpayment of producers has undoubtedly affected production, and the West African crop is an appreciable part of the world output. The new high market prices have encouraged the establishment of new capacity elsewhere, while the underpayment of producers in West Africa has discouraged it there. There is implicit here a serious threat to the long-run competitive position of the West African cocoa producers. This is another essential aspect of the system not mentioned in the mission's report.

[20]This is obvious when the surpluses are unspent. Where they are spent, the effect is more complex.

[21]It is suggested that the producer prices should not be varied by more than 10 per cent in either direction from one year to the next; but this does not meet the case if there is a marked trend in prices or if there are wide fluctuations. The report also presents a simple example to show that the reserves are sufficient to maintain producer prices over a number of years, even if prices fall severely (characteristically, the great depression is taken as an example), but this is quite meaningless.

[22][Footnote omitted.]

[23]In 1953 and 1954, the Nigeria Oil Palm Produce Marketing Board subsidized the producer prices of palm oil at a level of over £60 a ton; by doing so, it drew on reserves which had been accumulated partly over an earlier period when producer prices were about £30. Thus, so far from smoothing the fluctuations in producer prices or incomes by taxing producers in a period of high prices and subsidizing them in a period of low prices, the system taxed one group of producers in a period of low prices and used the proceeds to subsidize a different group in a period of high prices. For the other products there has been uninterrupted accumulation of surpluses, so that if the reserves were to be disbursed, the same anomaly would arise. As a matter of interest, oil palm produce in Nigeria is derived from wild trees not from planted trees, so that the adverse effect of underpayment of producers on long-term supply is much less important in this case than for other products. Yet palm oil is the only crop the producers of which have not been heavily underpaid in recent years.

[24]The so-called "improvement" in the quality of cocoa has come about partly by the prescription of grade differentials unrelated to market requirements and partly through prohibition of export of so-called "substandard" produce. (This latter factor is not mentioned in the report.) These measures necessarily affect adversely the interests of producers and of the economy as a whole, since they either (1) frustrate the export of substandard output already produced, (2) induce the uneconomic

expenditure of additional resources, or (3) deflect production into less valuable activities. A detailed discussion of these and similar measures will be found in an article, "The Economics of Marketing Reform," by Mr. B. S. Yamey and me, *Journal of Political Economy,* June, 1954.

[25]The mission frequently fails to recognize the significance of the concepts of waste and resources. For instance, it tends to regard nonutilization of materials as wasteful, without considering whether the cost of the co-operant resources would not exceed the value of the processed products; an example is the discussion of cottonseed processing on p. 375.

[26]In case the objection is made that this policy reflected a shortage of imports, it may be stated that, for the period reviewed by the mission, there was an ample supply of imports and for part of the period importers actually canceled commitments because of insufficient demand. (Cf. *West African Trade,* chaps. xxiii and xxiv, and *Journal of the Royal Statistical Society,* 1954, Part I, p. 27.)

30

A Reply to Mr. Bauer

by John H. Adler*

GOVERNMENT RECEIPTS AND EXPENDITURES IN AN UNDEVELOPED ECONOMY

THE only recommendations—as distinct from analysis—of the Nigeria report which Bauer challenges have to do with various aspects of fiscal policy.[1] Bauer's position may be summarized as follows: (a) The government's share of 7.5 per cent in the Nigerian gross national product is not, or not necessarily, "too low," as the mission has indicated, for this computation fails to take account of the fact that a substantial proportion of the gross national product is produced and consumed in the subsistence sector. Thus the tax burden falls upon the money sector of the economy alone and is therefore not only much heavier but "might retard the spread of production for sale."[2] (b) Export taxes are highly inequitable, because they impose a heavy burden on the small producer but do not affect the (presumably better-off) urban population.[3] (c) An increase in import duties, as proposed by the mission, is likewise inappropriate, since "higher prices (or reduced supply) of commodities to be purchased in the exchange sector diminish the attractiveness of work for that sector relative both to subsistence activity and to leisure."[4]

Before discussing these points, it is only fair to point out that there was not available either to the mission or, to the best of my knowledge, to Bauer the body of empirical evidence required to determine with any degree of exactness the ability to pay taxes, the incidence of taxation on people at various levels of income, the incidence of benefits of free government services on the various sectors of the economy, and so on. This lack of exact data is not peculiar to Nigeria; it is characteristic of virtually all underdeveloped countries. Bits and pieces of evidence, the "informed opinion" of persons familiar with

*John H. Adler, "The Economic Development of Nigeria," *Journal of Political Economy* (Chicago: The University of Chicago Press), LXIV (October, 1956), 425–32. Copyright 1956 by The University of Chicago. Reprinted with permission.

the country and the habits and attitudes of its people, and impressions and hunches frequently must take the place of "hard" data. Thus there is always room for doubt and disagreement about the most appropriate measures to be taken; this is particularly true in the field of public finance, the subject of *political* economy par excellence. There is, on the other hand, no room for dogmatic assertions.

In Nigeria, as in all countries, whether advanced or underdeveloped, any tax affects either consumption or savings or both, the volume of production or effort, and the direction of effort or the composition of production. In Nigeria, as elsewhere, taxes of any kind are likely to have an adverse effect on "investment" in the establishment, extension and improvement of agricultural holdings; and they affect the composition of output if export crops alone are taxed while crops sold in the domestic market remain tax-free. Similarly, an increase in the price of "incentive goods" brought about by an increase in import duties (as recommended by the mission) is likely to have *some* adverse effects, on both the volume and the composition of production.

I shall state later my reasons for believing that in Nigeria these disincentive effects are not so serious as Bauer seems to think. But another consideration is more important. Bauer has neglected to take into account, as an offset to the effects of the export taxes and import duties, the benefits of additional government expenditures which, like the taxes, have an effect on the volume and composition of production. To quote Bauer, "this neglect is crucial."[5] The largest part of the increases in expenditures which the mission recommended was for the expansion and improvement of transportation facilities, general and technical education, and agricultural facilities, such as research and experiment stations and extension services. Though an aggregate quantitative appraisal is obviously impossible, it was my conviction (and, I believe, that of all members of the mission) that an expansion of government services in these three categories, as well as in the field of medical services and public health, would be exceedingly "productive" in the sense of encouraging production to a far greater extent than the recommended taxes would discourage it.[6]

This conviction is based on the fact that Nigeria, like many other underdeveloped countries and particularly like many other dependent territories, has been "undergoverned." Because government receipts and expenditures are low and the government's share in the national product is small, the volume of communal services which only government can provide, or which can be provided much more economically by government, has been insufficient.

Until recently there was no public school system in Nigeria; even now only 7 per cent of the population of school age or over is literate. Of a network of 30,000 miles of roads, only 2,000 miles are hard-surfaced, although they must carry 26,200 motor vehicles. There are less than five hundred officials in the agricultural services—to care for the needs of six or seven million farm units. The view that there is a need for improving government services and the possibility of doing so is not merely a mistaken notion of the mission; it is borne out by the opinions of virtually all observers familiar with Nigeria, with tropical Africa, and, more generally, with underdeveloped countries. The benefits from an improved transportation system can be demonstrated partly in quantitative terms, simply by computing the extra cost of the transport allowances which the Groundnut Marketing Board used to pay per ton-mile for transportation on gravel and dirt roads over those paid on hard-surfaced roads and comparing this differential with the cost of road improvement; in the case of the railroads, by comparing the cost of more and better locomotives and rolling stock with the quantity and quality losses incurred in the prolonged storing of groundnuts at railheads because of the inability to transport them to the ports. On the importance of expanded agricultural services, Karl Pelzer recently commented: "The two great problems in Africa, as in other parts of the tropics, are (1) to develop farming systems which will permit higher yields per unit of land and per man-hour without adverse effects on the soil and (2) to devise effective channels of transmission down to the grass roots of the lesson learned in the research stations."[7]

There is no need to labor the importance of raising the educational level, both for economic reasons and for its effect on the social and political organization of a country on the verge of independence. But it seems worthwhile to mention the recent upsurge in the demand for education which has resulted this year in the introduction of free primary education for the first time in one region, to be followed in about three years by another region.

The incentive effects of additional government expenditures are likely to be strong enough to overcome the "discrimination" against export commodities or, more generally, against production for exchange, brought about by taxes on exports. Bauer himself refers to the deterrent effect of transport costs on production for the market. If transport costs are reduced, production for the market becomes relatively more attractive, and better agricultural production techniques introduced through extension services make it easier to produce a surplus over and above subsistence requirements.

Before leaving the subject of the disincentive and incentive effects of the mission's fiscal recommendations, a few more remarks should be made. First, there is the complex and perplexing question of the true magnitude of the price elasticity of supply of taxed commodities (which not only has an obviously important bearing on the Nigerian revenue structure but is of general interest, since export taxes are used extensively in many underdeveloped countries). Bauer cites as evidence of the response of output to prices the failure of export production to expand in the postwar period when the marketing boards "underpaid" the producers by withholding a large proportion of export proceeds. As a matter of fact, the figures he cites are rather misleading.[8] If marketing-board purchases for the crop years 1951–52 through 1953–54 (for which virtually complete information was available to the mission at the time of the completion of its report) are compared with the average annual exports in 1935–39, the picture shown in Table 1 emerges.

Thus, far from showing that exports have "increased little since the mid-1930's," the figures indicate a respectable, and in some instances spectacular, rise in the volume of exports. To be sure, they are cited here merely to show that the price policies of the marketing boards did not have a demonstrably adverse effect on production, as Bauer purports to show by his figures. This is not to deny that a still larger volume of output might have been obtained had higher prices been paid to the producers or, more exactly, had there been better terms of trade between export produce and the commodities which export producers bought (including not only imports, as Bauer implies, but domestic goods and services as well). But there is reason to believe

TABLE 1

PRINCIPAL EXPORT CROPS OF NIGERIA

(*In Thousands of Long Tons*)

	Average Annual Exports, 1935–37	Average Marketing Board Purchases, Crop Years 1951–52 to 1953–54[a]
Palm oil	150	218
Palm kernels	346	426
Groundnuts	242	427
Cocoa	91	104
Cotton	11	62

[a]The use of the export figures for the postwar period is misleading in the case of groundnuts, since a large proportion of what was purchased could not be moved to the ports because of transport difficulties. For all other commodities, marketing-board purchases and exports are vitually identical.

that in Nigeria, and probably in many other underdeveloped countries as well, supply elasticities are not large—certainly not as large as Bauer assumes on general grounds. To quote W. A. Lewis:

When people who have hitherto produced only for their own subsistence are first introduced to a price economy, their response is both limited and unskilled. They neglect opportunities; they do not know how to choose; they are easily defrauded; they do not know about seasonal and cyclical variations, or about quantity discounts; and so on. One has to learn how to respond to market prices just as one learns any other part of one's culture. The performance improves as generations grow up who have always known and used the market, and who are experienced in its tricks.[9]

Not all of Professor Lewis' points apply with equal force to Nigeria, because the Nigerian agricultural producer has already become accustomed to produce in part for the market. But there is no doubt that the response to price incentives is by and large spotty and slow.

One last remark about the effects of taxation on the supply of effort. Bauer dismisses in two sentences in a footnote the possibility that "higher prices of incentive goods may cause some people to work harder to earn the additional money income needed to maintain a desired level of consumption of these commodities."[10] I agree with Bauer that in the Nigerian scene, *in the aggregate,* the disincentive effects of taxation (and the substitution effects of taxes on specific commodities) are more important than the incentive effect incidental to attempts to maintain income and consumption notwithstanding tax liabilities. But this is not to say that this incentive effect can be disregarded. Because certain tax liabilities have to be discharged in money, and some commodities, particularly imports, can be acquired only for cash, there is a strong incentive to produce something for sale in the market economy. There is no doubt that in earlier periods taxes have acted as a powerful work incentive and have hastened the spread of the exchange economy.[11] The reason for my belief that the incentive effect of taxation is no longer of substantial importance in Nigeria is that the economy is already "shot through" with production for exchange. A scrutiny of the Nigerian national income estimates, together with information on external, interregional, and intraarea trade, indicates that perhaps half of the national output enters the exchange economy; one-third to two-fifths of total agricultural output is produced for sale.[12] But there are still some "backward" areas in the country where the need to raise cash to pay taxes and to buy imports is a strong work incentive.

BURDEN OF EXPORT DUTIES

A subsidiary argument running through Bauer's article is his contention that export duties are excessively high and therefore violate the principle of tax equity. He specifically mentions rates as high as 66 per cent for groundnuts and over 45 per cent for cocoa.[13] Bauer implies that rates of these magnitudes were indorsed by the mission. Were that so, the charge of irresponsibility or sheer ignorance would be justified.

Actually, the mission's recommendations are quite different. The mission (a) suggested that marketing boards follow a "neutral" price policy; that is, pay the producers the local equivalent of world market prices but mitigate excessive price fluctuations by keeping year-to-year changes within 10 per cent limits; and (b) projected prices of export commodities at which the export duties would be only 10 per cent of the f.o.b. price for all commodities except cocoa, for which they would amount to 18 per cent.[14]

So much by way of correction. There remains for discussion the more general problem of the place of export duties in the tax structure of underdeveloped countries or, at any rate, in countries whose structure of production bears some resemblance to that of Nigeria. Except in a few instances, the production of agricultural exports is not carried on in a separate "sector" of the economy but is intermingled with production for subsistence and for the internal market. There is a good deal of evidence—though, as indicated before, it is not susceptible of being put into exact quantitative terms—or a rather close positive correlation between total family income and the volume of production for export. A simple (and thus obviously oversimplified) "model" of the pattern of income distribution in the agricultural sector would look somewhat as follows. At the bottom of the income scale are the households which produce almost exclusively for their own subsistence; next are households which devote an appreciable proportion of their effort to production for the export or the domestic market; and so on. At the top of the scale are a small number of producing units specializing completely, or almost so, in the production of export commodities; for example, the "cocoa barons" of the West. As a consequence of this income distribution pattern, the incidence of export taxes is such that the tax exemption of subsistence production is equivalent to the "basic exemption" in an income tax system, and the incidence of a flat-rate export tax becomes progressive relative to total family income. To take Bauer's example of the small cocoa farmer who produces 7 cwt. of cocoa (and who would fall into my second income group), assuming a total household income corresponding to the average of the Western Region (that is, of the order of £170, in a five-person household), the tax on such a farmer's cocoa production would be at present £15, or less than 9 per cent. His total tax liability, assuming that he spends *all* cocoa income on imports (which is not likely) and allowing for the regional produce sales tax and for (local) direct taxes, would be of the order of £22–£25, or less than 15 per cent of his income.[15]

At first glance this seems a large tax burden on a family income equivalent to $476. But this level of income is two-thirds above the national average and corresponds on the income distribution scale to an American household income of $15,000.[16] The burden of other export taxes which falls on agricultural producers with lower average incomes should be substantially lower—according to the mission's recommendations and projections, they should not exceed 10 per cent of the f.o.b. value of exports; the total tax burden should also be correspondingly lower.

These comments should dispose of the question of the absolute level of the burden of export duties; they should also largely dispose of the issue of "discrimination" against production for sale, if they are read in conjunction with the preceding comments about the relatively small supply elasticity of export produce and the beneficial effects of additional government services. If, as I strongly believe, additional government services do stimulate total productive effort, then they must stimulate primarily production for sale because of the high income elasticity of demand for goods obtainable for money, as compared with the obviously very low income elasticity of demand for additional subsistence goods.

Export taxes, however, do discriminate against export products and thus favor the production of goods for sale in the domestic market. This is a serious drawback of export taxes unless there is a high elasticity of substitution of domestic goods for imports. Since Nigeria's imports consist almost exclusively of manufactured consumers' goods, capital goods, and raw materials not produced in Nigeria, the range of substitution possibilities is very limited.[17] It happens that for the time being this does not pose a balance-of-payments problem for Nigeria, since exchange reserves are equal to almost one-third of gross national product or to the value of imports for two years. But in some other countries export taxes, or adverse price policies equivalent to export taxes, can cause and in some instances have caused serious balance-of-payments difficulties.

INCIDENCE OF IMPORT DUTIES

I turn now to a brief discussion of the incidence of import duties. The mission suggested that duties should be raised, on the average by 50 per cent of the current tariff, for all commodities except food, tobacco, gasoline, and kerosene but that all imports of food (except confectionery and alcoholic beverages) and building materials should be exempt from duty.[18] This recommendation was made for two reasons, both mentioned in the report: (a) the prevailing duties are low and (b) there is considerable evidence that the incidence of the tariff, except for duties on such essentials as salt and kerosene, is on the whole progressive. The first point is generally accepted; the duty rates range between 15 and 20 per cent of the import price for most articles and amount to considerably less on the final sales price.[19] The second point follows directly from the relationship, set forth above, between income distribution and the degree of participation in the market economy.[20] It follows also from the presumably universal high income elasticity of demand for manufactured consumers' goods (most of which are imports in the case of Nigeria), and it is implied by Bauer himself by the use of the term "incentive goods."[21]

Compared with export taxes, import duties (as a revenue measure) have the additional advantage of imposing a tax liability on all sectors of the economy; they are therefore not discriminatory. (Because of the virtual absence of Nigerian domestic industries competing with imports, the protective effects of duties can be disregarded.) Nevertheless, I believe it would have been wrong to recommend to the Nigerian authorities the substitution of still higher import duties for export taxes. There is, I think, virtue in making use of more than one kind of levy rather than relying too heavily on one type alone. The doubling or tripling of import duties which would have been required were they to take the place of export duties undoubtedly would have had some undesirable effects, particularly on the urban cost of living and indirectly on the operating cost of private business and of government. But I do not press this point; I can easily conceive of situations—for example, a sharp deterioration in the Nigerian terms of trade—in which a reduction of export taxes, together with a further increase of import duties, would be appropriate.

There is one more point to be made in this connection: the proposed increase of duties on consumers' goods, together with duty exemptions for capital goods, is likely to have some effect on the aggregate expenditure pattern by diverting purchases from consumption into "investment," particularly toward the purchase of such items as agricultural tools and implements and fertilizer; it would thus contribute to the extension and improvement of agricultural holdings, which the mission, like Bauer, considered eminently important. This kind of substitution effect presumably would compensate in part for the undesirable substitution effects which Bauer mentions.

Use of Direct Taxes and its Limitations

In his review Bauer does not mention the fiscal recommendation of the mission which I believe is of the greatest general interest; namely, the recommendation to raise the level of direct local taxes substantially.[22] The reason for proposing an increase in these taxes was twofold. In the first place, the mission did not believe that an increase in the federal income tax, which applies only to non-Africans and to African residents of the federal capital of Lagos, was feasible or desirable. This tax is borne almost entirely by non-Africans, either government employees or employees of foreign-owned enterprises. Since in the next few years the development of Nigeria will depend to a considerable extent on the country's ability to attract foreign personnel,[23] and since Nigeria must compete with other overseas areas in the tight labor market of the United Kingdom and the European continent, it would have been folly to propose an increase in these income taxes.[24] There is thus a serious inequity in the Nigerian tax structure which is nevertheless unavoidable and even intentional as far as non-African salaried employees are concerned. The really unfortunate feature of the situation is that it also benefits a small number of well-to-do Africans in Lagos and some independent non-African businessmen.

But the main reason for relying on local direct taxes rather than on the federal income tax is the fact that in the Nigerian situation—and in that of many other underdeveloped countries as well—the willingness to pay taxes directly depends on the immediacy of the benefits of the government services which these taxes "buy." The rural areas of Nigeria abound with examples of virtually voluntary increases in taxes—where the taxpayer directly benefits from new or improved communal facilities such as schools, hospitals, community centers, and roads. In most instances the graduation of these direct taxes is still small and crude, and the system is thus a long way from reflecting ability to pay. But, with local pressures for better communal services growing and with rising over-all tax liabilities, a strong tendency is developing to make the tax burden progressive (or, at any rate, less regressive).

The other side of the coin is the impossibility, for social, political, and administrative reasons, of imposing and collecting regional or federal direct taxes. In the Nigerian social and cultural setting, where group allegiance in many parts of the country does not extend beyond the village level, the imposition of direct taxes by authorities higher than the local authority is regarded as equivalent to the imposition of a tribute, with all the connotations of injustice and inequity attached to that term. During the mission's stay in Nigeria, tax riots occurred in parts of the Western Region where the regional government had imposed a "Health and Education Levy" of 10s. 6d. per taxpayer, to be raised by making local tax assessments more progressive. The new levy was a complete failure until the government permitted local authorities to retain 7 shillings (out of the 10s. 6d.) for additional local expenditure.

In the long run, however, it should be possible to modify the tax structure gradually so as to increase the share of direct taxes and to reduce the reliance on custom duties and excise taxes. To hasten this development, the system of direct taxation will have to be built up in an unorthodox way—from the bottom up. But, as Mrs. Hicks remarked, "the country which can work a successful income tax may reasonably consider itself on the high road to development."[25]

NOTES TO SELECTION 30

[1]Although I trust that the members of the mission would agree with the substance of this comment, I cannot claim that I speak for the (now disbanded) mission. Likewise, what I have to say does not necessarily represent the views of the International Bank for Reconstruction and Development.

For simplicity, Bauer's article is referred to subsequently as "Bauer," and the mission's report, *The Economic Development of Nigeria,* is referred to as *"Report."*

[2]Bauer, p. 401 [see selection 29 above].

[3]Marketing-board profits may be considered equivalent to (additional) export taxes and are treated as such in this section; this in no way affects the argument.

[4]Bauer, p. 400 [see selection 29 above].

[5]Bauer states: "Three *semitechnical* points may be noted here. First, the discussion in the article does not allow for the effects of the expenditure of the receipts of taxation, since it is concerned with the implications of the proposal and *not with the incidence of the fiscal system as a whole* . . ." (p. 401, n. 9) (My italics.) The inadmissibility of an analysis which disregards the incidence of benefits of government services has been pointed out, among others, by G. F. Shirras and L. Rostas in *The Burden of British Taxation* (New York, 1943) as follows: "The estimates [of the tax burden] relate solely to the burden placed on the citizen by the finances of the state; they take no notice of the advantages he derives. Before any judgments in equity are entered, both sides must be considered" (p. xii). See also my paper, "The Fiscal System, the Distribution of Income and Public Welfare," in K. E. Poole, *Fiscal Policies and the American Economy* (New York, 1951), pp. 359–409.

[6]That is, the marginal benefits to be derived from additional public expenditures of these kinds would be far in excess of the marginal burden of additional taxation.

[7]In *Africa Today,* ed. C. Grove Haines (Baltimore, 1955), p. 415.

[8]Bauer, Table 1 and table in n. 31, p. 408 [not included in previous selection].

[9]*The Theory of Economic Growth* (London, 1955), p. 75.

[10]Bauer, p. 401 [see selection 29 above]. The quotation refers to taxation of imports, but it obviously applies also to export taxes and to the level of taxation in general.

[11]"In the case of the native, taxation introduces a money economy into his life which has no relation to his traditional ideas of wealth, and, where the incidence of taxation is based on his capacity for earning money rather than actual wealth or income, it causes a dislocation in his life, and forces him into an activity in which he would not otherwise engage. While it would not be correct to say that taxation is today the main reason which induces the native to seek work, the persistent and recurrent demand by the authorities for money for taxation necessitates a continual individual effort which has little counterpart with Europeans" (Lord Hailey, *An African Survey: A Study of Problems Arising in Africa South of the Sahara* [2d ed.; New York, 1945], p. 594).

[12]This admittedly rough estimate is based on the detailed data shown in A. R. Prest and I. G. Stewart, *The National Income of Nigeria, 1950–51* (London, 1953). A United Nations study, *Enlargement of the Exchange Economy in Tropical Africa* (New York, 1954), estimates (p. 14) that 41 per cent of the total area under cultivation is "under crops for market." It should be added that the distinction between the subsistence economy and the exchange economy which Bauer emphasizes so heavily is a rather thin one. Domestic goods (mostly foodstuffs) and imports are daily bought and sold in the thousands of village markets. There is no distinct "exchange sector" and no "subsistence sector." All households produce for the market, as well as for the satisfaction of their own wants. However, the proportion of total production (or effort) that is sold does vary greatly.

[13]These percentages include marketing-board profits.

[14]Plus somewhat less than 2 per cent for regional produce sales taxes effective in two of the three regions. At current prices (October, 1955) the "effective" tax rate on cocoa is 16.5 per cent, since the marketing boards apparently incur a loss of about £11 per ton. On groundnuts they are about breaking even or making a small profit of less than 10 shillings per ton; this means the "effective" tax rate is 10 per cent or slightly higher. On cotton, palm oil, and palm kernels, however, the marketing boards are apparently withholding a considerable share of the sales proceeds. Somewhere between 15 and 20 per cent is withheld; an exact computation is impossible because of the large number of grades and because, in the case of palm oil, prices vary among regions.

[15]This rough computation is based on estimates of regional income (*Report,* p. 616), the burden of import taxes relative to retail prices of imports (Prest and Stewart, *The National Income of Nigeria, 1950–51,* p. 84), the produce sales tax of £4 per ton, and the average direct tax liability applicable to the Western Region.

[16]The same point is made about the Gold Coast in B. M. Niculescu, "Fluctuations in Income of Primary Producers: Further Comment," *Economic Journal,* LXIV (December, 1954), 735: "There is no doubt that today, in the Gold Coast, the equivalent of the rich uncle from America is the uncle who owns a cocoa farm." Mr. Niculescu's article also throws considerable light on the relative importance of producer prices as a determinant of the volume of production and on other points raised by Bauer in his review article.

[17]There are a few minor exceptions (e.g., sugar), but these may be disregarded.

[18]*Report,* pp. 113–14. Most capital goods, including agricultural implements, are already duty-free.

[19]See n. 15 above.

[20]It is further borne out by observation: in the poorest parts of the country, such as the Plateau area, consumption of imports is limited to a narrow range of cheap goods, while it is in the "rich" cocoa area and in the commercial centers that one encounters the "snappy dresser" and the consumer of imported liquor.

[21]Lord Hailey writes: "The forms of native taxation are, in almost every case, insufficiently graduated as between richer and poorer individuals and areas, and need to be supplemented by a scheme of taxes which will fall upon those possessing exceptional capacity to pay; the purchase of imports is one important evidence of such capacity" (*op. cit.,* p. 1460). See also H. P. Wald and J. N. Froomkin (eds.), *Papers and Proceedings of the Conference on Taxation and Economic Development* (Cambridge, 1955), p. 30.

[22]*Report,* pp. 120–22. The recommended increase in direct taxes is *proportionately* much greater than the increase in customs and excise taxes (compare cols. 5 and 7 in Table 4, p. 111). Bauer, however, states that "the mission suggests higher import and excise duties as the principal source of additional revenue" (p. 399). [See selection 29 above.]

[23]*Report,* pp. 23–24 and 201–03.

[24]The views of the mission on this point have been amply confirmed by subsequent events. Following an official inquiry, government salaries have been raised, primarily to attract personnel to fill existing vacancies. The disincentive effect of high and progressive income taxes on recruitment of overseas personnel is analyzed in some detail by A. R. Prest, "Income Tax Can Check Development," *New Commonwealth,* XXIX (March 21, 1955), 270–72.

[25]Ursula Hicks, "The Search for Revenue in Underdeveloped Countries," *Revue de science et de legislation financières,* XLIV (1952), 40. In the article Mrs. Hicks strongly favors export taxes.

Part VII

Regional Integration, Tax Administration, and Technical Assistance

THE brief discussion by Carl Shoup of some of the possible problems of harmonizing the public finance systems of developing countries which are forming a common market or free trade area is suggestive of the way in which new problems arise in the field of taxation before we learn how to handle the old ones. Recent movements toward regional or international economic integration in both Latin America and Africa indicate the need for more thought along the lines indicated in this paper if serious problems are to be avoided in the future.

No book on the fiscal problems of the poor countries would be complete without an explicit treatment of tax administration, the level of which is in fact usually the overriding determinant of the kind of tax system a country now has and of the possibilities of changing it. The paper by Stanley Surrey, now Assistant Secretary of the United States Treasury, is an admirable survey of this important and complex field.

Finally, since we hope this book will be of some use to those interested in technical assistance work in the fiscal area, it seemed appropriate to conclude with a selection dealing with the problems and criteria of technical assistance missions. Dr. Papanek, Deputy Director of the Development Advisory Service of Harvard University, whose knowledge of technical assistance comes through extensive operating experience, is not concerned here with fiscal missions in particular; his article, however, is generally applicable to them and provides a fitting conclusion to this volume.

31

Tax Problems of Common
Markets in Latin America

by Carl S. Shoup*

WHEN nations join in a free trade area or a customs union, the
question arises whether differences among their several public finance
systems can continue without impairing operation of the common
market (for brevity, I shall use the term "common market" to cover
both a common market proper, that is, a customs union, and a free
trade area). Different proportions of gross national product are taken
in taxation, or spent on government outlays; the structure of the tax
system and of the expenditure system differs from one country to
another; the rate of income tax differs in each country, as well as the
level of personal exemptions, the treatment of corporate income, the
provisions for depreciation, and so on; sales taxes vary in rate and
type. Is all this a matter of little consequence, once the tariff barriers
have been removed? Or does removal of those barriers simply heighten
awareness of disparities that are inconsistent with, and even dangerous
for, a common market?

PUBLIC FINANCE SYSTEMS IN LATIN AMERICAN FREE
TRADE OR COMMON MARKET AREAS

I shall attempt some observations on this score, with respect to the
Latin American Free Trade Area (LAFTA) and the Central American Common Market. My remarks must be construed as invitations
to inquiry rather than considered conclusions; they are based on discussions with members of a research staff at Columbia University that
is beginning a three-year study of public finance problems in common
markets generally, and, in particular, the common markets of Europe,

*Tax Policy on United States Investment in Latin America (Princeton: Tax In-
stitute, Inc., 1963), pp. 181–88; and Carl S. Shoup, "Tax Problems of a Common
Market in Latin America," Tax Policy, XXIX (November, 1962), No. 11. Reprinted
with the kind permission of the publisher.

Latin America, and Africa.[1] Our staff has started to outline the issues that call for research, and we have the impression that this topic has been given little attention in academic, government, or business circles in Latin America.[2] In Europe, the discussion is much further advanced; the report of the Tinbergen Committee in 1953 to the Coal and Steel Authority, the papers in the Proceedings of the International Institute of Public Finance at its Frankfort meeting in 1953, and now the work of a special committee (Fiscal and Financial Committee) of the European Economic Community, under the chairmanship of Professor Neumark, together with recent scholarly books and articles on the issue, have laid a groundwork for more intensive research on certain aspects of the problem that we plan to pursue at Columbia. For Latin America, however, we must start almost at the beginning, except that the discussions of the European public finance disparities serve as a useful tool of comparison; and my remarks to follow will be cast largely in terms of just such a comparison, to inquire how the disparity problem differs in the Latin American common markets from its analogue in Europe.

In any event, the approach is not one of seeking a uniformity of public finance systems for uniformity's sake; instead, the question is, how much harmonization of the systems is necessary if the aims of the common market are to be achieved, and how far can the existing disparities be left untouched, so that the differing social, economic, and cultural values that they often reflect may not be needlessly contravened? Even if one attaches little value to these differences in background, he must distinguish between public finance reform, thought desirable for a given country regardless of what other countries are doing, and public finance harmonization, motivated by the desire to see a common market succeed.

DIFFERENCES BETWEEN LATIN AMERICAN AND EUROPEAN COMMON MARKETS

The first background difference that comes to mind between the European Economic Community (EEC) and the Latin American common markets is the difference in existing trade relations within the market. The EEC wishes to increase that which already exists on a considerable scale, namely, trade among the countries of the Community; Latin America must express the same aim in terms of bringing into being something (intra-market trade) that exists scarcely at all, or at least only to a modest degree. But this happens to be rather an advantage for tax harmonization, since it means that Latin America has chiefly to frame its tax laws so that future growth in intra-market trade is not hindered, while Europe has the difficult problem of removing hindrances of long standing, which are quantitatively important. If, for example, the European countries are to harmonize their systems of general sales taxation, especially if they are to consider moving from the destination principle to the origin principle, so that the sales tax rate of the country of origin governs, rather than that of the country where the goods are consumed, they must prepare for substantial shifts in existing trade, or pricing policies, or even investment flow. Latin America, on the other hand, can harmonize such taxes, if it wishes, with far less immediate disturbance to vested ways of doing business, or expectations.

A second background difference is geographical. Trade among the Latin American common market members moves, and will continue to move as it increases, largely by water (and to some extent by air) rather than overland. This fact indicates that one of the chief drives for harmonization of general sales taxes and excise taxes in Europe is lacking in Latin America, namely, the desire to remove the apparatus of border control, the desire to wipe out the petty annoyances and inconveniences that go with customs duties and that also go with compensating import duties and export exemptions. In a common market country most of whose imports come by sea, this hope has to be severely modified, for the port of entry must have some sort of customs apparatus to deal with goods that come from "third countries" (by this phrase I shall mean, countries outside the common market area). Hence we may say that Latin America unfortunately has less incentive for tax harmonization than Europe, so far as this single point, which of course must not be overrated, is concerned.

Export taxes are employed to a considerable degree in Latin America; but not at all by the European common market countries. Since trade among the Latin American countries is at present slight, giving up export taxes on goods moving only within the market will put little strain on the public revenues. Thus the Latin American countries have an important source of revenue that can be retained in virtually its present amount probably without standing in the way of such harmonization as proves necessary. But this conclusion is quite tentative; further research may uncover reasons why export taxes, even to third countries, must be harmonized within a common market.

A fourth difference between the circumstances of EEC the Latin American common markets is likely to prove very important with respect to harmonization, both of tax systems and expenditure systems, not to mention fiscal policies, including issuance or retirement of debt, and changes in the money stock. This is the fact that the EEC common market aims primarily at greater efficiency through heightened division of labor and through geographical flows of capital and labor, to equalize returns at the margins, while the Latin American countries are aiming first of all at development, which in this context seems to mean industrialization. In the European discussions, a strong flavor of economic neutrality pervades much of the analysis; although Europe, like everyone else, wants to "grow," they do not view the common market primarily as a means of reducing unproductive consumption in order to increase the proportion of GNP going to gross investment. In so far as the Latin American countries do have such an aim, it is conceivable that their plans for harmonizing their tax-expenditure systems would carry what might be called uniformity in bias, a deliberate bias to promote certain currents of economic activity, and discourage others. In this event, a much stricter degree of harmonization will be necessary than in Europe; no one country within the market is likely to be permitted to let its consumers go on as before, while the others carry the temporary burden of providing internal funds for growth.

Again, the issue can easily be overemphasized. Much of Latin America's lack of growth arises, in my view, from too low a level of consumption, not too high a level—but among the mass of low-income recipients only. In this connection I have just used the term "unproductive consumption" deliberately; economic growth will not be encouraged by building school houses for children who are too hungry to focus on their lessons, or by creating factories to be staffed by workers with a high rate of absenteeism because of illness. We need, then, to return to the classical school of economics with its distinction between productive and unproductive consumption. Tax systems will need to be harmonized to keep economic pressure off of such consumers, as well as allowing enough inducement to remain for the complementary capital stock with which the individuals, as producers, will work.

A fifth difference between Europe and Latin America is that, given their respective economic aims, Europe does not, but Latin America does, need to look forward to a rising proportion of government expenditures to total GNP. Once Europe has harmonized its existing systems of taxation and expenditure, its task will be largely done; in Latin America, on the contrary, harmonization measures adopted now may prove insufficient, or of an erroneous pattern, for the much larger role that governments will be destined to play in these economies, if stimulated industrialization rather than economic neutrality is to be the dominant policy. Europe's problems of public finance harmonization are large now, but will dwindle as steps are taken to meet them; Latin America's problems of public finance harmonization are small now, but will be growing indefinitely into the future.

A sixth distinction has to do with the flows of investment capital. Within the European common market it is important that intra-market movements of capital be not impeded, or distorted (allocated to less efficient use); such movements are important there. Accordingly, the income tax laws of the EEC must be harmonized in a way that will reduce double taxation, or undertaxation, of shareholders and corporations combined, when, for instance, the shareholders reside in one of the common market countries while their corporation does business in another. The problem is a technical one, its solution not likely to be obstructed by conflicting goals of high policy among the member states. A Latin American common market country, in contrast, gets little of its capital from the other countries of its common market. Third countries are an important source of capital. Given the aim of rapid industrialization, the Latin American countries have to guard against the danger of "tax wars" among themselves, in offering inducements to third-country capital by tax holidays, depreciation favors, and so on. Their income tax systems will have to be harmonized, and, more difficult perhaps, kept harmonized, with respect to such inducements. In the EEC countries, it is the treatment of each other's investors that is important; in the Latin American countries, it is the comparative treatment of third-country investors that makes urgent the harmonization of taxation of investment income.

Mention of the flow of capital brings to mind the possible flows of the other great factor of production, labor. Here, the question arises, whether the Latin American countries feel little pressure for harmonization of tax systems, social security systems, and distribution of public benefits; can these systems be fairly unequal without inducing a flow of labor from one of the market countries to another? In Europe, the comparative fiscal treatment of labor income, including the social security regime, is of some importance already and promises to become more so.

Finally, a uniform fiscal policy to combat unemployment and inflation is probably more significant in Europe than in Latin America, at least at the present time. This statement is based on the fact that the Latin American economies are more exposed economies, *vis-à-vis* the third-country world, than are the EEC economies. Being more exposed, they are somewhat less able to control their domestic employment and price levels by ordinary fiscal policy measures than are the EEC countries. Perhaps we should conclude that because the Latin American countries can do somewhat less, it is important that they coordinate even more closely than the European countries the measures that they can utilize. Moreover, there is clearly more room for improvement from the existing situation in the former group of countries than in the latter. And, as industrialization and intra-market trade grow in Latin America, harmonization of fiscal policy will become increasingly important and effective. On balance, perhaps there is not much distinction to be drawn after all between Europe and Latin America in the need for harmonization, though the pattern of fiscal measures utilized may well differ appreciably between the two groups.

In this appraisal of public finance problems in the Latin American markets, I have not distinguished between the free trade area of LAFTA and the common market of the Central American countries. The points made above apply to both markets, if not in precisely equal degree. More research is needed to ascertain whether, and if so, how, the need for public finance harmonization differs between these two groupings. A comparison of the two treaties (LAFTA and CACM) in this respect is not very helpful; neither one of them, quite naturally at this stage, devotes much attention to the harmonization problem, though the Central American treaty does provide for a Central American Trade Commission, which, among other duties, is to "take appropriate measures to ensure: . . . (ii) The establishment of a single fiscal system for articles under State monopoly and for goods subject to production, sales and consumption taxes; (iii) The conclusion of agreements designed to avoid double taxation in the matter of direct taxes; . . ."[3]

NOTES TO SELECTION 31

[1][The Research Program in International Economic Integration, sponsored by the School of International Affairs of Columbia University, of which Professor Shoup is now the director.]

[2]I am indebted to Professor Marion H. Gillim of Barnard College, Columbia University, and Mr. Esteban J. Karplus of Buenos Aires, who holds a Graduate Research Assistantship at Columbia University, for ideas and factual information on these issues, in the Latin American context.

[3]United Nations, Department of Economic and Social Affairs, *Multilateral Cooperation in Latin America* (New York, 1962), I, 21.

32

Tax Administration in Underdeveloped Countries

by Stanley S. Surrey*

INTRODUCTION

IN RECENT years considerable thought and attention have been devoted to the fiscal policies best suited to the economic development of the areas of the free world. As a part of this search for desirable fiscal policies, considerable stress is being placed on the role of tax policy. The various kinds of taxes—income, excise, property, import, export, succession—are being diligently surveyed. The combinations and alternatives within each class are all under scrutiny. Thus, in the income tax area, consideration is being given to individual and corporate taxes, to excess profits taxes, to taxes on increases in individual incomes, to taxes on dividends and other income payments, to the schedular and global forms of income taxes, and the like. In the excise area, there are sales taxes at the various levels of manufacture, wholesale or retail; taxes over the entire range of production and distribution, such as turnover and value added taxes; taxes on special pursuits such as mining or special products such as luxuries, and so on almost *ad infinitum*. Some countries are experimenting with an expenditure tax, which combines elements of income and excise taxation. The variety of taxes seems endless. Each must be considered in the light of particular fact situations and fiscal and economic goals. Each must be competitively analyzed against its rivals. And, when selected, the chosen tax must be imposed at the appropriate level of rates and scope of application.

*University of Miami Law Review, XII (Winter, 1958), 158–88. Mr. Surrey, at the time of this writing was professor of law and director of the International Program in Taxation, Harvard Law School.

This paper was originally prepared for the meeting of the International Institute of Public Finance at Rio de Janeiro, Brazil, September, 1954 and was published in the report of that meeting. It is reprinted here with the kind permission of the publisher. Some revisions have been made for the present article.

The problems of tax policy are difficult. Our knowledge of the effect and impact of various tax tools is not too impressive. We cannot talk with satisfactory confidence regarding such matters as tax incentives to economic development, the use of tax techniques to spur production, or consumption, or investment, or saving. But we are diligently striving to increase our knowledge about these matters, to indicate our confidence in the predictions regarding the results of one or another policy or tax technique. The efforts being made on these fronts are necessary and encouraging. However, a warning note seems appropriate. The concentration on tax policy—on the choice of taxes—may lead to insufficient consideration of the aspect of tax administration. In short, there may well be too much preoccupation with "what do do" and too little attention to "how to do it."

A survey of the available literature developing from the growing number of technical assistance missions underscores this warning. The administration of the tax system of the country involved generally receives relatively slight attention. Often the remarks devoted to administration are in the form of generalities, all of which notably come down to the repeated recommendation of "improvement." Exceptions may of course be found, as in the 1949–1950 Shoup Tax Mission to Japan.[1] But usually tax administration is off the beaten mission paths.

It is increasingly apparent, however, that tax administration must receive far greater attention if the goals of tax policy are to be attained. Much of tax policy is being directed to obtaining increased revenues to enable governments to carry out their economic planning. The search is for additional taxes, for new sources of revenue. Yet it is true in many countries that the successful administration of some of the existing taxes would provide a considerable part of the needed additional revenue. The diligent execution of existing taxes may well make unnecessary, or at least reduce, the multiplication of taxes in the search for revenue. It should be noted that this multiplication of taxes can, through a dispersion of administrative resources, result in a weakening of the entire tax structure. Moreover, the adoption of new taxes to compensate for the failure to enforce existing taxes may distort the equity of the system, for soon the rationale of the structure is lost in a complex maze of one set of taxes imposed to adjust for the defects in another set. Also, in the search of revenues, the rate of existing taxes may be pushed to such heights that the taxes cannot be enforced effectively and may cause undesirable economic effect.

In addition to the direct improvement in the revenue yields of existing taxes that could be achieved by effective tax administration, there are other factors pointing to the need for strengthening tax administration. The trend toward the progressive income tax is steadily growing. The reasons lie in the equity of the tax, with its roots in the public's strong acceptance of the ability-to-pay concept, and in its revenue strength as the economy expands. The income tax, however, presents formidable obstacles to effective enforcement. The stress on family status and on the net change of the taxpayer's economic position over a period of time demands a precision in the application of the income tax which is far greater than that required of other taxes. The need for precision grows in importance both as the rates climb upwards and as the base broadens with decreasing exemptions. The income tax may well be the favorite of the twentieth century, but it demands twentieth century administration. This requirement is even more urgent when one turns to the complex variations of that tax, such as a tax on excess profits or a tax on increases in individual incomes or a tax on expenditures: There are many who urge these variants without any comprehension of the complex legal and accounting problems which they create, without any recognition of the enormous difficulties being faced in the struggle to impose even the basic income tax, and without any realization that even countries with considerable experience in income tax administration have yet to master these specialized types of income taxation.

Another factor demanding emphasis on tax administration is the growing realization that the tax status of the agricultural sector of underdeveloped countries must be examined. There is strong support for the view that these sectors must furnish a substantial portion of the revenues if government is to carry out the social overhead projects necessary to economic development. But the tax devices to reach the agricultural sector are not fully developed and ready at hand to be utilized. One must explore the alternatives—the real property tax, the income tax, and excise taxes on agricultural products. Prominent in this examination must be a consideration of the aspect of administration with respect to these taxes.[2]

While many underdeveloped countries faced with dissatisfaction with their revenue systems are interested in making fundamental reforms, doing so may in some instances be putting the cart before the horse. Efforts to change the law may invoke sharp political and social struggles, whose effect might long delay any worthwhile changes. Also, desirable substantive reforms might be faced with the argument that they could not be administered and this could well be true given the present state of tax administration. Or, these changes if made might place such severe strains on an already weak administrative structure that the administration of the entire revenue system would be endangered. The sensible course in many countries may therefore be first to strengthen the existing administrative machinery and then when this had been accomplished to face the basic issues of tax reform.

We thus find, at least by comparison to substantive issues, insufficient consideration being paid to questions of tax administration at a time when the tax problems of underdeveloped countries accentuate the role of tax administration. Moreover, this lack of consideration is to be contrasted with the very acute difficulties which tax administrators face almost the world over. The tax administrator on the one hand sees new burdens falling on his shoulders—new taxes being imposed and existing levies becoming more severe. He must collect more taxes, at higher rates, and from an ever expanding body of taxpayers. On the other hand he finds himself saddled with a staff which is insufficient, inexperienced and poorly paid. He faces a public in large part unfamiliar with the tax knowledge and record keeping requirements which a developing state must inevitably demand of its citizens. He cannot obtain the needed support from the legal and accounting professions—the necessary allies for the successful administration of any complex tax system—either because of their lack of experience or sometimes because they are almost non-existent. Finally, he often must demand the taxes from businesses and individuals with a deep-rooted suspicion ranging to contempt of the tax collector, from a public whose antagonism to tax payment, arising from a basic lack of confidence in the government, is almost the very antithesis of the attitude which must be the cornerstone of every successful democratic tax system—that taxes are the price necessarily paid for civilized society.

So much for the background of this paper. While it can readily be concluded that the field of tax administration is of major importance, it must also be recognized that any such study would involved many facets and open up many difficult problems. The balance of this paper will briefly present some of these facets and problems. It may be pertinent to observe, in connection with the consideration of these matters, that while the issues and goals of fiscal policy may well differ from country to country, the problems of tax administration are quite likely to be very similar the world over. A multi-national meeting of tax administrators would much more quickly find common grounds respecting their problems and solutions than would a meeting of finance ministers.

CODIFICATION AND DRAFTING

Before a country considers how best to administer its tax system it must possess a clear picture of the scope of that tax system—what are the different taxes imposed, at what rates, and to whom do they apply. One would suppose that such knowledge is readily available, yet many countries really possess no such clear picture of their tax systems. Instead, there often exists a bewildering array of overlapping and contradictory taxes. Many of these taxes overlap so that a single commodity of transaction may be subject to a number of taxes, imposed at different or supplementary rates involving different tax bases with

different times of payment, different returns, and separate administrative and judicial procedures. Some of these taxes are obsolete,
yielding only a very small revenue or sometimes nothing at all, but
remain on the books to complicate the tax structure. Others are so
riddled with exemptions as to be scarcely applicable to anyone. Moreover, many tax measures are simply charges and fees for government
concessions or services. Often the administrative provisions and judicial procedures of an existing tax are applied without change to new
taxes as they are enacted, without any examination of the differing
requirements that the new taxes may warrant. In addition, the same
words will be used in the various tax laws, but with different definitions or without definition, so that only confusion in application can
result. Further, the controlling laws themselves may be extremely
difficult to locate. Very often there is a tangled mass of laws, regulations, decrees and the like reaching far into the past, jumbled together
with amendments and modifications. When the statutory picture is
so confused, it is extremely difficult for the government to know what
it must administer and for the taxpayers to know with what they
must comply.

A first step in the improvement of tax administration, as many
government are now recognizing, is thus the codification of the various
tax laws. This codification should be based on an orderly statutory
rearrangement of the entire tax system in accordance with a definite
outline. Thus, the various taxes should be classified among income
taxes, succession taxes, property taxes, excise and sales taxes, and so
on. Each field in turn should be subdivided, so that each tax is
separately identified. Overlapping among the taxes should be eliminated, with the various taxes applicable to a single article or transaction consolidated into one tax. The substantive provisions describing
the articles or persons taxed and fixing the rate and base of the tax
should be separated from the administrative provisions. The latter
should be divided functionally, as respects the returns to be filed, the
time for payment, the other duties of the taxpayer, the powers of the
administrator, the penalties imposed, etc. Thus, an excise tax codification recently enacted in one country has the following outline: [3]

   I. Definitions

       Effect of Definitions
       List of All Definitions Used in Act
       General Definitions

  II. Rates of Tax

       (In tabular form, giving only the name of the tax, the tax
       rate, and the section reference in Part III in which the tax
       is described.)

III. Description of Taxes
    A. Taxes on Articles and Merchandise
        Jewelry
        Luggage
        Sugar, etc.

    B. Taxes on Certain Transactions
        Public Documents
        Admissions, etc.

    C. License Taxes

    D. Exemptions

        (General or special exemptions in addition to those basic to the description of the particular tax.)

IV. Administrative Provisions
    A. Determination of Prices and Costs
    B. Determination of Taxpayer and Time of Payment
    C. Administration of Exemptions
    D. Duties of the Taxpayer and Other Persons
    E. Powers of the Secretary of the Treasury
    F. Miscellaneous Provisions

V. Penalties

VI. Effective Dates and Transition Provisions

Those familiar with the tax systems of underdeveloped countries will recognize that a serious obstacle to efficient codification lies in the pernicious habit of earmarking the revenues from a particular tax for a particular purpose. The revenues of a 10% tax on a commodity may go for relief purposes, the proceeds from an additional 5% tax on the same commodity may go for road building. This tax is earmarked for education, that tax for some health project, another tax for pensions, and so on. Earmarking may serve some short run political purposes, in that the function supported may make the tax less objectionable. Also, a bewildering array of taxes earmarked for many separate objectives may prevent the public from fully discerning the real impact of the tax burden. But it is generally agreed that the disadvantages of the system are serious. Proper budgeting and control of expenditures and receipts are made extremely difficult. The benefited institutions themselves are often greatly hampered in orderly planning since their revenues may depend not on their needs but on the particular taxes assigned to them. Moreover, the particular organization or institution benefited by the earmarking of revenue from a particular tax will often interfere in the administration of that tax.

Further, unless earmarking is dropped, the full benefits from a codification of the tax laws can scarcely be achieved since the overlapping and ramification of taxes would have to be preserved to support the earmarking. An elimination of the device of earmarking so that the revenues go into the general fund of the country as far as possible is thus a corollary of codification.

The task of codification would disclose another aspect of the tax structure which handicaps effective administration, that of poor legislative drafting. Once the tax policy is formulated, the task remains of expressing that policy in words of legal command, be they statute, decree, or administrative regulations. That task is not an easy one. The legal command should be precise, its boundaries defined, its exceptions clear, the possibilities of its abuse anticipated and blocked. The tax system is superimposed on the complex structures of business and family life with all their interwoven patterns. Its relationship to those complex structures in turn creates complex and interlocking patterns within the tax system. Yet very often the decisions on policy are regarded as the end of the tax job, with the drafting viewed as a simple and almost automatic process. Economists not experienced in drafting, or lawyers not versed in the technical ways of taxation, often act as the draftsmen of tax laws. A technique often adopted by these persons is simply to copy from other tax laws of the same or different countries. As a consequence the weaknesses of poorly drafted laws spread globally. The final result is often a hodge-podge of provisions poorly adapted to carrying out the policy decisions. Exceptions and provisions are piled on top of each other as each new problem is met by a new set of words put down without any analysis of the basic issues.

The solution here is to recognize that taxation requires skilled legal drafting by lawyers fully cognizant of the intricacies of the tax structure. Once such draftsmen are trained, continuity in drafting must be provided so that the developing tax policies can always be fitted into an orderly legal structure by draftsmen who at all times know the history and the exact contours of that structure.

Finally, codification by reducing the tax provisions to an orderly statutory and regulatory structure will permit the tax authorities to make available to those interested in taxation an authoritative, up-to-date, and manageable statement of tax rules. The legal, accounting and academic professions and the business groups will thus be enabled to participate more intelligently in the tax process. The statutory clarity that results from codification will also permit the tax administration to prepare for the lay public simplified explanations of the tax structure. These popular explanations will serve to increase the taxpayers' knowledge of their duties and thereby promote greater compliance.

SOME BASIC ASPECTS OF ADMINISTRATIVE PROCEDURE

Once the various components of the tax system are properly arranged and integrated, the task of carefully surveying their administration may appropriately follow. While the problems will vary from tax to tax, there are a number of basic aspects that usually occur under nearly any tax. The following comments relate to some of these basic aspects, with principal reference to the income tax.

Locating the Taxpayer

The beginnings of tax administration lie in seeing that the taxpayers are on the tax rolls. Unless the tax authorities know who are the individuals or units subject to the tax, the whole machinery of administration must necessarily function with incomplete coverage of the taxable area. Consequently, the first task is the preparation of lists or registers of taxpayers for each tax. Various registers may be compiled—property owners, business concerns, employers, investment owners—and combined where appropriate. The registers must be kept current, and maintained in an order—alphabetical, geographical, etc.—which proves most convenient for effective use. Every possible source of names for these registers must be combed—local property rolls, registration of voters, visual inspection of properties, records of new construction, records of other government departments, membership list of trade or merchants' associations and clubs, automobile registrations, etc. If other agencies of government have had air photographs or other surveys made of certain farm or city areas, these should be utilized. Once it is decided to keep adequate registers, sources of information will readily occur to the administration. The important tasks are to select among the various sources only those which promise to be productive of names likely to be taxpayers under the tax in question (thus in some places telephone books may be very useful, while elsewhere these lists may contain more non-taxpayers than taxpayers); to gather only so much information as can be efficiently processed; and to devise an efficient system for converting the selected information into a continuously current form usable for enforcement purposes.

Initial Taxpayer Compliance

Once the taxpayer is ascertained, the next step is that of obtaining initial compliance. In an income tax, unless the tax is withheld at the source, this will usually be the filing of a tax return on declaration. This return must provide the basic data for the assessment of the tax, and in some countries will also carry with it the taxpayer's computation and payment of his tax. In this sense, every effective income tax is basically a self-assessed tax. Hence, tax administration must aim for as high a degree of compliance at this stage as is possible. To achieve this compliance it must concentrate on several factors. The taxpayer must be furnished with the return by the tax authorities or provided with ready access to it, as through post offices, local agencies, and other centers of mass distribution. The geographical distribution of returns should take account of the distribution of taxpayers in the country, so that all areas receive sufficient returns. The return should be distributed free, not sold by the government or a private party having the concession for the distribution of the form. It might be mailed to all taxpayers on the tax rolls, but with publicity given to the fact that the failure to receive a return is not an excuse for a failure to file a return. The form should be arranged in as simple a manner and the steps on the return and the instructions written in as simple a style as is possible. Very often the effort to simplify the tax return will dramatically illustrate complexities inherent in the tax itself and force the simplification of these substantive aspects as a necessary prelude to simplification of the return. The return should be of convenient size on appropriate paper, and adaptable to type-written as well as handwritten use. The tax offices should be organized at return filing time to assist the taxpayer in every way possible. In fact, patient assistance will reveal those portions of the return which cause trouble to the taxpayers and thus enable their correction in subsequent forms. Newspapers and other media of public information should be utilized to explain the mechanics of the tax return and the requirements for filing. School children could be taught how to help their parents in filing out the returns. The filing dates for the various taxes should be coordinated, with concentration at one time wherever feasible of related taxes involving similar basic data.

If the tax is withheld, as is generally the case at least with wages and salaries, the initial steps relate to the withholding machinery. Here the employer must on the one hand secure the needed information from the employee as to his status and on the other hand obtain from the government exact instructions on the manner and extent of withholding. Here also the mechanics of withholding should be made as simple as possible, so that the employers can properly fulfill their role. Tables and other devices should be utilized which enable the employers themselves to compute the tax to be withheld, thereby making unnecessary the submission of the data in each case to the tax office for computation of the withheld tax. Care should be taken to see that employees are properly informed of the amount withheld from them and the employers promptly turn over to the government the sums collected.

Check on Taxpayer Compliance: Audit and Examination

After the taxpayer has performed the task of initial compliance, the tax authorities must take the next step. No tax will work effectively, especially an income tax, unless its administrators maintain an agressive attitude with respect to the correctness of the taxpayers' actions. Some taxpayers will fail to file or will make mistakes through ignorance or neglect; others will deliberately cheat. A passive attitude by the authorities toward these errors and falsifications will soon undermine the entire structure, since the diligent and honest taxpayers will almost in self-defense be forced to the level of the careless and dishonest. A tax administration which seeks compliance must protect those who comply or else compliance will not be forthcoming.

Consequently, the tax authorities must arrange systematically to check the compliance of the taxpayers. The taxpayer registers, if carefully prepared and matched against the returns, will reveal the failures to file. But after this step the path is difficult. Generally, limitations of personnel will make it impossible for each return to be given intensive scrutiny. A program of investigation and examination of returns must therefore be planned. Its objective should be an effective examination which both safeguards the government from major loss and instills in taxpayers a respect for the vigilance of the authorities. Moreover, the program must be capable of completion within the year, for the next year will inexorably bring a new set of returns to be examined.

There are no simple criteria to govern the selection of those returns to be investigated. Experience will suggest certain classifications and critical factors within those classifications. Thus, employee returns will usually not require much checking if the withholding procedure is effective, except as respects such factors as correctness of dependency claims or the expense accounts and disguised compensation of higher salaried employees and directors. Certain professions and businesses will warrant more scrutiny than others. It may be feasible to plan both for an annual examination of the most important returns and for reaching as much of the balance of the business returns on a schedule which insures that each business will be checked once in a period of years with all of the years in the period examined when that check is made. The period would vary with the length of the statute of limitations on additional assessments. Sources of information carefully collected in the tax offices—such as records of property sales, unusual bank transactions, large purchases of insurance, foreign currency transactions—will point to the selection of particular returns. The use of a system of estimated incomes, described later, will suggest other returns. Finally, a number of returns should simply be selected at random and examined, both to gauge the effectiveness of the planned programs and to make escape from detection of non-compliance more hazardous and less predictable. Of course, if the taxpayer is not initially required to compute and pay his tax, then in a sense every return must be "audited." But in these cases the "audit" can of necessity only be primarily a computation of the tax from the data appearing on the return. Consequently, as far as possible the system should call for initial taxpayer computation and payment.

When a return is selected for examination, the investigation may take several forms. Matters on the face of the return which appear suspicious or incorrect could be handled by correspondence, especially for the smaller returns. Or such matters may be handled on an "office audit," with the taxpayer requested to bring to the tax office the data necessary to verify certain items. The most effective audit, and thus the method to be used for the returns requiring a careful check, is the "field audit" at the taxpayer's place of business. This is an intensive check of the taxpayer's records and business and should be conducted by a trained accountant. It may be possible effectively to combine audits of related taxes whose returns contain similar information. With respect to these audits, the tax agent should be given a check list of items which experience indicates require scrutiny, such as the wrongful deduction of reserves, the charging to expense of expenditures which should be capitalized, reported gross profits margins varying with those customary in the trade, or any variation between the closing inventory for one year and the opening inventory for the next year. This type of investigation presupposes effective record keeping by the taxpayer. Consequently, its utility will vary directly with the ability of the tax office to impress upon taxpayers the need for keeping adequate records and to enforce record-keeping requirements imposed by the tax law. Experience indicates that this success comes easiest with large and medium sized business, hardest with small concerns. Often, in the case of these small concerns successful administration by either the national government or local governmental units of excise taxes involving gross receipts and other sales data will be the prelude to effective application of an income tax.

Where adequate taxpayer records are lacking, the ingenuity and resourcefulness of the administration are challenged. It is not without weapons, however. It may attempt to reconstruct an average week, even a typical day, for the taxpayer's business and apply the resulting profit reasonably to the entire year. It can resort to the use of "estimates," informed guesses as to what profit the taxpayer's business should yield in the light of a comparison of its characteristics with those of businesses whose profits are known. This technique of estimates is familiar to most administrators and is used with varying degrees of success. The variation is largely in the care and precision with which the estimates or standards are built up, and the degree of control possessed by the tax office in their application. Thus, a method which is crude but helpful in the sense that it does produce some check is that of the classification of businesses into various profit groups with the aid of trade associations or guilds. Too often, however, under this procedure the control rests with the trade association and not the tax office, with possibilities of favoritism among taxpayers or down-right bargaining between tax office and each trade operating as a unit to fix its share of the tax as compared with other trades. As rapidly as possible the tax office should pass beyond this stage to the compilation of its own standards, based on all of the workable data including investigations of taxpayers having proper records. With this refinement of standards accomplished, the next level of progress is to confine their use as far as possible to the selection of returns for individual audit rather than for the basis of the tax determination itself. Thus, the returns should initially be compared with the standards, and those returns showing considerable variation should be the subject of an office or field audit in which the taxpayer's actual situation would be decisive in the determination of his tax. It must never be forgotten that an income tax is an "individual" tax based on the particular taxpayer's net income and not on someone else's profit. The standards may help in approximating the determination of a taxpayer's net income, but the methods should not be confused with the goal. That goal is not the most accurate standards—it is the most accurate determination of the particular taxpayer's income.

A refined method of determining an individual's income in the absence of adequate records, but one requiring skill in its application, is the "net worth" technique. This may take several forms. If a taxpayer's net worth (assets less liabilities) is known with accuracy for a prior period, it can then be compared with his present net worth. The difference plus consumption items in the interval should represent his receipts. Or, expenditures over a period could be compared with sums stated to be available for spending and the excess of the former would then give a reasonable approximation of the income not disclosed. This "net worth" technique is obviously tailored to the individual's situation. Its effectiveness is balanced by the time and skill which it demands, and hence it can be used only in the most difficult and important cases. However, its utility could be greatly increased by a requirement that every individual with income over a certain level and every business be required annually to file a balance sheet along with the tax return. This would provide a starting point for net worth computations.[4]

The process of investigation can be materially assisted by statutory aids. Thus, tax offices should have the authority to obtain information from banks, insurance companies and other financial agencies, from stock brokers holding securities for clients, from corporations, and so on. "Information returns" should be required from those having significant financial relationships with the taxpayer, such as payors of dividends and interest where these items of income are not collected exclusively by withholding. The use of anonymous bank accounts, inadequate record keeping as to corporate shareholders, and other institutional devices facilitating tax evasion should be prohibited.

Resolution of Controversies between Taxpayers and Tax Offices

The process of audit and investigation described above will result in the determination of the taxpayer's tax liability as the tax office views it. The taxpayer will then be called upon for payment of this amount, either as the entire tax or in those countries in which the taxpayer initially pays and computes his own tax as an additional tax liability. In turn, some of the taxpayers will agree that the amounts requested are properly due. But others will disagree and thus controversies will spring into existence between the tax office and the taxpayer. Accordingly, a procedure for handling and resolving these controversies becomes the next stage of tax administration. The procedure will necessarily depend on the concepts of administrative law and judicial review of the particular country. But essentially the procedure should furnish internal methods of settlement within the administrative system and external methods of judicial consideration when a settlement at the administrative level is not reached. Whatever may be the precise steps adopted, however, one factor is paramount— the taxpayer must have complete confidence in the fairness and impartiality of the procedure as a whole. He cannot be placed at the mercy of a single tax official; he cannot be faced with arbitrary administrative action unchecked by judicial review. A fair albeit a firm system of resolving these controversies will instill taxpayer confidence in the tax administration. With that confidence will come an increase in voluntary taxpayer compliance, and thus a basic step forward in successful administration.

The internal administrative machinery for the settlement of these controversies should in essence consist of a series of hierarchal reviews of the case. The taxpayer should be able to discuss his case with the agent who investigated it, then with a supervisor of that agent, then with a higher administrative echelon. There cannot, however, be an endless series of successive considerations of a case, and hence the number of layers of review must be limited. Under such a system properly conducted, most controversies should be settled at the first stage and a majority of the balance at the next stage, leaving only a relatively small number to be considered at the highest administrative level of review. Here all but a very small percentage should prove capable of settlement—the remaining few cases, relatively speaking, must go on to the courts. The skill and experience of the administrative officials who consider these cases should, naturally, be the greatest at the top level, for only the most difficult cases should reach that stage. Where needed, checks against bribery or pressure for favoritism should be adopted. Thus, it might be required that the discussion with the investigating agent take place in the tax office with a higher official present so as to prevent a corrupt arrangement with the agent. Or, if the problem is pressure for favoritism at higher levels, the agent's original report would be sent to a special board for its information so that the higher officials are in a position to resist improper pressures to reverse the agent's report. The tax administration should be able at any stage of these reviews to assert any additional amount of tax that it believes owing on the basis of the information developed in the administrative review of the taxpayer's case. This will make the consideration a two-way street and thus discourage routine taxpayer appeals.

The discussion and consideration of a case should be on a conference basis rather than a formal hearing. There should be a full discussion of the issues and facts. The taxpayer should be given a clear statement of the issues, he should present his case, using the material, written or oral, that he believes pertinent, and after discussion the tax official should reach a decision. Very often the case will be "settled," that is each side will give way on doubtful points and a compromise of the issues in controversy thus reached. Many tax questions are clouded in uncertainty—the facts may be difficult to ascertain; the application of the law to the facts may be unclear; the issue may involve essentially an educated guess, as in the case of the determination of market values. The solution of these doubtful matters by a settlement is quite proper provided the settlement is reached by a careful weighing of the strength of the administrator's position and not by favoritism. Consequently, it is appropriate to have a special group check the quality of these settlements by a post-settlement sampling of the settled cases. Implicit in this procedure is a requirement that at each stage a report be written by the official handling the dispute. These reports should summarize the disputed issues, the basic evidence and arguments on each side, and the areas where agreement has been or is likely to be reached. These reports will aid in avoiding abuses by officials and will tend to assure greater uniformity in the application of the tax laws, provided an appropriate procedure is established for the review of the cases considered.

The proper resolution of a controversy will be more readily achieved if the taxpayer is represented by a person intelligently informed as to tax law and tax procedure. Hence, rules governing the qualifications of persons as taxpayers' representatives are needed. These rules should place stress on restricting taxpayer representation as far as possible to lawyers, accountants, and others who possess the requisite skill and tax knowledge, and on discouraging representation by those whose only stock in trade is influence.

In connection with this administrative procedure for the resolution of controversies it is often urged that fairness would be achieved by having the controversies heard by "citizen boards." It is said that these panels of prominent local citizens would prevent the taxpayers from being unfairly treated by an arbitrary administration. It is questionable whether this procedure is desirable. It might work where there is a long tradition of public duty and intelligent lay participation, and where the board's function is to aid in ascertaining the facts. But most likely the use of this system in countries attempting to improve tax administration would not be wise. At best, it divides responsibility between tax office and local citizenry, so that each can blame the other for any failures of administration. At worst, it could lend itself to placing the taxpayer at the mercy of local prejudices, to placing the tax administrator at the mercy of reciprocated favors among neighbors, and to strengthening tendencies in the cities or villages to domination by cliques. The responsibility for tax collection and administration is a government responsibility—it is dangerous to diffuse that responsibility among non-governmental officials, especially at the hearing level. The check against arbitrary, erroneous, or unfair administrative action lies with the judiciary and not with boards of local citizens.

As respects the judicial review of tax controversies, the procedure adopted will naturally be shaped by the judicial system of the country. Experience has definitely shown that tax cases require special procedures on the part of the judiciary. Tax cases are complex and difficult. Their resolution demands an informed knowledge of the intricacies of the statutory laws and regulations in the tax field. Hence, at the lower court level, it is preferable to have either specialized tax courts or at least tax judges who can concentrate on these cases. The avenues of appeal to the upper courts should be clear and efficient, so that differences among the lower courts may be readily resolved. The tax system applies to many taxpayers and it inexorably reaches those taxpayers year after year. Hence, unless controversies are speedily settled, tax cases will soon clog the judicial system. Any delay in decision, moreover, will rapidly create many new tax controversies as tax year succeeds tax year and as other taxpayers face similar problems. Also, as respects review by the upper courts, the taxpayer should, at least in important questions, be entitled to a review by an independent judicial tribunal.

Uniformity of judicial decisions and speed in reaching those decisions are essential to effective tax administration. The proper answer to the question of statutory interpretation in the tax field—which is the issue in most tax controversies that reach the courts—is generally debatable. What is needed, therefore, is a prompt and definite judicial answer rather than long delay in the search for the "true" answer. If the judicial answer is too wide of the mark, the legislature will correct it so that an erroneous answer is not fatal. But the system cannot function if no answer is forthcoming.[5]

Another important aspect in the treatment of controversies is the reduction of controversy through administrative interpretation of the tax laws. The tax administration should as far as possible anticipate doubtful points of statutory interpretation and make its view on those points clear. A taxpayer aware of that view is at least on notice of the tax consequences of conduct on his part. Very often he can in the light of that interpretation shape his affairs and plan his activities covered by the tax so that controversy is thereby avoided. In fact, successful tax administrations have a prospective "ruling" system under which a taxpayer can present a planned transaction to the tax authorities and obtain their view of the tax consequences. If the tax cost is too high, the plan may be dropped or altered and controversy avoided. At the same time the tax authorities are thus constantly kept informed of the areas of the tax law regarded as uncertain by taxpayers and of the problems thus created. They can as a result keep abreast of potential tax controversies and attempt to minimize or eliminate them by administrative action or statutory change. These rulings, however, should be published and made generally applicable, so that they cannot be used to provide special treatment for favored taxpayers.

Collection of Taxes

The final stage—in fact the goal—of tax procedure is the collection of the tax. The sure sign of ineffective tax administration is the presence of a very large delinquency in tax payments, for it indicates the lack of taxpayer respect for the tax system. The taxpayer in effect is acting on his belief that the administrative machinery may bark, but that it has no bite. In large part the solution for tax delinquency lies in providing the bite. In this sense effective tax collection is a facet of the larger problem of providing adequate penalties, to which reference will later be made. But tax collection has its special procedural aspects, and here also attention to proper techniques and routines is essential.

To begin with, the delinquency in payment must be recognized. Hence, the taxpayer lists and registers referred to earlier must be so maintained that a taxpayer's non-payment may immediately be noted. As soon as the payment date has passed, a formal demand should be made. If this step is not effective, prompt and firm procedures to follow that demand must be devised. The taxpayer must be made to see that his delinquency is known, that it is serious, and that it will not be tolerated. If the administration is casual and unconcerned about collection, the taxpayer will more than match that mood in his dilatory attitude toward payment. If the administration is alert and firm, taxpayers will react to that pressure and bring order into their payments.

Firmness requires the presence of sanctions and a resort to those sanctions when necessary. Hence the tax law must provide for the imposition of liens on real property where there is a registry system, for the distraint of property, for the garnishment of wages and salaries, and the like. It can also resort to collateral devices, such as the refusal of certain government services if taxes are unpaid. Above all, it must make non-payment expensive. The taxpayers should not through delay in payment in effect secure an interest-free loan from the government. Hence interest at a rate effectively higher than the commercial rate should be charged automatically for late payment. The tax administrator must, however, be intelligent in his firmness. Extensions of time, at interest, should be available to taxpayers who can show good cause for an extension. An honest but hard pressed taxpayer should be able to work out a schedule of installment payments arranged in the light of his financial condition. Where there are simply few or no assets available, the tax should be compromised, i.e., written-off, rather than carried for years in the future.

Another phase of the collection problem is proper integration between assessments and collection procedures. Those in charge of assessments should not permit unreliable assessments to be passed on to the collecting officials where the result can only be non-collection. It is simply a waste of effort all around to have most of the assessments returned for cancellation because they were unrealistic at the outset. On the other hand, the collection authorities should demonstrate initiative and enterprise in their search for the taxpayer. Sometimes a collector will return an assessment as uncollectible because of a "wrong address" without making any effort to locate the new address of the taxpayer. Also, bills which are for such a small amount that the cost of collection is out of all proportion to the tax involved should not be submitted for collection. In these and other ways proper working relations between these two branches of tax administration can promote the overall efficiency of the system. As indicated later, it is desirable to place these two activities under one agency.

The tax system itself should not be inherently conducive to tax delinquency. If the system attempts to collect last year's tax out of the current year's income, it is bound to run into collection difficulties when the income of the current year drops below that of the prior year. This may occur where the taxpayer becomes sick or unemployed, where his business or crops have suffered, or where there is an overall decline in the economic situation. Under such a system the taxpayer in a sense is always in debt to the government and any adversity in his fortunes will at once highlight that debt. As far as possible, therefore, the tax system should be placed on a current basis, with the current year's tax being collected at current tax rates out of current income. In the case of an income tax, this can be achieved by withholding on certain forms of income, such as wages, interest, and dividends, and by a system of estimated tax payments based on estimates of current income, with a reconciliation on the final tax return. In this fashion the taxpayer is largely current in his taxes and a tax debt cannot arise. Where the tax administration finds that taxpayers habitually do not report their full incomes, it can be provided that the estimated current income must at least be as high as the corrected income of the prior year. In addition, the law could provide for percentage increases or decreases in the base of prior year's income to match a general rise or decline in the economy for the current year. The objective here is a reasonable estimate of current income, with the final tax return for the year showing the actual income once the year is closed. The taxpayer may then owe some additional tax or be entitled to a refund if he has over-estimated his income. The refund in turn could be applied to the payment of the next year's estimated tax.

Penalties

The tax administrator must be equipped with a variety of effective penalties which he can wield intelligently and firmly. However, it is usually at this point that most tax laws are found wanting. The penalty provisions were established years ago, and quite often consist of small lump sum amounts which do not serve as effective deterrents. The entire system of tax penalties will thus generally require legislative overhauling. The various violations must be catalogued, such as failure to file a return; failure to pay the tax on time; failure to withhold taxes or to pay over withheld taxes; deliberate action to avoid the tax through the intentional filing of a false return; fraudulent record keeping; and so on. An appropriate civil penalty which takes account of the severity of the offense and can be administratively imposed must then be provided. Often as respects these civil monetary penalties, a combination of lump-sum penalties and percentage penalties varying with the amount of tax will be most desirable. The percentage penalty could operate over a range, with discretion in the administrator to choose the appropriate figure. Thus, a negligent failure to file a return could involve a five dollar flat penalty, plus a penalty of from ten to twenty-five per cent of the tax; an intentional failure to file return, a starting percentage of twenty-five per cent; the filing of a fraudulently incorrect return, a starting percentage of one hundred per cent.

For most taxpayers a civil monetary penalty which reaches the pocketbook is usually an effective deterrent, but for some these monetary penalties while unpleasant are not sufficient. Consequently, in most countries with effective tax administrations, willful evasion and fraudulent conduct are criminal offenses punishable by fine and imprisonment. Moreover, and certainly to the point, prosecutions are brought and jail sentences imposed. The failure to apply the criminal penalties on the statute books can have a demoralizing effect. In contrast, it is generally found that a few successful prosecutions and the attendant publicity can have a most exemplary effect. These two types of penalties, civil monetary penalties and criminal penalties, are not alternatives. Where criminal action is taken, the offending taxpayer should also be required to pay the tax and the accompanying civil penalty.

THE IMPORTANCE OF DETAILS

The preceding section has considered some of the essential steps in the overall procedure of tax administration. In a sense it has dealt with broad problems and with major issues of administration. But in a good part successful tax administration is the cumulative effect of hundreds of minor details properly executed. Too often these details are neglected in the planning of broad reforms and top level projects. Frequently it is only the office of the tax administrator and his immediate assistants which is "reorganized" and the details of the day-to-day work of the tax officials at the routine level completely overlooked. A few examples may illustrate the point.

Most taxpayers generally come into contact only with the tax officials in the local tax offices. Consequently, the daily operation and organization of these offices are important matters. But in many countries insufficient attention is paid to the routine operation of these offices. Once their situation is examined, however, many questions will arise. Are the offices properly arranged from the standpoint of space utilization? Is there a place for taxpayers to present their problems in a confidential, orderly way? Are the various work processes and the personnel so arranged as to location within the office that the daily work flows efficiently in an orderly current? Are such matters as the handling, sorting, and filing of documents properly organized so that the documents can be quickly stored and quickly located when needed? Are there mechanical shortcuts and aids available to facilitate these operations—such as the use of different colors for the different returns or documents, or the use of standard sized papers chosen with an eye to handling and filing? How efficient is the office equipment that is being used and are more modern devices available? Are equipment and personnel used effectively with an eye to the variation in peak periods and slack periods? Are appropriate travel facilities available for those officials who must make field investigations of returns or check on delinquent taxpayers?

The above questions are but illustrations of the type of details that require effective handling for the orderly conduct of the tax offices. One method of dramatizing the proper attention required for these details and of improving tax offices generally is to select a few offices as "model offices." These model offices should be overhauled and placed in effective daily operation. The officials of the other offices can then inspect and observe the model offices and carry back the improvements to their own offices. In effect the model offices serve both as guides to efficient operation and as targets to be attained by the remaining offices.

Finally, attention should be paid to the criticisms of taxpayers with respect to the operations of the tax procedures as they bear on the individual taxpayer affected. Too often these objections are regarded as mere resentment caused by the tax burden itself. But quite frequently the criticisms are occasioned by the irritations created through inefficient operation of the tax system rather than its monetary impact. Usually, persistent taxpayer complaints regarding "red tape" or inefficiency will be traceable to objectionable routines, though the complaints may have an exaggerated ring. Improvement in operation can be aided by an intelligent consideration of taxpayer reactions.

THE ASPECT OF PERSONNEL

It is often argued that the problems of administration in underdeveloped countries are basically problems of personnel. The foregoing discussion is an effort to demonstrate that the procedures and details of tax administration are highly significant, and that most tax systems could stand marked improvement in these respects. But it is obvious that procedures which are orderly and effective on paper are subject to the human factor of the personnel who administer those procedures. Hence the problem of personnel does occupy a key role in tax administration. Here, the surveys of technical missions usually contain the same critical catalogue of the faults to be found, such as poor pay, lack of training, inefficiency, understaffing as respects able people and overstaffing as respects incompetent political appointees, and so on. In many countries the talent has steadily been drawn away from the tax agencies and into the central banks and development authorities. The surveys urge higher salaries and more skilled personnel. Yet, while sympathetic and often optimistic, the surveys recognize that these goals are difficult to obtain. Although the future, viewed realistically, is indeed a troubled one, is it possible, in conjunction with the basic improvements suggested above and the changes in public attitudes considered later, to adopt measures which will improve the personnel aspect of administration?

First, as to the matter of pay scales. The results of inadequate salaries are obvious: for example, they attract mainly the incompetent; they lead to part-time employment with its problems of divided loyalties and inadequate attention to the government's work; they breed dishonesty, bribery and corruption. But with hard-pressed budgets, how can a government avoid the vicious circle of low pay—incompetent personnel—undesirability of increasing the salaries of an incompetent staff? There would seem to be some avenues of escape. Salaries higher than the norm could be justified for tax personnel on the ground that the resulting increase in efficiency will produce increased tax revenue. Where salary scales must be kept uniform among departments, the up-grading of the revenue positions is equally defensible. It is generally found in many countries that while the importance and difficulties of revenue tasks have increased, there has been little systematic re-grading of positions in the light of increased responsibilities. As a forerunner of the above, increases could be given to specially selected individuals to demonstrate the effectiveness of having skilled personnel working under appropriate salary scales. Proper travel allowances will often be a decisive factor and will eliminate the obvious distorted selection of cases that results when the cost of travel in investigating a case must be borne by the employee.

Attempts have been made to meet the salary problem by a bonus or commission system under which an individual receives a percentage of the additional taxes he assesses or collects. The disadvantages of this device are serious; the tendency toward arbitrary action, with resulting public hostility and overall inefficiency through the necessity of meeting the taxpayers' objections to the unfair assessments. Moreover, only those tax personnel engaged in assessment and collection can benefit from the plan.

If salary scales can be improved, then the recruitment of personnel must match those scales. Systematic procedures for attracting qualified and able individuals with an interest in the work must be adopted. Job standards must be devised, so that examinations and other objective testing of applicants can be substituted for political nomination. Close liaison should be maintained with universities and business schools so as to induce capable graduates to enter the tax service. Promotion policies should be coordinated with recruitment, so that recognition of talent and effort within the service is coupled with the flexibility obtained through the new ideas and talents of those chosen from outside the ranks.

The next step is the institution of appropriate training procedures. Tax work is technical and specialized. An effective recruitment policy will supply persons with the requisite intelligence and aptitudes, but it cannot be expected to yield fully-trained tax officials. Consequently, the personnel must through training be given an understanding of the operation of the system as a whole, of the relation of their specific jobs to that system, and of the requirements of their jobs. The training must be conducted in a systematic fashion by instructors qualified for the task and supervised by an official whose sole responsibility is that of the training program. The instruction should be regarded as a recognized part of the trainee's position, and not an added chore to be met at odd moments. It should offer incentives to advancement and new duties. The material should be suited to the personnel under instruction, with appropriate recognition of the differences in training required for non-specialist employees, supervisory personnel, technical personnel needing a knowledge of tax law and tax accounting, and so on. Various types of instructions must be utilized—full-time training schools for new employees or those selected for advancement, lectures and on-the-job training, instruction manuals, etc.

The aspect of delegation of authority is directly related to these personnel matters. The director of a tax office may consider himself as the sole person possessing capability and authority, a view sometimes rationalized on the basis of the responsibility he must bear. He then makes the decisions in each case and decides all the details of office management. This personalization of the tax office in the person of the director has important disadvantages. It adversely affects the morale and initiative of the other officials. It results in inefficiency and low output. It opens up avenues of abuse, since often the director is either chosen from the social and economic level of the wealthier taxpayers or is desirous of attaining that level, so that the concentration of authority makes for considerable pressure on the director as well as considerable opportunity for favoritism. Here also a vicious circle operates, in that the system is defended on the basis of inadequate personnel to warrant the delegation of duties from the director. One answer, building on the policies of recruitment and training described above, is that of manuals of procedure which recognize the necessary delegation of authority. These procedures should limit the authority of the director to inject himself into substantive decisions in particular cases, except under prescribed conditions. At the same time they should delineate the role of the director as a creative, energizing factor in the overall conduct of the office. The advantages that lie in freedom from routine, in the abandonment of procedures requiring him personally to sign every letter or document, should be emphasized.

Hovering over the entire field of tax administration is the spectre of dishonesty and corruption. As taxes rise, the opportunity to escape the tax by the payment of a lower amount in the form of a bribe is inevitably present. Moreover, as the taxes grow in complexity and as discretion and judgment on the part of the tax official play a greater role, the ability of an official to affect the result in a particular case without outward indicia of purchased favoritism is heightened. The personnel policies considered above are all antidotes to these temptations. Yet even countries with good personnel policies and traditions of fine administration have seen corruption in the form of bribery and influence emerge in unexpected places. Consequently, an effective system of discipline and personnel investigation becomes, unfortunately, a requisite to effective administration. But it must be recognized at the outset that unless it is crystal clear to all employees that complete honesty is demanded and that those in authority are unswervingly firm in that demand, no system of disciplinary procedures and methods will be effective. The most effective method of achieving honesty is the severe punishment of dishonesty. Moreover, the punishment must extend not only to the government employee but to the taxpayer or his representative who is a party to the dishonesty.

As to internal procedures, there should be a specifically trained corps of investigators acting as an inspection staff to check for possibilities of abuse and corruption, along with inspection for inefficiency. The work of the tax official should be sampled from time to time. Rumors and informers' tips should be pursued. Care must be taken, however, that these controls deter dishonesty but not the appropriate exercise of discretion. Officials should not feel that they will be "second-guessed" on every decision they make, or that the investigator will turn hindsight or a different view of the problems into a suspicion of dishonesty. If the investigatory process exceeds its proper bounds, then officials will fear to make any decisions in favor of taxpayers and effective administration will be stultified.

As a supplement to individual checking, it is desirable to require each employee to submit a net worth statement at the time of his employment and periodically thereafter. These statements are then available as the basis for an investigation when suspicion arises, as when an employee's standard of living is beyond that which his salary and previous wealth would indicate. While the net worth statement may not be popular with all employees, it acts as a deterrent to temptation since its mechancial impact is clearly obvious. As a further measure, care should be taken to audit the income tax returns of as many tax officials as possible. Generalized sources of income, such as gambling, should be carefully scrutinized. Finally, a proper system of penalties should be available, ranging from criminal action, dismissal, loss of pay or suspension to reprimands and warnings.

THE ASPECT OF MANAGEMENT

Given a proper framework of administrative procedures and capable tax officials to operate those procedures, the next aspect of tax administration is that of overall management. The functioning of the system must be viewed as a whole, the parts must fit together, the entire organization must constantly be scanned for defects and improvements, the machinery must be intelligently guided toward the effective fulfillment of the everincreasing burdens that will inevitably fall upon it.

Income tax administration starts as a highly centralized process involving relatively few taxpayers. Soon, however, especially in geographically large or heavily populated countries, the issue of centralization versus decentralization must be faced: How much of the detailed operations must go on at headquarters and how much may be properly conducted in the field? Which day-to-day decisions, especially those involving the application of law and regulations to particular cases, will be made at headquarters and which in the field? The answers to these questions, in the sense of the degree of decentralization that is appropriate for a given country, will largely turn on inexorable factors: the number of taxpayers, their geographical location, and the technical state of communications and transportation. Continual observation of these factors must be made to solve the basic problem in the decentralization issue, that of the rate at which decentralization should progress. The accompanying problems are the very complex ones of effective administrative management of a large-scale organization. As decentralization progresses, the problem of effective central direction becomes more important. Headquarters must now conduct a unified field operation—there must be uniformity in the procedures followed in the field, in interpretations applied, in assessments and settlements made. In practice, effective controls must rest on the adoption of orderly procedures, formulated in writing and made available to all of the offices involved. Manuals of operation which inform and instruct the field organization are thus essential to centralized direction. In effect, there must be an adequate and constant flow of information from headquarters to the field.

Coordination between the field and headquarters will not be achieved if the headquarters operations are themselves uncoordinated. Yet, in many countries effective central direction is lacking because authority is divided among several agencies. Audit and assessment is in one agency and collection is in another agency; some taxes are under one authority and other taxes under different control. This parceling out of the functions of tax administration must be reversed and one central agency given responsibility for the task. The various departments within that agency must in turn be operated on an integrated basis.

The flow of information and instruction from headquarters to the field offices has been mentioned above. But supervision is a two-way street, and there must be a flow of information back from the field to the central staff. This information essentially involves reports of the activities of the field offices, so that their performance may be understood and weighed. The reports must contain sufficient details to be informative, yet not so voluminous as to enmesh both field and headquarters in a mass of wasted data. The reports should, for example, indicate how many returns have been filed, how much tax paid, how many returns audited, how many added assessments made, how much additional tax collected, and so on. They should be arranged so that they can readily be filled out by the field offices and as readily comprehended at headquarters.

These reports will enable the central body to gauge quantitatively the effectiveness of field operations as a whole and to spot incipient danger points in advance. But such progress reports and charts must be amplified by detailed inspections of each office. The top officials themselves should annually visit a number of offices, both to retain the "feel" of the tasks and to improve morale. In addition, an inspection staff of competent officials should be maintained. Inspectors should visit each office to examine thoroughly the procedures followed, to check for compliance with instructions, to measure the overall quality of the work done and the general efficiency of personnel, and to catch weaknesses in instructions when tested by the problems of daily operation. The role of the inspectors is thus both critical and constructive, with an eye to desirable innovation and improvement as well as to substandard performance.

Finally, an extremely important phase of management, and the one that probably shapes the destiny of the entire system, is that of intelligent programing and planning for the administration as a whole. Effective administration is not achieved by accident. It must be reached by forethought and care. Hence, the headquarters should have a planning division, be it an individual or a unit, which is largely freed from the routine of daily tasks and which can thereby concentrate on future developments. Proper planning is not a matter to be fitted into the interstices of a director's busy day, but rather is a recognized task requiring adequate time and attention. As new taxes are considered, the planning unit can analyze their feasibility and requirements from the standpoint of administration—what kinds of returns will be needed, what instructions to taxpayers, how many additional tax personnel and with what training, what arrangement must be made for collection and payment, and so on. This advance planning permits a more informed decision as to the choice among possible new taxes, or as to the content of the tax selected. It also permits an orderly introduction of the tax into the activities of the taxpayers and the operations of the tax offices, instead of a confused and haphazard beginning. The planning unit should also constantly review existing operations in order to ascertain shortcomings and to introduce corrections. Thus, it can foresee the exchange of equipment and personnel among offices as the needs for them vary from place to place and time to time.

In another direction, the planning unit must seek ways to measure the effectiveness of the entire system. It must constantly ask itself such questions as: Just how effective are tax collections and taxpayer compliance? What is the correct number of taxpayers and what proportion of them are being reached by the administration? What is the degree of tax avoidance? These are difficult questions and even the most efficient of tax administrations do not as yet possess the statistical tools necessary to their answer. But progress is being made in the use of statistical analysis to reveal ways by which to measure present performance and realistic goals. Thus, analyses of national income and its components can provide some standards. The task of the planning unit, in cooperation with other agencies of government, is constantly to develop its statistical information, both as to coverage and accuracy, so that a realistic appraisal of tax administration is possible.

The Aspect of National Attitude towards the Tax System

The prior discussion has considered various aspects of tax administration and has indicated possible points of improvement with respect to existing procedures. But tax administration does not function in a vacuum. Its relationships at every turn are with the public, and since the combination of taxes reaches nearly every individual in one way or another, the administration finds itself dealing with the nation as a whole. Hence, inevitably its operations and effectiveness are affected by the attitudes of the nation towards the tax system. It is here that we enter on the broad currents of human affairs, on the play of history and tradition with respect to the interrelationship between citizenry and government. For present purposes we must acknowledge that national attitudes towards the tax system and tax administration differ, and that voluntary tax compliance will differ from country to country. We can appreciate that a full understanding of the nature, extent, and causes of these differences would be extremely helpful to the improvement of the existing situation. But that full understanding has yet to be achieved. Hence, as respects this larger problem, while not completely knowing the causes we must realistically face the effects. This means a recognition that in many countries the task of tax administration is adversely affected, and seriously so, by the prevailing tolerance of the public toward non-compliance and avoidance.

But while tax administration is thus affected by these national attitudes, it is equally true that the attitudes can in turn be affected by tax administration. All that has been said above is pertinent here. Rational and efficient procedures, higher personnel standards, better management, improvement in relations with the public and in the daily contacts between tax official and taxpayer, can operate to increase the public respect for the tax administration. Moreover, once the tax administration has been placed on a sound basis, it is in a position to assert that compliance must be forthcoming. Such an assertion would hardly be tolerated, or even taken seriously, as long as tax officials were themselves inefficient and corrupt. But if the administration has brought stability and honesty to its own operations, the self-respect thus achieved can form the foundation for its demand of respect and compliance from the taxpayer.

That demand will be considerably more effective if there are sanctions that can be applied when voluntary compliance is not forthcoming. It is here that the penalty provisions of the tax laws discussed above play a key role. But the presence of penalties on the books is not a self-operative sanction; there must be a will to enforce these penalties. And here the tax administrator must look to the heads of state for his answer. If there is a serious determination at the topmost political and governmental levels to bring about improvement in the tax system, then an affirmative answer to the use of penalties will be forthcoming and tax compliance will commence to improve. If that determination does not exist, the best that can be expected is that the machinery of administration will be at hand ready to be effectively utilized on that future day when the tide of government changes.

A tax administrator faced with the task of changing taxpayer attitudes should seek allies in those professions interested in the tax field. Primarily these are the legal and accounting professions, and the economists in the academic profession. All of these professional groups should interest themselves in the tax system and its administration. They should understand its operations and be able to criticize intelligently its activities, and they should aid in interpreting that system to the public. Such aid involves the writing of articles, the formation of professional organizations to conduct tax discussions, and the education of trade and business associations, as well as the advice given to individual clients. The universities should institute courses in the legal aspects of tax law as well as those in fiscal policy. The accounting profession should encourage the development of the role of independent certified or chartered public accountants. It should also assist in the standardization of accounting practices, and in the preparation of model record books and forms. These professional groups must realize that a significant share of the task of tax administration falls on them, and in these ways and many others they must aid the government in its striving for effective administration.

The foregoing is necessarily a brief summary of certain problems in the broad field of tax administration in underdeveloped countries. Even so, it may suffice to indicate both the importance of these problems and the need for intensive research respecting the many aspects of this part of the fiscal structure. In this connection the Harvard Law School International Program of Taxation, in cooperation with the Fiscal and Financial Branch of the United Nations Secretariat, is engaged in the preparation of a *Manual of Income Tax Administration* which is especially designed for use in underdeveloped countries. The training activities of the Harvard Program conducted for foreign tax officials, largely from underdeveloped countries, have also emphasized the problems of tax administration. The work on this *Manual* and the interchange of ideas and experiences in the training program have indicated many fruitful topics for further study. It may be appropriate here as a conclusion simply to refer to some of these topics in summary fashion. The following list is not intended as a complete agenda for research. Rather it is illustrative of what are believed to be useful lines of inquiry. These topics relate primarily to those problems of tax administration which lie at top levels and which are at the core of the relationships between substantive tax policy issues and tax administration.[6] They do not concern the day-to-day administrative operations and managerial problems which are primarily the concern of the *Manual of Income Tax Administration* mentioned earlier. The topics follow:

Organization for Tax Policy Formulation and Management

A consideration of some of the organizational factors essential to central formulation and direction of tax policy. The following are examples:

1. *Research Facilities and Technical Services*
    a) Effective use of statistics

    1) For forecasting revenue yields and for determining the distribution of the tax burden in relation to the distribution of national income, etc.

    2) For controlling tax audit operations through the selection of those geographical areas, income levels, taxpayer groups,

tax problems, etc. most appropriate for administrative scrutiny.

3) As a tool of management control, to gauge the effectiveness of tax administration in general and in its various detailed operations.

b) Economic Research

The techniques of economic research necessary to illuminate the various aspects of substantive tax policy.

c) Legislative drafting

The techniques of legislative drafting, including such aspects as codification of laws and regulations, the preparation of rulings, consideration of the limits of detail to be included in legislation and of the relationship between the degree of discretion granted (so as to avoid detail) and the fairness of the tax in the light of the actual exercise of that discretion. For example, what are the administrative problems involved in the exercise of discretion which policy planners must take into account in the final formulation of the laws?

2. *Organization of Government for Fiscal Management*

a) Coordination of the various revenue departments, such as the departments dealing with the customs and those administering the internal taxes, or the departments dealing with the assessment of taxes and those dealing with the collection of taxes.

b) Coordination of revenue and non-revenue departments on matters affecting tax policy, such as land reform and property taxation.

c) Coordination of the planning of tax laws with the administration of those laws—how can policy planners and administrators properly communicate so that the final product is an intelligent policy that can be effectively administered?

d) Coordination of the administration of federal taxes with that of state or regional taxes.

e) Problems relating to the decentralization of operational assessment and enforcement activities and the centralization of supervisory authority as respects the administration of taxes.

Institutional Factors Affecting the Tax Structure

1. *The effect of institutional economic factors on the shape of the tax structure.*

How do the economic organization of a country and the patterns of its economic life affect both the basic tax structure and the content and administration of the particular taxes making up that structure? Thus, what are the consequences for taxation of a predominance of small business concerns, of the existence of anonymous bank accounts and bearer shares, of the patterns of production and marketing in various industries, and the like?

2. *The effect of social and political institutions on the tax structure.*

What is the effect of the patterns of family life and community organization on the tax structure? How do the patterns of family property disposition affect the tax laws? What are the institutional factors that have an effect on the degree of compliance or evasion to be expected from the public?

3. *The effect of legal institutions on the tax structure.*

What are the points of interaction between tax law and the civil and commercial law? How do the regular processes of civil and criminal litigation interact with the enforcement of the tax laws? What are sound procedures for the resolution of disputes between government and taxpayers, as respects questions of fact and questions of law, and how do these procedures fit with the legal process generally? What is a proper system of civil and criminal tax penalties and how does this system fit with the legal process generally?

The Impact of Inflation and Other Instabilities on the Tax Structure

What problems are raised by the impact of inflation on the tax structure and its administration? Where are the stresses and strains of inflationary instability felt—in the consequences attendant upon a lack of currency in the timing of tax payments and collections; in the valuations of real property, inventories, and other assets; in the changing composition of income levels and tax brackets; in the changing importance of the types of taxes; in the need for revaluation of assets for depreciation and excess profits taxation, and so on?

What other instabilities are similarly important, such as sudden changes in export or import patterns?

What changes in substantive tax policies and tax administration are necessary to meet or ameliorate the effects of these instabilities?

The Modernization of the Tax Structure to Deal with Modern Industry and Finance

How do the organization and operation of modern industry and finance affect the administration of taxes? How can a tax administration so organize and operate that in its relationships with modern business it can both derive benefits from the efficiencies in operation and record keeping which the business world has achieved and avoid thrusting useless or annoying burdens on business? What are the significances for tax return and record requirements, for taxpayer audits and investigations, and the like, of the ways in which modern business manages its internal affairs and records its transactions?

The Role of Valuation in the Revenue System

Recognizing that the role of valuation, broadly conceived, is pervasive in a revenue system, what important problems of valuation can be identified and what techniques can be used to solve or ameliorate those problems? May average prices be substituted for actual prices under certain excise taxes; how may fluctuations in the price structure be met; may valuation problems be altered by changing the time or economic stage at which valuation is required? To what extent are valuation problems a limiting factor in the substantive shaping of real property taxes, net worth taxes, income taxes, excise taxes?

These are some of the issues whose exploration would contribute to a better understanding of the problems of tax administration and their solution. We have much to learn the world over about this vital sector of the fiscal field. But if those interested in tax policy and in the problems of underdeveloped countries will recognize that the administration of tax laws is as much a matter of prime concern as is the substantive content of those laws, then there is real hope for steady progress and improvement in tax administration everywhere.

NOTES TO SELECTION 32

[1]See also the United States Economic Survey Mission (Bell Mission) to the Philippines, 1950.

[2]See in general *Proceedings of Conference on Agricultural Taxation and Economic Development*, Harvard Law School International Program in Taxation (1954).

[3]Excise Tax Act of Puerto Rico, enacted January 26, 1956, and initially prepared in 1954 by Stanley S. Surrey for the Secretary of the Treasury, Department of Finance, Puerto Rico.

[4]Morag, "Some Economic Aspects of Two Administrative Methods of Estimating Taxable Income," *National Tax Journal*, Vol. 10 (1957), pp. 176, contains an interesting discussion of the consequences for tax policy in the utilization by administrators of presumptive estimates and net worth techniques.

[5]See papers on "Judicial Guarantees of Taxpayers," *International Fiscal Association Conference* (Rome, October, 1956).

[6]The formulation in the text of these topics draws in considerable part on an informal discussion of these matters in 1957 between members of the Harvard Program and staff members and consultants of the Fiscal and Financial Branch of the United Nations Secretariat.

33

Technical Assistance

by Gustav F. Papanek*

IT IS unnecessary to repeat that the priority of a development project is an important factor in the usefulness of the corresponding technical assistance project. The relationship between the two is particularly complex, however, when a development program has been poorly or haphazardly chosen or when there is a difference in the priority of a development project and the corresponding technical assistance project.

There is no need to consider the first of these problems in any detail. To meet it, an outside agency can either help to improve the development program or it can react by modifying its assistance program. Both steps are considered later in this study.

There are, inevitably, many cases where the second question arises. Extreme cases present no serious problems. If a development project is useless, a technical assistance project, even if itself sound, is of little value. In the opposite case, it is also clear that a development project of the highest priority will not be helped much by technical assistance if the latter is not a suitable technique. For instance, a project to improve fishing nets in Ceylon may have high priority, but may require only the supply of nylon twine. Most cases, however, are not so clear-cut. If malaria control has high priority and would be helped by technical assistance, while a less important cement plant would benefit very greatly from technical assistance, which of the two technical assistance projects should have priority? It does not seem possible to assign weights to express the relative importance of the priority of a development project and the usefulness of the corresponding technical assistance project. All one can say is that both need to be taken into account. Perhaps they should be considered about equally

*From "Framing a Development Program," *International Conciliation*, No. 527 (March, 1960), pp. 342–55, and used here with the permission of the publisher. *International Conciliation* is a publication of the Carnegie Endowment for International Peace. Dr. Papanek's article was also reproduced in June, 1963, by the Center for International Affairs at Harvard University, and copies may be obtained from the Center at a charge of one dollar.

important, but certainly neither alone is significant. The rest of this section is concerned only with the usefulness of technical assistance projects, since the previous chapter has already dealt with the priority of development projects.

In practice, governments and aid-giving agencies have often gone on the assumption that a good index to the usefulness of a technical assistance project is the receivers' interest and willingness to share its cost. It seems plausible that if a sponsoring body or country expects a technical assistance project to be particularly useful it will push harder for it and be willing to contribute to a greater extent. If its usefulness is sufficiently great, the country or body will presumably be willing to arrange and pay for the required technical competence without assistance from an outside agency.

The weakness of this criterion is similar to that of feasibility in appraising a development project—interest and participation, as well as feasibility, are related more to the strength and ability of the agencies carrying out a project than to its intrinsic importance. If interest and participation demonstrate usefulness, the bodies and countries already best supplied with personnel to plan projects, with managers to push them, and with funds to carry them out will be in the best position to demonstrate the "usefulness" of their projects, just as they are best able to show their feasibility. Their relative performance will improve further as they obtain more than their share of technical assistance, and gradually those best off will draw further ahead of those somewhat less well off.

Naturally, if a government or sponsoring body is not willing to share any costs and is not sufficiently interested to provide the minimum support necessary for the operation of any technical assistance project, it is not worth going into. Beyond the minimum level, support will vary, but in the long run this should not affect the priority of such a project. An assistance project has an intrinsic value, determined by the priority of the corresponding development project and the usefulness of the technical assistance technique. In the long run, bodies and countries can and should be strengthened so that they can provide the necessary support to useful technical assistance projects. This takes time, however, and in the short run the support provided for different projects helps determine their effectiveness and is a factor in their usefulness and priority.

Two factors influencing the value or priority of a technical assistance project have been mentioned—the priority of the development project being assisted and, in the short run, the support provided.

Three more are discussed below—the type of project, its benefits, and its costs.

There are three major types of technical assistance—assistance in carrying out an operation, in training or teaching, and in institution-building. These are not clear-cut, separate categories and many projects combine all aspects in various proportions, but they do have some usefulness in distinguishing major purposes.

Assistance in operation means that the technician's primary assignment is to substitute for an indigenous technician in the direct performance of some function. This may involve a foreign engineer building a dam or constructing a factory, a foreign doctor treating the sick, or a foreign extension agent who tries to introduce new agricultural techniques. He may be training subordinates or cultivators, but he is not training a replacement. The same is true of the foreign economist who serves a planning agency or the foreign specialist who is engaged in the widespread, and widely deplored, activity of preparing a report. In most cases there is an incidental training function—almost no one works in isolation, and something will rub off—but in all the instances cited the major purpose is not the training of a local technician to replace the foreigner.

Teaching or training means that the major purpose of technical assistance is to enable one or more individuals to do work previously done, or undone, by a foreigner. This was the major purpose of technical assistance as originally envisaged, and decriptions of most current technical assistance projects still emphasize this aspect. It involves the transfer of knowledge, of techniques, to individuals or groups, but without major concern with the organizations or institutions that are to use the newly trained individuals. Foreign training for persons from underdeveloped countries falls in this category, as well as such projects as the foreign technician assigned to train engineers in dam-building practices or malaria experts in spraying campaigns.

Institution-building adds to the training function the requirement that some organization be assisted. For instance, foreign technicians would not only help train engineers to build dams but would help and advise on how to establish a dam-building organization eventually capable of doing the whole job by itself.

Recently, there has been a great deal of emphasis on the importance of institution-building.[1] The impression left by some writing is that the usefulness of a technical assistance project is practically always greatest when it is designed to assist in building an institution, less when it helps to train, and least when its major objective is to help carry out an operation. This is an over-simplified and therefore often inaccurate conclusion. Each of the three types of technical assistance is useful if it is the appropriate one for dealing with the problem to which it is applied. For instance, if a country is building a fertilizer factory, plans to build no others in the foreseeable future, and has the people to do everything except buy equipment, a technical assistance project to help with this is very sensible even though no training or institution-building is involved. On the other hand, if the problem is to establish an agricultural extension service, a project limited to providing or training extension agents is not likely to be successful.

The first check—criterion might be too strong a word—on the usefulness of technical assistance would then be to see whether the type proposed is the type needed. One can to some extent determine the type of technical assistance required in relation to the number of times for which a particular skill, action, or activity is needed. For instance, if a country has a site for only one high dam, it is sensible to provide outside engineers to do the actual work on aspects that are unique to high-dam construction. It would not be efficient to train native engineers in these special techniques since there would be no further use for their training. However, if several high dams are to be built, or where aspects of construction will be duplicated on some other dams, it will be better to provide technical assistance whose major purpose is to train engineers rather than to do the actual construction. Finally, if a number of dams are to be built, the country will need an organization, not just some trained engineers who can be brought together anew for each piece of construction. Technical assistance in that case would mean not only helping to train individual engineers, but also assisting where necessary in providing an appropriate internal structure for the organization and appropriate relationships to other organizations, delimiting its functions and shape, and framing its policies and operating procedures. Some training would still be involved, perhaps even some direct operation by foreigners, but the major emphasis would be on helping with management and policy problems of establishing an institution.

BENEFITS OF TECHNICAL ASSISTANCE

The benefits of technical assistance can be measured in terms of the estimated losses that would result from its absence. Without technical assistance a development project may cost more, its returns may be less, or—what comes to the same thing—it may take longer to execute. It may not be possible to make precise quantitative estimates of these losses, but their magnitude is the relevant measure of the benefits of a technical assistance project. For instance, without technical assistance a dam might be built equally well but take three years longer to complete. The benefits of technical assistance then are given by the returns foregone for three years. Just as there are development projects whose benefits cannot be quantified, a large number of technical assistance projects have benefits that are not readily measurable. Nevertheless, the same concept applies to them. The benefits of a technical assistance project to help set up an agricultural extension service are given by the greater effectiveness of that service, even if it is not possible to express them in quantitative terms.

In addition, technical assistance can have some indirect benefits that are hard to measure. It can foster a general atmosphere of change, help to increase receptivity to new ideas, foster improved personnel procedures, and encourage a number of similar changes outside the confines of the particular development project it is to assist. These benefits may differ among projects, and, if significant, should be taken into account even though they cannot be quantified. Such differences may arise from the nature of the project itself or from differences in the persons available to staff them. For instance, a project to supply a grouting engineer is less likely to have indirect benefits (or costs) than one to provide an advisor on extension methods to a community development project.

Considered broadly, opinions about the benefits of technical assistance depend very much on one's view of the strategy of economic development. Those who consider inadequate savings the main obstacle to development regard technical assistance as an occasionally useful, but minor, aspect of the development process. On the other hand, those who regard the absence of technical competence as the significant obstacle view technical assistance as the most important technique for assisting underdeveloped countries.

Different views on development strategy affect not only the appraisal of the over-all importance of technical assistance but—what is more to the point here—the conception of the *type* that is most useful. Those who see development mainly as a problem in transferring knowledge, skills, and techniques would stress technical assistance projects that provide for either direct operations or training. It is usually argued, however, that of the two, technical assistance for direct operations is much less valuable or needed. In this type, the foreign technician can, and often does, have little contact with indigenous institutions and therefore has little impact on their operation. The history of technical assistance is full of stories, which have by now become almost traditional and are often told with relish to outsiders, of reports written but ignored, functions performed only as long as the foreign technician was available, and other examples of the failure of projects emphasizing direct operations by the foreigner.

Teaching and training, it is maintained, fill a more important need in development since they permit the foreign technician to multiply his effectiveness by training several persons, each one better able than a foreigner to function in the particular environment of his own country. However, there are other limits to the effectiveness of training projects. What is normally transferred are knowledge, techniques, and facts. But in many cases lack of knowledge is not the major obstacle. Stagnant agricultural production may not be due primarily to a lack of knowledge among technicians about fertilizers or improved seeds or the importance of credit, or even to lack of knowledge about techniques for distributing fertilizer or seeds or credit. What is more often missing, cultural factors aside, are the institutions or organizations to demonstrate to cultivators the benefits of and techniques for using fertilizer and seeds and to provide the necessary credit. Technicians from underdeveloped areas trained in developed countries at great expense often find on their return that there is no organization to use their training. Equally frequently, "counterparts" to foreign technicians find they cannot put their training or experience to use once the foreigner leaves, because there is no organization to use it and as individuals they have neither the prestige nor the ability to create their own organization. From these difficulties and disappointments stems the argument that the greatest benefits come from technical assistance in institution-building.

Three types of technical assistance were described early in this chapter, and it was concluded that one could not assign priorities by type, since operations, teaching, or institution-building could all be equally useful if they were appropriate to meet a particular problem. Here these three types have again been examined, but this time to see whether in general one type is likely to be more useful. One can conclude that assistance in institution-building meets the most urgent need of many development programs, and direct operation the least urgent. This does not determine the priority of individual technical assistance projects, which depends on their particular benefits, but it does provide a useful indication of broad differences.

Costs of Technical Assistance

So far the discussion has been concerned with the benefits of technical assistance. But technical assistance also has some costs, which naturally affect the priority of a given project.

Some costs are rather simple to measure. One can estimate the money costs of a technical assistance project and the number of people and amount of equipment likely to be needed. In addition, there are political and social costs. There is usually at least some resentment because outsiders have to be brought in, especially when they have privileges and remunerations much above those available to the indigenous technician or manager. Furthermore, the work of the foreign technician often results in making enemies as well as friends, since few recommendations or actions in economic development are not considered harmful by someone. These political and social liabilities vary from one technical assistance project to another.

There are other more direct costs to a development program. To some extent foreign technicians will do work that, if done by a native of the country, would have provided him with valuable experience. The local official may learn how to avoid some mistakes from the foreigner, but in at least some cases he would have learned more had he made the mistakes. Secondly, the foreigner inevitably makes some mistakes that the indigenous inhabitant might have avoided. Then, technical assistance sometimes serves as an excuse for postponing a decision or shifting the responsibility for it. Finally, a technical assistance program requires substantial efforts on the part of the recipient countries in negotiating agreements and providing administrative support and technical counterparts, and often calls for substantial attention from top government officials. Some of these efforts may be expended on projects because they are attractive to the outside agency, even if they are not accorded a high priority by the country. The result may be a dispersion of the country's effort on some marginal projects. The reduction in the opportunities to learn from doing, the possibility of postponing or shifting decisions, the mistakes of the foreigner, and the additional effort required from the recipient country are costs of technical assistance that are often overlooked.

The extent of some of these costs depends to a considerable degree on the suitability of the foreign technician involved in a particular project. His ability will in part determine whether they are significant or not. There has been much discussion of the need for flexibility and adaptability as well as competence on the part of technicians. Not much would be gained by trying to summarize work on personnel selection here, since this is a large field in itself with a considerable literature, much of it of some significance to the selection of technical assistance personnel.[2]

All of the costs—financial, social, political, and broadly economic— vary from project to project and these differences need to be taken into account in determining the priority of individual technical assistance projects, although they will often be difficult to estimate. Costs are also likely to vary among types of technical assistance projects. For instance, if a project involves a highly specialized technical task which clearly cannot be performed by an indigenous technician, and if it is to be carried out under the general supervision of a local official, non-monetary costs may be quite small. At the other end of the scale is the foreigner advising on a highly sensitive issue, such as the desirability of a steel plant or of land reform, or one brought in to replace a civil servant who is considered inefficient.

In general, a technical assistance project calling for operation by the foreigner and a narrow technical task is often the simplest and easiest to carry out successfully. When a grouting engineer is needed, it is simple to supply one, to have him check the dam site, make his recommendations, or even carry them out. His work is clearly defined and limited in time. He is likely to be effective, successful, and make few mistakes, regardless of the country where the dam is located, and its culture, history, or politics.

Where the major purpose is training or teaching rather than operation, technical assistance becomes more difficult and is more likely to result in costly failure, since it requires more attention to the background and motives of those taught or trained.

Assistance with institution-building is usually the most difficult. It requires not only a knowledge of and ability to deal with individuals but also an understanding of institutions and an ability to assist in changing them. To help build a credit system, for instance, is a very complex task, involving some knowledge of the particular country's land tenure, of cultivators' habits, past experience, motives and methods of operation, of politics and government administration, and a host of other factors. In addition, it requires the ability to help adapt techniques to new circumstances and a number of crucial personal characteristics. The foreign technician is most likely to make mistakes, to offend, and in general to encounter difficulties in this type of assignment. Institution-building is also the type of technical assistance that usually takes longest to achieve any measure of success and where continuity in personnel is most important. Otherwise, its costs are likely to increase sharply and its benefits decrease greatly.

In short, the difficulties, risks, and costs of technical assistance are usually least for simple operational assignments, greater in teaching or training projects, and greatest for those primarily involving institution-building. This is certainly one of the major reasons for the number of projects emphasizing direct operations and quite restricted problems, despite the nearly universal agreement on the limited usefulness of this type of assistance.

FUTURE WORK

Unfortunately, little seems to have been done to evaluate the applicability of technical assistance to different development projects.[3] For instance, although it was mentioned earlier that assistance in institution-building has been considered a major function of technical assistance, there seems to be no systematic analysis of whether technical assistance is an appropriate technique for facilitating this process.

Under what circumstances, if any, is technical assistance effective in helping to establish an agricultural credit system or a planning agency, an extension service or a changed system of education? It may be that in many cases cultural differences are so significant that most available foreigners can make little contribution to institution-building. The development of an agricultural extension service may be a crucial need in a particular country, but little is known about the effectiveness of foreign extension agents in helping with this problem and about the circumstances that influence their effectiveness. A related question is the applicability of any type of technical assistance in situations where a significant change in people's attitudes or values is involved. Is it worthwhile, for instance, to provide technical assistance in the field of nutrition, or do changes in this field involve such deeply held attitudes that a foreign nutritionist will accomplish little? If the technical assistance technique is usually not applicable to this type of problem, a project in this field, however good, may have low priority.

Sociology, anthropology, and related disciplines have been concerned with the problems arising from the impact of people from one culture or society on another.[4] Unfortunately, little of their work seems to provide specific guidance in deciding on the applicability of technical assistance under different circumstances. Where recommendations are made for the practitioner they are often confined to warnings that he should realize (1) that particular techniques will work differently in different cultures, and (2) that any change, even if it seems a small and simple technical innovation, can have far-reaching consequences difficult to foresee. It is certainly important to keep these warnings in mind, but they do not help much in determining the circumstances under which, and the projects for which, technical assistance is appropriate.

What is needed here is more research, more work on the development of criteria. A great deal of actual experience has been accumulated and could be analyzed to find out when and why particular technical assistance projects have been successful and others not. These studies would not be concerned with the question of how technical assistance should be administered, but with the kind of development project that can most effectively use it; with the circumstances that are relevant and the reasons for success or failure; with the type of technical assistance most useful to meet different problems; and with the kind of person most effective in providing different types of technical assistance. Some improvement in the composition of technical assistance programs would result if the experiences and knowledge of practitioners were exchanged. The major need, however, is for a systematic study, drawing on experience in different parts of the world, under different circumstances, and with different approaches to technical assistance.[5]

Conclusions

The criteria and general guidelines that are available to assist in deciding on the composition of a technical assistance program are not very satisfactory, but some general propositions can be stated. To summarize briefly and without the necessary qualifications:

First, the priority of a technical assistance project depends on two major factors—the priority of the development project being assisted and the usefulness of technical assistance in carrying out that development project. Both are important and might normally be given equal weight.

Second, the interest and willingness to share the cost shown by a sponsoring body is not a good indication of usefulness since they depend largely on the strength of the body. Used as criteria, they will reinforce the bodies and countries already best off. In the long run, technical assistance should be provided on the basis of the intrinsic usefulness of projects, and agencies should be strengthened so they can carry their share. However, in the short run, the effectiveness of technical assistance is inevitably affected by differences in the interest and support of sponsoring agencies, and this needs to be taken into account in evaluating the costs and benefits of a project.

Third, the benefits of technical assistance can be measured by the losses in terms of costs, benefits, and time that would be incurred on the corresponding development project in the absence of technical assistance. A good, accurate estimate will usually not be possible.

Fourth, costs of technical assistance are not only financial, but also social, political, and broadly economic. They include the effort and attention required from the recipient country, which may be a significant element. Differences in cost depend on the nature of the project, the availability of suitable personnel, and other factors.

And fifth, three types of technical assistance projects can be distinguished—assisting in operations, in teaching and training, and in institution-building. In general, the benefits are greatest for projects that aid in the creation of new institutions and organizations, while assistance in direct operations is least effective in meeting the problems of development. At the same time, assisting in operations involves the least danger of failure and of great political, social, and economic costs, while institution-building is the most difficult and calls for foreign personnel with particular personal characteristics as well as technical competences. Thus, the type of project with the greatest benefit may also be the one where costs and danger of failure are greatest. These general statements on the benefits and costs of different types do not, however, indicate the priority of a particular project. A technical assistance project in any category can and should have a high priority if that type of project is the appropriate one for meeting a particular problem. Failures arise when the problem calls for one type but another is supplied.

If all the variables above were measurable, one would be able to conceive of technical assistance projects being evaluated by giving equal weight to the priority of the corresponding development project and the usefulness of the technical assistance project itself—the latter being decided by weighing its benefits against its cost, subject to some correction for the extent of support by the sponsoring body.

A possible framework of concepts and criteria for determining the composition of a technical assistance program has been developed here, but the major conclusion that has emerged is the inadequate state of knowledge in this field, the need for further research, analysis of experience, and development of criteria before much progress can be made in their application.

NOTES TO SELECTION 33

[1]See Philip M. Glick, *The Administration of Technical Assistance* (Chicago: University of Chicago Press, 1957); Jonathan B. Bingham, *Shirt Sleeve Diplomacy* (New York: Day, 1954); and National Planning Association (NPA), Special Policy Committee on Technical Cooperation, Reports on Technical Cooperation in Latin America (Washington): *Administration of Bilateral Technical Cooperation* (January, 1956), *Recommendations for the Future* (June 1956), *The Role of Universities in Technical Cooperation* (July, 1955), *Technical Cooperation—Sowing the Seeds of Progress* (June, 1955), *Organizations of the U.S. Government for Technical Assistance* (May, 1955), and *Training through Technical Cooperation* (February, 1957).

[2]See *The American Overseas*, Hearing Before the Committee on Foreign Relations, United States Senate, 86th Cong., 1st Sess., February 18, 1959 (Washington, 1959); Harlan Cleveland and Gerard Mangone, eds., *The Art of Overseasmanship* (Syracuse University Press, 1957); Clarence E. Thurber, "Training Americans for Overseas Service in the U.S. Government Technical Assistance Programs" (Doctoral dissertation in public administration, Stanford University); Group for the Advancement of Psychiatry, *Working Abroad: A Discussion of Psychological Attitudes and Adaptation in New Situations*, Report No. 41 (New York, 1958): and U.S. Civil Service Commission, Examining and Placement Division, *Research Project on Selection Methods for Overseas Employees* (August, 1953).

[3]But see Glick, Bingham, NPA, works cited; and "Foreign Technical Assistance in Economic Development in a Newly Independent Country," *Economic Development and Cultural Change,* Vol. I (March, 1952), No. 1.

[4]See Bert F. Hoselitz, ed., *The Progress of Underdeveloped Areas* (Chicago: University of Chicago Press, 1952); and Marion J. Levy, Jr., "Some Social Obstacles to 'Capital Formation' in Underdeveloped Areas," *Capital Formation and Economic Growth* (Princeton, National Bureau of Economic Research, 1955).

[5]The United States International Cooperation Administration is considering such a study of its own technical assistance program. It could go far in meeting the need described above.

Selected Bibliography

Listed below are many of the books, articles, and official periodicals and documents, available in English, which deal with fiscal problems in developing countries. This is not intended to be a comprehensive list; a more complete listing may be found in the Harvard Law School International Program in Taxation's *Bibliography on Taxation in Underdeveloped Countries* (item 27 below). In particular, it should be noted that useful literature which does not deal explicitly with underdeveloped countries has been excluded. The main basis for including an item in this listing has been that the editors have personally found it useful; each student of the field will, of course, have such a list of his own. Brief annotations have been made to many but not all of the bibliographical references. These annotations occasionally include further references on the same topic. The main entries of the bibliography have been numbered to make cross-reference easier, and those works from which the selections in this volume of readings have been taken are, in addition, indicated by an asterisk.

Two works not included below are the forthcoming volumes (to be published in 1964 by The Johns Hopkins Press) containing the papers and proceedings of the Buenos Aires Conference on Tax Administration, held in October, 1961, and of the Santiago Conference on Tax Policy, held in December, 1962.* These conferences, originally stimulated by the Harvard Law School International Program in Taxation, were sponsored by the Joint Tax Program of the Organization of American States, the United Nations Economic Commission for Latin America, and the Inter-American Development Bank. Both of the conferences were oriented toward Latin American tax problems; each projected volume contains papers by noted experts from all over the world, comments chiefly by Latin American experts, and a summary of proceedings. While few of the papers are based upon new research on Latin America, many of them provide up-to-date surveys of the issues they treat, and some of them present new or reworked ideas for discussion. Both volumes will be valuable reference tools.

*The Spanish language versions of these conference volumes were published early in 1964 by the Joint Tax Program of the Organization of American States, the United Nations Economic Commission for Latin America, and the Inter-American Development Bank.

1. ADLER, JOHN H., "The Fiscal and Monetary Implementation of Development Programs," *American Economic Review, Papers and Proceedings,* XLII (May, 1952), 584–600. An exploration of the general use of fiscal tools in development planning. Note especially the suggestion for progressive property taxes.

2. *ADLER, JOHN H., "Fiscal Policy in a Developing Country," a paper presented at the Round Table on Economic Development with Special Reference to East Asia, April 2–9, 1960, at Gamagori, Japan; revised July 8, 1960. Copyright International Economic Association. Also to be published in 1964 by The Macmillan Company, London, as part of a volume entitled "Economic Development with Special Reference to East Asia."

3. ADLER, JOHN H., SCHLESINGER, E. R., and OLSON, E. C., *Public Finance and Economic Development in Guatemala* (Stanford: Stanford University Press, 1952). A companion volume to the study by WALLICH and ADLER on El Salvador (item 83) and, like it, a careful examination of the fiscal problems of a small, exposed, poor country.

4. *BAUER, PETER T., "The Economic Development of Nigeria," *Journal of Political Economy,* LXIII (October, 1955), 398–411. See also *ADLER, JOHN H., "The Economic Development of Nigeria: Comment," *Journal of Political Economy,* LXIV (October, 1956), 425–34.

5. BAUER, PETER T., and YAMEY, BASIL S., *The Economics of Underdeveloped Countries* (Chicago: University of Chicago Press, 1957). Especially Chapters 11 and 13. This pessimistic appraisal of the possibility of using tax policy to aid development is valuable material for all readers on the subject. Although many of the authors' criticisms of the usual writings on taxation and development ring true, their own argument—which is almost that those governments are best which attempts least—seems more to evade than to meet the real problems.

6. BLOCH, HENRY S., "Economic Development and Public Finance," HOSELITZ, BERT F., (ed), *The Progress of Underdeveloped Areas* (Chicago: University of Chicago Press, 1952), pp. 248–58. An excellent brief introductory survey of some of the problems in this field.

7. BLOCH, HENRY S., "The Relation of Tax Policy to Economic Growth," *The Limits of Taxable Capacity* (Princeton: Tax Institute, Inc., 1953), pp. 171–82. Another general survey.

8. BLOCH, HENRY S., *Revenue Administration and Policy in Israel* (United Nations, New York): (1) U.N. Sales No.: 1953.II.H.5; (2) U.N. Sales No.: 1955.II.H.3; (3) U.N. Sales No.: 1958.II.H.2. In some respects, Israel's system is the system most intentionally designed to encourage development of any in the world, a fact making these three reports containing a U.N. expert's appraisal of the system, at three different times, of special interest.

9. BRONFENBRENNER, MARTIN, "The Appeal of Confiscation in Economic Development," *Economic Development and Cultural Change,* III (April,

1955), 201–18; reprinted in AGARWALA, A. N., and SINGH, S. P. (eds.), *The Economics of Underdevelopment* (Bombay: Oxford University Press, 1958), pp. 472–94. Although confiscatory measures are not necessarily fiscal in nature, this article is included here for the stimulating effect it is likely to have on the thought of all readers.

10. BRONFENBRENNER, MARTIN, and KOGIKU, KIICHIRO, "The Aftermath of the Shoup Tax Reforms," *National Tax Journal*, X (1957), 236–54, 345–60. A detailed account of the effects of one of the most celebrated of modern fiscal missions (see item 58). In general, the authors feel that the mission was a success, measured by a realistic rather than idealistic standard, but in detail they feel much went wrong. Compare item 72.

11. BURKHEAD, JESSE, *Government Budgeting* (New York: John Wiley and Sons, Inc., 1956). Chapter 18 surveys the problem of budgeting for economic development. The book is an excellent treatment of budgeting procedures and problems. Other useful references on this subject are: (1) GOODE, RICHARD, and BIRNBAUM, EUGENE A., "Government Capital Budgets," *International Monetary Fund Staff Papers*, V (February, 1956), 23–46; (2) HICKS, U. K., "The Integration of the Budget and the Development Plan with Special Reference to the Spanish Situation," *Public Finance*, XVII (1962), No. 2, 120–53; (3) PUBLIC ADMINISTRATION SERVICE, *Modernizing Government Budget Administration* (Washington: Agency for International Development, 1962); and (4) such UNITED NATIONS reports on budgeting as: *A Manual for Programme and Performance Budgeting* (Document No.: E/CN.12/BRW.2/L.4); *A Manual for Economic and Functional Classification of Government Transactions* (U.N. Sales No.: 58.XVI.2); and *Report of the Workshop on Budgetary Classification and Management in South America* (Document No.: E/CN.12/634/Rev. 1) (1962).

12. *CHELLIAH, RAJA, J., *Fiscal Policy in Underdeveloped Countries with Special Reference to India* (London: George Allen & Unwin Ltd., 1960). Based on a doctoral dissertation, this book by a young Indian economist combines both a general account of the problem of fiscal policy for development and a careful appraisal of India's tax structure, with suggestions for reform. Chelliah's analysis of indirect taxation and support of a scheme exempting certain investments from income tax (see also selection 17 in this volume) is particularly noteworthy.

13. *CROCKETT, JOSEPH P., "Tax Pattern in Latin America," *National Tax Journal*, XV (March, 1962), 93–104.

14. DUE, JOHN, *Taxation and Economic Development in Tropical Africa* (Cambridge, Mass.: M.I.T. Press, 1963). A study of tax policy in eight African countries. Note especially the sections on the African personal taxes (also in *National Tax Journal*, XV [December, 1962], 385–98), and property taxes (also in *Land Economics*, XXXIX [February, 1963], 1–14).

15. *FROOMKIN, JOSEPH N., "Fiscal Management of Municipalities and Economic Development," *Economic Development and Cultural Change*, III

(July, 1955), 309–20; reprinted in *Journal of African Administration,* VIII (January, 1956), 15–26.

16. FROOMKIN, JOSEPH N., "Some Problems of Tax Policy in Latin America," *National Tax Journal,* X (December, 1957), 370–79. A study of some of the numerous tax incentives in existence in Mexico, Brazil, Colombia, and Argentina, with useful general comments. The variety of measures used and their general lack of effectiveness are worth noting.

17. *FROOMKIN, JOSEPH N., and LIDSTONE, H. K., "Tax Problems of Export Economies—Taxation of Coffee in El Salvador," *National Tax Journal,* VII (September, 1954), 264–73.

18. FUJITA, SEI, "Political Ceiling on Income Taxation," *Public Finance,* XVI (1961), No. 2, 183–98. A discussion of the problem of voluntary compliance under an income tax system and the limits imposed by tax consciousness on the extent to which income taxes can be used in less advanced countries. Mr. Fujita bases most of his conclusions on an analysis of Japanese experience since the war, with special reference to the Shoup Mission report (item 58).

19. GOODE, RICHARD, "New System of Direct Taxation in Ceylon," *National Tax Journal,* XIII (December, 1960), 329–40. A review of the fiscal changes in Ceylon resulting from Nicholas Kaldor's visit to that country, with comments on some novel devices in both income and expenditure taxation.

20. *GOODE, RICHARD, "Reconstruction of Foreign Tax Systems," National Tax Association, *Proceedings of the Forty-Fourth Annual Conference on Taxation* (held in Dallas, Texas, 1951) (Sacramento, 1952), pp. 212–22.

21. *GOODE, RICHARD, "Taxation of Saving and Consumption in Underdeveloped Countries, *National Tax Journal,* XIV (December, 1961), 305–21.

22. GOPAL, M. H., "Towards a Realistic Tax Policy for India," *Indian Economic Journal,* VI (January, 1959), 281–326. (See also his *A Realistic Tax Structure for India* [Bombay: Vora and Co., 1959].) An interesting view by an Indian scholar of the tax problems facing his country as it attempts to achieve its ambitious (though in absolute terms, still low) goal of development.

23. GOVERNMENT OF INDIA, *Report of the Direct Taxes Administration Enquiry Committee, 1958–59* (New Delhi: 1960). A thorough survey of how income taxation really works in the underdeveloped country with perhaps the highest level of competence—and complexity—in its direct tax administration.

24. GOVERNMENT OF INDIA, *Report of the Taxation Enquiry Commission, 1953–54* (3 vols.; New Delhi: 1955). A thorough survey of India's tax system, federal, state, and local, this report is one of the most comprehensive, if not particularly inspiring, documents of this type available. See also GOVERNMENT OF PAKISTAN, *Taxation Enquiry Committee Report* (Karachi, 1961).

25. *GOVERNMENT OF PAKISTAN, PLANNING COMMISSION, *The Second Five-Year Plan (1960–1965)* (Karachi, 1960), Chaps. 2–3. In addition to the excerpt in the present volume, these two chapters contain a survey of the problem of financing an ambitious development plan. The *Indian Third Five-Year Plan* (New Delhi, 1961) may be equally recommended for this purpose.

26. *HARVARD LAW SCHOOL INTERNATIONAL PROGRAM IN TAXATION, *Analysis of Draft Law No. 462 and Evaluation of Comments on Income Tax Reform: A Report to the Minister of Finance of the Republic of Colombia* (Cambridge, Mass., 1959) (mimeographed).

27. HARVARD LAW SCHOOL INTERNATIONAL PROGRAM IN TAXATION, *Bibliography on Taxation in Underdeveloped Countries* (Cambridge, Mass., 1962). An unselective bibliography of some 2,100 references, mostly in English, but with a number of foreign language items, chiefly on Latin America. Organized primarily by countries, the bibliography is almost complete through 1961.

28. HARVARD LAW SCHOOL INTERNATIONAL PROGRAM IN TAXATION, *World Tax Series: Taxation in India* (prepared by BRUDNO, COBB, and PALKHIVALA) (Boston: Little, Brown and Company, 1960) (Chicago: Commerce Clearing House, Inc., 1963). This volume of the World Tax Series is particularly interesting to students of taxation in developing countries for its detailed description of the expenditure and net wealth taxes and other aspects of India's advanced tax system. Other volumes of the series dealing with less-developed countries are *Taxation in Mexico* (prepared by GUMPEL and MARGÁIN, 1957), *Taxation in Brazil* (prepared by GUMPEL and GOMES DE SOUSA, 1957), and "Taxation in Colombia" (to be published in 1964). These volumes also describe the tax treatment of international income in the respective countries.

29. HELLER, JACK, and KAUFFMAN, KENNETH M., *Tax Incentives for Industry in Less Developed Countries* (Cambridge, Mass.: Harvard Law School International Program in Taxation, 1963). This book consists of several studies of tax incentive programs: incentive legislation is analyzed in detail; the aims and effects of income tax exemption programs are studied (this section is based on an article by DR. KAUFFMAN in the *National Tax Journal*, XIII [June and September, 1960], 141–62 and 252–69); and probable costs and benefits of different kinds of incentive programs are examined.

30. *HELLER, WALTER W., "Fiscal Policies for Underdeveloped Countries," in United Nations Technical Assistance Administration, *Taxes and Fiscal Policy in Under-developed Countries* (U.N. Sales No.: 1955.II.H.1) (New York, 1954), pp. 1–22; reprinted in WALD, HASKELL P., and FROOMKIN, JOSEPH N. (eds.), *Papers and Proceedings of the Conference on Agricultural Taxation and Economic Development* (Cambridge, Mass.: Harvard Law School International Program in Taxation, 1954), pp. 61–85.

31. *HICKS, J. R., and HICKS, U. K., *Report on Finance and Taxation in Jamaica* (Kingston: Government Printer, 1955). This short report is well worth reading in its entirety for many insights and ideas, in addition to those contained in the excerpt included in the present volume. See also the paper delivered in January, 1957, by PROFESSOR HICKS to the Economics Society of Nairobi, Kenya, "Unimproved Value Rating—the Case of East Africa," reprinted in HICKS, J. R., *Essays in World Economics* (London: Oxford University Press, 1959), pp. 237–44. In this gem of analysis, he further, but more generally, develops his views on the taxation of real property, but does not analyze proposals for partial exemption of improvements in as much detail as in the Jamaica report excerpt contained in this volume (selection 23).

32. HICKS, U. K., *Development from Below: Local Government and Finance in Developing Countries of the Commonwealth* (London: Oxford University Press, 1961). A thorough account of the development of local government institutions and practices in a number of former British territories in Asia, Africa, and the West Indies. Chapters 15 and 16 contain a more general discussion of a number of issues involved in taxing rural and urban real property.

33. HICKS, U. K., "The Search for Revenue in Underdeveloped Countries," *Revue de Science et de Législation Financières,* XLIV (January–March, 1952), 6–43. In this long article, Mrs. Hicks explores many possible sources of revenue and gives an especially enlightening discussion of export taxation.

34. HIGGINS, BENJAMIN, *Economic Development: Principles, Problems, and Policies* (New York: W. W. Norton & Company, Inc., 1959), Chapters 19–24. This well-known economic-development text contains a more extensive discussion of the fiscal problems of developing countries than any other text now available. Professor Higgins' own proposals for "a self-enforcing tax system," an elaboration of some suggestions made by Nicholas Kaldor (item 41), are contained in Chapter 23 (pp. 524–44).

35. HINRICHS, HARLEY H., "Certainty as Criterion: Taxation of Foreign Investment in Afghanistan," *National Tax Journal,* XV (June, 1962), 139–54. A stimulating study of the difference between form and substance in the tax treatment of foreign investment in a very poor country.

36. *HIRSCHMAN, ALBERT O., *Journeys Toward Progress: Studies of Economic Policy-Making in Latin America* (New York: Twentieth Century Fund, 1963).

37. HOLZMAN, F. D., "Financing Soviet Economic Development," in ABRAMOVITZ, MOSES (ed.), *Capital Formation and Economic Growth* (Princeton: Princeton University Press, 1955), pp. 229–87. Pages 229–46 are also reprinted in HOLZMAN, F. D. (ed.), *Readings on the Soviet Economy* (Chicago: Rand McNally & Company, 1962), pp. 553–70.

38. *INTERNATIONAL BANK FOR RECONSTRUCTION AND DEVELOPMENT, *The Basis of a Development Program for Colombia* (Sales No.: IBRD.1950.2)

(Washington: 1950) (Baltimore: The Johns Hopkins Press, 1952, 1953), Chapters 13 and 26. One of the earliest World Bank mission reports, the sections on public finance (summarized on pages 57–63 of item 79) are among the best. See selections 24 and 25 in this volume for this mission's recommendations on land taxation and the subsequent history of the proposal. Other World Bank mission reports devote varying amounts of attention to tax and public finance issues. For one of the more thorough treatments, see *The Economic Development of Kenya* (Baltimore: The Johns Hopkins Press, 1963), Chapter 10.

39. *INTERNATIONAL BANK FOR RECONSTRUCTION AND DEVELOPMENT, *The Economic Development of Nigeria* (Baltimore: The Johns Hopkins Press, 1955).

40. JOINT LEGISLATIVE-EXECUTIVE TAX COMMISSION, *Survey on Tax Consciousness in the Philippines* (Manila, 1962). A pioneering attempt to discover what the people of a developing country think of their tax system. Most of the information is statistical in form. The Joint Legislative-Executive Tax Commission, essentially a tax research group, is a recently created institution which has aroused considerable interest among students of taxation in developing countries and may be worthy of emulation in other such countries.

41. *KALDOR, NICHOLAS, *Indian Tax Reform: Report of a Survey* (New Delhi: Government of India, Ministry of Finance, Department of Economic Affairs, 1956). Mr. Kaldor's first fiscal report on an underdeveloped country, this stimulating report, with its unusual views, set the pattern for the reports that followed in Ceylon, Ghana, British Guiana, and elsewhere.

42. *KALDOR, NICHOLAS, "Tax Reform in India," *Economic Weekly (Annual)* (Bombay), XV (January, 1959), 195–98.

43. KUBINSKI, Z. M., *Public Finance for Stability and Growth in an Underdeveloped Export Economy* (Amsterdam: International Bureau of Fiscal Documentation, 1961). A discussion of the problems of fiscal policy in a very poor country, the Sudan.

44. *LEVIN, JONATHAN, *The Export Economies: Their Pattern of Development in Historical Perspective* (Cambridge, Mass.: Harvard University Press, 1960). In addition to extensive and penetrating historical studies of Peru in the Guano Age and of Burma's Rice-Marketing Board (Chapters 2 and 5), this book contains an able treatment of the problem of export economies and of fiscal methods of coping with them (Chapters 4, 6, and 7).

45. LOCKWOOD, WILLIAM W., *The Economic Development of Japan* (Princeton: Princeton University Press, 1954), pp. 521–28. A brief account of Japanese land taxation in the Meiji era, the most famous instance of deliberately squeezing the agricultural sector to finance industrialization. In addition to selection 26 in the present volume, the interested reader might also consult OSHIMA, HARRY T., "The Role of Land Taxes in

Japanese Development (1867–1912) and Its Relation to Underdeveloped Countries," in Joint Legislative-Executive Tax Commission, *Taxation and Socio-Economic Growth* (Manila, 1960), pp. 215–44.

46. *MARTIN, ALISON, and LEWIS, W. ARTHUR, "Patterns of Public Revenue and Expenditure," *Manchester School of Economic and Social Studies,* XXIV (September, 1956), 203–44. See also WILLIAMSON, JEFFREY G., "Public Expenditure and Revenue: An International Comparison," *Manchester School of Economic and Social Studies,* XXIX (January, 1961), 43–56, for a revision and broadening of the analysis in MARTIN and LEWIS' 1956 article; and LEWIS, JR., STEPHEN R., "Government Revenue from Foreign Trade: An International Comparison," *Manchester School of Economic and Social Studies,* XXXI (January, 1963), 39–46, for more information on the importance of foreign trade.

47. MORAG, AMOTZ, "Some Economic Aspects of Two Administrative Methods of Estimating Taxable Income," *National Tax Journal,* X (June, 1957), 176–85. This brief article, in discussing some of the economic effects of the net-worth and presumptive methods of estimating taxable income, provides one of the few examples of an economic appraisal of common administrative practices. More of this sort of analysis is necessary if tax policy is to be firmly based on reality.

48. MURRAY, J. F. N., *Report to the Government of Jamaica on Valuation, Land Taxation and Rating* (Kingston: Government Printer, 1957). A discussion of problems similar to those raised in selection 23 in this volume, with different conclusions, though based on less rigorous analysis.

49. NATIONAL COUNCIL OF APPLIED ECONOMIC RESEARCH, *Taxation and Private Investment* (New Delhi, 1961). A careful, though in parts scanty, review by a leading Indian economic research organization of the effects on private investment of India's high tax rates, this report is one of the very few empirical works in a field about which much is written.

50. NURKSE, RAGNAR, *Problems of Capital Formation in Underdeveloped Countries* (New York: Oxford University Press, 1957), pp. 99–103, 142–52. An early and still influential discussion of the role of public finance in effecting resource transfers to facilitate economic development.

51. OLDMAN, OLIVER, and TEMPLE, RALPH, "Comparative Analysis of the Taxation of Married Persons," *Stanford Law Review,* XII (May, 1960), 585–605. (See also United Nations, Commission on the Status of Women, *Tax Legislation Applicable to Women* [by OLDMAN and TEMPLE] [Document No.: E/CN.6/344, January 26, 1959].) A study of one of the most complex individual aspects of personal income tax systems. There is need for more such comparative analysis to provide firmer support for the generalizations that are so often made on the basis of a scanty knowledge of a very few systems.

52. *PAAUW, DOUGLAS S., *Financing Economic Development: The Indonesian Case* (Glencoe, Ill.: The Free Press, 1960). In addition to the excerpt on local finance reproduced in this volume, this book, a product of the

Massachusetts Institute of Technology's Center for International Studies, contains a careful investigation of most of the other aspects of Indonesia's fiscal experience and problems.

53. *PAPANEK, GUSTAV F., "Framing a Development Program," *International Conciliation* (No. 527 March, 1960), pp. 305–72. This issue of *International Conciliation* was also published separately in June, 1963, by the Center for International Affairs at Harvard University.

54. PERRY, J. HARVEY, *Taxation and Economic Development in Ghana* (Document No.: TAA/GHA/4/Rev. 1) (New York: United Nations, 1958). This U.N. report is especially useful for its discussion of tax incentives for industrial development.

55. PLASSCHAERT, SYLVAIN, "Taxable Capacity in Developing Countries," (Report No. EC–103) (Washington: International Bank for Reconstruction and Development, February, 1962) (Mimeographed). A pioneer study of an important subject; uneven but stimulating in its treatment.

56. PREST, A. R., *Public Finance in Under-developed Countries* (London: Weidenfeld and Nicolson, 1962). Based on lectures given in Portugal, supplemented by material from some of Dr. Prest's earlier work, this volume provides a well-presented introduction to this subject.

57. PUBLIC ADMINSTRATION SERVICE, *Modernizing Government Revenue Administration* (Washington: International Cooperation Administration, 1961). A brief survey of the issues involved in operating the tax system of an underdeveloped country. See also selection 32 in this volume.

58. *Report on Japanese Taxation by the Shoup Mission* (4 vols; Tokyo: General Headquarters, Supreme Commander for the Allied Powers, 1949). (See also *Second Report on Japanese Taxation by the Shoup Mission* [Tokyo, 1950].) Perhaps the most influential report of the postwar tax missions, this report remains an essential source for all those interested in technical assistance work. Parts of the subsequent history of the mission's recommendations are traced in items 10 and 72.

59. RIGGS, FREDERICK W., "Public Administration: A Neglected Factor in Economic Development," in HOSELITZ, BERT F. (ed.), *Agrarian Societies in Transition*, the Annals of the American Academy of Political and Social Science, Vol. 305, pp. 70–80 (1956). An introductory analysis of the subject, with special attention to tax administration.

60. ROSS, STANFORD G., and CHRISTENSEN, JOHN B., *Tax Incentives for Industry in Mexico* (Cambridge, Mass.: Harvard Law School International Program in Taxation, 1959). More legally oriented than Taylor's study of tax exemption in Puerto Rico (see items 69 and 70), this study concludes that Mexico's exemption program has had only a limited success in attaining its objectives.

61. SAHOTHA, G. S., *Indian Tax Structure and Economic Development* (New York: Asia Publishing House, 1961). An interesting, if insufficient, statistical examination of the way in which India's tax structure has reacted to changes in its economic structure. For a similar, though even less com-

plete, study on Pakistan, see CHOWDHURY, A. H. M. N., "The Predictability and Flexibility of Tax Revenues in Pakistan," *The Pakistan Development Review*, II (Summer, 1962), 189–214.

62. *SHOUP, CARL S., "Tax Problems of a Common Market in Latin America," *Tax Policy on United States Investment in Latin America* (Princeton: Tax Institute, Inc., 1963), pp. 181–88; also in *Tax Policy*, XXIX (November, 1962), No. 11.

63. *SHOUP, CARL S., ET AL., *The Fiscal System of Venezuela: A Report* (Baltimore: The Johns Hopkins Press, 1959). This comprehensive study includes, in addition to the sections on the income tax excerpted in the present volume, a careful account of almost every policy and technical issue that arises in connection with taxation in developing countries. Despite Venezuela's singular economic structure, this report is relevant in large part to many other countries and should be required reading for all interested in taxation and development.

64. SHOUP, CARL S., ET AL., *The Fiscal System of the Federal District of Venezuela: A Report* (New York, 1960). The most careful and thorough recent examination of the usually neglected problems of finance in a large metropolitan area in a poor country.

65. *SULLIVAN, CLARA K., "Concepts of Sales Taxation" (Cambridge, Mass.: Harvard Law School International Program in Taxation, 1964). This material appears in print for the first time in this volume of readings; it constitutes part of the materials experimentally used in the International Tax Research Seminar at the Harvard Law School.

66. *SURREY, STANLEY S., "Tax Administration in Underdeveloped Countries," *University of Miami Law Review*, XII (Winter, 1958), 158–88.

67. SURREY, STANLEY S., and OLDMAN, OLIVER, "Report of a Preliminary Survey of the Tax System of Argentina," *Public Finance*, XVI (1961), 155–82. A report of problem areas in Argentina's income tax system, with some suggested solutions.

68. TAYLOR, MILTON C., "Income Taxation in the Federation of Malaya," *National Tax Journal*, XIV (1961), 198–205. An optimistic appraisal of the possibility of using an income tax for at least limited purposes even in countries which are at a low level of development.

69. TAYLOR, MILTON C., *Industrial Tax-Exemption in Puerto Rico* (Madison: University of Wisconsin Press, 1957). The most careful examination of the famous "Puerto Rican success story," pointing out the very peculiar circumstances of the case.

70. *TAYLOR, MILTON C., "What Happens When Exemptions End: Retrospect and Prospect in Puerto Rico," *Taxation and Operations Abroad* (Princeton: Tax Institute, Inc., 1960), pp. 170–86; also in *Tax Policy*, XXVI (November–December, 1959), Nos. 11–12.

71. TRIPATHY, R. N., *Federal Finance in a Developing Economy* (Calcutta: The World Press Private Ltd., 1960). A review of practically every aspect of this important subject, concentrating on Indian problems.

72. UEMATSU, MORIO, and COLEMAN, REX, *Computation of Income in Japanese Income Taxation* (Cambridge, Mass.: Harvard Law School International Program in Taxation, 1963). Also in VON MEHREN, ARTHUR T. (ed.), *Law in Japan: The Legal Order in a Changing Society* (Cambridge, Mass.: Harvard University Press, 1963). A careful study by an experienced Japanese official, assisted by the American editor of the forthcoming World Tax Series volume on Japan. See items 10, 27, and 28.

73. *United Nations, Economic and Social Council, Fiscal Commission, *Corporate Tax Problems* (Document No.: E/CN.8/66, November 25, 1953), especially Chapter 6, pp. 57–75.

74. UNITED NATIONS, ECONOMIC COMMISSION FOR AFRICA, "Public Finance in African Countries," *Economic Bulletin for Africa,* I (June, 1961), 1–28. A comparative survey of a relatively unknown subject. See also item 14.

75. *UNITED NATIONS, ECONOMIC COMMISSION FOR ASIA AND THE FAR EAST, *Economic Survey of Asia and the Far East 1960* (Bangkok, 1961), pp. 53–119. An excellent review of postwar experience with public finance in a number of Asian countries.

76. UNITED NATIONS, ECONOMIC COMMISSION FOR ASIA AND THE FAR EAST, "Taxation and Economic Development in Asian Countries," *Economic Bulletin for Asia and the Far East,* IV (November, 1953), 1–15; reprinted in WALD, HASKELL P., and FROOMKIN, JOSEPH N. (eds.), *Papers and Proceedings of the Conference on Agricultural Taxation and Economic Development* (Cambridge, Mass.: Harvard Law School International Program in Taxation, 1954), pp. 86–109.

77. UNITED NATIONS, ECONOMIC COMMISSION FOR LATIN AMERICA, *Economic Survey of Latin America 1955* (New York, 1956), pp. 111–76. A survey of revenue and expenditure trends in Latin America, 1947–54.

78. *UNITED NATIONS, FOOD AND AGRICULTURAL ORGANIZATION, ECONOMIC AND SOCIAL COMMISSION, *Agricultural Development in Modern Japan,* Commission Papers: WFC/63/CP/IIC/1 (February 15, 1963). This paper, part of a larger report, was printed separately for the World Food Congress, organized by FAO, held in Washington, June, 1963.

79. *UNITED NATIONS TECHNICAL ASSISTANCE ADMINISTRATION, *Taxes and Fiscal Policy in Under-developed Countries* (U.N. Sales No.: 1955.II.H.1) (New York, 1954). Apart from the survey by WALTER HELLER (reprinted as the first selection in this volume), this document contains a report on the Technical Assistance Conference on Comparative Fiscal Administration held at Geneva in 1951 and eleven summaries of the recommendations of a number of technical assistance missions. The list of reports of fiscal missions to underdeveloped countries which concludes the volume has been supplemented in U.N. Document ST/TAA/M/8/Add. 1 (New York, 1961) to include information through 1960.

80. VAN PHILIPS, P. A. M., *Public Finance and Less Developed Economy, with Special Reference to Latin America* (The Hague: Martinus Nijhof, 1957).

81. WALD, HASKELL P., *Taxation of Agricultural Land in Underdeveloped Economies* (Cambridge, Mass.: Harvard University Press, 1959). In this book Dr. Wald has brought together almost all of the information available on his subject and has discussed practically every issue. Together with the 1954 Conference volume (item 82) Wald's book forms the indispensable starting point for study of the great and complex field of agricultural taxation, a field in which large areas remain unsurveyed.

82. WALD, HASKELL P., and FROOMKIN, JOSEPH N. (eds.), *Papers and Proceedings of the Conference on Agricultural Taxation and Economic Development* (Cambridge, Mass.: Harvard Law School International Program in Taxation, 1954). Essential reading in any investigation of this subject; the many questions raised in this 1954 volume are in general no nearer being answered now than then.

83. WALLICH, H. C., and ADLER, JOHN H., *Public Finance in a Developing Country: El Salvador, a Case Study* (Cambridge, Mass.: Harvard University Press, 1951). An early and very useful survey of the fiscal system of a small, export-oriented country.

READINGS ON TAXATION
IN DEVELOPING COUNTRIES
RICHARD BIRD AND OLIVER OLDMAN

designer:	Edward D. King
typesetter:	Monotype Composition Co., Inc.
typeface:	Text: Baskerville Display: Bodoni
printer:	J. H. Furst Company
paper:	Perkins and Squier SF
binder:	Moore and Company
cover material:	Columbia Riverside

DATE DUE

FACULTY			
APR 2 3 '67			
MAY 1 8 '67			
GAYLORD			PRINTED IN U.S.A.